Contemporary Sociological Thought

Contemporary Sociological Thought

Themes and Theories

Edited by Sean P. Hier

Canadian Scholars' Press Inc.
Toronto

Contemporary Sociological Thought: Themes and Theories
Edited by Sean P. Hier

First published in 2005 by
Canadian Scholars' Press Inc.
180 Bloor Street West, Suite 801
Toronto, Ontario
M5S 2V6

www.cspi.org

Canadian Scholars' Press gratefully acknowledges financial support for our publishing activities from the Government of Canada through the Book Publishing Industry Development Program (BPIDP).

Library and Archives Canada Cataloguing in Publication

Hier, Sean P. (Sean Patrick), 1971-
    Contemporary sociological thought : themes and theories / Sean P. Hier.

Includes bibliographical references and index.
ISBN 1-55130-288-8

    1. Sociology--Textbooks. 2. Sociology--Canada--Textbooks. I. Title.

HM586.H53 2005   301   C2005-903216-2

Cover design by Zack Taylor, www.zacktaylor.com
Cover photo: "Walking Through Change" by Jake Levin. Reprinted by permission of the
    photographer.
Page design and layout by Brad Horning

05 06 07 08 09   5 4 3 2 1

Printed and bound in Canada by Marquis Book Printing

Canadä

Dedicated to Stanley R. Barrett,
a sociological theorist trapped
in the body of an anthropologist

Table of Contents

Introduction: Themes and Theories in Contemporary Sociological Thought 1

SECTION 1: THEORETICAL OFFERINGS OF THE 20TH CENTURY

Part I: Structural Functionalism

Chapter 1
[Extracts from] *The Social System*
    TALCOTT PARSONS 11

Chapter 2
Introduction to *Social Theory and Social Structure*
    ROBERT K. MERTON 23

Part II: Class, Conflict, and the State

Chapter 3
Class and Power: The Major Themes
    JOHN PORTER.. 45

Chapter 4
The Intellectuals
    ANTONIO GRAMSCI 49

Chapter 5
The Rise and Future Demise of the World Capitalist System: Concepts for
Comparative Analysis
    IMMANUEL WALLERSTEIN... 59

Chapter 6
The Impoverishment of State Theory
    LEO PANITCH.. 73

Part III: Perspectives in Symbolic Interaction

Chapter 7
Society as Symbolic Interaction
HERBERT BLUMER 91

Chapter 8
Introduction to *The Presentation of Self in Everyday Life*
ERVING GOFFMAN 101

Chapter 9
Becoming a Marihuana User
HOWARD BECKER 111

Chapter 10
Symbolic Interactionism and Ethnomethodology: A Proposed Synthesis
NORMAN K. DENZIN.. 123

Part IV: Modernism, Culture, and Change

Chapter 11
The Metropolis and Mental Life
GEORG SIMMEL.. 145

Chapter 12
The New Forms of Control
HERBERT MARCUSE 153

Chapter 13
Modernity—An Incomplete Project
JÜRGEN HABERMAS 163

Chapter 14
The Dynamics of the Fields
PIERRE BOURDIEU 175

Chapter 15
Moral Capital
MARIANA VALVERDE 185

Part V: Feminist Social Thought

Chapter 16
The Social Relation of the Sexes: Methodological Implications of
Women's History
JOAN KELLY-GADOL.. 211

Chapter 17

Feminism and Marxism—A Place to Begin, a Way to Go

DOROTHY SMITH 225

Chapter 18

The Significance of Feminism

BELL HOOKS 233

SECTION II: CRITICAL THEMES FOR THE 21ST CENTURY

Part VI: Postmodernism and Its Critics

Chapter 19

Postmodernity: The History of an Idea

DAVID LYON... 255

Chapter 20

The End of Sociological Theory: The Postmodern Hope

STEVEN SEIDMAN 265

Chapter 21

Call Yourself a Sociologist—And You've Never Even Been Arrested?!

MARILYN PORTER 279

Chapter 22

Forward: On Being Light and Liquid

ZYGMUNT BAUMAN... 297

Chapter 23

[Extracts from] *The Spirit of Terrorism and Requiem for the Twin Towers*

JEAN BAUDRILLARD 307

Part VII: Society, Subjects, and the Self

Chapter 24

Reforming Foucault: A Critique of the Social Control Thesis

DANY LACOMBE.. 331

Chapter 25

The Emergence of Life Politics

ANTHONY GIDDENS 347

Chapter 26

Introduction: The Cosmopolitan Manifesto

ULRICH BECK... 357

Part VIII: Globalization and Global Consciousness

Chapter 27
Running Out of Control: Understanding Globalization
  R. ALAN HEDLEY 375

Chapter 28
[Extracts from] *Fences and Windows: Dispatches from the Front Lines of the Globalization Debate*
  NAOMI KLEIN 393

Chapter 29
Cosmopolitanism and the Future of Democracy: Politics, Culture, and the Self
  NICK STEVENSON 403

Part IX: Postcolonialism, Diaspora, Citizenship, and Identity

Chapter 30
Latent and Manifest Orientalism
  EDWARD SAID 423

Chapter 31
Cultural Identity and Diaspora
  STUART HALL 443

Chapter 32
Citizenship in an Era of Globalization
  WILL KYMLICKA 455

Chapter 33
The Politics of Recognition
  CHARLES TAYLOR 465

Copyright Acknowledgments 481

Themes and Theories in Contemporary Sociological Thought

FOR MANY SOCIOLOGY STUDENTS, TAKING A COURSE ON THEMES AND THEORIES IN contemporary sociological thought is a disciplinary requirement bitterly anticipated. Courses in sociological theory often entail an investigation of the ideas of men and, to a lesser extent, of women who wrote about a world far removed from social experiences in 21st-century Canada. These courses tend to be filled with concepts that are difficult to pronounce, let alone understand. Precisely how the dozens of theorists "fit" together in the sociological universe can be very difficult to grasp. Developing a strong understanding of contemporary sociological theory, in short, can be a very challenging—and, at times, frustrating—requirement.

Students who are about to begin their studies of contemporary sociological theory are presumably familiar with the history of social theory generally, and sociological theory particularly. This means that most students at this stage are somewhat familiar with the ideas of Karl Marx, Emile Durkheim, and Max Weber. A smaller number of students will have some understanding of the ideas of Plato, Aristotle, Descartes, Hobbes, Rousseau, Martineau, Webb, and Hegel, and will understand the significance of the Industrial and French revolutions, the Enlightenment, science, and the Age of Reason.

What connects contemporary theory to the long history of social thought, spanning Socrates to Weber and beyond, is a shared interest in understanding and explaining the characteristics and features of human group life. At the heart of sociological theory lies the concern to understand the relationship between the individual and society, the significance of social change, and the ways in which people come to perceive, act upon, and exist in the everyday world. Sociological theories have always focused on how the social world can be known or explained, and they have always been designed with the intention of explaining what makes human collective life possible. Although historical and contemporary contributions to sociological theory can sometimes be very difficult to comprehend, students should never lose sight of the fact that theories are always designed to explain the basic features of human group life.

The famous anthropologist Claude Levi-Stauss (1962) argued that cultural myths and symbols are *bon à penser* (or "good to think"). What he meant was neither that one culture's myths or symbols are inherently or naturally "better" than another culture's nor that myths become "better" as time passes. Rather, he maintained, they are "good to think"; that is, they are rich to contemplate, and they help us to think about the social world in many different ways. In 1984, the Canadian anthropologist Stanley R. Barrett applied this argument to socio-cultural theory, arguing that one theory is not inherently "better" than other theories, and that in the study of socio-cultural theory a limited number of concepts and ideas is continually recycled as new theories develop. Like Levi-Strauss explaining the value of studying cultural myths and symbols, Barrett argued that theories are *bon à penser* even if they do not always explain perfectly the social world in its contemporary form. Readers should not take from this argument that theory is apolitical or without practical application. Indeed, certain theories function as very powerful orienting frameworks for political praxis. It is likely, however, that students will find certain sociological themes and theories more appealing or attractive than others, and it is likely that students will find that certain themes and theories help to make sense of social events in the early 21st century more effectively than others. While certain theories will be preferred, this does not mean that other, perhaps older, theories are useless or redundant; all theories are, as they say, *bon à penser*.

This book is divided into two main sections and presented over nine parts. It may help to think of the section and part titles as general guidelines rather than clearly agreed-upon partitions and divisions in sociological theory. The titles represent nothing more than "road signs" that have been artificially imposed on contemporary sociological theories as a way to make sense of, and bring coherence to, an otherwise complex, rich, and, sometimes contradictory set of ideas. Sociologists often find themselves (and others) pledging theoretical allegiance to one theoretical orientation or another; they often find themselves (and others) in heated debates—about the merits of Marxian theory, for example, or about the insights of postmodernist thinkers. These remain important debates, but it would be irresponsible to dismiss outright all that an entire theoretical orientation has to offer. It would also be naive to deny that every theoretical orientation is in some ways connected to others.

The Section 1 of the book considers "Theoretical Offerings of the 20th Century." The contributions of 18 theorists are included over five parts: Structural Functionalism; Class, Conflict, and the State; Perspectives in Symbolic Interaction; Modernism, Culture, and Change; and Feminist Social Thought.

Section 2 is concerned with "Critical Themes for the 21st Century." The contributions of 15 theorists are included over four parts: Postmodernism and Its Critics; Society, Subjects, and the Self; Globalization and Global Consciousness; and Postcolonialism, Diaspora, Citizenship, and Identity. Throughout the book, the contributions of 13 Canadian theorists (or theorists working in Canada) are integrated with the ideas of influential European and American thinkers to demonstrate the significant contributions made by Canadian social scientists in international debates. Of course, not all major themes or theories in contemporary sociological theory could be presented. At the end of each chapter, students will find suggestions for further readings to better prepare for higher levels of study (if desired!).

REFERENCES

Barrett, Stanley R. 1984. *The Rebirth of Anthropological Theory*. Toronto: University of Toronto Press.
Levi-Strauss, Claude. 1962. *Totemism*. Boston: Beacon Press.

ACKNOWLEDGMENTS

I wish to thank my colleague Bill Carroll in the Department of Sociology at the University of Victoria for recommending me to Canadian Scholars' Press; Mary E. Leighton in the Department of English at the University of Victoria for taking the time to read the manuscript and to steady my fumbling prose; and Megan Mueller for encouraging the project and allowing me room to breathe. The book is dedicated to my first sociological theory teacher, Stan Barrett at the University of Guelph, who introduced me to the classics.

A NOTE FROM THE PUBLISHER

Thank you for selecting *Contemporary Sociological Thought: Themes and Theories*, edited by Sean P. Hier. The editor and publisher have devoted considerable time and careful development (including meticulous peer reviews) to this book. We appreciate your recognition of this effort and accomplishment.

Teaching Features

This volume distinguishes itself on the market in many ways. One key feature is the book's well-written and comprehensive part openers, which help to make the readings all the more accessible to undergraduate students. The part openers add cohesion to the section and to the whole book. The themes of the book are very clearly presented in these section openers.

The general editor, Sean Hier, has also greatly enhanced the book by adding pedagogy to close and complete each section. Each part ends with critical thinking questions pertaining to each reading, detailed annotated suggested readings, annotated related Web sites, and references.

SECTION I

Theoretical Offerings of the 20th Century

Part I: Structural Functionalism

Chapter 1
[Extracts from] *The Social System*
TALCOTT PARSONS

Chapter 2
Introduction to *Social Theory and Social Structure*
ROBERT K. MERTON

Part II: Class, Conflict, and the State

Chapter 3
Class and Power: The Major Themes
JOHN PORTER

Chapter 4
The Intellectuals
ANTONIO GRAMSCI

Chapter 5
The Rise and Future Demise of the World Capitalist System:
Concepts for Comparative Analysis
IMMANUEL WALLERSTEIN

Chapter 6
The Impoverishment of State Theory
LEO PANITCH

Part III: Perspectives in Symbolic Interaction

Chapter 7
Society as Symbolic Interaction
HERBERT BLUMER

Chapter 8
Introduction to *The Presentation of Self in Everyday Life*
ERVING GOFFMAN

Chapter 9
Becoming a Marihuana User
HOWARD BECKER

Chapter 10
Symbolic Interactionism and Ethnomethodology: A Proposed Synthesis
NORMAN K. DENZIN

Part IV: Modernism, Culture, and Change

Chapter 11
The Metropolis and Mental Life
GEORG SIMMEL

Chapter 12
The New Forms of Control
HERBERT MARCUSE

Chapter 13
Modernity—An Incomplete Project
JÜRGEN HABERMAS

Chapter 14
The Dynamics of the Fields
PIERRE BOURDIEU

Chapter 15
Moral Capital
MARIANA VALVERDE

Part V: Feminist Social Thought

Chapter 16
The Social Relation of the Sexes:
Methodological Implications of Women's History
JOAN KELLY-GADOL

Chapter 17
Feminism and Marxism—A Place to Begin, a Way to Go
DOROTHY SMITH

Chapter 18
The Significance of Feminism
BELL HOOKS

Structural Functionalism

THE SOCIOLOGICAL FOUNDATIONS FOR 20TH-CENTURY STRUCTURAL FUNCTIONALISM ARE to be found in the writings of men such as Auguste Comte, Herbert Spencer, and Emile Durkheim. Influential contributions also came from anthropologists, including Bronislaw Malinowski and A.R. Radcliffe-Brown. Early structural functionalists were interested, in different ways, to understand how societies pass through stages of development, how some societies "progress" more quickly than others, and the uniformity of social change across cultures. They assumed that institutions and social roles mesh together to form patterned and predictable social arrangements, and they examined the ways in which societies exhibit tendencies toward social equilibrium and cohesion.

At times referred to facetiously as the "big animal theory," structural functionalism sought to understand scientifically how social systems operate in a manner akin to living organisms. Just as the human body is comprised of functional components, including a heart, lungs, kidneys, etc., social institutions such as the educational system, government, law enforcement, and media outlets were explained as functioning *inter*dependently to form stable social systems. Structural functionalists argued that the achievement of functional interdependence took place over long periods of time, and one of the main goals of functionalism was to explain how social arrangements continually ascend to new levels of integration.

As the 20th century progressed, several important contributions to functionalist thought appeared. One prominent example is the so-called "caste school" of race relations, promoted by social anthropologists under the direction of W. Lloyd Warner (1930). Structural functionalism had enjoyed growing success in British anthropology since the 1850s, and it is little wonder that functionalism developed more quickly in American anthropology than it did in sociology. But it was in the two decades following the Second World War that functionalism assumed a position of authority and dominance in North American sociology. In fact, so confident were the post-war proponents of this theoretical orientation that Kingsley Davis proclaimed in his 1959 presidential address to the American Sociological Association that structural functionalism was not merely a special approach to the discipline; it was, he argued, the sociological model.

The end of the Second World War brought with it an optimistic future outlook in most industrializing capitalist nations. During the 1950s, industrial production intensified, labour market opportunities expanded, and a relative state of prosperity set in. The intensification of productive relations combined with progressive social reforms in areas such as health care and child care, unemployment insurance, medical coverage, and old age security. While the development of elaborate state welfare systems after 1945 can in some respects be explained as a compromise between the representatives of capital and organized labour, it also signified an international effort to stabilize political-economic relations to ensure the continuity of the social order (Li 1996). Post-war structural functionalism was shaped in the social, political, and economic climate of the times, and two of the most influential functionalists were Talcott Parsons and Robert Merton.

⊡ SECTION READINGS: TALCOTT PARSONS AND ROBERT MERTON

Although he had published *The Structure of Social Action* in 1937, it was not until *The Social System* (1951) and *Towards a General Theory of Action* (1951) were completed that Talcott Parsons (1902–1979) emerged as the most influential contributor to structural functionalism. There are important differences in Parsons's major writings, but constant throughout his career was the ambition to formulate a *systematic general theory* that he described as "… a conceptual scheme for the analysis of social systems in terms of the action frame of reference" (Parsons 1951: 3). For Parsons, the fundamental starting point for constructing any scientific theory is to establish an abstract frame of reference. In the scientific study of social action, the empirical basis for the frame of reference is a group of interacting individuals (social actors). Social actors have particular goals that they wish to achieve, and to realize those goals they must take advantage of opportunities (means) that are available under a particular set of conditions (situations). Parsons was clear that none of these elements can be reduced to the others, and he sought to formulate an action frame of reference for the study of social action that was capable of accounting for the individual and situational factors motivating people to act in the ways that they do.

As Parsons explains, an individual is always oriented toward particular courses of action. Individual actions take place in the context of actor situations. Actor situations are relational, in that they involve the individual ("ego") relating to, or interacting with, three primary classes of objects—social, cultural, and physical. The action situation has motivational significance to the individual—all gratifications and deprivations have "organic significance" for Parsons—yet motivation cannot be reduced to the "organic needs" of the individual/organism. That is, although human beings have basic organismic needs, the motivations for social action cannot be reduced to the basic physical needs of human beings. When deciding on a course of action (defining a situation), an individual may take into account one or more of the primary action elements in light of personality structures, as well as future anticipated gratifications and deprivations, to achieve desired goals. Social actions take place in the context of gratificational and orientational motivations, where the degree of an individual's desire (cathect) for something is based on what he or she knows about that particular object (cognition). The point that Parsons wishes to make is that actor situations cannot be understood scientifically if they are conceived of independently of orientations and motivations.

In the Parsonian scheme, relationships are interactive; the behaviour of individual actors has meaning in terms of motivations and orientations that take the form of social roles and cultural expectations. The functional prerequisites of interactive systems involve *adapting* to the basic needs of individuals, but individuals must also be sufficiently *motivated* to secure enough participation in systems to ensure their stability. The prerequisite of adequate motivation, in Parsons's view, presupposes a stable interactive system capable of proving reasonable *expectations that goals* will be attained. This involves the integration of individuals' behaviour with minimally compatible cultural and social systems to the extent that *maintaining the patterns* of interactive systems requires that a sufficient number of actors are motivated to conform to social roles. It is, for Parsons, the four component parts or subsystems in the action frame of reference—culture, society, personality, and behaviour/organic energy—that bring meaning to situations.

Before Parsons had started to make a serious impact on sociological thought, he trained several students at Harvard University, one of whom was Robert Merton. Merton (1910–2003) became one of Parsons's most influential collaborators in the structural functionalist orientation, but he also emerged as one of Parsons's most important critics. Merton believes that Parsons's emphasis on developing comprehensive theoretical systems did not facilitate the process of actually doing sociological research. In contrast to the abstraction and deduction that Parsons promotes, Merton argues that sociologists should work on testable and researchable hypotheses in specific situations. He also argues that sociologists should gradually develop theories from empirical evidence. What is lacking in functional analysis, insists Merton, is an integration of theory and research, a problem confounded by the failure in sociological discourse to distinguish progressively between "the history of theory" and "the systematics of theory."

For Merton, sociological theory is not to be constructed in the scientific tradition of a universal, "architectonic," methodologically empty conception of society. Rather, the development of sociological theory should consist of limited and modest working hypotheses that are applicable to the empirical world. Theories of the "middle range," he maintains, avoid speculating on general orientations of types of variables that structure the entire social world, emphasizing instead clear and verifiable relationships between specific variables. In Merton's view, one way to accomplish this is through empirical codification. Empirical codification takes place using the analytic device of the "theoretic paradigm." The paradigm not only helps to progress the discipline in a steady and orderly fashion, but it also facilitates brevity, precision, and objectivity. Whereas Parsons's functionalism is concerned with the functional integration of systems, then, Merton is inspired by social anthropologists' interest in how social systems function as a collection of component parts.

REFERENCES

Davis, Kingsley. 1959. "The Myth of Functional Analysis as a Special Method in Sociology and Anthropology." *American Sociological Review* 24: 757–772.

Li, Peter. 1996. *The Making of Post-war Canada*. Toronto: Oxford University Press.

Parsons, Talcott. 1937. *The Structure of Social Action*. New York: McGraw-Hill.

_____. 1951. *The Social System*. Glencoe: Free Press.

Parsons, Talcott, and Edward Shils (eds). 1951. *Towards a General Theory of Action*. Cambridge: Harvard University Press.

Warner, W.L. 1930. "American Caste and Class." *American Journal of Sociology* 42: 234–237.

CHAPTER 1

[Extracts from] *The Social System*

TALCOTT PARSONS

⑤ THE ACTION FRAME OF REFERENCE AND THE GENERAL THEORY OF ACTION SYSTEMS: CULTURE, PERSONALITY, AND THE PLACE OF SOCIAL SYSTEMS

* * * * *

The fundamental starting point is the concept of social systems of action. The interaction of individual actors, that is, takes place under such conditions that it is possible to treat such a process of *inter*action as a system in the scientific sense and subject it to the same order of theoretical analysis which has been successfully applied to other types of systems in other sciences.

The fundamentals of the action frame of reference have been extensively dealt with elsewhere and need only to be briefly summarized here.[1] The frame of reference concerns the "orientation" of one or more actors—in the fundamental individual case biological organisms—to a situation, which includes other actors. The scheme, that is, relative to the units of action and interaction, is a *relational* scheme. It analyzes the structure and processes of the systems built up by the relations of such units to their situations, including other units. It is not as such concerned with the *internal* structure of the units except so far as this directly bears on the relational system.

The situation is defined as consisting of objects of orientation, so that the orientation of a given actor is differentiated relative to the different objects and classes of them of which his situation is composed. It is convenient in action terms to classify the object world as composed of the three classes of "social," "physical," and "cultural" objects. A social object is an actor, which may in turn be any given other individual actor (alter), the actor who is taken as a point of reference himself (ego), or a collectivity which is treated as a unit for purposes of the analysis of orientation. Physical objects are empirical entities which do not "interact" with or "respond" to ego. They are means and conditions of his action. Cultural objects are

11

symbolic elements of the cultural tradition, ideas or beliefs, expressive symbols, or value patterns so far as they are treated as situational objects by ego and are not "internalized" as constitutive elements of the structure of his personality.

"Action" is a process in the actor–situation system which has motivational significance to the individual actor, or, in the case of a collectivity, its component individuals. This means that the orientation of the corresponding action processes has a bearing on the attainment of gratifications or the avoidance of deprivations of the relevant actor, whatever concretely in the light of the relevant personality structures these may be. Only in so far as his relation to the situation is in this sense motivationally relevant will it be treated in this work as action in a technical sense. It is presumed that the ultimate source of the energy or "effort" factor of action processes is derived from the organism, and correspondingly that in some sense all gratification and deprivation have an organic significance. But though it is rooted in them the concrete organization of motivation cannot for purposes of action theory be analyzed in terms of the organic needs of the organism. This organization of action elements is, for purposes of the theory of action, above all a function of the relation of the actor to his situation and the history of that relation, in this sense of "experience."

It is a fundamental property of action thus defined that it does not consist only of ad hoc "responses" to particular situational "stimuli" but that the actor develops a *system* of "expectations" relative to the various objects of the situation. These *may* be structured only relative to his own need-dispositions and the probabilities of gratification or deprivation contingent on the various alternatives of action which he may undertake. But in the case of interaction with social objects a further dimension is added. Part of ego's expectation, in many cases the most crucial part, consists in the probable reaction of alter to ego's possible action, a reaction which comes to be anticipated in advance and thus to affect ego's own choices.

On both levels, however, various elements of the situation come to have special "meanings" for ego as "signs" or "symbols" which become relevant to the organization of his expectation system. Especially where there is social interaction, signs and symbols acquire common meanings and serve as media of communication between actors. When symbolic systems which can mediate communication have emerged we may speak of the beginnings of a "culture" which becomes part of the action systems of the relevant actors.

It is only with systems of interaction which have become differentiated to a cultural level that we are here concerned. Though the term social system may be used in a more elementary sense, for present purposes this possibility can be ignored and attention confined to systems of interaction of a plurality of individual actors oriented to a situation and where the system includes a commonly understood system of cultural symbols.

Reduced to the simplest possible terms, then, a social system consists in a plurality of individual actors interacting with each other in a situation which has at least a physical or environmental aspect, actors who are motivated in terms of a tendency to the "optimization of gratification" and whose relation to their situations, including each other, is defined and mediated in terms of a system of culturally structured and shared symbols.

Thus conceived, a social system is only one of three aspects of the structuring of a completely concrete system of social action. The other two are the personality systems of the individual actors and the cultural system which is built into their action. Each of the three must be considered to be an independent focus of the organization of the elements of the action system in the sense that no one of them is theoretically reducible to terms of one or a combination of the other two. Each is indispensable to the other two in the sense that without personalities and culture there would be no social system and so on around the roster of logical possibilities. But this interdependence and interpenetration is a very different matter from reducibility, which would mean that the important properties and processes of one class of system could be theoretically *derived* from our theoretical knowledge of one or both of the other two. The action frame of reference is common to all three and this fact makes certain "transformations" between them possible. But on the level of theory here attempted they do not constitute a single system, however this might turn out to be on some other theoretical level.

Almost another way of making this point is to say that on the present level of theoretical systematization our dynamic knowledge of action-processes is fragmentary. Because of this we are forced to use these types of empirical system, descriptively presented in terms of a frame of reference, as an indispensable point of reference. In relation to this point of reference we conceive dynamic processes as "mechanisms"[2] which influence the "functioning" of the system. The descriptive presentation of the empirical system must be made in terms of a set of "structural" categories, into which the appropriate "motivational" constructs necessary to constitute a usable knowledge of mechanisms are fitted.

Before going further into some of these broad methodological problems of the analysis of systems of action with special reference to the social system, it is advisable to say something more about the more elementary components of action in general. In the most general sense the "need-disposition" system of the individual actor seems to have two most primary or elementary aspects which may be called the "gratificational" aspect and the "orientational" aspect. The first concerns the "content" of his interchange with the object world, "what" he gets out of his interaction with it, and what its "costs" to him are. The second concerns the "how" of his relation to the object world, the patterns or ways in which his relations to it are organized.

Emphasizing the relational aspect we may refer to the former as "cathectic" orientation, which means the significance of ego's relation to the object or objects in question for the gratification–deprivation balance of his personality. The most elementary and fundamental "orientational" category, on the other hand, seems to be the "cognitive" which in its most general sense may be treated as the "definition" of the relevant aspects of the situation in their relevance to the actor's "interests." This is then the cognitive orientation aspect, or cognitive mapping in Tolman's sense.[3] Both these aspects must be present in anything which could be considered a unit of an action system, a "unit act."

But acts do not occur singly and discretely, they are organized in systems. The moment even the most elementary system-level is brought under consideration a component of "system integration" must enter in. In terms of the action frame of reference again this integration is a selective ordering among the possibilities of orientation. Gratification needs have alternatively possible objects presented in the situation. Cognitive mapping has alternatives of judgment or interpretation as to what objects are or what they "mean." There must be ordered selection among such alternatives. The term "evaluation" will be given to this process of ordered selection. There is, therefore, an evaluative aspect of all concrete action orientation. The most elementary components of any action system then may be reduced to the actor and his situation. With regard to the actor our interest is organized about the cognitive, cathectic, and evaluative modes of his orientation; with regard to the situation, to its differentiation into objects and classes of them.

The three basic modes of motivational orientation along with the conception of an object system categorize the elements of action on the broadest level. They are all three implicated in the structure of what has been called "expectation." Besides cathectic interests, cognitive definition of the situation, and evaluative selection, an expectation has, as the term suggests, a time aspect in the orientation to future development of the actor–situation system and to the memory of past actions. Orientation to the situation is *structured*, that is, with reference to its developmental patterns. The actor acquires an "investment" in certain possibilities of that development. It matters to him how it occurs, that some possibilities should be realized rather than others.

* * * * *

⑤ THE FUNCTIONAL PREREQUISITES OF SOCIAL SYSTEMS[4]

Interactive relationships analyzed in terms of statuses and roles occur as we have seen in systems. If such a system is to constitute a persistent order or to undergo an orderly[5] process of developmental change, certain functional prerequisites must be met. A brief discussion of these functional prerequisites is in order because it provides the setting for a more extended analysis of the points of reference for analyzing the structure of social systems.

The problem of functional prerequisites is a protean problem because of the variety of different levels on which it may be approached. What we propose here is to start on the most general and therefore formal level of action theory and proceed to introduce specifications step by step. It should be possible to do this in a sufficiently orderly fashion.

The broadest framework of such an analysis is directly deducible from the considerations about action in general […]. The basis of this is the insight that action systems are structured about three integrative foci, the individual actor, the interactive system, and a system of cultural patterning.[6] Each implies the others and therefore the variability of any one is limited by its compatibility with the minimum conditions of functioning of each of the other two.

Looked at from the perspective of any one integrate of action such as the social system there are in turn two aspects of this reciprocal interrelation with each of the others. First, a social system cannot be so structured as to be radically incompatible with the conditions of functioning of its component individual actors as biological organisms and as personalities, or of the relatively stable integration of a cultural system. Secondly, in turn the social system, on both fronts, depends on the requisite minimum of "support" from each of the other systems. It must, that is, have a sufficient proportion of its component actors adequately motivated to act in accordance with the requirements of its role system, positively in the fulfillment of expectations and negatively in abstention from too much disruptive, i.e., deviant, behavior. It must, on the other hand, avoid commitment to cultural patterns which either fail to define a minimum of order or which place impossible demands on people and thereby generate deviance and conflict to a degree which is incompatible with the minimum conditions of stability or orderly development. These problems may be briefly taken up in turn.

We have tried to make clear that there is no simple relation between personalities and social systems. Because of this fact, in the present state of knowledge it is not possible to define precisely what are the minimum needs of individual actors, so only certain rather general things can be said. From the point of view of functioning of the social system, it is not the needs of all the participant actors which must be met, nor all the needs of any one, but only a sufficient proportion for a sufficient fraction of the population. It is indeed a very general phenomenon that social forces are directly responsible for injury to or destruction of some individuals and some of the wants or needs of all individuals, and though this may be reduced it is highly probable that it cannot be eliminated under realistic conditions. To cite a very simple case, a war cannot be won without casualties, and acceptance of war is sometimes a condition of survival of a social system as a distinctive system.

The elements of this class of functional prerequisites may be said to begin with the biological prerequisites of individual life, like nutrition and physical safety. They go on to the subtler problems of the conditions of minimum stability of personality. It seems to be reasonably well established that there are minimum conditions of socialization with respect for instance to the relation between affectional support and security, without which a functioning personality cannot be built up. The present task is not to attempt to analyze these borderline problems, but only to make clear where they fit in relation to the theory of the social system. These minimum needs of individual actors constitute a set of conditions to which the social system must be adapted. If the variation of the latter goes too far in a given direction this will tend to set up repercussions which will in turn tend to produce deviant behavior in the actors in question, behavior which is either positively disruptive or involves withdrawal from functionally important activities. Such a need, as a functional prerequisite, may be likened to a spring. The less adequately it is met, the more "pressure" it will take to realize certain patterns of social action in the face of it, and hence the less energy will be available for other purposes. At certain points for certain individuals or classes of them then the pressure may become too great and the spring may break — such persons no longer participate in the interactive system of personality and social system.[7]

The obverse of the functional prerequisite of meeting a minimum proportion of the needs of the individual actors is the need to secure adequate participation of a sufficient proportion of these actors in the social system, that is to motivate them adequately to the performances which may be necessary if the social system in question is to persist or develop. Indeed it is because it is a condition of this that the need to satisfy minimum needs of actors is a prerequisite at all.

The prerequisite of adequate motivation in turn subdivides into two main aspects, a negative and a positive. The negative is that of a minimum of control over potentially disruptive behavior. This means action which interferes with the action of others in their roles in the social system. It may involve either aggressive action toward others or merely action which has deleterious consequences for others or for an aspect of the system, without aggressive intent.

The field is highly complex, but perhaps one particular aspect of it may be singled out for special mention. This is that in terms of functional significance relative to the social system, the significance of an action or class of them is to be understood not directly and primarily in terms of its motivation but of its actual or probable consequences for the system. In this sense the pursuit of "private interests" may be highly disruptive under certain circumstances even though the content of the interests, for example in religious terms, may be such as to be rather generally ethically approved. Similarly conflict as such may be highly disruptive. If it becomes sufficiently severe the functional problem for the system becomes the control of the conflict as such. In such a case the merits of the "case" of one or the other of the parties may become of quite secondary importance.

In general terms the functional problem for a social system of minimizing potentially disruptive behavior and the motivation to it may be called the "motivational problem of order." Because of certain further features of social systems [...] the present discussion should lead up to consideration of certain relatively specific classes of potential disruption, notably the problem of opportunity, the problem of prestige allocation, and the problem of power. There is, that is to say, an immense variety of particular acts which are disruptive in that they interfere with the role-performance of one or more other actors. So long, however, as they remain nearly randomly distributed they may reduce the efficiency of the system by depressing levels of role performance, but still not constitute a threat to its stability. This latter may develop when disruptive tendencies become organized as a sub-system in such a way as to impinge on strategic points in the social system itself. It is as such strategic points that the problems of opportunity, prestige, and power will be treated below.[8]

The distinction between the negative and the positive aspects of the problem of adequate motivation is relative and gradual. Both present functional problems in terms of the operation of the social system, which focus attention on the mechanisms which fit into the relevant context. But in spite of this relativity there is an important distinction between action, which is positively disruptive of a going system of social relationships, and simple withdrawal of the individual from performance of his obligations. The principal criterion would be that in the latter case the only interference with others would consist in forcing them to do without the benefits expected from a person's actions. The possibility of withdrawal in fact defines one of the most important directions of deviant behavior, and enters as we shall see in most important ways into the structure of the problems and mechanisms of social control. Illness is, for example, one of the most important types of withdrawal behavior in our society [...].

Again in relation to withdrawal as a type of failure to be motivated to adequate role performance, it must be made clear that the negative aspect of withdrawal is *not* defined in motivational terms but in functional terms relative to the social system. Precisely because people are dependent on each other's performances, simple withdrawal from fulfillment of expectations may, motivationally speaking, be a highly aggressive act, and may in fact injure the other severely. But in part precisely because it does not correspond to the motivational distinction the functional distinction is highly significant as will become evident. It provides a point of reference for the analysis of the directions of deviant behavior and hence places such behavior in relation to problems of the mechanisms of operation of the social system.

The prerequisite of adequate motivation gives us one of the primary starting points for building up to the concepts of role and of institutionalization. Fundamentally the problem is, will the personalities developed within a social system, at whatever stage in the life cycle, "spontaneously" act in such ways as to fulfill the functional prerequisites of the social systems of which they are parts, or is it necessary to look for relatively specific mechanisms, that is, modes of organization of the motivational systems of personalities, which can be understood in direct relation to the socially structured level or role behavior? The older "psychological" view that societies are resultants of the independently determined "traits" of individuals would take the first alternative. The modern sociological view tends to emphasize the second.

Statement of the problem of adequate motivation not only poses in general the problems of the mechanisms of socialization and of social control and their relation to the dynamics of the social system, but it provides the setting for an approach to the analysis of the relevant mechanisms. Personality psychology, as we have seen, is becoming highly oriented to the actor's relational system, that is, his orientation to objects. When this fact is combined with the fundamental place of the concept of expectations in the theory of action, it becomes clear that one central aspect of the general and especially the cathectic orientation of the actor is his set of need-dispositions toward the fulfillment of role expectations, in the first place those of other significant actors but also his own. There is, in the personality structure of the individual actor a "conformity–alienation" dimension in the sense of a disposition to conform with the expectations of others or to be alienated from them. When these relevant expectations are those relative to the fulfillment of role-obligations, this conformity–alienation balance, in general or in particular role contexts, becomes a central focus of the articulation of the motivational system of the personality with the structure of the social system.   ·

It is furthermore in the present context of the problem of adequate motivation of role-expectation fulfillment that the basic significance for the social system of two fundamental properties of biological "human nature" may best be briefly brought to attention. The first of these is the much discussed "plasticity" of the human organism, its capacity to learn any one of a large number of alternative patterns of behavior instead of being bound by its genetic constitution to a very limited range of alternatives. It is, of course, within the limits of this plasticity that the independent determinant significance of cultural and social factors in action must be sought. The clear demonstration of determination in terms of the genes automatically narrows the range of relevance of the factors which are of theoretical interest in the sciences of action, except for their possible bearing on the problems of assortative mating which influence the processes of combination and recombination of genetic strains. The limits of plasticity are for the most part still unknown.[9]

The second characteristic of human nature in the biological sense is what may be called "sensitivity." By this is meant the accessibility of the human individual to influence by the attitudes of others in the social interaction process, and the resulting dependence on receiving relatively particular and specific reactions. What this provides essentially is the motivational basis for accessibility to influence in the learning process. Thus the attitudes of others are probably of first rate importance in all human learning, but are particularly crucial in motivating the acceptance of value-orientation patterns, with their legitimation of the renunciations which are essential to the achievement of a disciplined integration of personality. Without this discipline the stability of expectations in relation to their fulfillment, which is essential for a functioning social system, would not be possible. It is highly probable that one of the principal limitations on the social potentialities of animals on other than an instinct basis lies in the absence or weakness of this lever. The physiological dependency of the human infant is associated with its capacity for developing emotional dependency, which in turn is an essential condition of much of social learning.

It has not been common in discussions of the functional prerequisites of social systems to include explicit treatment of cultural prerequisites, but the need to do so seems to follow directly from the major premises of action theory as set forth above. The integration of cultural patterns as well as their specific content involve factors which at any given time are independent of the other elements for the action system and yet must be articulated with them. Such integration imposes "imperatives" on the other elements just as truly as is the case the other way around. This major functional problem area of the social system may be subdivided along the same lines as in the case of the motivational problem.

In the first place there are minimum social conditions necessary for the production, maintenance, and development of cultural systems in general and of particular types of cultural system. It may be presumed that disruption of the communication system of a society is ultimately just as dangerous as disruption of its system of order in the above sense of motivational integration. This is an aspect of "anomie" which deserves much more explicit analysis than it has received. Perhaps the most obvious specific example is provided by the role of language. We know quite definitely that the individual does not develop language spontaneously without undergoing a socially structured learning process in relation to others. It is quite definite that this process must be part of a system of social relations which is orderly within certain limits, however difficult it may be to specify the limits in detail. It is altogether probable that many protohuman groups failed to make the transition to the human socio-cultural level of action because of failure to fulfill the prerequisites of the emergence of language or of some other functionally essential aspects of culture.

Thus a social system in the present sense is not possible without language, and without certain other minimum patterns of culture, such as empirical knowledge necessary to cope with situational exigencies, and sufficiently integrated patterns of expressive symbolism and of value orientation. A social system which leads to too drastic disruption of its culture, for example through blocking the processes of its acquisition, would be exposed to social as well as cultural disintegration.

We do not accurately know the cultural limits of "human society," so exactly what the above limits may be remains to be determined. With respect to certain more specific types of cultural pattern, however, we have relatively detailed knowledge—we shall, for example, discuss modern science from this point of view below. In any case the determination of these conditions is an important field of sociological research.

One final remark in orientation to the general problem. Culture may, of course, be "embodied" in physical form independently of particular actors, e.g., knowledge in books, but it is a cardinal principle of the theory of action that culture is not merely "situational" relative to action but becomes directly constitutive of personalities as such through what personality psychologists now tend to call "internalization." The minimum cultural prerequisites of a social system may thus be said to operate at least in part through the functions of culture for personality. Without the requisite cultural resources to be assimilated through internalization it is not possible for a human level of personality to emerge and hence for a human type of social system to develop.

The other aspect of the problem of prerequisites on the cultural side is that of adequate cultural resources and organization for the maintenance of the social system. This has already been touched upon in the discussions above, but a few additional remarks may be made. Perhaps the most obvious type of case is instrumental knowledge. Without a minimum of technical lore which makes it possible to deal with the physical environment and with other human beings, no human society would be possible. This in turn presupposes language. But similar considerations also apply to the other departments of culture, to non-empirical existential ideas, to expressive symbol systems and, above all, to patterns of value-orientation about which much will have to be said in what follows.

It was pointed out above that tendencies to deviant behavior on the part of the component actors pose functional "problems" for the social system in the sense that they must be counteracted by "mechanisms of control" unless dysfunctional consequences are to ensue. The parallel on the cultural side is the case where the maintenance of certain cultural patterns as integral parts of the going system of action imposes certain strains. This may be true both on the personality and the social system levels. The most obvious cases are those of a value-orientation pattern and of cognitive beliefs which are motivationally difficult to conform with. Such difficulty might be attributable to a conflict with reality. Thus within the area covered by well-established medical science the maintenance of and action upon some beliefs of Christian Science may impose a serious strain on the actor especially where he cannot escape knowing the medical views. Or it may be a matter of difficulty in attaining con-formative motivation, as in the case where certain types of socialization tend to generate deeply anti-authoritarian sentiments so that at least some kinds of authority cannot be tolerated by some people. In particular a Utopian ideal, if accepted and institutionalized, imposes strains on the social system.

Though the limits in this as in the other cases are in general not known, it is safe to say not only that the social system must be able to keep a minimum of culture going, but vice versa, any given culture must be compatible with a social system to a minimum degree if its patterns are not to become extinct, and if the latter is to continue functioning unchanged. Analysis of the mediating mechanisms between the cultural patterns and the concrete action systems in its motivational aspect constitutes one of the most important problem areas of action theory and specifically of the theory of social systems [...].

* * * * *

NOTES

1. Cf. especially Parsons and Shils, *Values, Motives and Systems of Action* in *Toward a General Theory of Action.* Also Parsons, *Structure of Social Action,* and *Essays in Sociological Theory,* and, of course, Weber, *Theory of Social and Economic Organization.*

2. A mechanism as the term will here be used is an empirical generalization about motivational processes stated in terms of its relevance to the functional problems of an action system. [...]

3. Cf. E.C. Tolman, *Purposive Behavior in Animals and Men.*

4. On the general problem of functional prerequisites of the social system see Aberle, Cohen, Davis, Levy, Sutton, "The Functional Prerequisites of a Society," *Ethics,* IX (January, 1950), 100–111. The present treatment is indebted to their paper, but departs from it rather radically.

5. An orderly process in this sense is contrasted with the disintegration of a system. Disintegration in this sense means disappearance of the boundaries of the system relative to its environment. Cf. *Values, Motives, and Systems of Action,* Chapter I.

6. And also in a different sense about the non-action environment, the physical aspects of the situation.

7. It is, of course, highly important not to invent ad hoc generalizations about these prerequisites which allegedly explain certain classes of concrete social phenomena. This procedure is especially tempting because such an ad hoc hypothesis can serve to absolve the investigator from the difficult analysis of the internal balances and processes of the social system itself. In its cruder forms this procedure has played a very prominent part in the history of social thought, as in the currency of theories that virtually all social phenomena were determined by the genetic constitution of populations or their geographical environments. It is an index of the increasing maturity of our science that such sweeping formulae are no longer considered to merit even serious discussion. Both the positive role of such conditioning factors and of internal social processes are in general terms fully established. But the general formulae do not solve the specific problems. The task is to unravel the complex patterns of interaction between the two classes of factors.

8. It is in this kind of a context that the distinction between manifest and latent function becomes significant. In general only within limited ranges and to a limited extent are the consequences that the sociologist takes as his standard for the analysis of the systemic significance of actions explicitly intended by the actor, individual, or collective. It is these unintended consequences which constitute the latent functions or dysfunctions of the actions. Cf. Robert K. Merton, *Social Theory and Social Structure,* Chapter I.

9. From the point of view of action theory and specifically that of the social system, it may be said that the burden of proof rests upon him who would assert that what has been considered an action theory problem is adequately solved by invoking the role of such sub-action determinants of behavior. This will often turn out to be the case, but resort to ad hoc hypotheses on this level which have railed to stand up under criticism and further investigation has been so prominent in the history of social science that we must insist on this burden of proof maxim.

CHAPTER 2

Introduction to *Social Theory and Social Structure*

ROBERT K. MERTON

⑤ CONSOLIDATION OF SOCIAL THEORY AND RESEARCH

This announced interest in consolidating the reciprocal relations between social theory and social research is suspiciously irreproachable. Where will one find a social scientist disclaiming the desirability of the "integration" of theory and empirical research? Unless it is given some special force, this position will possess the same measure of trivial truth as the position held by Calvin Coolidge's preacher who was unexceptionably "against sin."

If it is to be more than another announcement of conventional faith, this interest in consolidation must be made *specific* and must be *concretely exemplified.* [...]

⑤ HISTORY OF THEORY AND SYSTEMATICS OF THEORY

[...] The attractive but fatal confusion of utilizable sociological theory with the history of sociological theory—who said what by way of speculation or hypothesis?—should long since have been dispelled by recognizing their very different functions. After all, schools of medicine do not confuse the history of medicine with current medical knowledge, nor do departments of biology identify the history of biology with the viable theory now employed in guiding and interpreting biological research. Once said, this seems obvious enough to be embarrassing. Yet the extraordinary fact is that in sociology, this plain distinction between the history of theory and currently operating theory has in many places not caught hold—at least, if we may judge from curricula and publications.

[...] Although the history and the systematics of sociological theory should both be of concern in training sociologists, this is no reason for merging and confusing the two. Systematic sociological theory [...] represents the highly selective accumulation of those small parts of earlier theory which have thus far survived the tests, of empirical research. But the history of theory includes also the far greater mass of conceptions which fell to bits when confronted with empirical test. It includes also the false starts, the archaic doctrines, and the fruitless errors of the past. Though acquaintance with all this may be a useful adjunct to the sociologist's training, it is no substitute for training in the actual use of theory in research. We can with profit study much of what the forefathers of sociology wrote as exercises in the conduct of intellectual inquiry, but this is quite another matter.

The clearly visible fact is that the early history of sociology—as represented, for example, in the speculations of a Comte or a Spencer, a Hobhouse, or a Ratzenhofer—is very far from cumulative. The conceptions of each seldom build upon the work of those who have gone before. They are typically laid out as alternative and competing conceptions rather than consolidated and extended into a cumulative product. Consequently, little of what these early forerunners wrote remains pertinent to sociology today. Their works testify to the large merits of talented men, but they do not often provide guidelines to the current analysis of sociological problems. They were grand achievements for their day, but that day is not ours. We sociologists of today may be only intellectual pigmies but, unlike the overly modest Newton, we are not pigmies standing on the shoulders of giants. The accumulative tradition is still so slight that the shoulders of the giants of sociological science do not provide a very solid base on which to stand. Whitehead's apothegm [...] is therefore all the more binding on sociology than on those physical sciences which have a larger measure of selectively accumulative advance: "a science which hesitates to forget its founders is lost."

⑤ THEORIES OF THE MIDDLE RANGE

Like so many words which are bandied about, the word *theory* threatens to become emptied of meaning. The very diversity of items to which the word is applied leads to the result that it often obscures rather than creates understanding. [...] The term *sociological theory* refers to logically interconnected conceptions which are limited and modest in scope, rather than all-embracing and grandiose. Throughout I attempt to focus attention on what might be called *theories of the middle range*: theories intermediate to the minor working hypotheses evolved in abundance during the day-by-day routines of research, and the all-inclusive speculations comprising a master conceptual scheme from which it is hoped to derive a very large number of empirically observed uniformities of social behavior.

[...] It must be admitted, I assume that the search for a total system of sociological theory, in which all manner of observations promptly find their preordained place, has the same large challenge and the same small promise as those all-encompassing philosophical systems which have fallen into deserved disuse. There are some who talk as though they expect, here and now, formulation of *the* sociological theory adequate to encompass vast ranges of precisely observed details of social behavior and fruitful enough to direct the attention of thousands of research workers to pertinent problems of empirical research. This I take to be a premature and apocalyptic belief. We are not ready. The preparatory work has not yet been done.

A sense of historical development may be sufficiently humbling to liberate these extravagant optimists from this clearly premature hope. Even they would not have expected Einstein to follow hard on the heels of Kepler. This could not be. Intervening centuries of research and systematic thought about the results of research were first needed to prepare the terrain. By all this I do not mean that sociology must uncritically adopt modest expectations simply because their elder and more experienced siblings among the sciences have done so with profit. Here, as elsewhere, unthinking imitation has little to commend it. But there are some pertinent features of the history of physical science which, properly understood, can be both instructive and encouraging. A proper appreciation of these would keep social scientists from permitting the very existence of the highly developed physical sciences to evoke these large and excessively optimistic hopes. We social scientists happen to live at a time in which some of the physical sciences have achieved comparatively great precision of theory and experiment, a great aggregate of instruments and tools, and an abundance of technological by-products. Looking about them, many social scientists take this as the standard for self-appraisal. Understandably, they want to compare biceps with their bigger brothers. They, too, want to *count*. And when it becomes evident to all who would look that they neither have the rugged physique nor pack the murderous wallop of their big brothers, the youngsters become afflicted with despair. They begin to ask: is a science of society *really* possible?

Not only would it be more modest and more realistic but also, perhaps, psychologically more rewarding to note the difference in age and hard-won experience. To perceive difference here would be to achieve proportion. It would be to avoid the error of assuming that *all cultural products existing at the same moment of history must have the same degree of intellectual maturity.* Because a discipline called physics and a discipline called sociology are both identifiable in the mid-twentieth century, it is gratuitously assumed that the achievements of the one must be the measure of the other. But this is to ignore the distinctive fore-history of each: between twentieth-century physics and twentieth-century sociology stand billions of man-hours of sustained, disciplined, and cumulative research. Perhaps sociology is not yet ready for its Einstein because it has not yet found its Kepler. Even the nonpareil Newton had, in his day, acknowledged the indispensable contribution of cumulative research, saying: "If I have seen farther, it is by standing on the shoulders of giants."

Nor is the comparison with the physical sciences the only source of this conviction among some sociologists that we must, here and now, achieve theoretical schemes on the grand scale. This belief, as premature as it is challenging, is, I believe, in part a response to the ambiguous status of sociology in contemporary West-European and American societies. (The present status of sociology in other societies is an altogether different matter: there, it is more difficult to identify the existence of sociology at all than to determine the functions of what little sociology does exist.) The very uncertainty of having accumulated knowledge adequate to the large demands now being laid upon sociology—by policymakers, reformers, and reactionaries, by business men and government men, by college presidents and college sophomores—this uncertainty provokes an overly zealous and defensive conviction among sociologists that they must somehow be equal to these demands, however premature and extravagant they may be.

Despite its psychological functions for the social scientist, this conviction involves the error of supposing that competence means adequacy to *any and all* demands, just or unjust, wise or stupid, which are made of him. Implicitly, it is the sacrilegious and masochistic error of assuming oneself to be omniscient. In effect, this belief holds that to admit less than universal knowledge is to admit failure. So it often happens in the early phases of a fledgling discipline that its exponents typically make extravagant claims to having evolved total systems of theory, adequate to the entire range of problems encompassed by the discipline. As Whitehead has observed, [...] "It is characteristic of a science in its earlier stages ... to be both ambitiously profound in its aims and trivial in its handling of details."

Complete sociological systems today, as in their day complete systems of medical theory or of chemical theory, must give way to less imposing but better grounded theories of the middle range. We cannot expect any individual to create an architectonic system of theory providing a manual for the solution of problems, social and sociological. Science, even sociological science, isn't that simple.

Like the social scientist who errs in thoughtlessly comparing himself with the *contemporary* physical scientist because of the accident that they both happen to be alive at the same instant of history, so the informed public, and strategic decision-makers in that public, often err in appraising social science, once and for all, on the basis of its present capacity to solve the large and urgent problems of society which press in on all of us. The misplaced masochism of the social scientist and the inadvertent sadism of the public both result from the same fault: failure to see that social science, like all civilization, is continually in the process of development and that there is no providential dispensation providing that, at any given moment, science must be adequate to the entire array of problems confronting men at that moment. Historical perspective might enable scientist and layman alike to see these facts of repeated experience in their fitting proportion. Otherwise it is as though the status and promise of medicine in the seventeenth century had been forever judged by its ability to produce, then and there, a preventive or cure for cardiac diseases. Suppose that the problem had been widely acknowledged to be urgent—look at the growing rate of death from coronary thrombosis!—and it might well have been that the very importance of the problem would have obscured the *entirely independent question* of the adequacy of the medical science of 1600 (or 1800 or 1900) for solving that particular problem. Yet it is precisely this illogic which lies behind so much of practical demands currently made of sociology (and the other social sciences). Because war and exploitation and poverty and discrimination and psychological insecurity are plaguing men in modern society, social science, if it is worth its salt, must provide solutions for each and all of them. It is possible, of course, that social scientists are as well equipped to solve these urgent problems *in 1955* as were Harvey or Sydenham to identify, study, and cure coronary thrombosis *in 1655*. Yet, as history shows, the inadequacy of seventeenth-century medicine in coping with this particular problem scarcely meant that it had no powers of development. If everyone were to back the sure thing, who would support the colt yet to come into his own?

This emphasis on the disproportion between the practical problems sometimes assigned the sociologist and the state of his accumulated skills and knowledge does not at all mean, of course, that the sociologist *should not* work on researches relevant for urgent practical problems, that he should deliberately seek out the pragmatically trivial problem. The emphasis is intended only to re-establish a historical sense of proportion. The urgency or immensity of a practical social problem does not entail the assurance of its solution. At any given moment, men are variously equipped to solve various problems. It should be remembered that, even by repeated popular testimony, necessity is only the mother of invention; socially accumulated knowledge is its father. Unless the two are brought together, necessity remains infertile. Yet present infertility does not mean that she may not conceive at some future time when she is properly mated. But the mate requires time (and sustenance) if he is to grow to the size and vigor needed for the demands which will be laid upon him.

From all this it would seem reasonable to suppose that sociology will advance in the degree that its major concern is with developing theories of the middle range and will be frustrated if attention centers on theory in the large. I believe that our major task *today* is to develop special theories applicable to limited ranges of data—theories, for example, of class dynamics, of conflicting group pressures, of the flow of power and the exercise of interpersonal influence—rather than to seek at once the "integrated" conceptual structure adequate to derive all these and other theories. The sociological theorist *exclusively* committed to the exploration of high abstractions runs the risk that, as with modern *decor*, the furniture of his mind will be sparse, bare, and uncomfortable. To say that both the general and the special theories are needed is to be correct and banal: the problem is one of allocating our scant resources. I am suggesting that the road to effective conceptual schemes in sociology will be the more effectively built through work on special theories, and that it will remain a largely unfulfilled plan if one seeks to build it directly at this time. So it is that in his inaugural address at the University of London, T.H. Marshall has lately put in a plea for "sociological stepping stones in the middle distance."

That this emphasis may be needed can be seen from a review of books on sociological theory. Note how few, how scattered, and, it must be said, how unimpressive the instances of specific sociological hypotheses which are *derived* from a master conceptual scheme. The basic theory (or speculation) runs so far ahead of confirmed special theories as to remain an unrealized program rather than a *consolidation* of apparently discrete theories. This is no dirge. As Talcott Parsons has indicated, much progress has lately been made. The gradual convergence of some streams of theory in social psychology, social anthropology, and sociology promises large theoretic gains. Yet, having said this, one must admit that a large part of what is now called sociological theory consists of *general orientations toward data, suggesting types of variables which need somehow to be taken into account, rather than clear, verifiable statements of relationships between specified variables.*[1] We have many concepts but few confirmed theories; many points of view, but few theorems; many "approaches," but few arrivals. Perhaps a shift in emphasis would be all to the good.

Sociological theory must advance on these interconnected planes: through special theories adequate to limited ranges of social data, and through the evolution of a more general conceptual scheme adequate to *consolidate* groups of special theories.

To concentrate entirely on special theories is to run the risk of emerging with unconnected *ad hoc* speculations consistent with a limited range of observations and inconsistent among themselves.

To concentrate entirely on the master conceptual scheme for deriving all subsidiary theories is to run the risk of producing twentieth-century sociological equivalents of the large philosophical systems of the past, with all their varied suggestiveness, all their architectonic splendor, and all their scientific sterility.

Men allocate their scant resources somehow, whether they know it or not, and this allocation reflects their workaday policies. This holds as much for the men concerned with the production of sociological theory as for the men concerned with the production of plumbing supplies. These observations, elicited by Parsons's paper on the position of sociological theory,[2] are intended to bring out one such policy decision faced by the men who practice sociological theory. Which shall have the greater share of our immediate energies and resources: the search for confirmed theories of the middle range or the search for all-inclusive conceptual schemes? I believe, and beliefs are, of course, notoriously subject to error, that for some time to come, it is the theories of the middle range which hold the largest promise,[3] *provided that,* underlying this modest search for social uniformities, there is an enduring and pervasive concern with *consolidating* the special theories into a more general set of concepts and mutually consistent propositions. Even so, we must adopt the provisional outlook of our big brothers, remembering with them, as with Tennyson, that

Our little systems have their day;
They have their day and cease to be.

* * * * *

⑤ CODIFICATION OF SOCIOLOGICAL THEORY

The second major concern [...] is that of codification, particularly the codification of substantive theory and of procedures of qualitative analysis in sociology. (Though there is no inherent reason why this should be the case, functional analysis in sociology has to this point been almost entirely qualitative in character.)

Codification involves orderly, disciplined reflection. [...] It entails the *discovery* of what has in fact been the strategic experience of scientific investigators, rather than the *invention* of new strategies of research. But the discovery of the one may facilitate the invention of the other. As here construed, codification is the orderly and compact arrangement of systematized fruitful experience with procedures of inquiry and with the substantive findings which result from the use of these procedures.

[...] I use the device of the *analytical paradigm* for presenting codified materials. [...]

Something should be said by way of explanation about the repeated use of formal paradigms such as these. I believe them to have great propaedeutic value. For one thing, they bring out into the open air for all to see the array of assumptions, concepts, and basic propositions employed in a sociological analysis. They thus minimize the inadvertent tendency to hide the hard core of analysis behind a veil of random and logically unconnected thoughts, ruminations, and comments. Sociology has few formulae, in the sense of highly abbreviated symbolic expressions of relationships between sociological variables. Consequently, sociological interpretations come to be highly discursive. The logic of procedure, the key concepts, and the relationships between variables not uncommonly become lost in an avalanche of words. They are then obscured from the reader and, at times, from the author as well, and in these instances, the critical reader must laboriously search out for himself the implicit assumptions of the author. The paradigm minimizes this tendency of the sociological theorist to deceive himself and others by the careless and unwitting employment of tacit concepts and assumptions.

Contributing to this tendency of sociological exposition to become lengthy rather than lucid is the received tradition—inherited slightly from philosophy, substantially from history, and greatly from literature—which holds that sociological accounts should be written vividly and intensely, conveying all the rich fullness of the human scene with which they deal. The sociologist who does not disavow this handsome but alien heritage becomes more intent on expressing the full individuality of his *response* to the sociological case in hand than on seeking out the generalizable, objective, and readily transmissible concepts and relationships pertinent to that case. In place of using objective concepts—the very core of a science as distinct from the arts—the sociologist who depends on his heritage from the humanities searches for the exceptional constellation of words which will best express the particularity of his experience. Too often, he is confirmed in this misplaced use of his genuine artistic skills by the plaudits of a lay public, gratefully assuring him that he writes like a novelist and not like an overly domesticated and academically henpecked Ph.D. Not infrequently, and of course not always, he pays for this popular applause, for the closer he approaches eloquence, the farther he retreats from sense. It must be acknowledged, however, as St. Augustine suggested in mild rebuttal long ago, that " ... a thing is not necessarily true because badly uttered, nor false because spoken magnificently."

Thus it is that ostensibly scientific reports become obscured by inclusion of the irrelevant. In extreme cases, the hard skeleton of fact, inference, and theoretic conclusion becomes overlaid with the soft flesh of stylistic ornamentation. Yet other disciplines—physics and chemistry are here in company with biology, geology, and statistics—have escaped this misplaced concern with the literary graces. Anchored to the purposes of science, these disciplines prefer brevity, precision, and objectivity to exquisitely rhythmic patterns of language, richness of connotation, and deep-felt verbal imagery. Because one does not subscribe to the unthinking doctrine that sociology must in all respects hew to the line laid down by chemistry, physics, or biology, one need not subscribe to the contrary doctrine that it must emulate history, discursive philosophy, or literature. Each to his last, and the last of the sociologist is that of lucidly presenting claims to logically interconnected and empirically confirmed propositions about the behavior of man in his relations with other men, and the social consequences of that behavior. Paradigms for sociological analysis are intended to help the sociologist work at his trade.

Since sound sociological interpretation inevitably *implies* some theoretic paradigm, it seems the better part of wisdom to bring it out into the open. If true art consists in concealing all signs of art, true science consists in revealing its scaffolding as well as its finished structure.

Without pretending that this tells the whole story, I suggest that paradigms for qualitative analysis in sociology have at least five closely related functions.[4]

First, paradigms have a notational function. They provide a compact parsimonious arrangement of the central concepts and their interrelations as these are utilized for description and analysis. Having one's concepts set out in sufficiently brief compass to permit their *simultaneous* inspection is an important aid to self-correction of one's successive interpretations, a result difficult to achieve when one's concepts are scattered and hidden in page after page of discursive exposition. (As may be seen from the work of Cajori on their history, this appears to be one of the major reasons for the importance of mathematical symbols: they permit the simultaneous inspection of all terms entering into the analysis.)

Second, the explicit statement of analytic paradigms lessens the likelihood of inadvertently importing hidden assumptions and concepts, since each new assumption and each new concept must be either logically *derivable* from the previous terms of the paradigm or explicitly *incorporated* in it The paradigm thus supplies a pragmatic and logical guide for the avoidance of *ad hoc* (i.e., logically irresponsible) hypotheses.

Third, paradigms advance the *cumulation* of theoretical interpretation. In this connection, we can regard the paradigm as the foundation upon which the house of interpretations is built. If a new story cannot be built directly upon the paradigmatic foundations, if it cannot be derived from the foundations, then it must be considered a new wing of the total structure, and the foundations (of concepts and assumptions) must be extended to support the new wing. Moreover, each new story which *can* be built upon the original foundations strengthens our confidence in their substantial quality just as every new extension, precisely because it requires additional foundations, leads us to suspect the soundness of the original substructure. To pursue the figure further: a paradigm in which we can justifiably repose great confidence will in due course support an interpretative structure of skyscraper dimensions, with each successive story testifying to the substantial and well-laid quality of the original foundations, whereas a defective paradigm will support only a rambling one-story structure, in which each new set of observations requires a new foundation to be laid, since the original cannot bear the weight of additional stories.

Fourth, paradigms, by their very arrangement, suggest the *systematic* cross-tabulation of presumably significant concepts and may thus sensitize the analyst to types of empirical and theoretic problems which might otherwise be overlooked. They promote *analysis* rather than concrete description. They direct our attention, for example, to the components of social behavior, to possible strains and tensions among these components, and thereby to sources of departure from the behavior which is socially expectable.

Fifth, and in this accounting, finally, paradigms make for the codification of methods of *qualitative* analysis in a manner approximating the logical, if not the empirical, rigor of *quantitative* analysis. The procedures for computing a standard deviation and the mathematical bases of these procedures are expressly codified as a matter of course: they are open to inspection by all, and the assumptions and procedures can be critically scrutinized by all who care to read. In frequent contrast to this public character of codified quantitative analysis, the sociological analysis of qualitative data is assumed to reside in a private world inhabited exclusively by penetrating but unfathomable insights and by ineffable understandings. Indeed, discursive expositions not based upon an explicit paradigm often involve perceptive interpretations; as the cant phrase has it, they are rich in "illuminating insights." But it is not always clear just which operations with analytic concepts were involved in these insights. There consequently results an aggregate of discrete insights rather than a codified body of knowledge, subject to reproducible research. In some quarters, the very suggestion that these intensely private experiences must be reshaped into publicly certifiable procedures if they are to be scientifically relevant is itself taken as a sign of blind impiety. Now, it is true that not all sociologists are blessed with the same degree of perceptiveness any more than all cabbage heads are blessed with the same degree of succulence as Brussels sprouts. Yet the procedures of even the most perceptive of sociologists must be standardizable and the results of their insights testable by others. Science, and this includes sociological science, is public, not private. It is not that we average sociologists wish to cut all talents to our own small stature; it is only, we suggest, that the contributions of the great and small alike must be codified if they are to advance the development of sociology.

Since all virtues can readily become vices merely by being carried to excess, the sociological paradigm can be abused almost as easily as it can be used. It is a temptation to mental indolence. Equipped with his paradigm, the sociologist may shut his eyes to strategic data not expressly called for in the paradigm. He may turn the paradigm from a sociological field-glass into a sociological blinker. Misuse results from absolutizing the paradigm rather than using it tentatively, as a point of departure.

The paradigms [...] are, without exception, provisional, undoubtedly destined to be modified in the immediate future as they have been in the recent past. But for the time being, these explicit paradigms seem preferable to tacit assumptions.

NOTES

1.   [...] For a recent suggestion that convergence rather than continued division has characterized recent developments in sociological theory, see George A. Lundberg, "The natural science trend in sociology," *American Journal of Sociology*, 1955, 61, 191–202. It must be acknowledged, however, that in substantial measure the convergence is that of general orientation rather than that of sociological theory. But manifestly, not everything can happen at once; the gain in convergence is real even though it is partial rather than complete.

2.   This refers to the paper later reprinted as Chapter I of Talcott Parsons, *Essays in Sociological Theory: Pure and Applied* (Glencoe: The Free Press, 1949); for further discussion, see Chapter XVII of the revised edition, 1954.

3.   For a careful formulation of logical requirements of theories of the middle range, see Hans L. Zetterberg, *On Theory and Verification in Sociology* (Stockholm: Almqvist & Wiksell; New York: The Tressler Press, 1954); for observations on the distinctive characteristics of theories of the middle range, see Frank H. Hankins, "A forty-year perspective," *Sociology and Social Research*, 1956, 40, 391–98; Jiri Nehnevajsa, "Reflections on theories and sociometric systems," *International Journal of Sociometry*, 1956, 1, 8–15; Peter H. Rossi, "Methods of social research, 1945–55," in *Sociology in the United States of America: A Trend Report,* edited by Hans L. Zetterberg (Unesco, 1956), 21–34, esp. at 23 ff. It should be noted, however, that the empirical testability of theories of the middle range is not their only or their major attribute. Rather, it is the double tact that the concepts in such theories involve a middling level of generality: that they are specific enough to be effectively utilized in organizing the evidence bearing upon determinate ranges of social phenomena and general enough to be consolidated into increasingly broader sets of generalizations.

4. The next few pages are a paraphrase and extension of the appendix to the paper on "Discrimination and the American creed," in *Discrimination and National Welfare*, edited by R.M. MacIver (New York: Harper & Brothers, 1948). For other discussions of the use of qualitative paradigms in sociology, see P.F. Lazarsfeld, "Some remarks on the typological procedure in social research," *Zeitschrift fur Sozialforschung*, 1937, 6, 119–139; C.G. Hempel and P. Oppenheim, *Der Typusbegriff im Lichte der neuen Logik* (Leiden: A. W. Sijthoff, 1936), esp. 44–101.

PART I

Structural Functionalism

CRITICAL THINKING QUESTIONS

Parsons

1. How can Parsons's distinction between positive and negative aspects of the problem of motivation be applied to contemporary social issues?
2. What are the functional prerequisites of social systems, and what characteristics do they exhibit?
3. What does Parsons mean by "situations"? What factors influence courses of action in different situations?

Merton

1. What are some of the ways in which Robert Merton's sociological theory differs from Talcott Parsons's?
2. What are theories of the "middle range," and how can Merton's conception of functionalism apply to North American politics today?
3. Using Merton's approach to sociological theory and research, how can sociologists investigate social problems such as homelessness, racism, or homophobia?

SUGGESTED READINGS

Camic, Charles. 1992. "Reputation and Predecessor Selection: Parsons and the Institutionalists." *American Journal of Sociology* 57: 421–445.

The writings of Talcott Parsons are often said to be indebted to Marx, Weber, Durkheim, and Marshall on the basis of an intellectual "fit" or fundamental compatibility. Camic argues, however, that reputational factors, particularly at Harvard University in the 1920s and 1930s, demonstrated a significant influence on Parsons's decision to align himself with European figures rather than with his American teachers (at Amherst College). The paper develops insight into "predecessor selection" as a process involving more than just "good ideas."

Kroeber, Alfred L., and Talcott Parsons. 1958. "The Concept of Culture and of Social System." *American Sociological Review* 23: 582–583.

In this classic article, anthropologist Alfred Kroeber, along with Talcott Parsons, defines culture as "transmitted and created content and patterns of values, ideas, and other symbolic-meaningful systems as factors in the shaping of human behavior and the artifacts produced through behavior" (p. 583). Their argument is that culture is tightly connected to interpersonal communications, and although they do not identify culture with values exclusively, they do emphasize the importance of values in cultural configurations. The article demonstrates some of Parsons's influence outside sociology.

Lackey, Pat N. 1987. *Invitation to Talcott Parsons' Theory*. Houston: CAP and Gown Press.

Lackey's book is unique in that it avoids treating Parsons's work in terms of divisions corresponding to the publications of his major writings. Rather, this analysis makes an effort to explicate the continuities of Parsons's theoretical work. Lackey offers a strong representation of Parsons's ideas, and he offers a critique in his final chapter. There is also a useful survey of Parsons's career and writing presented in the first chapter.

Merton, Robert. 1965. *On the Shoulders of Giants*. New York: New York Free Press.

In the 17th century, Sir Isaac Newton wrote: "If I have seen farther, it is by standing on the shoulders of giants." Reminiscent of 12th-century theology, this quotation addresses the simple argument that predecessors matter, that past knowledge is a useful foundation for present work, and, perhaps most important for Merton, that younger thinkers are the most capable of advancing levels of understanding and argumentation. Merton uses the quotation to embark on an analysis of creativity, tradition, progress, and knowledge dissemination in sociological research.

Turner, Bryan S. 1999. *The Talcott Parsons Reader*. Oxford: Blackwell Publishers.

This book takes a critical approach to Parsons's work, and it devotes particular attention to allegations concerning Parsons's conservative functional theory. It presents selections from Parsons's writings and offers an overview of his major contributions. The book is divided into several sections: religion and modern society; life, sex, and death; sociological theory; and American society and the world order.

RELATED WEB SITES

Biographies of Sociologists: Talcott Parsons
This Web site, run by the Department of Sociology and Anthropology at the University of Canterbury, not only offers biographical information on Parsons, but also offers links to other Web sites dealing with Parsons's life and works.
www.soci.canterbury.ac.nz/resources/biograph/parsons.shtml

Famous Sociologists
Perhaps meant as a reminder of Merton's "On the Shoulders of Giants," this Web site offers the subtitle "Strong Shoulders to Stand on." Part of SocioSite, based at the University of Amsterdam, the link offers an impressive range of social theorists. Links are offered to selections of Parsons's and Merton's writings.
www2.fmg.uva.nl/sociosite/topics/sociologists.html

Robert K. Merton's Functional Analysis Resource Page
This is a Web site designed for undergraduate students. There are links offered to resources on Merton, as well as a general glossary of sociological terms.
www.faculty.rsu.edu~felwell/Theorists/Merton

Robert Merton, 1910–2003
This Web site offers links to Merton's curriculum vitae, select publications, and a list of his writings. There are also useful links to Merton's papers that are available on-line.
www.garfield.library.upenn.edu/merton/list.html

Talcott Parsons, 1902–1979
This Web site offers a range of information on Parsons, from history and biography to his analytic approach. There is a PowerPoint slide show available. There is also a wide selection of theorists offered at the home site www.bolender.com/Sociological%20Theory/sociological%20Theorists.htm
www.bolender.com/Sociological%20Theory/Parsons,%20Talcott/parsons,_talcott.htm

PART II

Class, Conflict, and the State

ALTHOUGH STRUCTURAL FUNCTIONALISM REMAINED INFLUENTIAL IN AMERICAN sociology into the 1960s, a theoretical shift in sociological thought was on the horizon. In 1959, C. Wright Mills published *The Sociological Imagination*, in which he criticized Parsons for developing a "grand theory" that is neither "readily understandable nor altogether intelligible" (p. 27).[1] It is true, as we learn from the passages in the previous section, that Talcott Parsons's writings are not always so easy to understand—a characteristic realized by Parsons's critics and supporters alike. In fact, it is rumoured that after Parsons announced that one of his books had been translated into the nth language, the then-chairperson of Harvard Sociology, Pitirim Sorokin, sarcastically asked whether it had been translated into English yet (Lackey 1987).

The thrust of Mills's critique was that Parsons offered to American sociology a form of abstracted empiricism that failed to appreciate the significance of public issues and personal troubles in the context of asymmetrical power relations, conflict, and social inequality. Mills sought to invigorate sociological discourse with a form of radicalism that was critical of the status quo—distinguishing his critique from functionalists who took issue with Parsons's work—and he was inspired by a political orientation set in the Marxian tradition. This is to suggest neither that Mills was a Marxist nor that he should be credited with bringing Marxism to North American sociology. Throughout the early 1900s, Marxian themes were developed in the writings of thinkers associated with the Institute for Social Research at the University of Frankfurt, and there were certainly Marxian themes to be found in the contributions of W.E.B. Du Bois (1903) and Oliver Cromwell Cox (1948) concerning class relations and American racial politics. Nevertheless, Mills's book was significant because it enjoyed a position of influence: many sociologists were more familiar with his attack on Parsons than they were with Parsons's actual work (Ritzer 2000).

However much sociologists may have agreed with Mills's analysis—and however much influence the book had—it is undeniable that politics in America were changing. Throughout the 1950s, communism (and, by popular association, Marxism) was bitterly rejected, and the economic and political climate was hostile to deviations from post-war economic triumphalism. Sociological discourse mirrored this social conservativism not only with the kind of apolitical explanation for social inequality that explained social stratification as functionally necessary (Davis and Moore 1945), but also with an emphasis on developing a scientific sociology separate from value judgments and personal motivations. By the 1960s, however, the civil rights movement was gaining momentum in consort with anti-Vietnam protests, and advances in the women's movement and the student movement had been made. Critiques of value-free, objective sociological research appeared with greater frequency, and Marxian sociological contributions to the study of social inequality were beginning to make their way into mainstream sociology.

⌐ SECTION READINGS: JOHN PORTER, ANTONIO GRAMSCI, IMMANUEL WALLERSTEIN, AND LEO PANITCH

The opening passage is written by one of the most famous sociologists in Canadian history: John Porter. Porter (1921–1979) taught at Carleton University throughout the 1950s and 1960s when sociology in Canada was only beginning to develop. University-level sociology courses were offered in Canada as early as 1910, and McGill University was offering a sociology program by 1925. But Canadian sociologists in the 1950s were scarce; there were only 32 university-based sociologists in the country in 1956, and the two largest departments had no more than six members each (Helmes-Hayes 2002).

The dearth of Canadian sociologists was matched by a dearth of sociological research concerned with Canadian social structure. The Chicago-trained sociologist Everett Hughes had published *French Canada in Transition* in 1922 while working at McGill, and University of Toronto sociologist S.D. Clark published *The Social Development of Canada* in 1942. McGill's Carl Dawson had also published *An Introduction to Sociology* (1929) with Warner E. Gettys. But there existed neither a fully Canadian sociology textbook, nor a professional Canadian professional sociology journal devoted to analyses of distinctively Canadian sociological issues.[2]

Enter John Porter. Caught up in the expansion of post-secondary education in Canada, and the concomitant institutional development of the discipline of sociology, Porter published *The Vertical Mosaic: An Analysis of Class and Power* in 1965. Perhaps best conceptualized as the Canadian counterpart to C. Wright Mills's *The Power Elite* (1956), the publication of *TVM* was significant. The year following its appearance, the book was awarded the American Sociological Association's MacIver Award, the first and only book written by a Canadian and/or about Canada ever to win the award. It became the most cited book in Canadian sociological history, and it has sold more copies than any other sociology book published by the

University of Toronto Press (Helmes-Hayes and Curtis 1998). More important than the acclaim it received, however, was the book's substantive critique of Canadian social structure.

Porter introduces *The Vertical Mosaic* with the argument that one of the most persistent images that Canadians hold regarding their country is that it is not stratified along class lines. He explains that the affluence characterizing Canadian society after the Second World War was a major component in the consolidation of an image of middle-class uniformity. The social image of a unified middle class, he argues, was not only consolidated by, but continued to be reproduced through, outlets such as modern advertising, consumer magazines, and the work of intellectuals. The latter is particularly important for Porter because Canadian intellectuals in the 1960s neither originated in large numbers from the lower or upper classes, nor were they recruited in large numbers in Canada. For Porter, not only did this lead to an image of social equality, extracted from historical writings on the 19th-century Canadian frontier environment, but it also led to the exclusion of the experiences of members of the lower and upper class in Canada. The consequence, he reasons, is a continuing absence of intellectual criticism of the existing social order.

The theme of intellectuals in the production and maintenance of social order is crucial in the writings of Antonio Gramsci. For Gramsci (1891–1937), the notion of "intellectuals" as a social category existing independent of the class structure is nonsense. But so, too, is the conception of intellectuals as a special class of learned men pursuing objective truths and higher levels of understanding or insight. He explains that all men [sic] are potential intellectuals in the sense that all men have an intellect and use it. But not all men are intellectuals by social (class) function. What this means is that it is no more useful to look to the specific qualities of the labouring activities of the proletarian class(es) to understand the dynamics of capitalist production than it is to analyze the contents of intellectual work in an effort to understand the role of intellectuals in the wider relations of political and economic production.

Gramsci outlines two general categories of intellectuals by social function. First, the social category of the traditional intellectual encompasses a group of professional intellectuals of the variety students are most likely to encounter in the university. Also included in this group are clergymen, philosophers, and literary figures. Traditional intellectuals consider themselves, and are considered by the general population, to exist independently of historically specific dominant/ruling groups. Although they possess an aura of historical continuity independent of class relations, their contemporary institutional existence can be traced to the historical formation of the dominant social group at any given historical moment.

The second type of intellectual identified by Gramsci is the organic intellectual. Organic intellectuals are the thinking and organizing elements of the ruling class—the "deputies" who are entrusted with the organizing components of the social system. They grow "organically" with the dominant class, and it is this group of people that is most responsible for maintaining hegemonic relations. Because the organic intellectuals maintain hegemonic relations within the ruling class, the challenge for revolutionary political activity is the development of "permanent persuaders": a group of organic intellectuals that grows with the subordinated class(es). Organic intellectuals in the subordinated class(es) are defined by social function rather than the characteristics of formal education, cultural distinction, or social status. The creation of this new stratum of organic intellectual, Gramsci explains, must be an element of "general practical activity" that is closely bound to modern industrial labour. What he means is that the permanent pursuader is one who is engaged in practical (organic) activity, and who is able to evoke feeling and passion from within the subordinated class(es). He refers to feeling and passion because the consolidation of hegemony and, by implication, counter-hegemony involves more than the control of dominant ideas for Gramsci; the consolidation of mass consent necessitates that people identify with, and feel passionate about, the world in which they live (and the world they want to live in!).

Porter's and Gramsci's identification of a link between the perpetuation of social order and the production of conservative intellectual knowledge is related to arguments presented in the third reading passage. In this passage, Immanuel Wallerstein also identifies the role of intellectuals (ideologists) as an impediment to progressive scholarly insight. While he was professor of sociology at McGill University (1971–1975), Wallerstein (1930–) initiated a multi-decade study of the modern capitalist world system that culminated in numerous publications, a series of awards and accolades, a research centre, and a specialized journal (Hier 2001). The first argument that he makes in the reading passage is that the Industrial Revolution brought with it a number of ideologists whose methodological analyses of capitalism prioritized discrete categories or stages of social development (including some strands of Marxism) at the level of the nation-state. The problem with the ideologists and their contemporary counterparts is that they fail to appreciate the continuity and totality of social systems. The consequence, he contends, is a sequence of concepts that fail to capture the empirical reality of the world capitalist economy.

Wallerstein argues that since 1640, the social system has taken the form of a world system that exhibits a division of labour characterized by an economic interdependency within a framework of multiple polities and cultures. He maintains that over the duration of "the long sixteenth century" (1450–1640), the capitalist world system emerged in its first stage of development in northwest Europe. For Wallerstein, the analysis of capitalism as a world system necessitates a comparative conceptual apparatus capable of accounting for the importance of military force, ideological commitment, and social stratification, as well as the internal and external dilemmas of hegemony and rule. Wallerstein's approach is heavily materialist, in that mass legitimation of the world system is not as crucial to the survival of the system as the structural integrity of its gradations (core, periphery, semi-periphery).

He contends, however, that the decline of U.S. hegemony and gains made by countries in the semi-periphery after 1970 have polarized the system. Given the structural imperatives of the world economy, he projects that consolidation of the world economy brings with it two contradictions that raise important questions about the emergence of a socialist world government.

In the final passage, York University political scientist Leo Panitch (1945–) reflects on the new critical theory of the state that began to develop in Canadian academics in the late 1960s. The new theory of the state, he explains, was situated in the Marxian tradition of social transformation, but it addressed two additional imperatives for academic intellectuals. First, it prioritized the need for transformative academic politics to develop in conjunction with the working class. And second, it maintained a focus on the Marxian project of transformation and the imperative to resist analytic frameworks sympathetic to New Right conceptions of the state and market, particularly in the context of globalization. He contends that in the context of the New Right's accelerated integration of capital and the state, the reinvigoration of Marxian social theory can achieve a better understanding of the ways in which the state must be restructured, and the ways in which egalitarian reform may be achieved. For Panitch, one of the central imperatives before sociologists and political scientists is to overcome the impoverishment of state theory.

NOTES

1. *The Sociological Imagination* was the culmination of several studies that Mills published. See, for example, his critiques of American white-collar crime (1951) and economic and political power (1956).
2. *The Canadian Review of Sociology and Anthropology,* Canada's first sociology journal, was established in 1964.

REFERENCES

Clark, S.D. 1942. *The Social Development of Canada.* Toronto: University of Toronto Press.

Cox, Oliver C. 1948. *Caste, Class, and Race.* New York: Modern Reader Paperbacks.

Davis, Kingsley, and Wilbert Moore. 1945. "Some Principles of Stratification." *American Sociological Review* 10: 242–249.

Dawson, Carl, and Warner Gettys. 1948. *An Introduction to Sociology.* New York: Ronald.

Du Bois, W.E.B. 1903. *Souls of Black Folk.* Chicago: A.C. McClurg.

Helmes-Hayes, Rick. 2002. "John Porter: Canada's Most Famous Sociologist (and His Links to American Sociology)." *The American Sociologist* (Spring): 79–104.

Helmes-Hayes, Rick, and James Curtis. 1998. *The Vertical Mosaic Revisited.* Toronto: University of Toronto Press.

Hier, Sean P. 2001. "The Forgotten Architect: Cox, Wallerstein, and World-System Theory." *Race and Class* 42, 3: 69–86.

Hughes, Everett. 1943. *French Canada in Transition*. Chicago: University of Chicago Press.

Lackey, Pat N. 1987. *Invitation to Talcott Parsons' Theory*. Houston: Cap and Gown Press.

Mills, C.W. 1951. *White Collar*. New York: Oxford University Press.

_____. 1956. *The Power Elite*. New York: Oxford University Press.

_____. 1959. *The Sociological Imagination*. New York: Oxford University Press.

Porter, John. 1965. *The Vertical Mosaic: An Analysis of Class and Power*. Toronto: University of Toronto Press.

Ritzer, George. 2000. *Modern Sociological Theory* (5th ed.). New York: McGraw-Hill.

CHAPTER 3

Class and Power: The Major Themes

JOHN PORTER

🔲 THE CANADIAN MIDDLE CLASS IMAGE

One of the most persistent images that Canadians have of their society is that it has no classes. This image becomes translated into the assertion that Canadians are all relatively equal in their possessions, in the amount of money they earn, and in the opportunities which they and their children have to get on in the world. An important element in this image of classlessness is that, with the absence of formal aristocracy and aristocratic institutions, Canada is a society in which equalitarian values have asserted themselves over authoritarian values. Canada, it is thought, shares not only a continent with the United States, but also a democratic ideology which rejects the historical class and power structures of Europe.

Social images are one thing and social realities another. Yet the two are not completely separate. Social images are not entirely fictional characters with only a coincidental likeness to a real society, living or dead. Often the images can be traced to an earlier historical period of the society, its golden age perhaps, which, thanks to the historians, is held up, long after it has been transformed into something else, as a model way of life. As well as their historical sources, images can be traced to their contemporary creators, particularly in the world of the mass media and popular culture. When a society's writers, journalists, editors, and other image-creators are a relatively small and closely linked group, and have more or less the same social background, the images they produce can, because they are consistent, appear to be much more true to life than if their group were larger, less cohesive, and more heterogeneous in composition.

The historical source of the image of a classless Canada is the equality among pioneers in the frontier environment of the last century. In the early part of the present century there was a similar equality of status among those who were settlers in the west, although [...] these settlers were by no means treated equally. A rural, agricultural, primary producing society is a much less differentiated society than one which has highly concentrated industries in large cities. Equality in the rural society may be much more apparent than real, but the rural environment has been for Canada an important source of the image of equality. [...] The historical image has become out of date with the transformation of Canadian society from the rural to the urban type.

Although the historical image of rural equality lingers it has gradually given way in the urban industrial setting to an image of a middle level classlessness in which there is a general uniformity of possessions. For families these possessions include a separate dwelling with an array of electrical equipment, a car, and perhaps a summer cottage. Family members, together or as individuals, engage in a certain amount of ritualistic behaviour in churches and service clubs. Modern advertising has done much to standardize the image of middle-class consumption levels and middle-class behaviour. Consumers' magazines are devoted to the task of constructing the ideal way of life through articles on child-rearing, homemaking, sexual behaviour, health, sports, and hobbies. Often, too, corporations which do not produce family commodities directly will have large advertisements to demonstrate how general social well-being at this middle level is an outcome of their own operations.

That there is neither very rich nor very poor in Canada is an important part of the image. There are no barriers to opportunity. Education is free. Therefore, making use of it is largely a question of personal ambition. Even university education is available to all, except that it may require for some a little more summer work and thrift. There is a view widely held by many university graduates that they, and most other graduates, have worked their way through college. Consequently it is felt anyone else can do the same.

In some superficial respects the image of middle-class uniformity may appear plausible. The main values of the society are concerned with the consumption of commodities, and in the so-called affluence that has followed World War II there seem to have been commodities for everybody, except, perhaps, a small group of the permanently poor at the bottom. Credit facilities are available for large numbers of low-income families, enabling them, too, to be consumers of commodities over and above the basic necessities of life. The vast array of credit facilities, some of them extraordinarily ingenious, have inequalities built into them, in that the cost of borrowing money varies with the amount already possessed. There are vast differences in the quality of goods bought by the middle-income levels and the lower-income levels. One commodity, for instance, which low-income families can rarely purchase is privacy, particularly the privacy of a house to themselves. It is perhaps the value of privacy and the capacity to afford it which has become the dividing line between the real and the apparent middle class.

If low-income families achieve high consumption levels it is usually through having more than one income earner in the household. Often this is the wife and mother, but it may be an older child who has left school, and who is expected to contribute to the family budget. Alternatively, high consumption levels may be achieved at a cost in leisure. Many low-income family heads have two jobs, a possibility which has arisen with the shorter working day and the five-day week.

This "moonlighting," as it is called in labour circles, tends to offset the progress which has been made in raising the level of wages and reducing the hours of work. There is no way of knowing how extensive "moonlighting" is, except that we know that trade unions denounce it as a practice which tends to take away the gains which have been obtained for workers. For large segments of the population, therefore, a high level of consumption is obtained by means which are alien to a true middle-class standard. [...]

At the high end of the social class spectrum, also in contrast to the middle level image, are the families of great wealth and influence. They are not perhaps as ostentatious as the very wealthy of other societies, and Canada has no "celebrity world" with which these families must-compete for prestige in the way Mills has suggested is important for the very rich in American society.[1]

Almost every large Canadian city has its wealthy and prominent families of several generations. They have their own social life, their children go to private schools, they have their clubs and associations, and they take on the charitable and philanthropic roles which have so long been the "duty" of those of high status. Although this upper class is always being joined by the new rich, it still contributes [...] far more than its proportionate share to the elite of big business. The concentration of wealth in the upper classes is indicated by the fact that in Canada in 1955 the top one per cent of income recipients received about 40 per cent of all income from dividends.

Images which conflict with the one of middle-class equality rarely find expression, partly because the literate middle class is both the producer and the consumer of the image. Even at times in what purports to be serious social analysis, middle-class intellectuals project the image of their own class onto the social classes above and below them. There is scarcely any critical analysis of Canadian social life upon which a conflicting image could be based. The idea of class differences has scarcely entered into the stream of Canadian academic writing despite the fact that class differences stand in the way of implementing one of the most important values of western society, that is equality.[2] The fact [...] that Canada draws its intellectuals either from abroad or from its own middle class means that there is almost no one producing a view of the world which reflects the experience of the poor or the underprivileged. It was as though they did not exist. [...]

Closely related to differences in class levels are differences in the exercising of power and decision-making in the society. Often it is thought that once a society becomes an electoral democracy based on universal suffrage power becomes diffused throughout the general population so that everyone participates somehow in the selection of social goals. There is, however, a whole range of institutional resistances to the transfer of power to a democratic political system. [...] Class differences create very great differences in life chances, among which are the chances of individuals' reaching the higher levels of political, economic, and other forms of power. The structure of power reflects the structure of class, for class determines the routes and barriers to advancement up our institutional hierarchies. Power is used to perpetuate a given structure of class. [...] Class barriers act to prevent the full use of Canada's human resources in an age when high levels of skill are essential to future development.

* * * * *

NOTES

1.   C.W. Mills, *The Power Elite* (New York, 1956), chap. 4.
2.   Nor does class appear as a theme in Canadian literature. See R.L. McDougall, "The Dodo and the Cruising Auk," *Canadian Literature*, no. 18 (Autumn 1963).

CHAPTER 4

The Intellectuals

Antonio Gramsci

⑤ THE FORMATION OF THE INTELLECTUALS

Are intellectuals an autonomous and independent social group, or does every social group have its own particular specialised category of intellectuals? The problem is a complex one, because of the variety of forms assumed to date by the real historical process of formation of the different categories of intellectuals.

The most important of these forms are two:

1. Every social group, coining into existence on the original terrain of an essential function in the world of economic production, creates together with itself, organically, one or more strata[1] of intellectuals which give it homogeneity and an awareness of its own function not only in the economic but also in the social and political fields. The capitalist entrepreneur creates alongside himself the industrial technician, the specialist in political economy, the organisers of a new culture, of a new legal system, etc. It should be noted that the entrepreneur himself represents a higher level of social elaboration, already characterised by a certain directive [*dirigente*][2] and technical (i.e., intellectual) capacity: he must have a certain technical capacity, not only in the limited sphere of his activity and initiative but in other spheres as well, at least in those which are closest to economic production. He must be an organiser of masses of men; he must be an organiser of the "confidence" of investors in his business, of the customers for his product, etc.

If not all entrepreneurs, at least an *elite* amongst them must have the capacity to be an organiser of society in general, including all its complex organism of services, right up to the state organism, because of the need to create the conditions most favourable to the expansion of their own class; or at the least they must possess the capacity to choose the deputies (specialised employees) to whom to entrust this activity of organising the general system of relationships external to the business itself. It can be observed that the "organic" intellectuals, which every new class creates alongside itself and elaborates in the course of its development, are for the most part "specialisations" of partial aspects of the primitive activity of the new social type which the new class has brought into prominence.[3]

Even feudal lords were possessors of a particular technical capacity, military capacity, and it is precisely from the moment at which the aristocracy loses its monopoly of technico-military capacity that the crisis of feudalism begins. But the formation of intellectuals in the feudal world and in the preceding classical world is a question to be examined separately: this formation and elaboration follows ways and means which must be studied concretely. Thus it is to be noted that the mass of the peasantry, although it performs an essential function in the world of production, does not elaborate its own "organic" intellectuals, nor does it "assimilate" any stratum of "traditional" intellectuals, although it is from the peasantry that other social groups draw many of their intellectuals and a high proportion of traditional intellectuals are of peasant origin.[4]

2. However, every "essential" social group which emerges into history out of the preceding economic structure, and as an expression of a development of this structure, has found (at least in all of history up to the present) categories of intellectuals already in existence and which seemed indeed to represent an historical continuity uninterrupted even by the most complicated and radical changes in political and social forms.

The most typical of these categories of intellectuals is that of the ecclesiastics, who for a long time (for a whole phase of history, which is partly characterised by this very monopoly) held a monopoly of a number of important services: religious ideology, that is the philosophy and science of the age, together with schools, education, morality, justice, charity, good works, etc. The category of ecclesiastics can be considered the category of intellectuals organically bound to the landed aristocracy. It had equal status juridically with the aristocracy, with which it shared the exercise of feudal ownership of land, and the use of state privileges connected with property.[5] But the monopoly held by the ecclesiastics in the superstructural field[6] was not exercised without a struggle or without limitations, and hence there took place the birth, in various forms (to be gone into and studied concretely), of other categories, favoured and enabled to expand by the growing strength of the central power of the monarch, right up to absolutism. Thus we find the formation of the *noblesse de robe*, with its own privileges, a stratum of administrators, etc., scholars and scientists, theorists, non-ecclesiastical philosophers, etc.

Since these various categories of traditional intellectuals experience through an *"esprit de corps"* their uninterrupted historical continuity and their special qualification, they thus put themselves forward as autonomous and independent of the dominant social group. This self-assessment is not without consequences in the ideological and political field, consequences of wide-ranging import. The whole of idealist philosophy can easily be connected with this position assumed by the social complex of intellectuals and can be defined as the expression of that social Utopia by which the intellectuals think of themselves as "independent," autonomous, endowed with a character of their own, etc.

One should note, however, that if the Pope and the leading hierarchy of the Church consider themselves more linked to Christ and to the apostles than they are to senators Agnelli and Benni,[7] the same does not hold for Gentile and Croce, for example: Croce in particular feels himself closely linked to Aristotle and Plato, but he does not conceal, on the other hand, his links with senators Agnelli and Benni, and it is precisely here that one can discern the most significant character of Croce's philosophy.

What are the "maximum" limits of acceptance of the term "intellectual"? Can one find a unitary criterion to characterise equally all the diverse and disparate activities of intellectuals and to distinguish these at the same time and in an essential way from the activities of other social groupings? The most widespread error of method seems to me that of having looked for this criterion of distinction in the intrinsic nature of intellectual activities, rather than in the ensemble of the system of relations in which these activities (and therefore the intellectual groups who personify them) have their place within the general complex of social relations. Indeed the worker or proletarian, for example, is not specifically characterised by his manual or instrumental work, but by performing this work in specific conditions and in specific social relations (apart from the consideration that purely physical labour does not exist and that even Taylor's phrase of "trained gorilla"[8] is a metaphor to indicate a limit in a certain direction: in any physical work, even the most degraded and mechanical, there exists a minimum of technical qualification, that is, a minimum of creative intellectual activity). And we have already observed that the entrepreneur, by virtue of his very function, must have to some degree a certain number of qualifications of an intellectual nature, although his part in society is determined not by these, but by the general social relations which specifically characterise the position of the entrepreneur within industry.

All men are intellectuals, one could therefore say: but not all men have in society the function of intellectuals.[9]

When one distinguishes between intellectuals and non-intellectuals, one is referring in reality only to the immediate social function of the professional category of the intellectuals, that is, one has in mind the direction in which their specific professional activity is weighted, whether towards intellectual elaboration or towards muscular-nervous effort. This means that, although one can speak of intellectuals, one cannot speak of non-intellectuals, because non-intellectuals do not exist. But even the relationship between efforts of intellectual-cerebral elaboration and muscular-nervous effort is not always the same, so that there are varying degrees of specific intellectual activity. There is no human activity from which every form of intellectual participation can be excluded: *homo faber* cannot be separated from *homo sapiens*.[10] Each man, finally, outside his professional activity, carries on some form of intellectual activity, that is, he is a "philosopher," an artist, a man of taste, he participates in a particular conception of the world, has a conscious line of moral conduct, and therefore contributes to sustain a conception of the world or to modify it, that is, to bring into being new modes of thought.

The problem of creating a new stratum of intellectuals consists, therefore, in the critical elaboration of the intellectual activity that exists in everyone at a certain degree of development, modifying its relationship with the muscular-nervous effort towards a new equilibrium, and ensuring that the muscular-nervous effort itself, in so far as it is an element of a general practical activity, which is perpetually innovating the physical and social world, becomes the foundation of a new and integral conception of the world. The traditional and vulgarised type of the intellectual is given by the man of letters, the philosopher, the artist. Therefore, journalists, who claim to be men of letters, philosophers, artists, also regard themselves as the "true" intellectuals. In the modern world, technical education, closely bound to industrial labour even at the most primitive and unqualified level, must form the basis of the new type of intellectual.

On this basis the weekly *Ordine Nuovo*[11] worked to develop certain forms of new intellectualism and to determine its new concepts, and this was not the least of the reasons for its success, since such a conception corresponded to latent aspirations and conformed to the development of the real forms of life. The mode of being of the new intellectual can no longer consist in eloquence, which is an exterior and momentary mover of feelings and passions, but in active participation in practical life, as constructor, organiser, "permanent persuader" and not just a simple orator (but superior at the same time to the abstract mathematical spirit); from technique-as-work one proceeds to technique-as-science and to the humanistic conception of history, without which one remains "specialised" and does not become "directive"[12] (specialised and political).

Thus there are historically formed specialised categories for the exercise of the intellectual function. They are formed in connection with all social groups, but especially in connection with the more important, and they undergo more extensive and complex elaboration in connection with the dominant social group. One of the most important characteristics of any group that is developing towards dominance is its struggle to assimilate and to conquer "ideologically" the traditional intellectuals, but this assimilation and conquest is made quicker and more efficacious the more the group in question succeeds in simultaneously elaborating its own organic intellectuals.

The enormous development of activity and organisation of education in the broad sense in the societies that emerged from the medieval world is an index of the importance assumed in the modern world by intellectual functions and categories. Parallel with the attempt to deepen and to broaden the "intellectuality" of each individual, there has also been an attempt to multiply and narrow the various specialisations. This can be seen from educational institutions at all levels, up to and including the organisms that exist to promote so-called "high culture" in all fields of science and technology.

School is the instrument through which intellectuals of various levels are elaborated. The complexity of the intellectual function in different states can be measured objectively by the number and gradation of specialised schools: the more extensive the "area" covered by education and the more numerous the "vertical" "levels" of schooling, the more complex is the cultural world, the civilisation, of a particular state. A point of comparison can be found in the sphere of industrial technology: the industrialisation of a country can be measured by how well equipped it is in the production of machines with which to produce machines, and in the manufacture of ever more accurate instruments for making both machines and further instruments for making machines, etc. The country which is best equipped in the construction of instruments for experimental scientific laboratories and in the construction of instruments with which to test the first instruments can be regarded as the most complex in the technical-industrial field, with the highest level of civilisation, etc. The same applies to the preparation of intellectuals and to the schools dedicated to this preparation; schools and institutes of high culture can be assimilated to each other. In this field also, quantity cannot be separated from quality. To the most refined technical-cultural specialisation there cannot but correspond the maximum possible diffusion of primary education and the maximum care taken to expand the middle grades numerically as much as possible. Naturally this need to provide the widest base possible for the selection and elaboration of the top intellectual qualifications—i.e., to give a democratic structure to high culture and top-level technology—is not without its disadvantages: it creates the possibility of vast crises of unemployment for the middle intellectual strata, and in all modern societies this actually takes place.

It is worth noting that the elaboration of intellectual strata in concrete reality does not take place on the terrain of abstract democracy but in accordance with very concrete traditional historical processes. Strata have grown up which traditionally "produce" intellectuals and these strata coincide with those which have specialised in "saving," i.e., the petty and middle landed/ bourgeoisie and certain strata of the petty and middle urban; bourgeoisie. The varying distribution of different types of school (classical and professional)[13] over the "economic" territory and the varying aspirations of different categories within these strata determine, or give form to, the production of various branches of intellectual specialisation. Thus in Italy the rural bourgeoisie produces in particular state functionaries and professional people, whereas the urban bourgeoisie produces technicians for industry. Consequently it is largely northern Italy which produces technicians and the South which produces functionaries and professional men.

The relationship between the intellectuals and the world of production is not as direct as it is with the fundamental social groups but is, in varying degrees, "mediated" by the whole fabric of society and by the complex of superstructures, of which the intellectuals are, precisely, the "functionaries." It should be possible both to measure the "organic quality" [*organicita*] of the various intellectual strata and their degree of connection with a fundamental social group, and to establish a gradation of their functions and of the superstructures from the bottom to the top (from the structural base upwards). What we can do, for the moment, is to fix two major superstructural "levels": the one that can be called "civil society," that is the ensemble of organisms commonly called "private," and that of "political society" or "the State." These two levels correspond on the one hand to the function of "hegemony," which the dominant group exercises throughout society and on the other hand to that of "direct domination" or command exercised through the State and "juridical" government. The functions in question are precisely organisational and connective. The intellectuals are the dominant group's "deputies" exercising the subaltern functions of social hegemony and political government.

These comprise:

1. The "spontaneous" consent given by the great masses of the population to the general direction imposed on social life by the dominant fundamental group; this consent is "historically" caused by the prestige (and consequent confidence) which the dominant group enjoys because of its position and function in the world of production.

2. The apparatus of state coercive power which "legally" enforces discipline on those groups who do not "consent" either actively or passively. This apparatus is, however, constituted for the whole of society in anticipation of moments of crisis of command and direction when spontaneous consent has failed.

This way of posing the problem has, as a result, a considerable extension of the concept of intellectual, but it is the only way which enables one to reach a concrete approximation of reality. It also clashes with preconceptions of caste. The function of organizing social hegemony and state domination certainly gives rise to a particular division of labour and therefore to a whole hierarchy of qualifications in some of which there is no apparent attribution of directive or organisational functions. For example, in the apparatus of social and state direction there exist a whole series of jobs of a manual and instrumental character (non-executive work, agents rather than officials or functionaries).[14] It is obvious that such a distinction has to be made just as it is obvious that other distinctions have to be made as well. Indeed, intellectual activity must also be distinguished in terms of its intrinsic characteristics, according to levels which in moments of extreme opposition represent a real qualitative difference—at the highest level would be the creators of the various sciences, philosophy, art, etc., at the lowest the most humble "administrators" and divulgators of pre-existing, traditional, accumulated intellectual wealth.[15] In the modern world the category of intellectuals, understood in this sense, has undergone an unprecedented expansion. The democratic-bureaucratic system has given rise to a great mass of functions which are not all justified by the social necessities of production, though they are justified by the political necessities of the dominant fundamental group. Hence Loria's[16] conception of the unproductive "worker" (but unproductive in relation to whom and to what mode of production?), a conception which could in part be justified if one takes account of the fact that these masses exploit their position to take for themselves a large cut out of the national income.

Mass formation has standardised individuals both psychologically and in terms of individual qualification and has produced the same phenomena as with other standardised masses: competition which makes necessary organisations for the defence of professions, unemployment, over-production in the schools, emigration, etc.

* * * * *

NOTES

1. The Italian word here is *"ceti,"* which does not carry quite the same connotations as "strata," but which we have been forced to translate in that way for lack of alternatives. It should be noted that Gramsci tends, for reasons of censorship, to avoid using the word class in contexts where its Marxist overtones would be apparent, preferring (as for example in this sentence) the more neutral "social group." The word "group," however, is not always a euphemism for "class," and to avoid ambiguity Gramsci uses the phrase "fundamental social group" when he wishes to emphasise the fact that he is referring to one or other of the major social classes (bourgeoisie, proletariat) defined in strict Marxist terms by its position in the fundamental relations of production. Class groupings which do not have this fundamental role are often described as "castes" (aristocracy, etc.). The word "category," on the other hand, which also occurs on this page, Gramsci tends to use in the standard Italian sense of members of a trade or profession, though also more generally. [...] Throughout this edition [*Selections from the Prison Notebooks of Antonio Gransci*], we have rendered Gramsci's usage as literally as possible (see note on Gramsci's Terminology, p. xxiii).
2. See note on Gramsci's Terminology.
3. Mosca's *Elementi di Scienza Politica* (new expanded edition, 1923) are worth looking at in this connection. Mosca's so-called "political class" is nothing other than the intellectual category of the dominant social group. Mosca's concept of "political class" can be connected with Pareto's concept of the *élite,* which is another attempt to interpret the historical phenomenon of the intellectuals and their function in the life of the state and of society. Mosca's book is an enormous hotch-potch, of a sociological and positivistic character, plus the tendentiousness of immediate politics which makes it less indigestible and livelier from a literary point of view.

    [Note: "Political class" is] usually translated in English as "ruling class," which is also the title of the English version of Mosca's *Elementi* (G. Mosca, *The Ruling Class*, New York 1939). Gaetano Mosca (1858–1941) was, together with Pareto and Michels, one of the major early Italian exponents of the theory of political *élites.* Although sympathetic to fascism, Mosca was basically a conservative, who saw the *élite* in rather more static terms than did some of his fellows.
4. Notably in Southern Italy. "Rural-type intellectuals" [*Selections from the Prison Notebooks of Antonio Gramsci*] pp. 14–23. [...] Gramsci's general argument, here as elsewhere in

the *Quaderni,* is that the person of peasant origin who becomes an "intellectual" (priest, lawyer, etc.) generally thereby ceases to be organically linked to his class of origin. One of the essential differences between, say, the Catholic Church and the revolutionary party of the working class lies in the fact that, ideally, the proletariat should be able to generate its own "organic" intellectuals within the class and who remain intellectuals *of* their class.

5.   For one category of these intellectuals, possibly the most important after the ecclesiastical for its prestige and the social function it performed in primitive societies, the category of *medical men* in the wide sense, that is all those who "struggle" or seem to struggle against death and disease, compare the *Storia della medicina* of Arturo Castiglioni. Note that there has been a connection between religion and medicine, and in certain areas there still is: hospitals in the hands of religious orders for certain organisational functions, apart from the fact that wherever the doctor appears, so does the priest (exorcism, various forms of assistance, etc.). Many great religious figures were and are conceived of as great "healers": the idea of miracles, up to the resurrection of the dead. Even in the case of kings the belief long survived that they could heal with the laying on of hands, etc.

6.   From this has come the general sense of "intellectual" or "specialist" of the word *"chierico"* (clerk, cleric) in many languages of romance origin or heavily influenced, through church Latin, by the romance languages, together with its correlative *"laico"* (lay, layman) in the sense of profane, non-specialist.

7.   Heads of FIAT and Montecatini (Chemicals) respectively. For Agnelli, of whom Gramsci had direct experience during the *Ordine Nuovo* period, see note 11 on p. 286 [*Selections from the Prison Notebooks of Antonio Gramsci*].

8.   For Frederick Taylor and his notion of the manual worker as a "trained gorilla," see Gramsci's essay *Americanism and Fordism*, pp. 277–318 [*Selections from the Prison Notebooks of Antonio Gramsci*].

9.   Thus, because it can happen that everyone at some time fries a couple of eggs or sews up a tear in a jacket, we do not necessarily say that everyone is a cook or a tailor.

10.   I.e., Man the maker (or tool-bearer) and Man the thinker.

11.   The *Ordine Nuovo,* the magazine edited by Gramsci during his days as a militant in Turin, ran as a "weekly review of Socialist culture" in 1919 and 1920. See Introduction, pp. xxv ff. [*Selections from the Prison Notebooks of Antonio Gramsci*].

12.   *"Dirigente."* This extremely condensed and elliptical sentence contains a number of key Gramscian ideas: on the possibility of proletarian cultural hegemony through domination of the work process, on the distinction between organic intellectuals of the working class and traditional intellectuals from outside, on the unity of theory and practice as a basic Marxist postulate, etc.

13.   The Italian school system above compulsory level is based on a division between academic ("classical" and "scientific") education and vocational training for professional purposes. Technical and, at the academic level, "scientific" colleges tend to be concentrated in the Northern industrial areas.

14.   *"funzionari"*: in Italian usage the word is applied to the middle and higher echelons of the bureaucracy. Conversely "administrators" (*"amministratori"*) is used here (end

of paragraph) to mean people who merely "administer" the decisions of others. The phrase "non-executive work" is a translation of "[*impiego*] *di ordine e turn di concetto*," which refers to distinctions within clerical work.

15. Here again military organisation offers a model of complex gradations between subaltern officers, senior officers, and general staff, not to mention the NCOs, whose importance is greater than is generally admitted. It is worth observing that all these parts feel a solidarity and indeed that it is the lower strata that display the most blatant *esprit de corps*, from which they derive a certain "conceit" ["*boria*."] This is a reference to an idea of Vico (see note 41 on p. 151). [*Selections from the Prison Notebooks of Antonio Gramsci.*], which is apt to lay them open to jokes and witticisms.

16. For Loria see note 108 on p. 458. [*Selections from the Prison Notebooks of Antonio Gramsci*] The notion of the "unproductive labourer" is not in fact an invention of Loria's but has its origins in Marx's definitions of productive and unproductive labour in *Capital*, which Loria, in his characteristic way, both vulgarised and claimed as his own discovery.

CHAPTER 5

The Rise and Future Demise of the World Capitalist System: Concepts for Comparative Analysis

Immanuel Wallerstein

The growth within the capitalist world-economy of the industrial sector of production, the so-called "industrial revolution," was accompanied by a very strong current of thought which defined this change as both a process of organic development and of progress, There were those who considered these economic developments and the concomitant changes in social organization to be some penultimate stage of world development whose final working-out was but a matter of time. These included such diverse thinkers as Saint-Simon, Comte, Hegel, Weber, Durkheim. And then there were the critics, most notably Marx, who argued, if you will, that the nineteenth-century present was only an antepenultimate stage of development, that the capitalist world was to know a cataclysmic political revolution which would then lead in the fullness of time to a final societal form, in this case the classless society.

One of the great strengths of Marxism was that, being an oppositional and hence critical doctrine, it called attention not merely to the contradictions of the system but to those of its ideologists by appealing to the empirical evidence of historical reality, which unmasked the irrelevancy of the models proposed for the explanation of the social world. The Marxist critics saw in abstracted models concrete rationalization, and they argued their case fundamentally by pointing to the failure of their opponents to analyze the social whole. As Lukacs put it, "it is not the primacy of economic motives in historical explanation that constitutes the decisive difference between Marxism and bourgeois thought, but the point of view of totality."[1]

In the mid-twentieth century, the dominant theory of development in the core countries of the capitalist world-economy has added little to the theorizing of the nineteenth-century progenitors of this mode of analysis, except to quantify the models and to abstract them still further, by adding on epicyclical codas to the models in order to account for ever further deviations from empirical expectations.

What is wrong with such models has been shown many times over, and from many standpoints. I cite only one critic, a non-Marxist, Robert Nisfaet, whose very cogent reflections on what he calls the "Western theory of development" concludes with this summary:

> [We] turn to history and only to history if what we are seeking are the actual causes, sources, and conditions of overt changes of patterns and structures in society. Conventional wisdom to the contrary in modern social theory, we shall not find, the explanation of change in those studies which are abstracted from history; whether these be studies of small groups in the social laboratory, group dynamics generally, staged experiments in social interaction, or mathematical analyses of so-called social systems. Nor will we find the sources of change in contemporary revivals of the comparative method with its ascending staircase of cultural similarities and differences plucked from all space and time.[2]

Shall we then turn to the critical schools, in particular Marxism, to give us a better account of social reality? In principle yes; in practice there are many different, often contradictory, versions extant of "Marxism." But what is more fundamental is the fact that in many countries Marxism is now the official state doctrine. Marxism is no longer exclusively an oppositional doctrine as it was in the nineteenth century.

The social fate of official doctrines is that they suffer a constant social pressure towards dogmatism and apologia, difficult although by no means impossible to counteract, and that they thereby often fall into the same intellectual dead-end of ahistorical model-building. Here the critique of Fernand Braudel is most pertinent:

> Marxism is a whole collection of models .... I shall protest ..., more or less, not against the model, but rather against the use to which people have thought themselves entitled to put it. The genius of Marx, the secret of his enduring power, lies in his having been the first to construct true social models, starting out from the long term (la longue durée). These models have been fixed permanently in their simplicity; they have been given the force of law and they have been treated as ready-made, automatic explanations, applicable in all places to all societies .... In this way has the creative power of the most powerful social analysts of the last century been shackled. It will be able to regain its strength and vitality only in the long term.[3]

Nothing illustrates the distortions of ahistorical models of social change better than the dilemmas to which the concept of stages gives rise. If we are to deal with social transformations over long historical time (Braudel's "the long term"), and if we are to give an explanation of both continuity and transformation, then we must logically divide the long term into segments in order to observe the structural changes from time A to time B. These segments are, however, not discrete but continuous in reality; *ergo* they are "stages" in the "development" of a social structure, a development which we determine however not *a priori* but *a posteriori*. That is, we cannot predict the future concretely, but we can predict the past.

The crucial issue when comparing "stages" is to determine the units of which the "stages" are synchronic portraits (or "ideal types," if you will). And the fundamental error of ahistorical social science (including ahistorical versions of Marxism) is to reify parts of the totality into such units and then to compare these reified structures.

* * * * *

If we are to talk of stages, then—and we should talk of stages—it must be stages of social systems, that is, of totalities. And the only totalities that exist or have historically existed are mini-systems and world-systems, and in the nineteenth and twentieth centuries there has been only one world-system in existence, the capitalist world-economy.

We take the defining characteristic of a social system to be the existence within it of a division of labor, such that the various sectors or areas within are dependent upon economic exchange with others for the smooth and continuous provisioning of the needs of the area. Such economic exchange can clearly exist without a common political structure and even more obviously without sharing the same culture.

A mini-system is an entity that has within it a complete division of labor, and a single cultural framework. Such systems are found only in very simple agricultural or hunting-and-gathering societies. Such mini-systems no longer exist in the world. Furthermore, there were fewer in the past than is often asserted, since any such system that became tied to an empire by the payment of tribute as "protection costs"[4] ceased by that fact to be a "system," no longer having a self-contained division of labor. For such an area, the payment of tribute marked a shift, in Polanyi's language, from being a reciprocal economy to participating in a larger redistributive economy.[5]

Leaving aside the now defunct mini-systems, the only kind of social system is a world-system, which we define quite simply as a unit with a single division of labor and multiple cultural systems. It follows logically that there can, however, be two varieties of such world-systems, one with a common political system and one without. We shall designate these respectively as world-empires and world-economies.

It turns out empirically that world-economies have historically been unstable structures leading either towards disintegration or conquest by one group and hence transformation into a world-empire. Examples of such world-empires emerging from world-economies are all the so-called great civilizations of pre-modern times, such as China, Egypt, Rome (each at appropriate periods of its history). On the other hand, the so-called nineteenth-century empires, such as Great Britain or France, were not world-empires at all, but nation-states with colonial appendages operating within the framework of a world-economy.

World-empires were basically redistributive in economic form. No doubt they bred clusters of merchants who engaged in economic exchange (primarily long-distance trade), but such clusters, however large, were a minor part of the total economy and not fundamentally determinative of its fate. Such long-distance trade tended to be, as Polanyi argues, "administered trade" and not market trade, utilizing "ports of trade."[7]

It was only with the emergence of the modern world-economy in sixteenth-century Europe that we saw the full development and economic predominance of market trade. This was the system called capitalism. Capitalism and a world-economy (that is, a single division of labor but multiple polities and cultures) are obverse sides of the same coin. One does not cause the other. We are merely defining the same indivisible phenomenon by different characteristics.

* * * * *

By a series of accidents—historical, ecological, geographic—northwest Europe was better situated in the sixteenth century to diversify its agricultural specialization and add to it certain industries (such as textiles, shipbuilding, and metal wares) than were other parts of Europe. Northwest Europe emerged as the core area of this world-economy, specializing in agricultural production of higher skill levels, which favored [...] tenancy and wage-labor as the modes of labor control. Eastern Europe and the Western Hemisphere became peripheral areas specializing in export of grains, bullion, wood, cotton, sugar—all of which favored the use of slavery and coerced cash-crop labor as the modes of labor control. Mediterranean Europe emerged as the semi-peripheral area of this world-economy specializing in high-cost industrial products (for example, silks) and credit and specie transactions, which had as a consequence in the agricultural arena share-cropping as the mode of labor control and little export to other areas.

The three structural positions in a world-economy—core, periphery, and semi-periphery—had become stabilized by about 1640. How certain areas became one and not the other is a long story.[6] The key fact is that given slightly different starting-points, the interests of various local groups converged in northwest Europe, leading to the development of strong state mechanisms, and diverged sharply in the peripheral areas, leading to very weak ones. Once we get a difference in the strength of the state-machineries, we get the operation of "unequal exchange,"[7] which is enforced by strong states on weak ones, by core states on peripheral areas. Thus, capitalism involves not only appropriation of the surplus-value by an owner from a laborer, but an appropriation of surplus of the whole world-economy by core areas. And this was as true in the stage of agricultural capitalism as it is in the stage of industrial capitalism.

* * * * *

Capitalism was from the beginning an affair of the world-economy and not of nation-states. It is a misreading of the situation to claim that it is only in the twentieth century that capitalism has become "world-wide," although this claim is frequently made in various writings, particularly by Marxists. [...]

* * * * *

[...] Capital has never allowed its aspirations to be determined by national boundaries in a capitalist world-economy, and that the creation of "national" barriers—generically, mercantilism—has historically been a defensive mechanism of capitalists located in states which are one level below the high point of strength in the system. [...]

* * * * *

There have been three major mechanisms that have enabled world-systems to retain relative political stability (not in terms of the particular groups who will play the leading roles in the system, but in terms of systemic survival itself). One obviously is the concentration of military strength in the hands of the dominant forces. The modalities of this obviously vary with the technology, and there are to be sure political prerequisites for such a concentration, but nonetheless sheer force is no doubt a central consideration.

A second mechanism is the pervasiveness of an ideological commitment to the system as a whole. I do not mean what has often been termed the "legitimation" of a system because that term has been used to imply that the lower strata of a system feel some affinity with or loyalty towards the rulers, and I doubt that this has ever been a significant factor in the survival of world-systems. I mean rather the degree to which the staff or cadres of the system (and I leave this term deliberately vague) feel that their own well-being is wrapped up in the survival of the system as such and the competence of its leaders. It is this staff which not only propagates the myths; it is they who believe them.

But neither force nor the ideological commitment of the staff would suffice were it not for the division of the majority into a larger lower stratum and a smaller middle stratum. Both the revolutionary call for polarization as a strategy of change and the liberal encomium to consensus as the basis of the liberal polity reflect this proposition. The import is far wider than its use in the analysis of contemporary political problems suggests. It is the normal condition of either kind of world-system to have a three-layered structure. When and if this ceases to be the case, the world-system disintegrates.

In a world-empire, the middle stratum is in fact accorded the role of maintaining the marginally desirable long-distance luxury trade, while the upper stratum concentrates its resources on controlling the military machinery which can collect the tribute, the crucial mode of redistributing surplus. By providing, however, for an access to a limited portion of the surplus to urbanized elements who alone, in pre-modern societies, could contribute political cohesiveness to isolated clusters of primary producers, the upper stratum effectively buys off the potential leadership of coordinated revolt. And by denying access to political rights for this commercial-urban middle stratum, it makes them constantly vulnerable to confiscatory measures whenever their economic profits become sufficiently swollen so that they might begin to create for themselves military strength.

In a world-economy, such "cultural" stratification is not so simple because the absence of a single political system means the concentration of economic roles vertically rather than horizontally throughout the system. The solution then is to have three *kinds* of states, with pressures for cultural homogenization within each of them—thus, besides the upper stratum of core-states and the lower stratum of peripheral states, there is a middle stratum of semi-peripheral ones.

This semi-periphery is then assigned as it were a specific economic role, but the reason is less economic than political. That is to say, one might make a good case that the world-economy as an economy would function every bit as well without a semi-periphery. But it would be far less *politically* stable, for it would mean a polarized world-system. The existence of the third category means precisely that the upper stratum is not faced with the *unified* opposition of all the others because the *middle* stratum is both exploited and exploiter. It follows that the specific economic role is not all that important, and has thus changed through the various historical stages of the modern world-system. [...]

Where then does class analysis fit in all of this? And what in such a formulation are nations, nationalities, peoples, ethnic groups? First of all, [...] I would contend that all these latter terms denote variants of a single phenomenon which I will term "ethno-nations."

Both classes and ethnic groups, or status-groups, or ethno-nations are phenomena of world-economies and much of the enormous confusion that has surrounded the concrete analysis of their functioning can be attributed quite simply to the fact that they have been analyzed as though they existed within the nation-states of this world-economy, instead of within the world-economy as a whole. This has been a Procrustean bed indeed.

The range of economic activities being far wider in the core than in the periphery, the range of syndical interest groups is far wider there.[8] Thus, it has been widely observed that there does not exist in many parts of the world today a proletariat of the kind which exists in, say, Europe or North America. But this is a confusing way to state the observation. Industrial activity being disproportionately concentrated in certain parts of the world-economy, industrial wage-workers are to be found principally in certain geographic regions. Their interests as a syndical group are determined by their collective relationship to the world-economy. Their ability to influence the political functioning of this world-economy is shaped by the fact that they command larger percentages of the population in one sovereign entity than another. The form their organizations take have, in large part, been governed too by these political boundaries. The same might be said about industrial capitalists. Class analysis is perfectly capable of accounting for the political position of, let us say, French skilled workers if we look at their structural position and interests in the world-economy. Similarly with ethno-nations. The meaning of ethnic consciousness in a core area is considerably different from that of ethnic consciousness in a peripheral area precisely because of the different class position such ethnic groups have in the world-economy.[9]

Political struggles of ethno-nations or segments of classes within national boundaries of course are the daily bread and butter of local politics. But their significance or consequences can only be fruitfully analyzed if one spells out the implications of their organizational activity or political demands for the functioning of the world-economy. This also incidentally makes possible more rational assessments of these politics in terms of some set of evaluative criteria such as "left" and "right."

The functioning then of a capitalist world-economy requires that groups pursue their economic interests within a single world market while seeking to distort this market for their benefit by organizing to exert influence on states, some of which are far more powerful than others, but none of which controls the world-market in its entirety. Of course, we shall find on closer inspection that there are periods where one state is relatively quite powerful and other periods where power is more diffuse and contested, permitting weaker states broader ranges of action. We can talk then of the relative tightness or looseness of the world-system as an important variable and seek to analyze why this dimension tends to be cyclical in nature, as it seems to have been for several hundred years.

We are now in a position to look at the historical evolution of this capitalist world-economy itself and analyze the degree to which it is fruitful to talk of distinct stages in its evolution as a system. The emergence of the European world-economy in the "long" sixteenth century (1450–1640) was made possible by an historical conjuncture: on those long-term trends which were the culmination of what has been sometimes described as the "crisis of feudalism" was superimposed a more immediate cyclical crisis plus climatic changes, all of which created a dilemma that could only be resolved by a geographic expansion of the division of labor. Furthermore, the balance of inter-system forces was such as to make this realizable. Thus, a geographic expansion did take place in conjunction with a demographic expansion and an upward price rise.

The remarkable thing was not that a European world-economy was thereby created, but that it survived the Hapsburg attempt to transform it into a world-empire, an attempt seriously pursued by Charles V. The Spanish attempt to absorb the whole failed because the rapid economic-demographic-technological burst forward of the preceding century made the whole enterprise too expensive for the imperial base to sustain, especially given many structural insufficiencies in Castilian economic development. Spain could afford neither the bureaucracy nor the army that was necessary to the enterprise, and in the event went bankrupt, as did the French monarchs making a similar albeit even less plausible attempt.

Once the Hapsburg dream of world-empire was over—and in 1557 it was over forever—the capitalist world-economy was an established system that became almost impossible to unbalance. [...] By 1640, those in northwest Europe had succeeded in establishing themselves as the core-states; Spain and the northern Italian city-states declined into being semi-peripheral; northeastern Europe and Iberian America had become the periphery. At this point, those in semi-peripheral status had reached it by virtue of decline from a former more pre-eminent status.

It was the system-wide recession of 1650–1730 that consolidated the European world-economy and opened stage two of the modern world-economy. For the recession forced retrenchment, and the decline in relative surplus allowed room for only one core-state to survive. The mode of struggle was mercantilism, which was a device of partial insulation and withdrawal from the world market of *large* areas themselves hierarchically constructed—that is, empires within the world-economy (which is quite different from world-empires). In this struggle England first ousted the Netherlands from its commercial primacy and then resisted successfully France's attempt to catch up. As England began to speed up the process of industrialization after 1760, there was one last attempt of those capitalist forces located in France to break the imminent British hegemony. This attempt was expressed first in the French Revolution's replacement of the cadres of the regime and then in Napoleon's continental blockade. But it failed.

Stage three of the capitalist world-economy begins then, a stage of industrial rather than of agricultural capitalism. Henceforth, industrial production is no longer a minor aspect of the world market but comprises an ever larger percentage of world gross production—and, even more important, of world gross surplus. This involves a whole series of consequences for the world-system.

First of all, it led to the further geographic expansion of the European world-economy to include now the whole of the globe. This was in part the result of its technological feasibility both in terms of improved military firepower and improved shipping facilities which made regular trade sufficiently inexpensive to be viable. But, in addition, industrial production *required* access to raw materials of a nature and in a quantity such that the needs could not be supplied within the former boundaries. At first, however, the search for new markets was not a primary consideration in the geographic expansion since the new markets were more readily available within the old boundaries. [...]

* * * * *

The creation of vast new areas as the periphery of the expanded world-economy made possible a shift in the role of some other areas. Specifically, both the United States and Germany (as it came into being) combined formerly peripheral and semi-peripheral regions. The manufacturing sector in each was able to gain political ascendancy, as the peripheral subregions became less economically crucial to the world-economy. Mercantilism now became the major tool of semi-peripheral countries seeking to become core countries, thus still performing a function analogous to that of the mercantilist drives of the late seventeenth and eighteenth centuries in England and France. To be sure, the struggle of semi-peripheral countries to "industrialize" varied in the degree to which it succeeded in the period before the First World War: all the way in the United States, only partially in Germany, not at all in Russia.

The internal structure of core-states also changed fundamentally under industrial capitalism. For a core area, industrialism involved divesting itself of substantially all agricultural activities (except that in the twentieth century further mechanization was to create a new form of working the land that was so highly mechanized as to warrant the appellation industrial). Thus, whereas in the period 1700–40, England not only was Europe's leading industrial exporter but was also Europe's leading agricultural exporter—this was at a high point in the economy-wide recession—by 1900, less than 10 percent of England's population were engaged in agricultural pursuits.

At first under industrial capitalism, the core exchanged manufactured products against the periphery's agricultural products—hence, Britain from 1815 to 1873 as the "workshop of the world." Even to those semi-peripheral countries that had some manufacture (France, Germany, Belgium, the U.S.), Britain in this period supplied about half their needs in manufactured goods. As, however, the mercantilist practices of this latter group both cut Britain off from outlets and even created competition for Britain in sales to peripheral areas, a competition which led to the late nineteenth-century "scramble for Africa," the world division of labor was reallocated to ensure a new special role for the core: less the provision of the manufactures, more the provision of the machines to make the manufactures as well as the provision of infra-structure (especially, in this period, railroads).

The rise of manufacturing created for the first time under capitalism a large-scale urban proletariat. And in consequence for the first time there arose what Michels has called the "anti-capitalist mass spirit,"[10] which was translated into concrete organizational forms (trade-unions, socialist parties). This development intruded a new factor as threatening to the stability of the states and of the capitalist forces now so securely in control of them as the earlier centrifugal thrusts of regional anti-capitalist landed elements had been in the seventeenth century.

At the same time that the bourgeoisies of the core countries were faced by this threat to the internal stability of their state structures, they were simultaneously faced with the economic crisis of the latter third of the nineteenth century resulting from the more rapid increase of agricultural production (and indeed of light manufactures) than the expansion of a potential market for these goods. Some of the surplus would have to be redistributed to someone to allow these goods to be bought and the economic machinery to return to smooth operation. By expanding the purchasing power of the industrial proletariat of the core countries, the world-economy was unburdened simultaneously of two problems: the bottleneck of demand, and the unsettling "class conflict" of the core states—hence, the social liberalism or welfare-state ideology that arose just at that point in time.

The First World War was, as men of the time observed, the end of an era; and the Russian Revolution of October 1917 the beginning of a new one—our stage four. This stage was, to be sure, a stage of revolutionary turmoil, but it also was, in a seeming paradox, the stage of the *consolidation* of the industrial capitalist world-economy. The Russian Revolution was essentially that of a semi-peripheral country whose internal balance of forces had been such that as of the late nineteenth century it began on a decline towards a peripheral status. This was the result of the marked penetration of foreign capital into the industrial sector which was on its way to eliminating all indigenous capitalist forces, the resistance to the mechanization of the agricultural sector, the decline of relative military power (as evidenced by the defeat by the Japanese in 1905). The Revolution brought to power a group of state-managers who reversed each one of these trends by using the classic technique of mercantilist semi-withdrawal from the world-economy. In the process of doing this, the now U.S.S.R. mobilized considerable popular support, especially in the urban sector. At the end of the Second World War, Russia was reinstated as a very strong member of the semi-periphery and could begin to seek full core status.

Meanwhile, the decline of Britain, which dates from 1873, was confirmed and its hegemonic role was assumed by the United States. While the U.S. thus rose, Germany fell further behind as a result of its military defeat. Various German attempts in the 1920s to find new industrial outlets in the Middle East and South America were unsuccessful in the face of the U.S. thrust combined with Britain's continuing relative strength. Germany's thrust of desperation to recoup lost ground took the noxious and unsuccessful form of Nazism.

It was the Second World War that enabled the United States for a brief period (1945–65) to attain the same level of primacy as Britain had in the first part of the nineteenth century. United States growth in this period was spectacular and created a great need for expanded market outlets. The Cold War closure denied not only the U.S.S.R. but Eastern Europe to U.S. exports. And the Chinese Revolution meant that this region, which had been destined for much exploitative activity, was also cut off. [...]

But a world capitalist economy does not permit true imperium. Charles V could not succeed in his dream of world-empire. The Pax Britannica stimulated its own demise. So too did the Pax Americana. In each case, the cost of *political* imperium was too high economically, and in a capitalist system, over the middle run when profits decline, new *political* formulae are sought. In this case the costs mounted along several fronts. The efforts of the U.S.S.R. to further its own industrialization, protect a privileged market area (eastern Europe), and force entry into other market areas led to an immense spiralling of military expenditure, which on the Soviet side promised long-run returns, whereas for the U.S. it was merely a question of running very fast to stand still. The economic resurgence of western Europe, made necessary both to provide markets for U.S. sales and investments and to counter the U.S.S.R. military thrust, meant over time that the west European state structures collectively became as strong as that of the U.S., which led in the late 1960s to the "dollar and gold crisis" and the retreat of Nixon from the free-trade stance, which is the definitive mark of the self-confident leader in a capitalist market system. When the cumulated Third World pressures, most notably Vietnam, were added on, a restructuring of the world division of labor was inevitable, involving probably in the 1970s a quadripartite division of the larger part of the world surplus by the U.S., the European Common Market, Japan, and the U.S.S.R.

Such a decline in U.S. state hegemony has actually *increased* the freedom of action of capitalist enterprises, the larger of which have now taken the form of multinational corporations which are able to maneuver against state bureaucracies whenever the national politicians become too responsive to internal worker pressures. Whether some effective links can be established between multinational corporations, presently limited to operating in certain areas, and the U.S.S.R. remains to be seen, but it is by no means impossible.

* * * * *

What then have been the consequences for the world-system of the emergence of many states in which there is no private ownership of the basic means of production? To some extent, this has meant an internal reallocation of consumption. It has certainly undermined the ideological justifications in world capitalism, both by showing the political vulnerability of capitalist entrepreneurs and by demonstrating that private ownership is irrelevant to the rapid expansion of industrial productivity. But to the extent that it has raised the ability of the new semi-peripheral areas to enjoy a larger share of the world surplus, it has once again depolarized the world, recreating the triad of strata that has been a fundamental element in the survival of the world-system.

Finally, in the peripheral areas of the world-economy, both the continued economic expansion of the core (even though the core is seeing some reallocation of surplus internal to it) and the new strength of the semi-periphery has led to a further weakening of the political and hence economic position of the peripheral areas. The pundits note that "the gap is getting wider," but thus far no-one has succeeded in doing much about it, and it is not clear that there are very many in whose interests it would be to do so. Far from a strengthening of state authority, in many parts of the world we are witnessing the same kind of deterioration Poland knew in the sixteenth century, a deterioration of which the frequency of military coups is only one of many signposts. And all of this leads us to conclude that stage four has been the stage of the *consolidation* of the capitalist world-economy.

Consolidation, however, does not mean the absence of contradictions and does not mean the likelihood of long-term survival. We thus come to projections about the future, which has always been man's great game, his true *hybris*, the most convincing argument for the dogma of original sin. Having read Dante, I will therefore be brief.

There are two fundamental contradictions, it seems to me, involved in the workings of the capitalist world-system. In the first place, there is the contradiction to which the nineteenth-century Marxian corpus pointed, which I would phrase as follows: whereas in the short-run the maximization of profit requires maximizing the withdrawal of surplus from immediate consumption of the majority, in the long-run the continued production of surplus requires a mass demand which can only be created by redistributing the surplus withdrawn. Since these two considerations move in opposite directions (a "contradiction"), the system has constant crises which in the long-run both weaken it and make the game for those with privilege less worth playing.

The second fundamental contradiction, to which Mao's concept of socialism as process points, is the following: whenever the tenants of privilege seek to co-opt an oppositional movement by including them in a minor share of the privilege, they may no doubt eliminate opponents in the short-run, but they also up the ante for the next oppositional movement created in the next crisis of the world-economy. Thus, the cost of "co-option" rises ever higher and the advantages of co-option seem ever less worthwhile.

There are today no socialist systems in the world-economy any more than there are feudal systems because there is only *one* world-system. It is a world-economy and it is by definition capitalist in form. Socialism involves the creation of a new kind of world-system, neither a redistributive world-empire nor a capitalist world-economy but a socialist world-government. I don't see this projection as being in the least Utopian, but I also don't feel its institution is imminent. It will be the outcome of a long struggle in forms that may be familiar and perhaps in very new forms, that will take place in *all* the areas of the world-economy (Mao's continual "class struggle"). Governments may be in the hands of persons, groups, or movements sympathetic to this transformation, but *states* as such are neither progressive nor reactionary. It is movements and forces that deserve such evaluative judgments.

Having gone as far as I care to in projecting the future, let me return to the present and to the scholarly enterprise which is never neutral but does have its own logic and to some extent its own priorities. We have adumbrated as our basic unit of observation a concept of world-systems that have structural parts and evolving stages. It is within such a framework, I am arguing, that we can fruitfully make comparative analyses—of the wholes and of parts of the whole. Conceptions precede and govern measurements. I am all for minute and sophisticated quantitative indicators. I am all for minute and diligent archival work that will trace a concrete historical series of events in terms of all its immediate complexities. But the point of either is to enable us to see better what has happened and what is happening. For that we need glasses with which to discern the dimensions of difference, we need models with which to weigh significance, we need summarizing concepts with which to create the knowledge which we then seek to communicate to each other. And all this because we are men with hybris and original sin and therefore seek the good, the true, and the beautiful.

NOTES

1. George Lukacs, "The Marxism of Rosa Luxemburg," in *History and Class Consciousness* (London: Merlin Press, 1968), p. 27.
2. Robert A. Nisbet, *Social Change and History* (New York: Oxford University Press, 1969), pp. 302–3. I myself would exempt from this criticism the economic history literature.
3. Fernand Braudel, "History and the Social Sciences," in Peter Burke (ed.), *Economy and Society in Early Modern Europe* (London: Routledge and Kegan Paul, 1972), pp. 38–9.
4. See Frederic Lane's discussion of "protection costs," which is reprinted as Part Three of *Venice and History* (Baltimore: Johns Hopkins Press, 1966). For the specific discussion of tribute, see pp. 389–90, 416–20.
5. See Karl Polanyi, "The Economy as Instituted Process," in Karl Polanyi, Conrad M. Arsenberg, and Harry W. Pearson (eds.), *Trade and Market in the Early Empire* (Glencoe: Free Press, 1957), pp. 243–70.
6. I give a brief account or this in "Three Paths of National Development in the Sixteenth Century," *Studies in Comparative International Development*, VII, 2, Summer 1972, 95–101.
7. See Arghiri Emmanuel, *Unequal Exchange* (New York: Monthly Review Press, 1972).
8. Range in this sentence means the number of different occupations in which a significant proportion of the population is engaged. Thus, peripheral society typically is overwhelmingly agricultural. A core society typically has its occupations well distributed over all of Colin Clark's three sectors. If one shifted the connotation of range to talk of style of life, consumption patterns, even income distribution, quite possibly one might reverse the correlation. In a typical peripheral society, the differences between a subsistence farmer and an urban professional are probably far greater than those which could be found in a typical core state.
9. See my "The Two Modes of Ethnic Consciousness: Soviet Central Asia in Transition?" in Edward Atlworth (ed.), *The Nationality Question in Soviet Central Asia* (New York: Praeger, 1973), pp. 168–75.
10. Robert Michels, "The Origins of the Anti-Capitalist Mass Spirit," in *Man in Contemporary Society* (New York: Columbia University Press, 1955), Vol. 1, pp. 740–65.

CHAPTER 6

The Impoverishment of State Theory

Leo Panitch

Once upon a time, the capitalist state did not exist. I am not speaking of the period before the middle of the millennium that is now coming to a close, the era before the transition from feudalism to capitalism. I am speaking not of 500 years ago but of less than 50 years ago, the late 1950s and early 1960s; and when I say that the capitalist state did not exist, what I really mean to say is that it did not exist as a term within mainstream political discourse, even as this discourse was reflected in the concepts and theories which the discipline of political science uses to refer to the countries we live in. In the early 1960s, the term capitalism itself was rarely used in polite company. It was considered acceptable within the university classroom, even a mark of some intelligence, to point out that capitalism had once existed; it was even considered a plausible argument that back in the era of the robber barons there had actually existed a capitalist ruling class in North America. But that was all "once upon a time." We lived in a mixed economy with a pluralist political system. The term "state" itself was considered either vulgarly radical or tediously arcane as applied to the institutions of government in relation to society, and was rarely employed except to refer to the nation state in the international political system.

Students of a critical bent in the early and mid-1960s strained against this discourse. Just as we did not let the words *ceteris paribus* go unchallenged in our introductory economic courses (that is, we refused to accept that other things actually were equal), so we wrote essays challenging pluralism in political science, insisting, as Schattshneider already had way back in the 1940s, that the pluralist choir sang with a distinctly upper-class accent. But the exercise we were engaged in was negation. Even C. Wright Mills's *The Power Elite* [1956], or John Porter's *The Vertical Mosaic* [1965], or Galbraith's *New Industrial State* [1967] were mainly appreciated for the evidence they compiled and the tools they lent for tearing down the conceptual prison of mainstream social science. It was only with the emergence of the Marxist theory of the state in the late 1960s and early 1970s that we finally felt ourselves moving from a repetitive and increasingly tedious (because it was so easy) exercise of tearing down pluralism to actually participating in building up a new, far more sophisticated way of studying politics. We sensed, on reading Miliband [1969], Poulantzas [1968], and O'Connor [1973] that we were no longer confined to being just critics, constantly merely negating the old; we sensed that it might be possible to engage ourselves in developing an alternative and better theory, fashioning new conceptual tools for the purpose. It was a highly exhilarating feeling.

It needs to be stressed today that we did not at all see ourselves as falling back on a prefabricated Marxism; the new theory of the state had Marxist roots, but it was founded on the notion that nothing like an elaborated and coherent theory of the capitalist state (in contrast with the complex array of concepts and tendential laws that constituted Marxian economics and historical materialism) had been fashioned either by Marx himself or by his successors — up to and including Gramsci. And the new theory was concerned to displace the narrowly ideological official Marxism of the Communist Parties.

The recognition that the attempt to develop a Marxist theory of the state was a serious social scientific exercise yielded a certain toleration of the new theory in academic political science circles; indeed it even became rather fashionable. In the 1950s and into the 1960s, political science theory had been derivative of leading sociologists, but now it was sociologists who were drawing on political scientists like Miliband, Poulantzas, and their disciples. It appeared that what Gramsci had written a half-century before was finally being confirmed:

> If political science means science of the State, and the State is the entire complex of practical activities with which the ruling class not only justifies and maintains its dominance, but manages to win the active consent of those over whom it rules, then it is obvious that all the essential questions of sociology are nothing other than the questions of political science. [1971: 244]

All this meant that graduate students in political science and sociology who identified themselves with the new state theory were not often barred for that reason from academic employment or publication (provided, at least, they sanitised Miliband and Poulantzas as "neo-marxists"); sometimes it actually was a guarantee of visibility, which is usually what is meant in academic life by "success."

* * * * *

[...] Those who took up the new theory of the state recognised that imminent social transformation was not on the agenda for the advanced capitalist states, that it would likely not fall to our generation, despite May 1968, to build a new world. (I now wonder whether we learned this from reading Miliband and Poulantzas, or whether we were inclined to read them seriously because we already recognised this and thus saw little odds in joining the vanguard Trotskyist or Maoist parties.) Of course, we took very seriously the importance for long-term strategy of developing a new political science, but most of us knew that all the talk of strategy was empty so long as it remained within the halls of academe. As I put it in the preface to *The Canadian State*:

> One must of course cautiously avoid the illusion that by virtue of its strengths alone a Marxist theory of the state will gain prominence. The rise and fall of theories is not merely the product of intellectual competition with the most fruitful coming out on top. The acceptance of any particular theory and its conceptual elements rests on some consensus among intellectuals with regard to the importance of the "significant problems" it identifies. On the identification of those problems, questions of interest as well as objectivity, ideological hegemony as well as academic freedom, will inevitably play their part. Most important of all will be the question of whether the generation of Marxist theory will itself continue to be divorced from the working class in Canada. For without a working class helping to identify the "significant problems" by its own actions, and taking up cultural as well as political and economic struggle by re-examining its history and developing a theory and practice for future change, Marxist theory will lack a social base, which is finally the *sine qua non* for the sustenance of any body of ideas. [Panitch 1977: x]

That was written over twenty years ago. I don't think I realized just how little time we had, how contingent the further development of the Marxist theory of the state would be on immediately favourable political conditions. How quickly, in retrospect, it all passed. By the beginning of the 1980s, a strong reaction to the new Marxist state theory set in and it soon became quite unfashionable. This is, of course, one of the dangers of academic fashion. The advances made in Marxist state theory were swept away as part of the general post-marxist, post-structuralist, post-modernist trend, marked especially by the displacement (via Foucault and Derrida) of the academic "focus of attention from the state and class struggle to the micro-physics of power and the problems of identity formation" [Jessop 1991: 91]. But this is only one part of the story. Within political science and political sociology, one of the legacies of the new Marxist theory was actually that the state was firmly reestablished as part of the conceptual lexicon for the study of contemporary politics. In this respect, we might say that reaction against the new Marxist theory did not entail a shift of attention away from the state; on the contrary, research increasingly become determinedly and self-descriptively "state-centred."

There was a remarkable paradox in this development. The state autonomy perspective that emerged in the 1980s involved the theoretical assertion of the institutional autonomy of the state at the very time when the structural power of capital and the strategic and ideological reach of capitalist classes has become perhaps never more nakedly visible. The Marxist theory of the state had emerged to challenge the pretensions of social democratic reformism, epitomised in the claims like those advanced in Crosland's *The Future of Socialism* [1956] that business had lost its commanding position inside the state in the context of an irreversible shift of power from the business to the labouring classes. The development of the concept of relative autonomy was precisely about providing the tools of analysis to understand the distinct limits of the state's independence from capital, and one might have thought that the crisis of Social Democratic/New Deal regime in the face of the contradictions it gave rise to by the 1970s would have been taken as confirming and sustaining this approach to the study of the state. But the challenge to that regime posed by the new "free market" right instead produced two other responses. First, there was an insistence against Marxist state theory that, where deeply institutionally embedded, the social democratic regime would be able to withstand both the new right and the mass unemployment that everywhere (including in Sweden and Germany) accompanied the reemergence of severe crisis tendencies within capitalism. Second, there was an insistence against the free market theorists themselves that state intervention in the economy is *not* necessarily inefficient, inflationary, and so on.

These responses have often entailed accepting the new right's categories of analysis—states and markets, public and private—but assigning a positive rather than a negative evaluation to the role of the state in making markets work (and to the role of the public in making markets thrive), as well as in terms of making market economies more egalitarian and solidaristic. Resting one's hopes on the state in a world understood in terms of the simple categories of markets and states stemmed from a well-meaning concern that competitive market values alone should not determine the choices that govern our lives. But what emerged, [...] was a remarkable idealization of the state, alongside an implicit, if not explicit, assumption that the only historical choice for the left was that between less or more state intervention within the framework of capitalism.

The result has been a remarkable impoverishment of state theory. This is not the place to undertake anything like a comprehensive survey, but a critical examination of the "new paradigm," in the form advanced by even as radical a thinker as Fred Block, may help to clarify the nature of the problem. Block graced the "new paradigm" with the label of "market reconstruction" because it "emphasizes the degree of choice available in structuring markets and the possibility of reconstructing markets to achieve greater efficiency, greater equality, or other ends" [1994: 697]. Block made his own original contribution to the Marxist state theory literature in the 1970s, but he now lumped both liberalism and Marxism together into one "old paradigm." The "old paradigm" was allegedly structured in terms of a continuum of left and right prejudices ranging from distrust of the state on the right to distrust of the market on the left, but what was common to all positions on this spectrum — and which justified, for Block, representing Marxism and liberalism in terms of a common "paradigm"—was the incorrect treatment of "modernity" as a process of opening up more and more activities to market forces. The alleged originality of the "new paradigm" lies in its recognition that states and markets, while structured in different ways, have always been dependent on one another.

What is primarily notable about this type of argument is how historically vague are the conceptual categories of state and market. It [is] almost as though—in attempting to confound neo-classical economics' view of free markets—one is drawn into responding to them in their own categories of analysis, and thus we find even as sophisticated a thinker as Block slipping into a discourse which empties the categories of state and market of historical and comparative specificity. This is readily revealed in the absurdity of the notion that Marxism somehow "trusted" the state. But it is also revealed in the very abstractness and generality of the concept of markets. The alleged great insight of the "new paradigm"—that it is incorrect to see states as having more and more opened up societies to market forces—is based on the claim that modern history has seen as many markets closed down as opened up. The evidence offered in this respect is the Protestant church's banning of the selling [of] indulgences to the highest bidder, the ending of the international market in slaves, the restriction of child labour, the elimination of the sale of political offices. But this trivializes what is involved in capitalism's general commodification of social life (including the commodification of labour power and the development of the capitalist labour market).

Block tries to sustain his argument by arguing that the discontinuity between feudal and capitalist social relations has been exaggerated. He weakly offers as evidence a fictional family capitalist who, in trying to defy the local norms governing the treatment of his employees, would soon find his sources of credit and markets dry up in a community which regards him as a "deviant entrepreneur." And he claims that the corporate CEO within capitalism is as much restricted in his economic activity as the feudal lord and Soviet manager. Such gross categories of analysis must yield a sloppy historical sociology, as is revealed in the banal claim that in "feudal, capitalist and socialist property systems, the basic rights of employees and employers are established through state action" [Block 1994: 701]. What goes missing here, of course (revealed in the ahistorical transposition of the terms employer and employee back into feudalism), is the necessary discrimination between the class nature of one social order as opposed to another.

What also goes missing, as a result of adopting states and markets rather than social relations of class and class power as the basic units of analysis, is any pattern of determination regarding state action. The Marxist theory of the state was not only challenging pluralist and social democratic claims that the modern state had freed itself from the dynamics of capitalist accumulation, but was precisely trying to enrich the tools of class analysis so as to understand the (varying) patterns of determination of capitalist state structure and action. In contrast, "the point of the market reconstruction perspective," as Block puts it, is to stress "the extensive capacities of governments" and their "considerable scope to decide whether they want more price stability or economic growth." This is not only a vastly narrower perspective; even as such it is an impoverished one, for Block offers little guidance regarding the conjunctural and structural conditions—the variations and limits of such policy autonomy—in different states or in any given state at different periods or in different conjunctures. Nor does he systematically confront general claims about policy autonomy in relation to what he in the end admits is "the effect of the explosive growth of international financial transactions" in terms of the "powerful pressures on states to 'deregulate' those transactions" [Block 1994: 704].

* * * * *

It is, indeed, in the critical arena of what has come to be known as "globalization," which these powerful state institutions have played such a large role in sponsoring, that the impoverishment of state theory may be most readily recognised and lamented. This is especially evident in Paul Hirst and Grahame Thompson's much heralded *Globalization in Question* [1996]. The book has the virtue of understanding that one "key effect of the concept of globalization has been to paralyse radical reforming national strategies" and to insist that the processes associated with globalization were "at least in part policy driven" by states themselves. But while their concern to avoid the hysteria and defeatism associated with the term globalization is admirable, their claim that globalization is only "conjunctural" and that there is "nothing unprecedented about the levels of integration experienced at present" cannot be sustained. Even less acceptable is the claim that it is only "the political will that is lacking at present to gain extra leverage over undesirable and unjust aspects of international and domestic economic activity" (pp. 15–17). It is precisely this kind of trajectory from Althusserian superstructural determinism—for which Hirst was himself so famously criticised by E.P Thompson in *The Poverty of Theory* (1978)—to sheer liberal/social-democratic voluntarism that most clearly defines what I have called the impoverishment of state theory.

Hirst and Thompson define states as "communities of fate which tie together actors who share certain common interests in the success or failure of the national economies" (p. 146). This is not on the surface very different from Jessop's definition of the state as that "distinct ensemble of institutions and organizations whose socially accepted function is to define and enforce collectively binding decisions on the members of a society in the name of their common interest or general will" [Jessop 1990: 341]. But Jessop explicitly locates his definition within a conceptualisation of hegemonic class domination and in this light problematizes the contradictions and strategic dilemmas entailed in the state's performance of this function. Since they do not do this, it is difficult to know whether to take Hirst and Thompson's definition seriously in analytic terms (as opposed to mere idealism or wishful thinking) insofar as it is completely silent on the key issues of socio-economic inequality and power—and the conflicts of interest that have their roots therein. Their claim that "markets need to be embedded in social relations" and that "political authority remains central in assuring that markets are appropriately institutionalized and that the non-market conditions of economic success are present" is empty of content in relation to the actual social relations in question.

It is scarcely surprising, in face of this kind of theoretical evasion, that what was promised at the beginning of the book as a "radical reformist" strategy for the state turns out to amount to nothing more than a return to corporatist intermediation: the state's function is to bring about a "distributional coalition" and an "orchestration of social consensus" to the end of "promoting competitive manufacturing performance" (p. 146). Of course, it now turns out that there is more than political will involved even in achieving this modest goal. The chances of the USA or UK emulating the alleged successes of Germany and Japan in this respect are reckoned as slim. The reasons for this, however, only have to do with respective "political processes and interest group cultures." Shades of Easton and Almond (prominent mainstream political scientists of the 1950s): capitalist class strategies and the balance of class forces don't get a look in. It seems we are back, theoretically speaking, in the 1950s. The varying way states are constituted to reinforce capitalist class power is out of sight. Such is the conceptual impoverishment of state theory today.

* * * * *

In my own work on globalization and the state [Panitch 1994, 1996] I have also contested the widespread notion that capital has "by-passed" or "escaped" or "diminished" the power of the state. I have argued that this notion reflects a perspective which not only exaggerates the actual institutional autonomy of states from capital in the Keynesian/Bretton Woods era, but which also fails to see that globalization is a process that takes place under the aegis of states and is in many ways authored by states. But it will not advance our understanding very much if we merely assert the continuing importance of states amidst globalization, while failing to explore the determining patterns of state action in our era. To properly make sense of globalization, we cannot do without many of the tools of analysis of Marxist state theory.

By the early 1980s, with the rise of the Thatcher-Reagan regime, governments and bureaucrats proudly enveloped themselves in an ideology that proclaimed the necessity of the state's subordination to the requirements of capital accumulation and markets and even to the norms and opinions of capitalists themselves. Through the course of the decade, moreover, as social democratic regimes (including even Sweden's) found their freedom of manoeuvre restrained by lower rates of capitalist growth and a renewed ideological militancy on the part of capitalists, they soon abandoned all pretense that the mixed economy had not all along been a capitalist one and that the welfare state had not always been dependent on and necessarily contained within the limits of capital accumulation. What this suggests is that far from abandoning the kind of research on ideological links between state and capital that Miliband pioneered, we should have extended, enriched, and multiplied our investigations of ruling class-state "partnerships" (as Miliband termed them) in our time. Whatever the merits of theorizations that want to go beyond research on the ties between business and state elites to deeper structural factors, we can hardly ignore the significance of such linkages when they bulk as large as they do today.

Robert Reich's account of life inside the Clinton Administration, *Locked in the Cabinet*, contains a humorous passage [1998: 82–3] wherein Reich, after describing a lunch with Alan Greenspan at the Federal Reserve, reveals to his readers what he really had wanted (but did not have the courage) to ask Greenspan, and how he believes Greenspan would have replied had he been completely honest:

Q: What's your purpose in life?

A: To stamp out inflation.

Q: Even if that means high unemployment.

A: You bet.

Q: Even if it requires slow growth and stagnant wages?

A: Right you are.

Q: Even if it means drastic cuts in federal programs that help working people and the poor?

A: Absolutely, if that's what it takes to balance the budget and remove all temptation to inflate away the government debt.

Q: But why? A little inflation never hurt anybody.

A: You're wrong. It hurts bond traders and lenders.

Q: But why place their interests over everybody else's interest in good jobs?

A. Because I'm a capitalist and capitalism is driven by the filthy rich. They make their money off bonds. Your constituents are just plain filthy. They have to work for a living.

Q: You're the nation's central banker. You should be accountable to all Americans.

A: But I'm not and neither is the Fed ...

Q. Well you can take your crummy lunch and cram it, you robber-baron pimp.

A: Go suck on a pickle, you Bolshevik dwarf.

But what if Clinton made Reich head of the Federal Reserve rather than Greenspan? Would that have solved the problem? Don't start by imagining the reaction on Wall Street. Think first of all of the reaction inside the Federal Reserve itself. Reich knows this—that is why he has Greenspan say that not only is *he* primarily accountable to capitalists, but *so is the Fed*.

As Clyde Barrow (1993: 30) made clear in his useful book on state theory, even Miliband did not confine himself to the way in which capitalist class-state personnel linkages produced a common ideology, but explicitly tried to ground this ideology in relation to the practices of what he termed the "complex of institutions" that constitute the state, or what Poulantzas termed the "hierarchy of state apparatuses." And the time we now live in is one in which explicit theorizations and investigations of the increasingly close structural relationship between state and capital are more than ever required. Poulantzas was not wrong when he said: "The (capitalist) state, in the long run, can only correspond to the political interests of the dominant class or classes." (And he knew that he and Miliband were in agreement on this: since Miliband was "not some incorrigible Fabian, he of course knows this already.") The general capitalist definition of the nature of the state does not mean, however, that there are not variations among states in terms of their relative autonomy, and it was precisely this that needed to be empirically studied in each case:

> the degree, the extent, the forms, etc. ... of the relative autonomy of the state can only be examined ... with reference to a given capitalist state, and to the precise *conjuncture* of the class struggle (the specific configuration of the power bloc, the degree of hegemony within this bloc, the relations between the bourgeoisie and its different fractions on the one hand and the working classes and supporting classes on the other, etc.). [Poulantzas 1976: 72]

Poulantzas also insisted, of course, on the need to recognize and study the "pertinent effects" of working-class economism and reformism in any given conjuncture. But his overall strategic conclusion (one that Miliband also shared) has proved entirely correct: that is, that economistic/reformist policies were ineffectual, not only in the sense that "this policy could not lead to socialism," but also in the sense that the reforms were always reversible. We are living in a period when social democracy's "pertinent effects," as crystallized in institutional form and cultural values, have been undone in good part even in Sweden. As for those like Hirst and Thompson who now take Japan or Germany as their models, they not only ignore the negative aspects of these state-capitalist partnerships models in comparison with the old Swedish model, they also ignore the extent to which [...] Japan's and Germany's own institutional arrangements are increasingly being destabilised.

The study of the capitalist state today still must meet three requisites (see Panitch 1977: 5–9). It is necessary, first of all, to delineate the institutions of the state in terms of their "structural selectivity" *vis-à-vis* the field of political struggle. Second, it is necessary to maintain a constant stream of empirical research on the specific linkages between state institutions and class actors in terms of ideology, personnel, relations of dependence and influence, etc. Finally, it is always necessary to situate the first two in relation to the state's functions of promoting capital accumulation and the legitimating capitalist domination of the social order. As I have suggested before [Panitch 1994, 1996], what especially needs to be investigated in the context of globalization is whether the important shifts in the hierarchy of state apparatuses really are those, as Cox [1987] suggests, which bring to the fore those institutions, like central banks, most directly linked to the international "caretakers of the global economy," like the IMF and World Bank; or whether a more general process is at work, determined more from within the state itself, whereby all those agencies that directly facilitate capital accumulation and articulate a "competitiveness" ideology, are the ones that gain status, while those which fostered social welfare and articulated a class harmony orientation lose status. Ministries of labour, health, and welfare are perhaps not so much being subordinated as themselves being restructured. We need to investigate whether that loss of status is considerable, or even permanent; and this will partly depend on the transformations which these latter agencies are today going through in terms of being made, or making themselves, more attuned to the exigencies of global competitiveness and fiscal restraint.

* * * * *

REFERENCES

Barrow, Clyde [1993] *Critical Theories of the State*, Madison: University of Wisconsin.
Block, Fred [1994] "The Roles of the State in the Economy," *Handbook of Economic Sociology*,
        N.J. Smelser & R. Swedborg, eds., Princeton: Princeton University Press.
Cox, Robert [1987] *Production, Power and World Order*, New York: Columbia.   •
Crosland, Anthony [1956] *The Future of Socialism*, London: Jonathan Cape.
Galbraith, J.K. [1967] *The New Industrial State*, Boston: Houghton Mifflin.
Gramsci, Antonio [1971] *Selections from the Prison Notebooks*, Q. Hoare & G. Nowell Smith,
        eds., London: Lawrence & Wishart.
Jessop, Bob [1990] *State Theory: Putting Capitalist States in Their Place*, Cambridge: Polity.
Jessop, Bob [1991] "On the Originality, Legacy, and Actuality of Nicos Poulantzas," *Studies
        in Political Economy*, 34:1.
Miliband, Ralph [1969] *The State in Capitalist Society*, New York: Basic Books.
Mills, C. Wright [1956] *The Power Elite*, New York: Oxford University Press.
O'Connor, James [1973] *The Fiscal Crisis of the State*, New York: St. Martin's.
Panitch, Leo [1977] *The Canadian State*, Toronto: University of Toronto Press.
Panitch, Leo [1994] "Globalization and the State," *Socialist Register 1994*, London: Merlin.
Panitch, Leo [1996] "Rethinking the Role of the State," in J. Mittelman, ed., *Globalization:
        Critical Reflections*, Boulder: Lynn Rienner.
Porter, John [1965] *The Vertical Mosaic*, Toronto: University of Toronto Press.
Poulantzas, Nicos [1968] *Pouvoir politique et classes sociales*, Paris: Maspero.
Poulantzas, Nicos [1976] "The Capitalist State: A Reply to Laclau and Mouffe," *New Left
        Review* 95, January/February.
Reich, Robert [1998] *Locked in the Cabinet*, New York: Vintage.
Thompson, E.P. [1978] *The Poverty of Theory*, London: Merlin.

PART II

Class, Conflict, and the State

CRITICAL THINKING QUESTIONS

Porter

1. Why, according to Porter, do Canadians believe that they live in a classless society?
2. In Porter's assessment, in what ways does class position relate to decision-making power in Canada?
3. What role do intellectuals play in the formation of Canadians' perception of their society, according to Porter?

Gramsci

1. What are the major differences between traditional and organic intellectuals?
2. In the context of ethno-racial politics, can Afro-Caribbean Canadian rappers be understood as organic intellectuals?
3. What is a permanent persuader? Identify two permanent persuaders that are influential in North America today.

Wallerstein

1. In what ways does class analysis in Wallerstein's work differ from class analysis in the previous two readings?
2. Identify and explain three components of the capitalist world system. What is the relationship between these areas or regions?
3. How can the capitalist world system be linked to the consolidation of hegemony or cultural domination?

Panitch

1. What does Leo Panitch mean by "the impoverishment of state theory"?

2. What role does Panitch attribute to intellectuals in the development of
    a new theory of the state?
3. What is the relationship that Panitch identifies between intellectual
    state theory and contemporary politics?

SUGGESTED READINGS

Cox, Oliver. 1959. *The Foundations of Capitalism*. London: Peter Owen.

Unlike Marx and later Marxists, Cox argues that the first capitalist city
appeared in medieval Venice. The book details the internal and external
features of the capitalist system, and demonstrates how European capitalism
was one expression of a longer socio-historical process.

Dahrendorf, Ralf. 1959. *Class and Conflict in Industrial Society*. Stanford,
California: Stanford University Press.

Dahrendorf's classic study revises some of Marx's arguments in the
context of Weberian insights. He argues that divisions between people
cannot be explained exclusively in terms of access to property. Dahrendorf
contends that power should occupy the attention of sociologists, and that
power cannot be reduced to property and wealth.

Hamilton, Roberta. 1996. *Gendering the Vertical Mosaic: Feminist Perspectives
on Canadian Society*. Toronto: Copp Clark.

Hamilton's book is a feminist analysis of Canadian society. She argues
that gender is a social process affecting all areas of life in Canada. The book
is offered at an introductory reading level, but readers may benefit from
some preparation in feminist analyses.

Ogmundson, Rick. 1990. "Perspectives on the Class and Ethnic Origins of
Canadian Elites: A Methodological Critique of the Porter/Clement/Olsen
Tradition." *Canadian Journal of Sociology* 15, 2: 165–177.

Ogmundson contends that the work of "vertical mosaic" theorists on
the British upper-class origins of Canada's elites is inaccurate. He seeks
to show how Canada's elites are increasingly heterogeneous in social
characteristics.

Wolf, Eric. 1982. *Europe and the People without History*. Berkeley and Los
Angeles, California: University of California Press.

Wolf's study is an analysis of world capitalism set in the Marxian
tradition. He accounts in great detail for world history and particularly
the rise of European power as a complex web of interactions that existed

outside Europe. Great care is taken to develop a comprehensive theory of the development of capitalism since 1400, and he discusses in detail the people and experiences often left out of world capitalist theorization.

RELATED WEB SITES

Fernand Braudel Center
The Fernand Braudel Center is located at the State University of New York, Binghamton. It was founded by Immanuel Wallerstein in 1976. This Web site contains links to the *Journal of World System Research and Review*, and it offers information on contemporary world system research.
http://fbc.binghamton.edu/

Encyclopedia of Marxism
The Encyclopedia of Marxism was designed with the intention of becoming the most comprehensive reference guide to Marxism. Students will find the wide range of materials useful as a reference guide.
www.marxists.org/glossary/

Marxism Page
This site contains links to Marx and Engels's *Communist Manifesto*, as well as to contemporary Marxist materials. Other relevant materials are available through the links.
www.anu.edu.au/polsci/marx/marx.html

Marxist Internet Archive (Gramsci)
Part of the Marxist Internet Archive, this Web site offers information on Antonio Gramsci. Links are provided to sites containing information on Gramsci's life and works. Of special interest on this site is the link to Gramsci's pre-prison political writings (1910–1926).
www.marxists.org/archive/gramsci/

Youth for International Socialism
This Web site discusses and analyzes what is identified as the hypocrisy of the capitalist system. A wide range of materials is offered from numerous geographic locations.
www.newyouth.com/archives/marxisttheory.asp

PART III

Perspectives in Symbolic Interaction

T HE THIRD MAJOR THEORETICAL ORIENTATION TO DEMONSTRATE A SIGNIFICANT influence on sociological thought in the 20th century was the study of symbolic interaction. Like the theoretical orientations examined in previous chapters, symbolic interaction is comprised of several diverse and, at times, conflicting perspectives. Unlike the theories examined in the previous sections, however, the study of symbolic interaction represents one of several forms of interpretive sociology. Interpretive sociology, or interpretivism, is the study of lived human experience. It is centrally concerned with how people make sense of their life experiences, and the ways in which they derive meaning from, and attribute meaning to, everyday interactions. This is not to suggest that interpretive sociologists neglect social structure, but rather that they pay particular attention to the intersubjective human components involved in the construction and maintenance of social life.

The intellectual origins of symbolic interaction are found in the tradition of philosophical pragmatism. Although the pragmatists differ in some respects, their writings share an interest in the relationship between the individual and society (Stryker 1981). Represented by the philosophies of Charles Pierce, John Dewey, and William James (Prus 1996), philosophical pragmatists prioritize the individual's interpretation of the world to argue that human beings are the authors of their own realities. For the pragmatists, to truly understand reality is to understand processes of intersubjective interpretation and the symbolic construction of the social world.

One of the most influential—and recognizable—contributors to the study of symbolic interaction in the pragmatist tradition is George Herbert Mead (1863–1931). Influenced by the theoretical orientations of evolutionism and behaviorism prominent at the turn of the 20th century, Mead accepted that human beings are evolving biogenic organisms (evolutionism) that respond to various stimuli (behaviourism), but he also recognized that there is a fundamental piece of the puzzle missing both in evolutionism and behaviourism: the social realm. Mead understood communication/language as a component of human evolution that facilitates the survival of the species through the manipulation of shared symbols, gestures, role taking, and the continuous development of the human mind. Mead argued that the development of the human mind, as an evolutionary process, enables individuals to act, rather than simply react, to stimuli in the social world. Not only did this argument separate the study of symbolic interaction from the reductionism of evolutionism and behavioral psychology, but it also provided a viable theoretical alternative to Emile Durkheim's explanation of social facts as things.[1]

⑤ SECTION READINGS: HERBERT BLUMER, ERVING GOFFMAN, HOWARD BECKER, AND NORMAN DENZIN

The interpretive implications of George Herbert Mead's work have been realized in four varieties of, or perspectives on, symbolic interaction. The first perspective was developed in the writings of Herbert Blumer. Blumer (1900–1987) was a student of Mead, and it was Blumer who coined the term "symbolic interaction" in 1937. In Mead's work, Blumer finds the essential features or fundamental premises of the study of symbolic interaction. These include understanding society as comprised of interacting individuals who possess selves; recognizing individual action as a process of meaning construction; and acknowledging action as occurring in the context of manipulating shared symbols. What Blumer finds missing in Mead's account is a clear understanding of the methodological implications of symbolic interaction for sociological research.

Mead placed considerable faith in scientific concepts, and he aspired to nomothetism (generalization through scientific method). Blumer, by contrast, rejects the assumption that there exists sociological "truths" waiting to be unearthed through the use of scientific analyses. The social world, according to Blumer, cannot be understood "objectively" through scientific-deductive methods, and he argues that any methodological program that does not proceed inductively from the point of human experience (acting units) will inevitably (re)produce distorted understandings of social life. To interpret the process of acting units of individuals, Blumer dismisses conventional sociological theories that posit social forces that constrain individual behaviour in a determinant manner external to acting units. For Blumer, sociologists should pursue idiographic (non-generalizing) research through ethnographic methods that probe the life experiences and personal insights of human agents from the ground up.

While Blumer is probably the most influential contributor to symbolic interaction in the interpretive tradition, it was Erving Goffman's work that stimulated widespread interest in interpretivism and symbolic interaction. Goffman (1922–1982) was born in Manville, Alberta, and he received a bachelor's degree from the University of Toronto in 1945 (Goffman 1961). He attended graduate school at the University of Chicago in the late 1940s and early 1950s, where he interacted with Herbert Blumer and other important thinkers. Upon completing his doctorate, Goffman proceeded to write a series of books that portrayed how human behaviour is shaped by factors such as social expectation (Goffman 1959) and the normative constraints of social acceptance (Goffman 1963). He explained social action in terms of "social scripts," and he portrayed social actors as playing a role based on those scripts.

In the reading passage taken from his first manuscript, *The Presentation of Self in Everyday Life*, Goffman (1959) introduces the second variety of symbolic interaction: dramaturgy. The production of everyday life, Goffman argues, is best understood as a theatrical performance. He conceptualizes human beings as interactive performers who conduct their performances in "front settings." The front setting consists of a standard physical location, such as a university professor's office, which is typically lined with walls of books (a lesser number of which have actually been read). Front settings also involve personal fronts comprised of stimuli in the form of appearances and manners (such as a nose ring or tattoo). Fronts provide order in the mundane routines of everyday life, and they often become institutionalized in the form of abstract collective expectations. What is most interesting in Goffman's dramaturgical model is that, as human beings, we tend not to create our fronts, but rather select them from a number of already existing ones. When performing in everyday life, we take lines of action that give off impressions of appearance and manner. For Goffman, social life is about impression management.

While Goffman was working out his dramaturgical model in the 1950s and 1960s, a third variety of symbolic interaction developed under the auspices of "labelling theory." Labelling theory is primarily associated with the sociology of deviance. Sociologists in this tradition are interested in how people come to be labelled as deviant, what processes are involved in constituting deviant activities, and how people learn deviance in a particular social context. Labelling theorists argue that nothing is inherently deviant, and that attributions of deviance are social constructions that take place in particular social contexts.

In one of the classic statements on the social construction of deviance, Howard Becker (1899–1960) explains in the reading passage that all social groups make rules that they then attempt to enforce. Those who violate the rules become labelled as "outsiders." Becoming an outsider, however, involves more than simply being labelled as such by rule enforcers or moral entrepreneurs. It involves a sequence of interactions and exchanges, both verbal and non-verbal. Drawing from his studies of marihuana users and jazz musicians, Becker demonstrates the social construction of deviant identities. He also argues that a "high" in the context of marihuana use is not necessarily a property of the chemical substance; rather, highs are learned processes that come about through interactions with others.

The final variant of symbolic interaction dealt with in this chapter is ethnomethodology. Ethnomethodology was formalized with the publication of Harold Garfinkel's (1967) *Studies in Ethnomethodology*, and it is an effort to "treat practical activities, practical circumstances, and practical sociological reasoning as topics of empirical study ... by paying to the most commonplace activities of daily life the attention usually accorded extraordinary events." Garfinkel (1967: 1) makes it clear that he rejects those forms of Durkheimianism that teach the objective reality of social facts. For Garfinkel in particular, and ethnomethodologists in general, what is most important is the actor's interpretation of the social event. But in order to tap into the very nature of human interaction, Garfinkle believes that norms and rules must be violated. It is only when norms and rules are violated that social action can be separated from normative conformity.

How does ethnomethodology differ from more traditional (Mead) or mainstream (Goffman) currents in the study of symbolic interaction? As Norman Denzin explains in the reading passage, ethnomethodologists, like symbolic interactionists, take as their basic unit of analysis the individual. They criticize "traditional" sociologists for imposing their own sense of social reality on the world of lived experience, and they engage analyses of how social actors make sense of social life as it is revealed in the taken-for-granted everyday world of experience. However, one of the major points of contention between symbolic interactionism and ethnomethodology is that ethnomethodologists reject the notion that social order exists independent of actors' experiences and accounts. Both perspectives are rooted in the pragmatists' basic contention that reality is a human construct, and they both draw from the same lexicon ("meaning," "interpretation," "subjectivity," etc). But the underlying epistemological assumptions that each derives from these concepts is considerably diverse, and, to the ethnomethodologist, actors' interpretations of the rules that make collective activity possible are more important than symbolic interactionists' (implicit) presumption of social order. It is for these reasons that Denzin proposes that the two perspectives have much to offer one another.

NOTES

1. While one of Durkheim's primary concerns was to establish the scientific study of sociology, in his lectures of 1913–1914 he found the pragmatism of Dewey, Pierce, and Shilling tending toward a psychological reductionism that was at odds with sociological method. Prus (1996: 29) speculates that, had Durkheim read Cooley, Mead, or Dilthey, he would have been more favourably inclined to pragmatism and symbolic interaction.

REFERENCES

Garfinkel, Harold. 1967. *Ethnomethodology*. New Jersey: Prentice Hall.

Goffman, Erving. 1959. *The Presentation of Self in Everyday Life*. New York: Doubleday Anchor.

_____. 1961. *Asylums*. New York: Double Day Anchor.

_____. 1963. *Stigma*. Baltimore: Penguin.

Prus, Robert. 1996. *Symbolic Interaction and Ethnographic Research*. New York: State University of New York Press.

Stryker, Sheldon. 1981. *Symbolic Interactionism*. Menlo Park: Benjamin/Cummings.

CHAPTER 7

Society as Symbolic Interaction

HERBERT BLUMER

* * * * *

A view of human society as symbolic interaction has been followed more than it has been formulated. Partial, usually fragmentary, statements of it are to be found in the writings of a number of eminent scholars, some inside the field of sociology and some outside. Among the former we may note such scholars as Charles Horton Cooley, W.I. Thomas, Robert E. Park, E.W. Burgess, Florian Znaniecki, Ellsworth Faris, and James Mickel Williams. Among those outside the discipline we may note William James, John Dewey, and George Herbert Mead. None of these scholars, in my judgment, has presented a systematic statement of the nature of human group life from the standpoint of symbolic interaction. Mead stands out among all of them in laying bare the fundamental premises of the approach, yet he did little to develop its methodological implications for sociological study. Students who seek to depict the position of symbolic interaction may easily give different pictures of it. What I have to present should be regarded as my personal version. My aim is to present the basic premises of the point of view and to develop their methodological consequences for the study of human group life.

The term "symbolic interaction" refers, of course, to the peculiar and distinctive character of interaction as it takes place between human beings. The peculiarity consists in the fact that human beings interpret or "define" each other's actions instead of merely reacting to each other's actions. Their "response" is not made directly to the actions of one another but instead is based on the meaning which they attach to such actions. Thus, human interaction is mediated by the use of symbols, by interpretation, or by ascertaining the meaning of one another's actions. This mediation is equivalent to inserting a process of interpretation between stimulus and response in the case of human behavior.

The simple recognition that human beings interpret each other's actions as the means of acting toward one another has permeated the thought and writings of many scholars of human conduct and of human group life. Yet few of them have endeavored to analyze what such interpretation implies about the nature of the human being or about the nature of human association. They are usually content with a mere recognition that "interpretation" should be caught by the student, or with a simple realization that symbols, such as cultural norms or values, must be introduced into their analyses. Only G.H. Mead, in my judgment, has sought to think through what the act of interpretation implies for an understanding of the human being, human action, and human association. The essentials of his analysis are so penetrating and profound and so important for an understanding of human group life that I wish to spell them out, even though briefly.

The key feature in Mead's analysis is that the human being has a self. This idea should not be cast aside as esoteric or glossed over as something that is obvious and hence not worthy of attention. In declaring that the human being has a self, Mead had in mind chiefly that the human being can be the object of his own actions. He can act toward himself as he might act toward others. Each of us is familiar with actions of this sort in which the human being gets angry with himself, rebuffs himself, takes pride in himself, argues with himself, tries to bolster his own courage, tells himself that he should "do this" or not "do that," sets goals for himself, makes compromises with himself, and plans what he is going to do. That the human being acts toward himself in these and countless other ways is a matter of easy empirical observation. To recognize that the human being can act toward himself is no mystical conjuration.

Mead regards this ability of the human being to act toward himself as the central mechanism with which the human being faces and deals with his world. This mechanism enables the human being to make indication to himself of things in his surroundings and thus to guide his actions by what he notes. Anything of which a human being is conscious is something which he is indicating to himself—the ticking of a clock, a knock at the door, the appearance of a friend, the remark made by a companion, a recognition that he has a task to perform, or the realization that he has a cold. Conversely, anything of which he is not conscious is, *ipso facto,* something which he is not indicating to himself. The conscious life of the human being, from the time that he awakens until he falls asleep, is a continual flow of self-indications—notations of the things with which he deals and takes into account. We are given, then, a picture of the human being as an organism which confronts its world with a mechanism for making indications to itself. This is the mechanism that is involved in interpreting the actions of others. To interpret the actions of another is to point out to oneself that the action has this or that meaning or character.

Now, according to Mead, the significance of making indications to oneself is of paramount importance. The importance lies along two lines. First, to indicate something is to extricate it from its setting, to hold it apart, to give it a meaning or, in Mead's language, to make it into an object. An object—that is to say, anything that an individual indicates to himself—is different from a stimulus; instead of having an intrinsic character which acts on the individual and which can be identified apart from the individual, its character or meaning is conferred on it by the individual. The object is a product of the individual's disposition to act instead of being an antecedent stimulus which evokes the act. Instead of the individual being surrounded by an environment of pre-existing objects which play upon him and call forth his behavior, the proper picture is that he constructs his objects on the basis of his on-going activity. In any of his countless acts—whether minor, like dressing himself, or major, like organizing himself for a professional career—the individual is designating different objects to himself, giving them meaning, judging their suitability to his action, and making decisions on the basis of the judgment. This is what is meant by interpretation or acting on the basis of symbols.

The second important implication of the fact that the human being makes indications to himself is that his action is constructed or built up instead of being a mere release. Whatever the action in which he is engaged, the human individual proceeds by pointing out to himself the divergent things which have to be taken into account in the course of his action. He has to note what he wants to do and how he is to do it; he has to point out to himself the various conditions which may be instrumental to his action and those which may obstruct his action; he has to take account of the demands, the expectations, the prohibitions, and the threats as they may arise in the situation in which he is acting. His action is built up step by step through a process of such self-indication. The human individual pieces together and guides his action by taking account of different things and interpreting their significance for his prospective action. There is no instance of conscious action of which this is not true.

The process of constructing action through making indications to oneself cannot be swallowed up in any of the conventional psychological categories. This process is distinct from and different from what is spoken of as the "ego"—just as it is different from any other conception which conceives of the self in terms of composition or organization. Self-indication is a moving communicative process in which the individual notes things, assesses them, gives them a meaning, and decides to act on the basis of the meaning. The human being stands over against the world, or against "alters," with such a process and not with a mere ego. Further, the process of self-indication cannot be subsumed under the forces, whether from the outside or inside, which are presumed to play upon the individual to produce his behavior. Environmental pressures, external stimuli, organic drives, wishes, attitudes, feelings, ideas, and their like do not cover or explain the process of self-indication. The process of self-indication stands over against them in that the individual points out to himself and interprets the appearance or expression of such things, noting a given social demand that is made on him, recognizing a command, observing that he is hungry, realizing that he wishes to buy something, aware that he has a given feeling, conscious that he dislikes eating with someone he despises, or aware that he is thinking of doing some given thing. By virtue of indicating such things to himself, he places himself over against them and is able to act back against them, accepting them, rejecting them, or transforming them in accordance with how he defines or interprets them. His behavior, accordingly, is not a result of such things as environmental pressures, stimuli, motives, attitudes, and ideas but arises instead from how he interprets and handles these things in the action which he is constructing. The process of self-indication by means of which human action is formed cannot be accounted for by factors which precede the act. The process of self-indication exists in its own right and must be accepted and studied as such. It is through this process that the human being constructs his conscious action.

Now Mead recognizes that the formation of action by the individual through a process of self-indication always takes place in a social context. Since this matter is so vital to an understanding of symbolic interaction, it needs to be explained carefully. Fundamentally, group action takes the form of a fitting together of individual lines of action. Each individual aligns his action to the action of others by ascertaining what they are doing or what they intend to do—that is, by getting the meaning of their acts. For Mead, this is done by the individual "taking the role" of others—either the role of a specific person or the role of a group (Mead's "generalized other"). In taking such roles the individual seeks to ascertain the intention or direction of the acts of others. He forms and aligns his own action on the basis of such interpretation of the acts of others. This is the fundamental way in which group action takes place in human society.

The foregoing are the essential features, as I see them, in Mead's analysis of the bases of symbolic interaction. They presuppose the following: that human society is made up of individuals who have selves (that is, make indications to themselves); that individual action is a construction and not a release, being built up by the individual through noting and interpreting features of the situations in which he acts; that group or collective action consists of the aligning of individual actions, brought about by the individuals' interpreting or taking into account each other's actions. Since my purpose is to present and not to defend the position of symbolic interaction, I shall not endeavor in this essay to advance support for the three premises which I have just indicated. I wish merely to say that the three premises can be easily verified empirically. I know of no instance of human group action to which the three premises do not apply. The reader is challenged to find or think of a single instance which they do not fit.

I wish now to point out that sociological views of human society are, in general, markedly at variance with the premises which I have indicated as underlying symbolic interaction. Indeed, the predominant number of such views, especially those in vogue at the present time, do not see or treat human society as symbolic interaction. Wedded, as they tend to be, to some form of sociological determinism, they adopt images of human society, of individuals in it, and of group action which do not square with the premises of symbolic interaction. I wish to say a few words about the major lines of variance.

Sociological thought rarely recognizes or treats human societies as composed of individuals who have selves. Instead, they assume human beings to be merely organisms with some kind of organization, responding to forces which play upon them. Generally, although not exclusively, these forces are lodged in the make-up of the society, as in the case of "social system," "social structure," "culture," "status position," "social role," "custom," "institution," "collective representation," "social situation," "social norm," and "values." The assumption is that the behavior of people as members *of a society* is an expression of the play on them of these kinds of factors or forces. This, of course, is the logical position which is necessarily taken when the scholar explains their behavior or phases of their behavior in terms of one or other of such social factors. The individuals who compose a human society are treated as the media through which such factors operate, and the social action of such individuals is regarded as an expression of such factors. This approach or point of view denies, or at least ignores, that human beings have selves—that they act by making indications to themselves. Incidentally, the "self" is not brought into the picture by introducing such items as organic drives, motives, attitudes, feelings, internalized social factors, or psychological components. Such psychological factors have the same status as the social factors mentioned: they are regarded as factors which play on the individual to produce his action. They do not constitute the process of self-indication. The process of self-indication stands over against them, just as it stands over against the social factors which play on the human being. Practically all sociological conceptions of human society fail to recognize that the individuals who compose it have selves in the sense spoken of.

Correspondingly, such sociological conceptions do not regard the social actions of individuals in human society as being constructed by them through a process of interpretation. Instead, action is treated as a product of factors which play on and through individuals. The social behavior of people is not seen as built up by them through an interpretation of objects, situations, or the actions of others. If a place is given to "interpretation," the interpretation is regarded as merely an expression of other factors (such as motives) which precede the act, and accordingly disappears as a factor in its own right. Hence, the social action of people is treated as an outward flow or expression of forces playing on them rather than as acts which are built up by people through their interpretation of the situations in which they are placed.

These remarks suggest another significant line of difference between general sociological views and the position of symbolic interaction. These two sets of views differ in where they lodge social action. Under the perspective of symbolic interaction, social action is lodged in acting individuals who fit their respective lines of action to one another through a process of interpretation; group action is the collective action of such individuals. As opposed to this view, sociological conceptions generally lodge social action in the action of society or in some unit of society. Examples of this are legion. Let me cite a few. Some conceptions, in treating societies or human groups as "social systems," regard group action as an expression of a system, either in a state of balance or seeking to achieve balance. Or group action is conceived as an expression of the "functions" of a society or of a group. Or group action is regarded as the outward expression of elements lodged in society or the group, such as cultural demands, societal purposes, social values, or institutional stresses. These typical conceptions ignore or blot out a view of group life or of group action as consisting of the collective or concerted actions of individuals seeking to meet their life situations. If recognized at all, the efforts of people to develop collective acts to meet their situations are subsumed under the play of underlying or transcending forces which are lodged in society or its parts. The individuals composing the society or the group become "carriers," or media for the expression of such forces; and the interpretative behavior by means of which people form their actions is merely a coerced link in the play of such forces.

The indication of the foregoing lines of variance should help to put the position of symbolic interaction in better perspective. In the remaining discussion I wish to sketch somewhat more fully how human society appears in terms of symbolic interaction and to point out some methodological implications.

Human society is to be seen as consisting of acting people, and the life of the society is to be seen as consisting of their actions. The acting units may be separate individuals, collectivities whose members are acting together on a common quest, or organizations acting on behalf of a constituency. Respective examples are individual purchasers in a market, a play group or missionary band, and a business corporation or a national professional association. There is no empirically observable activity in a human society that does not spring from some acting unit. This banal statement needs to be stressed in light of the common practice of sociologists of reducing human society to social units that do not act—for example, social classes in modern society. Obviously, there are ways of viewing human society other than in terms of the acting units that compose it. I merely wish to point out that in respect to concrete or empirical activity human society must necessarily be seen in terms of the acting units that form it. I would add that any scheme of human society claiming to be a realistic analysis has to respect and be congruent with the empirical recognition that a human society consists of acting units.

Corresponding respect must be shown to the conditions under which such units act. One primary condition is that action takes place in and with regard to a situation. Whatever be the acting unit—an individual, a family, a school, a church, a business firm, a labor union, a legislature, and so on—any particular action is formed in the light of the situation in which it takes place. This leads to the recognition of a second major condition, namely, that the action is formed or constructed by interpreting the situation. The acting unit necessarily has to identify the things which it has to take into account—tasks, opportunities, obstacles, means, demands, discomforts, dangers, and the like; it has to assess them in some fashion and it has to make decisions on the basis of the assessment. Such interpretative behavior may take place in the individual guiding his own action, in a collectivity of individuals acting in concert, or in "agents" acting on behalf of a group or organization. Group life consists of acting units developing acts to meet the situations in which they are placed.

Usually, most of the situations encountered by people in a given society are defined or "structured" by them in the same way. Through previous interaction they develop and acquire common understandings or definitions of how to act in this or that situation. These common definitions enable people to act alike. The common repetitive behavior of people in such situations should not mislead the student into believing that no process of interpretation is in play; on the contrary, even though fixed, the actions of the participating people are constructed by them through a process of interpretation. Since ready-made and commonly accepted definitions are at hand, little strain is placed on people in guiding and organizing their acts. However, many other situations may not be defined in a single way by the participating people. In this event, their lines of action do not fit together readily and collective action is blocked. Interpretations have to be developed and effective accommodation of the participants to one another has to be worked out. In the case of such "undefined" situations, it is necessary to trace and study the emerging process of definition which is brought into play.

Insofar as sociologists or students of human society are concerned with the behavior of acting units, the position of symbolic interaction requires the student to catch the process of interpretation through which they construct their actions. This process is not to be caught merely by turning to conditions which are antecedent to the process. Such antecedent conditions are helpful in understanding the process insofar as they enter into it, but as mentioned previously they do not constitute the process. Nor can one catch the process merely by inferring its nature from the overt action which is its product. To catch the process, the student must take the role of the acting unit whose behavior he is studying. Since the interpretation is being made by the acting unit in terms of objects designated and appraised, meanings acquired, and decisions made, the process has to be seen from the standpoint of the acting unit. It is the recognition of this fact that makes the research work of such scholars as R.E. Park and W.I. Thomas so notable. To try to catch the interpretative process by remaining aloof as a so-called "objective" observer and refusing to take the role of the acting unit is to risk the worst kind of subjectivism—the objective observer is likely to fill in the process of interpretation with his own surmises in place of catching the process as it occurs in the experience of the acting unit which uses it.

By and large, of course, sociologists do not study human society in terms of its acting units. Instead, they are disposed to view human society in terms of structure or organization and to treat social action as an expression of such structure or organization. Thus, reliance is placed on such structural categories as social system, culture, norms, values, social stratification, status positions, social roles, and institutional organization. These are used both to analyze human society and to account for social action within it. Other major interests of sociological scholars center around this focal theme of organization. One line of interest is to view organization in terms of the functions it is supposed to perform. Another line of interest is to study societal organization as a system seeking equilibrium; here the scholar endeavors to detect mechanisms which are indigenous to the system. Another line of interest is to identify forces which play upon organization to bring about changes in it; here the scholar endeavors, especially through comparative study, to isolate a relation between causative factors and structural results. These various lines of sociological perspective and interest, which are so strongly entrenched today, leap over the acting units of a society and bypass the interpretative process by which such acting units build up their actions.

These respective concerns with organization on one hand and with acting units on the other hand set the essential difference between conventional views of human society and the view of it implied in symbolic interaction. The latter view recognizes the presence of organization in human society and respects its importance. However, it sees and treats organization differently. The difference is along two major lines. First, from the standpoint of symbolic interaction the organization of a human society is the framework inside of which social action takes place and is not the determinant of that action. Second, such organization and changes in it are the product of the activity of acting units and not of "forces" which leave such acting units out of account. Each of these two major lines of difference should be explained briefly in order to obtain a better understanding of how human society appears in terms of symbolic interaction.

From the standpoint of symbolic interaction, social organization is a framework inside of which acting units develop their actions. Structural features, such as "culture," "social systems," "social stratification," or "social roles," set conditions for their action but do not determine their action. People—that is, acting units—do not act toward culture, social structure or the like; they act toward situations. Social organization enters into action only to the extent to which it shapes situations in which people act, and to the extent to which it supplies fixed sets of symbols which people use in interpreting their situations. These two forms of influence of social organization are important. In the case of settled and stabilized societies, such as isolated primitive tribes and peasant communities, the influence is certain to be profound. In the case of human societies, particularly modern societies, in which streams of new situations arise and old situations become unstable, the influence of organization decreases. One should bear in mind that the most important element confronting an acting unit in situations is the actions of other acting units. In modern society, with its increasing criss-crossing of lines of action, it is common for situations to arise in which the actions of participants are not previously regularized and standardized. To this extent, existing social organization does not shape the situations. Correspondingly, the symbols or tools of interpretation used by acting units in such situations may vary and shift considerably. For these reasons, social action may go beyond, or depart from, existing organization in any of its structural dimensions. The organization of a human society is not to be identified with the process of interpretation used by its acting units; even though it affects that process, it does not embrace or cover the process.

Perhaps the most outstanding consequence of viewing human society as organization is to overlook the part played by acting units in social change. The conventional procedure of sociologists is (a) to identify human society (or some part of it) in terms of an established or organized form, (b) to identify some factor or condition of change playing upon the human society or the given part of it, and (c) to identify the new form assumed by the society following upon the play of the factor of change. Such observations permit the student to couch propositions to the effect that a given factor of change playing upon a given organized form results in a given new organized form. Examples ranging from crude to refined statements are legion, such as that an economic depression increases solidarity in the families of workingmen or that industrialization replaces extended families by nuclear families. My concern here is not with the validity of such propositions but with the methodological position which they presuppose. Essentially, such propositions either ignore the role of the interpretative behavior of acting units in the given instance of change, or else regard the interpretative behavior as coerced by the factor of change. I wish to point out that any line of social change, since it involves change in human action, is necessarily mediated by interpretation on the part of the people caught up in the change—the change appears in the form of new situations in which people have to construct new forms of action. Also, in line with what has been said previously, interpretations of new situations are not predetermined by conditions antecedent to the situations but depend on what is taken into account and assessed in the actual situations in which behavior is formed. Variations in interpretation may readily occur as different acting units cut out different objects in the situation, or give different weight to the objects which they note, or piece objects together in different patterns. In formulating propositions of social change, it would be wise to recognize that any given line of such change is mediated by acting units interpreting the situations with which they are confronted.

Students of human society will have to face the question of whether their preoccupation with categories of structure and organization can be squared with the interpretative process by means of which human beings, individually and collectively, act in human society. It is the discrepancy between the two which plagues such students in their efforts to attain scientific propositions of the sort achieved in the physical and biological sciences. It is this discrepancy, further, which is chiefly responsible for their difficulty in fitting hypothetical propositions to new arrays of empirical data. Efforts are made, of course, to overcome these shortcomings by devising new structural categories, by formulating new structural hypotheses, by developing more refined techniques of research, and even by formulating new methodological schemes of a structural character. These efforts continue to ignore or to explain away the interpretative process by which people act, individually and collectively, in society. The question remains whether human society or social action can be successfully analyzed by schemes which refuse to recognize human beings as they are, namely, as persons constructing individual and collective action through an interpretation of the situations which confront them.

CHAPTER 8

Introduction to *The Presentation of Self in Everyday Life*

ERVING GOFFMAN

When an individual enters the presence of others, they commonly seek to acquire information about him or to bring into play information about him already possessed. They will be interested in his general socio-economic status, his conception of self, his attitude toward them, his competence, his trustworthiness, etc. Although some of this information seems to be sought almost as an end in itself, there are usually quite practical reasons for acquiring it. Information about the individual helps to define the situation, enabling others to know in advance what he will expect of them and what they may expect of him. Informed in these ways, the others will know how best to act in order to call forth a desired response from him.

For those present, many sources of information become accessible and many carriers (or "sign-vehicles") become available for conveying this information. If unacquainted with the individual, observers can glean clues from his conduct and appearance which allow them to apply their previous experience with individuals roughly similar to the one before them or, more important; to apply untested stereotypes to him. They can also assume from past experience that only individuals of a particular kind are likely to be found in a given social setting. They can rely on what the individual says about himself or on documentary evidence he provides as to who and what he is. If they know, or know of, the individual by virtue of experience prior to the interaction, they can rely on assumptions as to the persistence and generality of psychological traits as a means of predicting his present and future behavior.

However, during the period in which the individual is in the immediate presence of the others, few events may occur which directly provide the others with the conclusive information they will need if they are to direct wisely their own activity. Many crucial facts lie beyond the time and place of interaction or lie concealed within it. For example, the "true" or "real" attitudes, beliefs, and emotions of the individual can be ascertained only indirectly, through his avowals, or through what appears to be involuntary expressive behavior. Similarly, if the individual offers the others a product or service, they will often find that during the interaction there will be no time and place immediately available for eating the pudding that the proof can be found in. They will be forced to accept some events as conventional or natural signs of something not directly available to the senses. In Ichheiser's terms,[1] the individual will have to act so that he intentionally or unintentionally *expresses* himself, and the others will in turn have to be *impressed* in some way by him.

The expressiveness of the individual (and therefore his capacity to give impressions) appears to involve two radically different lands of sign activity: the expression that he *gives*, and the expression that he *gives off*. The first involves verbal symbols or their substitutes which he uses admittedly and solely to convey the information that he and the others are known to attach to these symbols. This is communication in the traditional and narrow sense. The second involves a wide range of action that others can treat as symptomatic of the actor, the expectation being that the action was performed for reasons other than the information conveyed in this way. As we shall have to see, this distinction has an only initial validity. The individual does, of course, intentionally convey misinformation by means of both of these types of communication, the first involving deceit, the second feigning.

Taking communication in both its narrow and broad sense, one finds that when the individual is in the immediate presence of others, his activity will have a promissory character. The others are likely to find that they must accept the individual on faith, offering him a just return while he is present before them in exchange for something whose true value will not be established until after he has left their presence. (Of course, the others also live by inference in their dealings with the physical world, but it is only in the world of social interaction that the objects about which they make inferences will purposely facilitate and hinder this inferential process.) The security that they justifiably feel in making inferences about the individual will vary, of course, depending on such factors as the amount of information they already possess about him, but no amount of such past evidence can entirely obviate the necessity of acting on the basis of inferences. As William L. Thomas suggested:

> It is also highly important for us to realize that we do not as a matter of fact lead our lives, make our decisions, and reach our goals in everyday life either statistically or scientifically. We live by inference. I am, let us say, your guest. You do not know, you cannot determine scientifically, that I will not steal your money or your spoons. But inferentially I will not, and inferentially you have me as a guest.[2]

Let us now turn from the others to the point of view of the individual who presents himself before them. He may wish them to think highly of him, or to think that he thinks highly of them, or to perceive how in fact he feels toward them, or to obtain no clear-cut impression; he may wish to ensure sufficient harmony so that the interaction can be sustained, or to defraud, get rid of, confuse, mislead, antagonize, or insult them. Regardless of the particular objective which the individual has in mind and of his motive for having this objective, it will be in his interests to control the conduct of the others, especially their responsive treatment of him.[3] This control is achieved largely by influencing the definition of the situation which the others come to formulate, and he can influence this definition by expressing himself in such a way as to give them the kind of impression that will lead them to act voluntarily in accordance with his own plan. Thus, when an individual appears in the presence of others, there will usually be some reason for him to mobilize his activity so that it will convey an impression to others which it is in his interests to convey. Since a girl's dormitory mates will glean evidence of her popularity from the calls she receives on the phone, we can suspect that some girls will arrange for calls to be made, and Willard Waller's finding can be anticipated:

> It has been reported by many observers that a girl who is called to the telephone in the dormitories will often allow herself to be called several times, in order to give all the other girls ample opportunity to hear her paged.[4]

Of the two kinds of communication—expressions given and expressions given off—this report will be primarily concerned with the latter, with the more theatrical and contextual kind, the non-verbal, presumably unintentional kind, whether this communication be purposely engineered or not. As an example of what we must try to examine, I would like to cite at length a novelistic incident in which Preedy, a vacationing Englishman, makes his first appearance on the beach of his summer hotel in Spain:

> But in any case he took care to avoid catching anyone's eye. First of all, he had to make it clear to those potential companions of his holiday that they were of no concern to him whatsoever. He stared through them, round them, over them—eyes lost in space. The beach might have been empty. If by chance a ball was thrown his way, he looked surprised; then let a smile of amusement lighten his face (Kindly Preedy), looked round dazed to see that there *were* people on the beach, tossed it back with a smile to himself and not a smile *at* the people, and then resumed carelessly his nonchalant survey of space.
>
> But it was time to institute a little parade, the parade of the Ideal Preedy. By devious handlings he gave any who wanted to look a chance to see the title of his book—a Spanish translation of Homer, classic thus, but not daring, cosmopolitan too—and then gathered together his beach-wrap and bag into a neat sand-resistant pile (Methodical and Sensible Preedy), rose slowly to stretch at ease his huge frame (Big-Cat Preedy), and tossed aside his sandals (Carefree Preedy, after all).
>
> The marriage of Preedy and the sea! There were alternative rituals. The first involved the stroll that turns into a run and a dive straight into the water, thereafter smoothing into a strong splashless crawl towards the horizon. But of course not really to the horizon. Quite suddenly he would turn on to his back and thrash great

white splashes with his legs, somehow thus showing that he could have swum further had he wanted to, and then would stand up a quarter out of water for all to see who it was.

The alternative course was simpler, it avoided the cold-water shock and it avoided the risk of appearing too high-spirited. The point was to appear to be so used to the sea, the Mediterranean, and this particular beach, that one might as well be in the sea as out of it. It involved a slow stroll down and into the edge of the water—not even noticing his toes were wet, land and water all the same to *him!*—*with* his eyes up at the sky gravely surveying portents, invisible to others, of the weather (Local Fisherman Preedy).[5]

The novelist means us to see that Preedy is improperly concerned with the extensive impressions he feels his sheer bodily action is giving off to those around him. We can malign Preedy further by assuming that he has acted merely in order to give a particular impression, that this is a false impression, and that the others present receive either no impression at all, or, worse still, the impression that Preedy is affectedly trying to cause them to receive this particular impression. But the important point for us here is that the kind of impression Preedy thinks he is making is in fact the kind of impression that others correctly and incorrectly glean from someone in their midst.

* * * * *

There is one aspect of the others' response that bears special comment here. Knowing that the individual is likely to present himself in a light that is favorable to him, the others may divide what they witness into two parts; a part that is relatively easy for the individual to manipulate at will, being chiefly his verbal assertions, and a part in regard to which he seems to have little concern or control, being chiefly derived from the expressions he gives off. The others may then use what are considered to be the ungovernable aspects of his expressive behavior as a check upon the validity of what is conveyed by the governable aspects. In this a fundamental asymmetry is demonstrated in the communication process, the individual presumably being aware of only one stream of his communication, the witnesses of this stream and one other. For example, in Shetland Isle one crofter's wife, in serving native dishes to a visitor from the mainland of Britain, would listen with a polite smile to his polite claims of liking what he was eating; at the same time she would take note of the rapidity with which the visitor lifted his fork or spoon to his mouth, the eagerness with which he passed food into his mouth, and the gusto expressed in chewing the food, using these signs as a check on the stated feelings of the eater. The same woman, in order to discover what one acquaintance (A) "actually" thought of another acquaintance (B), would wait until B was in the presence of A but engaged in conversation with still another person (C). She would then covertly examine the facial expressions of

A as he regarded B in conversation with C. Not being in conversation with B, and not being directly observed by him, A would sometimes relax usual constraints and tactful deceptions, and freely express what he was "actually" feeling about B. This Shetlander, in short, would observe the unobserved observer.

Now given the fact that others are likely to check up on the more controllable aspects of behavior by means of the less controllable, one can expect that sometimes the individual will try to exploit this very possibility, guiding the impression he makes through behavior felt to be reliably informing.[6] For example, in gaining admission to a tight social circle, the participant observer may not only wear an accepting look while listening to an informant, but may also be careful to wear the same look when observing the informant talking to others; observers of the observer will then not as easily discover where he actually stands. A specific illustration may be cited from Shetland Isle. When a neighbor dropped in to have a cup of tea, he would ordinarily wear at least a hint of an expectant warm smile as he passed through the door into the cottage. Since lack of physical obstructions outside the cottage and lack of light within it usually made it possible to observe the visitor unobserved as he approached the house, islanders sometimes took pleasure in watching the visitor drop whatever expression he was manifesting and replace it with a sociable one just before reaching the door. However, some visitors, in appreciating that this examination was occurring, would blindly adopt a social face a long distance from the house, thus ensuring the projection of a constant image.

This kind of control upon the part of the individual reinstates the symmetry of the communication process, and sets the stage for a kind of information game—a potentially infinite cycle of concealment, discovery, false revelation, and rediscovery. It should be added that since the others are likely to be relatively unsuspicious of the presumably unguided aspect of the individual's conduct, he can gain much by controlling it. The others, of course, may sense that the individual is manipulating the presumably spontaneous aspects of his behavior, and seek in this very act of manipulation some shading of conduct that the individual has not managed to control. This again provides a check upon the individual's behavior, this time his presumably uncalculated behavior, thus re-establishing the asymmetry of the communication process. Here I would like only to add the suggestion that the arts of piercing an individual's effort at calculated unintentionality seem better developed than our capacity to manipulate our own behavior, so that regardless of how many steps have occurred in the information game, the witness is likely to have the advantage over the actor, and the initial asymmetry of the communication process is likely to be retained.

When we allow that the individual projects a definition of the situation when he appears before others, we must also see that the others, however passive their role may seem to be, will themselves effectively project a definition of the situation by virtue of their response to the individual and by virtue of any lines of action they initiate to him. Ordinarily the definitions of the situation projected by the several different participants are sufficiently attuned to one another so that open contradiction will not occur. I do not mean that there will be the kind of consensus that arises when each individual present candidly expresses what he really feels and honestly agrees with the expressed feelings of the others present. This kind of harmony is an optimistic ideal and in any case not necessary for the smooth working of society. Rather, each participant is expected to suppress his immediate heartfelt feelings, conveying a view of the situation which he feels the others will be able to find at least temporarily acceptable. The maintenance of this surface of agreement, this veneer of consensus, is facilitated by each participant concealing his own wants behind statements which assert values to which everyone present feels obliged to give lip service. Further, there is usually a kind of division of definitional labor. Each participant is allowed to establish the tentative official ruling regarding matters which are vital to him but not immediately important to others, e.g., the rationalizations and justifications by which he accounts for his past activity. In exchange for this courtesy he remains silent or non-committal on matters important to others but not immediately important to him. We have then a kind of interactional *modus vivendi*. Together the participants contribute to a single over-all definition of the situation which involves not so much a real agreement as to what exists but rather a real agreement as to whose claims concerning what issues will be temporarily honored. Real agreement will also exist concerning the desirability of avoiding an open conflict of definitions of the situation.[7] I will refer to this level of agreement as a "working consensus." It is to be understood that the working consensus established in one interaction setting will be quite different in content from the working consensus established in a different type of setting. Thus, between two friends at lunch, a reciprocal show of affection, respect, and concern for the other is maintained. In service occupations, on the other hand, the specialist often maintains an image of disinterested involvement in the problem of the client, while the client responds with a show of respect for the competence and integrity of the specialist. Regardless of such differences in content, however, the general form of these working arrangements is the same.

In noting the tendency for a participant to accept the definitional claims made by the others present, we can appreciate the crucial importance of the information that the individual *initially* possesses or acquires concerning his fellow participants, for it is on the basis of this initial information that the individual starts to define the situation and starts to build up lines of responsive action. The individual's initial projection commits him to what he is proposing to be and requires him to drop all pretenses of being other things. As the interaction among the participants progresses, additions and modifications in this initial informational state will, of course, occur, but it is essential that these later developments be related without contradiction to, and even built up from, the initial positions taken by the several participants. It would seem that an individual can more easily make a choice as to what line of treatment to demand from and extend to the others present at the beginning of an encounter than he can alter the line of treatment that is being pursued once the interaction is underway.

In everyday life, of course, there is a clear understanding that first impressions are important. Thus, the work adjustment of those in service occupations will often hinge upon a capacity to seize and hold the initiative in the service relation, a capacity that will require subtle aggressiveness on the part of the server when he is of lower socio-economic status than his client. W.F. Whyte suggests the waitress as an example:

> The first point that stands out is that the waitress who bears up under pressure does not simply respond to her customers. She acts with some skill to control their be-havior. The first question to ask when we look at the customer relationship is, "Does the waitress get the jump on the customer, or does the customer get the jump on the waitress?" The skilled waitress realizes the crucial nature of this question ....
>
> The skilled waitress tackles the customer with confidence and without hesitation. For example, she may find that a new customer has seated himself before she could clear off the dirty dishes and change the cloth. He is now leaning on the table studying the menu. She greets him, says, "May I change the cover, please?" and, without waiting for an answer, takes his menu away from him so that he moves back from the table, and she goes about her work. The relationship is handled politely but firmly, and there is never any question as to who is in charge.[8]

When the interaction that is initiated by "first impressions" is itself merely the initial interaction in an extended series of interactions involving the same participants, we speak of "getting off on the right foot" and feel that it is crucial that we do so. Thus, one learns that some teachers take the following view:

> You can't ever let them get the upper hand on you or you're through. So I start out tough. The first day I get a new class in, I let them know who's boss .... You've got to start off tough, then you can ease up as you go along. If you start out easy-going, when you try to get tough, they'll just look at you and laugh.[9]

Similarly, attendants in mental institutions may feel that if the new patient is sharply put in his place the first day on the ward and made to see who is boss, much future difficulty will be prevented.[10]

Given the fact that the individual effectively projects a definition of the situation when he enters the presence of others, we can assume that events may occur within the interaction which contradict, discredit, or otherwise throw doubt upon this projection. When these disruptive events occur, the interaction itself may come to a confused and embarrassed halt. Some of the assumptions upon which the responses of the participants had been predicated become untenable, and the participants find themselves lodged in an interaction for which the situation has been wrongly defined and is now no longer defined. At such moments the individual whose presentation has been discredited may feel ashamed while the others present may feel hostile, and all the participants may come to feel ill at ease, nonplussed, out of countenance, embarrassed, experiencing the kind of anomy that is generated when the minute social system of face-to-face interaction breaks down.

In stressing the fact that the initial definition of the situation projected by an individual tends to provide a plan for the co-operative activity that follows—in stressing this action point of view—we must not overlook the crucial fact that any projected definition of the situation also has a distinctive moral character. It is this moral character of projections that will chiefly concern us in this report Society is organized on the principle that any individual who possesses certain social characteristics has a moral right to expect that others will value and treat him in an appropriate way. Connected with this principle is a second, namely that an individual who implicitly or explicitly signifies that he has certain social characteristics ought in fact to be what he claims he is. In consequence, when an individual projects a definition of the situation and thereby makes an implicit or explicit claim to be a person of a particular kind, he automatically exerts a moral demand upon the others, obliging them to value and treat him in the manner that persons of his kind have a right to expect. He also implicitly forgoes all claims to be things he does not appear to be[11] and hence forgoes the treatment that would be appropriate for such individuals. The others find, then, that the individual has informed them as to what is and as to what they *ought* to see as the "is."

One cannot judge the importance of definitional disruptions by the frequency with which they occur, for apparently they would occur more frequently were not constant precautions taken. We find that preventive practices are constantly employed to avoid these embarrassments and that corrective practices are constantly employed to compensate for discrediting occurrences that have not been successfully avoided. When the individual employs these strategies and tactics to protect his own projections, we may refer to them as "defensive practices"; when a participant employs them to save the definition of the situation projected by another, we speak of "protective practices" or "tact." Together, defensive and protective practices comprise the techniques employed to safeguard the impression fostered by an individual during his presence before others. It should be added that while we may be ready to see that no fostered impression would survive if defensive practices were not employed, we are less ready perhaps to see that few impressions could survive if those who received the impression did not exert tact in their reception of it.

In addition to the fact that precautions are taken to prevent disruption of projected definitions, we may also note that an intense interest in these disruptions comes to play a significant role in the social life of the group. Practical jokes and social games are played in which embarrassments which are to be taken unseriously are purposely engineered.[12] Fantasies are created in which devastating exposures occur. Anecdotes from the past—real, embroidered, or fictitious—are told and retold, detailing disruptions which occurred, almost occurred, or occurred and were admirably resolved. There seems to be no grouping which does not have a ready supply of these games, reveries, and cautionary tales, to be used as a source of humor, a catharsis for anxieties, and a sanction for inducing individuals to be modest in their claims and reasonable in their projected expectations. The individual may tell himself through dreams of getting into impossible positions. Families tell of the time a guest got his dates mixed and arrived when neither the house nor anyone in it was ready for him. Journalists tell of times when an all-too-meaningful misprint occurred, and the paper's assumption of objectivity or decorum was humorously discredited. Public servants tell of times a client ridiculously misunderstood form instructions, giving answers which implied an unanticipated and bizarre definition of the situation.[13] Seamen, whose home away from home is rigorously he-man, tell stories of coming back home and inadvertently asking mother to "pass the fucking butter."[14] Diplomats tell of the time a near-sighted queen asked a republican ambassador about the health of his king.[15]

* * * * *

NOTES

1. Gustav Ichheiser, "Misunderstandings in Human Relations," Supplement to *The American Journal of Sociology*, LV (September, 1949), pp. 6–7.
2. Quoted in E.H. Volkart, editor, *Social Behavior and Personality*, Contributions of W. I. Thomas to Theory and Social Research (New York: Social Science Research Council, 1951).
3. Here I owe much to an unpublished paper by Tom Burns of the University of Edinburgh. He presents the argument that in all interaction a basic underlying theme is the desire of each participant to guide and control the responses made by the others present. A similar argument has been advanced by Jay Haley in a recent unpublished paper, but in regard to a special kind of control, that having to do with defining the nature of the relationship of those involved in the interaction.
4. Willard Waller, "The Rating and Dating Complex," *American Sociological Review*, II, p. 730.
5. William Sansom, *A Contest of Ladies* (London: Hogarth, 1956), pp. 230–32.
6. The widely read and rather sound writings of Stephen Potter are concerned in part with signs that can be engineered to give a shrewd observer the apparently incidental cues he needs to discover concealed virtues the gamesman does not in fact possess.
7. An interaction can be purposely set up as a time and place for voicing differences in opinion, but in such cases participants must be careful to agree not to disagree on the proper tone of voice, vocabulary, and degree of seriousness in which all arguments are to be phrased, and upon the mutual respect which disagreeing participants must carefully continue to express toward one another. This debaters' or academic definition

of the situation may also be invoked suddenly and judiciously as a way of translating a serious conflict of views into one that can be handled within a framework acceptable to all present.

8. W.F. Whyte, "When Workers and Customers Meet," Chap. VII, *Industry and Society*, ed. W.F. Whyte (New York: McGraw-Hill, 1946), pp. 132–33.

9. Teacher interview quoted by Howard S. Becker, "Social Class Variations in the Teacher-Pupil Relationship," *Journal of Educational Sociology*, XXV, p. 459.

10. Harold Taxel, "Authority Structure in a Mental Hospital Ward" (unpublished Master's thesis, Department of Sociology, University of Chicago, 1953).

11. This role of the witness in limiting what it is the individual can be has been stressed by Existentialists, who see it as a basic threat to individual freedom. See Jean-Paul Sartre, *Being and Nothingness*, trans. by Hazel E. Barnes (New York: Philosophical Library, 1956), p. 365 ff.

12. Goffman, *op. cit.*, pp. 319–27.

13. Peter Blau, "Dynamics of Bureaucracy" (Ph.D. dissertation, Department of Sociology, Columbia University, forthcoming, University of Chicago Press), pp. 127–29.

14. Walter M. Beattie, Jr., "The Merchant Seaman" (unpublished M.A. Report, Department of Sociology, University of Chicago, 1950), p. 35.

15. Sir Frederick Ponsonby, *Recollections of Three Reigns* (New York: Button, 1952), p. 46.

CHAPTER 9

Becoming a Marihuana User

HOWARD BECKER

An unknown, but probably quite large, number of people in the United States use marihuana. They do this in spite of the fact that it is both illegal and disapproved.

The phenomenon of marihuana use has received much attention, particularly from psychiatrists and law enforcement officials. The research that has been done, as is often the case with research on behavior that is viewed as deviant, is mainly concerned with the question: why do they do it? Attempts to account for the use of marihuana lean heavily on the premise that the presence of any particular kind of behavior in an individual can best be explained as the result of some trait which predisposes or motivates him to engage in that behavior. In the case of marihuana use, this trait is usually identified as psychological, as a need for fantasy and escape from psychological problems the individual cannot face.[1]

I do not think such theories can adequately account for marihuana use. In fact, marihuana use is an interesting case for theories of deviance, because it illustrates the way deviant motives actually develop in the course of experience with the deviant activity. To put a complex argument in a few words: instead of the deviant motives leading to the deviant behavior, it is the other way around; the deviant behavior in time produces the deviant motivation. Vague impulses and desires—in this case, probably most frequently a curiosity about the kind of experience the drug will produce—are transformed into definite patterns of action through the social interpretation of a physical experience which is in itself ambiguous. Marihuana use is a function of the individual's conception of marihuana and of the uses to which it can be put, and this conception develops as the individual's experience with the drug increases.[2]

The research reported in this and the next chapter deals with the career of the marihuana user. In this chapter, we look at the development of the individual's immediate physical experience with marihuana. In the next, we consider the way he reacts to the various social controls that have grown up around use of the drug. What we are trying to understand here is the sequence of changes in attitude and experience which lead to *the use of marihuana for pleasure*. This way of phrasing the problem requires a little explanation. Marihuana does not produce addiction, at least in the sense that alcohol and the opiate drugs do. The user experiences no withdrawal sickness and exhibits no ineradicable craving for the drug.[3] The most frequent pattern of use might be termed "recreational." The drug is used occasionally for the pleasure the user finds in it, a relatively casual kind of behavior in comparison with that connected with the use of addicting drugs. The report of the New York City Mayor's Committee on Marihuana emphasizes this point:

> A person may be a confirmed smoker for a prolonged period, and give up the drug voluntarily without experiencing any craving for it or exhibiting withdrawal symptoms. He may, at some time later on, go back to its use. Others may remain infrequent users of the cigarette, taking one or two a week, or only when the "social setting" calls for participation. From time to time we had one of our investigators associate with a marihuana user. The investigator would bring up the subject of smoking. This would invariably lead to the suggestion that they obtain some marihuana cigarettes. They would seek a "tea-pad," and if it was closed the smoker and our investigator would calmly resume their previous activity, such as the discussion of life in general or the playing of pool. There were apparently no signs indicative of frustration in the smoker at not being able to gratify the desire for the drug. We consider this point highly significant since it is so contrary to the experience of users of other narcotics. A similar situation occurring in one addicted to the use of morphine, cocaine or heroin would result in a compulsive attitude on the part of the addict to obtain the drug. If unable to secure it, there would be obvious physical and mental manifestations of frustration. This may be considered presumptive evidence that there is no true addiction in the medical sense associated with the use of marihuana.[4]

In using the phrase "use for pleasure," I mean to emphasize the noncompulsive and casual character of the behavior. (I also mean to eliminate from consideration here those few cases in which marihuana is used for its prestige value only, as a symbol that one is a certain kind of person, with no pleasure at all being derived from its use.)

The research I am about to report was not so designed that it could constitute a crucial test of the theories that relate marihuana use to some psychological trait of the user. However, it does show that psychological explanations are not in themselves sufficient to account for marihuana use and that they are, perhaps, not even necessary. Researchers attempting to prove such psychological theories have run into two great difficulties, never satisfactorily resolved, which the theory presented here avoids. In the first place, theories based on the existence of some predisposing psychological trait have difficulty in accounting for that group of users, who turn up in sizable numbers in every study,[5] who do not exhibit the trait or traits which are considered to cause the behavior. Second, psychological theories have difficulty in accounting for the great variability over time of a given individual's behavior with reference to the drug. The same person will at one time be unable to use the drug for pleasure, at a later stage be able and willing to do so, and still later again be unable to use it in this way. These changes, difficult to explain from a theory based on the user's needs for "escape," are readily understandable as consequences of changes in his conception of the drug. Similarly, if we think of the marihuana user as someone who has learned to view marihuana as something that can give him pleasure, we have no difficulty in understanding the existence of psychologically "normal" users.

In doing the study, I used the method of analytic induction. I tried to arrive at a general statement of the sequence of changes in individual attitude and experience which always occurred when the individual became willing and able to use marihuana for pleasure, and never occurred or had not been permanently maintained when the person was unwilling to use marihuana for pleasure. The method requires that *every* case collected in the research substantiate the hypothesis. If one case is encountered which does not substantiate it, the researcher is required to change the hypothesis to fit the case which has proven his original idea wrong.[6]

To develop and test my hypothesis about the genesis of marihuana use for pleasure, I conducted fifty interviews with marihuana users. I had been a professional dance musician for some years when I conducted this study and my first interviews were with people I had met in the music business. I asked them to put me in contact with other users who would be willing to discuss their experiences with me. Colleagues working on a study of users of opiate drugs made a few interviews available to me which contained, in addition to material on opiate drugs, sufficient material on the use of marihuana to furnish a test of my hypothesis.[7] Although in the end half of the fifty interviews were conducted with musicians, the other half covered a wide range of people, including laborers, machinists, and people in the professions. The sample is, of course, in no sense "random"; it would not be possible to draw a random sample, since no one knows the nature of the universe from which it would have to be drawn.

In interviewing users, I focused on the history of the person's experience with marihuana, seeking major changes in his attitude toward it and in his actual use of it, and the reasons for these changes. Where it was possible and appropriate, I used the jargon of the user himself.

The theory starts with the person who has arrived at the point of willingness to try marihuana. He knows others use marihuana to "get high," but he does not know what this means in any concrete way. He is curious about the experience, ignorant of what it may turn out to be, and afraid it may be more than he has bargained for. The steps outlined below, if he undergoes them all and maintains the attitudes developed in them, leave him willing and able to use the drug for pleasure when the opportunity presents itself.

⑤ LEARNING THE TECHNIQUE

The novice does not ordinarily get high the first time he smokes marihuana, and several attempts are usually necessary to induce this state. One explanation of this may be that the drug is not smoked "properly," that is, in a way that insures sufficient dosage to produce real symptoms of intoxication. Most users agree that it cannot be smoked like tobacco if one is to get high:

> Take in a lot of air, you know, and ... I don't know how to describe it, you don't smoke it like a cigarette, you draw in a lot of air and get it deep down in your system and then keep it there. Keep it there as long as you can.

Without the use of some such technique,[8] the drug will produce no effects, and the user will be unable to get high:

> The trouble with people like that [who are not able to get high] is that they're just not smoking it right, that's all there is to it. Either they're not holding it down long enough, or they're getting too much air and not enough smoke, or the other way around or something like that. A lot of people just don't smoke it right, so naturally nothing's gonna happen.

If nothing happens, it is manifestly impossible for the user to develop a conception of the drug as an object which can be used for pleasure, and use will therefore not continue. The first step in the sequence of events that must occur if the person is to become a user is that he must learn to use the proper smoking technique so that his use of the drug will produce effects in terms of which his conception of it can change.

Such a change is, as might be expected, a result of the individual's participation in groups in which marihuana is used. In them the individual learns the proper way to smoke the drug. This may occur through direct teaching:

> I was smoking like I did an ordinary cigarette. He said, "No, don't do it like that." He said, "Suck it, you know, draw in and hold it in your lungs till you ... for a period of time."
>   I said, "Is there any limit of time to hold it?"
>   He said, "No, just till you feel that you want to let it out, let it out." So I did that three or four times.

Many new users are ashamed to admit ignorance and, pretending to know already, must learn through the more indirect means of observation and imitation:

> I came on like I had turned on [smoked marihuana] many times before, you know. I didn't want to seem like a punk to this cat. See, like I didn't know the first thing

about it—how to smoke it, or what was going to happen, or what. I just watched him like a hawk—I didn't take my eyes off him for a second, because I wanted to do everything just as he did it. I watched how he held it, how he smoked it, and everything. Then when he gave it to me I just came on cool, as though I knew exactly what the score was. I held it like he did and took a poke just the way he did.

No one I interviewed continued marihuana use for pleasure without learning a technique that supplied sufficient dosage for the effects of the drug to appear. Only when this was learned was it possible for a conception of the drug as an object which could be used for pleasure to emerge. Without such a conception marihuana use was considered meaningless and did not continue.

⑤ LEARNING TO PERCEIVE THE EFFECTS

Even after he learns the proper smoking technique, the new user may not get high and thus not form a conception of the drug as something which can be used for pleasure. A remark made by a user suggested the reason for this difficulty in getting high and pointed to the next necessary step on the road to being a user:

> As a matter of fact, I've seen a guy who was high out of his mind and didn't know it.
> [How can that be, man?]
> Well, it's pretty strange, I'll grant you that, but I've seen it. This guy got on with me, claiming that he'd never got high, one of those guys, and he got completely stoned. And he kept insisting that he wasn't high. So I had to prove to him that he was.

What does this mean? It suggests that being high consists of two elements: the presence of symptoms caused by marihuana use and the recognition of these symptoms and their connection by the user with his use of the drug. It is not enough, that is, that the effects be present; alone, they do not automatically provide the experience of being high. The user must be able to point them out to himself and consciously connect them with having smoked marihuana before he can have this experience. Otherwise, no matter what actual effects are produced, he considers that the drug has had no effect on him: "I figured it either had no effect on me or other people were exaggerating its effect on them, you know. I thought it was probably psychological, see." Such persons believe the whole thing is an illusion and that the wish to be high leads the user to deceive himself into believing that something is happening when, in fact, nothing is. They do not continue marihuana use, feeling that "it does nothing" for them.

Typically, however, the novice has faith (developed from his observation of users who do get high) that the drug actually will produce some new experience and continues to experiment with it until it does. His failure to get high worries

him, and he is likely to ask more experienced users or provoke comments from
them about it. In such conversations he is made aware of specific details of his
experience which he may not have noticed or may have noticed but failed to identify
as symptoms of being high:

> I didn't get high the first time .... I don't think I held it in long enough. I probably let it
> out, you know, you're a little afraid. The second time I wasn't sure, and he [smoking
> companion] told me, like I asked him for some of the symptoms or something, how
> would I know, you know .... So he told me to sit on a stool. I sat on—I think I sat
> on a bar stool—and he said, "Let your feet hang," and then when I got down my
> feet were real cold, you know.
>
> And I started feeling it, you know. That was the first time. And then about a week
> after that, sometime pretty close to it, I really got on. That was the first time I got
> on a big laughing kick, you know. Then I really knew I was on.

One symptom of being high is an intense hunger. In the next case the novice becomes
aware of this and gets high for the first time:

> They were just laughing the hell out of me because like I was eating so much. I just
> scoffed [ate] so much food, and they were just laughing at me, you know. Sometimes
> I'd be looking at them, you know, wondering why they're laughing, you know,
> not knowing what I was doing. [Well, did they tell you why they were laughing
> eventually?] Yeah, yeah, I come back, "Hey, man, what's happening?" Like, you
> know, like I'd ask, "What's happening?" and all of a sudden I feel weird, you know.
> "Man, you're on, you know. You're on pot [high on marihuana]." I said, "No, am
> I?" Like I don't know what's happening.

The learning may occur in more indirect ways:

> I heard little remarks that were made by other people. Somebody said, "My legs are
> rubbery," and I can't remember all the remarks that were made because I was very
> attentively listening for all these cues for what I was supposed to feel like.

The novice, then, eager to have this feeling, picks up from other users some
concrete referents of the term "high" and applies these notions to his own
experience. The new concepts make it possible for him to locate these symptoms
among his own sensations and to point out to himself a "something different" in
his experience that he connects with drug use. It is only when he can do this that he
is high. In the next case, the contrast between two successive experiences of a user
makes clear the crucial importance of the awareness of the symptoms in being high
and re-emphasizes the important role of interaction with other users in acquiring
the concepts that make this awareness possible:

[Did you get high the first time you turned on?] Yeah, sure. Although, come to think of it, I guess I really didn't. I mean, like that first time it was more or less of a mild drunk. I was happy, I guess, you know what I mean. But I didn't really know I was high, you know what I mean. It was only after the second time I got high that I realized I was high the first time. Then I knew that something different was happening.

[How did you know that?] How did I know? If what happened to me that night would of happened to you, you would've known, believe me. We played the first tune for almost two hours—one tune! Imagine, man! We got on the stand and played this one tune, we started at nine o'clock. When we got finished I looked at my watch, it's a quarter to eleven. Almost two hours on one tune. And it didn't seem like anything.

I mean, you know, it does that to you. It's like you have much more time or something. Anyway, when I saw that, man, it was too much. I knew I must really be high or something if anything like that could happen. See, and then they explained to me that that's what it did to you, you had a different sense of time and everything. So I realized that that's what it was. I knew then. Like the first time, I probably felt that way, you know, but I didn't know what's happening.

It is only when the novice becomes able to get high in this sense that he will continue to use marihuana for pleasure. In every case in which use continued, the user had acquired the necessary concepts with which to express to himself the fact that he was experiencing new sensations caused by the drug. That is, for use to continue, it is necessary not only to use the drug so as to produce effects, but also to learn to perceive these effects when they occur. In this way marihuana acquires meaning for the user as an object which can be used for pleasure.

With increasing experience the user develops a greater appreciation of the drug's effects; he continues to learn to get high. He examines succeeding experiences closely, looking for new effects, making sure the old ones are still there. Out of this there grows a stable set of categories for experiencing the drug's effects whose presence enables the user to get high with ease.

Users, as they acquire this set of categories, become connoisseurs. Like experts in fine wines, they can specify where a particular plant was grown and what time of year it was harvested. Although it is usually not possible to know whether these attributions are correct, it is true that they distinguish between batches of marihuana, not only according to strength, but also with respect to the different kinds of symptoms produced.

The ability to perceive the drug's effects must be maintained if use is to continue; if it is lost, marihuana use ceases. Two kinds of evidence support this statement. First, people who become heavy users of alcohol, barbiturates, or opiates do not continue to smoke marihuana, largely because they lose the ability to distinguish between its effects and those of the other drugs.[9] They no longer know whether the marihuana gets them high. Second, in those few cases in which an individual uses marihuana in such quantities that he is always high, he is apt to feel the drug has no effect on him, since the essential element of a noticeable difference between feeling high and feeling normal is missing. In such a situation, use is likely to be given up completely, but temporarily, in order that the user may once again be able to perceive the difference.

⑤ LEARNING TO ENJOY THE EFFECTS

One more step is necessary if the user who has now learned to get high is to continue use. He must learn to enjoy the effects he has just learned to experience. Marihuana-produced sensations are not automatically or necessarily pleasurable. The taste for such experience is a socially acquired one, not different in kind from acquired tastes for oysters or dry martinis. The user feels dizzy, thirsty; his scalp tingles; he misjudges time and distances. Are these things pleasurable? He isn't sure. If he is to continue marihuana use, he must decide that they are. Otherwise, getting high, . while a real enough experience, will be an unpleasant one he would rather avoid.

The effects of the drug, when first perceived, may be physically unpleasant or at least ambiguous:

> It started taking effect, and I didn't know what was happening, you know, what it was, and I was very sick. I walked around the room, walking around the room trying to get off, you know; it just scared me at first, you know. I wasn't used to that kind of feeling.

In addition, the novice's naive interpretation of what is happening to him may further confuse and frighten him, particularly if he decides, as many do, that he is going insane:

> I felt I was insane, you know. Everything people done to me just wigged me. I couldn't hold a conversation, and my mind would be wandering, and I was always thinking, oh, I don't know, weird things, like hearing music different .... I get the feeling that I can't talk to anyone. I'll goof completely.

Given these typically frightening and unpleasant first experiences, the beginner will not continue use unless he learns to redefine the sensations as pleasurable:

> It was offered to me, and I tried it. I'll tell you one thing. I never did enjoy it at all. I mean it was just nothing that I could enjoy. [Well, did you get high when you turned on?] Oh, yeah, I got definite feelings from it. But I didn't enjoy them. I mean I got plenty of reactions, but they were mostly reactions of fear. [You were frightened?] Yes. I didn't enjoy it. I couldn't seem to relax with it, you know. If you can't relax with a thing, you can't enjoy it, I don't think.

In other cases the first experiences were also definitely unpleasant, but the person did become a marihuana user. This occurred, however, only after a later experience enabled him to redefine the sensations as pleasurable:

> [This man's first experience was extremely unpleasant, involving distortion of spatial relationships and sounds, violent thirst, and panic produced by these symptoms.] After the first time I didn't turn on for about, I'd say, ten months to a year .... It wasn't a moral thing; it was because I'd gotten so frightened, bein' so high. An' I didn't want to go through that again, I mean, my reaction was, "Well, if this is what they call bein' high, I don't dig [like] it." ... So I didn't turn on for a year almost, accounta that ....
>
> Well, my friends started, an' consequently I started again. But I didn't have any more, I didn't have that same initial reaction, after I started turning on again.
>
> [In interaction with his friends, he became able to find pleasure in the effects of the drug and eventually became a regular user.]

In no case will use continue without a redefinition of the effects as enjoyable.

This redefinition occurs, typically, in interaction with more experienced users who, in a number of ways, teach the novice to find pleasure in this experience which is at first so frightening.[10] They may reassure him as to the temporary character of the unpleasant sensations and minimize their seriousness, at the same time calling attention to the more enjoyable aspects. An experienced user describes how he handles newcomers to marihuana use:

> Well, they get pretty high sometimes. The average person isn't ready for that, and it is a little frightening to them sometimes. I mean, they've been high on lush [alcohol], and they get higher that way than they've ever been before, and they don't know what's happening to them. Because they think they're going to keep going up, up, up till they lose their minds or begin doing weird things or something. You have to like reassure them, explain to them that they're not really flipping or anything, that they're gonna be all right. You have to just talk them out of being afraid. Keep talking to them, reassuring, telling them it's all right. And come on with your own story, you know: "The same thing happened to me. You'll get to like that after awhile." Keep coming on like that; pretty soon you talk them out of being scared. And besides they see you doing it and nothing horrible is happening to you, so that gives them more confidence.

The more experienced user may also teach the novice to regulate the amount he smokes more carefully, so as to avoid any severely uncomfortable symptoms while retaining the pleasant ones. Finally, he teaches the new user that he can "get to like it after awhile." He teaches him to regard those ambiguous experiences formerly defined as unpleasant as enjoyable. The older user in the following incident is a person whose tastes have shifted in this way, and his remarks have the effect of helping others to make a similar redefinition:

> A new user had her first experience of the effects of marihuana and became frightened and hysterical. She "felt like she was half in and half out of the room" and experienced a number of alarming physical symptoms. One of the more experienced users present said, "She's dragged because she's high like that. I'd give anything to get that high myself. I haven't been that high in years."

In short, what was once frightening and distasteful becomes, after a taste for it is built up, pleasant, desired, and sought after. Enjoyment is introduced by the favorable definition of the experience that one acquires from others. Without this, use will not continue, for marihuana will not be for the user an object he can use for pleasure.

In addition to being a necessary step in becoming a user, this represents an important condition for continued use. It is quite common for experienced users suddenly to have an unpleasant or frightening experience, which they cannot define as pleasurable, either because they have used a larger amount of marihuana than usual or because the marihuana they have used turns out to be of a higher quality than they expected. The user has sensations which go beyond any conception he has of what being high is and is in much the same situation as the novice, uncomfortable and frightened. He may blame it on an overdose and simply be more careful in the future. But he may make this the occasion for a rethinking of his attitude toward the drug and decide that it no longer can give him pleasure. When this occurs and is not followed by a redefinition of the drug as capable of producing pleasure, use will cease.

The likelihood of such a redefinition occurring depends on the degree of the individual's participation with other users. Where this participation is intensive, the individual is quickly talked out of his feeling against marihuana use. In the next case, on the other hand, the experience was very disturbing, and the aftermath of the incident cut the person's participation with other users to almost zero. Use stopped for three years and began again only when a combination of circumstances, important among which was a resumption of ties with users, made possible a redefinition of the nature of the drug:

> It was too much, like I only made about four pokes, and I couldn't even get it out of my mouth, I was so high, and I got real flipped. In the basement, you know, I just couldn't stay in there anymore. My heart was pounding real hard, you know, and I was going out of my mind; I thought I was losing my mind completely. So I cut out of this basement, and this other guy, he's out of his mind, told me, "Don't, don't leave me, man. Stay here." And I couldn't.
>
> I walked outside, and it was five below zero, and I thought I was dying, and I

had my coat open; I was sweating, I was perspiring. My whole insides were all ...,
and I walked about two blocks away, and I fainted behind a bush. I don't know how
long I laid there. I woke up, and I was feeling the worst, I can't describe it at all, so I
made it to a bowling alley, man, and I was trying to act normal, I was trying to shoot
pool, you know, trying to act real normal, and I couldn't lay and I couldn't stand up
and I couldn't sit down, and I went up and laid down where some guys that spot
pins lay down, and that didn't help me, and I went down to a doctor's office. I was
going to go in there and tell the doctor to put me out of my misery ... because my
heart was pounding so hard, you know.... So then all weekend I started nipping,
seeing things there and going through hell, you know, all kinds of abnormal things
.... I just quit for a long time then.

[He went to a doctor who defined the symptoms for him as those of a nervous
breakdown caused by "nerves" and "worries." Although he was no longer using
marihuana, he had some recurrences of the symptoms which led him to suspect
that "it was all his nerves."] So I just stopped worrying, you know; so it was about
thirty-six months later I started making it again. I'd just take a few pokes, you know.
[He first resumed use in the company of the same user-friend with whom he had
been involved in the original incident.]

A person, then, cannot begin to use marihuana for pleasure, or continue its use
for pleasure, unless he learns to define its effects as enjoyable, unless it becomes and
remains an object he conceives of as capable of producing pleasure.

In summary, an individual will be able to use marihuana for pleasure only when
he goes through a process of learning to conceive of it as an object which can be used
in this way. No one becomes a user without (1) learning to smoke the drug in a way
which will produce real effects; (2) learning to recognize the effects and connect
them with drug use (learning, in other words, to get high); and (3) learning to enjoy
the sensations he perceives. In the course of this process he develops a disposition
or motivation to use marihuana which was not and could not have been present
when he began use, for it involves and depends on conceptions of the drug which
could only grow out of the kind of actual experience detailed above. On completion
of this process he is willing and able to use marihuana for pleasure.

He has learned, in short, to answer "Yes" to the question: "Is it fun?" The
direction his further use of the drug takes depends on his being able to continue to
answer "Yes" to this question and, in addition, on his being able to answer "Yes"
to other questions which arise as he becomes aware of the implications of the fact
that society disapproves of the practice: "Is it expedient?" "Is it moral?" Once he
has acquired the ability to get enjoyment by using the drug, use will continue to
be possible for him. Considerations of morality and expediency, occasioned by
the reactions of society, may interfere and inhibit use, but use continues to be a
possibility in terms of his conception of the drug. The act becomes impossible only
when the ability to enjoy the experience of being high is lost, through a change in the
user's conception of the drug occasioned by certain kinds of experience with it.

NOTES

1. See, as examples of this approach, the following: Eli Marcovitz and Henry J. Meyers, "The Marihuana Addict in the Army," *War Medicine*, VI (December, 1944), 382–391; Herbert S. Gaskill, "Marihuana, an Intoxicant," *American Journal of Psychiatry*, CII (September, 1945), 202–204; Sol Charen and Lois Perelman, "Personality Studies of Marihuana Addicts," *American Journal of Psychiatry*, CII (March, 1946), 674–682.
2. This theoretical point of view stems from George Herbert Mead's discussion of objects in *Mind, Self, and Society* (Chicago: University of Chicago Press, 1934), pp. 277–280.
3. Cf. Rogers Adams, "Marihuana," *Bulletin of the New York Academy of Medicine*, XVIII (November, 1942), 705–730.
4. The New York City Mayor's Committee on Marihuana, *The Marihuana Problem in the City of New York* (Lancaster, Pennsylvania: Jacques Cattell Press, 1944), pp. 12–13.
5. Cf. Lawrence Kolb, "Marihuana," *Federal Probation*, II (July, 1938), 22–25; and Walter Bromberg, "Marihuana: A Psychiatric Study," *Journal of the American Medical Association*, CXIII (Jury 1, 1939), 11.
6. The method is described in Alfred R. Lindesmith, *Opiate Addiction* (Bloomington, Indiana: Principia Press, 1947), chap. 1. There has been considerable discussion of this method in the literature. See, particularly, Ralph H. Turner, "The Quest for Universals in Sociological Research," *American Sociological Review*, 18 (December, 1953), 604–611, and the literature cited there.
7. I wish to thank Solomon Kobrin and Harold Finestone for making these interviews available to me.
8. A pharmacologist notes that this ritual is in fact an extremely efficient way of getting the drug into the bloodstream. See R.P. Walton, *Marihuana: America's New Drug Problem* (Philadelphia: J.B. Lippincott, 1938), p. 48.
9. "Smokers have repeatedly stated that the consumption of whiskey while smoking negates the potency of the drug. They find it very difficult to get 'high' while drinking whiskey and because of that smokers will not drink while using the 'weed.'" (New York City Mayor's Committee on Marihuana, *The Marihuana Problem in the City of New York*, *op. cit.*, p. 13.)
10. Charen and Perelman, *op. cit.*, p. 679.

CHAPTER 10

Symbolic Interactionism and Ethnomethodology: A Proposed Synthesis

NORMAN K. DENZIN

* * * * *

The development of a theoretical perspective appropriate for the joint analysis of social psychological and sociological problems has long concerned the sociologist. The methodology that would permit such an analysis has also remained an issue. Although various alternatives have been offered, ranging from the use of models taken from economics and psychology to structural-functionalism, none has proven completely satisfactory. My intent is to take two perspectives in contemporary sociology, one old and one relatively new, and to examine their potential for meeting the above issues. Specifically, I shall examine symbolic interactionism and ethnomethodology. Because both focus in some way on the individual, they provide a view of social organization that may be termed subjective and social psychological in nature. Analysis of the degree of convergence between the two should permit an expanded treatment of how individuals are linked to, shaped by, and in turn create social structure. These two perspectives are especially relevant to the above problems because they also propose special views of methodology.

⑤ THE PERSPECTIVES DEFINED

The ethnomethodology of Garfinkel (1967) and Cicourel (1968) proposes an analysis of the routine, taken-for-granted expectations that members of any social order regularly accept. Basic to this perspective is the attempt to sharply distinguish scientific from everyday activity. The problems of penetrating everyday perspectives and giving them sociological explanations are repeatedly addressed and the method of documentary analysis is set forth as a preferred strategy. The abiding concern, however, is with the relationship between everyday, taken-for-granted meanings, and the organization of these meanings into routine patterns of interaction.

Symbolic interactionism takes as a fundamental concern the relationship between individual conduct and forms of social organization. This perspective asks how selves emerge out of social structure and social situations.

Both perspectives posit a link between the person and social structure that rests on the role of symbols and common meanings. To this extent they share a great deal in common with the structural-functional perspective. Locating the unit of analysis in the individual and interaction separates interactionism and ethnomethodology from other points of view.

⑤ SYMBOLIC INTERACTIONISM

The interactionist assumes that human beings are capable of making their own thoughts and activities objects of analysis, that is, they can routinely, and even habitually, manipulate symbols and orient their own actions towards other objects. A great deal of human conduct is of this routine nature. Once the meanings of objects have been agreed upon, conduct can flow along lines of custom, tradition, and ritual.

Because humans also possess the ability to self-consciously direct their own activities, the interaction process may be classified into those behaviors that are routinely organized and those that are actively constructed in a self-conscious and interpretative fashion (Blumer, 1966: 537–538). Granted this assumption, a fundamental empirical question becomes the identification of the shifting modes of interpretation that characterize the interaction process. Clearly, interaction cannot be so grossly divided into either interpretative or noninterpretative elements. There are many levels and shades of difference between these two, and the extent to which action and objects move between these points remains to be identified.

* * * * *

These meanings typically derive from a group or organized interactional perspective. Human life is group life, and concerted action arises out of the ability of persons to be objects of both their own activity and others'. Joint actions, which represent the generic form of all interaction, rest on the ability of the human to grasp the direction of the acts of others (Blumer, 1966). For consensual lines of action to emerge there must exist a common community of symbols. Because the definitions of certain objects within a group's perspective are subject to continual negotiation, at least certain features of group life are subject to negotiation and change. The basic object for all interaction is the self. Because the self carries a multitude of differing interpretations, shifts in these definitions often give group life its changing character.

When selves are consensually denned, stable patterns of action will be observed. At the heart of group life lies a series of social selves that have been lodged in that structure. Through the process of self-lodging, humans translate crucial features of their own identity into the selves, and into the memories and imaginations of relevant others. In this way Cooley's proposition that the other exists in "our imaginations of him" comes to life. By lodging the self in interaction, and in the selves of others, a reciprocal bond is created, and the firm foundations for future relationships are established. Self-lodging stands in distinction to what Goffman (1959) has termed the process of presenting a self. It is certainly the case that selves have to be presented, but at some point in the cycle of recurrent interactions, the self moves from the presentational to the lodging phase. [...]

* * * * *

5 THE METHODOLOGICAL ASSUMPTIONS OF INTERACTIONISM

Because human interaction involves behavior of both the covert and overt variety, and because the meanings attached to objects often change during an encounter, the interactionist endeavors to relate covert symbolic behavior with overt patterns of interaction. This additionally demands a concern for the unfolding meaning objects assume during an interactional sequence. The usual strategy is to work from overt behaviors (Mead, 1934: 1–8) back to the meaning attached to those behaviors and objects. This feature of interactionist methodology suggests that behavioral analyses alone (see, for example, Webb et al., 1966) are insufficient to establish valid explanations of human conduct. Similarly, an analysis of the meanings, or definitions held by a set of persons and carried into a real or proposed interaction, will not supply the needed link between those symbols and interaction. Thus, our first methodological principle asserts that covert and overt forms of conduct must be examined before an investigation is complete. Because this principle suggests that meaning shifts during interaction, a basic problem for research is the identification of interpretational phases. Studies must be conducted which determine at which point during an encounter objects cease to be negotiated.

A second principle focuses on the self as an object and a process. The investigator is directed to examine behavior from the perspective of those being studied, and he must indicate the shifting meanings and statuses assigned the self. At certain times the self ceases to be a negotiated object, assumes an agreed-upon meaning, and interaction then turns to other concerns. This may be observed in many ritual encounters where the basic activity lies above the self, or in the interaction process. Social games, routine work, and even participation in a religious ceremony represent such occasions. By making the self a central object of study, analysis can quickly establish what is taken for granted and what is problematic for the respective interactants. A commitment to this principle permits the researcher to escape the fallacy of objectivism which is the substitution of the scientist's perspective for those studied.

Taking the role of the acting other leads to a third principle. The researcher must link his subjects' symbols and meanings to the social circles and relationships that furnish those perspectives. Unless meanings are linked to larger social perspectives, analysis remains largely psychological. This suggests a two-step process for any study; meanings at both the individual and interactional levels must be examined.

A fourth methodological principle directs researchers to consider the "situated aspects" of human conduct. If behavior occurs within social situations and if the meaning attached to those situations influences subsequent behavior, then the situation becomes a dimension of analysis. Four components of the situation may be distinguished: the interactants as objects, the concrete setting, the meanings brought into the situation, and the time taken for the interaction. Variations in behavior can arise from definitions given the respective selves, the other objects that constitute the situation (e.g., furniture, lighting), the meanings and definitions for action that are held before interaction occurs, and the temporal sequencing of action.

The situation as an intrusive variable cannot be ignored. The entry of alien others, the failure of mechanical equipment (Gross and Stone, 1963), or shifts in levels of mutual involvement, all relate to interaction as a situated process. In this way concrete situations become both places for interaction and objects of negotiation. It is impossible to separate the two from situational analysis.

Because the interaction process is characterized by both stability and change, a fifth principle demands that research strategies be capable of reflecting both aspects of group life. Research methods can be judged by their ability to yield both kinds of information. Because of the interaction between the observer and his environment, we mention parenthetically that the act of making observations becomes symbolic and subject to personal bias and even ideological preference.

For the interactionist the preferred concepts are sensitizing. This does not mean that operationalization is avoided—it merely suggests that the point of operationalization is delayed until the situated meaning of concepts are [sic] discovered. At this point standard methods of observation can be employed. Another feature of this process is the use of multiple methods of observation. Commonly termed triangulation (Webb et al., 1966), this directs the researcher to utilize different tools in the observational process. This strategy assumes that no single method can adequately treat all the problems of discovery and verification. Each method has restrictions, and if several different methods are combined in the same study, the restrictions of one are often the strength of another.

The triangulation process assumes the following elements: a series of common data bases; a reliable sampling model that recognizes interaction; a series of empirical indicators for each data base; a series of hypotheses; and a continual reciprocation between data and hypotheses.

A final methodological principle relates to theory. Formal theory (Simmel, 1950) is a common goal of interactionist research. Although historically, or situationally, specific propositions are recognized, propositions with the greatest universal relevance are sought. This assumes that human affairs, wherever they occur, rest on the same interactional processes. Formal theory, in this sense, extends Merton's view of middle-range theory to a position that calls for soundly grounded empirical propositions of an all-inclusive, universal nature (see Glaser and Strauss, 1967). Properly speaking, the interactionist has not achieved this goal; interactionism remains a perspective or conceptual framework and is not a theory in the strict meaning of the term.

⑤ ETHNOMETHODOLOGY

The ethnomethodologist directs attention to the question of how a social order is possible. For Garfinkel (1967) the answer merges a Durkheimian concern for large collective representations with an interactionist conception of the rules, norms, and meanings that members of any social order daily take for granted.

These rules, which any bonafide member of a social order is aware of, include the following assumptions: (1) interaction flows in a temporal sequence and statements in any encounter cannot be understood without reference to the actual flow of events; (2) persons in any situation will talk about many things that are only tacitly recognized, if at all; (3) normal background affairs and conditions in any situation are taken for granted and typically go unchallenged during an encounter; (4) once a situation is defined, this definition holds for the duration of the encounter; (5) any object present in the situation is what it is presented as being; (6) the meanings given an object on one occasion will hold for future occasions, suggesting that definitions of one set of interactants will be the same as those any other person, or persons would develop were they in the same situation; (7) interactants identify and attach meaning to objects by the use of standard terms, symbols, and labels; (8) while persons base their definitions of situations on their own biographies and past experiences, any discrepancies that would arise in an encounter because of variations in biography or experience are held in abeyance. In short, situations are defined through the process of interaction; therefore, persons will often feel a degree of conflict between their public and private definitions.

A basic interest of the ethnomethodologist has been the penetration of normal situations of interaction to uncover these taken-for-granted rules. This is typically phrased in terms of how one could disrupt normal social events so that any person's conception of the normal, real, and the ordinary would be challenged. In Garfinkel's studies (1967: 54) the common strategy has been to design quasi-experimental field studies in which three conditions are created. First, the situation is structured so that the subject studied could not interpret it as a game, an experiment, a deception, or a play. Second, the subject is given insufficient time to reconstruct the situation in his own terms. Third, he is given no aid in forging new definitions.

At several points Garfinkel reports experiments which meet the above three conditions. On one occasion students were asked to play as boarders in their own homes; on another, they were told to overpay and underpay for objects purchased in a store; in one experiment medical students were given discrepant information regarding an application for medical school; and in another study students were told to violate the usual rules of tick-tack-toe.

In all of these studies, which Garfinkel insists are only exploratory and illustrative, it was found that persons who act as "everyday experimenters" find it difficult to challenge the routine rules of interaction. Feelings of distrust, hostility, anger, frustration, and persecution were reported by his student experimenters. The focus of interaction was soon lost when the "experimenter" attitude was assumed, and for all practical purposes the students were unable to carry on normal interaction. Garfinkel explains this inability with the concept of trust, which he defines as one's assumption that all others he encounters will share the same expectations and definitions of the situation and that the other person will act on the basis of these assumptions, even in problematic situations.

This concept suggests that when one or more interactants are forced to distrust the other, the normal background features of the situation suddenly become problematic, and the organization of joint action soon collapses. These experiments represent small-scale studies concerning the basis of collective behavior. They also offer data on the interpretational phases of encounters.

Another broad concern of the ethnomethodologist has been with the routine productions of persons in social organizations. The basic hypothesis guiding these studies, which have ranged from analyses of mental health clinics, to hospitals, police departments, juvenile courts, and suicide prevention centers, is that members of any social organization develop a special perspective for handling their clients. It is argued that the perspectives of any given organization will be sufficiently different from any similar organization to make comparisons between such agencies problematic. Ethnomethodological studies have suggested that (1) organizations perpetuate themselves through time by generating fictitious records; (2) comparable organizations differ in the meanings they assign to the same events (e.g., birth, death, mental illness, cured, etc.); (3) the production of organizational records is basically an interactional process based on rumor, gossip, overheard conversations, discrepant information, and biographically imperfect bookkeeping. Cicourel (1968), for example, noted that agencies created to process juvenile delinquency routinely produced delinquents by piecing together long series of conversations between the predelinquent, his parents, the arresting officer, the counselor, and the judge. The sum total of these conversations, translated into official reports, represented the organizational documentation that a delinquent act had or had not occurred. And (4) in piecing together these organizational reports, it was found that members routinely relied on open-ended categories to classify cases. What Garfinkel (1967: 73–75) calls the "et cetera clause" refers to this tendency of persons to fit events into a pattern that complements their on-going action.

It is important to note that these studies amplify the research of interactionists on the labeling process. Becker (1963) has suggested that deviance does not reside in social acts, but must be traced to definitions that arise during interaction. Cicourel's research suggests that deviance may be as much organizational as interactional in nature and must be related to the working perspectives of members of social control agencies. Garfinkel's studies propose that disruptions of everyday perspectives can create feelings of distrust which become translated into deviant labels.

* * * * *

Perhaps the most important claim of the ethnomethodologist is the statement that the productions of the sociologist are similar to those in everyday life. This echoes the concern of Mead and others for distinguishing scientific from everyday activities.

The ethnomethodologist's argument involves the following points. First, all sociologists are (or should be) concerned with depicting the taken-for-granted affairs of actors in any social order. The sociologist will find that he is forced to make decisions regarding the relationship between his concepts and his observations. In making these decisions, he will note that unclassifiable instances appear, that coding schemes become too narrow, that statistical tests are inappropriate, or that observations bear little, if any, relationship to central concepts and hypotheses. In the process of deciding when an observation fits or does not fit a conceptual category Garfinkel (1967: 78–79) suggests the sociologist make use (even if unconsciously) of the documentary method of analysis. In applying this method it will be found that any instance of classifying an observation rests on the earlier discussed assumptions of daily interaction. That is, events will be placed in a temporal sequence, certain statements will be ignored, and common vocabularies will be assumed. If the method of data collection rests on interviews, it is argued that the researcher must give attention to the interaction that occurs between himself and the respondent. In this context Garfinkel (1967) and Cicourel (1967) suggest that while it is commonly assumed that interviewers and respondents achieve a "rapport" during the interview, this hypothesis is problematic. Data gathered via interviews and questionnaires are viewed by the ethnotnethodologist as collaborative products created by the sociologist and his subject. To understand such productions demands a knowledge of the routine meanings held by subjects.

* * * * *

🔄 A VIEW OF SOCIAL ORGANIZATION AND THE INTERACTION PROCESS: A PROPOSED SYNTHESIS

If face-to-face interaction is characterized by shifting modalities of interpretation, then a major point of convergence between ethnomethodology and interactionism is the treatment of the meanings given to social objects.

The Interpretational Process
This suggests several hypotheses concerning the movement of objects from interpretative to non-interpretative roles. The first suggests that any event challenging

normal interpretation creates pressures to bring that event into the flow of interaction. When an object is taken out of its non-interpretative status and held up for consideration, frustration and groping will be observed at a rate proportionate to the importance assigned the object. Thus, some objects can be quickly settled upon if they occupy a relatively low position in the interaction. This would be the case with breakdowns in mechanical equipment at sociable gatherings; they can either be replaced with other objects, or ignored.

A second hypothesis suggests that the fundamental objects for any interaction involve those that must be negotiated over. In short, taken-for-granted objects will not account for the complete variance in behavior. Those objects which are accorded explicit interpretative status will significantly determine the flow of events. On the other hand, taken-for-granted objects cannot be ignored, and I would hypothesize that objects in this class receive earliest attention in any encounter. Once their meaning can be taken for granted, they cease to operate as problematic elements.

The nature of the interaction process is such that a complete *a priori* classification of objects cannot be given. Earlier I suggested that the self represents the most significant object for interpretation. To this should be added the meanings brought into the situation and perhaps the situation as well although the situation, in a concrete sense, is likely to contain the greatest proportion of non-problematic objects.

The problem of meaning still remains vague in both perspectives. As a point of empirical inquiry, meaning can be treated as an element of the covert symbolic act, and by self-reports measured in terms of the expectations for action that are brought into the interactions (e.g., McHugh, 1968). Following Garfinkel, such expectations would include assumptions concerning who was going to be present, the length of time to be spent, the types of selves one was going to present, the degree of knowledge held about the occasion, and the types of objects that were going to be encountered. Once the interaction begins, overt activities could be linked to the shifts in meaning that the participants were constructing as they interacted.

In this way interaction could be measured by the frequency of joined actions. The emergent effect of interaction would be represented by the frequency of disrupted plans of action; that is, how frequently participants had to alter plans of action brought into the encounter. Interactions could then be examined in terms of their emergent qualities. Those that flowed basically along non-interpretative lines would be judged less emergent, and so on.

Deviance, the Labeling Process, and Agents of Social Control

Because interactionism and ethnomethodology have focused on the deviance and labeling process, an additional series of hypotheses can be offered. If Garfinkel's conception of trust is redefined to specify those situations where two or more actors assume that the other will abide by decisions mutually agreed upon, then violations of trust become violations of these agreements. Examples would include entrusting another with a dark secret about the self, withholding salient information from outsiders, or simply continuing to interact along consensual lines. Breakdowns in joint action could be partially traced to breakdowns in the trust-taking attitude and would be vividly displayed in the betrayal process that characterizes interactions between normals and persons denned as mentally ill (e.g., Sampson, Messinger, and Towne (1962: 88–96).

A first hypothesis emerges: continued violations of trust create strains in the relationship which culminate in attributions of deviance directed toward the trust-violator. This suggests that only certain breakdowns in consensual interaction will produce a deviant label. Violations of the relational order would lead to a greater proportion of deviant labels than would violations of polite-interactional and civil-legal codes. Thus, a failure to abide by rules of deference and demeanor, refusals to act in terms of an agreed upon division of labor, or leaking of crucial information to outsiders would represent significant concerns around which trust would have to be sustained.

If the labeling process is raised to the organizational level, the readiness of members within social control agencies to validate a deviant label would vary by their perception of the degree of trust-violation attributed to the potential deviant. That is, the extent to which the member of a social relationship can validate a claim of trust-violation increases the readiness of members of social control agencies to accept and process the potential deviant. This hypothesis must be conditioned by the fact that social control agencies continually monitor their deviant populations in terms of the ability of those populations to meet perceived organizational needs. As Cicourel (1968) indicates, this monitoring process serves collective organizational needs as well as the concerns of individual members. When these concerns converge with the attributions of deviance among members of social relationships, greater rates of labeling would be expected, suggesting that members of social control agencies may turn away valid instances of deviance simply because they do not meet the needs of the organization. On the other hand, deviants may be created by such agencies when valid attributions of deviance are not given within the social relationship. This would be especially so when members of the social relationship are in conflict with the social control agency. Current examples include police monitoring of ghetto areas, and police enforcement of drug abuse laws among college youth. In these instances the labeling process becomes a political and ideological issue with members of social control agencies responding more to political demands than to socially validated instances of deviance.

Social Relationships, Socialization, and the Languages of Interaction

Returning the discussion to social relationships and trust, breakdowns in consensual action often arise because persons hold conflicting definitions of the salient objects in their environment. If a wife persists in directing interaction around objects which a husband regards as taken for granted, consensus may soon collapse and joint action becomes problematic. A sense of dissatisfaction with the interactional partner may be created which soon eventuates in reciprocal alienation; this in turn produces a situation of deviance attribution. The outcome may be divorce.

Another area of mutual concern is the language of interaction. It appears that at least two languages, one silent, and one vocal, characterize the interaction process. On the silent level, rules regarding body spacing, gesturing, the control of body noises, and aromas, and the ordering of words can be observed (Sommer, 1968). These often remain unstated, and represent the "background expectancy set" of the interactants. On the vocal level, prescriptions concerning proper address, naming, tone of voice, and choice of vocabulary are observable. These represent the overt aspects of interaction and their expression displays the salient features of the silent dialogue (Goffman, 1963).

If interaction involves both languages, then ethnomethodology and inter-actionism provide a perspective for analyzing the contingencies of face-to-face encounters. An important line of investigation becomes the problem of socialization. How are persons taught rules that are seldom vocalized? How are sanctions brought to bear upon perceived violations of the silent language? At what point in the socialization process are children assumed to be responsible for their silent behaviors?

These questions are cross-cut by a particular image of socialization. Contrary to some theories which regard socialization as a discontinuous learning process into well-defined roles, ethnomethodology and symbolic interactionism suggest that socialization is never-ending, and often involves more of what is not said than what is stated (e.g., Olesen and Whittaker, 1968; and Clausen 1968: 130–181). Socialization thus represents a ubiquitous feature of all interactions—the apprehension of another's perspective so that joint action can occur. Indeed, if interaction is regarded as a potentially emergent event, socialization is one aspect of the role-taking process. If success at joint action is measured by the ability of persons to fit lines of action together, then this success represents the quality of the ongoing socialization process.

The Study of Social Organization

Because both perspectives provide a similar view of the interaction and socialization process, they offer a powerful strategy for organizational analysis. The following points can be indicated. First, organizations become territories of interaction that are focused around complex spoken and unspoken languages. These languages represent the salient organizational concerns, often work-related, and they offer prescriptions for action that frequently run counter to formally stated organizational goats. Each organizational role position can be seen as having its own special language, both silent and vocal. This language will communicate special socializa-tion strategies which are daily tested and reaffirmed through interaction. These languages will tend to cluster within, and indeed give focus to, special social orders that exist hand-in-hand with other social orders. The organization is then conceived in terms of competing perspectives and social orders, each of which rests on its own language. The sum of these languages represents the organization's collective perspective. The sum of the social or moral orders becomes the behavioral representation of the organization.

In this way organizations are broken down into interactional units, each of which offer special ways of thinking and acting. It becomes difficult to speak of one organization, or one organizational perspective. An organization represents a multitude of shifting and competing languages and social orders: a social order that is held together, if at all, by a few very salient symbols such as university X, or mental hospital V. The name of the organization perhaps represents the only salient symbol all participants would agree upon.

Methodology and the Study of Scientific Conduct

Both perspectives offer a series of hypotheses relevant to the analysis of scientific conduct and the development of sociological methodology. The scientist is judged by his ability to challenge accepted perspectives—that is, by his ability to be self-consciously interpretative. Developments in science reflect growth stimulated by this challenging stance. In this way Mead partially anticipated Thomas Kuhn's notion of the paradigm model of scientific development. Of equal importance was Mead's ability to separate the rationalities of scientific conduct from the perspectives of everyday life, a point more fully elaborated by Garfinkel in his analysis of the forms of rationality (also see Blumer, 1931). A hypothesis which runs slightly counter to the Mertonian and Parsonian image of scientific behavior emerges (Kaplan, 1964: 855–857). Scientific conduct is so imbued with elements from everyday life that unless the scientist self-consciously directs his activity in terms of the norm of discovery, his behavior is unfavorably judged. The norms of the scientific institution parallel those of other enterprises, most notably art, theology, and philosophy (Swanson, 1968: 123). Consequently, Merton's (1957) four norms of universalism, communism, disinterestedness, and organized skepticism are not unique to science.

In this way Mead and Garfinkel have opened the way for a more open discourse of the value-free problem. It is now impossible to view science as other than a value-laden enterprise—a position similarly reached by Gouldner (1962) and Becker (1967). It can be no other way if the assumption that science as a human enterprise is granted. Consequently, the scientific norms of rationality which include (1) official neutrality toward the meaning of objects; (2) an irrelevancy for the real world; (3) an indifference to chronological time; (4) perfect communication; (5) standards of publicity, remain norms that are imperfectly realized (Swanson, 1968: 123). This is the thrust of Garfinkel's critique of modern sociology. The sociologist's belief in a perfect system of rationalities has led him further away from the world of social events. The sociologist has pursued his normative system at the expense of concrete behavioral analyses of face-to-face interaction. By forgetting that he is responsive to social demands, the sociologist has overlooked the irrational elements of his own conduct—most notably his inability to make sound observations, to reliably code documents, to conduct face-to-face interviews and so on.

The thrust of ethnomethodology and interactionism becomes clear—the sociologist can never ignore the interactional features of his own conduct. Interactionism and ethnomethodology offer some recipes for corrective action. They may be stated as hypotheses.

If the scientific observer is subject to interactional demands, and hence less than perfect as a recorder of social events, then multiple observers and multiple methods, which overcome one another's restrictive biases, become the most valid and reliable strategies of observation. This suggests that any observation based on the triangulation principle will yield data that are more reliable and valid than an investigation that is not so based.

Because the scientist brings unique interpretations to bear upon his own conduct, a major source of variance in any investigation becomes the nature of these interpretations. Specifically, this predicts that two experimenters, for example, will produce different findings to the extent that they conceive their role differently (see Friedman, 1967). This would also hold for interviewers, coders, and unobtrusive observers.

Third, the interaction process between an observer and a subject must be examined for its effect on the data. Whenever interaction is emergent, observational encounters become noncomparable events for purposes of collective analysis. If an encounter proceeds along taken-for-granted lines, which is a measure of the degree of nonemergence, similar observational encounters could be pooled for collective analysis. This proposition directs investigators to record carefully the nature of the interaction process with a special eye to events that they judge to be unique within each encounter.

Additional hypotheses could be offered, but space restricts their elaboration. The basic point is that both interactionism and ethnomethodology direct scientific interest in the scientific process itself.

In concluding this proposed synthesis, I would offer as a final point the convergence of ethnomethodology's interest in the study of face-to-face interaction with the methodological principles of symbolic interactionism discussed earlier. The documentary method, as a strategy of pointing to empirical instances of theoretical concepts, can be easily merged with the use of analytic induction, sensitizing concepts, the method of role taking, and the strategies of linking individual perspectives with larger social units.

Similarly, Garfinkel's use of the quasi-experiment in natural field settings can become a model for more rigorous studies of face-to-face encounters. This is especially so if recent findings on experimenter effect and subject perceptions are incorporated into the experimental design (e.g., Friedman, 1967).

REFERENCES

Becker, Howard S.
    1963   *Outsiders: Studies in the Sociology of Deviance*. New York: The Free Press.
    1967   "Whose side are we on." *Social Problems* 14 (Winter): 239–248.
Blumer, Herbert.
    1931   "Science without concepts." *American Journal of Sociology* 36 (January): 515–531.
    1966   "Sociological implications of the thought of George Herbert Mead." *American Journal of Sociology* 71 (March): 535–544.
Cicourel, Aaron V.
    1967   "Fertility, family planning and the social organization of family life: Some methodological issues." *The Journal of Social Issues* 23 (October): 57–81.
    1968   *The Social Organization of Juvenile Justice*. New York: John Wiley and Sons, Inc.
Clausen, John A. (ed.).
    1968   *Socialization and Society*. Boston: Little, Brown.
Friedman, Neil J.
    1967   *The Social Nature of Psychological Research*. New York: Basic Books.
Garfinkel, Harold.
    1967   *Studies in Ethnomethodology*. Englewood Cliffs, N.J.: Prentice-Hall.
Glaser, Barney G. and Anselm L. Strauss.
    1967   *The Discovery of Grounded Theory*. Chicago: Aldine.
Goffman, Erving.
    1959   *The Presentation of Self in Everyday Life*. Garden City, N.Y.: Doubleday.
    1963   *Behavior in Public Places*. New York: The Free Press.
Gouldner, Alvin W.
    1962   "Anti-minotaur: The myth of a value-free sociology." *Social Problems* 9 (Winter, 1962): 199–213.
Gross, Edward and Gregory P. Stone.
    1963   "Embarrassment and the analysis of role requirements." *American Journal of Sociology* 70 (July): 1–15.
Kaplan, Norman.
    1964   "Sociology of science." Pp. 852–881 in Robert E.L. Fans (ed.), *Handbook of Modern Sociology*. Chicago: Rand McNally.
McHugh, Peter.
    1968   *Defining the Situation*. Indianapolis, Ind.: Bobbs-Merrill.
Mead, George Herbert.
    1934   *Mind, Self and Society*. Chicago: University of Chicago Press.
Merton, Robert K.
    1957   *Social Theory and Social Structure*. Glencoe, Ill.: The Free Press.
Olesen, Virginia and Elvi Whittaker.
    1968   *The Silent Dialogue*. San Francisco: Jossey-Bass.
Sampson, Harold, Sheldon L. Messinger, and Robert D. Towne.
    1962   "Family processes and becoming a mental patient." *American Journal of Sociology* 62 (July): 88–96.

Simmel, Georg.
    1950   *The Sociology of Georg Simmel.* Kurt H. Wolff (ed. and tr.). Glencoe, Ill: The Free
            Press.
Sommer, Robert.
    1968   *Personal Space.* Englewood Cliffs, N.J.: Prentice-Hall
Swanson, Guy E.
    1968   "Review symposium of Harold Garfinkel, studies in ethnomethodology." *American
            Sociological Review* 33 (February): 122–124.
Webb, Eugene J., Donald T. Campbell, R.D. Schwartz, and L. Sechrest.
    1966   *Unobtrusive Measures: Nonreactive Research in the Social Sciences.* Chicago: Rand
            McNally.

PART III

Perspectives in Symbolic Interaction

CRITICAL THINKING QUESTIONS

Blumer

1. What, according to Blumer, is the self?
2. According to Blumer, can the self be studied using standard sociological methods?
3. According to Blumer, can the self be "known" in any final sense? Why or why not?

Goffman

1. How do people present "the self" in everyday life? Are there contradictions between selves?
2. Does Goffman understand the self to be a property unique to each person? Why or why not?
3. What are "settings," and can settings have different meanings to different people from diverse socio-cultural backgrounds?

Becker

1. In Becker's assessment, what is "deviance"?
2. How would Becker's argument apply to seemingly objective social problems such as murder, terrorism, or HIV/AIDS?
3. Can you think of different ways that "outsiders" are constructed? Can you think of instances in which the same act or behaviour perpetrated by two different people results in different assessments of a person's "outsider" status?

Denzin

1. What are three main differences between symbolic interactionism and ethnomethodology?

2. What are three main similarities between symbolic interactionism and ethnomethodology?
3. Choose a social issue or problem. Can you think of the different ways that an ethnomethodologist would study the issue/problem compared to a symbolic interactionist?

SUGGESTED READINGS

Atkinson, Michael. 2003. *Tattooed: The Sociogenesis of a Body Art.* Toronto: University of Toronto Press.

A study of how tattoo enthusiasts negotiate their differences as they relate to the social stigma and symbolic feelings of inclusiveness or belonging. The book argues that tattoos have become a part of the shared experiences of diverse people.

Goffman, Erving. 1961. *Asylums.* Chicago: University of Chicago Press.

Asylums is Goffman's famous study of total institutions. In this book, he analyzes institutional life in the closed world of places such as prison, hospitals, and boarding schools. Four essays are presented in the book.

Lemert, Charles, and Ann Branaman. 1999. *The Goffman Reader.* Oxford: Blackwell.

The Goffman Reader details Goffman's life and works. An argument is made for Goffman as a major contemporary theorist, demonstrating his innovation and diversity. Chapters focus on the constitution and character of the self.

Mead, George Herbert. 1934. *Mind, Self and Society.* Chicago: University of Chicago Press.

As a classic study of symbolic interaction, this book is a compilation of Mead's lectures at the University of Chicago. In these lectures, Mead detailed what came to be associated with the position of "social behaviourism," a term that Mead did not actually use.

Shaffir, William, and Jack Hass. 1991. *Becoming Doctors: Adopting the Cloak of Confidence.* Connecticut: JAI Press.

This book portrays professional socialization processes at McMaster University Medical School. Using interviewing and participant observation techniques, the authors offer some disturbing arguments about medicine, training, and personal and professional fronts.

RELATED WEB SITES

Changing Minds.org—Symbolic Interaction Theory
This site offers a description of symbolic interactionist theory and links to other sites.
http://changingminds.org/explanations/theories/symbolic_interaction.htm

Mead Project
The Mead Project Web site is run from Brock University. This site has many links to Mead and other interactionists.
http://spartan.ac.brocku.ca/%7Elward/

Moral Panic
This is a Web site, set in the tradition of the social construction of deviance, that centres on moral panics. Many links are offered to concepts such as urban legends and mods and rockers. There are also specific instances of panics offered.
www.fact-index.com/m/mo/moral_panic.html

Society for the Study of Symbolic Interaction
The SSSI is an international organization for scholars interested in qualitative and particularly interactionist research. The Web site offers information on symbolic interactionism today.
http://sun.soci.niu.edu/~sssi/

Theory Library: Interactionists
This is a Web site run from Black Hills State University. The link offers a range of other resources. There is a general theory library as well.
www.bhsu.edu/artssciences/asfaculty/dpeterson/theorylibrary.htm#Interactionists

PART IV

Modernism, Culture, and Change

A S THE DISCIPLINE OF SOCIOLOGY DEVELOPED THROUGH THE 19ᵀᴴ AND 20ᵀᴴ CENTURIES, one of the defining features of sociological thought was a concern with the social implications of modernization, industrialization, and social change. Focusing on the massive transformations transpiring in social, cultural, political, and religious life following the Enlightenment period (spanning approximately the 16ᵗʰ century through the 18ᵗʰ century), early sociologists sought to explain the importance of emerging urban, industrial lifestyles.

Of particular sociological interest have been the "social discontents" of urbanism and modernization: anonymity, isolation, and individualism, as well as moral pretensions to judgments of character, aesthetics, and taste. Emile Durkheim (1893), for example, contrasted mechanical to organic forms of solidarity in his treatise, *The Division of Labour in Society*. Theorizing that the system of links in which the bonds that hold individuals to society vary according to the division of labour, he explored the importance of social rules, interdependency, specialization, and levels of social integration in the context of changes to social density, volume, and anonymity. Karl Marx (1976) approached questions of social solidarity and change differently, theorizing that industrial production in England emerged from processes of primitive accumulation to produce various forms of alienation in the context of capitalist wage labour relations. And related themes pertaining to the individual, society, and social change were captured vividly by Max Weber's (1978) image of the modern bureaucracy as a dehumanizing iron cage. Rather than theorizing the dynamics of class struggle or the intricacies of social solidarity, Weber explored how individuals could be administered through bureaucratic processes such as the development of paper files, dossiers, and other rationally calculable modern organizational procedures.

Theorization on modernism and social change, while comprising a significant component of the history of sociological thought, is by no means unique to the writings of our canonical disciplinary forerunners. Interest in these sociological themes captured the analytic attention of important women who have either been marginal to mainstream sociological history or absent from it. Fascinating

141

women—such as Harriet Martineau, Beatrice Webb, Jane Addams, Mary Wollstonecraft, and Harriet Taylor Mill—each wrote, in their own ways, on different aspects of modernism, culture, and change (see McDonald 1994). More popular contemporary assessments of these foundational concerns appear in assessments of the "McDonaldization of Society" (Ritzer 1995) and the surveillance capacities of the modern nation-state (Dandeker 1990). Indeed, Charles Baudelaire's famous portrayal of the Flâneur in the middle of the 19th century was conceived through the social conditions of anonymity afforded by modern city living.

⑤ SECTION READINGS: GEORG SIMMEL, HERBERT MARCUSE, JÜRGEN HABERMAS, PIERRE BOURDIEU, AND MARIANA VALVERDE

In the first reading passage, Georg Simmel (1858–1918) identifies one of the greatest problems of modern metropolitan life as that of maintaining autonomy and individuality in the context of "overwhelming social forces." City dwellers, Simmel explains, think of themselves as the highest expression of civilization, a form of "sociation" unparalleled in history. But in a society of strangers, marked by social distance and superficial associations, he seeks to identify how the human personality accommodates itself as it adjusts to the "superindividual" contents of social life in the city. Inspired by the fact that people in the city are faced with ever-changing impressions that exist in sharp contrast to small-town rural settings (a larger population, uncertainty, anonymity), Simmel contends that the metropolitan man [sic] develops a heightened sense of intellectual consciousness that works against emotion and feeling to preserve the inner subjective life in the modern metropolitan culture.

The role of the money economy, for Simmel, is key to understanding the changing nature of human relations in the metropolis. The use of money creates interactions based on rational calculation and formal exchange. Whereas previous forms of sociation (e.g., face-to-face interactions in rural towns) were characterized by a greater degree of feeling and emotion, modern city life stimulates a decline in genuine human interaction or individuality. Money neutralizes human individuality and prioritizes only what is common to all rational people in metropolitan life. The money economy thrives on the calculation of exchange, and it fosters depersonalizing forces that lead to egoistic consumerism. But the metropolitan money economy, Simmel contends, carries with it merely a cloak of human despair; the money economy actually affords to the individual a level of freedom not found in any other social forms. For Simmel, people gain personal freedom by remaining separate from others, and the city dweller is spiritually free, although he or she does not often enjoy emotional comfort.

When Karl Marx wrote the "Economic and Philosophic Manuscripts of 1844," one of his central interests concerned the relationship between human nature, alienation, and modern social relations—indeed, themes found throughout his writings. For Marx, labour was the primary activity through which human beings realize their fundamental nature because labour enables the individual to achieve self-definition and self-realization by actively engaging the material environment. For Marx, labour must be oriented toward the satisfaction of basic material needs. When an individual's labour is not under his or her own control, however, or when material resources necessary to meet basic material needs are not available to the individual, the person cannot to realize full human potential. The consequence, Marx argued, was several levels of alienation.

Freedom and alienation are issues addressed by Herbert Marcuse in the second passage. Marcuse (1898–1979) argues that the technologies predominant in advanced industrial society have effectively eliminated conflict through affluence. In early stages of industrialism, freedom of speech, thought, and conscience were critical social goals in that they involved replacing outmoded material and intellectual culture with higher degrees of democratic human rationalization and individual freedom. Paradoxically, the achievement of those democratic goals ushered in a state of democratic "unfreedom." For Marcuse, however, democratic unfreedom is not a tool or a mechanism of the bourgeoisie, and power does not rest in the hands of any one social group. It is the totality of the industrial mechanization of society that is of greatest consequence to the suppression of human freedom. As Marcuse writes, "The most enduring and effective form of warfare against liberation is the implanting of material and intellectual needs that perpetrate obsolete forms of the struggle for existence" (p. 4) ("false needs"). For Marcuse, freedom is industrial society's mystifying ideological mechanism that sustains various levels of alienation. New forms of social control produce a pattern of one-dimensional thought interlinked with the ideology of rational-technical progress.

The third reading passage is written by Jürgen Habermas (1929–), who addresses a form of aesthetic modernity that first appeared in the 19th century. He explains how "the modern form" has functioned to distinguish past from present social relations since the 5th century. But it was with the emergence of the most recent interpretation of "modernism" that a stronger distinction has been enforced between the present and the past. Addressing the tensions between historical continuity and social change, Habermas rejects recent attempts in social theory to diagnose a postmodern social form (see Section 2, Part VI). The so-called postmodern reaction against tradition, he argues, is not new. Such a tension is found in the long history of art, and it traces most clearly to the critical project of the Enlightenment. What is new, Habermas continues, is that the avant-garde has become infected with modernism, engrossed in the very culture it sought to criticize. As art increasingly developed apart from the everyday world of laypeople, its strivings for self-justification were thwarted. So, too, were the emancipatory possibilities of art. For Habermas, the completion of the project of modernity consequently involves fusing the system and the lifeworld through art and aesthetic culture.

In the next selection, the late French sociologist Pierre Bourdieu (1930–2002) writes on "the dynamics of the fields." Bourdieu, who is recognized for his efforts to establish culture as a legitimate object of scientific study, is specifically interested in the ways in which the production and consumption of art as a cultural object determines social relations in the context of fields. Fields, for Bourdieu, are sites of power struggles between dominant and subordinate classes, whereby various forms of capital (economic, cultural, social, symbolic) are used to legitimate knowledge, relations, tastes, etc., between groups of people. Explained by Bourdieu as networks of relations existing within and between objective social-structural positions, fields operate in conjunction with systems of acquired dispositions (habitus) to describe the environment where class struggles take place.

Bourdieu examines how works of art represent the objectification of a relationship of distinction. He argues that every appropriation of a work of art, which is the embodiment of a more general relation of social distinction, is structured objectively by the cultural distinctions inscribed in it. For Bourdieu, the production of art operates within a field of existing tastes that is selected from a system of "stylistic possibilities," and experiences are, in turn, shaped in the field.

The final reading passage is drawn from the work of Mariana Valverde. Valverde (1945–), who is a professor of criminology at the University of Toronto, invokes Bourdieu's distinction between economic and cultural capital to formulate a third concept: moral capital. Moral capital refers to an "elusive inward essence" (often understood as "character") that is involved in creating, naturalizing, and maximizing certain human dispositions and habits. Valverde contends that moral capital is best understood as one of three "circuits" in civil society that interacts with economic and cultural capital to create a "mixed economy." This mixed economy, however, does not exclusively or even primarily involve changing the behaviour of people through repressive, heavy-handed, top-down forms of social sanctions. Rather, moral capital operates in conjunction with the other circuits to generate certain kinds of subjectivities that people come to understand as natural and normal (see Section 2, Part VII). Valverde offers the example of late-Victorian philanthropy to illustrate how moral capital encouraged the character formation of the poor beyond the simple act of dispensing sums of money through charitable acts. She also points to important dialectical processes in the formation of the self.

REFERENCES

Dandeker, Christopher. 1990. *Surveillance, Power, and Modernity*. Cambridge: Polity.

Durkheim, Emile. 1984. *The Division of Labour in Society*. New York: The Free Press.

Marx, Karl. 1976. *Capital*, vol. 1. London: Penguin Books.

McDonald, Lynn. 1994. *The Women Founders of the Social Sciences*. Ottawa: Carleton University Press.

Ritzer, George. 1995. *The McDonaldization of Society: An Investigation into the Changing Character of Contemporary Social Life*. Thousand Oaks, California: Pine Forge Press.

Weber, Max. 1978. *Economy and Society*, vol. 2. Berkeley: University of California Press.

CHAPTER 11

The Metropolis and Mental Life

GEORG SIMMEL

The deepest problems of modern life derive from the claim of the individual to preserve the autonomy and individuality of his existence in the face of overwhelming social forces, of historical heritage, of external culture, and of the technique of life. The fight with nature, which primitive man has to wage for his bodily existence, attains in this modern form its latest transformation. The eighteenth century called upon man to free himself of all the historical bonds in the state and in religion, in morals and in economics. Man's nature, originally good and common to all, should develop unhampered. In addition to more liberty, the nineteenth century demanded the functional specialization of man and his work; this specialization makes one individual incomparable to another, and each of them indispensable to the highest possible extent. However, this specialization makes each man the more directly dependent upon the supplementary activities of all others. Nietzsche sees the full development of the individual conditioned by the most ruthless struggle of individuals; socialism believes in the suppression of all competition for the same reason. Be that as it may, in all these positions the same basic motive is at work: the person resists to being leveled down and worn out by a social-technological mechanism. An inquiry into the inner meaning of specifically modern life and its products, into the soul of the cultural body, so to speak, must seek to solve the equation which structures like the metropolis set up between the individual and the super-individual contents of life. Such an inquiry must answer the question of how the personality accommodates itself in the adjustments to external forces. This will be my task today.

The psychological basis of the metropolitan type of individuality consists in the *intensification of nervous stimulation*, which results from the swift and uninterrupted change of outer and inner stimuli. Man is a differentiating creature. His mind is stimulated by the difference between a momentary impression and the one which preceded it. Lasting impressions, impressions which differ only slightly from one another, impressions which take a regular and habitual course and show regular and habitual contrasts—all these use up, so to speak, less consciousness than does the rapid crowding of changing images, the sharp discontinuity in the grasp of a single glance, and the unexpectedness of onrushing impressions. These are the psychological conditions which the metropolis creates. With each crossing of the street, with the tempo and multiplicity of economic, occupational and social life, the city sets up a deep contrast with small town and rural life with reference to the sensory foundations of psychic life. The metropolis exacts from man as a discriminating creature a different amount of consciousness than does rural life. Here the rhythm of life and sensory mental imagery flows more slowly, more habitually, and more evenly. Precisely in this connection the sophisticated character of metropolitan psychic life becomes understandable—as over against small town life, which rests more upon deeply felt and emotional relationships. These latter are rooted in the more unconscious layers of the psyche and grow most readily in the steady rhythm of uninterrupted habituations. The intellect, however, has its locus in the transparent, conscious, higher layers of the psyche; it is the most adaptable of our inner forces. In order to accommodate to change and to the contrast of phenomena, the intellect does not require any shocks and inner upheavals; it is only through such upheavals that the more conservative mind could accommodate to the metropolitan rhythm of events. Thus, the metropolitan type of man—which, of course, exists in a thousand individual variants—develops an organ protecting him against the threatening currents and discrepancies of his external environment which would uproot him. He reacts with his head instead of his heart. In this an increased awareness assumes the psychic prerogative. Metropolitan life, thus, underlies a heightened awareness and a predominance of intelligence in metropolitan man. The reaction to metropolitan phenomena is shifted to that organ which is least sensitive and quite remote from the depth of the personality. Intellectuality is thus seen to preserve subjective life against the overwhelming power of metropolitan life, and intellectuality branches out in many directions and is integrated with numerous discrete phenomena.

The metropolis has always been the seat of the money economy. Here the multiplicity and concentration of economic exchange gives an importance to the means of exchange which the scantiness of rural commerce would not have allowed. Money economy and the dominance of the intellect are intrinsically connected. They share a matter-of-fact attitude in dealing with men and with things; and, in this attitude, a formal justice is often coupled with an inconsiderate hardness. The intellectually sophisticated person is indifferent to all genuine individuality, because relationships and reactions result from it which cannot be exhausted with logical operations. In the same manner, the individuality of phenomena is not commensurate with the pecuniary principle. Money is concerned only with what is common to all: it asks for the exchange value, it reduces all quality and individuality to the question: How much? All intimate emotional relations between persons are founded in their individuality, whereas in rational relations man is reckoned with like a number, like an element which is in itself indifferent. Only the objective measurable achievement is of interest. Thus metropolitan man reckons with his merchants and customers, his domestic servants and often even with persons with whom he is obliged to have social intercourse. These features of intellectuality contrast with the nature of the small circle in which the inevitable knowledge of individuality as inevitably produces a warmer tone of behavior, a behavior which is beyond a mere objective balancing of service and return. In the sphere of the economic psychology of the small group it is of importance that under primitive conditions production serves the customer who orders the good, so that the producer and the consumer are acquainted. The modern metropolis, however, is supplied almost entirely by production for the market, that is, for entirely unknown purchasers who never personally enter the producer's actual field of vision. Through this anonymity the interests of each party acquire an unmerciful matter-of-factness; and the intellectually calculating economic egoisms of both parties need not fear any deflection because of the imponderables of personal relationships. The money economy dominates the metropolis; it has displaced the last survivals of domestic production and the direct barter of goods; it minimizes, from day to day, the amount of.work ordered by customers. The matter-of-fact attitude is obviously so intimately interrelated with the money economy, which is dominant in the metropolis, that nobody can say whether the intellectualistic mentality first promoted the money economy or whether the latter determined the former. The metropolitan way of life is certainly the most fertile soil for this reciprocity, a point which I shall document merely by citing the dictum of the most eminent English constitutional historian: throughout the whole course of English history, London has never acted as England's heart but often as England's intellect and always as her moneybag!

In certain seemingly insignificant traits, which lie upon the surface of life, the same psychic currents characteristically unite. Modern mind has become more and more calculating. The calculative exactness of practical life which the money economy has brought about corresponds to the ideal of natural science: to transform the world into an arithmetic problem, to fix every part of the world by mathematical formulas. Only money economy has filled the days of so many people with weighing, calculating, with numerical determinations, with a reduction of qualitative values to quantitative ones. Through the calculative nature of money a new precision, a certainty in the definition of identities and differences, an unambiguousness in agreements and arrangements has been brought about in the relations of life-elements—just as externally this precision has been effected by the universal diffusion of pocket watches. However, the conditions of metropolitan life are at once cause and effect of this trait. The relationships and affairs of the typical metropolitan usually are so varied and complex that without the strictest punctuality in promises and services the whole structure would break down into an inextricable chaos. Above all, this necessity is brought about by the aggregation of so many people with such differentiated interests, who must integrate their relations and activities into a highly complex organism. If all clocks and watches in Berlin would suddenly go wrong in different ways, even if only by one hour, all economic life and communication of the city would be disrupted for a long time. In addition an apparently mere external factor: long distances, would make all waiting and broken appointments result in an ill-afforded waste of time. Thus, the technique of metropolitan life is unimaginable without the most punctual integration of all activities and mutual relations into a stable and impersonal time schedule. Here again the general conclusions of this entire task of reflection become obvious, namely, that from each point on the surface of existence—however closely attached to the surface alone—one may drop a sounding into the depth of the psyche so that all the most banal externalities of life finally are connected with the ultimate decisions concerning the meaning and style of life. Punctuality, calculability, exactness are forced upon life by the complexity and extension of metropolitan existence and are not only most intimately connected with its money economy and intellectualistic character. These traits must also color the contents of life and favor the exclusion of those irrational, instinctive, sovereign traits and impulses which aim at determining the mode of life from within, instead of receiving the general and precisely schematized form of life from without. [...]

The same factors which have thus coalesced into the exactness and minute precision of the form of life have coalesced into a structure of the highest impersonality; on the other hand, they have promoted a highly personal subjectivity. There is perhaps no psychic phenomenon which has been so unconditionally reserved to the metropolis as has the blasé attitude. The blasé attitude results first from the rapidly changing and closely compressed contrasting stimulations of the nerves. From this, the enhancement of metropolitan intellectuality, also, seems originally to stem. Therefore, stupid people who are not intellectually alive in the first place usually are not exactly blasé. A life in boundless pursuit of pleasure makes one blasé because it agitates the nerves to their strongest reactivity for such a long time that they finally cease to react at all. In the same way, through the rapidity and contradictoriness of their changes, more harmless impressions force such violent responses, tearing the nerves so brutally hither and thither that their last reserves of strength are spent; and if one remains in the same milieu they have no time to gather new strength. An incapacity thus emerges to react to new sensations with the appropriate energy. This constitutes that blasé attitude which, in fact, every metropolitan child shows when compared with children of quieter and less changeable milieus.

This physiological source of the metropolitan blasé attitude is joined by another source which flows from the money economy. The essence of the blasé attitude consists in the blunting of discrimination. This does not mean that the objects are not perceived, as is the case with the half-wit, but rather that the meaning and differing values of things, and thereby the things themselves, are experienced as insubstantial. They appear to the blasé person in an evenly flat and gray tone; no one object deserves preference over any other. This mood is the faithful subjective reflection of the completely internalized money economy. By being the equivalent to all the manifold things in one and the same way, money becomes the most frightful leveler. For money expresses all qualitative differences of things in terms of "how much?" Money, with all its colorlessness and indifference, becomes the common denominator of all values; irreparably it hollows out the core of things, their individuality, their specific value, and their incomparability. All things float with equal specific gravity in the constantly moving stream of money. All things lie on the same level and differ from one another only in the size of the area which they cover. In the individual case this coloration, or rather discoloration, of things through their money equivalence may be unnoticeably minute. However, through the relations of the rich to the objects to be had for money, perhaps even through the total character which the mentality of the contemporary public everywhere imparts to these objects, the exclusively pecuniary evaluation of objects has become quite considerable. The large cities, the main seats of the money exchange, bring the purchasability of things to the fore much more impressively than do smaller localities. That is why cities are also the genuine locale of the blasé attitude. In the blasé attitude the concentration of men and things stimulate the nervous system of the individual to its highest achievement so that it attains its peak. Through the mere quantitative intensification of the same conditioning factors this achievement is transformed into its opposite and appears in the peculiar adjustment of the blasé attitude. In this phenomenon the nerves find in the refusal to react to their stimulation the last possibility of accommodating to the contents and forms of metropolitan life. The self-preservation of certain personalities is brought at the price of devaluating the whole objective world, a devaluation which in the end unavoidably drags one's own personality down into a feeling of the same worthlessness.

Whereas the subject of this form of existence has to come to terms with it entirely for himself, his self-preservation in the face of the large city demands from him a no less negative behavior of a social nature. This mental attitude of metropolitans toward one another we may designate, from a formal point of view, as reserve. If so many inner reactions were responses to the continuous external contacts with innumerable people as are those in the small town, where one knows almost everybody one meets and where one has a positive relation to almost everyone, one would be completely atomized internally and come to an unimaginable psychic state. Partly this psychological fact, partly the right to distrust which men have in the face of the touch-and-go elements of metropolitan life, necessitates our reserve. As a result of this reserve we frequently do not even know by sight those who have been our neighbors for years. And it is this reserve which in the eyes of the small-town people makes us appear to be cold and heartless. Indeed, if I do not deceive myself, the inner aspect of this outer reserve is not only indifference but, more often than we are aware, it is a slight aversion, a mutual strangeness and repulsion, which will break into hatred and fight at the moment of a closer contact, however caused. The whole inner organization of such an extensive communicative life rests upon an extremely varied hierarchy of sympathies, indifferences, and aversions of the briefest as well as of the most permanent nature. The sphere of indifference in this hierarchy is not as large as might appear on the surface. Our psychic activity still responds to almost every impression of somebody else with a somewhat distinct feeling. The unconscious, fluid, and changing character of this impression seems to result in a state of indifference. Actually this indifference would be just as unnatural as the diffusion of indiscriminate mutual suggestion would be unbearable. From both these typical dangers of the metropolis, indifference and indiscriminate suggestibility, antipathy protects us. A latent antipathy and the preparatory stage of practical antagonism effect the distances and aversions without which this mode of life could not at all be led. The extent and the mixture of this style of life, the rhythm of its emergence and disappearance, the forms in which it is satisfied—all these, with the unifying motives in the narrower sense, form the inseparable whole of the metropolitan style of life. What appears in the metropolitan style of life directly as dissociation is in reality only one of its elemental forms of socialization.

This reserve with its overtone of hidden aversion appears in turn as the form or the cloak of a more general mental phenomenon of the metropolis: it grants to the individual a kind and an amount of personal freedom which has no analogy whatsoever under other conditions. The metropolis goes back to one of the large developmental tendencies of social life as such, to one of the few tendencies for which an approximately universal formula can be discovered. The earliest phase of social formations found in historical as well as in contemporary social structures is this: a relatively small circle firmly closed against neighboring, strange, or in some way antagonistic circles. However, this circle is closely coherent and allows its individual members only a narrow field for the development of unique qualities and free, self-responsible movements. Political and kinship groups, parties, and religious associations begin in this way. The self-preservation of very young associations requires the establishment of strict boundaries and a centripetal unity. Therefore, they cannot allow the individual freedom and unique inner and outer development. From this stage social development proceeds at once in two different, yet corresponding, directions. To the extent to which the group grows—numerically, spatially, in significance, and in content of life—to the same degree the group's direct, inner unity loosens, and the rigidity of the original demarcation against others is softened through mutual relations and connections. At the same time, the individual gains freedom of movement, far beyond the first jealous delimitation. The individual also gains a specific individuality to which the division of labor in the enlarged group gives both occasion and necessity. [...]

* * * * *

It is not only the immediate size of the area and the number of persons which, because of the universal historical correlation between the enlargement of the circle and the personal inner and outer freedom, has made the metropolis the locale of freedom. It is rather in transcending this visible expanse that any given city becomes the seat of cosmopolitanism. The horizon of the city expands in a manner comparable to the way in which wealth develops; a certain amount of property increases in a quasi-automatical way in ever more rapid progression. As soon as a certain limit has been passed, the economic, personal, and intellectual relations of the citizenry, the sphere of intellectual predominance of the city over its hinterland, grow as in geometrical progression. Every gain in dynamic extension becomes a step, not for an equal, but for a new and larger extension. From every thread spinning out of the city, ever new threads grow as if by themselves, just as within the city the unearned increment of ground rent, through the mere increase in communication, brings the owner automatically increasing profits. At this point, the quantitative aspect of life is transformed directly into qualitative traits of character. The sphere of life of the small town is, in the main, self-contained and autarchic. For it is the decisive nature of the metropolis that its inner life overflows by waves into a far-flung national or international area. [...]

* * * * *

The most profound reason, however, why the metropolis conduces to the urge for the most individual personal existence—no matter whether justified and successful—appears to me to be the following: the development of modern culture is characterized by the preponderance of what one may call the "objective spirit" over the "subjective spirit." This is to say, in language as well as in law, in the technique of production as well as in art, in science as well as in the objects of the domestic environment, there is embodied a sum of spirit. The individual in his intellectual development follows the growth of this spirit very imperfectly and at an ever-increasing distance. If, for instance, we view the immense culture which for the last hundred years has been embodied in things and in knowledge, in institutions and in comforts, and if we compare all this with the cultural progress of the individual during the same period—at least in high-status groups—a frightful disproportion in growth between the two becomes evident. Indeed, at some points we notice a retrogression in the culture of the individual with reference to spirituality, delicacy, and idealism. This discrepancy results essentially from the growing division of labor. For the division of labor demands from the individual an ever more one -sided accomplishment, and the greatest advance in a one-sided pursuit only too frequently means death to the personality of the individual. In any case, he can cope less and less with the overgrowth of objective culture. The individual is reduced to a negligible quantity, perhaps less in his consciousness than in his practice and in the totality of his obscure emotional states that are derived from this practice. The individual has become a mere cog in an enormous organization of things and powers which tear from his hands all progress, spirituality, and value in order to transform them from their subjective form into the form of a purely objective life. It needs merely to be pointed out that the metropolis is the genuine arena of this culture which outgrows all personal life. Here in buildings and educational institutions, in the wonders and comforts of space-conquering technology, in the formations of community life, and in the visible institutions of the state, is offered such an overwhelming fullness of crystallized and impersonalized spirit that the personality, so to speak, cannot maintain itself under its impact. On the one hand, life is made infinitely easy for the personality in that stimulations, interests, uses of time, and consciousness are offered to it from all sides. They carry the person as if in a stream, and one needs hardly to swim for oneself. On the other hand, however, life is composed more and more of these impersonal contents and offerings which tend to displace the genuine personal colorations and incomparabilities. This results in the individual's summoning the utmost in uniqueness and particularization, in order to preserve his most personal core. He has to exaggerate this personal element in order to remain audible even to himself. [...]

* * * * *

CHAPTER 12

The New Forms of Control

HERBERT MARCUSE

A comfortable, smooth, reasonable, democratic unfreedom prevails in advanced industrial civilization, a token of technical progress. Indeed, what could be more rational than the suppression of individuality in the mechanization of socially necessary but painful performances; the concentration of individual enterprises in more effective, more productive corporations; the regulation of free competition among unequally equipped economic subjects; the curtailment of prerogatives and national sovereignties which impede the international organization of resources. That this technological order also involves a political and intellectual coordination may be a regrettable and yet promising development.

The rights and liberties which were such vital factors in the origins and earlier stages of industrial society yield to a higher stage of this society: they are losing their traditional rationale and content. Freedom of thought, speech, and conscience were—just as free enterprise, which they served to promote and protect—essentially *critical* ideas, designed to replace an obsolescent material and intellectual culture by a more productive and rational one. Once institutionalized, these rights and liberties shared the fate of the society of which they had become an integral part. The achievement cancels the premises.

To the degree to which freedom from want, the concrete substance of all freedom, is becoming a real possibility, the liberties which pertain to a state of lower productivity are losing their former content. Independence of thought, autonomy, and the right to political opposition are being deprived of their basic critical function in a society which seems increasingly capable of satisfying the needs of the individuals through the way in which it is organized. Such a society may justly demand acceptance of its principles and institutions, and reduce the opposition to the discussion and promotion of alternative policies *within* the status quo. In this respect, it seems to make little difference whether the increasing satisfaction of needs is accomplished by an authoritarian or a non-authoritarian system. Under the conditions of a rising standard of living, non-conformity with the system itself appears to be socially useless, and the more so when it entails tangible economic and

153

political disadvantages and threatens the smooth operation of the whole. Indeed, at least in so far as the necessities of life are involved, there seems to be no reason why the production and distribution of goods and services should proceed through the competitive concurrence of individual liberties.

Freedom of enterprise was from the beginning not altogether a blessing. As the liberty to work or to starve, it spelled toil, insecurity, and fear for the vast majority of the population. If the individual were no longer compelled to prove himself on the market, as a free economic subject, the disappearance of this kind of freedom would be one of the greatest achievements of civilization. The technological processes of mechanization and standardization might release individual energy into a yet uncharted realm of freedom beyond necessity. The very structure of human existence would be altered; the individual would be liberated from the work world's imposing upon him alien needs and alien possibilities. The individual would be free to exert autonomy over a life that would be his own. If the productive apparatus could be organized and directed toward the satisfaction of the vital needs, its control might well be centralized; such control would not prevent individual autonomy, but render it possible.

This is a goal within the capabilities of advanced industrial civilization, the "end" of technological rationality. In actual fact, however, the contrary trend operates: the apparatus imposes its economic and political requirements for defense and expansion on labor time and free time, on the material and intellectual culture. By virtue of the way it has organized its technological base, contemporary industrial society tends to be totalitarian. For "totalitarian" is not only a terroristic political coordination of society, but also a non-terroristic economic-technical coordination which operates through the manipulation of needs by vested interests. It thus precludes the emergence of an effective opposition against the whole. Not only a specific form of government or party rule makes for totalitarianism, but also a specific system of production and distribution which may well be compatible with a "pluralism" of parties, newspapers, "countervailing powers," etc.[1]

Today political power asserts itself through its power over the machine process and over the technical organization of the apparatus. The government of advanced and advancing industrial societies can maintain and secure itself only when it succeeds in mobilizing, organizing, and exploiting the technical, scientific, and mechanical productivity available to industrial civilization. And this productivity mobilizes society as a whole, above and beyond any particular individual or group interests. The brute fact that the machine's physical (only physical?) power surpasses that of the individual, and of any particular group of individuals, makes the machine the most effective political instrument in any society whose basic organization is that of the machine process. But the political trend may be reversed; essentially the power of the machine is only the stored-up and projected power of man. To the extent to which the work world is conceived of as a machine and mechanized accordingly, it becomes the potential basis of a new freedom for man.

Contemporary industrial civilization demonstrates that it has reached the stage at which "the free society" can no longer be adequately defined in the traditional terms of economic, political, and intellectual liberties, not because these liberties have become insignificant, but because they are too significant to be confined within the traditional forms. New modes of realization are needed, corresponding to the new capabilities of society.

Such new modes can be indicated only in negative terms because they would amount to the negation of the prevailing modes. Thus, economic freedom would mean freedom *from* the economy—from being controlled by economic forces and relationships; freedom from the daily struggle for existence, from earning a living. Political freedom would mean liberation of the individuals *from* politics over which they have no effective control. Similarly, intellectual freedom would mean the restoration of individual thought now absorbed by mass communication and indoctrination, abolition of "public opinion" together with its makers. The unrealistic sound of these propositions is indicative, not of their Utopian character, but of the strength of the forces which prevent their realization. The most effective and enduring form of warfare against liberation is the implanting of material and intellectual needs that perpetuate obsolete forms of the struggle for existence.

The intensity, the satisfaction, and even the character of human needs, beyond the biological level, have always been preconditioned. Whether or not the possibility of doing or leaving, enjoying or destroying, possessing or rejecting something is seized as a *need* depends on whether or not it can be seen as desirable and necessary for the prevailing societal institutions and interests. In this sense, human needs are historical needs and, to the extent to which the society demands the repressive development of the individual, his needs themselves and their claim for satisfaction are subject to overriding critical standards.

We may distinguish both true and false needs. "False" are those which are superimposed upon the individual by particular social interests in his repression: the needs which perpetuate toil, aggressiveness, misery, and injustice. Their satisfaction might be most gratifying to the individual, but this happiness is not a condition which has to be maintained and protected if it serves to arrest the development of the ability (his own and others) to recognize the disease of the whole and grasp the chances of curing the disease. The result then is euphoria in unhappiness. Most of the prevailing needs to relax, to have fun, to behave and consume in accordance with the advertisements, to love and hate what others love and hate, belong to this category of false needs.

Such needs have a societal content and function which are determined by external powers over which the individual has no control; the development and satisfaction of these needs is heteronomous. No matter how much such needs may have become the individual's own, reproduced and fortified by the conditions of his existence; no matter how much he identifies himself with them and finds himself in their satisfaction, they continue to be what they were from the beginning—products of a society whose dominant interest demands repression.

The prevalence of repressive needs is an accomplished fact, accepted in ignorance and defeat, but a fact that must be undone in the interest of the happy individual as well as all those whose misery is the price of his satisfaction. The only needs that have an unqualified claim for satisfaction are the vital ones—nourishment, clothing, lodging at the attainable level of culture. The satisfaction of these needs is the prerequisite for the realization of *all* needs, of the unsublimated as well as the sublimated ones.

For any consciousness and conscience, for any experience which does not accept the prevailing societal interest as the supreme law of thought and behavior, the established universe of needs and satisfactions is a fact to be questioned—questioned in terms of truth and falsehood. These terms are historical throughout, and their objectivity is historical. The judgment of needs and their satisfaction, under the given conditions, involves standards of *priority*—standards which refer to the optimal development of the individual, of all individuals, under the optimal utilization of the material and intellectual resources available to man. The resources are calculable. "Truth" and "falsehood" of needs designate objective conditions to the extent to which the universal satisfaction of vital needs and, beyond it, the progressive alleviation of toil and poverty, are universally valid standards. But as historical standards, they do not only vary according to area and stage of development, they also can be defined only in (greater or lesser) *contradiction* to the prevailing ones. What tribunal can possibly claim the authority of decision?

* * * * *

The more rational, productive, technical, and total the repressive administration of society becomes, the more unimaginable the means and ways by which the administered individuals might break their servitude and seize their own liberation. To be sure, to impose Reason upon an entire society is a paradoxical and scandalous idea—although one might dispute the righteousness of a society which ridicules this idea while making its own population into objects of total administration. All liberation depends on the consciousness of servitude, and the emergence of this consciousness is always hampered by the predominance of needs and satisfactions which, to a great extent, have become the individual's own. The process always replaces one system of preconditioning by another; the optimal goal is the replacement of false needs by true ones, the abandonment of repressive satisfaction.

The distinguishing feature of advanced industrial society is its effective suffocation of those needs which demand liberation—liberation also from that which is tolerable and rewarding and comfortable—while it sustains and absolves the destructive power and repressive function of the affluent society. Here, the social controls exact the overwhelming need for the production and consumption of waste; the need for stupefying work where it is no longer a real necessity; the need for modes of relaxation which soothe and prolong this stupefication; the need for maintaining such deceptive liberties as free competition at administered prices, a free press which censors itself, free choice between brands and gadgets.

Under the rule of a repressive whole, liberty can be made into a powerful instrument of domination. The range of choice open to the individual is not the decisive factor in determining the degree of human freedom, but *what* can be chosen and what *is* chosen by the individual. The criterion for free choice can never be an absolute one, but neither is it entirely relative. Free election of masters does not abolish the masters or the slaves. Free choice among a wide variety of goods and services does not signify freedom if these goods and services sustain social controls over a life of toil and fear—that is, if they sustain alienation. And the spontaneous reproduction of superimposed needs by the individual does not establish autonomy; it only testifies to the efficacy of the controls.

Our insistence on the depth and efficacy of these controls is open to the objection that we overrate greatly the indoctrinating power of the "media," and that by themselves the people would feel and satisfy the needs which are now imposed upon them. The objection misses the point. The preconditioning does not start with the mass production of radio and television and with the centralization of their control. The people enter this stage as preconditioned receptacles of long standing; the decisive difference is in the flattening out of the contrast (or conflict) between the given and the possible, between the satisfied and the unsatisfied needs. Here, the so-called equalization of class distinctions reveals its ideological function. If the worker and his boss enjoy the same television program and visit the same resort places, if the typist is as attractively made up as the daughter of her employer, if the Negro owns a Cadillac, if they all read the same newspaper, then this assimilation indicates not the disappearance of classes, but the extent to which the needs and satisfactions that serve the preservation of the Establishment are shared by the underlying population.

Indeed, in the most highly developed areas of contemporary society, the transplantation of social into individual needs is so effective that the difference between them seems to be purely theoretical. Can one really distinguish between the mass media as instruments of information and entertainment, and as agents of manipulation and indoctrination? Between the automobile as nuisance and as convenience? Between the horrors and the comforts of functional architecture? Between the work for national defense and the work for corporate gain? Between the private pleasure and the commercial and political utility involved in increasing the birth rate?

We are again confronted with one of the most vexing aspects of advanced industrial civilization: the rational character of its irrationality. Its productivity and efficiency, its capacity to increase and spread comforts, to turn waste into need, and destruction into construction, the extent to which this civilization transforms the object world into an extension of man's mind and body makes the very notion of alienation questionable. The people recognize themselves in their commodities; they find their soul in their automobile, hi-fi set, split-level home, kitchen equipment. The very mechanism which ties the individual to his society has changed, and social control is anchored in the new needs which it has produced.

The prevailing forms of social control are technological in a new sense. To be sure, the technical structure and efficacy of the productive and destructive apparatus has been a major instrumentality for subjecting the population to the established social division of labor throughout the modern period. Moreover, such integration has always been accompanied by more obvious forms of compulsion: loss of livelihood, the administration of justice, the police, the armed forces. It still is. But in the contemporary period, the technological controls appear to be the very embodiment of reason for the benefit of all social groups and interests—to such an extent that all contradiction seems irrational and all counteraction impossible.

No wonder then that, in the most advanced areas of this civilization, the social controls have been introjected to the point where even individual protest is affected at its roots. The intellectual and emotional refusal "to go along" appears neurotic and impotent. This is the socio-psychological aspect of the political event that marks the contemporary period: the passing of the historical forces which, at the preceding stage of industrial society, seemed to represent the possibility of new forms of existence.

But the term "introjection" perhaps no longer describes the way in which the individual by himself reproduces and perpetuates the external controls exercised by his society. Introjection suggests a variety of relatively spontaneous processes by which a Self (Ego) transposes the "outer" into the "inner." Thus, introjection implies the existence of an inner dimension distinguished from and even antagonistic to the external exigencies—an individual consciousness and an individual unconscious *apart from* public opinion and behavior.[2] The idea of "inner freedom" here has its reality: it designates the private space in which man may become and remain "himself."

Today this private space has been invaded and whittled down by technological reality. Mass production and mass distribution claim the entire individual, and industrial psychology has long since ceased to be confined to the factory. The manifold processes of introjection seem to be ossified in almost mechanical reactions. The result is, not adjustment but *mimesis:* an immediate identification of the individual with *his* society and, through it, with the society as a whole.

This immediate, automatic identification (which may have been characteristic of primitive forms of association) reappears in high industrial civilization; its new "immediacy," however, is the product of a sophisticated, scientific management and organization. In this process, the "inner" dimension of the mind in which opposition to the status quo can take root is whittled down. The loss of this dimension, in which the power of negative thinking—the critical power of Reason—is at home, is the ideological counterpart to the very material process in which advanced industrial society silences and reconciles the opposition. The impact of progress turns Reason into submission to the facts of life, and to the dynamic capability of producing more and bigger facts of the same sort of life. The efficiency of the system blunts the individuals' recognition that it contains no facts which do not communicate the repressive power of the whole. If the individuals find themselves in the things which shape their life, they do so, not by giving, but by accepting the law of things—not the law of physics but the law of their society.

I have just suggested that the concept of alienation seems to become questionable when the individuals identify themselves with the existence which is imposed upon them and have in it their own development and satisfaction. This identification is not illusion but reality. However, the reality constitutes a more progressive stage of alienation. The latter has become entirely objective; the subject which is alienated is swallowed up by its alienated existence. There is only one dimension, and it is everywhere and in all forms. The achievements of progress defy ideological indictment as well as justification; before their tribunal, the "false consciousness" of their rationality becomes the true consciousness.

This absorption of ideology into reality does not, however, signify the "end of ideology." On the contrary, in a specific sense advanced industrial culture is *more* ideological than its predecessor, inasmuch as today the ideology is in the process of production itself.[3] In a provocative form, this proposition reveals the political aspects of the prevailing technological rationality. The productive apparatus and the goods and services which it produces "sell" or impose the social system as a whole. The means of mass transportation and communication, the commodities of lodging, food, and clothing, the irresistible output of the entertainment and information industry carry with them prescribed attitudes and habits, certain intellectual and emotional reactions which bind the consumers more or less pleasantly to the producers and, through the latter, to the whole. The products indoctrinate and manipulate; they promote a false consciousness which is immune against its falsehood. And as these beneficial products become available to more individuals in more social classes, the indoctrination they carry ceases to be publicity; it becomes a way of life. It is a good way of life—much better than before—and as a good way of life, it militates against qualitative change. Thus emerges a pattern of *one-dimensional thought and behavior* in which ideas, aspirations, and objectives that, by their content, transcend the established universe of discourse and action are either repelled or reduced to terms of this universe. They are redefined by the rationality of the given system and of its quantitative extension.

* * * * *

One-dimensional thought is systematically promoted by the makers of politics and their purveyors of mass information. Their universe of discourse is populated by self-validating hypotheses which, incessantly and monopolistically repeated, become hypnotic definitions or dictations. For example, "free" are the institutions which operate (and are operated on) in the countries of the Free World; other transcending modes of freedom are by definition either anarchism, communism, or propaganda. "Socialistic" are all encroachments on private enterprises not undertaken by private enterprise itself (or by government contracts), such as universal and comprehensive health insurance, or the protection of nature from all too sweeping commercialization, or the establishment of public services which may hurt private profit. This totalitarian logic of accomplished facts has its Eastern counterpart. There, freedom is the way of life instituted by a communist regime, and all other transcending modes of freedom are either capitalistic, or revisionist, or leftist sectarianism. In both camps, non-operational ideas are non-behavioral and subversive. The movement of thought is stopped at barriers which appear as the limits of Reason itself.

Such limitation of thought is certainly not new. Ascending modern rationalism, in its speculative as well as empirical form, shows a striking contrast between extreme critical radicalism in scientific and philosophic method on the one hand, and an uncritical quietism in the attitude toward established and functioning social institutions. Thus, Descartes' *ego cogitans* was to leave the "great public bodies" untouched, and Hobbes held that "the present ought always to be preferred, maintained, and accounted best." Kant agreed with Locke in justifying revolution *if and when* it has succeeded in organizing the whole and in preventing subversion.

However, these accommodating concepts of Reason were always contradicted by the evident misery and injustice of the "great public bodies" and the effective, more or less conscious rebellion against them. Societal conditions existed which provoked and permitted real dissociation from the established state of affairs; a private as well as political dimension was present in which dissociation could develop into effective opposition, testing its strength and the validity of its objectives.

With the gradual closing of this dimension by the society, the self-limitation of thought assumes a larger significance. The interrelation between scientific-philosophical and societal processes, between theoretical and practical Reason, asserts itself "behind the back" of the scientists and philosophers. The society bars a whole type of oppositional operations and behavior; consequently, the concepts pertaining to them are rendered illusory or meaningless. Historical transcendence appears as metaphysical transcendence, not acceptable to science and scientific thought. The operational and behavioral point of view, practiced as a "habit of thought" at large, becomes the view of the established universe of discourse and action, needs and aspirations. The "cunning of Reason" works, as it so often did, in the interest of the powers that be. The insistence on operational and behavioral concepts turns against the efforts to free thought and behavior *from* the given reality and *for* the suppressed alternatives. Theoretical and practical Reason, academic and social behaviorism meet on common ground: that of an advanced society which makes scientific and technical progress into an instrument of domination.

"Progress" is not a neutral term; it moves toward specific ends, and these ends are defined by the possibilities of ameliorating the human condition. Advanced industrial society is approaching the stage where continued progress would demand the radical subversion of the prevailing direction and organization of progress. This stage would be reached when material production (including the necessary services) becomes automated to the extent that all vital needs can be satisfied while necessary labor time is reduced to marginal time. From this point on, technical progress would transcend the realm of necessity, where it served as the instrument of domination and exploitation which thereby limited its rationality; technology would become subject to the free play of faculties in the struggle for the pacification of nature and of society.

Such a state is envisioned in Marx's notion of the "abolition of labor." The term "pacification of existence" seems better suited to designate the historical alternative of a world which—through an international conflict which transforms and suspends the contradictions within the established societies—advances on the brink of a global war. "Pacification of existence" means the development of man's struggle with man and with nature, under conditions where the competing needs, desires, and aspirations are no longer organized by vested interests in domination and scarcity—an organization which perpetuates the destructive forms of this struggle.

Today's fight against this historical alternative finds a firm mass basis in the underlying population, and finds its ideology in the rigid orientation of thought and behavior to the given universe of facts. Validated by the accomplishments of science and technology, justified by its growing productivity, the status quo defies all transcendence. Faced with the possibility of pacification on the grounds of its technical and intellectual achievements, the mature industrial society closes itself against this alternative. Operationalism, in theory and practice, becomes the theory and practice of *containment*. Underneath its obvious dynamics, this society is a thoroughly static system of life: self-propelling in its oppressive productivity and in its beneficial coordination. Containment of technical progress goes hand in hand with its growth in the established direction. In spite of the political fetters imposed by the status quo, the more technology appears capable of creating the conditions for pacification, the more are the minds and bodies of man organized against this alternative.

The most advanced areas of industrial society exhibit throughout these two features: a trend toward consummation of technological rationality, and intensive efforts to contain this trend within the established institutions. Here is the internal contradiction of this civilization: the irrational element in its rationality. It is the token of its achievements. The industrial society which makes technology and science its own is organized for the ever-more-effective domination of man and nature, for the ever-more-effective utilization of its resources. It becomes irrational when the success of these efforts opens new dimensions of human realization. Organization for peace is different from organization for war; the institutions which served the struggle for existence cannot serve the pacification of existence. Life as an end is qualitatively different from life as a means.

Such a qualitatively new mode of existence can never be envisaged as the mere by-product of economic and political changes, as the more or less spontaneous effect of the new institutions which constitute the necessary prerequisite. Qualitative change also involves a change in the *technical* basis on which this society rests—one which sustains the economic and political institutions through which the "second nature" of man as an aggressive object of administration is stabilized. The techniques of industrialization are political techniques; as such, they prejudge the possibilities of Reason and Freedom.

To be sure, labor must precede the reduction of labor, and industrialization must precede the development of human needs and satisfactions. But as all freedom depends on the conquest of alien necessity, the realization of freedom depends on the *techniques* of this conquest. The highest productivity of labor can be used for the perpetuation of labor, and the most efficient industrialization can serve the restriction and manipulation of needs.

When this point is reached, domination—in the guise of affluence and liberty— extends to all spheres of private and public existence, integrates all authentic opposition, absorbs all alternatives. Technological rationality reveals its political character as it becomes the great vehicle of better domination, creating a truly totalitarian universe in which society and nature, mind and body are kept in a state of permanent mobilization for the defense of this universe.

NOTES

1. See p. 50, *One Dimensional Man: Studies in the Ideology of Advanced Industrial Society.*
2. The change in the function of the family here plays a decisive role: its "socializing" functions are increasingly taken over by outside groups and media. See my *Eros and Civilization* (Boston: Beacon Press, 1955), p. 96ff.
3. Theodor W. Adorno, *Prismen. Kulturkritik und Gesellschaft.* (Frankfurt: Suhrkamp, 1955), p. 24f.

CHAPTER 13

Modernity—An Incomplete Project

JÜRGEN HABERMAS

In 1980, architects were admitted to the Biennial in Venice, following painters and filmmakers. The note sounded at this first Architecture Biennial was one of disappointment. I would describe it by saying that those who exhibited in Venice formed an avant-garde of reversed fronts. I mean that they sacrificed the tradition of modernity in order to make room for a new historicism. Upon this occasion, a critic of the German newspaper, *Frankfurter Allgemeine Zeitung*, advanced a thesis whose significance reaches beyond this particular event; it is a diagnosis of our times: "Postmodernity definitely presents itself as Antimodernity." This statement describes an emotional current of our times which has penetrated all spheres of intellectual life. It has placed on the agenda theories of postenlightenment, postmodernity, even of posthistory.

From history we know the phrase, "The Ancients and the Moderns." Let me begin by defining these concepts. The term "modern" has a long history, one which has been investigated by Hans Robert Jauss.[1] The word "modern" in its Latin form "modernus" was used for the first time in the late 5th century in order to distinguish the present, which had become officially Christian, from the Roman and pagan past. With varying content, the term "modern" again and again expresses the consciousness of an epoch that relates itself to the past of antiquity, in order to view itself as the result of a transition from the old to the new.

Some writers restrict this concept of "modernity" to the Renaissance, but this is historically too narrow. People considered themselves modern during the period of Charles the Great in the 12th century, as well as in France of the late 17th century at the time of the famous "Querelle des Anciens et des Modernes." That is to say, the term "modern" appeared and reappeared exactly during those periods in Europe when the consciousness of a new epoch formed itself through a renewed relationship to the ancients—whenever, moreover, antiquity was considered a model to be recovered through some kind of imitation.

The spell which the classics of the ancient world cast upon the spirit of later times was first dissolved with the ideals of the French Enlightenment. Specifically,

163

the idea of being "modern" by looking back to the ancients changed with the belief, inspired by modern science, in the infinite progress of knowledge and in the infinite advance towards social and moral betterment. Another form of modernist consciousness was formed in the wake of this change. The romantic modernist sought to oppose the antique ideals of the classicists; he looked for a new historical epoch and found it in the idealized Middle Ages. However, this new ideal age, established early in the 19th century, did not remain a fixed ideal. In the course of the 19th century, there emerged out of this romantic spirit that radicalized conscious-ness of modernity which freed itself from all specific historical ties. This most recent modernism simply makes an abstract opposition between tradition and the present; and we are, in a way, still the contemporaries of that kind of aesthetic modernity which first appeared in the midst of the 19th century. Since then, the distinguishing mark of works which count as modern is "the new" which will be overcome and made obsolete through the novelty of the next style. But, while that which is merely "stylish" will soon become outmoded, that which is modern preserves a secret tie to the classical. Of course, whatever can survive time has always been considered to be a classic. But the emphatically modern document no longer borrows this power of being a classic from the authority of a past epoch; instead, a modern work becomes a classic because it has once been authentically modern. Our sense of modernity creates its own self-enclosed canons of being classic. In this sense we speak, e.g., in view of the history of modern art, of classical modernity. The relation between "modern" and "classical" has definitely lost a fixed historical reference.

⑤ THE DISCIPLINE OF AESTHETIC MODERNITY

The spirit and discipline of aesthetic modernity assumed clear contours in the work of Baudelaire. Modernity then unfolded in various avant-garde movements and finally reached its climax in the Café Voltaire of the dadaists and in surrealism. Aesthetic modernity is characterized by attitudes which find a common focus in a changed consciousness of time. This time consciousness expresses itself through metaphors of the vanguard and the avant-garde. The avant-garde understands itself as invading unknown territory, exposing itself to the dangers of sudden, shocking encounters, conquering an as yet unoccupied future. The avant-garde must find a direction in a landscape into which no one seems to have yet ventured.

But these forward gropings, this anticipation of an undefined future, and the cult of the new mean in fact the exaltation of the present. The new time consciousness, which enters philosophy in the writings of Bergson, does more than express the experience of mobility in society, of acceleration in history, of discontinuity in everyday life. The new value placed on the transitory, the elusive, and the ephemeral, the very celebration of dynamism, discloses a longing for an undefiled, immaculate, and stable present.

This explains the rather abstract language in which the modernist temper has spoken of the "past." Individual epochs lose their distinct forces. Historical memory is replaced by the heroic affinity of the present with the extremes of history—a sense of time wherein decadence immediately recognizes itself in the barbaric, the wild, and the primitive. We observe the anarchistic intention of blowing up the continuum of history, and we can account for it in terms of the subversive force of this new aesthetic consciousness. Modernity revolts against the normalizing functions of tradition; modernity lives on the experience of rebelling against all that is normative. This revolt is one way to neutralize the standards of both morality and utility. This aesthetic consciousness continuously stages a dialectical play between secrecy and public scandal; it is addicted to a fascination with that horror which accompanies the act of profaning, and yet is always in flight from the trivial results of profanation.

On the other hand, the time consciousness articulated in avant-garde art is not simply ahistorical; it is directed against what might be called a false normativity in history. The modern, avant-garde spirit has sought to use the past in a different way; it disposes those pasts which have been made available by the objectifying scholarship of historicism, but it opposes at the same time a neutralized history which is locked up in the museum of historicism.

Drawing upon the spirit of surrealism, Walter Benjamin constructs the relationship of modernity to history in what I would call a posthistoricist attitude. He reminds us of the self-understanding of the French Revolution: "The Revolution cited ancient Rome, just as fashion cites an antiquated dress. Fashion has a scent for what is current, whenever this moves within the thicket of what was once." This is Benjamin's concept of the *Jetztzeit*, of the present as a moment of revelation; a time in which splinters of a messianic presence are enmeshed. In this sense, for Robespierre, the antique Rome was a past laden with momentary revelations.[2]

Now, this spirit of aesthetic modernity has recently begun to age. It has been recited once more in the 1960s; after the 1970s, however, we must admit to ourselves that this modernism arouses a much fainter response today than it did fifteen years ago. Octavio Paz, a fellow-traveller of modernity, noted already in the middle of the 1960s that "the avant-garde of 1967 repeats the deeds and gestures of those of 1917. We are experiencing the end of the idea of modern art." The work of Peter Burger has since taught us to speak of "post-avant-garde" art; this term is chosen to indicate the failure of the surrealist rebellion.[3] But what is the meaning of this failure? Does it signal a farewell to modernity? Thinking more generally, does the existence of a post-avant-garde mean there is a transition to that broader phenomenon called postmodernity?

This is in fact how Daniel Bell, the most brilliant of the American neoconservatives, interprets matters. In his book, *The Cultural Contradictions of Capitalism*, Bell argues that the crises of the developed societies of the West are to be traced back to a split between culture and society. Modernist culture has come to penetrate the values of everyday life; the life-world is infected by modernism. Because of the forces of modernism, the principle of unlimited self-realization, the demand for authentic self-experience and the subjectivism of a hyperstimulated sensitivity have come to be dominant. This temperament unleashes hedonistic motives irreconcilable with the discipline of professional life in society, Bell says. Moreover, modernist culture is altogether incompatible with the moral basis of a purposive, rational conduct of life. In this manner, Bell places the burden of responsibility for the dissolution of the Protestant ethic (a phenomenon which had already disturbed Max Weber) on the "adversary culture." Culture in its modern form stirs up hatred against the conventions and virtues of everyday life, which has become rationalized under the pressures of economic and administrative imperatives.

I would call your attention to a complex wrinkle in this view. The impulse of modernity, we are told on the other hand, is exhausted; anyone who considers himself avant-garde can read his own death warrant. Although the avant-garde is still considered to be expanding, it is supposedly no longer creative. Modernism is dominant but dead. For the neoconservative the question then arises: how can norms arise in society which will limit libertinism, reestablish the ethic of discipline and work? What new norms will put a brake on the levelling caused by the social welfare state so that the virtues of individual competition for achievement can again dominate? Bell sees a religious revival to be the only solution. Religious faith tied to a faith in tradition will provide individuals with clearly defined identities and existential security.

5 CULTURAL MODERNITY AND SOCIETAL MODERNIZATION

One can certainly not conjure up by magic the compelling beliefs which command authority. Analyses like Bell's, therefore, only result in an attitude which is spreading in Germany no less than in the States: an intellectual and political confrontation with the carriers of cultural modernity. I cite Peter Steinfels, an observer of the new style which the neoconservatives have imposed upon the intellectual scene in the 1970s:

> The struggle takes the form of exposing every manifestation of what could be considered an oppositionist mentality and tracing its "logic" so as to link it to various forms of extremism: drawing the connection between modernism and nihilism ... between government regulation and totalitarianism, between criticism of arms expenditures and subservience to communism, between Women's liberation or homosexual rights and the destruction of the family ... between the Left generally and terrorism, anti-semitism, and fascism ...[4]

The *ad hominem* approach and the bitterness of these intellectual accusations have also been trumpeted loudly in Germany. They should not be explained so much in terms of the psychology of neoconservative writers; rather, they are rooted in the analytical weaknesses of neoconservative doctrine itself.

Neoconservatism shifts onto cultural modernism the uncomfortable burdens of a more or less successful capitalist modernization of the economy and society. The neoconservative doctrine blurs the relationship between the welcomed process of *societal* modernization on the one hand, and the lamented cultural development on the other. The neoconservative does not uncover the economic and social causes for the altered attitudes towards work, consumption, achievement, and leisure. Consequently, he attributes all of the following—hedonism, the lack of social identification, the lack of obedience, narcissism, the withdrawal from status, and achievement competition—to the domain of "culture." In fact, however, culture is intervening in the creation of all these problems in only a very indirect and mediated fashion.

In the neoconservative view, those intellectuals who still feel themselves committed to the project of modernity are then presented as taking the place of those unanalyzed causes. The mood which feeds neoconservatism today in no way originates from discontent about the antinomian consequences of a culture breaking from the museums into the stream of ordinary life. This discontent has not been called into life by modernist intellectuals. It is rooted in deep-seated reactions against the process of societal modernization. Under the pressures of the dynamics of economic growth and the organizational accomplishments of the state, this social modernization penetrates deeper and deeper into previous forms of human existence. I would describe this subordination of the life-worlds under the system's imperatives as a matter of disturbing the communicative infrastructure of everyday life.

Thus, for example, neopopulist protests only express in pointed fashion a widespread fear regarding the destruction of the urban and natural environment and of forms of human sociability. There is a certain irony about these protests in terms of neoconservatism. The tasks of passing on a cultural tradition, of social integration, and of socialization require adherence to what I call communicative rationality. But the occasions for protest and discontent originate precisely when spheres of communicative action, centered on the reproduction and transmission of values and norms, are penetrated by a form of modernization guided by standards of economic and administrative rationality—in other words, by standards of rationalization quite different from those of communicative rationality on which those spheres depend. But neoconservative doctrines turn our attention precisely away from such societal processes: they project the causes, which they do not bring to light, onto the plane of a subversive culture and its advocates.

To be sure, cultural modernity generates its own aporias as well. Independently from the consequences of *societal* modernization and within the perspective of *cultural* development itself, there originate motives for doubting the project of modernity. Having dealt with a feeble kind of criticism of modernity—that of neoconservatism—let me now move our discussion of modernity and its discontents into a different domain that touches on these aporias of cultural modernity—issues that often serve only as a pretense for those positions which either call for a postmodernity, recommend a return to some form of premodernity, or throw modernity radically overboard.

⑤ THE PROJECT OF ENLIGHTENMENT

The idea of modernity is intimately tied to the development of European art, but what I call "the project of modernity" comes only into focus when we dispense with the usual concentration upon art. Let me start a different analysis by recalling an idea from Max Weber. He characterized cultural modernity as the separation of the substantive reason expressed in religion and metaphysics into three autonomous spheres. They are: science, morality, and art. These came to be differentiated because the unified world-views of religion and metaphysics fell apart. Since the 18th century, the problems inherited from these older world-views could be arranged so as to fall under specific aspects of validity: truth, normative rightness, authenticity, and beauty. They could then be handled as questions of knowledge, or of justice and morality, or of taste. Scientific discourse, theories of morality, jurisprudence, and the production and criticism of art could in turn be institutionalized. Each domain of culture could be made to correspond to cultural professions in which problems could be dealt with as the concern of special experts. This professionalized treatment of the cultural tradition brings to the fore the intrinsic structures of each of the three dimensions of culture. There appear the structures of cognitive-instrumental, of moral-practical, and of aesthetic-expressive rationality, each of these under the control of specialists who seem more adept at being logical in these particular ways than other people are. As a result, the distance grows between the culture of the experts and that of the larger public. What accrues to culture through specialized treatment and reflection does not immediately and necessarily become the property of everyday praxis. With cultural rationalization of this sort, the threat increases that the life-world, whose traditional substance has already been devalued, will become more and more impoverished.

The project of modernity formulated in the 18th century by the philosophers of the Enlightenment consisted in their efforts to develop objective science, universal morality and law, and autonomous art according to their inner logic. At the same time, this project intended to release the cognitive potentials of each of these domains from their esoteric forms. The Enlightenment philosophers wanted to utilize this accumulation of specialized culture for the enrichment of everyday life—that is to say, for the rational organization of everyday social life.

Enlightenment thinkers of the cast of mind of Condorcet still had the extravagant expectation that the arts and sciences would promote not only the control of natural forces but also understanding of the world and of the self, moral progress, the justice of institutions, and even the happiness of human beings. The 20th century has shattered this optimism. The differentiation of science, morality, and art has come to mean the autonomy of the segments treated by the specialist and their separation from the hermeneutics of everyday communication. This splitting off is the problem that has given rise to efforts to "negate" the culture of expertise. But the problem won't go away: should we try to hold on to the *intentions* of the Enlightenment, feeble as they may be, or should we declare the entire project of modernity a lost cause? I now want to return to the problem of artistic culture, having explained why, historically, aesthetic modernity is only a part of cultural modernity in general.

🖅 THE FALSE PROGRAMS OF THE NEGATION OF CULTURE

Greatly oversimplifying, I would say that in the history of modern art one can detect a trend towards ever greater autonomy in the definition and practice of art. The category of "beauty" and the domain of beautiful objects were first constituted in the Renaissance. In the course of the 18th century, literature, the fine arts, and music were institutionalized as activities independent from sacred and courtly life. Finally, around the middle of the 19th century an aestheticist conception of art emerged, which encouraged the artist to produce his work according to the distinct consciousness of art for art's sake. The autonomy of the aesthetic sphere could then become a deliberate project: the talented artist could lend authentic expression to those experiences he had in encountering his own de-centered subjectivity, detached from the constraints of routinized cognition and everyday action.

In the mid-19th century, in painting and literature, a movement began which Octavio Paz finds epitomized already in the art criticism of Baudelaire. Color, lines, sounds, and movement ceased to serve primarily the cause of representation; the media of expression and the techniques of production themselves became the aesthetic object. Theodor W. Adorno could therefore begin his *Aesthetic Theory* with the following sentence: "It is now taken for granted that nothing which concerns art can be taken for granted any more: neither art itself, nor art in its relationship to the whole, nor even the right of art to exist." And this is what surrealism then denied: *das Existenzrecht der Kunst als Kunst*. To be sure, surrealism would not have challenged the right of art to exist, if modern art no longer had advanced a promise of happiness concerning its own relationship "to the whole" of life. For Schiller, such a promise was delivered by aesthetic intuition, but not fulfilled by it. Schiller's *Letters on the Aesthetic Education of Man* speaks to us of a Utopia reaching beyond art itself. But by the time of Baudelaire, who repeated this *promesse de bonheur* via art, the Utopia of reconciliation with society had gone sour. A relation of opposites had come into being; art had become a critical mirror, showing the irreconcilable nature of the aesthetic and the social worlds. This modernist transformation was all the more painfully realized, the more art alienated itself from life and withdrew into the untouchableness of complete autonomy. Out of such emotional currents finally gathered those explosive energies which unloaded in the surrealist attempt to blow up the autarkical sphere of art and to force a reconciliation of art and life.

But all those attempts to level art and life, fiction and praxis, appearance and reality to one plane; the attempts to remove the distinction between artifact and object of use, between conscious staging and spontaneous excitement; the attempts to declare everything to be art and everyone to be an artist, to retract all criteria and to equate aesthetic judgment with the expression of subjective experiences—all these undertakings have proved themselves to be sort of nonsense experiments. These experiments have served to bring back to life, and to illuminate all the more glaringly, exactly those structures of art which they were meant to dissolve. They gave a new legitimacy, as ends in themselves, to appearance as the medium of fiction, to the transcendence of the artwork over society, to the concentrated and planned character of artistic production as well as to the special cognitive status of judgments of taste. The radical attempt to negate art has ended up ironically by giving due exactly to these categories through which Enlightenment aesthetics had circumscribed its object domain. The surrealists waged the most extreme warfare, but two mistakes in particular destroyed their revolt. First, when the containers of an autonomously developed cultural sphere are shattered, the contents get dispersed. Nothing remains from a desublimated meaning or a destructured form; an emancipatory effect does not follow.

Their second mistake has more important consequences. In everyday communication, cognitive meanings, moral expectations, subjective expressions, and evaluations must relate to one another. Communication processes need a cultural tradition covering all spheres—cognitive, moral-practical, and expressive. A rationalized everyday life, therefore, could hardly be saved from cultural impoverishment through breaking open a single cultural sphere—art—and so providing access to just one of the specialized knowledge complexes. The surrealist revolt would have replaced only one abstraction.

In the spheres of theoretical knowledge and morality, there are parallels to this failed attempt of what we might call the false negation of culture. Only they are less pronounced. Since the days of the Young Hegelians, there has been talk about the negation of philosophy. Since Marx, the question of the relationship of theory and practice has been posed. However, Marxist intellectuals joined a social movement; and only at its peripheries were there sectarian attempts to carry out a program of the negation of philosophy similar to the surrealist program to negate art. A parallel to the surrealist mistakes becomes visible in these programs when one observes the consequences of dogmatism and of moral rigorism.

A reified everyday praxis can be cured only by creating unconstrained interaction of the cognitive with the moral-practical and the aesthetic-expressive elements. Reification cannot be overcome by forcing just one of those highly stylized cultural spheres to open up and become more accessible. Instead, we see under certain circumstances a relationship emerge between terroristic activities and the over-extension of any one of these spheres into other domains: examples would be tendencies to aestheticize politics, or to replace politics by moral rigorism or to submit it to the dogmatism of a doctrine. These phenomena should not lead us, however, into denouncing the intentions of the surviving Enlightenment tradition as intentions rooted in a "terroristic reason."[5] Those who lump together the very project of modernity with the state of consciousness and the spectacular action of the individual terrorist are no less short-sighted than those who would claim that the incomparably more persistent and extensive bureaucratic terror practiced in the dark, in the cellars of the military and secret police, and in camps and institutions, is the *raison d'être* of the modern state, only because this kind of administrative terror makes use of the coercive means of modern bureaucracies.

⑤ ALTERNATIVES

I think that instead of giving up modernity and its project as a lost cause, we should learn from the mistakes of those extravagant programs which have tried to negate modernity. Perhaps the types of reception of art may offer an example which at least indicates the direction of a way out.

Bourgeois art had two expectations at once from its audiences. On the one hand, the layman who enjoyed art should educate himself to become an expert. On the other hand, he should also behave as a competent consumer who uses art and relates aesthetic experiences to his own life problems. This second, and seemingly harmless, manner of experiencing art has lost its radical implications exactly because it had a confused relation to the attitude of being expert and professional.

To be sure, artistic production would dry up, if it were not carried out in the form of a specialized treatment of autonomous problems and if it were to cease to be the concern of experts who do not pay so much attention to exoteric questions. Both artists and critics accept thereby the fact that such problems fall under the spell of what I earlier called the "inner logic" of a cultural domain. But this sharp delineation, this exclusive concentration on one aspect of validity alone, and the exclusion of aspects of truth and justice, break down as soon as aesthetic experience is drawn into an individual life history and is absorbed into ordinary life. The reception of art by the layman, or by the "everyday expert," goes in a rather different direction than the reception of art by the professional critic.

Albrecht Wellmer has drawn my attention to one way that an aesthetic experience which is not framed around the experts' critical judgments of taste can have its significance altered: as soon as such an experience is used to illuminate a life-historical situation and is related to life problems, it enters into a language game which is no longer that of the aesthetic critic. The aesthetic experience then not only renews the interpretation of our needs in whose light we perceive the world. It permeates as well our cognitive significations and our normative expectations and changes the manner in which all these moments refer to one another. Let me give an example of this process.

This manner of receiving and relating to art is suggested in the first volume of the work *The Aesthetics of Resistance* by the German-Swedish writer Peter Weiss.

Weiss describes the process of reappropriating art by presenting a group of politically motivated, knowledge-hungry workers in 1937 in Berlin.[6] These were young people who, through an evening high-school education, acquired the intellectual means to fathom the general and social history of European art. Out of the resilient edifice of this objective mind, embodied in works of art which they saw again and again in the museums in Berlin, they started removing their own chips of stone, which they gathered together and reassembled in the context of their own milieu. This milieu was far removed from that of traditional education as well as from the then existing regime. These young workers went back and forth between the edifice of European art and their own milieu until they were able to illuminate both.

In examples like this which illustrate the reappropriation of the expert's culture from the standpoint of the life-world, we can discern an element which does justice to the intentions of the hopeless surrealist revolts, perhaps even more to Brecht's and Benjamin's interests in how art works, which having lost their aura, could yet be received in illuminating ways. In sum, the project of modernity has not yet been fulfilled. And the reception of art is only one of at least three of its aspects. The project aims at a differentiated relinking of modern culture with an everyday praxis that still depends on vital heritages, but would be impoverished through mere traditionalism. This new connection, however, can only be established under the condition that societal modernization will also be steered in a different direction. The life-world has to become able to develop institutions out of itself which set limits to the internal dynamics and imperatives of an almost autonomous economic system and its administrative complements.

If I am not mistaken, the chances for this today are not very good. More or less in the entire Western world a climate has developed that furthers capitalist modernization processes as well as trends critical of cultural modernism. The disillusionment with the very failures of those programs that called for the negation of art and philosophy has come to serve as a pretense for conservative positions. Let me briefly distinguish the anti-modernism of the "young conservatives" from the premodernism of the "old conservatives" and from the postmodernism of the neoconservatives.

The "young conservatives" recapitulate the basic experience of aesthetic modernity. They claim as their own the revelations of a decentered subjectivity, emancipated from the imperatives of work and usefulness, and with this experience they step outside the modern world. On the basis of modernistic attitudes they justify an irreconcilable antimodernism. They remove into the sphere of the far-away and the archaic the spontaneous powers of imagination, self-experience, and emotion. To instrumental reason they juxtapose in Manichean fashion a principle only accessible through evocation, be it the will to power or sovereignty, Being or the Dionysiac force of the poetical. In France this line leads from Georges Bataille via Michel Foucault to Jacques Derrida.

The "old conservatives" do not allow themselves to be contaminated by cultural modernism. They observe the decline of substantive reason, the differentiation of science, morality, and art, the modern world view and its merely procedural rationality, with sadness and recommend a withdrawal to a position *anterior* to modernity. Neo-Aristotelianism, in particular, enjoys a certain success today. In view of the problematic of ecology, it allows itself to call for a cosmological ethic. (As belonging to this school, which originates with Leo Strauss, one can count the interesting works of Hans Jonas and Robert Spaemann.)

Finally, the neoconservatives welcome the development of modern science, as long as this only goes beyond its sphere to carry forward technical progress, capitalist growth, and rational administration. Moreover, they recommend a politics of defusing the explosive content of cultural modernity. According to one thesis, science, when properly understood, has become irrevocably meaningless for the orientation of the life-world. A further thesis is that politics must be kept as far aloof as possible from the demands of moral-practical justification. And a third thesis asserts the pure immanence of art, disputes that it has a Utopian content, and points to its illusory character in order to limit the aesthetic experience to privacy. (One could name here the early Wittgenstein, Carl Schmitt of the middle period, and Gottfried Benn of the late period.) But with the decisive confinement of science, morality, and art to autonomous spheres separated from the life-world and administered by experts, what remains from the project of cultural modernity is only what we would have if we were to give up the project of modernity altogether. As a replacement one points to traditions which, however, are held to be immune to demands of (normative) justification and validation.

This typology is like any other, of course, a simplification, but it may not prove totally useless for the analysis of contemporary intellectual and political confrontations. I fear that the ideas of antimodernity, together with an additional touch of premodernity, are becoming popular in the circles of alternative culture. When one observes the transformations of consciousness within political parties in Germany, a new ideological shift (*Tendenzwende*) becomes visible. And this is the alliance of postmodernists with premodernists. It seems to me that there is no party in particular that monopolizes the abuse of intellectuals and the position of neoconservatism. I therefore have good reason to be thankful for the liberal spirit in which the city of Frankfurt offers me a prize bearing the name of Theodor Adorno, a most significant son of this city, who as philosopher and writer has stamped the image of the intellectual in our country in incomparable fashion, who, even more, has become the very image of emulation for the intellectual.

NOTES

1. Jauss is a prominent German literary historian and critic involved in "the aesthetics of reception," a type of criticism related to reader-response criticism in this country. For a discussion of "modern" see Jauss, *Asthetische Normen und geschichtliche Reflexion in der Querelle desAnciens et desModernes* (Munich, 1964). For a reference in English, see Jauss,

"History of Art and Pragmatic History," *Toward an Aesthetic of Reception*, trans. Timothy Bahti (Minneapolis: University of Minnesota Press, 1982), pp. 46–8. [Ed.]

2. See Benjamin, "Theses on the Philosophy of History," *Illuminations*, trans. Harry Zohn (New York: Schocken, 1969), p. 261. [Ed.]

3. For Paz on the avant-garde, see in particular *Children of the Mire: Modern Poetry from Romanticism to the Avant-Garde* (Cambridge: Harvard University Press, 1974), pp. 148–64. For Burger, see *Theory of the Avant-Garde* (Minneapolis: University of Minnesota Press, Fall 1983). [Ed.]

4. Peter Steinfels, *The Neoconservatives* (New York: Simon and Schuster, 1979), p. 65.

5. The phrase "to aestheticize politics" echoes Benjamin's famous formulation of the false social program of the fascists in "The Work of Art in the Age of Mechanical Reproduction." Habermas's criticism here of Enlightenment critics seems directed less at Adorno and Max Horkheimer than at the contemporary *nouveaux philosophes* (Bernard-Henri Levy, etc.) and their German and American counterparts. [Ed.]

6. The reference is to the novel *Die Asthetik des Widerstands* (1975–78) by the author perhaps best known here for his 1965 play *Marat/Sade.* The work of art "reappropriated" by the workers is the Pergamon altar, emblem of power, classicism, and rationality. [Ed.]

CHAPTER 14

The Dynamics of the Fields

PIERRE BOURDIEU

There are thus as many fields of preferences as there are fields of stylistic possibles. Each of these worlds—drinks (mineral waters, wines, and aperitifs) or automobiles, newspapers, or holiday resorts, design or furnishing of house or garden, not to mention political programmes—provides the small number of distinctive features which, functioning as a system of differences, differential deviations, allow the most fundamental social differences to be expressed almost as completely as through the most complex and refined expressive systems available in the legitimate arts; and it can be seen that the total field of these fields offers well-nigh inexhaustible possibilities for the pursuit of distinction.

If, among all these fields of possibles, none is more obviously predisposed to express social differences than the world of luxury goods, and, more particularly, cultural goods, this is because the relationship of distinction is objectively inscribed within it, and is reactivated, intentionally or not, in each act of consumption, through the instruments of economic and cultural appropriation which it requires. It is not only a matter of the affirmations of difference which writers and artists profess ever more insistently as the autonomy of the field of cultural production becomes more pronounced,[1] but also of the intention immanent in cultural objects. One could point to the socially charged nature of legitimate language and, for example, the systems of ethical and aesthetic values deposited, ready for quasi-automatic reactivation, in pairs of contrasting adjectives; or the very logic of literary language, whose whole value lies in an *écart*, i.e., a distance from simple, common ways of speaking. Rhetorical figures, as modifications of ordinary usage, are in a sense the objectifications of the social relationship in which they are produced and function, and it is futile to seek, in the intrinsic nature of the tropes catalogued in the "Arts of Rhetoric," properties which, like all properties of distinction, exist only in and through the relationship, in and through difference. A figure of words or style is always only an alteration of usage, and consequently a distinctive mark which may consist in the absence of any mark when the intention of distinguishing oneself from a would-be distinction that is held to be "excessive" (the vulgarity of "pretension") or simply "worn out" or "outmoded" leads to the double negations which underlie so many spurious encounters between the opposite extremes of social space. It is well known that all dominant aesthetics set a high value on the virtues of sobriety, simplicity, economy of means, which are as much opposed to first-degree poverty and simplicity as to the pomposity or affectation of the "half-educated."

It is scarcely necessary to establish that the work of art is the objectification of a relationship of distinction and that it is thereby explicitly predisposed to bear such a relationship in the most varied contexts. As soon as art becomes self-conscious, in the work of Alberti, for example, as Gombrich demonstrates, it is defined by a negation, a refusal, a renunciation, which is the very basis of the refinement in which a distance is marked from the simple pleasure of the senses and the superficial seductions of gold and ornaments that ensnare the vulgar taste of the Philistines: "In the strict hierarchic society of the sixteenth and seventeenth centuries the contrast between the 'vulgar' and the 'noble' becomes one of the principal preoccupations of the critics .... Their belief was that certain forms or modes are 'really' vulgar, because they please the low, while others are inherently noble, because only a developed taste can appreciate them."[2] The aim of distinction, expressing the specific interest of the artists, who are increasingly inclined to claim exclusive control over form at the risk of disappointing their clients' "bad taste," is far from incompatible with the functions really conferred on works of art by those who commission them or conserve them in their collections: these "cultural creations which we usually regard purely aesthetically, as variants of a particular style, were perceived by their contemporaries," as Norbert Elias reminds us, referring to the society of the Grand Siècle, as "the highly differentiated expression of certain social qualities."[3]

This means that, like art as defined by Yeats ("Art is a social act of a solitary man"), every appropriation of a work of art which is the embodiment of a relation of distinction is itself a social relation and, contrary to the illusion of cultural communism, it is a relation of distinction. Those who possess the means of symbolically appropriating cultural goods are more than willing to believe that it is only through their economic dimension that works of art, and cultural goods in general, acquire rarity. They like to see symbolic appropriation—the only legitimate sort, in their view—as a kind of mystical participation in a common good of which each person has a share and which everyone has entirely, as a paradoxical appropriation, excluding privilege and monopoly, unlike material appropriation, which asserts real exclusivity and therefore exclusion. "If I contemplate a painting by Poussin or read a Platonic dialogue, that doesn't imply that I am depriving anyone and that we need to produce as many Poussins and Platos as there are possible beholders or readers" (Philosophy teacher, age 30).

The love of art is conceived as a secularized form of the "intellectual love of God," a love, according to Spinoza, that is "the greater as more men enjoy it." There is no doubt that the works of art inherited from the past and deposited in museums and private collections and, beyond them, all objectified cultural capital, the product of history accumulated in the form of books, articles, documents, instruments, which are the trace or materialization of theories or critiques of these theories, problematics, or conceptual systems, present themselves as an autonomous world which, although it is the product of historical action, has its own laws, transcending individual wills, and remains irreducible to what each agent or even the whole population of agents can appropriate (i.e., to internalized cultural capital), just as the language objectified in dictionaries and grammars remains irreducible to the language really appropriated, that is, to what is internalized by each speaker or even the whole population. However, contrary to theories of the autonomy of the world of ideas or of "objective knowledge without a knowing subject" and "subjectless processes" (in which Louis Althusser and Karl Popper concur), it has to be pointed out that objectified cultural capital only exists and subsists in and through the struggles of which the fields of cultural production (the artistic field, the scientific field, etc.) and, beyond them, the field of the social classes, are the site, struggles in which the agents wield strengths and obtain profits proportionate to their mastery of this objectified capital, in other words, their internalized capital.[4]

Because the appropriation of cultural products presupposes dispositions and competences which are not distributed universally (although they have the appearance of innateness), these products are subject to exclusive appropriation, material or symbolic, and, functioning as cultural capital (objectified or internalized), they yield a profit in distinction, proportionate to the rarity of the means required to appropriate them, and a profit in legitimacy, the profit par excellence, which consists in the fact of feeling justified in being (what one is), being what it is right to be.[5] This is the difference between the legitimate culture of class societies, a product of domination predisposed to express or legitimate domination, and the culture of little-differentiated or undifferentiated societies, in which access to the means of appropriation of the cultural heritage is fairly equally distributed, so that culture is fairly equally mastered by all members of the group and cannot function as cultural capital, i.e., as an instrument of domination, or only so within very narrow limits and with a very high degree of euphemization.

The symbolic profit arising from material or symbolic appropriation of a work of art is measured by the distinctive value which the work derives from the rarity of the disposition and competence which it demands and which determines its class distribution.[6] Cultural objects, with their subtle hierarchy, are predisposed to mark the stages and degrees of the initiatory progress which defines the enterprise of culture, according to Valery Larbaud. Like "Christian's progress towards the heavenly Jerusalem," it leads from the "illiterate" to the "literate," via the "non-literate" and "semi-literate," or the "common reader" (lecteur)—leaving aside the "bibliophile"—to the truly cultivated reader (liseur). The mysteries of culture have their catechumens, their initiates, their holy men, that "discrete elite" set apart from ordinary mortals by inimitable nuances of manner and united by "a quality, something which lies in the man himself, which is part of his happiness, which may be indirectly very useful to him but which will never win him a sou, any more than his courtesy, his courage or his goodness."[7]

Hence the incessant revisions, reinterpretations, and rediscoveries which the learned of all religions of the book perform on their canonical texts: since the levels of "reading" designate hierarchies of readers, it is necessary and sufficient to change the hierarchy of readings in order to overturn the hierarchy of readers.

It follows from what has been said that a simple upward displacement of the structure of the class distribution of an asset or practice (i.e., a virtually identical increase in the proportion of possessors in each class) has the effect of diminishing its rarity and distinctive value and threatening the distinction of the older possessors. Intellectuals and artists are thus divided between their interest in cultural proselytism, that is, winning a market by widening their audience, which inclines them to favour popularization, and concern for cultural distinction, the only objective basis of their rarity; and their relationship to everything concerned with the "democratization of culture" is marked by a deep ambivalence which may be manifested in a dual discourse on the relations between the institutions of cultural diffusion and the public.

When asked in a survey how they thought works of art in museums might be better presented, and whether the "supply level" ought to be made more accessible by providing technical, historical, or aesthetic explanations, members of the dominant class—and especially the teachers and art specialists—endeavour to escape from the contradiction by dissociating what is desirable for others from what is desirable for themselves. It is because the museum is as it is that it is their exclusive privilege; so it is as it should be for people like them, i.e., people made for it. But they cannot fail to be sensitive to the fact that they, the habitués, are being consulted first about what should be done, because this recognizes their privilege of granting part of their privilege to others. In accepting educational improvements, it is *their* museum, the one that they alone can enjoy, austere, ascetic, and noble, which they graciously open to others. (An analysis of the debates which occurred when cheap paperbacks came onto the market—a promise of popularity for the author, a threat of vulgarization for the reader—would reveal the same ambivalence.)

Because the distinctive power of cultural possessions or practices—an artifact, a qualification, a film culture—tends to decline with the growth in the absolute number of people able to appropriate them, the profits of distinction would wither away if the field of production of cultural goods, itself governed by the dialectic of pretension and distinction, did not endlessly supply new goods or new ways of using the same goods.

5 THE CORRESPONDENCE BETWEEN GOODS PRODUCTION AND TASTE PRODUCTION

In the cultural market—and no doubt elsewhere—the matching of supply and demand is neither the simple effect of production imposing itself on consumption nor the effect of a conscious endeavour to serve the consumers' needs, but the result of the objective orchestration of two relatively independent logics, that of the fields of production and that of the field of consumption. There is a fairly close homology between the specialized fields of production in which products are developed and the fields (the field of the social classes or the field of the dominant class) in which tastes are determined. This means that the products developed in the competitive struggles of which each of the fields of production is the site, and which are the source of the incessant changing of these products, meet, without having expressly to seek it, the demand which is shaped in the objectively or subjectively antagonistic relations between the different classes or class fractions over material or cultural consumer goods or, more exactly, in the competitive struggles between them over these goods, which are the source of the changing of tastes. This objective orchestration of supply and demand is the reason why the most varied tastes find the conditions for their realization in the universe of possibles which each of the fields of production offers them, while the latter find the conditions for their constitution and functioning in the different tastes which provide a (short- or long-term) market for their different products.[8]

The field of production, which clearly could not function if it could not count on already existing tastes, more or less strong propensities to consume more or less clearly defined goods, enables taste to be realized by offering it, at each moment, the universe of cultural goods as a system of stylistic possibles from which it can select the system of stylistic features constituting a life-style. It is always forgotten that the universe of products offered by each field of production tends in fact to limit the universe of the forms of experience (aesthetic, ethical, political, etc.) that are objectively possible at any given moment.[9] It follows from this, among other things, that the distinction recognized in all dominant classes and in all their properties takes different forms depending on the state of the distinctive signs of "class" that are effectively available. In the case of the production of cultural goods at least, the relation between supply and demand takes a particular form: the supply always exerts an effect of symbolic imposition. A cultural product—an avant-garde picture, a political manifesto, a newspaper—is a constituted taste, a taste which has been raised from the vague semi-existence of half-formulated or unformulated experience, implicit or even unconscious desire, to the full reality of the finished product, by a process of objectification which, in present circumstances, is almost always the work of professionals. It is consequently charged with the legitimizing, reinforcing capacity which objectification always possesses, especially when, as is the case now, the logic of structural homologies assigns it to a prestigious group so that it functions as an authority which authorizes and reinforces dispositions by giving them a collectively recognized expression.[10] Taste, for its part, a classification system constituted by the conditionings associated with a condition situated in a determinate position in the structure of different conditions, governs the relationship with objectified capital, with this world of ranked and ranking objects which help to define it by enabling it to specify and so realize itself.[11]

Thus, the tastes actually realized depend on the state of the system of goods offered; every change in the system of goods induces a change in tastes. But conversely, every change in tastes resulting from a transformation of the conditions of existence and of the corresponding dispositions will tend to induce, directly or indirectly, a transformation of the field of production, by favouring the success, within the struggle constituting the field, of the producers best able to produce the needs corresponding to the new dispositions. There is therefore no need to resort to the hypothesis of a sovereign taste compelling the adjustment of production to needs, or the opposite hypothesis, in which taste is itself a product of production, in order to account for the quasi-miraculous correspondence prevailing at every moment between the products offered by a field of production and the field of socially produced tastes. The producers are led by the logic of competition with other producers and by the specific interests linked to their position in the field of production (and therefore by the habitus which have led them to that position) to produce distinct products which meet the different cultural interests which the consumers owe to their class conditions and position, thereby offering them a real possibility of being satisfied. In short, if, as they say, "There is something for everyone," if each fraction of the dominant class has its own artists and philosophers, newspapers and critics, just as it has its hairdresser, interior decorator, or tailor, or if, as an artist put it, "Everyone sells," meaning that paintings of the most varied styles always eventually find a purchaser, this is not the result of intentional design but of the meeting between two systems of differences.

The functional and structural homology which guarantees objective orchestration between the logic of the field of production and the logic of the field of consumption arises from the fact that all the specialized fields (haute couture or painting, theatre or literature) tend to be governed by the same logic, i.e., according to the volume of the specific capital that is possessed (and according to seniority of possession, which is often associated with volume), and from the fact that the oppositions which tend to be established in each case between the richer and the less rich in the specific capital—the established and the outsiders, veterans and newcomers, distinction and pretension, rear-guard and avant-garde, order and movement, etc.—are mutually homologous (which means that there are numerous invariants) and also homologous to the oppositions which structure the field of the social classes (between dominant and dominated) and the field of the dominant class (between the dominant fraction and the dominated fraction).[12] The correspondence which is thereby objectively established between the classes of products and the classes of consumers is realized in acts of consumption only through the mediation of that sense of the homology between goods and groups which defines tastes. Choosing according to one's tastes is a matter of identifying goods that are objectively attuned to one's position and which "go together" because they are situated in roughly equivalent positions in their respective spaces, be they films or plays, cartoons or novels, clothes or furniture; this choice is assisted by institutions—shops, theatres (left- or right-bank), critics, newspapers, magazines—which are themselves defined by their position in a field and which are chosen on the same principles.

For the dominant class, the relationship between supply and demand takes the form of a pre-established harmony. The competition for luxury goods, emblems of "class," is one dimension of the struggle to impose the dominant principle of domination, of which this class is the site; and the strategies it calls for, whose common feature is that they are oriented towards maximizing the distinctive profit of exclusive possessions, must necessarily use different weapons to achieve this common function. On the supply side, the field of production need only follow its own logic, that of distinction, which always leads it to be organized in accordance with a structure analogous to that of the symbolic systems which it produces by its functioning and in which each element performs a distinctive function.

* * * * *

NOTES

1. A few examples all the same: "What is Equality if not the negation of all liberty, all superiority, and nature itself? Equality is slavery. That is why I love art" (Flaubert to Louise Colet, 15–16 May 1852, *Correspondence* [Paris, Conard, 1926–1933]. "In the reign of equality, and it is almost upon us, everything that is not covered with warts will be flayed alive. The masses couldn't give a damn for Art, poetry, style. Give them vaudeville, treatises on prison labour, on housing estates and the material interests of the moment. There is a permanent conspiracy against originality" (20 June 1853, ibid.). "But it seems to me that one truth has emerged: that we have no need of the vulgar, of the numerous element of majorities, of approval, of consecration; '89 destroyed royalty and the nobility, '48 the bourgeoisie, and '51 the people. There's nothing left, except a loutish, imbecile mob. We are all wading in universal mediocrity. Social equality rules the roost. Books for everyone, Art for everyone, science for everyone, just like railways and warming-rooms. Humanity is furiously intent on moral abasement and I resent being part of it" (28–29 September 1853, ibid.). One could also cite Mallarmé's "L'Art pour tous" or "Le mystère dans les lettres," *Oeuvres completes* (Paris, Gallimard, 1945), pp. 257–260, 382–387.
2. E.H. Gombrich, *Meditations on a Hobby Horse* (London, Phaidon Press, 1963), pp. 17–18.
3. N. Elias, *Die hofische Gesellschaft* (Darmstadt, Luchterhand, 1975), p. 92.
4. Durkheim, unlike Popper, for example, whose theses he anticipates—cf. K. Popper, *Objective Knowledge: An Evolutionary Approach* (Oxford, Oxford University Press, 1972),

esp. ch. 3—poses the problem of the relationship between the world of science, "the result of concentrated, accumulated human existence," and individual reason; but immediately obscures it by answering it in the language of participation, the basis of the illusion of cultural communism: "Philosophers have often speculated that, beyond the bounds of human understanding, there is a kind of universal and impersonal understanding in which individual minds seek to participate by mystical means; well, this kind of understanding exists, and it exists not in any transcendent world but in this world itself. It exists in the world of science; or at least that is where it progressively realises itself; and it constitutes the ultimate source of logical vitality to which individual human rationality can attain." E. Durkheim, *The Evolution of Educational Thought* (London, Routledge and Kegan Paul, 1977), pp. 341–342.

5. Because the possession of works of art is supposed to attest not only the owner's wealth but also his good taste, it tends to be perceived as merited and to constitute a guarantee of legitimacy in its own right.

6. The more "modern" a work of "high" art is, the rarer is the competence it demands. "Modernity" is defined in terms of the stages of the relatively autonomous history of the fields of production. This history is quasi-cumulative because belonging in the field and the history of the field ("epoch-making") implies a self-definition by reference to, and generally in opposition to, the immediately previous art. (In the field of music, for example, this leads in certain periods to a constant extension of the field of accepted harmonies or the range of acceptable modulations.) This explains why the history of individual tastes tends to reproduce, with a few deviations, the history of the corresponding art.

7. I am grateful to Jean-Daniel Reynaud for this reference.

8. Thus, E.B. Henning has been able to show that the constitution of a relatively autonomous field of artistic production offering stylistically diversified products depends on the existence of two or more patrons with different artistic needs and an equal power to choose works corresponding to their needs. E.B. Henning, "Patronage and Style in the Arts: A suggestion concerning their Relations," *The Journal of Esthetics and Art Criticism*, 18 (June 1960), 464–471.

9. This system of the ethical, aesthetic, or political "possibles," which are effectively available at a given moment, is no doubt an essential dimension of what makes up the historicity of ways of thinking and world views, and the contemporaneity of individuals and groups linked to the same period and place.

10. Advertising for luxury goods systematically exploits the association of a product with a group. In no other field are institutions more overtly defined by their clientele than in the luxury trades, no doubt because here the virtually exclusive function of the products is to classify their owners. The link between the value of emblems and the value of the group which owns them is very clear in the antiques market, in which the value of an object may derive from the social standing of its previous owners.

11. The internalized classifications of taste have to reckon, at every moment, with the classifications objectified in institutions, such as the agencies of cultural consecration

and conservation, and with all the objectified hierarchies of which they are always partly the product. But in return, the dominant taxonomies are constantly challenged and revised in the classification struggles through which the different classes or class fractions endeavour to impose their own taxonomy as legitimate, either directly or through the professionals who compete in the specialized fields of production.

12. Rather than elaborate here all the presuppositions of analysis in terms of field (in particular, the interdependence between specific capital and the field in which it is valid and produced its effects), I shall merely refer the reader to earlier texts in which these ideas are developed. See, in particular: P. Bourdieu, "Le marché des biens symboliques," *L'Année Sociologique*, 22 (1971), 49–126; "Genèse et structure du champ religieux," *Revue Franchise de Sociologie*, 12 (1971), 295–334; "Champ du pouvoir, champ intellectuel et habitus de classe," *Scolies*, 1 (1971), 7–26; "Le couturier et sa griffe," *Actes*, 1 (1975), 7–36; "L'invention de la vie d'artiste," *Actes*, 2 (1975), 67–93; "L'ontologie politique de Martin Heidegger," *Actes*, 5–6 (1975), 109–156; "The Specificity of the Scientific Field," *Social Science Information*, 14 (December 1975), 19–47; and especially "The Production of Belief," *Media, Culture and Society*, 2 (July 1980), 261–293.

CHAPTER 15

Moral Capital*

MARIANA VALVERDE

* * * * *

In his landmark work, *Distinction: A Social Critique of the Judgement of Taste*,[1] Pierre Bourdieu explored the dynamics of the primitive accumulation, investment, and transformation of what he called "cultural capital." Through a large-scale quantitative study of the minute but significant differences in cultural tastes and consumption among various occupational, class, and status groups, Bourdieu provides a total picture of the French class system which takes into account the relative predominance of economic *versus* cultural assets in each group's total capital (schoolteachers, for instance, rank low on their ability to control means of economic production, but they have quite a bit of cultural capital). Bourdieu's framework, while solidly materialist, suggests that economic production is not the only social site upon which classes are formed (something which has also been explored, for very different purposes, in feminist analyses of domestic and reproductive labour in capitalist societies). I will here argue in a similar vein that the study of moral regulation and the formation of ethical identities does not preclude, and may in fact complement and revise, the critical study of capitalist social formations.[2]

One characteristic of cultural capital relevant to a theory of moral capital is that, while the circuit of economic capital is notoriously unpredictable, cultural tastes rise and fall in value at a much more sedate pace. Key to the greater stability of cultural capital is that it is not made up of tangible commodities; rather, the books or paintings one owns are merely material tokens of a "habitus," a style, a set of desires, which is the true capital. One can be too poor to go to the opera, but derive comfort (and status) from knowing opera: cultural capital thus helps the educated elites to compensate for the notorious vagaries of the economic marketplace.

A habitus, like the social and sexual identities analyzed by Foucault, is the product of regulatory processes, but this production process is often invisible to the individuals concerned: they imagine that they are born with innate good taste. While Bourdieu's interest is in unmasking the social process creating, certifying,

185

and maximizing forms of cultural capital, my interest lies in the parallel process by which certain moral dispositions and "habits" are constituted and naturalized. The aim of moral reform in a moral-capitalist setting, I will argue, is not so much to change behaviour as to generate certain ethical subjectivities that appear as inherently "moral." Correct actions will, of course, follow; but the subjectivity is more important than the behaviour, as it is in the realm of cultural capital.

In addition, just as cultural capital usually requires certification by academic or artistic authorities, moral capital requires a similar certification process. At one time official churches had a quasi-monopoly on the certification of moral capital, but today a variety of professional groups are involved in this. Many people believe that we now live in a post-moralistic era, but a case could be made that moral regulation has simply become more secular and formalistic. The practice of writing letters of reference, for example, could be analyzed as a form of moral regulation, insofar as such letters, contemporary versions of the 19th-century "character" required of servants, act to certify the general moral status of the people in question, not just narrowly professional accomplishments. The term "moral" is hence used here·not in the narrow religious sense, but in a broader sense.

⑤ THE CIRCUIT OF MORAL CAPITAL

Despite the high status conferred on those possessing and certifying cultural capital, particularly in continental Europe, the middle classes have been simultaneously fearful of excesses of culture. The mad genius, the degenerate artist, and the immoral intellectual are, in bourgeois European cultures, recurring symbols of what can go wrong when the accumulation of intellectual/cultural capital runs amok.[3]

Now, how can one have "too much culture"? There is nothing in the logic of cultural capital to suggest that any one person can ever acquire too much culture: one of bourgeois society's most cherished myths is that both truth and good taste are perpetually receding ideals, and that the acquisition of culture is a constant striving. There is also nothing in the relationship of economic to cultural capital to set any necessary limits on the acquisition of cultural capital by those with economic capital.

The judgement that some people have too much cultural capital and have therefore become "effete" or degenerate[4] can only be made from a standpoint outside both the economic and the cultural. This is the standpoint of morality, grounded in what I shall call the circuit of moral capital. The immoral artist or intellectual (represented a century ago by Oscar Wilde or Nietzsche, and today by Robert Mapplethorpe and Foucault) contravenes no laws of motion other than those of moral capital. If the overly cultured risk falling into immorality, so do the overly rich. Victorian fantasies about aristocratic brothels and contemporary accounts of the leisure-time habits of the Kennedy family both point to a middle-class view, turned into "common sense" by the combined action of Christianity and popular culture, to the effect that those who have too much wealth (especially if unearned) are morally suspect. Since it is the essence of capital to expand indefinitely, the perception of "excess" can only be made from outside the logic of capital, from a location in the circuit of moral capital. The relationship between morality and the other two types of capital accumulation thus produces a kind of Aristotelian warning against excess, an emphasis on balance and moderation that continually undermines the infinite-accumulation dynamic of both economic and cultural capital.

The view that the morally debilitating effects of static wealth need to be counteracted by the bracing effects of hard work, deferred gratification, and investment, probably dates back to the Protestant Reformation,[5] as does the twin view that extreme poverty is a reliable indicator of vice. This idea about the relationship between economic and moral capital, central to middle-class philanthropy, was developed in Britain in the second half of the 18th century and achieved its greatest triumph in the late 19th century, but continues to be popular into our own days. Moral regulation, which I argue is not a "cover" for economic power but is a distinct mode of regulation, is alive and well today. It is now more likely to use the language of biomedical science or of social work than the narratives of evangelism or Victorian melodrama: but it remains moral, in the sense of being aimed at the production of individual ethical subjectivity and the reproduction of the nation's moral capital.

Is moral capital, that intangible resource known as "character," simply an ideological result or precondition of economic capital accumulation? The idea of the "relative autonomy" of the cultural has been adopted by both neo-Marxists and anti-Marxists, and more recently there have been discussions of the relative autonomy of the moral sphere. But, in the moral as well as in the cultural sphere, relative autonomy is more easily advocated than defined. My own view is that there are no universal answers to such abstract questions, for although the circuit of economic capital in many ways provides the fundamental paradigm for all social processes under capitalism, Max Weber's insights about the relative autonomy of the moral can still be quite useful in concrete historical and sociological analysis (as long as they are not used, as they often are, as sticks to beat Marx with). But perhaps the old unsolved questions about the relative importance of "base" and "superstructure" can be circumvented if we simply abandon the architectural metaphor which gave rise to the dilemma in the first place. If we cease imagining social relations as fixed and solid and building-like, and think of them in more fluid terms, then primacy is not so much of an issue.

Civil society can usefully be envisioned as constituted through the interaction of three circuits: economic, cultural, and moral. These, in turn, are not separate from the relations of power originating in and sustaining the state; as John Keane and others have pointed out, the separation of civil society from the state is often more rhetorical than real.[6] For the purposes of administering people, private and public institutions often cooperate in the social equivalent of a "mixed economy."

Of course, one could well extend the present model into the sphere of the state in order to argue that the workings of both government and other state institutions can be theorized as processes for the accumulation of political capital; but here we shall only consider the state and governmental action insofar as they are involved in constituting and regulating civil society, and will leave the analysis of political capital for another occasion.

This three-circuit model of civil society has the advantage of avoiding positing quasi-geographical separate "realms" or "spheres" ("the public" *versus* "the private," "the family" *versus* "the market"). The term "circuit" is employed here precisely as a metaphor bringing into view the dynamism of social processes. The circuits are not located in distinct social sites, but are rather fluid-like processes taking place throughout the social.

In trying to specify the dynamics of various circuits, one could begin by arguing that even the circuit of economic capital is not aimed at producing tangible commodities but rather (as Marx pointed out) increasingly rarified, even "spiritual" forms of value. Modern capital divorced itself from the mercantilist crass concern for piles of gold and numbers of people, just as Protestant inwardness replaced the Catholic emphasis on the material mediations of religious value.[7] In our own day, much as other Marxian predictions have failed to come true, it is indisputable that capital has become virtually intangible, abstract, and extra-local.[8] But it is in the cultural and moral circuits that the process of "spiritualization" or abstraction is most complete. Bourdieu's analysis shows that the endpoint and final cause of the circuit of cultural capital is not an amount of commodities but rather an intangible and continually self-reproducing capital embodied in the soul: the cultured personality, reflected in one's goods and one's actions but not exhausted by them. Similarly, as Foucault so eloquently argued (following, perhaps unwittingly, Luther's emphasis on faith as opposed to "good works"), being moral is not so much a set of visible actions as the cultivation of a particular subjectivity requiring constant self-supervision.[9]

Clearly, then, the dynamics of all three circuits resemble each other. Marx would, of course, say this is because the circuit of capital is the basis and model for all other social processes, something which Foucault denies (or refuses to address). I take the view that it is not necessary, and may even be harmful, to develop a general theory of the relation between the economy in general, culture in general, and morality in general, since this may blind us to the ways in which the three circuits interact in specific situations. What I would like to study are not hypothetical general structures but rather the constant struggles in civil society to "fix" certain events within the discourse of a particular circuit. The persistence of these struggles suggests that social processes do not "naturally" fall into one of three separate categories which are statically linked in a hierarchical system. If, say, Sunday shopping were "really" a labour issue, or "really" an issue of morality and family life, or "really" an issue of the freedom of capital, Protestant cultures would not have been struggling with its regulation for a long century. The history of social regulation shows social actors constantly involved in jurisdictional disputes not just over specific regulations but, more radically, over the prior categorization of the social that is the precondition of any particular regulation.

In these disputes to categorize the social, certain collective or institutional actors make regular appearances. While economics as a collective actor provides an analysis of any and all social processes as if they were economic, the collective actor which, since the rise of capitalism, has been key in attempting to define any and all social processes as moral has been philanthropy. Philanthropy is here defined not as proto-welfare but rather as a set of practices, which take place within State welfare agencies as well as in private charities, aimed at restoring and maximizing the moral capital of the urban poor in capitalist countries. This process sometimes involves providing small amounts of both economic and cultural capital (e.g., buying tools for workers, providing free classes), but these are generally means to the aim of re-moralization.

Philanthropy, as has often been pointed out, saw itself as scientific, by opposition to old-fashioned, non-scientific charity.[10] While charity-givers expect a return for their alms from God, and the value of this exchange of money for spiritual goods is realized instantly, philanthropy resembles a capitalist investment more than a simple commodity exchange. As Max Weber said, the idea of gain is quite transhistorical, but the idea of profit is specifically capitalist;[11] similarly, all forms of charity seek moral gain, but only philanthropy seeks moral profit over the long run. Although earning points in Heaven may still motivate the modern philanthropist, he/she tries to ensure an earthly result, which, like the return on economic capital, is necessarily risky and delayed. Organized charities are incorporated precisely to minimize and evenly distribute the risk that is an inherent element in moral as well as economic investment. The investment of both money and the philanthrophist's own moral capital is supposed to generate a moral profit, an idea foreign to alms-giving. While the charity giver does not care whether the beggar uses the money "wisely" or not, for giving is good in itself and the beggar will square his/her own accounts with God, the philanthropist is obsessed with getting social and moral returns. Aid — increasingly taking the form of services or advice rather than money — is now supposed to "moralize" the poor, to make them thrifty, clean, hard-working, and sober. This subjective transformation is portrayed as owing to the philanthropist personally; philanthropists' reports often reveal profound disappointment when the delayed exchange does not realize the right kind and amount of moral profit.[12] The currency with which the poor pay back what they have received is that elusive inward essence, "character" (also known as "moral fibre").

A quick phenomenological experiment bears out the depth and breadth of morally capitalist values: most of us today have internalized the moral-capitalist ethic so well that we feel guilty if, in a fit of old-fashioned charity, we give a beggar a few coins. Moral capitalism demands that we give only to well-administered corporate bodies that, as the saying goes, helps only those who help themselves. We feel we have a duty to ensure that the money we give purchases not a coffee or a bottle of wine but rather moral commodities such as independence or good character.

Philanthropy models itself on capitalist production, but it is not always subordinate to it, having historically acted as a check on the most inhumane tendencies of capitalism. It is a tribute to its influence that bourgeois states, even the most classically liberal ones, have at times agreed that the need to produce and reproduce moral capital takes precedence over the needs of "real" capital: for instance, child labour was banned in Britain in the 1830s and 1840s, and until recently, women in many countries were banned from night-work and many "dirty" jobs for philanthropic reasons, despite their lower cost to employers.

But while philanthropy can act as an external limit on the accumulation of economic capital, it is itself shaped by extra-moral considerations to varying degrees. As Donna Andrew's study of 18th-century charities shows, during the major imperial wars Lying-in and Foundling hospitals were set up to boost the population (not to reform their "clients"); but after the Malthusian revolution, saving poor people's babies became unpopular and gave way to the more "modern" concern with the quality, not the number, of the poor.[13] Thus, changes in philanthropic practice reflect and are to a certain extent shaped by, extra-moral considerations—in Andrew's study, political economy's shifting evaluation of the value of "mere" human life. Furthermore, philanthropy may have interfered with free enterprise in the case of child-labour laws, but the philanthropists in question were usually organized in what were known as "joint-stock" charities, with boards of directors and procedures modelled on those of emerging capitalist enterprises.

The investment/return imperative was applied to both the finances of the agencies and the "moral results" being sought: traditional charities that gave money or goods without ensuring some kind of return from the poor in moral currency were perceived as unprofitable in all senses of the word—and thus as somehow immoral.[14] Modern philanthropy was and is based on a consensus about the inability of economics and culture to alone maintain the social and moral fabric of bourgeois society, together with a rejection of the old idea that poverty was a divinely ordained condition enabling the wealthy to exercise charity. Put in positive terms, philanthropy is based on the felt need for specific institutions and regulations ensuring the continued reproduction of the nation's moral capital.

⑤ THE EARLY 19TH CENTURY: THE CRISIS IN THE ACCUMULATION OF MORAL CAPITAL AND THE RISE OF PHILANTHROPY

As Jacques Donzelot and other Foucaultian historians have pointed out, European cities in the period after the Napoleonic wars witnessed the rise of a number of phenomena collected under the umbrella term "la question sociale."[15] In France and in England, political economy was criticized from the new perspective of "social science," in France sometimes known as "economie sociale." Social science promised to provide a more human-centred view of social processes than classical political economy: it aimed to integrate moral considerations into economic rationality. At the theoretical level, social science counterposed its more holistic views to the narrow wealth-oriented perspectives of political economy; at the level of practice, social science was often coterminous with the replacement of market economics by a more moral system such as socialism. Louis Blanc, the most famous socialist of the 1848 generation, defined "socialism" using the philanthropic trope of a "point of view" outside of, and acting as, limit to the circuit of economic capital:

> [À] la différence de l'économie politique, qui est la science de la formation des richesses, mais qui n'est que cela, et qui décrit le mécanisme de la production, sans égard à son influence sur la condition des producteurs, le socialisme a pour objet d'étudier la constitution économique de la société en se plaçant au point de vue de l'amélioration intellectuelle, morale et physique de la classe la plus nombreuse et la plus pauvre.[16]

The main object for social economy was not wealth but rather "the poor," or more specifically the theoretical object named "misère" or "paupérisme." The social economists ranged from conservative critics of political economy's free market (Villeneuve-Bargemont, Eugene Buret, some English Romantics) to socialists like Blanc and his friend Francois Vidal, who wrote a major manifesto of social economy in 1846, proclaiming the "death" of political economy. In this work, Vidal argues that political economy is only interested in the accumulation of wealth, and should therefore be subordinated to "economie sociale" or "philosophic sociale," studying moral needs and demands.[17] This focus on the moral was not necessarily indicative of a failure of theoretical nerve, as "scientific socialists" have claimed since Marx: it was rather a considered effort to theorize the specifically moral effects of capitalism and industrialism.

The Australian historical sociologist Mitchell Dean has recently taken this argument even further, showing that right in the heart of classical liberalism lies a profound concern for the moral/social preconditions of the accumulation of economic capital and the reproduction of wage labour.[18] Malthus' catastrophic economics presupposed and legitimized an absolute moral code in which male breadwinners made all the economic and reproductive decisions within the working class (indeed it was their monopoly over such decisions that constituted them as breadwinners). Similarly, post-Malthusian liberalism, Dean argues, ought not to be seen as "laissez-faire," as non-regulation, but rather as a very specific system of moral and economic regulation, a system in which both the pauper and the "honest" wage labourer were constituted through moral categories. The male breadwinner, the chaste and economically dependent wife, the disciplined young male worker

... these and other social identities made up the moral capital of the poor, a capital whose reproduction was perceived as happening "naturally" in good conditions but as requiring philanthropic intervention in times of crisis.

The prime object of the new sciences of the social was pauperism or "misère," theorized as a historical break from previous forms of scarcity. "Poverty" denotes an inability to satisfy certain economic needs, the social economists argued, but misery or pauperism is the subspecies of poverty involving moral degradation. Blanc wrote: "La misère conseille incessamment le sacrifice de la dignité personnelle, et presque toujours la commande. La misère crée une dépendance de condition ...."[19] And the earlier social economist Eugène Buret (whose 1840 magnum opus was heavily referenced in Marx's 1844 manuscripts), wrote that while savages may be poor because they lack economic resources, only civilized peoples can be miserable (or pauperized, as the English would say): "La misère est un phénomène de la civilisation: ... la misère, c'est la pauvreté moralement sentie."[20]

English observers, from conservative philanthropists to Frederick Engels, also agreed that lack of money was not the basic problem. The new poor, the urban poor of industrial capitalism, had become dehumanized by losing their morality: they had become a new/old race of barbarians threatening to destroy not just themselves but the combined moral and cultural capital of European civilization.[21] Moralizing remedies, ranging from "moral architecture" and new sewers all the way to a socialist revolution, were advocated in order to re-moralize the urban miserables. In Britain, the first efforts toward housing reform, public health, and urban planning were made in the 1840s from this moralizing perspective.[22] The vast 19th-century literature on urban hygiene used as a constant refrain the idea that dirtiness produced vice and immorality as surely as rotten garbage produced disease, and for the Victorians the moral decay was as visible as its physical counterpart.

⑤ LATE VICTORIAN DEBATES ON MORALIZING THE URBAN POOR: "MODERN" METHODS OF MAXIMIZING MORAL CAPITAL

In the late Victorian period, there was a re-discovery of pauperism.[23] The most detailed and influential study of urban poverty at the turn of the century, Charles Booth's *Life and Labour of the People of London*, used the following list of "causes of pauperism" to categorize its massive quantitative data: "Crime, vice, drink, laziness, pauper association, heredity, mental disease, temper (queer), incapacity, early marriage, large family, extravagance, lack of work, trade misfortune, restlessness ... sickness, accident, ill luck, old age."[24] Economic factors were acknowledged, but only as relatively minor factors in a sea of moral causes.

The standpoint of moral capital is similarly evident on almost every page of an influential set of articles published from 1866 to 1872 and collected in 1883: Octavia Hill's *Homes of the London Poor*. Hill depicts herself exercising a moralizing influence on each and every one of the tenants under her management—she was a rent collector cum social worker for several blocks of "model" tenements—and claims that practical experience shows that what the poor need is not more money (she thought the *Poor Law* was often far too generous) but moralization. When she states that her key aim is not to help the poor but to "develop the resources of the poor themselves,"[25] what she means is their moral resources: the duty of charity workers is to "raise" the poor "to be energetic, self-reliant, provident and industrious."[26] The moral impetus behind late Victorian housing reform is also visible in the way that poor people's housing became a major political concern only after the publication of the much-read 1883 exposé *The Bitter Cry of Outcast London*. This pamphlet, and particularly its prim and yet salacious allusion to the commonness of incest, was widely credited with motivating the 1884–1885 Royal Commission on the Housing of the Urban Poor.[27]

As historians have pointed out, scientific philanthropy in the late Victorian period was primarily concerned with building "character" among the poor.[28] The desire to maximize opportunities for building character and to ensure a return for the philanthropist's moral capital led to the accepted view that the "drunken and idle people should be offered the workhouse only,"[29] while those meriting investment were subjected to a time-consuming but ultimately rewarding process of investigation and habit reform. As Hill says, in a description evoking the Foucaultian understanding of power but also echoing the capitalist manager's day-to-day work:

> For the work is one of detail. Looking back over the years as they pass, one sees a progress that is not small; but day after day the work is one of such small things, that if one did not look beyond and through them they would be trying—locks to be mended, notices to be served, the missing shillings of the week's rent to be called for three or four times, petty quarrels to be settled, small rebukes to be spoken, the same remonstrances to be made again and again.
>
> But it is on these things and their faithful execution that the life of the whole matter depends, and by which steady progress is ensured.[30]

Attempting to reconcile the circuits of moral and economic capital, Octavia Hill built her fame on managing housing blocks, built by philanthropists not as charity but as an admittedly low-profit business.[31] Denouncing the new municipal partly subsidized housing for failing to moralize the tenants, she argued that low-cost housing could be run "on a thoroughly sound commercial principle,"[32] though she uneasily admitted that clearing condemned houses and hygiene hazards would have to be done out of public funds because there was no economic profit in it.

Hill saw clearly that if philanthropy were only concerned to alleviate poverty it would undertake large-scale, impersonal measures; but since its object was the maximization of moral capital, and moral capital is necessarily composed of habits embodied in individuals, then those who would manage moral capital have to individualize as they manage. One of the basic principles of a key institution to which Hill belonged, the Charity Organization Society (COS), was "that if the poor are to be raised to a permanently better condition, they must be dealt with as individuals and by individuals ...."[33] The phrase "as individuals" has been sufficiently theorized in Foucault's analysis of discipline or modern power; but the second phrase, "by individuals," refers to the less remarked upon process by which philanthropists invested their personal moral capital in their work. As they shaped the individual subjectivity of the poor, they too exercised and confirmed their individual moral identity through their "work of detail," expecting a return from the people then known as objects and now known as clients.

In Hill's case, the return took the mixed moral/economic form of on-time rents and clean, respectable homes. These tokens of successful reform were perceived as owing not so much to the tenement owners but to her personally: the "first" principle with which to "rule these people," she writes, is "to demand a strict fulfillment of their duties to me—one of the chief of which would be the punctual payment of rent."[34] Since she did not own the houses, it is clear that she was holding the tenants accountable for a moral debt to her as much as an economic debt to the landlords.

Hill was, of course, on the right wing of the late Victorian social reform movement. She and her colleagues at the Charity Organization Society were classic liberals: they had an absolute faith in self-regulating economic and moral markets which was not shaken by their recognition of the dire need for both philanthropic and state intervention. They attempted to circumvent this regulatory dilemma by arguing that, as long as most intervention was voluntary and short-term, and involved lots of advice but very little if any money, the mythical "independence" of the poor was not being undermined. Universal entitlement, even to a plank bed in the workhouse, was perceived as undermining the circuit of moral capital because the paupers checked out of the house whenever they wanted, without any thought of repayment. The inmates of workhouses did not acquire a moral debt to the guardians, and therefore any efforts made by the authorities (locks mended, shillings collected, etc.) were for nought, morally speaking.[35]

Hill's views regarding the accumulation of moral capital among the underclasses, however, were shared by many in liberal and labour circles, who disagreed with her on the division of moralizing work between philanthropy and expert state agencies but who also defined pauperism as a moral condition. This can best be seen by a brief consideration of the role of moralization in the proposals about the social regulation of the poor put forward by the influential team of Beatrice and Sidney Webb. In their work the term "pauperism" was purposively avoided; this was because the British *Poor Law* created a legal category of paupers, and one of the Webbs' key projects was to abolish legal pauperism and "break up the *Poor Law*." But the term they used instead, "destitution," denoted not an economic status but rather "mental degradation" or "moral malaria."[36] While condemning many of their immediate enemies, notably the Charity Organization Society, for imposing moralistic criteria on the operations of public and private relief, the Webbs nevertheless retained a strong sense of the need to maximize moral capital. For instance, they decried the Salvation Army's non-investigative charity practices as leading to "de-moralisation"[37] because the Army's soup kitchens and shelters did not exact any behavioural or attitudinal payment, and thus were not morally capitalistic even though they were explicitly moralizing. They went so far as to oppose universal old age pensions (thus missing the historical boat of Lloyd George's pension and insurance schemes) because unconditionally given payments, whether contributory or not, would inevitably lead to the "insidious deterioration of personal character" and to "slowly spreading habits of malingering."[38] They favoured the introduction of a "national minimum," but insisted that the state ought to expect a return on its investment of moral capital.

The rhetoric about a return on investment did not mean that relief was at bottom an economic measure geared to producing more efficient workers through health and welfare measures.[39] The proposals for children's medical care might be construed as long-term investments in human capital or labour power, but no economic explanation accounts for the demands the Webbs (Beatrice in particular) wanted to place on the elderly and on full-time mothers. Pensions should only be granted to "the destitute aged who live decent lives"; this went against Lloyd George's non-moralistic pension plan, but was in agreement with the view of the Charity Organization Society (COS) that even old age pensions should be reserved for those who live "respectable lives in decent houses."[40]

The COS, represented by Octavia Hill and other members of the Royal Commission on the Poor Laws of 1905–1909, presented a diagnosis of "the problem" that differed from the Fabian/Webb perspective a great deal less than one would think from Beatrice's partisan account of her machinations as a Royal Commissioner. (She was, with Sidney, responsible for the Commission's Minority Report, heralded by many as a blueprint for the post-1945 welfare state.[41]) The problem of pauperism or destitution was partly economic, it was agreed, with the precise role of structural economic factors remaining a major bone of contention between the two sides. But all agreed that, fundamentally, pauperism was caused by the fact that the circuits of moral capital were not functioning smoothly, and that in large parts of urban England "normal" socialization processes were failing to reproduce moral capital both individually and in the aggregate.

In their recommendations, the two sides presented different views of what needed to be done in order to re-establish the circuits of moral capital. The COS assigned a much larger role to private initiative in the circuit of moral capital, in keeping with their myth of self-regulating marketplaces. The Webbs, by contrast, believed that most types of moralization should be accomplished by state agencies, specifically local education and public health authorities, with occasional back-up by private religious agencies specializing in the moral reform of the vicious. Their critique of classic liberal modes of regulation has often been regarded simply as a socialist call for more and better social services.[42] This is inaccurate: if they wanted to replace the frankly punitive but non-compulsory *Poor Law of 1834* by the gaze of public health inspectors and school attendance officials, this was not necessarily because they trusted the poor and wanted to treat them benevolently. On the contrary: the problem with the *Poor Law*, they state, is that it does not exercise enough surveillance. In the context of arguing for universal maternal and child health care, they put forward a model of social regulation that echoes Bentham's panopticon as well as the worst dystopias of scientific management:

> What is needed [...] is *continuous* observation of the household both before and after birth. The Destitution Authority, by the very nature of its work, has, and can have, no such continuity of knowledge. The Local Health Authority, on the other hand is—by its ubiquitous machinery of health visitors, and house to house visitations—continuously observing the circumstances of the household, irrespective of temporary destitution. By its staff of Sanitary Inspectors it knows the character, of the street, and even of the house, in which the expectant mother is living [...][43]

The regulation of motherhood through continuous surveillance is supposed to ensure that the work of mothering—the reproduction of the physical and moral capital of the working class—is properly done. The implication is that without expert supervision it would not be properly done.

Throughout their much-vaunted Minority Report, the Webbs agreed with right-wing philanthropists that the aim of both charity and social welfare was not to supplant but rather to foster the independence and moral autonomy of the family unit. Aid to the poor should be seen to produce a mysterious moral quality known as "a sense of personal responsibility" or "an increased feeling of personal obligation"[44]—all different ways of naming that elusive essence, "character." The "character" produced by the "continuous" surveillance of sanitary inspectors and other expert officials was the currency with which the poor paid back for what they had received by way of services or monetary payments, though the Webbs put less stress than the COS on the personal moral investment of philanthropists and more emphasis on the corporate moral investment of the state. The specific content of "character" varied by age, gender, and personal situation: mothers had character if they looked properly after their children, male adults had character if they provided for dependants, old people had character if they refrained from drinking and led orderly, thrifty lives. But the imperative to return, in moral currency, the investment that charity or the state had initially made, was universal.

Where the Webbs differed from classic liberalism and contributed to laying the basis of social-democratic social policy was in their perception that both economic and moral "private" spheres needed a permanent regulatory structure. COS publications, among which one could include the Majority Report of the Poor

Law Commission, were crammed with anecdotes illustrating how particular poor families benefited from wise philanthropic investment and became independent, a stylistic choice fostering the illusion that the moral economy could be self-regulating. (This parallels the liberal myth that state regulation of the economy is short-term and is only designed to return the market to its "natural" state). By contrast, the Webbs—and the Fabians as a whole—eschew tales of family regeneration in favour of technocratic descriptions of efficiently functioning state organizations.[45] For the Fabians, as for social democrats generally, continuous surveillance and permanent regulation are necessary, not contingent, features of social regulation under capitalist conditions. Just as the Webbs recognized that the economic marketplace required permanent regulation, and thus proposed national labour exchanges, a pro-active Ministry of Labour, and a permanent system of public works, so too the moral dimension of capitalist society was envisioned as requiring permanent systems for the surveillance of the poor and the constant production of "character." The poor family, headed by that flawed creature usually referred to by Beatrice Webb as "the average sensual man," would not achieve moral independence even after philanthropic intervention. Moral capital was, for Webb, chronically scarce,[46] and vast bureaucracies were required in order to ensure its reproduction in the aggregate.

⑤ CURRENT REGULATORY DILEMMAS

Although the bulk of this article is devoted to a historical account of the rise of philanthropy/welfare as practices aimed at the constitution and reproduction of moral character among the poor, given the current crisis in capitalist welfare States and the renewed popularity of voluntary social agencies, it is perhaps appropriate to conclude with a few remarks about the contemporary situation.

The historical debates between liberals and social democrats about the size and responsibilities of the State are, of course, haunting us today, since post-war welfare States have proven to be much more easily discredited and dismantled than anyone in 1950 probably thought possible. Even as one fights to maintain the Fabian position that the State has a responsibility to provide a "national minimum," it is worth taking a closer look at the terms of the debate, the underlying assumptions that both sides of the welfare wars often take for granted. A key assumption is that moral capital has its proper circuit, and that those in whom the State invests owe something in return, something embodied in the poor's moral currency, character. In Canada that assumption was somewhat successfully contested for a time, for instance by those who argued that the family allowance was not a reward for moral mothering but rather a universal entitlement. But the ease with which the Mulroney government, cheered on by a media chorus, attacked the principle of universality makes one wonder whether the challenge to the moral capitalist perspective was ever as radical and broad-based as the optimistic writings of progressive social policy experts had led us to believe.

Progressives have very recently been forced to acknowledge that the idea of ensuring that the investment of welfare capital is returned in the shape of "decent" individual habits is not a remnant of the Victorian past: we see it every day both in bourgeois pronouncements and in the populist working-class contempt for "scroungers." It is therefore an appropriate time to re-examine the historical development of the relationship between economic and moral regulation. This re-examination, to which this article seeks to contribute, may well reveal that modern social welfare's image of itself as completely different from Victorian philanthropy is a self-serving and hence distorted image. Further work on the way in which social programmes (even those, like unemployment insurance, originally touted as non-moralistic) are actually administered may shed new light upon the depth and breadth of moral regulation in contemporary society.

NOTES

*   Thanks to Lorna Weir and Richard Ericson for their comments on an earlier draft.

1.   P. Bourdieu, *Distinction: A Social Critique of the Judgement of Taste*, trans. R. Nice (Cambridge, Mass: Harvard University Press, 1984).

2.   A similar aim moves Corrigan & Sayer (P. Corrigan and D. Sayer, *The Great Arch: State English State Formations as Cultural Revolution*, Oxford: Blackwell, 1979) in that they ground the central process studied, moral regulation, in English/British liberal state formation. This, however, while helping to avoid a transhistorical concept of moral regulation, makes invisible agencies of moral regulation outside the state (charities, professional bodies, etc.). The account presented here owes a great deal to Corrigan and Sayer, but seeks to develop the theorization of moral regulation by using a "society-centred" rather than a "state-centric" approach.

3.   For a parallel between *fin-de-siècle* fears about artists and moral degeneration and similar contemporary fears, see E. Showalter, *Sexual Anarchy* (New York: Viking, 1990).

4.   One of the finest literary explorations of this theme is found in Henry James' *Portrait of a Lady*, where we see the character, Gilbert Osmond, become increasingly empty morally as he pursues and achieves perfect "taste." James appears to agree with Bourdieu, since Osmond's acquisition of cultural goods—from furniture to a wife—is only the tangible representation of the more fundamental process of achieving the perfectly "tasteful" personality.

5.   M. Weber's classic study, *The Protestant Ethic and the Spirit of Capitalism* (New York: Scribner's, 1958, orig. 1904–1905), highlights the ways in which the Reformation sanctified saving and investment, that is, the expanded reproduction of capital. What it also points out, however, though this is not generally stressed in Weber commentaries, is the way in which the older Christian suspicion of wealth was now focussed on static wealth (namely, money or commodities, as distinct from capital). Being a capitalist may have become morally praiseworthy, but being rich continued and continues to pose moral problems.

6. J. Keane, *Democracy and Civil Society* (London: Verso, 1988). Keane does not argue that there can ever be an abolition of the distinction between civil society and the state; in fact, he is highly critical of orthodox Marxism for imagining that the distinction is merely a capitalist one. What he does argue is that civil society and the state are not antagonistic or even external to each other. A very different theorization sharing some common concerns is found in N. Rose, "Beyond the Public/Private Division: Law, Power and the Family" (1987) 14:1 *Journal of Law and Society* 61.

7. The economic characteristics of capital, in Marx's view, lead to the pernicious social consequence that what is abstract (money, for instance) is perceived as more concrete than actual things. In times of crisis, he writes, money becomes the "summum bonum"; "compared with it all other commodities—just because they are use values—appear to be useless, mere baubles and toys, or as our Dr. Martin Luther says, mere ornament and gluttony." See K. Marx, *Contribution to the Critique of Political Economy* (Moscow: Progress, 1970, orig. 1857) at 146. The same point is made in the discussion of "modern" credit systems: "The monetary system is essentially a Catholic institution, the credit system essentially Protestant, 'The Scotch hate gold' ... It is Faith [not Catholic good works] that brings salvation. Faith in money-value and the immanent spirit of commodities, faith in the mode of production and its predestined order, faith in the individual agents of production ...." K. Marx, *Capital* (New York: International, 1967) vol. 3 at 592.

8. The new capitalism, located nowhere and often producing nothing tangible, requires the work of bourgeois women to locate itself and create a culturally distinct class, a point often neglected in analyses of postmodern capitalism. See D. Smith, "Women, Class and Family," reprinted in V. Burstyn & D. Smith, eds., *Women, Class, Family and the State* (Toronto: Garamond, 1985).

9. The most influential theorization of the key distinction between subjective identity and objective behaviour in the moral/sexual realm is, of course, that of Foucault; see especially *History of Sexuality*, vol. 1 (New York: Pantheon, 1979).

10. See, for example, J. Donzelot, *The Policing of Families* (New York: Pantheon, 1979).

11. M. Weber, *The Protestant Ethic and the Spirit of Capitalism*, trans. T. Parsons (New York: Scribner's, 1958) at 17.

12. One of the few turn-of-the-century social reformers to question this idea of the poor's debt to philanthropists was Jane Addams, who argued that the purpose of social/moral reform was not moral regeneration as much as a healthier democracy. J. Addams, *Democracy and Social Ethics* (New York: Macmillan, 1905).

13. D. Andrew, *Philanthropy and Police: Charity in 18th-century London* (Princeton: Princeton University Press, 1989). For similar developments during France's pronatalist panic, see R. Fuchs, *Poor and Pregnant in Paris: Strategies for Survival in the Nineteenth Century* (New Brunswick, N.J.: Rutgers University Press, 1992).

14. Andrew points out that while in the early 18th century, bequests were the most common form of donation, by the 19th century many philanthropists, even those very active in particular agencies, left them no money in their wills, preferring to exercise more control over their investment by means of annual subscriptions and involvement in

the boards and committees (see Andrew, *supra* note 13 at c. 2). A century later, scientific philanthropists bemoaned the existence of endowed charities precisely because they lacked flexibility and gave the poor too much security; they preferred to be constantly evaluating and changing their investments.

15. See essays by J. Donzelot, G. Procacci, and M. Foucault in G. Burchell, C. Gordon, & P. Miller, eds., *The Foucault Effect: Studies in Governmentality* (Chicago: University of Chicago Press, 1991).

16. L. Blanc, *Organisation du travail* (Paris: Bureau du Nouveau Monde, 1850) at 4.

17. F. Vidal, *De la repartition des richesses, pour de la justice distributive en economie sociale* (Paris: Capelle, 1846) esp. at 25, 78 ff.

18. M. Dean, The *Constitution of Poverty: Toward a Genealogy of Liberal Governance* (London: Routledge, 1991).

19. L. Blanc, *supra* note 16 at 4.

20. E. Buret, *De la misère des classes laborieuses en Anglelerre et en France*, vol. 1 (Paris: Paulin, 1840) at 113.

21. The classic study of middle-class fear of the "new barbarians" in the 1830s and 1840s is still L. Chevalier, *Classes laborieuses et classes dangereuses à Paris pendant la première moitié du XIXe siècle* (Paris: Plon, 1958).

22. See F. Mort's analysis of early Victorian reformers, Edwin Chadwick and James Kay-Shuttleworth, in his *Dangerous Sexualities: Medico-Moral Politics in England Since 1800* (London: Routledge, 1987).

23. There are numerous sources on this. Prominent among left-wing analyses is G. Stedman Jones, *Outcast London* (Oxford: Oxford University Press, 1971). A recent right-wing survey is G. Himmelfarb, *Poverty and Compassion: The Moral Imagination of the Late Victorians* (New York: Knopf, 1991).

24. C. Booth et al., *Life and Labour of the People of London*, vol. 8 (London: Macmillan, 1896) at 395, Appendix B.

25. O. Hill, *Homes of the London Poor*, rev. ed. (London: Frank Cass, 1970) at 74.

26. Ibid., at 75.

27. See A. Wohl, *The Bitter Cry of Outcast London* (New York: Humanities, 1970), introduction to reprint and A. Wohl, "Sex and the Single Room" in A. Wohl, ed., *The Victorian Family: Structure and Stress* (London: Croom Helm, 1978).

28. On the centrality of "character" as the product sought by the Charity Organization Society, in which Octavia Hill was a prominent leader, see J. Fido, "The COS and Social Casework in London 1869–1900" in A.P. Donajgrodzki, ed., *Social Control in 19th-century Britain* (London: Croom Helm, 1977) at 207.

29. *Supra* note 25 at 74.

30. Ibid., at 52.

31. See J.N. Tarn, *Five Percent Philanthropy: An Account of Housing in Urban Areas Between 1840 and 1914* (Cambridge: Cambridge University Press, 1973).

32. Ibid., at 7.

33. *Supra* note 25 at 56.

34. Ibid., at 41.

35. The convolutions made by poor law guardians, especially masters of workhouses, in order to incorporate a "test" element into the administration of a poor law that also acknowledged a universal entitlement to not starve, are well described (though not analyzed) in the massive reports and studies of the 1909 Royal Commission on the Poor Laws, about which more below.

36. S. & B. Webb, *The Prevention of Destitution* (London: Longmans, 1912) at 1–2.

37. Ibid., at 239.

38. Ibid., at 39.

39. This is J. Donzelot's interpretation, in his influential work on philanthropy and social policy, *The Policing of Families, supra* note 10. The late-19th-century shift in interest from old people to children is taken to be a rational economic measure, insofar as children represent future economic values and old people do not; while this is true, it does not prove that separate moral considerations were not at work.

40. The Webb statement on pensions is from their jointly written "Minority Report of the Royal Commission on the Poor Laws," on which Beatrice sat (alongside her rival Octavia Hill and other COS representatives), U.K. (H.C. *Parliamentary Papers* (1909) vol. 37,941, henceforth "Minority Report"). The phrase "respectable lives in decent houses" is found throughout the Majority Report's very lengthy discussion of the conditions of outdoor relief.

41. See B. Webb, *The Diary of Beatrice Webb*, vol. 3 (London: Virago, 1984) and B. Webb, *Our Partnership* (New York: Longmans, 1948). Some recent commentators have pointed out that the majority and the minority in the Royal Commission "had more in common than divided them." See P. Thane, *The Foundations of the Welfare State* (London: Longmans, 1982) at 8; also P. Squires, *Anti-Social Policy: Welfare, Ideology and the Disciplinary State* (Brighton: Harvester, 1990).

42. The Minority Report "became part of a Socialist charter .... Nearly forty years after its first publication, the first Labour government with a clear majority in the House of Commons was to make it the basis for the 'Welfare state' legislation of the late 1940s." See K. Jones, *The Making of Social Policy in Britain* (London: Athlone, 1991) at 94.

43. *Supra* note 40 at 816. Emphasis in original.

44. Ibid., at 815, 905. This is repeated at 846, in the section on social welfare for school-age children, which praises the "constant supervision of unfit parents" as a means not to undermine parenting but "to induce them [poor parents] to continuously fulfil their parental responsibilities."

45. The Webbs' obliviousness to popular culture was more than just a personal prejudice; as Sally Alexander has pointed out, it was indicative of the Fabian Society's lack of popular base. See S. Alexander, ed., *Women's Fabian Tracts* (London: Routledge, 1988) introduction.

46. Beatrice Webb's personal life was dominated, from the tender age of 15, by a constant struggle against what she perceived as her "lower" passions. Sensual love, the pleasures of eating and drinking, and even those of listening to religious music or reading anything

not geared to social research, were enemies to be defeated in the service of a pure life of public service. Even her own moral capital seemed constantly imperilled. See *The Diary of Beatrice Webb, supra* note 41.

PART IV

Modernism, Culture, and Change

CRITICAL THINKING QUESTIONS

Simmel
1. In the context of modern city life, does the impersonal nature of economic exchange foster emotional detachment? Are people numb to the social realities of poverty, bigotry, or war?
2. What are some of the positive and negative aspects of modern living in terms of Simmel's comments on individual freedom?
3. In what respects does Canadian society today resemble the metropolis that Simmel discusses?

Marcuse
1. How does social control operate in society, according to Marcuse?
2. In what ways do you think modern institutions such as education or media shape ideology through consumption?
3. What, in Marcuse's opinion, is one-dimensionality?

Habermas
1. What, according to Habermas, is aesthetic modernity?
2. In what ways do you think art matters to modernity?
3. In Habermas's view, is the avant-garde a positive force of change?

Bourdieu
1. What does Bourdieu imply by the concept of "field"?
2. What factors contribute to the field?
3. In Bourdieu's assessment, does power co-exist with wealth? Explain.

Valverde
1. What is moral capital? Is it related to other forms of capital?

2. In what ways does/did scientific philanthropy differ from charity?
3. In what ways does a mixed economy operate today through media
    reporting on juvenile crime, homelessness, or terrorism?

SUGGESTED READINGS

Martineau, Harriet. 1839. *Society in America*. London: Saunders and Otley.
     It is becoming increasingly common to acknowledge Martineau as the
first woman sociologist. This book analyzes the contradictions of democracy
in America. Particular attention is granted to neglected women's rights.

Kincaid, Jamaica. 1988. *A Small Place*. New York: Penguin Books.
     Kincaid's book is an emotionally gripping discussion of social change
and tourism in Antigua. This is a short, plainly written book of only 81
pages.

Ritzer, George. 1995. *The McDonaldization of Society: An Investigation into the
Changing Character of Contemporary Social Life*. Thousand Oaks, California:
Pine Forge Press.
     Ritzer's book is an analysis of social change and rationalization in the
spirit of Weber. He argues that the organizational processes of the typical
fast-food restaurant are sweeping modern society.

Dandeker, Christopher. 1990. *Surveillance, Power, and Modernity*. Cambridge:
Polity.
     Inspired by Max Weber's writing on bureaucracy, this book focuses
on surveillance, the state, and economy. The discussion explicates the
relationship between power, modern societies, and the surveillance
capacities of the state.

Gandy, Oscar. 1993. *The Panoptic Sort: A Political Economy of Personal
Information*. Oxford: Westview Press.
     A blend of Weber and Foucault, this book analyzes how personal data
in the modern world function to sort and categorize the population. Gandy
grants particular attention to computer power and modern governance.

RELATED WEB SITES

Bourdieu Forum
At the time of writing, this Web site was being constructed. It is to become
a forum for the discussion of topics related to Bourdieu and his work in

all its aspects: aesthetic, artistic, cultural, scientific, social, philosophical, and political.
http://lists.village.virginia.edu/~spoons/bourdieu/

Georg Simmel: The Stranger
This Web site contains Simmel's writing on the stranger. This will be of interest to students interested in Simmel's ideas.
www2.pfeiffer.edu/~lridener/DSS/Simmel/STRANGER.HTML

Habermas Links
"Habermas Links" is a Web site offering annotated links to Jürgen Habermas's work.
www.helsinki.fi/~amkauppi/hablinks.html

Max Weber
This is a Web site offering numerous links to Max Weber's work on bureaucracy, rationality, and social change. This is an important resource for students interested in social change and modernization.
http://cepa.newschool.edu/het/profiles/weber.htm

Surveillance and Society
Surveillance and Society is a new on-line journal. The Web site offers many resources pertaining to surveillance, social change, and rationalization.
www.surveillance-and-society.org

PART V

Feminist Social Thought

Feminist social thought, like other forms of social thought, critically analyzes the social world by questioning taken-for-granted assumptions, perceptions, and beliefs. What is different about feminist social thought, however, is that it maintains a distinct emphasis on the experiences, positions, and imperatives of women in society.

Feminist social thought traces at least as far back as the "women controversy" of the 17th century. Caught up in debates over the first two creation stories presented in the Book of Genesis, certain Christian-patriarchal interpretations of human nature understood women to be immoral and deceptive (contemporary embodiments of Eve). The social subordination of women was predicated on divine foundations of male superiority, and religious and legal definitions of gender roles were prescribed on the basis of God's will. But women were far from silent in this debate. At the beginning of the 17th century, Marie de Gourney wrote essays on women's equality. Mary Astell joined the debate later in the century, and others such as Mary Wortley Montagu, Mary Hays, and Mary Wollstonecraft offered important works as well.

Despite the rather long history of research and writing on the rights of women, neither feminist sociology nor feminist sociologists made significant (that is, widely acknowledged and recognized) gains in mainstream sociological theory until the 1970s. This was a period of time in the industrial West when women were entering the labour force at an unprecedented rate, when civil rights infrastructures that had been developing since 1945 began to secure a greater number of rights for women, and when gender became a recognized category of theorization and debate. Emergent academic feminist theorization, however, was neither unique to sociology nor homogeneous across the disciplines. Whereas one set of multidisciplinary feminist writers found inspiration in Marx's argument that the social relations of production (e.g., gender division of labour in society) are tied to the material relations of production (e.g., mode of production), for example, others emphasized interpretive perspectives and focused on the experiences and actions of women. What feminist sociological theorists did share was an interest in how basic physical differences between men and women assumed social and cultural importance. They also shared an interest in eradicating or subverting those interpretations.

⑤ SECTION READINGS: JOAN KELLY-GADOL, DOROTHY SMITH, AND BELL HOOKS

Historian Joan Kelly-Gadol's work (1928–1982) introduces the chapter by outlining three basic concerns of historical thought for women's history at a time when historians were beginning to recognize (or acknowledge) the need to study women and gender. She explains that feminist historiography problematizes the notion that the history of women is similar to the history of men. By conflating the experiences of men and women in the periodization of history (e.g., the events of the French Revolution), Kelly-Gadol contends that the historical experiences of women as unique from men are lost. This is because women form a distinct social group whose essence cannot be ascribed to a fundamental female nature. Created and maintained through economic, political, and cultural forces, Kelly-Gadol maintains, "woman" is a social category that develops relationally to the category of "man" under particular social circumstances. As a consequence, she concludes that an historical understanding of the formation of the category of "woman" necessitates an understanding of how relationships between the sexes/genders have developed in the context of social changes generally. This is particularly the case with respect to family, private property, and the domestic realm.

Similar themes appear in the work of Dorothy Smith (1926–). Smith, who currently teaches in the Department of Sociology at the University of Victoria, became famous for her work on topics including feminism, standpoint, institutional ethnography, and sociological theory. In the next reading passage, Smith addresses the uneasy relationship between Marxism and feminism. She offers the concept, indeed what she understands as the reality, of "sisterhood" as a place to begin. Sisterhood, for Smith, does not refer to an emotional bond or a sentimental grouping. Sisterhood foremost involves the grounded standpoint of the collective position of women in social and political ruling relations. It involves the shared experience of social oppression as the common starting point for an understanding of all the differences that women possess. What this means for Smith is that there are common external social, political, and economic constraints on all women's lives, regardless of the myriad of women's individual experiences. The problem with much feminist social thought, she contends, is that it tends to take as a place to begin the personal experiences of women—the experiences of women that are shaped through relations of subordination. This is problematic for Smith because it transposes the oppression of women in the private/personal realm to the political domain without addressing the political and economic bases of patriarchy. That is, women experience oppression based on social and economic processes in the form of gender relations, sexual roles, and domestication, but often that oppression is explained on the basis of mystifying notions of what it means to be a woman rather than the essential material relations of subordination.

To demonstrate how women can emerge from these oppressive relations to make progressive change, she turns to the women's movement in Canada. Acknowledging important feminist struggles taking place with respect to pay equity, matrimonial property laws, and abortion laws, for example, she maintains that there are more fundamental processes at work in Canadian capitalism. Pointing to the reality of gender differences manifested in examples such as underemployment rates in B.C., the different ways that welfare cuts are felt, and social support for women's health care, she suggests that there are wider external forces that need to be addressed.

bell hooks (1952–) addresses issues of accountability and significance in feminist movement(s) in the final reading passage. The issue of accountability pertains to the tendency she identifies in the feminist movement for White, vocal, middle-class women to universalize their own experiences and assume that their experiences are representative of women everywhere. The issue of significance pertains to the failure of feminist movements to articulate why feminism matters to all people. Rather than accentuating the positive implications of feminism, the result has been twofold: the marginalization of feminism as a reactionary, restrictive movement, and the imposition of limitations on mass [non-White] women's participation within the feminist movement.

hooks concentrates her attention on sexual oppression. She does so not because it is the most important or fundamental form of oppression in the West, but rather because she believes sexual oppression to be the first form of oppression that is learned in the Western family. Sexual oppression, hooks contends, distorts the positive functions of the family in two ways. The first is that it reinforces relations of subordination and superordination on the grounds of a natural order. Second, it has led feminists to call for the eradication of the family. The latter is particularly important because for hooks it represents one further manifestation of the universalization of White, middle-class feminism. She explains that for women of colour, the family is the least oppressive of social institutions. Devaluations of the family in the feminist movement, she maintains, are not based on the inherent structure of the family but on the class structure of the feminist movement itself. The significance of the feminist movement, as she sees it, is to affirm the positive and liberating potential of the family structure, as well as to contribute to the eradication of all forms of (interlocking) oppression.

CHAPTER 16

The Social Relation of the Sexes: Methodological Implications of Women's History

JOAN KELLY-GADOL

* * * * *

Women's history has a dual goal: to restore women to history and to restore our history to women. In the past few years, it has stimulated a remarkable amount of research as well as a number of conferences and courses on the activities, status, and views of and about women. The interdisciplinary character of our concern with women has also newly enriched this vital historical work. But there is another aspect of women's history that needs to be considered: its theoretical significance, its implications for historical study in general.[1] In seeking to add women to the fund of historical knowledge, women's history has revitalized theory, for it has shaken the conceptual foundations of historical study. It has done this by making problematical three of the basic concerns of historical thought: (1) periodization, (2) the categories of social analysis, and (3) theories of social change.

Since all three issues are presently in ferment, I can at best suggest how they may be fruitfully posed. But in so doing, I should also like to show how the conception of these problems expresses a notion which is basic to feminist consciousness, namely, that the relation between the sexes is a social and not a natural one. This perception forms the core idea that upsets traditional thinking in all three cases.

⬚ PERIODIZATION

Once we look to history for an understanding of woman's situation, we are, of course, already assuming that woman's situation is a social matter. But history, as we first came to it, did not seem to confirm this awareness. Throughout historical time, women have been largely excluded from making war, wealth, laws, governments, art, and science. Men, functioning in their capacity as historians, considered exactly those activities constitutive of civilization: hence, diplomatic history, economic history, constitutional history, and political and cultural history. Women figured chiefly as exceptions, those who were said to be as ruthless as, or wrote like, or had the brains of men. In redressing this neglect, women's history recognized from the start that what we call compensatory history is not enough. This was not to be a history of exceptional women, although they too need to be restored to their rightful places. Nor could it be another subgroup of historical thought, a history of women to place alongside the list of diplomatic history, economic history, and so forth, for all these developments impinged upon the history of women. Hence feminist scholarship in history, as in anthropology, came to focus primarily on the issue of women's status. I use "status" here and throughout in an expanded sense, to refer to woman's place and power—that is, the roles and positions women hold in society by comparison with those of men.

In historical terms, this means to look at ages or movements of great social change in terms of their liberation or repression of woman's potential, their import for the advancement of her humanity as well as "his." The moment this is done—the moment one assumes that women are a part of humanity in the fullest sense—the period or set of events with which we deal takes on a wholly different character or meaning from the normally accepted one. Indeed, what emerges is a fairly regular pattern of relative loss of status for women precisely in those periods of so-called progressive change. Since the dramatic new perspectives that unfold from this shift of vantage point have already been discussed at several conferences, I shall be brief here.[2] Let me merely point out that if we apply Fourier's famous dictum— that the emancipation of women is an index of the general emancipation of an age—our notions of so-called progressive developments, such as classical Athenian civilization, the Renaissance, and the French Revolution, undergo a startling re-evaluation. For women, "progress" in Athens meant concubinage and confinement of citizen wives in the gynecaeum. In Renaissance Europe it meant domestication of the bourgeois wife and escalation of witchcraft persecution, which crossed class lines. And the Revolution expressly excluded women from its liberty, equality, and "fraternity." Suddenly we see these ages with a new, double vision—and each eye sees a different picture.

Only one of these views has been represented by history up to now. Regardless of how these periods have been assessed, they have been assessed from the vantage point of men. Liberal historiography in particular, which considers all three periods as stages in the progressive realization of an individualistic social and cultural order, expressly maintains—albeit without considering the evidence—that women shared these advances with men. In Renaissance scholarship, for example, almost all historians have been content to situate women exactly where Jacob Burckhardt placed them in 1890: "on a footing of perfect equality with men." For a period that rejected the hierarchy of social class and the hierarchy of religious values in its restoration of a classical, secular culture, there was also, they claim, "no question of 'woman's rights' or female emancipation, simply because the thing itself was a matter of course."[2] Now while it is true that a couple of dozen women can be assimilated to the humanistic standard of culture which the Renaissance imposed upon itself, what is remarkable is that *only* a couple of dozen women can. To pursue this problem is to become aware of the fact that there was no "renaissance" for women—at least not during the Renaissance. There was, on the contrary, a marked restriction of the scope and powers of women. Moreover, this restriction is a consequence of the very developments for which the age is noted.[3]

What feminist historiography has done is to unsettle such accepted evaluations of historical periods. It has disabused us of the notion that the history of women is the same as the history of men and that significant turning points in history have the same impact for one sex as for the other. Indeed, some historians now go so far as to maintain that, because of woman's particular connection with the function of reproduction, history could, and women's history should, be rewritten and periodized from this point of view, according to major turning points affecting childbirth, sexuality, family structure, and so forth.[4] In this regard, Juliet Mitchell refers to modern contraception as a "world-historic event"—although the logic of her thought, and my own, protests against a periodization that is primarily geared to changes in reproduction. Such criteria threaten to detach psychosexual development and family patterns from changes in the general social order, or to utterly reverse the causal sequence. Hence I see in them a potential isolation of women's history from what has hitherto been considered the mainstream of social change.

To my mind, what is more promising about the way periodization has begun to function in women's history is that it has become relational. It relates the history of women to that of men, as Engels did in *The Origin of the Family, Private Property and the State*, by seeing in common social developments institutional reasons for the advance of one sex and oppression of the other. Handled this way, traditional periodizing concepts may well be retained—and ought to be insofar as they refer to major structural changes in society. But in the evaluation of such changes we need to consider their effects upon women as distinct from men. We expect by now that those effects may be so different as to be opposed and that such opposition will be socially explicable. When women are excluded from the benefits of the economic, political, and cultural advances made in certain periods, a situation which gives women a different historical experience from men, it is to those "advances" we must look to find the reasons for that separation of the sexes.

⑤ SEX AS A SOCIAL CATEGORY

Two convictions are implicit in this more complete and more complex sense of periodization: one, that women do form a distinctive social group and, second, that the invisibility of this group in traditional history is not to be ascribed to female nature. These notions, which clearly arise out of feminist consciousness, effect another, related change in the conceptual foundations of history by introducing sex as a category of social thought.

Feminism has made it evident that the mere fact of being a woman meant having a particular kind of social and hence historical experience, but the exact meaning of "woman" in this historical or social sense has not been so dear. What accounts for woman's situation as "other," and what perpetuates it historically? The "Redstockings Manifesto" of 1969 maintained that "women are an oppressed class" and suggested that the relations between men and women are class relations, that "sexual politics" are the politics of class domination. The most fruitful consequence of this conception of women as a social class has been the extension of class analysis to women by Marxist feminists such as Margaret Benston and Sheila Rowbotham.[5] They have traced the roots of woman's secondary status in history to economics inasmuch as women as a group have had a distinctive relation to production and property in almost all societies. The personal and psychological consequences of secondary status can be seen to flow from this special relation to work. As Rowbotham and Benston themselves make clear, however, it is one thing to extend the tools of class analysis to women and quite another to maintain that women are a class. Women belong to social classes, and the new women's history and histories of feminism have borne this out, demonstrating, for example, how class divisions disrupted and shattered the first wave of the feminist movement in nonsocialist countries, and how feminism has been expressly subordinated to the class struggle in socialist feminism.[6]

On the other hand, although women may adopt the interests and ideology of men of their class, women as a group cut through male class systems. Although I would quarrel with the notion that women of all classes, in all cultures, and at all times are accorded secondary status, there is certainly sufficient evidence that this is generally, if not universally, the case. From the advent of civilization, and hence of history proper as distinct from prehistorical societies, the social order has been patriarchal. Does that then make women a caste, a hereditary inferior order? This notion has its uses, too, as does the related one drawn chiefly from American black experience, which regards women as a minority group.[7] The sense of "otherness," which both these ideas convey, is essential to our historical awareness of women as an oppressed social group. They help us appreciate the social formation of "femininity" as an internalization of ascribed inferiority which serves, at the same time, to manipulate those who have the authority women lack. As explanatory concepts, however, notions of caste and minority group are not productive when applied to women. *Why* should this majority be a minority? And why is it that the members of this particular caste, unlike all other castes, are not of the same rank throughout society? Clearly the minority psychology of women, like their caste status and quasi-class oppression, has to be traced to the universally distinguishing feature of all women, namely their sex. Any effort to understand women in terms of social categories that obscure this fundamental fact has to fail, only to make more appropriate concepts available. As Gerda Lerner put it, laying all such attempts to rest: "All analogies—class, minority group, caste—approximate the position of women, but fail to define it adequately. Women are a category unto themselves: an adequate analysis of their position in society demands new conceptual tools."[8] In short, women have to be defined as women. We are the social opposite, not of a class, a caste, or of a majority, since we are a majority, but of a sex: men. We are a sex, and categorization by gender no longer implies a mothering role and subordination to men, except as social role and relation recognized as such, as socially constructed and socially imposed.

A good part of the initial excitement in women's studies consisted of this discovery, that what had been taken as "natural" was in fact man-made, both as social order and as description of that order as natural and physically determined. Examples of such ideological reasoning go back to the story of Eve, but the social sciences have been functioning the same way, as myth reinforcing partriarchy. A feminist psychologist argues: "It is scientifically unacceptable to advocate the natural superiority of women as child-rearers and socializers of children when there have been so few studies of the effects of male–infant or father–infant interaction on the subsequent development of the child."[9] An anthropologist finds herself constrained to reject, and suspect, so-called scientific contentions that the monogamous family and male dominance belong to primates in general. In fact, she points out, "these features are *not* universal among non-human primates, including some of those most closely related to humans." And when male domination and male hierarchies do appear, they "seem to be adaptations to particular environments."[10]

* * * * *

I find the idea of the social relation of the sexes, which is at the core of this conceptual development, to be both novel and central in feminist scholarship and in works stimulated by it. An art historian, Carol Duncan, asks with respect to modern erotic art, "what are the male-female relations it implies," and finds those relations of domination and victimization becoming more pronounced precisely as women's claims for equality were winning recognition.[11] Michelle Zimbalist Rosaldo, coeditor of a collection of studies by feminist anthropologists, speaks of the need for anthropology to develop a theoretical context "within which the social relation of the sexes can be investigated and understood."[12] Indeed almost all the essays in this collective work are concerned with the structure of the sexual order—patriarchal, matrifocal, and otherwise—of the societies they treat. In art history, anthropology, sociology, and history, studies of the status of women necessarily tend to strengthen the social and relational character of the idea of sex. The activity, power, and cultural evaluation of women simply cannot be assessed except in relational terms: by comparison and contrast with the activity, power, and cultural evaluation of men, and in relation to the institutions and social developments that shape the sexual order. To conclude this point, let me quote Natalie Zemon Davis's address to the Second Berkshire Conference on the History of Women in October 1975:

> It seems to me that we should be interested in the history of both women and men, that we should not be working only on the subjected sex any more than an historian

of class can focus exclusively on peasants. Our goal is to understand the significance of the *sexes*, of gender groups in the historical past. Our goal is to discover the range in sex roles and in sexual symbolism in different societies and periods, to find out what meaning they had and how they functioned to maintain the social order or to promote its change.[13]

⑤ THEORIES OF SOCIAL CHANGE

If the relationship of the sexes is as necessary to an understanding of human history as the social relationship of classes, what now needs to be worked out are the connections between changes in class and sex relations.[14] For this task, I suggest that we consider significant changes in the respective roles of men and women in the light of fundamental changes in the mode or production. I am not here proposing a simple socioeconomic scheme. A theory of social change that incorporates the relation of the sexes has to consider how general changes in production affect and shape production in the family and, thereby, the respective roles of men and women. And it has to consider, as well, the flow in the other direction: the impact of family life and the relation of the sexes upon psychic and social formations.

The study of changes in the social relation of the sexes is new, even if we trace it as far back as Bachhofen, Morgan, and Engels. Engels, in particular, solidly established the social character of woman's relation to man, although it was only one change in that relation—albeit the major one—that concerned him: the transition to patriarchy with the advance from kin society to civilization, and the overthrow of patriarchy with the advent of socialism. His analysis of the subordination of women in terms of the emergence of private property and class inequality is basic to much of feminist scholarship today. Engels had almost no effect upon historical scholarship, except for socialist theorists such as August Bebel, and historians of women such as Emily James Putnam and Simone de Beauvoir, but contemporary efforts to understand the social causes of patriarchy, and the reasons for the various forms it takes, tend to confirm his ideas on the social relation of the sexes. Certain conclusions, which in turn open new directions for historical and anthropological research, can already be drawn from this recent work. One is that "woman's social position has not always, everywhere, or in most respects been subordinate to that of men."[15] I am quoting here from an anthropologist because the historical case for anything other than a patriarchal sexual order is considerably weaker. The dominant causal feature that emerges from anthropological studies of the sexual order (in the Rosaldo and Lamphere collection I have mentioned) is whether, and to what extent, the domestic and the public spheres of activity are separated from each other. Although what constitutes "domestic" and what "public" varies from culture to culture, and the lines of demarcation are differently drawn, a consistent pattern emerges when societies are placed on a scale where, at one end, familial and public activities are fairly merged, and, at the other, domestic and public activities are sharply differentiated.

Where familial activities coincide with public or social ones, the status of women is comparable or even superior to that of men. This pattern is very much in agreement with Engels's ideas, because in such situations the means of subsistence and production are commonly held and a communal household is the focal point of both domestic and social life. Hence it is in societies where production for exchange is slight and where private property and class inequality are not developed that sex inequalities are least evident. Women's roles are as varied as men's, although there are sex-role differences; authority and power are shared by women and men rather than vested in a hierarchy of males; women are highly evaluated by the culture; and women and men have comparable sexual rights.

The most one can say about the sexual division of labor in societies at this end of the scale is that there is a tendency toward mother/child or women/children grouping and toward male hunting and warfare. This "natural" division of labor, if such it is, is not yet socially determined. That is, men as well as women care for children and perform household tasks, and women as well as men hunt. The social organization of work, and the rituals and values that grow out of it, do not serve to separate out the sexes and place one under the authority of the other. They do just that at the opposite end of the scale where the domestic and public orders are clearly distinguished from each other. Women continue to be active producers all the way up the scale (and must continue to be so until there is considerable wealth and class inequality), but they steadily lose control over property, products, and themselves as surplus increases, private property develops, and the communal household becomes a private economic unit, a family (extended or nuclear) represented by a man. The family itself, the sphere of women's activities, is in turn subordinated to a broader social or public order—governed by a state—which tends to be the domain of men. This is the general pattern presented by historical or civilized societies.[16]

As we move in this direction on the scale, it becomes evident that sexual inequalities are bound to the control of property. It is interesting to note in this regard that in several societies class inequalities are expressed in sexual terms. Women who have property, in livestock, for example, may use it for bridewealth to purchase "wives" who serve them.[17] This example, which seems to confound sex and class, actually indicates how sex and class relations differ. Although property establishes a class inequality among such women, it is nevertheless "wives," that is, women as a group, who constitute a propertyless serving order attached to a domestic kind of work, including horticulture.

How does this attachment of women to domestic work develop, and what forms does it take? This process is one of the central problems confronting feminist anthropology and history. By definition, this query rejects the traditional, simple/biological "reasons" for the definition of woman-as-domestic. The privatizing of child rearing and domestic work and the sex typing of that work are social, not natural, matters. I suggest, therefore, that in treating this problem, we continue to look at *property relations* as the basic determinant of the sexual division of labor and of the sexual order. The more the domestic and the public domains are differentiated, the more work, and hence property, are of two clearly distinguishable kinds. There is production for subsistence and production for exchange. However the productive system of a society is organized, it operates, as Marx pointed out, as a continuous process which reproduces itself: that is, its material means and instruments, its people, and the social relations among them. Looked at as a continuous process (what Marx meant by reproduction), the productive work of society thus includes procreation and the socialization of children who must find their places within the social order.[18] I suggest that what shapes the relation of the sexes is the way this work of procreation and socialization is organized in relation to the organization of work that results in articles for subsistence and/or exchange. In sum, what patriarchy means as a general social order is that women function as the property of men in the maintenance and production of new members of the social order; that these relations of production are worked out in the organization of kin and family; and that other forms of work, such as production of goods and services for immediate use, are generally, although not always, attached to these procreative and socializing functions.[19]

Inequalities of sex as well as class are traced to property relations and forms of work in this scheme, but there are certain evident differences between the two. In the public domain, by which I mean the social order that springs from the organization of the general wealth and labor of society, class inequalities are paramount. For the relation of the sexes, control or lack of control of the property that separates people into owners and workers is not significant. What is significant is whether women *of either class* have equal relations to work or property with men of their class.

In the household or family, on the other hand, where ownership of all property resides in historic societies characterized by private property, sex inequalities are paramount and they cut through class lines. What is significant for the domestic relation is that women in the family, like serfs in feudal Europe, can both have and be property. To quote from an ancient description of early Roman law,

a woman joined to her husband by a holy marriage, should share in all his possessions and sacred rites .... This law obliged both the married women, as having no other refuge, to conform themselves entirely to the temper of their husbands and the husbands to rule their wives as necessary and inseparable possessions. Accordingly, if a wife was virtuous and in all things obedient to her husband, she was mistress of the house to the same degree as her husband was master of it, and after the death of her husband she was heir to his property in the same manner as a daughter .... But if she did any wrong, the injured party was her judge, and determined the degree of her punishment .... [20]

Regardless of class, and regardless of ownership (although these modify the situation in interesting ways), women have generally functioned as the property of men in the procreative and socializing aspect of the productive work of their society. Women constitute part of the means of production of the private family's mode of work.

Patriarchy, in short, is at home at home. The private family is its proper domain. But the historic forms that patriarchy takes, like its very origin, are to be traced to the society's mode of production. The sexual order varies with the general organization of property and work because this shapes both family and public domains and determines how they approach or recede from each other.

These relations between the domestic and the public orders, in turn, account for many of the unexpected oppositions and juxtapositions expressed by our new sense of historical periods.[21] Blurring the lines between family and society diminished a number of sexual inequalities, including the double standard, for feudal noblewomen, for example, as well as for women in advanced capitalistic societies. The status of the feudal noblewoman was high before the rise of the state when the family order *was* the public order of her class; and the scope that familial political power gave women included the Church where aristocratic women also commanded a sphere of their own. Again today, the two domains approach each other as private household functions—child rearing, production of food and clothing, nursing, and so forth—become socially organized. Women can again work and associate with each other outside the household, and the sexual division of labor, although far from overcome, appears increasingly irrational.

Where domestic and public realms pulled apart, however, sexual inequalities became pronounced as did the simultaneous demand for female chastity and prostitution. This was the case with Athens of the classical period, where the private household economy was the basic form of production and the social or public order of the polis consisted of many such households which were subordinated to and governed by it. Wives of the citizenry were confined to the order of the household to production of legitimate heirs and supervision of indoor slave production of goods and services for use. Although necessary to the public order, wives did not directly belong to or participate in it, and free women who fell outside the domestic order and its property arrangements fell outside the public order as well. The situation of women was much the same in the middle classes of modern Europe, although here capitalist commodity production moved out of the home and became socially organized. What capitalist production did was to turn the working-class family, too, after an initial, almost disastrous onslaught upon it, into a complement of social production. The family in modern society has served as the domain for the production and training of the working class. It has been the alleged reason for women having to function as underpaid, irregular laborers whose wages generally had to be supplemented by sexual attachment to a man, inside or outside family arrangements. And it has served to compensate the worker whose means of subsistence were alienated from him but who could have private property in his wife.

Such has been the institutionally determined role of the family under capitalism, and women of both the owning and the working classes, women both in and outside the family, have had their outer and inner lives shaped by the structure of its social relations.

Surely a dominant reason for studying the social relation of the sexes is political. To understand the interests, aside from the personal interests of individual men, that are served by the retention of an unequal sexual order is in itself liberating. It detaches an age-old injustice from the blind operation of social forces and places it in the realm of choice. This is why we look to the organization of the productive forces of society to understand the shape and structure of the domestic order to which women have been primarily attached.

But women's history also opens up the other half of history, viewing women as agents and the family as a productive and social force. The most novel and exciting task of the study of the social relation of the sexes is still before us: to appreciate how we are all, women and men, initially humanized, turned into social creatures by the work of that domestic order to which women have been primarily attached. Its character and the structure of its relations order our consciousness, and it is through this consciousness that we first view and construe our world.[22] To understand the historical impact of women, family, and the relation of the sexes upon society serves a less evident political end, but perhaps a more strictly feminist one. For if the historical conception of civilization can be shown to include the psychosocial functions of the family, then with that understanding we can insist that any reconstruction of society along just lines incorporate reconstruction of the family—all kinds of collective and private families, and all of them functioning, not as property relations, but as personal relations among freely associating people.

NOTES

1. Conference of New England Association of Women Historians, Yale University (October 1973): Marilyn Arthur, Renate Bridenthal, Joan Kelly-Gadol; Second Berkshire Conference on the History of Women, Radcliffe (October 1974): panel on "The Effects of Women's History upon Traditional Historiography," Renate Bridenthal, Joan Kelly-Gadol, Gerda Lemer, Richard Vann (papers deposited at Schlesinger Library); Sarah Lawrence symposium (March 1975): Marilyn Arthur, Renate Bridenthal, Gerda Lemer, Joan Kelly-Gadol (papers available as *Conceptual Frameworks in Women's History* [Bronxville, N.Y.: Sarah Lawrence Publications, 1976]). For some recent comments along some of these same lines, see Carl N. Degler, *Is There a History of Women?* (Oxford: Clarendon Press, 1975). As I edit this paper for printing, the present economic crisis is threatening the advances of feminist scholarship once again by forcing the recently arrived women educators out of their teaching positions and severing thereby the professional connections necessary to research and theory, such as the conferences mentioned above.

2. *The Civilization of the Renaissance in Italy* (London: Phaidon Press, 1950), p. 241. With the exception of Ruth Kelso, *Doctrine for the Lady of the Renaissance* (Urbana: University of Illinois Press, 1956), this view is shared by every work I know of on Renaissance women

except for contemporary feminist historians. Even Simone de Beauvoir, and, of course, Mary Beard, regard the Renaissance as advancing the condition of women, although Burckhardt himself pointed out that the women of whom he wrote "had no thought of the public; their function was to influence distinguished men, and to moderate male impulse and caprice."

3. See the several contemporary studies recently or soon to be published on Renaissance women: Susan Bell, "Christine de Pizan," *Feminist Studies* (Winter 1975/76); Joan Kelly-Gadol, "Notes on Women in the Renaissance and Renaissance Historiography," in *Conceptual Frameworks in Women's History* (n. 1 above); Margaret Leah King, "The Religious Retreat of Isotta Nogarola, 1418–66," *Signs* 3:4 (1978); an article on women in the Renaissance by Kathleen Casey in *Liberating Women's History*, Berenice Carroll, ed. (Urbana: University of Illinois Press, 1976); Joan Kelly-Gadol, "Did Women Have a Renaissance?" in *Becoming Visible*, ed. R. Bridenthal and C. Koonz (Boston: Houghton Mifflin Co., 1976).

4. Vann (n. 1 above).

5. "Redstockings Manifesto," in *Sisterhood Is Powerful*, ed. Robin Morgan (New York: Random House, 1970), pp. 533–36. Margaret Benston, *The Political Economy of Women's Liberation* (New York: Monthly Review reprint, 1970). Sheila Rowbotham, *Woman's Consciousness, Man's World* (Middlesex: Pelican Books, 1973), with bibliography of the periodical literature. A number of significant articles applying Marxist analysis to the oppression of women have been appearing in issues of *Radical America* and *New Left Review*.

6. Eleanor Flexner, *Century of Struggle* (New York: Atheneum, 1970); Sheila Rowbotham, *Women, Resistance and Revolution* (New York: Random House, 1974); panel at the Second Berkshire Conference on the History of Women, Radcliffe (n. 1 above), on "Clara Zetkin and Adelheid Popp: The Development of Feminist Awareness in the Socialist Women's Movement—Germany and Austria, 1890–1914." with Karen Honeycutt, Ingurn LaFleur, and Jean Quataert. Karen Honeycutf's paper on Clara Zetkin is in *Feminist Studies* (Winter 1975/76).

7. Helen Mayer Hacker did interesting work along these lines in the 1950s, "Women as a Minority Group," *Social Forces* 30 (October 1951–May 1952): 60–69, and subsequently, "Women as a Minority Group: Twenty Years Later" (Pittsburgh: Know, Inc., 1972). Degler has recently taken up these classifications and also finds he must reject them (see n. 1 above).

8. "The Feminists: A Second Look," *Columbia Forum* 13 (Fall 1970): 24–30.

9. Rochelle Paul Wortis, "The Acceptance of the Concept of Maternal Role by Behavioral Scientists: Its Effects on Women," *American Journal of Orthopsychiatry* 41 (October 1971): 733–46.

10. Kathleen Gough, "The Origin of the Family," *Journal of Marriage and the Family* 33 (November 1971): 760–71.

11. Unpublished paper on "The Esthetics of Power" to appear in *The New Eros*, ed. Joan Semmel (New York: Hacker Art Books, 1975). See also Carol Duncan, "Virility and

Domination in Early 20th Century Vanguard Painting," *Artforum* 12 (December 1973): 30–39.

12. Michelle Zimbalist Rosaldo and Louise Lamphere, eds. *Women, Culture and Society*, (Stanford, Calif.: Stanford University Press, 1974), p. 17.

13. "Women's History in Transition: The European Case," *Feminist Studies* 3:3–4 (1976): 83–103.

14. See panel papers, *Conceptual Framework in Women's History* (n. 1 above).

15. Karen Sacks, "Engels Revisited," in Rosaldo and Lamphere, p. 207. See also Eleanor Leacock's introduction to Engels, *The Origin of the Family, Private Property and the State* (New York: International Publishers, 1972); also Leacock's paper delivered at Columbia University Seminar on Women in Society, April 1975.

16. On this point, one would like to see many more specific studies as in n. 15 above, which trace in detail the process of social change that fosters male control of the new means of production for exchange, and with the new wealth, control of the broader social or public order and of the family as well. Historical studies of civilized societies would be useful for examples of extended processes of social change, including those of our own society.

17. E.g., among the Ibo, Mbuti, and Lovedu (see Rosaldo and Lamphere, pp. 149, 216).

18. In *Woman's Estate* (New York: Random House, 1973), Juliet Mitchell (developing an earlier essay) offered the categories of reproduction/production within which to consider the history of women. This is roughly equivalent to the domestic/public categorization, except that she added sexuality and socialization as two further socially ordered functions which need not be attached to reproduction universally, although they have been under capitalism. I believe we must consider sexuality and socialization in any study of the sexual order: what are the relations among love, sex, and marriage in any society, for women and for men, heterosexual and homosexual, and who socializes which groups of children, by sex and by age, so that they find their places in the social order— including their sexual places. I also believe, as Juliet Mitchell does, that the evidence clearly warrants working out relations between the dominant mode of production in a society and the forms of reproduction, sexuality, and socialization. However, certain difficulties emerge, not in using this scheme so much as in using its terms—especially when we deal with the capitalist societies. Neither cultural nor political activities have a clearly definable place under the heading of production, as they do, e.g., when we use the terms domestic/public or, more simply, family and society. Another reason I prefer family/society or domestic/public, is that the terms production/reproduction tend to confound biological reproduction with social reproduction, and this obscures the essentially *productive* work of the family and the property relation between husband and wife. See my review of Rowbotham in *Science and Society* 39, no. 4 (Winter 1975/76): 471–74, and Use Vogel's review essay on Juliet Mitchell, "The Earthly Family," *Radical America* 7 (Fall 1973): 9–50.

19. Ideas along these lines have been developed by Rowbotham, *Woman's Consciousness, Man's World*; Bridget O'Laughlin, "Mediation of Contradiction: Why Mbum Women Do Not Eat Chicken," in Rosaldo and Lamphere, pp. 301–20.

20. Dionysius of Halicarnassus, *The Roman Antiquities*, trans. E. Cary (Cambridge, Mass.: Harvard University Press), 1: 381–82. Milton extended the property relationship between husband and wife to the Garden of Eden where Adam's possession of Eve constitutes the first example of private property: "Hail, wedded Love, mysterious law, true source/Of human offspring, sole propriety/In Paradise of all things common else!" (*Paradise Lost*, pt. 4, lines 750–51). Needless to say, where Eve serves Adam while he serves God, the "propriety" is not a mutual relation.

21. For examples given here, see the articles on the periods in question in Bridenthal and Koonz, *Becoming Visible*.

22. This is one of Rowbotham's points in *Woman's Consciousness, Man's World*. I believe it should lead to development of the genre of psychohistorical studies and studies in family history exemplified by Philippe Aries, *Centuries of Childhood: A Social History of Family Life* (New York: Alfred A. Knopf, 1965); Nancy Chodorow, "Family Structure and Feminine Personality," in Rosaldo and Lamphere, pp. 43–67; David Hunt, *Parents and Children in History* (New York: Harper & Row, 1972); the Frankfort school in *Autorität und Familie*, ed. Max Horkheimer (Paris: Alcan, 1936); Wilhelm Reich, *The Mass Psychology of Fascism* (New York: Farrar, Straus & Giroux, 1970); and Eli Zaretsky, "Capitalism, the Family and Personal Life," *Socialist Revolution* nos. 13, 14, 16 (1973). See the excellent article on this mode of historical inquiry by Lawrence Stone, in the *New York Review of Books* 21 (November 14, 1974): 25.

CHAPTER 17

Feminism and Marxism—A Place to Begin, a Way to Go

DOROTHY SMITH

I want to dissociate myself from any notion that what I'm doing here is a performance. This is partly because I'd like to treat it as part of a political work and partly because preparing for this has been, for me, a process of trying to work through some of the difficulties I've experienced as a Marxist feminist, both in relation to Marxists and in relation to feminists ... and feminism. I needed to try and locate for myself, and hopefully for other feminists, a base in Marxism, which has been difficult to establish. This is what I'm doing here. It is a work in progress.

Therefore as an introduction, I want to talk about my personal experience in becoming a feminist. It has been for me an important basis for my own political commitment as a Marxist. Earlier in my life when I lived in England, when I was a young woman, I worked as a socialist. I've realized since then that I had no idea what that meant. I certainly had no understanding of Marxism. I had very little idea of what I was doing, and indeed I think that few people with whom I worked at that particular time had either. Since then I've done a great deal of work, thought a great deal, and worked in various ways within the women's movement, and I feel that I have some better grounding for a political position, some better basis for working. This began for me with discovering what feminism meant. So that has been very personal for me as it is indeed for all women—the discovery of what oppression means. It is the discovery that many aspects of my life which I had seen privately—perhaps better, experienced privately as guilt, or as pathology, or that I'd learned to view as aspects of my biological inferiority—that all these things could be seen as aspects of an objective organization of a society—as features that were external to me, as they were external to other women. This is the discovery that the inner experiences which also involved our exercise of oppression against ourselves were ones that had their location in the society outside and originated there. Insofar as we co-operated in our oppression, we co-operated as people who did not know what we were doing. We were convinced by our own belief in the defectiveness of womanhood. The experience of this change—the discovery of these as objective aspects of the society and the world—was also the discovery of sisterhood.

Sisterhood has become something that is decried increasingly both in the women's movement and elsewhere. Yet it is a very important basis for feminists because it is in sisterhood that we discover the objectivity of our oppression. That discovery is made in the relation to other women, in our discussion with other women, in exploring with other women the dimensions of the oppression. For we discover oppression in learning to speak of it as such, not as something which is peculiar to yourself, not as something which is an inner weakness, nor as estrangement from yourself, but as something which is indeed imposed upon you by the society and which is experienced in common with others. Whatever else sisterhood means, it means this opportunity. But what it also means is the discovery of women as your own people ... as my people ... as the people I stand with ... as the people whose part I take.

Being a Marxist has for me developed in large part, though not entirely, out of this experience of discovering feminism. It has come to stand for me as an emblematic moment in my life that when I moved here to the University of British Columbia, I moved into an office vacated by Lionel Tiger. For many years I couldn't bring myself to read his book *Men in Groups* because I was afraid he might be right. Part of the work I've done in learning how to be a Marxist originated because I wanted to understand how the society could be put together so that the relations among men and women and between men and women could be fictionalized into Lionel Tiger's account of men in groups. I was very happy when I finally came to read Lionel Tiger's book because by that time I had the beginnings of an understanding of women's oppression under capitalism and because I saw that it was, among other things, a trivial and insignificant piece of work, and totally inadequate as any kind of account of either men's experience of contemporary capitalism or of women's. And if men like to dwell on their likeness to baboons, they are welcome to.

So becoming a Marxist has been an enterprise in trying to discover and trying to understand the objective social, economic, and political relations which shape and determine women's oppression in this kind of society. What has shaped this experience of mine as a woman? What has shaped the experience of other women? What are the social and economical determinations of this? These questions led me almost imperceptibly into an attempt to work with a Marxist framework as a way of understanding how society is put together. This was not a willful choice nor an accidental one. It was made on the basis of a sense that the kind of understanding Marx and Engels offered tells you something about how the determinations of your particular space could be seen as arising as aspects of a social and economic process, of social relations outside it. I think that Marxism is the only method of understanding the world which allows you to do this. That was my first reason, rather than its political relevance in other ways, for working to grasp Marxism.

But trying to become engaged politically in other ways on the "left" and in relation to Marxists has been an extremely painful and difficult experience. What you generally find among Marxists is a rejection of feminism. It is exactly the same rejection we experience in almost every other encounter that we have outside the women's movement. How Marxists, whether Social Democrats or Marxist-Leninists, responded to us as feminists does not differ from how we are responded to by the ruling class—the "upstairs" people. This difficulty is, of course, a very serious one if you have become committed as a Marxist because it does not enable you to locate your work with those who are basing their work on a similar analysis, a similar approach, a similar understanding. This has been a really serious difficulty for the women's movement in Canada and I assume the women's movement in the United States as well—although it might be worth recognizing that in Britain, for example, this kind of difficulty does not appear to exist in the same way. There the women's movement appears to be more deeply anchored in the various Marxist groups than it is almost anywhere else, as well as having substantial roots in the working class. So these difficulties seem not to be fundamental to the relationship between Marxism and feminism, but are presumably structured by historically special features of contemporary capitalism in North America as we know it.

I'd like now to try to define what I see as distinctive about a feminist position. I want to do this in a way that doesn't commit me to any particular feminist theory because it must be clear to you that I would reject many of the theoretical positions identified as feminist. Yet I want to say that I am a feminist and I want to say what I think that to be, in ways that don't commit me to a determinate political position underlying the ideological formulations. I see perhaps three things here. One is that a feminist takes the standpoint of women. That is, we begin from this place and it is the place where we are. This is something that is very distinctive about feminism as a place to begin from politically—that we begin with ourselves, with our sense of what we are, our own experience. The second thing is that we oppose women's oppression. That is, we struggle against the oppression of women. And the third thing is the recognition of sisterhood. That is something that I find difficult to describe. It is difficult if you make it merely a sentimental basis for relations among women because it doesn't work for very long. It doesn't work if you treat sisterhood as something that organizes a political basis across class, across time, because you can't unite with all women politically. It certainly doesn't make sense to Marxists, and it has proved in our experience of working in the women's movement not to make sense in practice. Nevertheless sisterhood is that understanding of your relation to other women which comes prior to taking up a political position. Before the women's movement we did not see ourselves as women politically at all. We did not organize or speak as women and for women. Sisterhood is that first moment of discovery on which everything else depends. It is the discovery that women's experience matters to us, that women are people we are concerned to work with as women and that is how we also work for ourselves as women. We did not have that before. When we worked politically or otherwise organized or were active outside the little domestic space into which we were meant to squash our lives, we were neutered, we did not act as women, we worked in relation to and in enterprises organized by men. We did not "identify" as women. We did not have a sisterhood.

Sisterhood is the change from being an outsider in, say, reading books, seeing movies and images, or hearing tell of, what has happened in the past or is happening in the world to women in their struggles and suffering, to locating yourself on their side and in their position. Sisterhood means a different understanding of women as they have experienced slavery and struggled against it, as they have been persecuted for speaking as women and for working politically as women for women, as they have struggled for the survival of their children in many different ways, as they have been oppressed as women by imperialist wars and have fought as the women of Vietnam fought against US imperialism. Sisterhood is a relocation. You take up a different place in the world. It is one in which the character and form of the oppression and the oppressor begin to take shape. As it takes shape, it becomes clearer whose side you are on. There's a difference then in hearing women tell of their oppression when you are detached from that and do not understand how you are related to their experience, and acknowledging sisterhood and finding yourself on their side and opposed to what oppresses them. The experience of sisterhood is a very powerful experience—a very great change in our experience of the world. It forces us to grasp our identity with those who are also oppressed and also more savagely oppressed, not as an altruistic and disinterested concern but because the basis of their oppression is or was their sex and you share that with them.

This is the fundamental experience of being a feminist. It is a political moment simply because without first a basis in sisterhood we can't understand the divergences and differences among women or the things we share, nor see with whom we can work and with whom we are fundamentally in conflict. Far from sisterhood proving a basis of spurious agreement in the women's movement, the discovery of sisterhood and the first experimental efforts to unify politically on that basis alone was precisely the context in which we learned about our differences. We could not see these until we first saw women as those we had to learn these things from and with. Shifts in the women's movement came about in part as women from other spaces than those originating the movement began to be heard and to be listened to—housewives, for example, who refused to be despised, women who had children or wanted children and could not accept the negation of motherhood that was important in the early stages. Sisterhood forced women in the movement to be open to other women and their experience. Issues and analyses had to shift and deepen accordingly. The narrow original focus—such as seeing the key to women's oppression in the control of their bodies and thence making abortion-law reform the central objective of struggle—came to be seen as only one aspect of a more general and grosser oppression. As other women made themselves heard and became part of the circle of authoritative voices, new experience sought political voice. Political alignments changed. Modes of organizing changed. New forms were innovated, sometimes discarding, sometimes incorporating the old. We had to shift from the simple and rather magical thinking of our first struggles and to take up aspects of women's experience which hadn't counted for us before. We had no choice—though we often tried to work as if we had. (I think this is what we were doing when we trashed or were trashed.) Women had to be relevant to us, they *had* to matter, they *had* to be those whose experience counted for us. Once sisterhood was our basis, once we took the standpoint of women, once we were feminists, we had to deal with that. This then is what sisterhood means—not well or clearly defined, I realize, but described as I understand it as an actual experience, as *my* actual experience.

When we come to feminism in its varieties as a political theory, we run into difficulties of a different kind. One of the problems is exactly that we do begin from the personal inner understanding, from this personal experience which is distinctive to women's experience of oppression. We begin from the ways in which oppression is not just an external constraint but part of our personal lives, part of our inter-personal relations, part of our sexuality, part of how we relate to men as individuals as well as in institutional context. In feminism as a political theory, the problem is that the political formulations are transposed by a metaphorical procedure from these personal locations, to the world as a way to talk about it. These personal locations are the bounded, powerless, and domesticated position from which women begin and their political formulations as radical feminism preserve this structure. Our personal experience of oppression becomes the analogue of a political theory. We talk about patriarchy as a political relation by going directly from personal situations of oppression and direct personal relations with men to treating that as a political form. In this way we are prevented from seeing that patriarchy is and must be located in a political and economic process. The formulation of oppression as patriarchal simply skips over this because our experience as women skips over it. We talk about the domination of men and of how men oppress women, as if the personal experience of oppression could be seen as the general and dominant mode in which the society is organized. And then we talk about a golden age of matriarchy in compensation. It is a means of restoring to us some sense of our power—a power women are supposed to have had some two thousand years ago, who knows when? It is a magical way of giving ourselves a sense that we as women truly have the possibility of overcoming our oppression. What was once, can be again. We need only to dip into that deep source, to draw on it, to take up our power, to act and we shall overcome. But then we do not see that power cannot exist apart from actual individuals organizing and working concertedly and hence that the power oppressing us is an actual organization of the work and energies of actual people, both women and men, and that our power to struggle depends also upon working together with others confronting the same bases of oppression. When we call on the magic of a distant matriarchy as a source of power we depend upon a mythology, a mythology rather than an analysis of actual relations, a mythology rather than an attempt to grasp the actual character of the social and economic relations of the society oppressing us now. We must grasp the oppression of women in *this* society, the oppression of women elsewhere in the world *today*. Our oppression is now and this is what concerns us now. It must not be seen as something that you could spread like butter over the bread of time by using the term "patriarchy"; and treating it as something which has always been there ever since the departure of the golden time. We have to see what's happening to us as what's happening to us now. It's happening to us here. It's part of what's happening to other women—other people—elsewhere in the world. And here and now for sure is the only place to begin. So we have to start to try to see what in hell is going on now. Why is it happening to us as it does happen? This is the only way we can begin to know how to act, how to organize, how to work, how to struggle against oppression.

⬒ WOMEN ARE LOSING GROUND

Women are confronting a difficult time now. The women's movement is confronting a difficult time. So I wanted to say something at this point about the achievements of the women's movement. I want to say something about the work women have done here in British Columbia, the work that has been done moving outwards from women's understanding of their experience as oppression in this society to attempt to make issues and to make changes. These have been first very straightforwardly related to doing something about women's oppression. Many of you here in this room have been part of efforts to make changes, to change the abortion laws, to establish adequate child care for women of all classes in B.C., to struggle against the ways in which the professions have oppressed women by establishing a health collective, by working in relation to the law, both attempting to secure legal changes in marriage laws and also trying to make legal help available to women in a form which is not just a further means of oppression. Women have established organizations such as Transition House, which provides a refuge for women who are beaten by their husbands. (Because Transition House exists, we have learned how much more of this type of support for women is needed.) Women have done immense organizational work, in establishing women's studies courses throughout the province, in setting up feminist publishing collectives publishing magazines and books and other feminist literature. Women have created feminist media in film and television. We have created political organization and political networks throughout the province. The organizing of unions for clerical and service workers which the established unions would never actively take up has been taken up by feminists. We have done an incredible amount of work in the last six years in this province as well as elsewhere in Canada. It has been an enormous and often exhausting effort. It has had many failures as well as successes. But the greatest gain has been what women have learned about themselves and their capacities to work politically and how to do that. We have learned a great deal about how to organize, how to work, how to work outside the establishment, outside the recognized institutions of the society. This kind of learning is very important and must be seen as a major gain by feminists. It is particularly important because it is hard to see other kinds of consolidated and lasting gain. It is hard to see how we have made gains in terms of the kinds of changes we aimed to bring about, at least as permanent and lasting changes in women's situation. We would like to see equality in pay. We would like to see equality of access of women to employment of all kinds. We would like to see the widespread introduction of child care. We would like to see repeal of anti-abortion laws. We would like to see changes in the matrimonial property laws. We would like to see many changes of this kind and we do not see them. But what women have done, what women's organizations have developed, and the progress we have made in doing this is something that has to be remembered because this is an achievement and this is the basis on which it is possible for us to go forward, to work. I want to put this before you as something that must be seen as a background to what I believe to be otherwise a gloomy picture, and that is that as times are hard in general, they are specially difficult for women and difficult for the women's movement. There is a crisis in capitalism and changes are taking place which, as you look at them, can be seen as women being put back into the places that we were trying to escape from. That "we" is not just this group here, but women in general in this society.

When the media begin to lay the death penalty on the women's movement one can treat this as a sign-off, not of the women's movement but of media interest in the women's movement. The media are closing down on the women's movement. It is not news any more—in so far as it ever was. There is a pervasive change in the women's pages. I don't know whether you look at the kinds of dressmaking patterns that are presented, but they've gone back from pant suits to being dress patterns again. The styles are changing, make-up is coming back, red-painted fingernails, brilliantly painted lips, and the frontiers of the deodorant continue to advance. "Feminine" styles of being a woman that the women's magazines had laid on us are coming back. The media have worked over the women's movement so that its revolutionary implications are transposed into a particular "feminine" style—careerism, the new marriage, couples without children. What remains of the fundamental critique is the style of the new woman. And the women's movement is over. It's had its day. It was a fad. Sexist advertising can be slipped back in if it ever in fact disappeared. Now we can get down to the kind of society we had before.

We can see the kind of retreat that is taking place if we look at the unemployment figures among women. If you do so, you will find that the unemployment rates among women in this province have gone up and that they are substantially higher than rates among men. When you look at the welfare crunch you see also how that is placed on women, remembering that the majority of single-parent families are women and that the majority of single-parent families fall below the so-called "poverty-line" in income. If you begin to think through the implications of the withdrawal of funds not only from child care, which has a clear and direct impact, but in general from services to the handicapped, to the old—to all those who depend directly on others for their subsistence and daily care—these are all things that tend to fall back on women's work in the home. Look at the implications of the decline in real wages in terms of what that means for women's work in the home. There women's work must take up the slack that is created by the depreciation of the value of wages and the irregularity and uncertainty of income from wages when rates of unemployment are high. At the same time as married women must often try to get work because the family needs her wage, the difficulties of doing so are increased, and the burdens of work in the home are increased. When money is short, women's work in the home substitutes for labour embodied in goods bought at the store. There is a very straightforward relation here. You put more time in. You do more darning. You do more mending. You make more of your own clothes. You do more processing of food if you can't afford to buy that labour embodied in commodities. All these things are happening.

In addition there are those things that directly affect the women's movement in terms of women's ability to put forward the position of women and their oppression so that others can understand it and organize in struggle against it. Funds supporting women's magazines and media ventures are drying up. Funds supporting the organization of women for equality in all areas are getting harder to find. Financing for women's health care, for rape relief, is increasingly difficult to find. Women's studies courses in community colleges and universities are under pressure because of budgetary cuts. It's hard to maintain women's studies in the University of British Columbia. Though Simon Fraser University will have a women's studies program by virtue of the lucky accident of having a woman president, nevertheless even there budgetary cuts are experienced. And in many community colleges the established courses are under continual pressure. In all these areas, many of the concrete gains that we made are in the process of being eroded. This is the situation we are confronted with. As for the successes of International Women's Year, it's nice to know that they've changed some of the nomenclature of government forms and documents.

* * * * *

CHAPTER 18

The Significance of Feminism

BELL HOOKS

Contemporary feminist movement in the United States called attention to the exploitation and oppression of women globally. This was a major contribution to feminist struggle. In their eagerness to highlight sexist injustice, women focused almost exclusively on the ideology and practice of male domination. Unfortunately, this made it appear that feminism was more a declaration of war between the sexes than a political struggle to end sexist oppression, a struggle that would imply change on the part of women and men. Underlying much white women's liberationist rhetoric was the implication that men had nothing to gain by feminist movement, that its success would make them losers. Militant white women were particularly eager to make feminist movement privilege women over men. Their anger, hostility, and rage were so intense that they were unable to resist turning the movement into a public forum for their attacks. Although they sometimes considered themselves "radical feminists," their responses were reactionary. Fundamentally, they argued *that all men are the enemies of all women* and proposed as solutions to this problem a Utopian woman nation, separatist communities, and even the subjugation or extermination of all men. Their anger may have been a catalyst for individual liberatory resistance and change. It may have encouraged bonding with other women to raise consciousness. It did not strengthen public understanding of the significance of authentic feminist movement.

Sexist discrimination, exploitation, and oppression have created the war between the sexes. Traditionally the battle-ground has been the home. In recent years, the battle ensues in any sphere, public or private, inhabited by women and men, girls and boys. The significance of feminist movement (when it is not co-opted by opportunistic, reactionary forces) is that it offers a new ideological meeting ground for the sexes, a space for criticism, struggle, and transformation. Feminist movement can end the war between the sexes. It can transform relationships so that the alienation, competition, and dehumanization that characterize human interaction can be replaced with feelings of intimacy, mutuality, and camaraderie.

Ironically, these positive implications of feminist movement were often ignored by liberal organizers and participants. Since vocal bourgeois white women were

233

insisting that women repudiate the role of servant to others, they were not interested in convincing men or even other women that feminist movement was important for everyone. Narcissistically, they focused solely on the primacy of feminism in their lives, universalizing their own experiences. Building a mass-based women's movement was never the central issue on their agenda. After many organizations were established, leaders expressed a desire for greater participant diversity; they wanted women to join who were not white, materially privileged, middle-class, or college-educated. It was never deemed necessary for feminist activists to explain to masses of women the significance of feminist movement. Believing their emphasis on social equality was a universal concern they assumed the idea would carry its own appeal. Strategically the failure to emphasize the necessity for mass-based movement, grassroots organizing, and sharing with everyone the positive significance of feminist movement helped marginalize feminism by making it appear relevant only to those women who joined organizations.

Recent critiques of feminist movement highlight these failures without stressing the need for revision in strategy and focus. Although the theory and praxis of contemporary feminism with all its flaws and inadequacies has become well established, even institutionalized, we must try and change its direction if we are to build a feminist movement that is truly a struggle to end sexist oppression. In the interest of such a struggle we must, at the onset of our analysis, call attention to the positive, transformative impact the eradication of sexist oppression could have on all our lives.

Many contemporary feminist activists argue that eradicating sexist oppression is important because it is the primary contradiction, the basis of all other oppressions. Racism as well as class structure is perceived as stemming from sexism. Implicit in this line of analysis is the assumption that the eradication of sexism, "the oldest oppression," "the primary contradiction," is necessary before attention can be focused on racism or classism. Suggesting a hierarchy of oppression exists, with sexism in first place, evokes a sense of competing concerns that is unnecessary. While we know that sex role divisions existed in the earliest civilizations, not enough is known about these societies to conclusively document the assertion that women were exploited or oppressed. The earliest civilizations discovered so far have been in archaic black Africa where presumably there was no race problem and no class society as we know it today. The sexism, racism, and classism that exist in the West may resemble systems of domination globally but they are forms of oppression which have been primarily informed by Western philosophy. They can be best understood within a Western context, not via an evolutionary model of human development. Within our society, all forms of oppression are supported by traditional Western thinking. The primary contradiction in Western cultural thought is the belief that the superior should control the inferior. In *The Cultural Basis of Racism and Group Oppression*, the authors argue that Western religious and philosophical thought is the ideological basis of all forms of oppression in the United States.

Sexist oppression is of primary importance not because it is the basis of all other oppression, but because it is the practice of domination most people experience, whether their role be that of discriminator or discriminated against, exploiter or exploited. It is the practice of domination most people are socialized to accept before they even know that other forms of group oppression exist. This does not mean that eradicating sexist oppression would eliminate other forms of oppression. Since all forms of oppression are linked in our society because they are supported by similar institutional and social structures, one system cannot be eradicated while the others remain intact. Challenging sexist oppression is a crucial step in the struggle to eliminate all forms of oppression.

Unlike other forms of oppression, most people witness and/or experience the practice of sexist domination in family settings. We tend to witness and/or experience racism or classism as we encounter the larger society, the world outside the home. In his essay, "Dualist Culture and Beyond," philosopher John Hodge stresses that the family in our society, both traditionally and legally, "reflects the Dualist values of hierarchy and coercive authoritarian control," which are exemplified in the parent–child, husband–wife relationships:

> It is in this form of the family where most children first learn the meaning and practice of hierarchical, authoritarian rule. Here is where they learn to accept group oppression against themselves as non-adults, and where they learn to accept male supremacy and the group oppression of women. Here is where they learn that it is the male's role to work in the community and control the economic life of the family and to mete out the physical and financial punishments and rewards, and the female's role to provide the emotional warmth associated with motherhood while under the economic rule of the male. Here is where the relationship of superordination–subordination, of superior–inferior, or master–slave is first learned and accepted as "natural."[1]

Even in families where no male is present, children may learn to value dominating, authoritative rule via their relationship to mothers and other adults, as well as strict adherence to sexist-defined role patterns.

In most societies, family is an important kinship structure, a common ground for people who are linked by blood ties, heredity, or emotive bonds; an environment of care and affirmation, especially for the very young and the very old who may be unable to care for themselves; a space for communal sharing of resources. In our society, sexist oppression perverts and distorts the positive function of family. Family exists as a space wherein we are socialized from birth to accept and support forms of oppression. In his discussion of the cultural basis of domination, John Hodge emphasizes the role of the family:

The traditional Western family, with its authoritarian male rule and its authoritarian adult rule, is the major training ground which initially conditions us to accept group oppression as the natural order.[2]

Even as we are loved and cared for in families, we are simultaneously taught that this love is not as important as having power to dominate others. Power struggles, coercive authoritarian rule, and brutal assertion of domination shapes family life so that it is often the setting of intense suffering and pain. Naturally, individuals flee the family. Naturally, the family disintegrates.

Contemporary feminist analyses of family often implied that successful feminist movement would either begin with or lead to the abolition of family. This suggestion was terribly threatening to many women, especially non-white women.[3] While there are white women activists who may experience family primarily as an oppressive institution (it may be the social structure wherein they have experienced grave abuse and exploitation), many black women find the family the least oppressive institution. Despite sexism in the context of family, we may experience dignity, self-worth, and a humanization that is not experienced in the outside world wherein we confront all forms of oppression. We know from our lived experiences that families are not just households composed of husband, wife, and children or even blood relations; we also know that destructive patterns generated by belief in sexism abound in varied family structures. We wish to affirm the primacy of family life because we know that family ties are the only sustained support system for exploited and oppressed peoples. We wish to rid family life of the abusive dimensions created by sexist oppression without devaluing it.

Devaluation of family life in feminist discussion often reflects the class nature of the movement. Individuals from privileged classes rely on a number of institutional and social structures to affirm and protect their interests. The bourgeois woman can repudiate family without believing that by so doing she relinquishes the possibility of relationship, care, protection. If all else fails, she can buy care. Since many bourgeois women active in feminist movement were raised in the modern nuclear household, they were particularly subjected to the perversion of family life created by sexist oppressions; they may have had material privilege and no experience of abiding family love and care. Their devaluation of family life alienated many women from feminist movement. Ironically, feminism is the one radical political movement that focuses on transforming family relationships. Feminist movement to end sexist oppression affirms family life by its insistence that the purpose of family structure is not to reinforce patterns of domination in the interest of the state. By challenging Western philosophical beliefs that impress on our consciousness a concept of family life that is essentially destructive, feminism would liberate family so that it could be an affirming, positive kinship structure with no oppressive dimensions based on sex differentiation, sexual preference, etc.

Politically, the white supremacist, patriarchal state relies on the family to indoctrinate its members with values supportive of hierarchical control and coercive authority. Therefore, the state has a vested interest in projecting the notion that feminist movement will destroy family life. Introducing a collection of essays, *Re-thinking the Family: Some Feminist Questions*, sociologist Barrie Thorne makes the point that feminist critique of family life has been seized upon by New Right groups in their political campaigns:

> Of all the issues raised by feminists, those that bear on the family—among them, demands for abortion rights, and for legitimating an array of household and sexual arrangements, and challenges to men's authority, and women's economic dependence and exclusive responsibility for nurturing—have been the most controversial.[4]

Feminist positions on the family that devalue its importance have been easily co-opted to serve the interests of the state. People are concerned that families are breaking down, that positive dimensions of family life are overshadowed by the aggression, humiliation, abuse, and violence that characterizes the interaction of family members. They must not be convinced that anti-feminism is the way to improve family life. Feminist activists need to affirm the importance of family as a kinship structure that can sustain and nourish people; to graphically address links between sexist oppression and family disintegration; and to give examples, both actual and visionary, of the way family life is and can be when unjust authoritarian rule is replaced with an ethic of communalism, shared responsibility, and mutuality. The movement to end sexist oppression is the only social change movement that will strengthen and sustain family life in all households.

Within the present family structure, individuals learn to accept sexist oppression as "natural" and are primed to support other forms of oppression, including heterosexist domination. According to Hodge:

> The domination usually present within the family—of children by adults, and of female by male—are forms of group oppression which are easily translated into the "rightful" group oppression of other people defined by "race" (racism), by nationality (colonialism), by "religion," or by "other means."[5]

Significantly, struggle to end sexist oppression that focuses on destroying the cultural basis for such domination strengthens other liberation struggles. Individuals who fight for the eradication of sexism without supporting struggles to end racism or classism undermine their own efforts. Individuals who fight for the eradication of racism or classism while supporting sexist oppression are helping to maintain the cultural basis of all forms of group oppression. While they may initiate successful reforms, their efforts will not lead to revolutionary change. Their ambivalent relationship to oppression in general is a contradiction that must be resolved or they will daily undermine their own radical work.

Unfortunately, it is not merely the politically naive who demonstrate a lack of awareness that forms of oppression are interrelated. Often brilliant political thinkers have had such blind spots. Men like Franz Fanon, Albert Memmi, Paulo Freire, and Aime Cesaire, whose works teach us much about the nature of colonization, racism, classism, and revolutionary struggle, often ignore issues of sexist oppression in their own writing. They speak against oppression, but then define liberation in terms that suggest it is only oppressed "men" who need freedom. Frantz Fanon's important work, *Black Skin, White Masks*, draws a portrait of oppression in the first chapter that equates the colonizer with white men and the colonized with black men. Towards the end of the book, Fanon writes of the struggle to overcome alienation:

> The problem considered here is one of time. Those Negroes and white men will be disalienated who refuse to let themselves be sealed away in the materialized Tower of the Past. For many other Negroes, in other ways, disalienation will come into being through their refusal to accept the present definitive.
>
> I am a man, and what I have to recapture is the whole past of the world. I am not responsible solely for the revolt in Santo Domingo.
>
> Every time a man has contributed to the victory of dignity of the spirit, every time a man has said no in an attempt to subjugate his fellows, I have felt solidarity with his act.[6]

In Paulo Freire's book, *Pedagogy of the Oppressed*, a text which has helped many of us to develop political consciousness, there is a tendency to speak of people's liberation as male liberation:

> Liberation is thus a childbirth, and a painful one. The man who emerges is a new man, viable only as the oppressor–oppressed contradiction is superseded by the humanization of all men. Or to put it another way, the solution of this contradiction is borne in the labor which brings into the world this new man: no longer oppressor, no longer oppressed, but man in the process of achieving freedom.[7]

The sexist language in these translated texts does not prevent feminist activists from identifying with or learning from the message content. It diminishes without negating the value of the works. It also does support and perpetuate sexist oppression.

Support of sexist oppression in much political writing concerned with revolutionary struggle as well as in the actions of men who advocate revolutionary politics undermines all liberation struggles. In many countries wherein people are engaged in liberation struggle, subordination of women by men is abandoned as the crisis situation compels men to accept and acknowledge women as comrades in struggle, e.g., Cuba, Angola, Nicaragua. Often when the crisis period has passed, old sexist patterns emerge, antagonism develops, and political solidarity is weakened. It would strengthen and affirm the praxis of any liberation struggle if a commitment to eradicating sexist oppression was a foundation principle shaping all political work. Feminist movement should be of primary significance for all groups and individuals who desire an end to oppression. Many women who would like to participate fully in liberation struggles (the fight against imperialism, racism, classism) are drained of their energies because they are continually confronting and coping with sexist discrimination, exploitation, and oppression. In the interest of continued struggle, solidarity, and sincere commitment to eradicating all forms of domination, sexist oppression cannot continue to be ignored and dismissed by radical political activists.

An important stage in the development of political consciousness is reached when individuals recognize the need to struggle against all forms of oppression. The fight against sexist oppression is of grave political significance—it is not for women only. Feminist movement is vital both in its power to liberate us from the terrible bonds of sexist oppression and in its potential to radicalize and renew other liberation struggles.

* * * * *

Feminism in the United States has never emerged from the women who are most victimized by sexist oppression; women who are daily beaten down, mentally, physically, and spiritually—women who are powerless to change their condition in life. They are a silent majority. A mark of their victimization is that they accept their lot in life without visible question, without organized protest, without collective anger or rage. Betty Friedan's *The Feminine Mystique* is still heralded as having paved the way for contemporary feminist movement—it was written as if these women did not exist. Friedan's famous phrase "the problem that has no name," often quoted to describe the condition of women in this society, actually referred to the plight of a select group of college-educated, middle-, and upper-class, married white women—housewives bored with leisure, with the home, with children, with buying products, who wanted more out of life. Friedan concludes her first chapter by stating: "We can no longer ignore that voice within women that says: 'I want something more than my husband and my children and my house.'" That "more" she defined as careers. She did not discuss who would be called in to take care of the children and maintain the home if more women like herself were freed from their house labour and given equal access with white men to the professions. She did not speak of the needs of women without men, without children, without homes. She ignored the existence of all non-white women and poor white women. She did not tell readers whether it was more fulfilling to be a maid, a babysitter, a factory worker, a clerk, or a prostitute, than to be a leisure-class housewife.[8]

She made her plight and the plight of white women like herself synonymous with a condition affecting all American women. In so doing, she deflected attention away from her classism, her racism, her sexist attitudes towards the masses of American women. In the context of her book, Friedan makes clear that the women she saw as victimized by sexism were college-educated, white women who were compelled by sexist conditioning to remain in the home. She contends:

> It is urgent to understand how the very condition of being a housewife can create a sense of emptiness, non-existence, nothingness in women. There are aspects of the housewife role that make it almost impossible for a woman of adult intelligence to retain a sense of human identity, the firm core of self or "I" without which a human being, man or woman, is not truly alive. For women of ability, in America today, I am convinced that there is something about the housewife state itself that is dangerous.[9]

Specific problems and dilemmas of leisure-class white housewives were real concerns that merited consideration and change, but they were not the pressing political concerns of masses of women. Masses of women were concerned about economic survival, ethnic and racial discrimination, etc. When Friedan wrote *The Feminine Mystique*, more than one third of all women were in the work force. Although many women longed to be housewives, only women with leisure time and money could actually shape their identities on the model of the feminine mystique. They were women who, in Friedan's words, were "told by the most advanced thinkers of our time to go back and live their lives as if they were Noras, restricted to the doll's house by Victorian prejudices."[10]

From her early writing, it appears that Friedan never wondered whether or not the plight of the college-educated, white housewives was an adequate reference point by which to gauge the impact of sexism or sexist oppression on the lives of women in American society. Nor did she move beyond her own life experience to acquire an expanded perspective on the lives of women in the United States. I say this not to discredit her work. It remains a useful discussion of the impact of sexist discrimination on a select group of women. Examined from a different perspective, it can also be seen as a case study of narcissism, insensitivity, sentimentality, and self-indulgence which reaches its peak when Friedan, in a chapter titled "Progressive Dehumanization," makes a comparison between the psychological effects of isolation on white housewives and the impact of confinement on the self-concept of prisoners in Nazi concentration camps.[11]

Friedan was a principal shaper of contemporary feminist thought. Significantly, the one-dimensional perspective on women's reality presented in her book became a marked feature of the contemporary feminist movement, like Friedan before them, white women who dominate feminist discourse today rarely question whether or not their perspective on women's reality is true to the lived experience of women as a collective group. Nor are they aware of the extent to which their perspectives reflect race and class biases, although there has been a greater awareness of biases in recent years. Racism abounds in the writings of white feminists, reinforcing white supremacy and negating the possibility that women will bond politically across ethnic and racial boundaries. Past feminist refusal to draw attention to and attack racial hierarchies suppressed the link between race and class. [...]

* * * * *

A central tenet of modern feminist thought has been the assertion that "all women are oppressed." This assertion implies that women share a common lot, that factors like class, race, religion, sexual preference, etc., do not create a diversity of experience that determines the extent to which sexism will be an oppressive force in the lives of individual women. Sexism as a system of domination is institutionalized, but it has never determined in an absolute way the fate of all women in this society. Being oppressed means the *absence of choices*. It is the primary point of contact between the oppressed and the oppressor. Many women in this society do have choices (as inadequate as they are), therefore exploitation and discrimination are words that more accurately describe the lot of women collectively in the United States. Many women do not join organized resistance against sexism precisely because sexism has not meant an absolute lack of choices. They may know they are discriminated against on the basis of sex, but they do not equate this with oppression. Under capitalism, patriarchy is structured so that sexism restricts women's behaviour in some realms even as freedom from limitations is allowed in other spheres. The absence of extreme restrictions leads many women to ignore the areas in which they are exploited or discriminated against; it may even lead them to imagine that no women are oppressed.

* * * * *

NOTES

1. John Hodge, "Dualist Culture and Beyond" in J. Hodge et al., *The Cultural Basis of Racism and Group Oppression* (Two Riders, 1975): 233.
2. Ibid.
3. In their essay, "Challenging Imperial Feminism," *Feminist Review* (Autumn 1984) Valerie Amos and Pratibha Parmar examine the way in which Euro-American feminist discussions of family are ethnocentric and alienate black women from feminist movement.
4. Barrie Thorne, "Feminist Rethinking of the Family: An Overview" in *Re-Thinking the Family: Some Feminist Questions*, eds. B. Thorne and M. Yalom (New York: Longman, 1981): 1.
5. Hodge, *op. cit.*

6. Frantz Fanon, *Black Skin, White Masks*, tr. Charles L. Markman (Grove, 1988): 226.

7. Paulo Freire, *Pedagogy of the Oppressed*, tr. Myra B. Ramos (Continuum, 1970): 33. In a discussion with Freire on this issue, he supported wholeheartedly this criticism of his work and urged me to share this with readers.

8. Although *The Feminine Mystique* has been criticized and even attacked from various fronts, I call attention to it again because certain biased premises about the nature of woman's social status put forth initially in this context continue to shape the tenor and direction of feminist movement.

9. Betty Friedan, *The Feminist Mystique* (New York: Norton, 1963): 15.

10. Ibid.: 32.

11. Betty Friedan, "Progressive Dehumanization," 305.

PART V

Feminist Social Thought

CRITICAL THINKING QUESTIONS

Kelly-Gadol

1. Do you believe that women form a distinct group? What are some of the implications of this argument in terms of other social identifications like class or race?
2. In what ways do dominant gender relations develop? Can you think of ways in which those relations can be (or are being) changed?
3. What should be the goals of an historical inquiry into gender(ed) relations?

Smith

1. In what ways, according to Smith, does feminism reproduce patterns of social inequality?
2. What does Marxism have to offer feminism?
3. What are some of the class-based difficulties facing the women's movement in Canada?

hooks

1. How does hooks believe that feminism can help to understand the role(s) of women in society?
2. What problems are posed by feminist analyses of the family?
3. What cleavages or tensions does hooks identify within feminism generally?

SUGGESTED READINGS

Butler, Judith. 1990. *Gender Troubles: Feminism and the Subversion of Identity.* New York: Routledge.

    Butler argues that to base contemporary gender analyses on essentialized notions of "woman" and "man" is to minimize the empirical complexities of identity. She demonstrates how this is problematic for feminism because it fails to understand gender roles as performances.

Chodorow, Nancy. 1978. *The Reproduction of Mothering: Psychoanalysis and the Sociology of Gender.* Berkeley: University of California Press.

    Set in the psychoanalytic tradition, this book offers an explanation of sexism and sex roles. In all societies, Chodorow contends, the primary responsibility for child rearing is assigned to women. She argues that the universal custom of female child rearing affects the internal psychic structures of human beings and their psychological development.

Dworkin, Andrea. 1981. *Pornography: Men Possessing Women.* London: The Women's Press.

    As an example of a more radical version of contemporary feminism, Dworkin argues for pornography as a form of women's sexual subordination. This was one of her more popular and critically evaluated books on sexual politics and women's subordination.

Smith, Dorothy. 1987. *The Everyday World as Problematic: A Feminist Sociology.* Boston: Northeastern University Press.

    This book won the John Porter Award in 1990. Smith argues that traditional sociological research marginalizes the voices of women. For Smith, research must express the voices of women explicitly.

Wollstonecraft, Mary. 1992. *A Vindication of the Rights of Woman.* New York: Alfred Knopf.

    Originally published in 1792, *Vindication* is a classic feminist analysis that takes seriously the imperative of women's education. The book maintains certain gendered roles, i.e., women's role in the private sphere, but it seeks to conflate public and private life. Wollstonecraft admirably grants attention to male and female gender roles.

RELATED WEB SITES

Canadian Women's Studies Association

The Canadian Women's Studies Association is a bilingual feminist association. Its members are women's studies faculty and students, as well

as policy researchers and community activists. The CWSA intends to build a women's studies network across Canada, and to promote women's studies as a multidisciplinary study.
www.yorku.ca/cwsaacef/cwsaacef/cwsa.htm

Canadian Women's Studies On-line
This is a Canadian Web site offering information on undergraduate and graduate programs in women's studies. A Web resource guide is offered, and there is a library link.
www.utoronto.ca/womens/cdnwomen.htm

Feminism and the Net
Feminism and the Net is a Web site with links to activism, distribution lists, and general communication.
www.eskimo.com/~feminist/nownetin.html

Feminism in Canada
This Web site offers general information on feminism in Canada, as well as information on aesthetics, history, literature, multiculturalism, politics, and religion.
www.cddc.vt.edu/feminism/can.html

Feminist Theory
The Feminist Theory Web site provides research materials on women's conditions and struggles around the world.
www.cddc.vt.edu/feminism/enin.html

*In the summer of 2005, The Orlando Project will be launched on the Web. Many feminist resources will be made available.
www.ualberta.ca/ORLANDO/

SECTION II

Critical Themes for the 21ˢᵗ Century

Part VI: Postmodernism and Its Critics

Chapter 19
Postmodernity: The History of an Idea
DAVID LYON

Chapter 20
The End of Sociological Theory: The Postmodern Hope
STEVEN SEIDMAN

Chapter 21
Call Yourself a Sociologist—And You've Never Even Been Arrested?!
MARILYN PORTER

Chapter 22
Forward: On Being Light and Liquid
ZYGMUNT BAUMAN

Chapter 23
[Extracts from] *The Spirit of Terrorism and Requiem for the Twin Towers*
JEAN BAUDRILLARD

Part VII: Society, Subjects, and the Self

Chapter 24
Reforming Foucault: A Critique of the Social Control Thesis
DANY LACOMBE

Chapter 25
The Emergence of Life Politics
ANTHONY GIDDENS

Chapter 26
Introduction: The Cosmopolitan Manifesto
ULRICH BECK

Part VIII: Globalization and Global Consciousness

Chapter 27
Running Out of Control: Understanding Globalization
R. ALAN HEDLEY

Chapter 28
[Extracts from] *Fences and Windows: Dispatches from the
Front Lines of the Globalization Debate*
NAOMI KLEIN

Chapter 29
Cosmopolitanism and the Future of Democracy: Politics, Culture, and the Self
NICK STEVENSON

Part IX: Postcolonialism, Diaspora, Citizenship, and Identity

Chapter 30
Latent and Manifest Orientalism
EDWARD SAID

Chapter 31
Cultural Identity and Diaspora
STUART HALL

Chapter 32
Citizenship in an Era of Globalization
WILL KYMLICKA

Chapter 33
The Politics of Recognition
CHARLES TAYLOR

PART VI

Postmodernism and Its Critics

WHAT IS COMMONLY RECOGNIZED AS "MODERN SOCIOLOGICAL THEORY" DEVELOPED between 1750 and 1920 primarily in the writings of Karl Marx, Emile Durkheim, and Max Weber. Although not always identifying themselves as sociologists, these writers reflected critically on changes to "modern" cultural, political, and economic arrangements that appeared to many people as normal and natural—even inevitable—ways of living. These changes were related to the fall of feudalism and the rise of industrialism and capitalism, as well as to corresponding changes to the relationship between individuals and society.

In a manner akin to modern sociological theory, postmodern theory represents a sequence of attempts to explain changes in human social organization. While postmodern theorists are by no means homogeneous, what they share is an interest in explaining the social, cultural, economic, and political changes following what is usually understood as the end of the modern period. Committed to developing insights into social life beyond grand metanarratives (of the variety we would find in the writings of Talcott Parsons, for example), postmodernists emphasize the role of interpretation in the explanation of social life. Postmodernists generally maintain that knowledge is partial, fragmentary, and incomplete; they problematize the authority of the traditional author to speak for any social group entirely; and they challenge the authority of the written text to represent social phenomena fully. Postmodernists also prioritize the importance of personal expression, individual voices, and cultural particularism in explaining social life.

There are at least two ways in which the term "postmodern" is put to use in sociological theory. The first refers to a set of cultural shifts or transformations beyond what are understood as "modern" forms of social organization. Postmodern theorists often reduce the social phenomena that made up (or make up) modernity to a sequence of forces based on cultural beliefs in reason, progress, and human advancement. For many postmodernists, this translates to (or translated to) sociological theorization on urbanization, industrialism, and the expansion of capitalism, as well as on widespread human interventions into nature, the

249

application of scientific knowledge to control and alter the physical universe, and the rationalization of social life. "Postmodernity," then, is a term used to identify a shift away from what are understood as older and perhaps outdated markers of modernity.

The second way that the concept of "postmodern" is put to use is in the context of cultural and intellectual transformations. Referring to postmodernism (rather than postmodernity), some theorists argue that the production of Western scientific knowledge, which can be traced to the Enlightenment, has falsely universalized cultural understandings of the human and physical world. Postmodernists argue that modernism gave rise to a sequence of social processes that have contributed to, rather than alleviated, human suffering and inequality, and that claims to "objectivity" under the guise of science and expertise should be rejected. Postmodernism in sociological theory, therefore, is oriented toward revising and deconstructing grand theoretical discourses on humanity, nature, and society.

⑤ SECTION READINGS: DAVID LYON, STEVE SEIDMAN, MARILYN PORTER, ZYGMUNT BAUMAN, AND JEAN BAUDRILLARD

The section opens with a passage written by David Lyon. Lyon (1948–), who is a professor of sociology at Queen's University (Kingston, Ontario), outlines the "pre-postmodern progenitors" of postmodernism. In doing so, he raises interesting questions about the relationship between modernity and postmodernity (and modernism and postmodernism), suggesting that postmodernity may be better conceptualized as a component part of modernity rather than as a distinct historical epoch (a theme addressed by Zygmunt Bauman in this chapter). The ideas that make up postmodernism in social theory, says Lyon, can be traced to Marx, Nietzsche, and Heidegger. It was in the writings of these theorists that the themes of nihilism, Being, multiple realities, and the rejection of absolute truth-claims emerged as sustained topics of theorization. Interestingly, Lyon also identifies Georg Simmel as the sole postmodern thinker who diagnosed the loss of meaning in the modern world—themes addressed in Section 1, Part IV.

Lyon proceeds to consider contemporary contributions to postmodern sociological (and social) thought. Importantly, he explains that the term "postmodern" came into popular usage with the appearance of Jean-Francois Lyotard's (1979) *The Postmodern Condition*. In that work, Lyotard argues that the postmodern condition is best summarized as "incredulity towards meta-narratives." What he means is that a disbelief in claims to science and progress as the solution to social and human problems marks postmodernism. Lyotard's ideas inspired, as Lyon explains, many other important contributions such as those offered by Jacques Derrida, Michel Foucault, and Jean Baudrillard.

In the next passage, Steven Seidman writes on "the end of sociological theory." He could have justifiably written on "the imperative for the return or resurrection of social theory." In Seidman's assessment, there is an important distinction to be maintained between social theory and sociological theory. Whereas he understands social theory as a critical set of discourses aimed at bringing coherence to, and shaping, various social configurations, he explains sociological theory as a product of Western modernity that seeks universal answers to specific social questions. Although social theory and sociological theory have been linked since the 18th century, he contends, the post-1945 era has witnessed the triumph of sociological theory over social theory. However, he continues to argue that the failure of modern Western "foundational" efforts has opened space for dialogue on situated knowledges and partial perspectives. He explains that postmodernism rejects grand social metanarratives and emphasizes instead the importance of local struggles pertaining to race, class, gender, sexuality, and status. The postmodern hope, for Seidman, is to recognize the inherent biases of universal knowledge construction and the fallacies of totalizing general theory and disciplinary foundationalism.

The reading passage to follow was written by Marilyn Porter. Porter (1942–) is a professor of sociology at Memorial University and the current editor of the *Canadian Review of Sociology and Anthropology*. In the reading, she assesses the "radical roots" of sociology to understand the usefulness of postmodern theory. She argues that the kind of sociology that Marx, Weber, and Durkheim helped to develop was motivated by a passionate engagement with, and a commitment to, social and political change. By the 1960s, however, at the same time that Western universities were experiencing an increased radicalism, sociological theories emphasizing value neutrality and objectivity were all the rage.

Porter proceeds to explore developments in Canadian sociology in the 1970s and 1980s. She argues that feminism has been the dominant paradigm in Canadian sociology. By the 1980s, however, developments both within and outside the university began to jeopardize the radical roots of sociology. In particular, she identifies postmodern theory as a hostile force. Acknowledging certain useful contributions of postmodern theory, she concludes that postmodernism is a theoretical development that exists at too great a distance from the empirical/material world, and that it represents a closure on the thrust of radical sociology. For Porter, what is needed is a return to passion and engagement in sociological theory and praxis.

The reading passage by Porter ends with commentary on the work of Zygmunt Bauman (the author of the next reading selection). Bauman (1925–) is emeritus professor of sociology at the University of Leeds and the University of Warsaw. He is world-renowned for his many contributions to theoretical debates. Bauman's recent writings have focused on the political and cultural dynamics of postmodernity (or liquid modernity). Some of his most interesting contributions have pertained to contemporary politics in the context of the declining significance of traditional political structures and institutions.

In the reading, Bauman uses an interesting metaphor to conceptualize the postmodern condition (or what he terms the fluid/liquid modern condition). He argues that modernity has always been a fluid process, in constant motion and always susceptible to the forces of change. Although social organization may at times seem impossibly static (e.g., capitalism, dictatorship, tyranny), Bauman suggests that the history of modernity can be characterized as a process of "melting the solids" of social structure.

He explains how throughout modernity, relations of time and space have existed in tension. Despite the fact that time is continuous, he contends, modern social structure (and, hence, modern sociological theory) has tried to control, regulate, and routinize time. This, for Bauman, carries implications for space. If one is to regulate time in, for example, a manufacturing factory, then that form of regulation depends on the mutual presence of "the regulator" and "the regulated." Both time and space are held constant, and this is what the modern era has been about for Bauman: maintaining the "solidity" of space in the presence of time. But what Bauman understands to be "melting" today is the "solid" bond that fuses the individual and society, which is the hallmark of modern sociological thought. In a world where co-presence is not required, where communication systems (e.g., video-surveillance cameras, biometrically encoded identification cards) are used to regulate workers, citizens, migrants, and travellers, time-space relations dissolve (or melt). This is what Bauman calls fluid modernity, and he reflects on the dynamics of a "liquid" society.

In the final passage, French philosopher Jean Baudrillard writes on the symbolism of the collapsing World Trade Center's twin towers (11 September 2001). Baudrillard (1929–) has become famous for his arguments pertaining to simulations and simulacra. Simulations are representations of real events, and simulations lead to simulacra, the reproduction of objects or events that no longer correspond to an original form. While simulation can be understood as a "copy" or "analogue" form of the real object or event, Baudrillard argues that, in postmodern times, simulations often precede real world events. Consider, for example, the popular Hollywood movie *The Matrix*. In *The Matrix*, the lead-character Neo (played by Keanu Reeves) is confronted with "the reality" that all he has known his whole life is a computer simulation—a simulacrum. The physical sensations and experiences he has, even the air he breathes, are revealed as nothing more than a set of computer-generated images. When he is finally confronted with true reality beyond the computer simulation/simulacrum, he is forced to make certain decisions about remaining in the domain of the real (or outside the Matrix).

In the reading, Baudrillard explains that, while popular political discourses conceive of terrorism in terms of good versus evil, morality versus immorality, us versus them—as President George W. Bush so famously put it following the terrorist attacks on Washington and New York, "You are either with us or against us"—Baudrillard sees immorality/evil/them/terrorists as a product of "us." Using the concept of "terroristic situational transfer" in the context of globalization and hegemonic world domination, he refers to the fallacy of Western philosophy explaining "evil" as the antithesis of "good." This antagonism, for Baudrillard, is a false opposition, as good and evil grow organically together. Good and evil are dialectic: one cannot be understood in the absence of the other. Baudrillard argues that the terrorist imagination is inherent in everyone. Any power that reaches hegemonic status, he insists, taps into desires of its own annihilation. The World Trade Center's twin towers stood as the symbol of power. But until 11 September 2001, there had not transpired any symbolic event that marked a setback for globalization. The terrorist attacks, argued Baudrillard, confront(ed) people with the pure event that concentrates in itself all the events that have never taken place. The simulacrum, in effect, confronts the real. Indeed, it is telling that Warner Brothers had produced a feature film starring Arnold Schwarzenegger (*Collateral Damage*) that depicted terrorism and the death of American civilians prior to the events of 9/11.

CHAPTER 19

Postmodernity: The History of an Idea

DAVID LYON

* * * * *

THE PROGENITORS

In order to understand the main currents of postmodern thought, it helps to step back and interrogate those thinkers who anticipated postmodernity. Undoubtedly the single most significant figure is Friedrich Nietzsche (1844–1900), a postmodern *avant la lettre.* He announced in 1888 that "nihilism stands at the door." This, the "uncanniest of all guests," was indeed eyed suspiciously and with some trepidation in Europe. Why? For Nietzsche, truth was "only the solidification of old metaphors." This had to be understood in the Europe of the Enlightenment. The metaphors must be melted again to reveal them as human belief and the opinion of this or that social group. He devoted his days to exposing the hollowness of Enlightenment hopes. But his work has only come home, with a vengeance, a century later.[1]

One of the most basic themes of postmodern debate revolves around reality, or lack of reality, or multiplicity of realities. Nihilism is the Nietzschean concept corresponding most closely to this fluid and anchorless sense of reality.[2] When the restless, doubting attitude of modern reason turns on reason itself, nihilism results. Rationality, whether in art, philosophy, or in science, is attacked by nihilism. So-called systems of reason, asserts Nietszche, are actually systems of persuasion. Thus, claims to have discovered truth are unmasked as what Nietzsche called the "will to power." Those making such claims place themselves above those to whom the claims are made, thus dominating them.

Nietzsche achieved notoriety for proclaiming the "death of God." Though some take this merely as a trope for the loss of philosophical foundations, arguably it also represents serious anti-theism. At any rate, Nietzsche's slogan "the death of God" means that we can no longer be sure of anything. Morality is a lie, truth is fiction. The Dionysian option of accepting nihilism, of living with no illusions or pretence, but doing so enthusiastically, joyfully, is all that remains. Following on from this,

255

nothing is left of the difference between truth and error; it is mere delusion. No guarantee of grounds for difference—such as God—remains beyond our language and its concepts. Difference is also revealed as part of the will to power, a point that connects Nietzsche's thought with that of Heidegger, to whom we shall turn in a moment.

While cosmic traumas such as the death of God may seem somewhat abstract and ethereal, it should be noted that a generation before Nietzsche, Karl Marx viewed the same process in a much more mundane light. What Nietzsche saw as a predicament for science, rationality, and metaphysics, Marx attributed to the "banal everyday workings of the bourgeois economic order."[3] In other words, under capitalism people allow the market to organize life, including our inner lives. By equating everything with its market value—commodifying—we end up seeking answers to questions about what is worthwhile, honourable, and even what is real in the marketplace. Nihilism can also be understood in this practical, everyday sense. In the postmodern context, Marx and Engels' use of Prospero's words in *The Tempest*, "All that is solid melts into air," have become the new favoured text quoted from *The Communist Manifesto*.[4]

A second character in the prehistory of postmodernity is Martin Heidegger (1889–1976). Most famous for his 1927 book, *Being and Time*, Heidegger was concerned above all with the nature of thought in existing human beings. From his reading of Brentano, Dostoevsky, and Kierkegaard, he concluded that attending to concrete and relevant historical problems showed the way forward for philosophy. These other figures grappled with the same set of existential questions as Nietzsche, though they came to different conclusions. Dostoevsky wrestled with the issue of whether one could claim that "since there is no God, everything is permitted," while Kierkegaard sought authentic human existence in relation to God, which he saw as an ongoing quest of faith and commitment. Like Heidegger, these two tried to face the challenge of the modern world, expressed in the dominance of natural science and the rise of technology, which seemed to squeeze out concern with real-life individuals.[5]

Heidegger shares Nietzsche's interest in "philosophy of difference," but also goes beyond Nietzsche in declaring that Being, not truth, is what should concern philosophers. Heidegger disputes Nietzsche's assertion that difference is just a product of the will to power. "Being" is prior to all the many "beings" we encounter on earth, including humans. So it is not our human wills but Being itself that produces difference. The mistake of philosophers, including Nietzsche, is to focus on truth in exploring the relationship between beings. Their prior existence should rather be the central concern.

Today, humanism finds itself in crisis precisely because it replaces God with humanity at the centre of the universe, says Heidegger. Humans take themselves to be the measure of all things rather than recognizing the difference of Being. In this sense, humanism is not opposed to technology. On the contrary, technology expresses the controlling, dominating approach that comes from putting humans at the centre of things. "The essence of technology is not something technological," insists Heidegger. Acknowledging this is the only escape route from the clutches of modern technological constraint.

For Heidegger, the way forward is to come to terms with our condition; neither metaphysics nor humanism nor technology will do as a basis for life. This "coming to terms with" (as opposed to "overcoming") Heidegger summarized in the word *Verwindung*. Such an approach is followed in the debate over postmodernity by Gianni Vattimo in particular, who resists the apocalyptic effusions of some who see the end of modernity as decadent decline and cultural collapse. Heidegger sees a "twilight" in Western thought, but regards it as an opportunity for reconstruction, not a terminus.

There is no point in pretending that these giants of so-called existential thought were not engaged in a search for a post-Christian basis for interpreting history. As Vattimo says:

> Only modernity, in developing and elaborating in strictly worldly and secular terms the Judeo-Christian heritage—i.e., the idea of history as the history of salvation, articulated in terms of creation, sin, redemption, and waiting for the Last Judgement—gives ontological, weight to history and a determining sense to our position within it.[6]

The question raised by Heidegger and, for that matter, Kierkegaard, is whether the critique of the old foundations locks us into a purely secular alternative.[7]

The selfsame question lurks within a third account of the "tragedy of culture," that of Georg Simmel (1858–1918). Now widely recognized not merely as a founding father of sociology, but also as the "sole postmodern thinker" among them,[8] Simmel straddles the worlds of sociology and cultural analysis. This tragedy, or crisis of culture, was for him the widening gap between the objective culture, seen in technology for instance, and the increasingly alienated individual, frustrated in the quest for genuine individuality. Simmel began his analysis, not with some grand total view of society, but with the fragments of social reality.

Simmel's sociology of culture emphasizes the apparent loss of meaning in the modern world of industrialism, a loss that he associated with, among other things, the "decline of Christianity." He regarded contemporary movements such as socialism in politics or impressionism in art as the response to a felt need for a "final object" in life, "above everything relative, above the fragmentary character of human existence."[9] But in his own diagnosis of modernity he tried to paint a picture of the "passing moment" of life, in all its seeming disconnectness.

For Simmel, the social experiences of modernity were especially strongly felt in the growing urban metropolis and in the alienation of a mature money economy.[10] And they were best understood in terms of the inner lives of individuals, thus providing a sort of social psychological counterpoint to Marx's analysis of capitalist society. Simmel prefigured some of the central discussions of postmodernity.[11] Unlike Marx, Simmel sees the sphere of circulation, exchange, and consumption as relatively autonomous, a law to itself. It is the symbolic significance of money and commodities that fascinates Simmel. The growing attachment to this "world of things" steadily devalues the human world.

Simmel also commented on the autonomy of the cultural sphere. As objective culture—form—increasingly militates against life, Simmel develops a tragic vision in which, for instance, marriage becomes merely oppressive and lifeless or religion loses contact with distinct beliefs and degenerates into mysticism. And thirdly, the aesthetic is accented. For Simmel himself, art was a means of overcoming the contradictions of modernity, and he believed that in times of confusion and uncertainty a more general shift towards the aesthetic would occur. Both these motifs—noting the withdrawal from form, and seeking meaning or even morality in art—reappear in the debate over postmodernity.

* * * * *

The term "postmodern" came into popular usage above all after Jean-Francois Lyotard's *The Postmodern Condition* appeared.[12] Once established, however, other—mainly French—authors were also associated with this tendency. During the 1980s, and despite the fact that several of these discarded, denied or distanced themselves from the term, the postmodern came to be linked with their names. Most prominent within this debate are Jean Baudrillard, Jacques Derrida, Michel Foucault, and, of course, Lyotard himself. To simplify matters I shall refer mainly to them, although I certainly do not want to overlook others such as Gianni Vattimo or Luce Irigaray. Simplicity also dictates that we focus on one or two relevant ideas of each author so that when I refer to them later the reader will not have too hard a time disentangling the threads.

"Simplifying to the extreme," says Lyotard, "I define *postmodern* as incredulity towards metanarratives."[13] Innocently posing as a report on the status of knowledge in the advanced societies for the Conseil des Universites de Quebec, Lyotard's book plunges right into the fate of Enlightenment thought in an age of globalized high technology. The main "metanarrative" in question follows the Enlightenment line that science legitimates itself as the bearer of emancipation. *Modern* knowledge justifies itself in relation to grand narratives such as wealth creation or workers' revolution. We will be freed as we understand our world better. Lyotard knocks the bottom out of this by his claim that we can no longer fall back on such discourses. Why not?

Science, once taken to be the touchstone of legitimate knowledge, has lost its assumed unity. As science spawns disciplines and sub-disciplines, it becomes harder to maintain that they are all part of the same enterprise. Each form of discourse is forced to generate what home-made authority it can. Scientists must be much more modest than hitherto; so far from stating definitively how things are, only opinions can be offered. As Zygmunt Bauman puts it, intellectuals no longer legislate, they just interpret.[14] All that remains is "flexible networks of language games."[15] The traditional sense of "knowledge" is thus decomposed. Lyotard does not explore in depth the sociological aspects of his argument, though he does refer to economic and political factors.

Although the seeds of delegitimation were sown during the nineteenth century, when, for example, Nietzsche turned the truth requirement of science back on itself, the harvest has been ripened by the advent of computer technologies in the later twentieth century. These have helped shift the emphasis to "performativity," the efficiency and productivity of systems, and away from the issues of intrinsic value or purposes of knowledge. Computer printouts are trusted as indicators of "reliable" data and become the guide for styles of research and investigation. Indeed, Lyotard observes that the rationales or purposes of knowledge are seldom sought beyond the immediate. "Who needs metanarratives when management will do?" might be asked by those who have not yet woken up to the dissolution of the "metanarratives" themselves.

This is linked with another postwar development, the resurgence of liberal capitalism, "a renewal that has eliminated the communist alternative and valorized the individual enjoyment of goods and services."[16] In one phrase Lyotard thus points out how the collapse of communism as an ideology (and, after 1989, as a political system) further clears the way for the "atomization of the social," this time into consumer clusters of taste and fashion, a theme we shall pursue in a moment. First, however, it is worth commenting that the collapse of communism is of more than passing interest to Lyotard, for whom the future of Marxism is a vital aspect of the postmodern question. Marxism, after all, represents one of the grandest metanarratives ever. For Lyotard, while Marxist analysis retains some of its relevance—computer-generated information itself is now a commodity—he acknowledges that Marxism has lost forever its claim to universality.

If for Lyotard the atomization of the social means we are each bound up in our local language games, for Jacques Derrida it is a question of "texts." Like Lyotard, however, Derrida raises crucial queries concerning what he calls the Western philosophical tradition. Cultural life involves texts we produce, says Derrida, intersecting with other texts that influence ours in ways we cannot ever unravel. The task of "deconstruction," a strategy gleaned from Derrida's reading of Heidegger, is to raise persistent questions about our own texts and those of others, to deny that any text is settled or stable. The logocentric stance of modernity is radically disrupted by stressing the indeterminacy of language. Though some, such as Richard Rorty, take Derrida to be arguing that the modern era of Enlightenment is over, others insist that he should be seen as still working within those parameters.[17]

Whether or not Derrida would accept that his is a postmodern account, it is certainly the case that his concept of deconstruction has entered the canon of postmodern critique. Just as Lyotard's description shows how scientists have lost status, so Derrida's indicates how authority itself has waned. Literally, the "authors" of texts—any cultural artifacts—cannot impose their own meanings on their texts when they are clearly not their sole product. Popular participation in cultural production becomes more of an option in this view, such that texts are reworked and recombined by their consumers. Collage becomes the postmodern style. TV soap opera audiences are polled for their preferred episode outcomes. Colonial, ranch, and row houses sit together in the suburbs. Scott Joplin, Georg Telemann, and Joni Mitchell meet on the radio. But the danger, equally, is mass-market manipulation.[18]

Nietzsche's "truth" as merely the "solidification of old metaphors" is but a short step away from Derrida's contingent world of textuality. Boundaries between knowledge and world or text and interpretation no longer exist; the mind is always renewing and redefining the texts it tries to contain. This implies that science can no longer presume on logical coherence or the discoverability of truth. This includes social science, of course, long riven by disputes over positivist and hermeneutic—interpretative—approaches. The conclusion drawn by Bauman for sociology is that it simply has to accept its "insider" status, not attempting to "correct" laypersons' views but trying to discover opportunities such study offers.[19]

Other inferences have been drawn especially from Derrida's work by feminists, notably Luce Irigaray, for whom the issue of women and language is central. Debates have raged, following Irigaray's work, over whether or not a unique women's language exists. Derrida defends *différance* against the tyranny of sameness, and wants to deconstruct the male-female dichotomy. But Irigaray apparently harks back to the dichotomy in claiming feminine subjectivity as a means of empowerment.[20]

[...]

Riding on what are in many ways parallel tracks, Michel Foucault's work touches on themes similar to Derrida's. But while Derrida focuses on the literary and the philosophical, Foucault refers more to the human sciences. I hinted a moment ago that the very notion of a "history of ideas" would be unacceptable to most postmodern theorists. To suggest a linear progression of concepts and to explore the connection between each in terms of their antecedents is a hopelessly modernist enterprise. For Foucault, building on Nietzsche, *genealogy* is rather what should be pursued. Knowledge is still in question, but linked with—or melded with—power and also with bodies. In genealogy, a line of descent is traced, but no causal connections are assumed and no origins are sought. Whereas for Nietzsche the body could be used to explain behaviour, Foucault thinks of bodies as being worked upon. Bodies are passive.[21]

In Foucault's scheme, two main *epistemes*—as he calls them—may be discerned in Western thought. Classical thought, dating from the seventeenth century, had no special place for human beings. But the modern *episteme*, on the other hand, characterizing the nineteenth century onwards, actually constitutes "man" as both object and subject. As language becomes detached from representation so the distinctive possibilities of the human sciences are born.[22] But if their birth can be traced, then by the same token so can their death. Foucault exposes what he sees as the deep limitations of sociology and psychology and shows how humans may also be "unmade" by disciplines such as psychoanalysis. His work lent strong credence to the idea not only that the modern *episteme* was crumbling, but also that its object—"man"—was dead.

* * * * *

If Foucault offers few clues about what might lie beyond, his compatriot Jean Baudrillard offers even less. Indeed, he advises us to "forget Foucault."[23] What he does offer shifts the focus once more, this time to the media of modern communication. Whereas earlier eras depended on either face-to-face symbolic exchanges or, in the modern period, print, the contemporary world is dominated by images from the electronic mass media. Immediate communication takes place over vast distances unimaginable to dwellers in traditional societies, and takes the form of montage—piecing together for effect—which distinguishes it from print. In the process, our understanding of reality is radically revised.[24]

Along with several other postmodern thinkers, Baudrillard's work is forged in part out of a debate with the ghost of Karl Marx. Near the centre of the storm of student revolt in 1968, he was then involved with anarchism, structural Marxism, and media theory. But in *The Consumer Society* his work clearly split away from orthodox Marxism in its emphasis on consumption as the overriding feature of class domination. Within monopoly capitalism people are mobilized as consumers; "their needs become as essential as their labour power."[25] Commodity exchange is not unimportant, he said, but the *symbolic* exchange of the consumer order represents the real basis of radical critique of capitalism.[26]

How, then, can such a critique be mounted? Certainly not on the basis of Marxist "foundations" or the rationalist idea that concepts can somehow grasp their object. These are, in Lyotard's terms, fallen metanarratives. Now, says Baudrillard, our situation is one of "hyperreality." With distinctions dissolved between objects and their representations, we are left only with "simulacra." These refer to nothing but themselves. Media messages, such as TV ads, are prime examples. This self-referentiality goes far beyond Max Weber's fears for a disenchanted, detraditionalized world. Signs lose contact with things signified; the late twentieth century is witness to unprecedented destruction of meaning. The quest for some division between the moral and immoral, the real and the unreal, is futile.

Can this count as critique? It would appear that the very term "critique" loses its salience when there is no position from which to assess, evaluate, judge. Yet more than one social theorist sees Baudrillard's ideas—albeit with the apocalyptic volume turned down several degrees—as potentially fruitful for just such social critique.[27]

Others, admittedly, think he so recklessly overstates his case—that everything can be understood in terms of the TV simulacra, or that in our meaningless digitalized societies melancholy is the norm—that critique is impossible without more radically modifying his stance.[28] Yet others, such as Arthur Kroker, pick up his "panic" as the "key psychological mood of postmodern culture," marked by its *fin-de-millénium* swings from deep euphoria to deep despair.[29]

Perhaps the truth of the matter is that Baudrillard's own quest for the real is not over. The world of pure simulacra, of apocalyptic artificiality, is seen most clearly in Baudrillard's searing study of *America*. Its hyperreal setting, a highway in the desert, supposedly sums up American civilization. Some things, he affirms, simply cannot be exported, so the nostalgia of many American intellectuals towards European ideas and culture is pointless. But Europeans are not without nostalgia, in this case for failed revolutions. Perhaps, Bryan Turner hints, a "submerged religious paradigm" lingers on here that makes Baudrillard not just postmodern, but *anti*-modern. Maybe "his own work can be read as a quest for the real, which disappears before his eyes like a mirage in the desert."[30]

* * * * *

NOTES

1.   Many understand the relevance of Nietzsche through Gianni Vattimo's *The End of Modernity* (Cambridge: Polity Press) published in this English translation in 1988, 100 years after the original edition of Nietzsche's *The Will to Power*.

2.   Jean-Francois Lyotard, *The Postmodern Condition: A Report on Knowledge* (Minneapolis: University of Minnesota Press, and Manchester: Manchester University Press, 1984), p. 77.

3.   Marshall Berman, *All That Is Solid Melts into Air* (London and New York: Penguin, 1988), p. 111.

4.   William Shakespeare, *The Tempest*, Act 4, Scene 1, 1.150.

5.   See C. Stephen Evans, *Passionate Reason: Making Sense of Kierkegaard's Philosophical Fragments* (Bloomington: Indiana University Press, 1992).

6.   Vattimo, *The End of Modernity*, p. 4.

7.   See the comments of Jon R. Snyder in the translator's introduction to Vattimo, *The End of Modernity*, p. lvi.

8.   Zygmunt Bauman, *Intimations of Postmodernity* (London and Boston: Routledge, 1992), p. 31.

9.   Quoted in David Frisby, *Fragments of Modernity* (Cambridge, MA: MIT Press, 1986), p. 43.

10. Simmel's best-known work is *The Philosophy of Money* (London and Boston: Routledge, 1978).

11. David Frisby, *Simmel and Since* (London and New York: Routledge, 1992), p. 169.

12. The original French edition of Lyotard's book, *La Condition post-moderne: rapport sur le savoir*, appeared in 1979, but the English translation was not available until 1984.

13. Lyotard, *The Postmodern Condition*, p. xxiv.

14. Zygmunt Bauman, *Legislators and Interpreters* (Cambridge: Polity Press, 1987).

15. Lyotard, *The Postmodern Condition*, p. 17. The notion of "language games" comes from Ludwig Wittgenstein who, along with Ferdinand de Saussure, is a tremendously important influence upon postmodern discussions of "discourse."

16. Ibid., p. 38.

17. See, for example, Christopher Norris, "Deconstruction, Postmodernism and Philosophy" in David Wood (ed.), *Derrida: A Critical Reader* (Oxford, UK, and Cambridge, MA: Blackwell, 1992), pp. 167–92.

18. David Harvey, *The Condition of Postmodernity* (Cambridge, MA, and Oxford: Blackwell), 1990, p. 51.

19. Bauman, *Intimations*, p. 133.

20. Luce Irigaray, *Speculum of the Other Woman* (Ithaca, NY: Cornell University Press, 1985).

21. See Scott Lash, *Sociology of Postmodernism* (London and New York: Routledge, 1990), pp. 55ff.

22. Michel Foucault, *The Order of Things: An Archeology of the Human Sciences* (New York: Vintage Books, 1973).

23. Jean Baudrillard, *Forget Foucault* (New York: Semiotext(e), 1987).

24. The best introduction to Baudrillard in his own words is Mark Poster, *Jean Baudrillard: Selected Writings* (Cambridge: Polity Press, and Stanford, CA: Stanford University Press, 1988).

25. Jean Baudrillard, *The Mirror of Production* (St Louis, MO: Telos, 1975), p. 144. First published in French in 1973.

26. See Jean Baudrillard, *For a Critique of the Political Economy of the Sign* (St Louis, MO: Telos, 1981). First published in French in 1972.

27. See, for example, Mark Poster, *The Mode of Information* (Cambridge: Polity Press, 1990), Chapter 2.

28. See, for example, Martin Jay, *Forcefields* (London and New York: Routledge, 1993), pp. 90–8; Bauman, *Intimations*, p. 155; and Bryan Turner and Chris Rojek (eds.), *Forget Baudrillard* (London and New York: Routledge, 1993).

29. The quotation is from Arthur Kroker, Marielouise Kroker, and David Cook (eds.), *Panic Encyclopedia* (Montreal: New World Perspectives, 1989), pp. 13, 16. Kroker is probably best known for his *The Postmodern Scene: Excremental Culture and Hyper-Aesthetics* (Montreal: New World Perspectives, 1988).

30. Bryan Turner (ed.), *Theories of Modernity and Postmodernity* (London and Beverly Hills, CA: Sage, 1990), p. 10; and Barry Smart, "Europe/America: Baudrillard's fatal comparison" in Turner and Rojek, *Forget Baudrillard*.

CHAPTER 20

The End of Sociological Thought: The Postmodern Hope

STEVEN SEIDMAN

Sociological theory has gone astray. It has lost most of its social and intellectual importance; it is disengaged from the conflicts and public debates that have nourished it in the past; it has turned inward and is largely self-referential. Sociological theory today is produced and consumed almost exclusively by sociological theorists.[1] Its social and intellectual insularity accounts for the almost permanent sense of crisis and malaise that surrounds contemporary sociological theory. This distressing condition originates, in part, from its central project: the quest for foundations and for a totalizing theory of society.[2]

To revitalize sociological theory requires that we renounce scientism—that is, the increasingly absurd claim to speak the Truth, to be an epidemically privileged discourse. We must relinquish our quest for foundations or the search for the one correct or grounded set of premises, conceptual strategy, and explanation. Sociological theory will be revitalized if and when it becomes "social theory." My critique of sociological theory and advocacy of social theory as a social narrative with a moral intent will be advanced from the standpoint of postmodernism.[3]

Anticipating the end of sociological theory entails renouncing the millennial social hopes that have been at the center of modernist sociological theory.[4] Postmodernism carries no promise of liberation—of a society free of domination. Postmodernism gives up the modernist idol of human emancipation in favor of deconstructing false closure, prying open present and future social possibilities, detecting fluidity and porousness in forms of life where hegemonic discourses posit closure and a frozen order. The hope of a great transformation is replaced by the more modest aspiration of a relentless defense of immediate, local pleasures and struggles for justice. Postmodernism offers the possibility of a social analysis that takes seriously the history of cruelty and constraint in Western modernity without surrendering to the retreat from criticalness that characterizes much current conservative and liberal social thought.

⑤ SOCIOLOGICAL THEORY/SOCIAL THEORY: A DIFFERENCE THAT MATTERS

I'd like to posit a distinction between social theory and sociological theory. Social theories typically take the form of broad social narratives. They relate stories of origin and development, tales of crisis, decline, or progress. Social theories are typically closely connected to contemporary social conflicts and public debates. These narratives aim not only to clarify an event or a social configuration but also to shape its outcome—perhaps by legitimating one outcome or imbuing certain actors, actions, and institutions with historical importance while attributing to other social forces malicious, demonic qualities. Social theory relates moral tales that have practical significance; they embody the will to shape history. Marx wrote *The Communist Manifesto* and the successive drafts of his critique of political economy in response to current social conflicts, as a practical intervention for the purpose of effecting change—to wit, contributing to the transformation of wage labor into the proletariat (i.e., into self-identified members of the working class antagonistic to capitalism). Weber wrote *The Protestant Ethic and the Spirit of Capitalism* in part to stimulate the building of a politicized German middle class willing to seize power. Durkheim wrote *The Division of Labor in Society* in order to legitimate and shape the Third Republic against attacks from the right and the left. Social theories might be written to represent the truth of social matters, but they arise out of ongoing contemporary conflicts and aim to affect them. Their moral intent is never far from the surface. They are typically evaluated in terms of their moral, social, and political significance.

Sociological theory, by contrast, intends to uncover a logic of society; it aims to discover the one true vocabulary that mirrors the social universe. Sociological theorists typically claim that their ideas arise out of humanity's self-reflection as social beings. They position theory in relation to a legacy of social discourse, as if theorizing were simply humanity's continuous dialogue on "the social." Sociological theorists aim to abstract from current social conflicts to reflect on the conditions of society everywhere, to articulate the language of social action, conflict, and change in general. They seek to find a universal language, a conceptual casuistry that can assess the truth of all social languages. Sociological theory aims to denude itself of its contextual embeddedness; to articulate humanity's universal condition. Insofar as sociological theory speaks the language of particularity, it is said to have failed. It must elevate itself to the universal, to the level of theoretical logics or central problems, or to the study of social laws or the structure of social action. The intent of sociological theorists is to add to the stock of human knowledge in the hope that this will bring enlightenment and social progress.

The story I wish to tell is not that of a movement from social theory to sociological theory. Social theory and sociological theory, at least since the eighteenth century, have lived side by side and frequently have been intertwined. Marx wrote social theory but also sociological theory; Weber may have penned the *Protestant Ethic*, but he also wrote methodological essays that attempted to offer ultimate grounds for his conceptual strategies. Durkheim wrote the *Division of Labor in Society* but also the *Rules of Sociological Method,* which set out a logic of sociology; Parsons wrote the *Structure of Social Action* but also *The American University.* Although sociological and social theory intermingle in the history of social thought, I want to suggest that within the discipline of sociology, especially since the post-World War II period, the emphasis has been on sociological theory. Indeed, social theory is often devalued; it is described as ideological. Sociological theorists are encouraged to do sociological theory, not social theory. In the discipline of sociology, sociological theorists stake their claim to prestige and privilege on their ability to produce new analytic approaches to supposedly universal problems. I want to claim further that the hegemony of sociological theory within sociology has contributed to rendering sociological theorists insular and making their products—theories—socially and intellectually obscure and irrelevant to virtually everyone except other theorists. As sociological theorists have moved away from social theory, they have contributed to the enfeeblement of public moral and political debate.

⑤ A CRITIQUE OF SOCIOLOGICAL THEORY AS A FOUNDATIONALIST DISCOURSE

Many sociological theorists have accepted a concept of theory as a foundational discourse (Seidman 1989, 1990, 1991a, 1991b). We have come to define our principal task as providing foundations for sociology. This entails giving ultimate reasons why sociology should adopt a specific conceptual strategy. We have assigned ourselves the task of defining and defending the basic premises, concepts, and explanatory models of sociology. We have assumed the role of resolving disciplinary disputes and conceptual conflicts by presuming to be able to discover a universal epistemic rationale that provides objective, value-neutral standards of conflict resolution. Sociological theorists have stepped forward as the virtual police of the sociological mind. In the guise of maintaining rationality and safeguarding intellectual and social progress, we have proposed to legislate codes of disciplinary order by providing a kind of epistemological casuistry that can serve as a general guide to conceptual decision making.

The quest for foundations has rendered sociological theory a metatheoretical discourse. Its disputes are increasingly self-referential and epistemological. Theory discussions have little bearing on major social conflicts and political struggles or on important public debates over current social affairs. Sociological theory has diminished impact on crucial public texts of social commentary, criticism, and analysis. And if I'm not mistaken, sociological theory functions as little more than a legitimating rhetoric for ongoing research programs and empirical analyses. Theory texts and conferences are preoccupied with foundational disputes regarding the logic of the social sciences, the respective merits of a conflict versus an order paradigm, the nature of social action and order, the conceptual link between agency and structure or a micro and macro level of analysis, the problem of integrating structural with cultural analysis, and so on. These discussions are rehearsed endlessly and use a short list of rhetorical tropes, such as the appeal to classic texts or to the higher values of humanism or scientism, to legitimate a favored vocabulary or conceptual strategy.

Has this discursive proliferation produced a centered, evolving vital theoretical tradition? No. Instead of a concentrated, productive discourse focused on a limited set of problems that exhibits sustained elaboration, we find a dispersed, discursive clamoring that covers a wide assortment of ever-changing issues in a dazzling diversity of languages. These vocabularies of social discourse typically imply divergent (if not incommensurable) philosophical, moral, and ideological standpoints. In this discursive clamor there is virtually no standardization of language, no agreement on what are central problems or standards of evaluation. There is a virtual babble of different vocabularies addressing a heterogeneous cluster of changing disputes. Indeed, a good deal of this discourse involves struggles to authorize a particular dispute or a particular conceptual vocabulary or a specific justificatory rationale (e.g., empirical adequacy or explanatory comprehensiveness). Typically, a text backed by a social network briefly captures the attention of some of the principal players in the field. A discussion ensues; local skirmishes break out in journals, books, and conferences; a particular vocabulary may acquire salience among sociological theorists. Such coherence, however, is typically short-lived because the field is always divided, and rival theorists with their own agendas and networks clamor for recognition and reward. This metatheoretical proliferation has yielded little, if any, conceptual order or progress.

* * * * *

If one conclusion to date seems painstakingly clear, even if resisted equally painstakingly, it is that metatheoretical disputes do not appear to be resolvable by appeals to abstract or formal reason. Rival ontological and epistemological claims seem meaningful only insofar as they are tied to practical interests or specific forms of life. Yet if this is true—and I am claiming only that from my historical and social vantage point this point seems compelling—then foundational discourses can hardly escape being local and ethnocentric. This point suggests that the search for ultimate or universal grounds for our conceptual strategies should be abandoned in favor of local, pragmatic justifications.

The notion that foundational discourses cannot avoid being local and ethnocentric is pivotal to what has come to be called postmodernism (Rorty 1979, 1982, 1991). Postmodernists have evoked the suspicion that the products of the human studies—concepts, explanations, theories—bear the imprint of the particular prejudices and interests of their creators. This suspicion may be posed as follows:

How can a knowing subject, who has particular interests and prejudices by virtue of living in a specific society at a particular historical juncture and occupying a specific social position defined by his or her class, gender, race, sexual orientation, and ethnic and religious status, produce concepts, explanations, and standards of validity that are universally valid? How can we both assert that humans are constituted by their particular socio-historical circumstances and also claim that they can escape their embeddedness by creating nonlocal, universally valid concepts and standards? How can we escape the suspicion that every move by culturally bound agents to generalize their conceptual strategy is not simply an effort to impose particular, local prejudices on others?

Postmodernism elicits the suspicion that science is tied to the project of Western modernity and to a multiplicity of more local, more specific struggles around class, status, gender, sexuality, race, and so on. Thus, feminists have not only documented the androcentric bias of sociology but have analyzed critically the politics of science in its normative constructions of femininity and womanhood (e.g., Andersen 1983; Harding 1986; Harding and Hintikka 1983; Jagger and Bordo 1989; Keller 1985; Millman and Kanter 1975; Smith 1979, 1989; Westcott 1979). Because this relentless epistemological suspicion is turned against disciplinary discourses by, say, feminists, and because the same trope is rehearsed among African-Americans, gay men and lesbians, Latinos, Asians, the differently abled, and so on, no social discourse can escape the doubt that its claims to truth are tied to and yet mask an ongoing social interest to shape the course of history. Once the veil of epistemic privilege is torn away by postmodernists, science appears as a social force enmeshed in particular cultural and power struggles. The claim to truth, as Foucault has proposed, is inextricably an act of power—a will to form humanity.

This epistemic suspicion is at the core of postmodernism. Postmodernists challenge the charge of theory as a foundational discourse. The postmodern critique does not deny the possibility of success in the quest for foundations. I urge only that from the standpoint of the history of such foundational efforts, and from the vantage point of modern consciousness, which itself has generated this relentless eptstemic doubt, this project does not seem compelling or credible.

Aside from this epistemic doubt, there are practical and moral reasons to consider in assessing the value of the foundational project. Postmodernists view such discourses as exhibiting a bad faith: concealed in the will to truth is a will to power. To claim that there are universal and objective reasons to warrant a social discourse, to claim that a discourse speaks the language of truth, is to privilege that discourse, its carriers, and its social agenda. Insofar as we believe that social discourses are social practices which, like other social forces, shape social life and history, privileging a discourse as true authorizes its social values and agenda (Brown 1990).

Social discourses, especially the broad social narratives of development produced by sociological theorists, but also the specialized discourses produced by demographers, criminologists, organizational sociologists, and so on, shape the social world by creating normative frameworks of racial, gender, sexual, national, and other types of identity, social order, and institutional functioning that carry the intellectual and social authority of science. A discourse that bears the stamp of scientific knowledge gives its normative concepts of identity and order an authority while discrediting the social agendas produced by other (scientific and nonscientific) discourses. To claim to have discovered the true language of society delegitimates rival paradigms—now described as merely ideological or, at best, as precursors—and their social agendas and carriers. It entails a demand to marginalize or withdraw privilege and its rewards from these rivals. Indeed, to claim epistemic privilege for a social discourse is to demand social authority not only for its social agenda but also for its producers and carriers. To assert that a social discourse speaks a universally valid language of truth confers legitimacy on its social values and its carriers. In a word, the politics of epistemology is bound up with social struggles to shape history.

When one appeals solely to the truth of a discourse to authorize it intellectually and socially, one represses reflection on its practical-moral meaning and its social consequences. A discourse that justifies itself solely by epistemic appeals will not be compelled to defend its conceptual decisions on moral and political grounds. The practical and moral significance of the discourse will go unattended or else will be considered only in the most cursory way. On the other hand, if theorists—as postmodernists—believe that all appeals to universal standards or justificatory strategies are not ultimately compelling, they will be forced to offer "local" moral, social, and political reasons for their conceptual decisions. Disputes between rival theories or conceptual strategies would not concern epistemic first principles—e.g., individualism versus holism, materialism versus idealism, micro-versus macro-level analysis, instrumental versus normative concepts of action and order. Instead theorists would argue about the intellectual, social, moral, and political consequences of choosing one conceptual strategy or another.

A pragmatic turn has distinct advantages. It expands the number of parties who may participate more or less as equals in a debate about society. Where a discourse is redeemed ultimately by metatheoretical appeals, experts step forward as the authorities. This situation contributes to the enfeeblement of a vital public realm of moral and political debate because social questions are deemed the domain of experts. By contrast, when a discourse is judged by its practical consequences or its moral implications, more citizens are qualified to assess it by considering its social and moral implications. A pragmatic move, in principle, implies an active, politically engaged citizenry participating in a democratic public realm.

Postmodernism contests a representational concept of science whose legitimacy hinges on an increasingly cynical belief in science's enlightening and empowering role. This Enlightenment legitimation obscures the social entanglement of the disciplines and permits them to abandon moral responsibility for their own social efficacy. Postmodernism underscores the practical and moral character of science. It sees the disciplines as implicated in heterogeneous struggles around gender, race, sexuality, the body, and the mind, to shape humanity.

⑤ THE POSTMODERN HOPE: SOCIAL NARRATIVE WITH A MORAL INTENT

Foundational theorizing is by no means a product of the social scientific disciplines. The attempt to resolve conceptual disputes or to authorize a particular conceptual strategy by appealing to some presumably universal or objective justification has accompanied modern social thought. Yet the institutionalization of social science and the phenomenal growth of the disciplines in the twentieth century has contributed greatly to the rise of theory specialists whose expertise revolves around metatheoretical or foundational concerns. Although foundational discourses may play a beneficial role at certain sociohistorical junctures (e.g., during periods of epochal transition, such as the 18th century), my view is that today they contribute to the social and intellectual insularity and irrelevance of much sociological theory. Moreover, I have voiced an epistemological doubt about the likely success of the foundational project. This suspicion has been a systematic feature of modern Western social consciousness at least since Marx's time. Postmodernism evokes this suspicion as current.

From a postmodern perspective, justifications of conceptual strategies appear to be unable to avoid a local, ethnocentric character. This is not an argument denying the possibility of foundations; I offer no proof of the impossibility of achieving a grounded social discourse. My epistemic doubt is local, if you will. It stems from my reflection on the historical failure of foundational efforts; it reflects a sympathy for the relentless epistemic doubt generated by modernist social science itself. If a genius comes along tomorrow and proves to the satisfaction of the social scientific community that he or she has succeeded in providing foundations, I will relinquish my standpoint. Until then, however, I propose that we renounce the quest for foundations in favor of local rationales for our conceptual strategies. Instead of appealing to absolutist justifications, instead of constructing theoretical logics and epistemic casuistries to justify a conceptual strategy, to lift them out of contextual embeddedness and elevate them to the realm of universal truths, I propose that we be satisfied with local, pragmatic rationales for our conceptual approaches. Instead of asking what is the nature of reality or knowledge in the face of conflicting conceptual strategies—and therefore going metatheoretical—I suggest we evaluate conflicting perspectives by asking what are their intellectual, social, moral, and political consequences. Does a conceptual strategy promote precision or conceptual economy? Does it enhance empirical predictability? What social values or forms of life does it promote? Does it lead to relevant policy-related information? Postmodern justifications shift the debate from that of Truth and abstract rationality to that of social and intellectual consequences.

The quest for foundations has been connected intimately to the project of creating a general theory (Seidman and Wagner 1991). Many modern social theorists have sought to elaborate an overarching totalizing conceptual framework that would be true for all times and all places. The search, for the one right vocabulary or language that would mirror the social world, that would uncover the essential structures and dynamics or laws of society, has been integral to sociological theory. In *The German Ideology*, Marx and Engels believed that they had uncovered a universally valid language of history and society. In their view, the categories of labor, mode of production, class, and class conflict crystallized what they considered to be a general theory that captured the essential structure and dynamics of history. Durkheim proposed in *The Division of Labor in Society* and *In The Rules of the Sociological Method* the dual categories of collective representations and social morphology as the conceptual basis for a universal theory of society; Parsons wrote *The Structure of Social Action* and *The Social System* to reveal a universal set of premises and concepts that would unify and guide all social inquiry. This quest to discover the one true language of the social world, to uncover its laws, general structure, and universal logic, has been an abiding aim of sociological theory.

The quest for a totalizing general theory, in my view, is misguided. My reasoning parallels my reservations about foundationalism. General theories have not succeeded; their basic premises, concepts, and explanatory models, along with their metatheoretical rationales, consistently have been shown to be local, ethnocentric projections (Turner and Wardell 1986). The project of general theory has pushed theorists into the realm of metatheory as theorists attempt to specify an epistemic rationale to resolve conceptual or paradigm disputes; it has isolated theorists from vital ongoing research programs and empirical analyses; the quest for foundations and for a totalizing theory has marginalized theorists in regard to the major social events and public debates of the times. Moreover, when concepts are stretched to cover all times and places or to be socially inclusive, they become so contentless as to lose whatever explanatory value they have. These flat, contentless general categories seem inevitably to ignore or repress social differences (Nicholson 1991). For example, the categories of labor, mode of production, or class conflict may be useful in explaining nineteenth-century England, but are much less so, I think, in explaining nineteenth-century France or Germany or the United States and are virtually irrelevant for societies that are more kinship-centered or politically centered (e.g., Balbus 1982; Baudrillard 1975; Habermas 1977, 1984, 1987; Nicholson 1986; Rubin 1975).

If social theorists renounce the project of foundationalism and the quest for general theories, as I am recommending, what's left for us? Undoubtedly some theorists will want to argue that a more modest version of the project of general theory is still feasible, such as Merton's middle range theories or some variant, say, in the mold of Skocpol's *States and Social Revolution*. I won't dispute here the value of these alternatives, although I believe that they remain tied too closely to scientism and the modernist ideology of enlightenment and progress that have been suspect for decades. Instead I wish to propose that when theorists abandon the foundationalist project in the broad sense—elaborating general theories and principles of justification—what they have left is social theory as social narrative. When we strip away the foundationalist aspects of Marx's texts, what remain are stories of social development and crisis; when we purge Durkheim's *Division of Labor in Society* of its foundationalist claims, we have a tale of the development of Western modernity. The same applies to Parsons, Luhmann, Munch, or Habermas. I am not recommending that we simply return to the grand stories of social evolution from Condorcet to Habermas. If social theory is to return to its function as social narrative, I believe it must be a narrative of a different sort than those of the great modernists. […]

The postmodern social narrative I advocate is event-based and therefore careful about its temporal and spatial boundaries. By event-based, I mean that the primary reference points of postmodern narratives are major social conflicts or developments. As event-based narratives, postmodern social analyses also would be densely contextual. Social events always occur in a particular time and place, related to both contemporary and past developments in a specific social space.

The grand narratives of the great modernist social theorists responded to the major events of the day but typically disregarded their temporal and spatial settings. Instead of locating events in their specific sociohistorical setting, these grand narratives framed events as world historical and evolved stories of the course of Western, if not human, history. Instead of telling the story of capitalism or secularization in, say, England or Italy, they analyzed these events as part of a sketch of "Western" or human development. Thus, instead of analyzing the unique industrial development of England or Germany, which had "capitalistic" aspects, by being attentive to their dramatic differences and singular histories, Marx proposed a theory of capitalism that purported to uncover essential, uniform processes in all "capitalist" social formations. His "theory of capitalism" outlined a history of Western and ultimately human development that disregarded the specificity of particular "Western" and non-Western societies. To be sure, Marx counseled that the uniform operation of capitalism would vary in different societies even if the essential dynamics and direction of history were set by the "laws of capitalism." Marx assumed that the fact that different societies have divergent national traditions, geopolitical positions, and political, cultural, familial-kinship, gender, racial, and ethnic structures would not seriously challenge the utility of his model of capitalism as setting out the essential dynamics and direction of human history.

In my view, this was a serious mistake. Even if one takes Marx's model of capitalism to be of some utility for analyzing nineteenth-century dynamics of socioeconomic change, I believe that the immense sociohistorical differences among European and Anglo-American societies and between them and non-Western societies would affect seriously the form and functioning of industrializing dynamics. Individual societies evolve their own unique configurations and historical trajectories, which are best analyzed historically, not from the heights of general theory.

The Eurocentrism of these grand narratives has been exposed thoroughly (e.g., Baudrillard 1975). Human history in these modernist tales really meant Western history. Non-Western societies were relegated to a marginal position in past, present, and future history; their fate was presumed to be tied to that of Europe and the United States. The West, in these stories, was the principal agent of history; it showed the future to all of humanity. Behind this conceit was the arrogance of the Western theorists, with their claim that the Western breakthrough to "modernity" carried world historical significance. The great modernists claimed not only that Western modernity unleashed processes which would have world impact, but also that modernization contained universally valid forms of life (e.g., science, bureaucracy, socialism, organic solidarity, secularism). Not much effort is required to see that behind the aggrandizing intellectualism of the modernists were the expansionist politics of the age of colonialism.

These grand narratives seem to bear the mark of their own national origin. They contain an element of national chauvinism. Modernists projected their own nations' unique development and conflicts onto the globe as if their particular pattern were of world historical importance. These totalizing conceptual strategies that attempted to sketch a world historical story seem today extremely naive and misguided. The grand narratives of industrialization, modernization, secularization, democratization, these sweeping stories that presume to uncover a uniform social process in a multitude of different societies, these stories with their simplistic binary schemes (e.g., Tonnies's *Gemeinschaft* to *Gesellschaft*, Durkheim's mechanical to organic solidarity), which purport to relate a story of change over hundreds of years, should be abandoned. They repress important differences between societies; they perpetuate Western-world hegemonic aspirations and national chauvinistic wishes; they are, in short, little more than myths that aim to authorize certain social patterns.

Although I believe we should abandon the great modernist narratives, general stories are still needed. This is so because in all societies there occur certain events and developments that prompt highly charged social, moral, and political conflicts. The various parties to these conflicts frequently place them in broad conceptual or narrative frameworks. In order to imbue an event with national moral and political significance or to legitimate a specific social agenda, advocates elaborate social narratives that link the event to the larger history and fate of their society or humanity. This process is clear, for example, in the case of the AIDS epidemic: the spread of HIV in the United States occasioned social discourses that relate a fairly broad story of the failure of the "sexual revolution" or, indeed, the failure of a liberal, permissive society (Seidman 1988; Sontag 1988; Watney 1987). The construction of broad social narratives by theorists still has an important role.

These narratives offer alternative images of the past, present, and future; they can present critical alternatives to current dominant images; they can provide symbolic cultural resources on which groups can draw in order to redefine themselves, their social situation, and their possible future. [...]

Postmodern social narratives will depart from those of the great modernists in an additional way: such narratives abandon the centrality of the ideas of progress or decadence that have served as the unifying themes of modernist social thought. From *philosophes* like Condorcet or Turgot to Comte, Marx, Durkheim, and Parsons, these stories of social development are little more than variations on the motif of human advancement. They amount to millennial, salvationist tales. In reaction to the stories of the enlighteners, there appeared the great tales of lament or decadence by Rousseau, Bonald, Schiller, Weber, Simmel, Spengler, Adorno, and Horkheimer. Both the great modernist narratives of progress and the counterenlightenment motif of decadence are decidedly Eurocentric. In all cases the site of the fateful struggles of humanity is the West. Indeed, national histories are important in these grand narratives only insofar as they exhibit a pattern of progress or decadence. These stories typically disregard the enormous social complexities and heterogeneous struggles and strains within a specific society at a specific time. They have one story to tell, which they rehearse relentlessly on a national and world historical scale. They utterly fail to grasp the multisided, heterogeneous, morally ambiguous social currents and strains that make up the life of any society. In the end they amount to little more than rhetorics of national and Eurocentric chauvinism or rhetorics of world rejection.

* * * * *

Recognizing that all social narratives have a socially effective character, we would not try to purge them of this character but would try to acknowledge it and, indeed, to seize it as a fruitful source of an elaborated social reason. How so? Not, as I've said, by simply offering a general criticism or defense of social forms from the high ground of some abstract moral values or standpoint. And certainly not by trying to ground one's moral standpoint in an appeal to some objective universal element (e.g., nature, God, natural law). Rather, I have recommended a pragmatic, socially informed moral analysis in which the critic is compelled to defend social arrangements by analyzing their individual and social consequences in light of local traditions, values, and practices. The values of the community of which the critic is a part stands as the "ultimate" realm of moral appeal.

* * * * *

NOTES

1. Discontent about the state of sociological theory is becoming more and more evident. See, for example, Geertz (1983), Sica (1989), Skocpol (1986), and Turner and Wardell (1986).
2. For an argument exploring the institutional sources of intellectual distress among the disciplines, see Jacoby (1987).
3. For useful discussions of postmodernism, especially as it pertains to social theory, see Bauman (1988), Brown (1990), Kellner (1988), Kroker and Cook (1986), Lash (1985, 1988), Lemert (1991), Nicholson (1990), and Seidman and Wagner (1991).
4. This antimillennial theme is prominent in Baudrillard (1975, 1981), Foucault (1978, 1980), and Lyotard (1984).

REFERENCES

Andersen, Margaret. 1983. *Thinking about Women*. New York: Macmillan.

Balbus, Isaac. 1982. *Marxism and Domination*. Princeton: Princeton University Press.

Baudrillard, Jean. 1975. *The Mirror of Production*. St. Louis: Telos.

_____. 1981. *For a Critique of the Political Economy of the Sign*. St. Louis: Telos.

Bauman, Zygmunt. 1988. "Is There a Postmodern Sociology?" *Theory, Culture, and Society* 5: 217–38.

Brown, Richard. 1990. "Rhetoric, Textuality, and the Postmodern Turn." *Sociological Theory* 8 (Fall): 188–98.

Foucault, Michel. 1978. *The History of Sexuality: An Introduction*. New York: Pantheon.

_____. 1980. *Power/Knowledge*. New York: Pantheon.

Geertz, Clifford. 1983. *Local Knowledge*. New York: Basic Books.

Habermas, Jürgen. 1977. *Communication and the Evolution of Society*. Boston: Beacon.

_____. 1984. *The Theory of Communicative Action*, Vol. 1. Boston: Beacon.

_____. 1987. *The Theory of Communicative Action*, Vol. 2. Boston: Beacon.

Harding, Sandra. 1986. *The Science Question in Feminism*. Ithaca: Cornell University Press.

Harding, Sandra and Merrill Hintikka (eds.). 1983. *Discovering Reality*. London: D. Reidel.

Jacoby, Russell. 1987. *The Last Intellectuals*. New York: Basic Books.

Jagger, Alison and Susan Bordo (eds.). 1989. *Gender/Body/Knowledge*. New Brunswick: Rutgers University Press.

Keller, Evelyn Fox. 1985. *Science and Gender*. New Haven: Yale University Press.

Kellner, Douglas. 1988. "Postmodernism as Social Theory: Some Challenges and Problems." *Theory, Culture, and Society* 5: 2 39–69.

Kroker, Arthur and David Cook. 1986. *The Postmodern Scene*. New York: St. Martin's.

Lash, Scott. 1985. "Postmodernity and Desire." *Theory & Society* 14: 1–33.

_____. 1988. "Discourse or Figure? Postmodernism as a Regime of Signification." *Theory, Culture & Society* 5: 311–36.

Lemett, Charles. 1991. "Social Theory? Theoretical Play after Difference." Pp. 17–46 in *Postmodernism and Social Theory*, edited by Steven Seidman and David Wagner. Cambridge: Blackwell.

Lyotard, Jean-Francois. 1984. *The Postmodern Condition*. Minneapolis: University of Minnesota Press.

Millman, Marcia and Rosabeth Moss Kanter (eds.). 1975. *Another Voice*. New York: Anchor.

Nicholson, Linda. 1986. *Gender and History*. New York: Columbia University Press.

_____. (ed.) 1990. *Feminism/Postmodernism*. New York: Routledge.

_____. 1991. "On the Postmodern Barricades: Feminism, Politics and Theory." Pp. 82–100 in *Postmodernism & Social Theory*, edited by Steven Seidman and David Wagner. Cambridge: Blackwell.

Rorty, Richard. 1979. *Philosophy and the Mirror of Nature*. Princeton: Princeton University Press.

_____. 1982. *Consequences of Pragmatism*. Minneapolis: University of Minnesota Press.

_____. 1991. *Objectivity, Relativism, and Truth*. Cambridge: Cambridge University Press.

Rosaldo, Renato. 1989. *Culture and Truth*. Boston: Beacon.

Rubin, Gayle. 1975. "The Traffic in Women." Pp. 157–210 in *Towards an Anthropology of Women*, edited by Rayna Reiter. New York: Monthly Review.

Seidman, Steven. 1988. "Transfiguring Sexual Identity: AIDS & the Contemporary Construction of Homosexuality." *Social Text* 19/20 (Fall): 187–205.

_____. 1989. "The Tedium of General Theory." *Contemporary Sociology* 18.

_____. 1990. "Against Theory as a Foundationalist Discourse." *Perspectives* (Spring): 1–3.

_____. 1991a. "Theory as Social Narrative with a Moral Intent: A Postmodern Intervention." Pp. 47–81 in *Postmodernism & Social Theory*, edited by Steven Seidman and David Wagner. New York: Blackwell.

_____. 1991b. *Romantic Longings: Love in America, 1830–1980*. New York: Routledge.

Seidman, Steven and David Wagner (eds.). 1991. *Postmodernism & Social Theory*. New York: Blackwell.

Sica, Alan. 1989. "Social Theory's Constituents." *The American Sociologist* 20: 227–41.

Skocpol, Theda. 1986. "The Dead End of Metatheory." *Contemporary Sociology* 16: 10–12.

Smith, Dorothy. 1979. "A Sociology for Women." Pp. 133–87 in *The Prism of Sex*, edited by Julia Sherman and Evelyn Torton. Madison: University of Wisconsin Press.

_____. 1989. "Sociological Theory: Methods of Writing Patriarchy." Pp. 34–64 in *Feminism and Sociological Theory*, edited by Ruth Wallace. Newbury Park, CA: Sage.

Sontag, Susan. 1988. *AIDS and Its Metaphors*. New York: Farrar, Strauss, and Giroux.

Turner, Stephen and Mark Wardell, eds. 1986. *The Transition in Sociological Theory*. Boston: Allen & Unwin.

Vance, Carole (ed.). 1984. *Pleasure and Danger*. New York: Routledge.

Watney, Simon. 1987. *Policing Desire*. Minneapolis: University of Minnesota Press.

Westcott, Marcia. 1979. "Feminist Criticism of the Social Sciences." *Harvard Educational Review*, 49: 422–30.

CHAPTER 21

Call Yourself a Sociologist—
And You've Never Even Been
Arrested?!

MARILYN PORTER

* * * * *

🆖 THE RADICAL ROOTS OF SOCIOLOGY

Why do I feel so uneasy and yet so compelled to refer to Marx, Weber, and Durkheim and other early luminaries? It is only partly because I claim no expertise in this area. It is partly because I resist the notion that the classics/founders/canon have authority over how we think now. But I suspect that both my ignorance and my suspicion derive from the way in which our 19th and early-20th-century predecessors have been used by precisely the kind of sociology that I want to argue has worked against a radical development of the discipline, and against the principles that should inform that development. It is therefore salutary to do a little reclaiming of the history of radicalism in sociology. It is, of course, normal (or it was until a year or two ago) to treat Marx and his writings as the epitome of the radical sociologist at work, and as blueprints for revolution. The collapsing of these two categories caused certain difficulties. They would have caused more were it not for the fact that—in the United Kingdom, at least—Marxism and sociology were virtually coterminous for most of the late 1960s, 1970s, and early 1980s or, as Philip Abrams put it: "It would have been difficult to establish that British sociology was very much more than the academic wing of British Marxism" (Abrams, 1981:66). Despite the contradictions inherent in the use of Marx, the simple message absorbed in the 1960s was that sociology was radical because it was Marxist. But this begs the question of whether Marx was a radical, a word notoriously difficult to define. Its obvious botanical meaning tends to confuse—certainly if the metaphor is pushed too far. Raymond Williams, as so often, is provocative rather than prescriptive. However, in this case he is useful in uncovering a contradictory shift in interpretation, which parallels one I think I discern in sociology. In the early 19th century, "Radical is a word in very bad odour here being used to denote a set of blackguards," and "the term Radical, once employed as a name of low reproach, has found its way into high places, and is gone forth as the title of a class, who glory in their designation," but, as Williams notes, "the word then had a curious subsequent history, and was by the second half of the 19th century almost as respectable as liberal." In the 20th century the picture becomes more complicated, as instanced by phrases such as "Radical Right," but as Williams suggests, "Radical seemed to offer a way of avoiding dogmatic and factional associations while reasserting the need for vigorous and fundamental change" (Williams, 1976: 210).

I'm not sure if this allows us to conflate "radical" with "committed" or "passionate," but it surely permits some association and provides an a priori case for Marx to be both a "founding father" of sociology *and* a radical. It is probably easier to demonstrate that Marx was a radical than that he was a sociologist, rather than being simply "sociologically relevant," as Bottomore puts it (1956: 44).[1] To be brief and direct, I think that the evidence for Marx's radicalism lies less in his painstaking and illuminating analysis of capitalism and capitalist society than in the passion, anger, and frustration that inform his writing on, say, the conditions in the factories or the collapse of the Paris Commune in 1870. I opened my *Capital*, Vol. 1 more or less at random to find this:

> Three railway men are standing before a London coroner's jury—a guard, an engine-driver, a signalman. A tremendous railway accident has hurried hundreds of passengers into another world. The negligence of employees is the cause of the misfortune. They declare with one voice before the jury that ten or twelve years before, their labour only lasted eight hours a day. During the last five or six years it had been screwed up to 14, 18, and 20 hours, and under a specially severe pressure of holiday-makers, at times of excursion trains, it often lasted for 40 or 50 hours without a break. They were ordinary men, not Cyclops. At a certain point their labour-power failed. Torpor seized them. Their brains ceased to think, their eyes to see. The thoroughly "respectable" British jurymen answered by a verdict that sent them to the next assizes on a charge of manslaughter, and, in a gentle "rider" to their verdict, expressed the pious hope that the capitalistic magnates of the railways would, in future, be more extravagant in the purchase of a sufficient quantity of labour power, and more "abstemious," more "self-denying," more "thrifty," in the draining of paid labour-power ... the motley crowd of labourers of all callings, ages, sexes, that press on us more busily than the souls of the slain on Ulysses, on whom ... we see at a glance the mark of over-work ... (Marx, 1929: 238).[2]

I think we tend to forget how much of Marx's writing was informed by this kind of passion and commitment to vigorous and fundamental change. Notice that the aspect of Marx's work that I am highlighting here is "sociologically relevant," to be sure, but it also springs from, and leads back to, his *political* convictions. Marx clearly cared less about whether what he wrote was sociology than whether it would help him confront the evils of capitalism.

Marx's radical credentials are often seen in contra-distinction to those of Durkheim and Weber—not least by Marxist students of sociology. Yet careful and sympathetic reading has attempted to rescue both Weber and Durkheim (and others) from the designation "reactionary." In 1964, John Horton contributed an essay called "The dehumanization of anomie and alienation" (Horton, 1964), in which he argued that both concepts were equally rooted in a sense of moral outrage at aspects of the societies in which the authors lived: "The classical definitions have in common their condemnation of economic individualism and its rationalization in the middle class doctrines of economic and political liberalism"; he goes on to say that "a radical criticism cannot be derived from a description of the facts alone; it rests on standards which transcend them" (286). Horton then argues that one source of both Marx's and Durkheim's radicalism was the emerging discipline of sociology.

Horton's argument, then, ascribes a recognizable radicalism and social involvement to at least two of the early contenders for "founder" status, and also inextricably links such extra-academic concerns with the development of the discipline. But the clarity and passion of Marx's and Durkheim's original insights, which were embodied in the *related* concepts of alienation and anomie, were later transformed into pallid and innocuous shadows in the name of "objective" sociology. Horton focusses his especial ire on what he sees happening in his own country[3] when he states that "American sociologists have made a concerted effort to cleanse alienation and anomie of the messy conditions of their birth in the polemical writings of Marx and Durkheim."[4] And lest we should think that Horton's argument smacks of 1960s zeal, Stephen Crook (1991) situates his description of Durkheim as a "modernist radical" firmly within the project of establishing a "post-foundational radicalism."[5]

There is not space here to extend the argument to the more problematic case of Weber's radicalism (or that of other notable precursors). What is not in doubt is that Weber both chose the topics for his work and applied the results of his studies to the social and political situation he was involved in, and that his writing reveals a passionate commitment to seeing certain changes in German society.[6] My point is not to demonstrate that one can discover redeeming/radical features in the most unpromising material, but rather to point out that *even* the most respectable of the 19th-century founding fathers brought passion and commitment to their sociology— unashamedly—and that the source of their passion lay in their involvement in the worlds they lived in. This brings me to some documents of the 1960s that develop the argument one stage further.

▣ THE 1960S: WHY SOCIOLOGISTS?

While Becker and Horton were fighting their way out of the prevailing miasmic gloom of 1950s "value-free" sociology and the Procrustean bed of "objectivity," a much more wholesale attack on what sociology had become was brewing on the other side of the Atlantic. "Why sociologists?" asked the Nanterre students in 1969, led by Daniel Cohn-Bendit. It is a good question, and one that we might attend to today. The Hawthorne experiments in the United States crystallized their disgust: "Mayo initiated the age of large-scale collaboration of sociologists with all the powers of the bourgeois world .... Henceforth, the rise of sociology is increasingly tied to the social demand for rationalized practice in the service of bourgeois ends: money, profit, the maintenance of order" (Nanterre Students, 1969: 373). While they concede that in France, sociology professors were not quite as bad as those in other disciplines, they were more reprehensible because they knew where it was all leading—to "organisation, rationalization, production of human commodities made to order for the economic needs of organised capitalism" (376).

And one should not dismiss that outburst as a trivial relic of a hysterical yesteryear. The same little volume also contains Perry Anderson's famous essay "Components of a national culture" and one by Robin Blackburn called "A brief guide to Bourgeois ideology." In it, he conducts a sustained attack on sociology as it was then practised in British universities, caught unequivocally in a prevailing ideology that "consistently defends the existing social arrangements of the capitalist world." He goes on: "Critical concepts are either excluded or emasculated .... [It] is systematically pessimistic about the possibilities of attacking repression and inequality: on this basis it constructs theories of the family, of bureaucracy, of social revolution, of 'pluralist' democracy all of which imply that existing social institutions cannot be transcended." In short, "bourgeois social science tries to mystify social consciousness by imbuing it with fatalism and by blunting any critical impulse. Those aspects of this social science which are not directly aimed at conserving the social order are concerned with the techniques of running it" (Blackburn, 1969: 164). In the course of the next 50 pages (it is not a *very* brief guide) he demonstrates his case.

Given the torpor of British sociology in the late 1950s and early 1960s, it was not all that difficult.[7] But by the end of his essay, Blackburn has effectively substituted Marxism, pure and unadulterated, for what he clearly regards as a hopelessly contaminated sociology. Indeed, the takeover of sociology in Britain by a hegemonic Marxism was swift and effective. Abrams describes the intrusion as "remarkably rapid and comprehensive" and "given the already established effects of very rapid growth, profoundly disconcerting and distracting." Indeed, "the ambiguity of the relationship was such ... that by 1978 one could see Sociology as a profession entirely staffed by Marxists all devoted to proving that Sociology was a form of bourgeois ideology—an army consisting only of a fifth column, as it were" (Abrams, 1981: 65).

Whatever the other consequences, the swiftness of the conquest obscures something just as important. The writers I have just quoted represent a whole generation of radicals who argued that the addiction to objectivity and value-free sociology, the increasing conflation of intellectual and corporate agendas, the growth of the profession and the "professionalism" of sociology deprived the discipline of the passion, commitment, radicalism, and concern with social change that had marked at least some of its origins. That passion returned in the 1960s, but masked as the revolutionary programme of Marxism. It was no longer sociology that commanded allegiance, but the Marxist cuckoo in the nest. The Marxism that established itself in British universities rapidly denied its own passionate roots, becoming preoccupied with being a "science," with practising scientific methods of analysis, with ever more abstruse theorizing, and with a concomitant hard-eyed rejection of "bourgeois" or "infantile" concerns with anything other than the analysis of "objective class structures and relations and the over-riding goal of class struggle."[8] Certainly anything that smacked of emotion and caring was clearly a bourgeois deviation. It was at just this point that feminism first fell out with Marxism.

* * * * *

THE LIBERIAN FLAG STAGE IN SOCIOLOGY

We need now to return to the question of how and in what ways a form of radicalism is constitutive of the sociological enterprise, and whether the difficult decade of the 1980s has seen its decline. I have argued that a strand of passion and commitment informs early sociology on both sides of the Atlantic, but that this had wavered and dwindled to nothingness by the 1960s—precisely the time of radical upsurge in Western universities, but also the time when sociology in Canada came into existence. On both sides of the Atlantic, similar preoccupations were being expressed, albeit in different contexts. I came to sociology with a generation that felt that if we were going to enter sociology, then it was because it could be relevant to our concerns in the political and social world outside the University. In other words, we entered sociology already equipped with values, commitments, and passion and determined to integrate them with their intellectual practice. Sociology was *about* being able to do something worthwhile. In this it was unlike most, if not all, other disciplines.

In Canada, also, there was a covert case being made that sociology not only was different from other disciplines, but that it *should* be different. This approach is reflected in the three papers in *Fragile Truths: 25 Years of Sociology and Anthropology in Canada* (Carroll et al., 1992) by Ester Reiter, Pat and Hugh Armstrong, and Barb Neis—all of them, not coincidentally, Marxists, and all of them feminists. Neis describes 30 years of research by sociologists and anthropologists in Newfoundland on issues of significant and immediate concern to the province. Furthermore, there is little attempt, at least in the earlier work, to disguise the passionate involvement of the academics in the issues of the day (e.g., resistance to Smallwood's resettlement programme in the 1960s). More recently, such involvement only comes over clearly in the work of the "advocacy researchers," and this raises a point I will return to later. The Armstrongs' essay is a plea for just such committed work as I am describing, and points to the feminist work as a shining example—but warns of the dangers of incorporation. Again, I detect a shift between the period in which the Armstrongs came to intellectual maturity and the later period that clearly causes them concern. Ester Reiter's essay on academic work in and for the labour movement is actually called "The price of legitimacy," and carries a similar message. In all three cases, the authors have clearly been formed in the interventionist, radical mould, and are distressed by a falling-away from their earlier standards.

We have always been troubled by identity and boundaries in sociology. There have been many, largely futile, efforts to demonstrate how distinctive is sociology's approach, method, subject area, theories, or whatever, and many and violent have been the defences of what has been seen as "our" territory. Much of this has been, in my view, wrong-headed. I am supported in this view by John Urry. Urry avers that beyond the generally acknowledged ambiguous nature of sociology it is a parasitic discipline "since it has no essence, no essential unity" (Urry, 1981: 25). He argues the case in considerable detail, using the example of the state to show how much sociological analysis originates outside mainstream sociology. Such arguments are not new, but Urry goes on to argue that (1) sociology develops in part through *appropriating* theoretical and empirical work conducted in neighbouring disciplines and related social movements; (2) that it can never be understood in terms of a paradigm or even of a scientific community (Kuhn); and (3) that—paradoxically—its intellectual strength predominantly lies in its parasitism, its openness, and relative lack of authority and control. "Sociology's central concepts neither generate a discursive unity nor demarcate it in a strong sense from neighboring disciplines" (Urry, 1981: 26). I would argue that it is *this* characteristic (or lack of it) that made sociology a safe space for first Marxists and then feminists to enter and to develop and enrich both themselves and the discipline.

For all activists, Marxist, feminist, or other in Britain, it was thus *counter* sociology we were attracted to, the space left by the defeated discipline of conventional sociology. In the next few years it became, clearly, the place where one could import, develop, and practise one's politics. In Canada there was no defeated giant, but much of the rage around Canadianization depended on a similar agenda. It was assumed that one's research would be informed by and directed toward some political project (though there were some raised eyebrows when these turned out to be *feminist* projects). Furthermore—and I think that this is crucial—there was an assumed obligation that the "radical" faculty would at least facilitate and make space for new kinds of both radical activism and theoretical ideas. It thus became the most comfortable academic space for feminists to gather and argue our pitch. It is no accident that one of the first major theoretical feminist conferences in Britain was the British Sociology Association (BSA) Conference on Sexual Divisions and Society, organized by Sheila Allen and Diana Leonard in 1974. This was the heyday of the period when sociology became the academic equivalent of the Liberian flag—a registry of convenience that made few rules and under which one could get into all kinds of constructive mischief. It is certainly my experience that sociology *did* provide that kind of space to Marxists, feminists, and others, willingly or not, and it is Urry's contention that sociology was not the loser.

This kind of experience is relatively well documented (Oakley, 1981; Rowbotham, 1973; Barker and Allen, 1976). What is more questionable is whether the same process took place in Canada. The crucial difference seems to lie in the place of Marxism, which was clearly less dominant in Canadian sociology. My reading of the sociological work of that era seems to indicate that much the same kinds of people entered sociology with much the same agendas—but they did not come to cast them so strictly or universally in the Marxist framework. Canadian sociology may thus have escaped some of the problems that beset British sociology as a result of its wholesale subsumption under the Marxist rubric.

This is well illustrated when we look at the differences in the career of feminism in sociology in the U.K. and Canada. While feminist sociological work is just as rich in Britain as in Canada, its institutional presence both in professional associations and in the universities is much weaker. The BSA's retrospective volume *Practice and Progress: British Sociology 1950–1980* included a single paper by Meg Stacey on one aspect of feminist work; the parallel Canadian volume includes five, with several focussing on issues of institutionalized feminism; there is no British counterpart to the Social Science and Humanities Research Council's (SSHRC) strategic theme "Women and Social Change" ... and so on. This is the moment to examine the achievement of feminism in Canadian sociology, and its consequence for what kind of sociology we have.

I really do not need to belabour the point about the scale and significance of feminism's contribution to sociology in Canada. I need only cite, for example, the documentation contained in the special issue of *The Canadian Review of Sociology and Anthropology* (Vol. 25, No. 2), edited by Pat Armstrong and Roberta Hamilton (1988); Margrit Eichler's "And the work never ends: Feminist contributions" (1985) in the CRSA's special issue on anglophone sociology and her article in *Fragile Truths*, "The unfinished transformation: Women and feminist approaches in sociology and anthropology" (1992a). Together with their associated references and bibliographies, these three works alone document a large, growing, and significant body of feminist sociological work (sociologically feminist work, perhaps?).

The other half of feminists' contribution has been the roles they have played in the Canadian Sociology and Anthropology Association (CSAA) as teachers and researchers in university departments, and more generally in the discipline. This contribution began as a sheer fight for space, for example, as described by Eleanor Maticka-Tyndale and Janice Drakich (1992), but went on to mount profound challenges to the established methodological and epistemological paradigms, as illustrated by Dorothy Smith's two articles in *Fragile Truths*, one of which—"Whistling women" (Smith, 1992)—was the Hawthorne Lecture in the anniversary year.

It has, in fact, become a platitude to acknowledge feminism's place in, and contribution, to sociology. But I would go further and argue that it is feminism *rather* than Marxism that has become the dominant paradigm in sociology in Canada, though it has not dominated in the same kind of way.[9] The contrast with the situation in the U.S. is also instructive. As in Britain, there is no shortage of excellent feminist work, yet it seems neither to have permeated the institutional structures of sociology nor to have been recognized by the upper echelons of the discipline as being a distinguished and progressive force. It bears notice that Sally Hacker's work, for example, is much better known among feminists than among her fellow sociologists. Nor do I find it irrelevant that her obituary, written by her military historian husband, contains as good a definition of "radical" as I could hope to find: "Research without action—without potential to advance social justice—was not research she deemed worth doing. In her ceaseless effort to seek and destroy the roots of oppression, Sally was radical in the word's literal, and best, sense" (Hacker, 1989: 154).

There are clear similarities between the reasons that both Marxism and feminism found relatively safe havens in sociology and the consequences for the discipline. Both Marxism and feminism are profoundly doctrines of political involvement, and not only actually so, but as a moral imperative. As Robyn Rowland has put it: "If we lose touch or fail to be accountable to the basic concept of changing women's oppression, we betray that source of our strength" (Rowland, 1987: 519).[10] And while Eichler's article on the relationship between women's studies and the women's movement in Canada is entitled "Not always an easy alliance," the results of her study on women's studies professors shows a massive involvement in women's movement activism, and the connection between their academic and political work is seen as vital.

* * * * *

While such open political assaults are less common in Canada, the concomitant adulation of the "hard sciences" and business-oriented disciplines has much the same effect on our self-confidence and our budget.[11] To add insult to injury, we have also lost the intellectual high ground. Whatever the actual political success (or more often, the failure) of the Left on either side of the Atlantic, at least (and here I speak of both the hard and soft versions of Marxist sociology), we had the only political analysis of any substance. The Right concentrated on power and we analysed how they did it. But now, the Right has its own theorists and ideologues. In a variety of disciplines, writers such as Hajek, Milton Friedman, Scruton, and others not only have the ear of governments, but have also come to anew pre-eminence in intellectual circles. Sociology has been less affected by this tendency, although more extremely conservative ideas do seem to be gaining credibility. I wonder, sometimes, if it was entirely accidental that Freeman's article, which appeared in the *Canadian Journal of Physics*, was published as "Sociology."[12] Nor is it entirely paranoid to see the failed attempt to merge the SSHRC with the Canada Council as an act unfriendly to the social sciences, including sociology.

⑤ THE WRONG ANSWER: POSTMODERNISM

Faced with all this, what have we done? It may seem strange to turn at this point to talk about the development of postmodern theories. The picture is complex and it would be impossible to even sketch the debates surrounding postmodernism in this paper. In any case, relatively small numbers of sociologists have taken the total vows of postmodernism. Nevertheless, I think it is important that this new intellectual force, especially an interdisciplinary one, is attracting increasing allegiance. I do not think that postmodernism in any of its expressions will take over the responsibilities held by either Marxism or feminism. In fact, I think it likely that its influence will be in the opposite direction.

I have made the case against at least some aspects of postmodernism in other places (Porter, 1995). The crux of my concern here is that unlike Marxism or feminism, postmodernism is *not* rooted in involvement outside the academy and it is manifestly *not* informed by commitment or passion—far from it. Such Enlightenment concepts, and certainly the political projects to which they lead, are unrecognizable in postmodern discourse. They do not exclude such concerns explicitly so much as simply walk right through them as if they didn't exist—which, for them, they don't. I am, of course, sensible to the many arguments put forward for the emancipatory potential of postmodernism. In particular, I find the cavalier approach to boundaries and limitations of all kinds exciting. I find the dethroning of the white, middle-class, heterosexual hegemony of the Enlightenment, and the consequent validation of the diverse experience and accounts of other "voices," such as women's, to be exhilarating (Nicholson, 1990). But even at its liberatory best, postmodernism denies the connection with activity leading to social change. It thus denies the heart of sociology.

It is beyond my reach in this paper to demonstrate this point fully. The very diversity of postmodern writing would militate against it. Instead, I want to examine the work of one sociologist who has become increasingly enthralled with postmodern ideas. The trajectory taken by Zygmunt Bauman is exemplary.

In answer to the question—a good one—"Is there a postmodern sociology?" Bauman (1988) gives us an essay on the changing conditions of intellectuals in Western societies and their (collective) response to them. He ends with a cogent recognition of the "supreme position allotted to the *social relevance* [his emphasis] of social discourse" (231), and with some explicitly modernist recipes for sociological theorizing, providing only that we recognize that our premises are only assumptions and that we must do without the comfort of history being on our side. "Such a sociology," he says, "would not pretend that its preoccupations, however skillfully pursued, would offer it the centrality in the 'historical process' to which it once aspired" (236). In this essay, Bauman is already contracting the prospects for effective sociology and already referring to the "age of postmodernity" and "specifically postmodern phenomena." Both these tendencies gain greater salience in his subsequent essays. His essay "A sociological theory of postmodernity" (Bauman, 1991), for example, asserts that "the term postmodernity renders accurately the defining traits of the social condition that emerged throughout the affluent countries of Europe and of European descent in the course of the 20th century" (33).

After a complex argument, which I have discussed elsewhere, Bauman describes what happens to politics under "the postmodern condition":

> ... grievances which in the past would cumulate into a collective political process and address themselves to the state, stay difiuse and translate into self-reflexivity of the agents, stimulating further dissipation of policies and the autonomy of postmodern agencies (41).

He goes on to enumerate the typically postmodern forms of politics, presenting a depressing vision of political futility — tribal politics, entailing the creation of tribes as "imagined communities" to help agents in their self-constructing efforts; the politics of desire, aimed at establishing the relevance of a certain type of conduct for self-constitution; the politics of fear, which arises from "uncertainty as to the soundness of advice offered through the politics of desire" and leads to a series of panics about the risks of maiming or damaging the body (the real human body — that precious instrument of self-confirmation), through AIDS, environmental pollution, ozone depletion, etc., and finally the ever more despairing "politics of certainty — the desperate search for social confirmation of the agents choices in the face of endless pluralism and fluidity." In fact, the sum of postmodern forms of politics is reduced to the agents' increasingly desperate and hopeless search for "self-confirmation," for identity, and for some form of stability.

One of Bauman's most recent essays, "Survival as a social construct," carries tendencies that disconcert me even further. His very topic — the changing nature of death in Western society, and our less-than-competent ways of dealing with it — is hardly likely to tend toward an invigorating call to arms. Here is his description of the way with which we deal with death under postmodern conditions — which are now so taken for granted that Bauman no longer even encloses them in quotation marks. In fact it is no longer "us" that deals with it, but postmodernism itself:

> [A] new, specifically postmodern strategy of survival [...] attempts to resolve the haunting issue of survival by doing its best to take it off the life agenda. Instead of trying (in vain) to colonise the future, it dissolves it in the present [and] it rehearses mortality, so to speak, by practising it day by day. Daily life becomes a perpetual dress rehearsal for death. What is being rehearsed in the first place is the ephemerality and evanescence of things (Bauman, 1992: 29).

I always enjoy exposure to Bauman's learned and subtle thinking. What bothers me about his recent writing is that gradually he has become first convinced of the reality of the "postmodern condition"—a reality I would deny, except in special circumstances—and then absorbed into it. His work represents what happens to political energy, passion, and involvement in sociology under postmodernism. It simply drains away.

I must look for my champions elsewhere. Christopher Norris is not a sociologist; he is a professor of English, but he shares that characteristic I have come to see as defining a sociologist—of being unable to separate his intellectual work from the central concerns of his life—and a commitment to using his work to change the world for the better.

In one of his most recent books, Norris relates the present deplorable state of theory to the wholesale reactionary shift to the right in both political programmes and its related ideological retrenchment, which among other things is currently bent upon destroying the universities as centres of independent thought. "In short, we have reached a point where theory has effectively turned against itself, generating a form of extreme epistemological scepticism which reduces everything—philosophy, politics, criticism and theory" alike—[note the exclusion of sociology from this list] to a dead level of suasive or rhetorical effect ...." (Norris, 1990: 4).

Theory has collapsed into a

> retreat to a "post-modern" stance of all-out sceptical indifference, a stance that involves (as in Baudrillard's case) the willingness to jettison every last notion of truth, justice, or critical understanding. Another—exemplified by Lyotard—is the more refined version of postmodernist thinking that preserves those ideas but only on conditions of driving a wedge between judgements of a speculative (ethical) order and cognitive truth claims of whatever kind. Then again, there is the turn toward that thoroughly depoliticised version of deconstructionist thought that reduces all concepts to metaphors, all philosophy to and undifferentiated "kind of writing," and hence all history to a play of ungrounded figural representations. In each case—so I have argued—theory has served as an escape-route from pressing political questions and a pretext for avoiding any serious engagement with real-world historical events" (Norris, 1990: 44).[13]

My thoughts exactly. I rest my case.

⑤ SOCIOLOGY: LESS A DISCIPLINE THAN A METAPHOR

If postmodernism is not the answer, what is? The drift of my argument is surely clear. To help me bring it together I want to enlist another non-sociologist, Terry Eagleton, and to refer again to John Urry.

In his essay *The Significance of Theory* (Eagleton, 1990), which is a sustained defence of emancipatory theorists, including "socialists, feminists and others," Eagleton has this to say:

> Children make the best theorists, since they have not yet been educated into accepting our routine social practices as "natural," and so insist on posing to those practices the most embarrassingly general and fundamental questions, regarding them with a wondering estrangement which we adults have long forgotten. Since they do not yet grasp our social practices as inevitable, they do not see why we might not do things entirely differently. "Where does capitalism come from, mummy?" is thus the prototypical theoretical question, one which usually receives what one might term a Wittgensteinian reply: "This is just the way we do things, dear." It is those children who remain discontented with this shabby parental response who tend to grow up to be emancipatory theorists, unable to conquer their amazement at what everyone else seems to take for granted (Eagleton, 1990: 34).

This surely is a recipe for decent sociology, and so, buoyed up by amazement (which also carries etymological connotations of wonder, of creative dreaming), let me remind the reader of John Urry's description of sociology as a parasite, a condition he regards as virtuous and creative—but also vulnerable. Significantly, he refers to the need to defend a space for sociology—that is, for sociology with the characteristics of a parasite that he has described. Thus, he comes full circle with my own concerns in this paper.

Sociology, in my view, is less a discipline than a space. It is a space in which enormously exciting things can happen when new ideas meet, clash, and develop. It is manifestly obvious that this has happened with both Marxism and feminism. But it only happened because sociology, which means practising sociologists such as you and me, created, defended, and developed that space. We refused restraints, refused to stay politely within disciplinary boundaries. We have scrabbled in our neighbours' garbage and found pearls; we have challenged their icons and found them hollow.

Sociology has also been a redoubt, a vessel under the Liberian flag—a safe place from which our innovators and activists could go out and return to be fed, watered, and restored. And when they go out, we cannot, and should not, predetermine the direction in which they go. If they come back bloodied and muddy, having got into scrapes we don't want to know the details of, so be it. The drift of my argument, and of Urry's description of sociology as parasite, is that all bets are off. Some innovations will lead nowhere, but sociology will lose its best advantage if it predetermines the issue.

But to return to my original concern, and to shift to another geographical metaphor, sociology is a gateway or arch between the academy and the world outside. Of course, more than the other social sciences, we have made it our task to analyse it, but what I have been arguing goes much further than that, to assert the central, inescapable, essential dialectical relationship between sociology and the world—society, if you will—whereby the experience, involvement, and commitment become the stuff of theory and are then returned to the world with informed passion. We block up that arch at our peril, for it would deny us access to "that untravelled world, whose margin fades for ever and for ever when I move," as Tennyson put it. More than that, it would deny our students, our research, and our discipline the range and richness of a fully developed "radical sociology."

NOTES

1.   There has been too easy an assumption of Marx into the sociological canon. Bottomore, for example, seems uncertain. In his 1956 *Karl Marx: Selected Writings in Sociology and Social Philosophy,* he never actually refers to Marx as a sociologist, but as "sociologially relevant." In a 1960 article, he refers to the founders of sociology as Comte, Spencer, and Marx. However, in the entry under "Sociology" in *A Dictionary of Marxist Thought* (1983), he flatly denies it—distinguishing the Marxism of just after Marx's death as having had a "close but often antagonistic relationship (with) sociology" from the "founding fathers of sociology—Weber and Durkheim" (1983: 450).

2.   Here he is commenting on the findings of a House of Commons' Committee on the adulteration of food: "His report, together with the evidence given, roused not only the heart of the public but its stomach. Englishmen, always well up in the Bible, knew well enough that man, unless by elective grace a capitalist, or landlord or sinecurist, is commanded to eat his bread in the sweat of his brow, but they did not know that he had to eat daily in his bread a certain quantity of human perspiration mixed with the discharge of abscesses, cobwebs, dead black-beetles, and putrid German yeast ... and by the same Act of Parliament, work from 9 in the evening to 5 in the morning was forbidden for journeyman bakers under the age of 18. The last clause speaks volumes as to the over-work in this old-fashioned, homely line of business" (Marx, 1889: 233).

3.   Whether sociology in the USA *was* more conservative and incorporated into the capitalist agenda than elsewhere is another matter, and one which becomes relevant in the discussion of the effects of American influence on Canadian sociology. It was the received wisdom in Britain at the time, and it is no accident that Horton's article was published in the *British Journal of Sociology.*

4.   Interestingly, Horton also suggests that this subversion of Marx's and Durkheim's radical views was caused by the changing class positions of sociologists and the organization of the discipline.

5.   In this context it is interesting to watch the progression of writers such as Baehr, who move from a relatively traditional dependence on the authority structures of "founding fathers," classics, and the like, to a rejection of the idea of founders of discourses (allowing the foundations of *institutions* and of any notion of a secular canon and an exploration of the much less authoritarian concept of "classics." See Baehr and O'Brien, 1994).

6.   I am not doing justice to a wealth of material on this topic, but briefly see Weber (1948) and Tribe (1989), especially the translation of Weber's speech on Germany as an industrial state.

7.   Of course, there were notable exceptions on both sides of the Atlantic. The U.S. had its Chicago school, and their associates, as well as such luminaries as C. Wright Mills, who resisted the iron mantle of McCarthyism to produce work that is still respected today. In the U.K., one might point to the work of Tawney, Titmuss, and Worsley to give one courage. But I think it is incontrovertible that these few were bucking a prevailing stream of incorporation and all the ills ascribed to it by the critics of the 1960s.

8.   This is best documented in the increasing aridness of the Domestic Labour Debate (see, for example, Himmelweit and Mohun, 1977) or issues of *Capital and Class*. One of the most effective challenges was mounted by Sheila Rowbotham et al. in their appeal for a socialism "Beyond the Fragments" (Rowbotham et al., 1979).

9.   When I first arrived in 1980, it was noticeable that the circumstances under which it was O.K. to be a Marxist in Britain were the same ones as those under which it was not O.K. to confess to Marxism in Canada—but it *was* O.K. to be a feminist. It was also surprising how little translation it required to change identities.

10. See also Thorne (1978).

11. In my own university we have just had a classic case of this: despite pleas from the social sciences, including sociology, the *Report on the Merger of the Marine Institute with Memorial* provided only a minuscule place for any of the social science disciplines in the proposed new Faculty of Marine Science—and this in a province where sociology and anthropology have a long and distinguished record of studying the fishery and maritime communities as well as other social and economic factors concerning the marine environment (see Mercer, 1993).

12. The *CAUT Bulletin*, Vol. 40, No. 3 (March 1993) contains a useful summary account of this affair.

13. Norris is not as sweepingly dismissive of all postmodern tendencies—only what he calls the "postmodern-pragmatist" malaise. He engages with writers such as Derrida, de Man, Bhaskar, and Habermas critically and seriously as exponents of a "continuing critical impulse."

REFERENCES

Abrams, P. 1981. "The collapse of British sociology?" In *Practice and Progress: British Sociology, 1950–1980*. P. Abrams et al. (eds). London: Allen and Unwin, pp. 53–70.

Abrams, P., R. Deem, J. Finch, and P. Rock (eds.). 1981. *Practice and Progress: British Sociology, 1950–1980*. London: Allen and Unwin.

Armstrong, P. and H. Armstrong. 1992. "Better irreverent than irrelevant." In *Fragile Truths*. Ottawa: Carleton University Press, pp. 339–348.

Armstrong, P. and R. Hamilton (eds.). 1988. "25th Anniversary Issue: Feminist Scholarship." *The Canadian Review of Sociology and Anthropology*, Vol. 25, No. 2.

Backhouse, C. and D. Flaherty (eds.). 1992. *Challenging Times: The Women's Movement in Canada and the United States.* Montreal and Kingston: McGill-Queen's University Press.

Baehr, P. and M. O'Brien. 1994. "Founders, classics and the concept of a canon." *Current Sociology,* Vol. 42, No. 1, pp. 1–149.

Baehr, P. Forthcoming. "Mundane foundationalism and the limits of 'radical' social theory."

Barker, D.L. and S. Allen (eds.). 1976. *Sexual Divisions and Society: Process and Change.* London: Tavistock.

Barnes, J.A. et al. (eds.). 1981. *Professionalism in British Sociology.* N.p.

Bauman, Z. 1988. "Is there a postmodern Sociology?" *Theory, Culture and Society,* Vol. 5, Nos. 2–3, pp. 217–317.

Bauman, Z. 1991. "A sociological theory of postmodernity." *Thesis Eleven,* No. 29, pp 33–46.

Bauman, Z. 1992. "Survival as a social construct." *Theory, Culture and Society,* Vol. 9, pp. 1–36.

Blackburn, R. 1969. "A brief guide to bourgeois ideology" In *Student Power.* Harmondsworth: Penguin, pp. 163–213.

Bottomore, T. (ed.). 1956. *Karl Marx: Selected Writings in Sociology and Social Philosophy.* Harmondsworth: Penguin.

Bottomore, T. 1960. "The ideas of the founding fathers." *European Journal of Sociology,* Vol. 1, No. 1, pp. 33–49.

Bottomore, T. 1983. *A Dictionary of Marxist Thought.* Oxford: Basil Blackwell.

Breton, R. 1989. "Quebec sociology: Agendas from society or from sociologists?" *The Canadian Review of Sociology and Anthropology,* Vol. 26, No. 3, pp. 557–570.

Carroll, W., L. Christiansen-Ruffman, R. Curries, and D. Harrison (eds.). 1992. *Fragile Truths: 25 Years of Sociology and Anthropology in Canada.* Ottawa: Carleton University Press.

Cassin, A.M. and J.G. Morgan. 1992. "The professoriate and the market-driven university: Transforming the control of work in the academy." In *Fragile Truths.* Ottawa: Carleton University Press, pp. 247–260.

Cockburn, A. and R. Blackburn (eds.). 1969. *Student Power: Problems, Diagnosis, Action.* Middlesex: Penguin.

Crook, S. 1991. *Modernist Radicalism and Its Aftermath: Foundationalism and Anti-Foundationalism in Radical Social Theory.* London and New York: Routledge.

Eagleton, T. 1990. *The Significance of Theory.* Oxford and Cambridge, Mass.: Basil Blackwell.

Eichler, M. 1985. "And the work never ends: Feminist contributions." *The Canadian Review of Sociology and Anthropology,* Vol. 22, No. 5., pp. 619–644.

Eichler, M. 1992a. "The unfinished transformation: Women and feminist approaches in Sociology and Anthropology." In *Fragile Truths.* Ottawa: Carleton University Press, pp. 71–101.

Eichler, M. 1992b. "Not always an easy alliance: The relationship between Women's Studies and the Women's Movement in Canada." In *Challenging Times: The Women's Movement in Canada and the United States.* C. Backhouse and D. Flaherty (eds.). Montreal and Kingston: McGill-Queen's University Press, pp. 120–135.

Forcese, D. and S. Richer. 1975. *Issues in Canadian Society: An Introduction to Sociology.* Scarborough, Ont.: Prentice-Hall Canada.

Hacker, S. 1989. *Pleasure, Power and Technology.* Boston: Unwin Hyman.

Himmelweit, S. and S. Mohun. 1977. "Domestic labour and capital." *Cambridge Journal of Economics,* Vol. 1, No. 2, pp. 15–31.

Horton, J. 1964. "The dehumanization of anomie and alienation: A problem in the ideology of Sociology." *British Journal of Sociology,* Vol. 15, pp. 283–300.

Marx, K. 1929. *Capital, a Critique of Political Economy; the Crisis of Capitalist Production.* Tr. E. Paul and C. Paul. D. Torr (ed.). London: Allen and Unwin.

Maticka-Tyndale, E. and J. Drakich. 1992. "Striking a balance: Women organizing for change in the CSAA." In *Fragile Truths.* Ottawa: Carleton University Press, pp. 43–55.

Mercer, M. 1993. *A Sea Change: Development of the Marine Institute as a Faculty of Memorial University.* St. John's: Memorial University of Newfoundland.

Nanterre Students. 1969. "Why Sociologists?" In *Student Power: Problems, Diagnosis, Action.* A. Cockburn and R. Blackburn (eds.). Harmondsworth: Penguin, pp. 373–378.

Neis, B. 1992. "The uneasy marriage of academic and policy work: Reflections on the Newfoundland and Labrador experience." In *Fragile Truths.* Ottawa: Carleton University Press, pp. 321–337.

Newson, J. 1992. "The decline of faculty influence: Confronting the effects of the corporate agenda." In *Fragile Truths.* Ottawa: Carleton University Press, pp. 227–246.

Nicholson, L.J. 1990. *Feminism/Postmodernism.* London and New York: Routledge.

Norris, C. 1990. *What's Wrong with Postmodernism: Critical Theory and the Ends of Philosophy.* Baltimore: Johns Hopkins University Press.

Oakley, A. 1986. *Subject Women.* New York: Pantheon.

Porter, M. 1995. "Are some countries more postmodern than others?" *Journal of Canadian Studies,* Vol. 30, No. 2, forthcoming.

Reiter, E. 1992. "The price of legitimacy: Academics and the labour movement." In *Fragile Truths.* Ottawa: Carleton University Press, pp. 349–362.

Rowbotham, S. 1973. *Woman's Consciousness, Man's World.* Harmondsworth: Penguin.

Rowbotham, S., L. Segal, and H. Wainwright. 1979. *Beyond the Fragments: Feminism and the Making of Socialism.* London: Merlin.

Rowland, R. 1987. "What are the key questions which could be addressed in Women's Studies?" *Women's Studies International Forum,* Vol. 10, No. 5, pp. 519–524.

Smith, D. 1987. *The Everyday World as Problematic: A Feminist Sociology.* Boston: Northeastern University Press

Smith, D. 1992. "Whistling women: Reflections on rage and rationality." In *Fragile Truths.* Ottawa: Carleton University Press, pp. 207–226.

Stacey, M. 1981. "The two Adams: Sexual divisions revisited." In *Practice and Progress.* London: Allen and Unwin, pp. 172–190.

Thorne, B. 1978. "Contradictions and a glimpse of Utopia: Daily life in a university women's studies program." *Women's Studies International Quarterly,* Vol. 1, No. 2, pp. 201–206.

Tremblay, M.-A. (ed.). 1983. *Conscience et enquête: l'ethnologie des réalités canadiennes.* Ottawa: Musées nationaux du Canada.

Tribe, K. 1989. *Governing Economy: The Reformation of German Economic Discourse, 1750–1840.* Cambridge and New York: Cambridge University Press.

Urry, J. 1981. "Sociology as a parasite: Some vices and virtues." In *Practice and Progress.* London: Allen and Unwin, pp. 25–38.

Williams, R. 1976. *Keywords: A Vocabulary of Culture and Society.* London: Croom Helm.

CHAPTER 22

Foreword: On Being Light and Liquid

Zygmunt Bauman

Interruption, incoherence, surprise are the ordinary conditions of our life. They have even become real needs for many people, whose minds are no longer fed ... by anything but sudden changes and constantly renewed stimuli .... We can no longer bear anything that lasts. We no longer know how to make boredom bear fruit.

So the whole question comes down to this: can the human mind master what the human mind has made?

— *Paul Valéry*

"Fluidity" is the quality of liquids and gases. What distinguishes both of them from solids, as the *Encyclopaedia Britannica* authoritatively informs us, is that they "cannot sustain a tangential, or shearing, force when at rest" and so undergo "a continuous change in shape when subjected to such a stress."

This continuous and irrecoverable change of position of one part of the material relative to another part when under shear stress constitutes flow, a characteristic property of fluids. In contrast, the shearing forces within a solid, held in a twisted or flexed position, are maintained, the solid undergoes no flow and can spring back to its original shape.

Liquids, one variety of fluids, owe these remarkable qualities to the fact that their "molecules are preserved in an orderly array over only a few molecular diameters"; while "the wide variety of behaviour exhibited by solids is a direct result of the type of bonding that holds the atoms of the solid together and of the structural arrangements of the atoms." "Bonding," in turn, is a term that signifies the stability of solids—the resistance they put up "against separation of the atoms."

So much for the *Encyclopaedia Britannica*—in what reads like a bid to deploy "fluidity" as the leading metaphor for the present stage of the modern era.

What all these features of fluids amount to, in simple language, is that liquids, unlike solids, cannot easily hold their shape. Fluids, so to speak, neither fix space nor bind time. While solids have clear spatial dimensions but neutralize the impact, and thus downgrade the significance, of time (effectively resist its flow or render it irrelevant), fluids do not keep to any shape for long and are constantly ready (and prone) to change it; and so for them it is the flow of time that counts, more than the space they happen to occupy: that space, after all, they fill but "for a moment." In a sense, solids cancel time; for liquids, on the contrary, it is mostly time that matters. When describing solids, one may ignore time altogether; in describing fluids, to leave time out of account would be a grievous mistake. Descriptions of fluids are all snapshots, and they need a date at the bottom of the picture.

Fluids travel easily. They "flow," "spill," "run out," "splash," "pour over," "leak," "flood," "spray," "drip," "seep," "ooze"; unlike solids, they are not easily stopped—they pass around some obstacles, dissolve some others, and bore or soak their way through others still. From the meeting with solids they emerge unscathed, while the solids they have met, if they stay solid, are changed—get moist or drenched. The extraordinary mobility of fluids is what associates them with the idea of "lightness." There are liquids which, cubic inch for cubic inch, are heavier than many solids, but we are inclined nonetheless to visualize them all as lighter, less "weighty" than everything solid. We associate "lightness" or "weightlessness" with mobility and inconstancy: we know from practice that the lighter we travel, the easier and faster we move.

These are reasons to consider "fluidity" or "liquidity" as fitting metaphors when we wish to grasp the nature of the present, in many ways *novel*, phase in the history of modernity.

I readily agree that such a proposition may give a pause to anyone at home in the "modernity discourse" and familiar with the vocabulary commonly used to narrate modern history. Was not modernity a process of "liquefaction" from the start? Was not "melting the solids" its major pastime and prime accomplishment all along? In other words, has modernity not been "fluid" since its inception?

These and similar objections are well justified, and will seem more so once we recall that the famous phrase "melting the solids," when coined a century and a half ago by the authors of *The Communist Manifesto*, referred to the treatment which the self-confident and exuberant modern spirit awarded the society it found much too stagnant for its taste and much too resistant to shift and mould for its ambitions—since it was frozen in its habitual ways. If the "spirit" was "modern," it was so indeed in so far as it was determined that reality should be emancipated from the "dead hand" of its own history—and this could only be done by melting the solids (that is, by definition, dissolving whatever persists over time and is negligent of its passage or immune to its flow). That intention called in turn for the "profaning of the sacred": for disavowing and dethroning the past, and first and foremost "tradition"—to wit, the sediment and residue of the past in the present; it thereby called for the smashing of the protective armour forged of the beliefs and loyalties which allowed the solids to resist the "liquefaction."

Let us remember, however, that all this was to be done not in order to do away with the solids once and for all and make the brave new world free of them for ever, but to clear the site for *new and improved solids*; to replace the inherited set of deficient and defective solids with another set, which was much improved and preferably perfect, and for that reason no longer alterable. When reading de Tocqueville's *Ancien Régime*, one might wonder in addition to what extent the "found solids" were resented, condemned, and earmarked for liquefaction for the reason that they were already rusty, mushy, coming apart at the seams, and altogether unreliable. Modern times found the pre-modern solids in a fairly advanced state of disintegration; and one of the most powerful motives behind the urge to melt them was the wish to discover or invent solids of—for a change—*lasting* solidity, a solidity which one could trust and rely upon and which would make the world predictable and therefore manageable.

The first solids to be melted and the first sacreds to be profaned were traditional loyalties, customary rights, and obligations which bound hands and feet, hindered moves, and cramped the enterprise. To set earnestly about the task of building a new (truly solid!) order, it was necessary to get rid of the ballast with which the old order burdened the builders. "Melting the solids" meant first and foremost shedding the "irrelevant" obligations standing in the way of rational calculation of effects; as Max Weber put it, liberating business enterprise from the shackles of the family-household duties and from the dense tissue of ethical obligations; or, as Thomas Carlyle would have it, leaving solely the "cash nexus" of the many bonds underlying human mutuality and mutual responsibilities. By the same token, that kind of "melting the solids" left the whole complex network of social relations unstuck—bare, unprotected, unarmed, and exposed, impotent to resist the business-inspired rules of action and business-shaped criteria of rationality, let alone to compete with them effectively.

That fateful departure laid the field open to the invasion and domination of (as Weber put it) instrumental rationality, or (as Karl Marx articulated it) the determining role of economy: now the "basis" of social life gave all life's other realms the status of "superstructure"—to wit, an artefact of the "basis" whose sole function was to service its smooth and continuing operation. The melting of solids led to the progressive untying of economy from its traditional political, ethical, and cultural entanglements. It sedimented a new order, defined primarily in economic terms. That new order was to be more "solid" than the orders it replaced, because—unlike them—it was immune to the challenge from non-economic action. Most political or moral levers capable of shifting or reforming the new order have been broken or rendered too short, weak, or otherwise inadequate for the task. Not that the economic order, once entrenched, will have colonized, re-educated, and converted to its ways the rest of social life; that order came to dominate the totality of human life because whatever else might have happened in that life has been rendered irrelevant and ineffective as far as the relentless and continuous reproduction of that order was concerned.

That stage in modernity's career has been well described by Claus Offe (in "The Utopia of the Zero Option," first published in 1987 in *Praxis International*): "complex" societies "have become rigid to such an extent that the very attempt to reflect normatively upon or renew their 'order,' that is, the nature of the coordination of the processes which take place in them, is virtually precluded by dint of their practical futility and thus their essential inadequacy." However free and volatile the "subsystems" of that order may be singly or severally, the way in which they are intertwined is "rigid, fatal, and sealed off from any freedom of choice." The overall order of things is not open to options; it is far from clear what such options could be, and even less clear how an ostensibly viable option could be made real in the unlikely case of social life being able to conceive it and gestate. Between the overall order and every one of the agencies, vehicles, and stratagems of purposeful action there is a cleavage—a perpetually widening gap with no bridge in sight.

Contrary to most dystopian scenarios, this effect has not been achieved through dictatorial rule, subordination, oppression, or enslavement; nor through the "colonization" of the private sphere by the "system." Quite the opposite: the present-day situation emerged out of the radical melting of the fetters and manacles rightly or wrongly suspected of limiting the individual freedom to choose and to act. *Rigidity of order is the artefact and sediment of the human agents' freedom.* That rigidity is the overall product of "releasing the brakes": of deregulation, liberalization, "flexibilization," increased fluidity, unbridling the financial, real estate and labour markets, easing the tax burden, etc. (as Offe pointed out in "Binding, Shackles, Brakes," first published in 1987); or (to quote from Richard Sennett's *Flesh and Stone*) of the techniques of "speed, escape, passivity"—in other words, techniques which allow the system and free agents to remain radically disengaged, to by-pass each other instead of meeting. If the time of systemic revolutions has passed, it is because there are no buildings where the control desks of the system are lodged and which could be stormed and captured by the revolutionaries; and also because it is excruciatingly difficult, nay impossible, to imagine what the victors, once inside the buildings (if they found them first), could do to turn the tables and put paid to the misery that prompted them to rebel. One should be hardly taken aback or puzzled by the evident shortage of would-be revolutionaries: of the kind of people who articulate the desire to change their individual plights as a project of changing the order of society.

The task of constructing a new and better order to replace the old and defective one is not presently on the agenda—at least not on the agenda of that realm where political action is supposed to reside. The "melting of solids," the permanent feature of modernity, has therefore acquired a new meaning, and above all has been redirected to a new target—one of the paramount effects of that redirection being the dissolution of forces which could keep the question of order and system on the political agenda. The solids whose turn has come to be thrown into the melting pot and which are in the process of being melted at the present time, the time of fluid modernity, are the bonds which interlock individual choices in collective projects and actions—the patterns of communication and co-ordination between individually conducted life policies on the one hand and political actions of human collectivities on the other.

* * * * *

What is happening at present is, so to speak, a redistribution and reallocation of modernity's "melting powers." They affected at first the extant institutions, the frames that circumscribed the realms of possible action-choices, like hereditary estates with their no-appeal-allowed allocation-by-ascription. Configurations, constellations, patterns of dependency, and interaction were all thrown into the melting pot to be subsequently recast and refashioned; this was the "breaking the mould" phase in the history of the inherently transgressive, boundary-breaking, all-eroding modernity. As for the individuals, however—they could be excused for failing to notice; they came to be confronted by patterns and figurations which, albeit "new and improved," were as stiff and indomitable as ever.

Indeed, no mould was broken without being replaced with another; people were let out from their old cages only to be admonished and censured in case they failed to relocate themselves, through their own, dedicated and continuous, truly life-long efforts, in the ready-made niches of the new order: in the *classes*, the frames which (as uncompromisingly as the already dissolved *estates*) encapsulated the totality of life conditions and life prospects and determined the range of realistic life projects and life strategies. The task confronting free individuals was to use their new freedom to find the appropriate niche and to settle there through conformity: by faithfully following the rules and modes of conduct identified as right and proper for the location.

It is such patterns, codes, and rules to which one could conform, which one could select as stable orientation points and by which one could subsequently let oneself be guided, that are nowadays in increasingly short supply. It does not mean that our contemporaries are guided solely by their own imagination and resolve and are free to construct their mode of life from scratch and at will, or that they are no longer dependent on society for the building materials and design blueprints. But it does mean that we are presently moving from the era of pre-allocated "reference groups" into the epoch of "universal comparison," in which the destination of individual self-constructing labours is endemically and incurably underdetermined, is not given in advance, and tends to undergo numerous and profound changes before such labours reach their only genuine end: that is, the end of the individual's life.

These days patterns and configurations are no longer "given," let alone "self-evident"; there are just too many of them, clashing with one another and contradicting one another's commandments, so that each one has been stripped of a good deal of compelling, coercively constraining powers. And they have changed their nature and have been accordingly reclassified: as items in the inventory of individual tasks. Rather than preceding life-politics and framing its future course, they are to follow it (follow *from* it), to be shaped and reshaped by its twists and turns. The liquidizing powers have moved from the "system" to "society," from "politics" to "life-policies" —or have descended from the "macro" to the "micro" level of social cohabitation.

Ours is, as a result, an individualized, privatized version of modernity, with the burden of pattern-weaving and the responsibility for failure falling primarily on the individual's shoulders. It is the patterns of dependency and interaction whose turn to be liquefied has now come. They are now malleable to an extent unexperienced by, and unimaginable for, past generations; but like all fluids they do not keep their shape for long. Shaping them is easier than keeping them in shape. Solids are cast once and for all. Keeping fluids in shape requires a lot of attention, constant vigilance, and perpetual effort—and even then the success of the effort is anything but a foregone conclusion.

It would be imprudent to deny, or even to play down, the profound change which the advent of "fluid modernity" has brought to the human condition. The remoteness and unreachability of systemic structure, coupled with the unstructured, fluid state of the immediate setting of life-politics, change that condition in a radical way and call for a rethinking of old concepts that used to frame its narratives. Like zombies, such concepts are today simultaneously dead and alive. The practical question is whether their resurrection, albeit in a new shape or incarnation, is feasible; or—if it is not—how to arrange for their decent and effective burial.

* * * * *

Modernity means many things, and its arrival and progress can be traced using many and different markers. One feature of modern life and its modern setting stands out, however, as perhaps that "difference which make[s] the difference"; as the crucial attribute from which all other characteristics follow. That attribute is the changing relationship between space and time.

Modernity starts when space and time are separated from living practice and from each other and so become ready to be theorized as distinct and mutually independent categories of strategy and action, when they cease to be, as they used to be in long pre-modern centuries, the intertwined and so barely distinguishable aspects of living experience, locked in a stable and apparently invulnerable one-to-one correspondence. In modernity, time has history, it has history because of the perpetually expanding "carrying capacity" of time—the lengthening of the stretches of space which units of time allow to "pass," "cross," "cover"—or *conquer*. Time acquires history once the speed of movement through space (unlike the eminently inflexible space, which cannot be stretched and would not shrink) becomes a matter of human ingenuity, imagination, and resourcefulness.

The very idea of speed (even more conspicuously, that of acceleration), when referring to the relationship between time and space, *assumes* its variability, and it would hardly have any meaning at all were not that relation truly changeable, were it an attribute of inhuman and pre-human reality rather than a matter of human inventiveness and resolve, and were it not reaching far beyond the narrow range of variations to which the natural tools of mobility—human or equine legs—used to confine the movements of pre-modern bodies. Once the distance passed in a unit of time came to be dependent on technology, on artificial means of transportation, all extant, inherited limits to the speed of movement could be in principle transgressed. Only the sky (or, as it transpired later, the speed of light) was now the limit, and modernity was one continuous, unstoppable, and fast accelerating effort to reach it.

Thanks to its newly acquired flexibility and expansiveness, modern time has become, first and foremost, the weapon in the conquest of space. In the modern struggle between time and space, space was the solid and stolid, unwieldy and inert side, capable of waging only a defensive, trench war—being an obstacle to the resilient advances of time. Time was the active and dynamic side in the battle, the side always on the offensive: the invading, conquering, and colonizing force. Velocity of movement and access to faster means of mobility steadily rose in modern times to the position of the principal tool of power and domination.

Michel Foucault used Jeremy Bentham's design of Panopticon as the archmetaphor of modern power. In Panopticon, the inmates were tied to the place and barred from all movement, confined within thick, dense, and closely guarded walls and fixed to their beds, cells, or work-benches. They could not move because they were under watch; they had to stick to their appointed places at all times because they did not know, and had no way of knowing, where at the moment their watchers—free to move at will—were. The surveillants' facility and expediency of movement was the warrant of their domination; the inmates' "fixedness to the place" was the most secure and the hardest to break or loose of the manifold bonds of their subordination. Mastery over time was the secret of the managers' power—and immobilizing their subordinates in space through denying them the right to move and through the routinization of the time-rhythm they had to obey was the principal strategy in their exercise of power. The pyramid of power was built out of velocity, access to the means of transportation, and the resulting freedom of movement.

Panopticon was a model of mutual engagement and confrontation between the two sides of the power relationship. The managers' strategies of guarding their own volatility and routinizing the flow of time of their subordinates merged into one. But there was tension between the two tasks. The second task put constraints on the first—it tied the "routinizers" to the place within which the objects of time routinization had been confined. The routinizers were not truly and fully free to move: the option of "absentee landlords" was, practically, out of the question.

Panopticon is burdened with other handicaps as well. It is an expensive strategy: conquering space and holding to it as well as keeping its residents in the surveilled place spawned a wide range of costly and cumbersome administrative tasks. There are buildings to erect and maintain in good shape, professional surveillants to hire and pay, the survival and working capacity of the inmates to be attended to and provided for. Finally, administration means, willy-nilly, taking responsibility for the overall well-being of the place, even if only in the name of well-understood self-interest and responsibility again means being bound to the place. It requires presence, and engagement, at least in the form of a perpetual confrontation and tug-of-war.

What prompts so many commentators to speak of the "end of history," of post-modernity, "second modernity," and "surmodernity," or otherwise to articulate the intuition of a radical change in the arrangement of human cohabitation and in social conditions under which life-politics is nowadays conducted, is the fact that the long effort to accelerate the speed of movement has presently reached its "natural limit." Power can move with the speed of the electronic signal—and so the time required for the movement of its essential ingredients has been reduced to instantaneity. For all practical purposes, power has become truly *exterritorial*, no longer bound, not even slowed down, by the resistance of space (the advent of cellular telephones may well serve as a symbolic "last blow" delivered to the dependency on space: even the access to a telephone socket is unnecessary for a command to be given and seen through to its effect. It does not matter any more where the giver of the command is—the difference between "close by" and "far away," or for that matter between the wilderness and the civilized, orderly space, has been all but cancelled.) This gives the power-holders a truly unprecedented opportunity: the awkward and irritating aspects of the panoptical technique of power may be disposed of. Whatever else the present stage in the history of modernity is, it is also, perhaps above all, *post-Panoptical*. What mattered in Panopticon was that the people in charge were assumed always to "be there," nearby, in the controlling tower. What matters in post-Panoptical power-relations is that the people operating the levers of power on which the fate of the less volatile partners in the relationship depends can at any moment escape beyond reach into sheer inaccessibility.

The end of Panopticon augurs *the end of the era of mutual engagement*: between the supervisors and the supervised, capital and labour, leaders and their followers, armies at war. The prime technique of power is now escape, slippage, elision, and avoidance, the effective rejection of any territorial confinement with its cumbersome corollaries of order-building, order-maintenance, and the responsibility for the consequences of it all as well as of the necessity to bear their costs.

* * * * *

Throughout the solid stage of the modem era, nomadic habits remained out of favour. Citizenship went hand in hand with settlement, and the absence of "fixed address" and "statelessness" meant exclusion from the law-abiding and law-protected community and more often than not brought upon the culprits legal discrimination, if not active prosecution. While this still applies to the homeless and shifty "underclass," which is subject to the old techniques of panoptical control (techniques largely abandoned as the prime vehicle of integrating and disciplining the bulk of the population), the era of unconditional superiority of sedentarism over nomadism and the domination of the settled over the mobile is on the whole grinding fast to a halt. We are witnessing the revenge of nomadism over the principle of territoriality and settlement. In the fluid stage of modernity, the settled majority is ruled by the nomadic and exterritorial elite. Keeping the roads free for nomadic traffic and phasing out the remaining check-points has now become the meta-purpose of politics, and also of wars, which, as Clausewitz originally declared, are but "extension of politics by other means."

The contemporary global elite is shaped after the pattern of the old-style "absentee landlords." It can rule without burdening itself with the chores of administration, management, welfare concerns, or, for that matter, with the mission of "bringing light," "reforming the ways," morally uplifting, "civilizing," and cultural crusades. Active engagement in the life of subordinate populations is no longer needed (on the contrary, it is actively avoided as unnecessarily costly and ineffective)—and so the "bigger" is not just not "better" any more, but devoid of rational sense. It is now the smaller, the lighter, the more portable that signifies improvement and "progress." Travelling light, rather than holding tightly to things deemed attractive for their reliability and solidity—that is, for their heavy weight, substantiality, and unyielding power of resistance—is now the asset of power.

Holding to the ground is not that important if the ground can be reached and abandoned at whim in a short time or in no time. On the other hand, holding too fast, burdening one's bond with mutually binding commitments, may prove positively harmful and the new chances crop up elsewhere. Rockefeller might have wished to make his factories, railroads, and oilrigs big and bulky and own them for a long, long time to come (for eternity, if one measures time by the duration of human or human family life). Bill Gates, however, feels no regret when parting with possessions in which he took pride yesterday; it is the mind-boggling speed of circulation, of recycling, ageing, dumping, and replacement which brings profit today—not the durability and lasting reliability of the product. In a remarkable reversal of the millennia-long tradition, it is the high and mighty of the day who resent and shun the durable and cherish the transient, while it is those at the bottom of the heap who—against all odds—desperately struggle to force their flimsy and paltry, transient possessions to last longer and render durable service. The two meet nowadays mostly on opposite sides of the jumbo-sales or used-car auction counters.

The disintegration of the social network, the falling apart of effective agencies of collective action is often noted with a good deal of anxiety and bewailed as the unanticipated "side effect" of the new lightness and fluidity of the increasingly mobile, slippery, shifty, evasive, and fugitive power. But social disintegration is as much a condition as it is the outcome of the new technique of power, using disengagement and the art of escape as its major tools. For power to be free to flow, the world must be free of fences, barriers, fortified borders, and checkpoints. Any dense and tight network of social bonds, and particularly a territorially rooted tight network, is an obstacle to be cleared out of the way. Global powers are bent on dismantling such networks for the sake of their continuous and growing fluidity, that principal source of their strength and the warrant of their invincibility. And it is the falling apart, the friability, the brittleness, the transcience, the until-further-noticeness of human bonds and networks which allow these powers to do their job in the first place.

Were the intertwined trends to develop unabated, men and women would be reshaped after the pattern of the electronic mole, that proud invention of the pioneering years of cybernetics immediately acclaimed as the harbinger of times to come: a plug on castors, scuffling around in a desperate search for electrical sockets to plug into. But in the coming age augured by cellular telephones, sockets are likely to be declared obsolete and in bad taste as well as offered in ever shrinking quantity and ever shakier quality. At the moment, many electric power suppliers extol the advantages of plugging into their respective networks and vie for the favours of the socket-seekers. But in the long run (whatever "the long run" means in the era of instantaneity) sockets are likely to be ousted and supplanted by disposable batteries individually bought in the shops and on offer in every airport kiosk and every service station along the motorway and country road.

This seems to be a dystopia made to the measure of liquid modernity—one fit to replace the fears recorded in Orwellian and Huxleyan-style nightmares.

June 1999

CHAPTER 23

[Extracts from] *The Spirit of Terrorism and Requiem for the Twin Towers*

JEAN BEAUDRILLARD

When it comes to world events, we had seen quite a few. From the death of Diana to the World Cup. And violent, real events, from wars right through to genocides. Yet, when it comes to symbolic events on a world scale—that is to say not just events that gain worldwide coverage, but events that represent a setback for globalization itself—we had had none. Throughout the stagnation of the 1990s, events were "on strike" (as the Argentinian writer Macedonio Fernandez put it). Well, the strike is over now. Events are not on strike any more. With the attacks on the World Trade Center in New York, we might even be said to have before us the absolute event, the "mother" of all events, the pure event uniting within itself all the events that have never taken place.

The whole play of history and power is disrupted by this event, but so, too, are the conditions of analysis. You have to take your time. While events were stagnating, you had to anticipate and move more quickly than they did. But when they speed up this much, you have to move more slowly—though without allowing yourself to be buried beneath a welter of words, or the gathering clouds of war, and preserving intact the unforgettable incandescence of the images.

All that has been said and written is evidence of a gigantic abreaction to the event itself, and the fascination it exerts. The moral condemnation and the holy alliance against terrorism are on the same scale as the prodigious jubilation at seeing this global superpower destroyed—better, at seeing it, in a sense, destroying itself, committing suicide in a blaze of glory. For it is that superpower which, by its unbearable power, has fomented all this violence which is endemic throughout the world, and hence that (unwittingly) terroristic imagination which dwells in all of us.

The fact that we have dreamt of this event, that everyone without exception has dreamt of it—because no one can avoid dreaming of the destruction of any power that has become hegemonic to this degree—is unacceptable to the Western moral conscience. Yet it is a fact, and one which can indeed be measured by the emotive violence of all that has been said and written in the effort to dispel it.

At a pinch, we can say that they *did it*, but we *wished for* it. If this is not taken into account, the event loses any symbolic dimension. It becomes a pure accident, a purely arbitrary act, the murderous phantasmagoria of a few fanatics, and all that would then remain would be to eliminate them. Now, we know very well that this is not how it is. Which explains all the counterphobic ravings about exorcizing evil: it is because it is there, everywhere, like an obscure object of desire. Without this deep-seated complicity, the event would not have had the resonance it has, and in their symbolic strategy the terrorists doubtless know that they can count on this unavowable complicity.

This goes far beyond hatred for the dominant world power among the disinherited and the exploited, among those who have ended up on the wrong side of the global order. Even those who share in the advantages of that order have this malicious desire in their hearts. Allergy to any definitive order, to any definitive power, is — happily — universal, and the two towers of the World Trade Center were perfect embodiments, in their very twinness, of that definitive order.

No need, then, for a death drive or a destructive instinct, or even for perverse, unintended effects. Very logically — and inexorably — the increase in the power of power heightens the will to destroy it. And it was party to its own destruction. When the two towers collapsed, you had the impression that they were responding to the suicide of the suicide-planes with their own suicides.

It is probable that the terrorists had not foreseen the collapse of the Twin Towers (any more than had the experts!), a collapse which — much more than the attack on the Pentagon — had the greatest symbolic impact. The symbolic collapse of a whole system came about by an unpredictable complicity, as though the towers, by collapsing on their own, by committing suicide, had joined in to round off the event. In a sense, the entire system, by its internal fragility, lent the initial action a helping hand.

The more concentrated the system becomes globally, ultimately forming one single network, the more it becomes vulnerable at a single point (already a single little Filipino hacker had managed, from the dark recesses of his portable computer, to launch the "I love you" virus, which circled the globe devastating entire networks). Here it was eighteen suicide attackers who, thanks to the absolute weapon of death, enhanced by technological efficiency, unleashed a global catastrophic process.

When global power monopolizes the situation to this extent, when there is such a formidable condensation of all functions in the technocratic machinery, and when no alternative form of thinking is allowed, what other way is there but a *terroristic situational transfer*? It was the system itself which created the objective conditions for this brutal retaliation. By seizing all the cards for itself, it forced the Other to change the rules. And the new rules are fierce ones, because the stakes are fierce. To a system whose very excess of power poses an insoluble challenge, the terrorists respond with a definitive act which is also not susceptible of exchange. Terrorism is the act that restores an irreducible singularity to the heart of a system of generalized exchange. All the singularities (species, individuals, and cultures) that have paid with their deaths for the installation of a global circulation governed by a single power are taking their revenge today through this *terroristic situational transfer*.

This is terror against terror—there is no longer any ideology behind it. We are far beyond ideology and politics now. No ideology, no cause—not even the Islamic cause—can account for the energy which fuels terror. The aim is no longer even to transform the world, but (as the heresies did in their day) to radicalize the world by sacrifice. Whereas the system aims to realize it by force.

Terrorism, like viruses, is everywhere. There is a global perfusion of terrorism, which accompanies any system of domination as though it were its shadow, ready to activate itself anywhere, like a double agent. We can no longer draw a demarcation line around it. It is at the very heart of this culture which combats it, and the visible fracture (and the hatred) that pits the exploited and the underdeveloped globally against the Western world secretly connects with the fracture internal to the dominant system. That system can face down any visible antagonism. But against the other kind, which is viral in structure—as though every machinery of domination secreted its own counterapparatus, the agent of its own disappearance—against that form of almost automatic reversion of its own power, the system can do nothing. And terrorism is the shock wave of this silent reversion.

This is not, then, a clash of civilizations or religions, and it reaches far beyond Islam and America, on which efforts are being made to focus the conflict in order to create the delusion of a visible confrontation and a solution based on force. There is, indeed, a fundamental antagonism here, but one which points past the spectre of America (which is, perhaps, the epicentre, but in no sense the sole embodiment, of globalization) and the spectre of Islam (which is not the embodiment of terrorism either), to *triumphant globalization battling against itself*. In this sense, we can indeed speak of a world war—not the Third World War, but the Fourth and the only really global one, since what is at stake is globalization itself. The first two world wars corresponded to the classical image of war. The first ended the supremacy of Europe and the colonial era. The second put an end to Nazism. The third, which has indeed taken place, in the form of cold war and deterrence, put an end to Communism. With each succeeding war, we have moved further towards a single world order. Today that order, which has virtually reached its culmination, finds itself grappling with the antagonistic forces scattered throughout the very heartlands of the global, in all the current convulsions. A fractal war of all cells, all singularities, revolting in the form of antibodies. A confrontation so impossible to pin down that the idea of war has to be rescued from time to time by spectacular set-pieces, such as the Gulf War or the war in Afghanistan. But the Fourth World War is elsewhere. It is what haunts every world order, all hegemonic domination—if Islam dominated the world, terrorism would rise against Islam, *for it is the world, the globe itself, which resists globalization*.

Terrorism is immoral. The World Trade Center event, that symbolic challenge, is immoral, and it is a response to a globalization which is itself immoral. So, let us be immoral; and if we want to have some understanding of all this, let us go and take a little look beyond Good and Evil. When, for once, we have an event that defies not just morality, but any form of interpretation, let us try to approach it with an understanding of Evil.

This is precisely where the crucial point lies—in the total misunderstanding on the part of Western philosophy, on the part of the Enlightenment, of the relation between Good and Evil. We believe naively that the progress of Good, its advance in all fields (the sciences, technology, democracy, human rights), corresponds to a defeat of Evil. No one seems to have understood that Good and Evil advance together, as part of the same movement. The triumph of the one does not eclipse the other—far from it. In metaphysical terms, Evil is regarded as an accidental mishap, but this axiom, from which all the Manichaean forms of the struggle of Good against Evil derive, is illusory. Good does not conquer Evil, nor indeed does the reverse happen: they are at once both irreducible to each other and inextricably interrelated. Ultimately, Good could thwart Evil only by ceasing to be Good since, by seizing for itself a global monopoly of power, it gives rise, by that very act, to a blowback of a proportionate violence.

In the traditional universe, there was still a balance between Good and Evil, in accordance with a dialectical relation which maintained the tension and equilibrium of the moral universe, come what may—not unlike the way the confrontation of the two powers in the Cold War maintained the balance of terror. There was, then, no supremacy of the one over the other. As soon as there was a total extrapolation of Good (hegemony of the positive over any form of negativity, exclusion of death and of any potential adverse force—triumph of the values of Good all along the line), that balance was upset. From this point on, the equilibrium was gone, and it was as though Evil regained an invisible autonomy, henceforward developing exponentially.

Relatively speaking, this is more or less what has happened in the political order with the eclipse of Communism and the global triumph of liberal power: it was at that point that a ghostly enemy emerged, infiltrating itself throughout the whole planet, slipping in everywhere like a virus, welling up from all the interstices of power: Islam. But Islam was merely the moving front along which the antagonism crystallized. The antagonism is everywhere, and in every one of us. So, it is terror against terror. But asymmetric terror. And it is this asymmetry which leaves global omnipotence entirely disarmed. At odds with itself, it can only plunge further into its own logic of relations of force, but it cannot operate on the terrain of the symbolic challenge and death—a thing of which it no longer has any idea, since it has erased it from its own culture.

Up to the present, this integrative power has largely succeeded in absorbing and resolving any crisis, any negativity, creating, as it did so, a situation of the deepest despair (not only for the disinherited, but for the pampered and privileged too, in their radical comfort). The fundamental change now is that the terrorists have ceased to commit suicide for no return; they are now bringing their own deaths to bear in an effective, offensive manner, in the service of an intuitive strategic insight which is quite simply a sense of the immense fragility of the opponent — a sense that a system which has arrived at its quasi-perfection can, by that very token, be ignited by the slightest spark. They have succeeded in turning their own deaths into an absolute weapon against a system that operates on the basis of the exclusion of death, a system whose ideal is an ideal of zero deaths. Every zero-death system is a zero-sum-game system. And all the means of deterrence and destruction can do nothing against an enemy who has already turned his death into a counterstrike weapon. "What does the American bombing matter? Our men are as eager to die as the Americans are to live!" Hence the non-equivalence of the four thousand deaths inflicted at a stroke on a zero-death system.

Here, then, it is all about death, not only about the violent irruption of death in real time — "live," so to speak — but the irruption of a death which is far more than real: a death which is symbolic and sacrificial — that is to say, the absolute, irrevocable event.

This is the spirit of terrorism.

Never attack the system in terms of relations of force. That is the (revolutionary) imagination the system itself forces upon you — the system which survives only by constantly drawing those attacking it into fighting on the ground of reality, which is always its own. But shift the struggle into the symbolic sphere, where the rule is that of challenge, reversion, and outbidding. *So that death can be met only by equal or greater death.* Defy the system by a gift to which it cannot respond except by its own death and its own collapse.

The terrorist hypothesis is that the system itself will commit suicide in response to the multiple challenges posed by deaths and suicides. For there is a symbolic obligation upon both the system and power [*le pouvoir*], and in this trap lies the only chance of their catastrophic collapse. In this vertiginous cycle of the impossible exchange of death, the death of the terrorist is an infinitesimal point, but one that creates a gigantic suction or void, an enormous convection. Around this tiny point the whole system of the real and of power [*la puissance*] gathers, transfixed; rallies briefly; then perishes by its own hyperefficiency.

It is the tactic of the terrorist model to bring about an excess of reality, and have the system collapse beneath that excess of reality. The whole derisory nature of the situation, together with the violence mobilized by the system, turns around against it, for terrorist acts are both the exorbitant mirror of its own violence and the model of a symbolic violence forbidden to it, the only violence it cannot exert — that of its own death.

This is why the whole of visible power can do nothing against the tiny, but symbolic, death of a few individuals.

We have to face facts, and accept that a new terrorism has come into being, a new form of action which plays the game, and lays hold of the rules of the game, solely with the aim of disrupting it. Not only do these people not play fair, since they put their own deaths into play—to which there is no possible response ("they are cowards")—but they have taken over all the weapons of the dominant power. Money and stock-market speculation, computer technology and aeronautics, spectacle and the media networks—they have assimilated everything of modernity and globalism, without changing their goal, which is to destroy that power.

They have even—and this is the height of cunning—used the banality of American everyday life as cover and camouflage. Sleeping in their suburbs, reading and studying with their families, before activating themselves suddenly like time bombs. The faultless mastery of this clandestine style of operation is almost as terroristic as the spectacular act of September 11, since it casts suspicion on any and every individual. Might not any inoffensive person be a potential terrorist? If *they* could pass unnoticed, then each of us is a criminal going unnoticed (every plane also becomes suspect), and in the end, this is no doubt true. This may very well correspond to an unconscious form of potential, veiled, carefully repressed criminality, which is always capable, if not of resurfacing, at least of thrilling secretly to the spectacle of Evil. So the event ramifies down to the smallest detail—the source of an even more subtle mental terrorism.

The radical difference is that the terrorists, while they have at their disposal weapons that are the system's own, possess a further lethal weapon: their own deaths. If they were content just to fight the system with its own weapons, they would immediately be eliminated. If they merely used their own deaths to combat it, they would disappear just as quickly in a useless sacrifice—as terrorism has almost always done up to now (an example being the Palestinian suicide attacks), for which reason it has been doomed to failure.

As soon as they combine all the modern resources available to them with this highly symbolic weapon, everything changes. The destructive potential is multiplied to infinity. It is this multiplication of factors (which seem irreconcilable to us) that gives them such superiority. The "zero-death" strategy, by contrast, the strategy of the "clean" technological war, precisely fails to match up to this transfiguration of "real" power by symbolic power.

The prodigious success of such an attack presents a problem, and if we are to gain some understanding of it, we have to slough off our Western perspective to see what goes on in the terrorists' organization, and in their heads. With us, such efficiency would assume a maximum of calculation and rationality that we find hard to imagine in others. And, even in this case, as in any rational organisation or secret service, there would always have been leaks or slip-ups.

So, the secret of such a success lies elsewhere. The difference is that here we are dealing not with an employment contract, but with a pact and a sacrificial obligation. Such an obligation is immune to any defection or corruption. The miracle is to have adapted to the global network and technical protocols, without losing anything of this complicity "unto death." Unlike the contract, the pact does not bind individuals—even their "suicide" is not individual heroism, it is a collective sacrificial act sealed by an ideal demand. And it is the combination of two mechanisms—an operational structure and a symbolic pact—that made an act of such excessiveness possible.

We no longer have any idea what a symbolic calculation is, as in poker or potlatch: with minimum stakes, but the maximum result. And the maximum result was precisely what the terrorists obtained in the Manhattan attack, which might be presented as quite a good illustration of chaos theory: an initial impact causing incalculable consequences; whereas the Americans' massive deployment ("Desert Storm") achieved only derisory effects—the hurricane ending, so to speak, in the beating of a butterfly's wing.

Suicidal terrorism was a terrorism of the poor. This is a terrorism of the rich. This is what particularly frightens us: the fact that they have become rich (they have all the necessary resources) without ceasing to wish to destroy us. Admittedly, in terms of our system of values, they are cheating. It is not playing fair to throw one's own death into the game. But this does not trouble them, and the new rules are not ours to determine.

So any argument is used to discredit their acts. For example, calling them "suicidal" and "martyrs"—and adding immediately that martyrdom proves nothing, that it has nothing to do with truth, that it is even (to quote Nietzsche) the enemy number one of truth. Admittedly, their deaths prove nothing, but in a system where truth itself is elusive (or do we claim to possess it?), there is nothing to prove. Moreover, this highly moral argument can be turned around. If the voluntary martyrdom of the suicide bombers proves nothing, then the involuntary martyrdom of the victims of the attack proves nothing either, and there is something unseemly and obscene in making a moral argument out of it (this is in no way to deny their suffering and death).

Another argument in bad faith: these terrorists exchanged their deaths for a place in paradise; their act was not a disinterested one, hence it is not authentic; it would be disinterested only if they did not believe in God, if they saw no hope in death, as is the case with us (yet Christian martyrs assumed precisely such a sublime equivalence). There again, then, they are not fighting fair, since they get salvation, which we cannot even continue to hope for. So we mourn our deaths while they can turn theirs into very high-definition stakes.

Fundamentally, all this—causes, proof, truth, rewards, ends, and means—is a typically Western form of calculation. We even evaluate death in terms of interest rates, in value-for-money terms. An economic calculation that is a poor man's calculation—poor men who no longer even have the courage to pay the price.

What can happen now—apart from war, which is itself merely a conventional safety shield [*écran de protection*]? There is talk of bio-terrorism, bacteriological warfare, or nuclear terrorism. Yet that is no longer of the order of the symbolic challenge, but of annihilation pure and simple, with no element of risk or glory:

it is of the order of the final solution. Now, it is a mistake to see terrorist action as obeying a purely destructive logic. It seems to me that the action of the terrorists, from which death is inseparable (this is precisely what makes it a symbolic act), does not seek the impersonal elimination of the other. Everything lies in the challenge and the duel—that is to say, everything still lies in a dual, personal relation with the opposing power. It is that power which humiliated you, so it too must be humiliated. And not merely exterminated. It has to be made to lose face. And you never achieve that by pure force and eliminating the other party: it must, rather, be targeted and wounded in a genuinely adversarial relation. Apart from the pact that binds the terrorists together, there is also something of a dual pact with the adversary. This is, then, precisely the opposite of the cowardice of which they stand accused, and it is precisely the opposite of what the Americans did in the Gulf War (and which they are currently beginning again in Afghanistan), where the target is invisible and is liquidated operationally.

In all these vicissitudes, what stays with us, above all else, is the sight of the images. This impact of the images, and their fascination, are necessarily what we retain, since images are, whether we like it or not, our primal scene. And, at the same time as they have radicalized the world situation, the events in New York can also be said to have radicalized the relation of the image to reality. Whereas we were dealing before with an uninterrupted profusion of banal images and a seamless flow of sham events, the terrorist act in New York has resuscitated both images and events.

Among the other weapons of the system which they turned round against it, the terrorists exploited the "real time" of images, their instantaneous worldwide transmission, just as they exploited stock-market speculation, electronic information, and air traffic. The role of images is highly ambiguous. For, at the same time as they exalt the event, they also take it hostage. They serve to multiply it to infinity and, at the same time, they are a diversion and a neutralization (this was already the case with the events of 1968). The image consumes the event, in the sense that it absorbs it and offers it for consumption. Admittedly, it gives it unprecedented impact, but impact as image-event.

How do things stand with the real event, then, if reality is everywhere infiltrated by images, virtuality, and fiction? In the present case, we thought we had seen (perhaps with a certain relief) a resurgence of the real, and of the violence of the real, in an allegedly virtual universe. "There's an end to all your talk about the virtual—this is something real!" Similarly, it was possible to see this as a resurrection of history beyond its proclaimed end. But does reality actually outstrip fiction? If it seems to do so, this is because it has absorbed fiction's energy, and has itself become fiction. We might almost say that reality is jealous of fiction, that the real is jealous of the image .... It is a kind of duel between them, a contest to see which can be the most unimaginable.

The collapse of the World Trade Center towers is unimaginable, but that is not enough to make it a real event. An excess of violence is not enough to open on to reality. For reality is a principle, and it is this principle that is lost. Reality and fiction are inextricable, and the fascination with the attack is primarily a fascination with the image (both its exultatory and its catastrophic consequences are themselves largely imaginary).

In this case, then, the real is superadded to the image like a bonus of terror, like an additional *frisson*; not only is it terrifying, but, what is more, it is real. Rather than the violence of the real being there first, and the *frisson* of the image being added to it, the image is there first, and the *frisson* of the real is added. Something like an additional fiction, a fiction surpassing fiction. Ballard (after Borges) talked like this of reinventing the real as the ultimate and most redoubtable fiction.

The terrorist violence here is not, then, a blowback of reality, any more than it is a blowback of history. It is not "real." In a sense, it is worse: it is symbolic. Violence in itself may be perfectly banal and inoffensive. Only symbolic violence is generative of singularity. And in this singular event, in this Manhattan disaster movie, the twentieth century's two elements of mass fascination are combined: the white magic of the cinema and the black magic of terrorism; the white light of the image and the black light of terrorism.

We try retrospectively to impose some kind of meaning on it, to find some kind of interpretation. But there is none. And it is the radicality of the spectacle, the brutality of the spectacle, which alone is original and irreducible. The spectacle of terrorism forces the terrorism of spectacle upon us. And, against this immoral fascination (even if it unleashes a universal moral reaction), the political order can do nothing. This is our theatre of cruelty, the only one we have left—extraordinary in that it unites the most extreme degree of the spectacular and the highest level of challenge .... It is at one and the same time the dazzling micro-model of a kernel of real violence with the maximum possible echo—hence the purest form of spectacle—and a sacrificial model mounting the purest symbolic form of defiance to the historical and political order.

We would forgive them any massacre if it had a meaning, if it could be interpreted as historical violence—this is the moral axiom of good violence. We would pardon them any violence if it were not given media exposure ("terrorism would be nothing without the media"). But this is all illusion. There is no "good" use of the media; the media are part of the event, they are part of the terror, and they work in both directions.

The repression of terrorism spirals around as unpredictably as the terrorist act itself. No one knows where it will stop, or what turnabouts there may yet be. There is no possible distinction, at the level of images and information, between the spectacular and the symbolic, no possible distinction between the "crime" and the crackdown. And it is this uncontrollable unleashing of reversibility that is terrorism's true victory. A victory that is visible in the subterranean ramifications and infiltrations of the event—not just in the direct economic, political, financial slump in the whole of the system—and the resulting moral and psychological downturn—but in the slump in the value-system, in the whole ideology of freedom, of free circulation, and so on, on which the Western world prided itself, and on which it drew to exert its hold over the rest of the world.

To the point that the idea of freedom, a new and recent idea, is already fading from minds and mores, and liberal globalization is coming about in precisely the opposite form—a police-state globalization, a total control, a terror based on "law-and-order" measures. Deregulation ends up in a maximum of constraints and restrictions, akin to those of a fundamentalist society.

A fall-off in production, consumption, speculation, and growth (but certainly not in corruption!): it is as though the global system were making a strategic fallback, carrying out a painful revision of its values—in defensive reaction, as it would seem, to the impact of terrorism, but responding, deep down, to its secret injunctions: enforced regulation as a product of absolute disorder, but a regulation it imposes on itself—internalizing, as it were, its own defeat.

Another aspect of the terrorists' victory is that all other forms of violence and the destabilization of order work in its favour. Internet terrorism, biological terrorism, the terrorism of anthrax and rumour—all are ascribed to Bin Laden. He might even claim natural catastrophes as his own. All the forms of disorganization and perverse circulation operate to his advantage. The very structure of generalized world trade works in favour of impossible exchange. It is like an "automatic writing" of terrorism, constantly refuelled by the involuntary terrorism of news and information. With all the panic consequences which ensue; if, in the current anthrax scare,* the hysteria spreads spontaneously by instantaneous crystallization, like a chemical solution at the mere contact of a molecule, this is because the whole system has reached a critical mass which makes it vulnerable to any aggression.

There is no remedy for this extreme situation, and war is certainly not a solution, since it merely offers a rehash of the past, with the same deluge of military forces, bogus information, senseless bombardment, emotive and deceitful language, tech-nological deployment, and brainwashing. Like the Gulf War: a non-event, an event that does not really take place.

And this indeed is its *raison-d'être:* to substitute, for a real and formidable, unique and unforeseeable event, a repetitive, rehashed pseudo-event. The terrorist attack corresponded to a precedence of the event over all interpretative models; whereas this mindlessly military, technological war corresponds, conversely, to the model's precedence over the event, and hence to a conflict over phoney stakes, to a situation of "no contest." War as continuation of the absence of politics by other means.

* * * * *

The September 11 attacks also concern architecture, since what was destroyed was one of the most prestigious of buildings, together with a whole (Western) value-system and a world order.[1] It may, then, be useful to begin with a historical and architectural analysis of the Twin Towers, in order to grasp the symbolic significance of their destruction.

First of all, why the *Twin* Towers? Why *two* towers at the World Trade Center?

All Manhattan's tall buildings had been content to confront each other in a competitive verticality, and the product of this was an architectural panorama reflecting the capitalist system itself—a pyramidal jungle, whose famous image stretched out before you as you arrived from the sea. That image changed after 1973, with the building of the World Trade Center. The effigy of the system was no longer the obelisk and the pyramid, but the punch card and the statistical graph. This architectural graphism is the embodiment of a system that is no longer competitive, but digital and countable, and from which competition has disappeared in favour of networks and monopoly.

Perfect parallelepipeds, standing over 1,300 feet tall, on a square base. Perfectly balanced, blind communicating vessels (they say terrorism is "blind," but the towers were blind too—monoliths no longer opening on to the outside world, but subject to artificial conditioning²). The fact that there were two of them signifies the end of any original reference. If there had been only one, monopoly would not have been perfectly embodied. Only the doubling of the sign truly puts an end to what it designates.

There is a particular fascination in this reduplication. However tall they may have been, the two towers signified, none the less, a halt to verticality. They were not of the same breed as the other buildings. They culminated in the exact reflection of each other. The glass and steel facades of the Rockefeller Center buildings still mirrored each other in an endless specularity. But the Twin Towers no longer had any facades, any faces. With the rhetoric of vertically disappears also the rhetoric of the mirror. There remains only a kind of black box, a series closed on the figure two, as though architecture, like the system, was now merely a product of cloning, and of a changeless genetic code.

New York is the only city in the world that has, throughout its history, tracked the present form of the system and all its many developments with such prodigious fidelity. We must, then, assume that the collapse of the towers—itself a unique event in the history of modern cities—prefigures a kind of dramatic ending and, all in all, disappearance both of this form of architecture and of the world system it embodies. Shaped in the pure computer image of banking and finance, (ac)countable and digital, they were in a sense its brain, and in striking there the terrorists have struck at the brain, at the nerve-centre of the system.

The violence of globalization also involves architecture, and hence the violent protest against it also involves the destruction of that architecture. In terms of collective drama, we can say that the horror for the 4,000 victims of dying in those towers was inseparable from the horror of living in them—the horror of living and working in sarcophagi of concrete and steel.

These architectural monsters, like the Beaubourg Centre, have always exerted an ambiguous fascination, as have the extreme forms of modern technology in general—a contradictory feeling of attraction and repulsion, and hence, somewhere, a secret desire to see them disappear. In the case of the Twin Towers, something particular is added: precisely their symmetry and their twin-ness. There is, admittedly, in this cloning and perfect symmetry an aesthetic quality, a kind of perfect crime against form, a tautology of form which can give rise, in a violent reaction, to the temptation to break that symmetry, to restore an asymmetry, and hence a singularity.

Their destruction itself respected the symmetry of the towers: a double attack, separated by a few minutes' interval, with a sense of suspense between the two impacts. After the first, one could still believe it was an accident. Only the second impact confirmed the terrorist attack. And in the Queens air crash a month later, the TV stations waited, staying with the story (in France) for four hours, waiting to broadcast a possible second crash "live." Since that did not occur, we shall never know now whether it was an accident or a terrorist act.

The collapse of the towers is the major symbolic event. Imagine they had not collapsed, or only one had collapsed: the effect would not have been the same at all. The fragility of global power would not have been so strikingly proven. The towers, which were the emblem of that power, still embody it in their dramatic end, which resembles a suicide. Seeing them collapse themselves, as if by implosion, one had the impression that they were committing suicide in response to the suicide of the suicide planes.

Were the Twin Towers destroyed, or did they collapse? Let us be clear about this: the two towers are both a physical, architectural object and a symbolic object[3] (symbolic of financial power and global economic liberalism). The architectural object was destroyed, but it was the symbolic object which was targeted and which it was intended to demolish. One might think the physical destruction brought about the symbolic collapse. But in fact no one, not even the terrorists, had reckoned on the total destruction of the towers. It was, in fact, their symbolic collapse that brought about their physical collapse, not the other way around.

As if the power bearing these towers suddenly lost all energy, all resilience; as though that arrogant power suddenly gave way under the pressure of too intense an effort: the effort always to be the unique world model.

So the towers, tired of being a symbol which was too heavy a burden to bear, collapsed, this time physically, in their totality. Their nerves of steel cracked. They collapsed vertically, drained of their strength, with the whole world looking on in astonishment.

The symbolic collapse came about, then, by a kind of unpredictable complicity— as though the entire system, by its internal fragility, joined in the game of its own liquidation, and hence joined in the game of terrorism. Very logically, and inexorably, the increase in the power of power heightens the will to destroy it. But there is more: somewhere, it was party to its own destruction. The countless disaster movies bear witness to this fantasy, which they attempt to exorcize with images and special effects. But the fascination they exert is a sign that acting-out is never very far away—the rejection of any system, including internal rejection, growing all the stronger as it approaches perfection or omnipotence. It has been said that "Even God cannot declare war on Himself." Well, He can. The West, in the position of God (divine omnipotence and absolute moral legitimacy), has become suicidal, and declared war on itself.

Even in their failure, the terrorists succeeded beyond their wildest hopes: in bungling their attack on the White House (while succeeding far beyond their objectives on the towers), they demonstrated unintentionally that that was not the essential target, that political power no longer means much, and real power lies elsewhere. As for what should be built in place of the towers, the problem is insoluble. Quite simply because one can imagine nothing equivalent that would be worth destroying—that would be worthy of being destroyed. The Twin Towers were worth destroying. One cannot say the same of many architectural works. Most things are not even worth destroying or sacrificing. Only works of prestige deserve that fate, for it is an honour. This proposition is not as paradoxical as it sounds, and it raises a basic issue for architecture: one should build only those things which, by their excellence, are worthy of being destroyed. Take a look around with this radical proposition in mind, and you will see what a pass we have come to. Not much would withstand this extreme hypothesis.

This brings us back to what should be the basic question for architecture, which architects never formulate: is it normal to build and construct? In fact it is not, and we should preserve the absolutely problematical character of the undertaking. Undoubtedly, the task of architecture—of good architecture—is to efface itself, to disappear as such. The towers, for their part, have disappeared. But they have left us the symbol of their disappearance, their disappearance as symbol. They, which were the symbol of omnipotence, have become, by their absence, the symbol of the possible disappearance of that omnipotence—which is perhaps an even more potent symbol. Whatever becomes of that global omnipotence, it will have been destroyed here for a moment.

Moreover, although the two towers have disappeared, they have not been annihilated. Even in their pulverized state, they have left behind an intense awareness of their presence. No one who knew them can cease imagining them and the imprint they made on the skyline from all points of the city. Their end in material space has borne them off into a definitive imaginary space. By the grace of terrorism, the World Trade Center has become the world's most beautiful building—the eighth wonder of the world![4]

NOTES

*   This text was written in October 2001 and published in *Le Monde* on November 3 2001.

1. In the New York debate, Baudrillard prefaced his talk with the following comments: "There is an absolute difficulty in speaking of an absolute event. That is to say, in providing an analysis of it that is not an explanation—as I don't think there is any possible explanation of this event, either by intellectuals or by others—but its *analogon*, so to speak; an analysis which might possibly be as unacceptable as the event, but strikes the ... let us say, symbolic imagination in more or less the same way."

2. In New York, Baudrillard here glossed: "Air conditioning, but mental conditioning too."

3. In New York, Baudrillard added: "symbolic in the weak sense, but symbolic, for all that."

4. After delivering a slightly modified version of this last paragraph in New York, Baudrillard closed with the comment: "So I set out to produce a Requiem, but it was also, in a way, a Te Deum."

Postmodernism and Its Critics

CRITICAL THINKING QUESTIONS

Lyon

1. Does postmodernism represent a distinct break from modern sociological theory, or do important continuities flow from modern to postmodern thought?
2. What practical benefits can postmodern sociological theory bring to struggles for ethno-racial equality, gender equality, or equal treatment of people of diverse sexualities?
3. Do you see any limitations to postmodern sociological theory?

Seidman

1. Why does Steven Seidman theorize "the end of sociological theory"?
2. In Seidman's view, how should sociologists explain the social world?
3. What is the difference between social theory and sociological theory, and why does this distinction matter? (Or does it matter?)

Porter

1. What major difference(s) do(es) Porter identify between the roots of sociological theory and postmodern theory?
2. In what ways does Porter see feminism as more sociologically and politically fruitful than postmodernism?
3. What do you think Porter wishes to imply with the title of her paper?

Bauman

1. What is liquid modernity?
2. Why does Bauman use the metaphors of liquids and solids to theorize social process? Do you think this is useful for understanding social process?

3. How does Bauman theorize Panopticon in the context of time and space relations?

Baudrillard

1. What major cultural institutions do you see shaping simulations in everyday life?
2. In what way(s) does Baudrillard see reality and simulation coming together in the context of the mediation of the collapsing twin towers?
3. In what ways can the attacks on the twin towers be understood to symbolize other socio-political, psychological, or cultural phenomena?

SUGGESTED READINGS

Baudrillard, Jean. 1994. *Simulacra and Simulations*. Ann Arbor: University of Michigan Press.

In Baudrillard's famous analysis, he argues that the concept of simulacra is the creation of the real through conceptual or "mythological" models that have no origin in reality. He contends that people come to understand reality through social perceptions consolidated in and through media. For Baudrillard, the boundary between the image and reality has dissolved, leaving us with a world of "hyperreality."

Lyon, David. 1994. *Jesus in Disneyland: Religion in Postmodern Times*. Cambridge: Polity Press.

This book focuses on religion in the era of postmodernity (or through the lens of postmodernism). Lyon shows how contemporary disciples of Jesus have used Disneyland for religious events, and he argues that Disney characters are better known worldwide than many biblical figures. He argues, furthermore, that this is an innovative feature of contemporary spirituality.

Lyotard, Jean-Francois. 1979. *The Postmodern Condition: A Report on Knowledge*. Manchester: Manchester University Press.

Lyotard's book departs from Marx's and Parsons's "grand meta-discourses" to theorize partiality and incomplete knowledge. He seeks to theorize multiplicity, and he explains postmodern knowledge as a toolkit for understanding "localized" or small social phenomena.

Nicholson, Linda (ed.). 1990. *Feminism/Postmodernism*. New York: Routledge.

This is an edited volume on postmodern feminism. It analyzes questions of epistemology, the politics of location, identity, and difference.

Rosenau, Pauline Marie. 1992. *Postmodernism and the Social Sciences: Insights, Inroads and Intrusions*. Princeton: Princeton University Press.

This is a good introduction to postmodern theory in the social sciences. The book traces the origins of postmodernism in the humanities, and it shows how postmodernism is restructuring the social sciences.

RELATED WEB SITES

Contemporary Philosophy, Critical Theory, and Postmodern Thought
This is a Web site that offers links to many postmodern theorists, as well as theorists whose ideas have influenced certain aspects of postmodern thought. There is a very useful section with several links on the basics of postmodernism.
http://carbon.cudenver.edu/~mryder/itc_data/postmodern.html

Everything Postmodern
The "Everything Postmodern" Web site offers links to resources, publications, and thinkers concerned with postmodernism.
www.ebbflux.com/postmodern/

Our Postmodern Life
This is a different type of Web site from the others. It offers links to architecture, art, and fiction in the postmodern context, as well as to commentary on poststructuralism. Several links are in preparation.
www.pixcentrix.co.uk/pomo/

Postmodernism
The Postmodernism Web site contains interactive links to postmodernism and photography, art and the body.
http://losthighway.dcu.ie/solas/index3.html

Postmodernism and Its Critics
This is a Web site that, while not inspiring the title of this chapter, offers many interesting links to explanations, critiques, methods, and leading figures in postmodernism.
www.as.ua.edu/ant/Faculty/murphy/436/pomo.htm

REFERENCES

Lyotard, Jean-Francois. 1979. *The Postmodern Condition: A Report on Knowledge.*
    Manchester: Manchester University Press.

Society, Subjects, and the Self

A CONSIDERABLE AMOUNT OF SOCIOLOGICAL THEORY HAS BEEN CONCERNED, IMPLICITLY or explicitly, with explaining the concept of ideology and how it "works" or operates. Karl Marx (1947), for example, developed a theory of ideology in *The German Ideology*, where he argued that [wo]men experience the phenomenal world (the world of perception) in or through a realm of consciousness that inverts reality, as in a camera obscura. For Marx, social relations appear "upside-down," distorted, and mystified in everyday life. In Marx's sense, ideology is explained as a one-sided, false perception of the world that serves the interests of the dominant class in the context of struggles over material resources.

Although Marx's analysis of ideology has been very influential in social analyses and the political struggles of oppressed groups, it is unable to explain fully how social subjectivity is formed. Are members of the working class always subjected (or subjugated) to the ideas of the ruling class in particular historical epochs? Does control over social resources, such as media outlets, literary production, and educational institutions, place so many limitations on human subjectivity that resistance to dominant ideology is futile? How does an oppressed class transform itself, in Marx's words, from "a class in itself" to "a class for itself" if ideology (as a component of the economic system of production) exists prior to the act of communication, to interaction, and to discourse (that is, if an individual's subjective perception of class consciousness remains dependent on objective changes to social structure rather than on basic human communication and interaction)?

One attempt to explain more fully how ideology operates is found in Louis Althusser's (1971) writings. Althusser, a structural Marxist, theorized the workings of ideology through a process he termed "interpellation." By interpellation Althusser referred to the mechanisms through which ideology constitutes human beings as subjects. The constitution of subjects concerns the ways in which individuals come to define themselves and to make sense of their own subjectivity through social positions such as "taxpayer," "citizen," or "middle class." If, for example, you understand your essence as a human being in terms of social positions such as "student," "Canadian," or "Republican," then you have become conscious of your presence in the social world through socio-historical, shared identifications. For Althusser, ideological state apparatuses such as media, education, and the church interpellate or "hail" individuals in a way that situates them in certain subject positions. Those subject positions, in turn, fall in line with the desires and aspirations of the ruling class.

Although Althusser understood ideology to constitute subject positions in a deterministic manner (he theorized ideology as always already present, suggesting that ideology and subject positions precede the act of communication), what is found in his work is the often-overlooked dynamic of recognition. The dynamic of recognition means that the process of interpellation, when thought through to its logical end, entails an active process of awareness and consciousness on the part of the person being interpellated. Ideology does not always or even regularly interpellate human beings passively into certain subject positions, and individuals are not simply subjected or subjugated to the particular contents or features of ruling-class ideology. For example, Canadian newspapers play an important role in influencing how people understand the social world, and the structure of newspaper ownership matters to the ideological contents of daily reporting. But it would be presumptuous to assume that Canadians are not able to question and to reflect critically on what they read in newspapers; it would be presumptuous to assume that Canadian newspaper readers are "ideological dupes." Subject formation involves a process of conscious recognition on the part of the interpellated subject, and people are capable of rejecting attempts at interpellation.

Theoretical work on interpellation has, since Althusser's writings, tried to explain how people occupy multiple and sometimes contradictory subject positions (Hall 1988), as well as how the process of interpellation is never complete (Butler, Laclau, and Žižek 2000). Although not always using the language of interpellation and subject formation, sociological interest in social subjectivity, self-formation, and the structural influences on human consciousness continues in contemporary theoretical discourse.

🖻 SECTION READINGS: DANY LACOMBE, ANTHONY GIDDENS, AND ULRICH BECK

It was the closure on human agency and the deterministic emphasis on the workings of ideology, power, and social control that captured the attention of one of Althusser's most famous students, Michel Foucault. In his writings, Foucault (1926–1984) sought to understand how the exercise of power is dispersed, multifaceted, and fluid. Power, for Foucault, is not a "thing" that is wielded through dominant ideology; rather, power is a process, at once constraining and liberating. Power in a social setting can be oppressive, says Foucault, but the relations of power always present possibilities for resistance. Although Foucault granted much attention to power and resistance, in one of his most famous statements he proclaimed:

I would like to say, first of all, what has been the goal of my work during the last twenty years. It has not been to analyse the phenomena of power, nor to elaborate the foundations of such an analysis. My objective, instead, has been to create a history of the different modes by which, in our culture, human beings are made subjects. (Foucault 1982: 208–209)

Foucault's work is widely interpreted as an explication of a new form of power and social control that emerged in the late 17th and early 18th centuries. In *Discipline and Punish: The Birth of the Modern Prison* (1979), he explains how, in a relatively short period of time, the act of punishing criminals using torture and public spectacle was replaced by a more humanizing process of social control that took place in the "closed context" of the modern prison (beyond the gaze of the public).[1] Whereas "sovereign" expressions of power and social control entailed prisoners enduring gruesome torture through public spectacle (students may recall the depiction of such events in the 1995 Hollywood movie *Braveheart*), a new form of "disciplinary" power had emerged that involved the governance of criminals through rules, procedures, and the centralization of supervision. In the "panoptic prison," Foucault argues, prisoners were to be monitored by prison guards from a centralized "inspection lodge" surrounded by a semi-circular building housing inmates in separate cells. The inspection lodge was to be equipped with a mechanism resembling venetion blinds; prisoners would not know when they were being watched, which would create in them a sense of constant uncertainty. The assumption was that through these processes prisoners would begin to regulate their own behaviour. For Foucault, the 18th-century trends toward practices of punishment and social control could be used metaphorically to explain a new kind of "disciplinary power" sweeping over society as a whole.

In the first reading, Simon Fraser University's Dany Lacombe argues that Foucault's work has been misinterpreted and wrongly applied in the sociology of law and criminology. Maintaining a focus on Foucault's interest in how individuals are transformed into subjects, she outlines how Foucault's work is best understood in terms of "mechanisms of life" that both enable and constrain human subjectivity. In one sense, power is dominating, Lacombe explains. But she also explains how power in Foucault's assessment is not owned or controlled by any one individual. Power is not a thing but a relation, inscribed in relations of both domination and liberation. Power can always be subverted in what Foucault calls the "strategic reversibility" of power relations. For Lacombe, then, it is more effective for sociologists and criminologists to understand Foucault's work in its entirety, with particular attention granted to his writings on subjectification.

The second reading passage is written by Anthony Giddens. Giddens (1938–) is one of the world's most recognized sociologists. In the reading, he begins with the simple assertion that there has emerged a "reflexive self" in the period of "late modernity." The reflexive self, says Giddens, is symptomatic of a structural transition in core social institutions and processes. To better understand the emergence of the late modern reflexive self, he differentiates "emancipatory politics" from "life politics." In their many forms, Giddens argues, emancipatory forms of politics have historically been oriented toward freeing individuals from both traditional and hierarchical social constraints that negatively affect their life chances. For Giddens, this has involved a break from traditional social constraints (e.g., class position, family, gender roles) as well as illegitimate social constraints (e.g., one social group's monopoly of valued resources and efforts by the disadvantaged group(s) to seek emancipation from exploitative social arrangements).

What happens, Giddens wonders, when individuals are freed from the traditional and hierarchical constraints of the past? Emancipatory politics, he explains, can be understood as a politics of life chances. This means that the success of emancipatory politics "loosens" systemic patterns of inequality. By contrast, Giddens uses the concept of life politics as a politics of *life choices*. The emergence of life politics is caught up in social structural forces that have increasingly freed individuals from traditional and hierarchical forms of constraint, and Giddens contends that people today regularly engage with social issues that are globally significant. He argues that in the past an individual's self-identity (or subjectivity) was strongly shaped by place, space, and rank or status. Today, however, self-formation has become a reflexive process that involves a radical alteration of how people "live in the world." This can involve an alteration in the relationship between self and lifestyle, but also in that between self and planetary needs.

The themes touched on by Giddens are salient in the third passage, written by Ulrich Beck. Beck (1944–) is a German theorist who has made a profound impact on contemporary sociological theory around the world. Since the early 1990s, he has devoted much attention to developing new ways of thinking about the social world, the social sciences, and social theory. Beck believes that transformations taking place in the social and material world have rendered "zombie categories" in the social sciences historically obsolete. He defines zombie categories as sociological concepts that are widely used across the social sciences—such as class, family, relationships, and territorial states (nation-states)—but that no longer correspond to real-world phenomena. These analytic concepts are, for Beck, like zombies: they are empirically dead, yet still "alive" and being put to use in social scientific analysis. By continuing to rely on "zombie sociology," Beck maintains, sociologists and other social scientists continue to produce sociological theory and discourse that exist at too great a distance from the empirical realities of social life in the age of "second modernity."

In the reading passage, Beck argues that we are living in transformative times. He contends that the intersection of "individualization," "globalization," and "manufactured uncertainties" has combined with the cultural forces of gender revolution and underemployment to bring about the end of "simple linear modernity." What has emerged in its place, Beck continues, is the age of "second modernity." The age of second modernity is an historical epoch that requires social scientists to reinvent concepts and disciplinary resources that are able to account accurately for contemporary global political, economic, and societal relations. He argues that as the bipolar world of first modernity—a world that for decades was explained sociologically in debates concerning society versus nature, traditional versus modern, North versus South—becomes increasingly unable to represent the empirical realities of life in the 21st century, there is a need to rethink the concepts and resources that sociologists use to explain the social world.

Beck refers to contemporary transformative processes using the concept of "world risk society." He argues that world risk society connects individual autonomy and insecurity in the domain of labour relations or gender politics to the techno-scientific complex. What is emerging in world risk society, he continues, is a new sequence of transitional politics that usher in the "democratization of democracy" (a praise coined by Giddens). For Beck, this complex set of behaviours entails the "release" of individuals from the social constraints of the past. Upon this release, says Beck, people confront a new cosmopolitan society comprised of those who share an interest in material and ethical questions of global significance beyond "traditional" sources of division (class, state, geography).

NOTES

1. Foucault's comments on the panoptic prison were borrowed from Jeremy Bentham. While Foucault's interpretation of Bentham's writings on the panoptic prison involves a system of punishment removed from public view, there is some debate over how "closed" Bentham envisioned the panoptic prison. Bentham had argued that the panoptic prison would be open to the "great tribunal of the world," suggesting that the prison itself would be open to public inspection. This is a point that is not entirely appreciated by Foucault.

CHAPTER 24

Reforming Foucault: A Critique of the Social Control Thesis

DANY LACOMBE

* * * * *

For the past fifteen years, Michel Foucault's groundbreaking account of the birth of the prison has exerted a powerful influence on the social sciences. Indeed, "to write today about punishment and classification without Foucault," says criminologist Stanley Cohen "is like talking about the unconscious without Freud" (1985: 10). In *Discipline and Punish: The Birth of the Prison* (1979), Foucault provided concepts that radically transformed the discourse in which penal reform was typically thought (e.g., Garland 1986). These concepts—"power/knowledge," "disciplinary society," "micro-powers"—have allowed analysts to deconstruct both the liberal conception of the birth of the prison as a humanistic advance over the brutal punishments administered in pre-modern societies, and the Marxist conception of penality as an epiphenomenon of the mode of production. Under Foucault's influence, scholars have rewritten the history of penal reform as the history of the dispersion of a new mode of domination called "disciplinary power," a power exercised through techniques of objectification, classification, and normalization, a power deployed through the whole social body.

Moreover, Foucault's concepts have enabled criminology and the sociology of law to study the way various welfare state institutions "regulate life." Thus, analysts have shown not only how "coercive" institutions (the prison, the asylum, and the courts) discipline society, but also how other institutions that on the surface simply facilitate everyday life (education, health, social security, etc.) actually also have a disciplinary function. Simply put, these analysts have studied the way these institutions control and objectify the individual. However, most of their work is marred by its simplistic understanding of Foucault. While their studies are ostensibly based on Foucault's concept of penality as a *productive* technique of power/knowledge, at bottom, they simply reinscribe a functionalist and instrumentalist account of law reform.[1] Hence, in the social sciences, we witness a surfeit of studies glibly demonstrating that all attempts to ameliorate the social system, in particular

331

the criminal justice system, only lead to the dispersion and extension of social control.[2]

* * * * *

Revisionist accounts of the "enlightened" penal policies that swept Europe and North America at the turn of the nineteenth century have had a tremendous impact on the way analysts of contemporary law reform undertake their research (Rushe and Kircheimer 1968; Rothman 1971, 1980; Ignatieff 1978, 1983; Melossi and Pavarani 1981; Garland 1985). The realization that the prison was far from the enlightened, rational, and humane solution to the barbaric system of punishment preceding it led analysts of contemporary reforms to distrust all attempts to "do good." As the prison was at its birth, contemporary reforms are often celebrated by their makers as progressive: according to them, we move from barbarism to enlightenment, from ignorance to guided intervention, from cruel to humane treatment. Analysts of contemporary reforms try to deconstruct this narrative of humanitarianism, benevolence, and improvement. In its place they present a story of failure: alternatives to prison or the asylum neither ameliorate nor humanize—whatever that would mean. In fact, the result of those reforms are gloomy, with more and more people becoming enmeshed in new forms of control and regulation. The realization that not only past but contemporary attempts to reform the law have failed to bring social justice encouraged the following grim academic consensus: rather than modifying the oppressive practices of the social system, law reforms simply reproduce (or "re-form") those practices in ways that are less obvious. In other words, when it comes to law reform "nothing works!"

Stanley Cohen succinctly describes the failure of new penal policies and agencies to transform the criminal justice system: "the most fundamental fact about what is going on in the new agencies is that it is much the same as what went on and is still going on in the old system" (1985: 79). Cohen refers, here, to the failure of recent prison alternatives, such as half-way houses, probation, and parole, to radically change the way our society punishes criminal activity. "What is going on" nowadays, however, for Cohen is more than a simple failure to adequately punish and redeem the criminal. Drawing on Foucault's thesis about the gradual refinement and expansion of mechanisms of control and discipline in modern society, Cohen argues that contemporary penal reforms result in the "blurring" of the boundaries between formal and informal social control (1979, 1983, 1985). Consequently, alternatives to the social control system result in "a gradual expansion and intensification of the system; a dispersal of its mechanisms from more closed to more open sites and a consequent increase in the invisibility of social control and the degree of its penetration into the social body" (1985: 83–4). Following Foucault, Cohen describes modern penal reform as a "technology of power," a mechanism producing a type of control that becomes more and more difficult to grasp, that blurs the boundary between formal and informal control. Thus, law reform is a paradoxical process, involving both "the thinning of the mesh" and the "widening of the net" of social control (Cohen, 1983, 1985).

The thesis of the dispersion of control in the whole of the social body—best encapsulated in the idea of the "disciplinary society"—has expanded the field of criminology and the sociology of law beyond the study of formal control. Their object of study became the larger society, understood, however, in terms of a "carceral" body. Analysts in those fields quickly began to reveal all the micro-powers and technologies of control at work both inside and outside the criminal justice system. For example, Ericson and Baranek (1982), in their analysis of the accused in the criminal justice system, compare his/her position of total dependency to that of the ordinary citizen in relationship to the law: human rights, justice, and "due process" are all reduced to technologies of power reproducing social control (see also McBarnett 1981). Ericson (1985, 1987) subsequently affirms that law reform is nothing more than a rhetorical tool ("reform talk") used to ensure the reproduction of the necessarily oppressive "order of things." In his analysis, the *Canadian Charter of Rights and Freedom* amounts to "social control talk" promulgated by the state to produce social control.[3] Similarly, but from a feminist perspective, Carol Smart (1989) cautions women against resorting to law to fight current gender inequalities because of law's "androcentric" and "juridogenic" mechanisms of control. In other words, law's logic of control simply reproduces strategies of patriarchal domination. It subverts the original intent of feminist demands and de-radicalizes women's efforts to gain equality. Conceived as a technology of patriarchal power, or power *tout court*, law appears as simply a weapon to deceive and oppress people. The implication is that we would be better off without it.

Drawing on Foucault, then, analysts have constructed a knowledge of law reform founded in a specific conception of power, as an energy that fatally deploys itself throughout the social body. Hence, every attempt to reform society, to give people more freedom, ineluctably becomes its opposite—a technique of domination. No matter where or when, it is the same as it ever was—social control.

The conventional wisdom about law reform is based on a circular logic: on the one hand, law reform produces control, and on the other hand, the social control system needs law reform to perpetuate itself. This logic is made possible by an essentialist conception of the social world. Most accounts of law reform conceive society as a totality controlled by the state or some dominant group that, amoeba-like, regenerates itself through perpetual absorption. In this story, "power" is simply repressive and, law reform, as a technique of power, produces only practices of domination. As stated above, this view of law reform is based on an essentialist reading of the work of Foucault that must be abandoned. While *Discipline and Punish* describes a "police state" shot through with disciplinary techniques and normalizing practices, Foucault does not simply reduce the "police" and disciplinary techniques in general to apparatuses used in the maintenance of order. In fact, he rejects such an idea describing the "police" as an ensemble of mechanisms insuring the "public good."

* * * * *

5 FOUCAULT'S PRODUCTIVE AND RELATIONAL CONCEPTION OF POWER

a) Discipline and Punish and Power-knowledge

> Power in the substantive sense, *le pouvoir*, doesn't exist. What I mean is this. The idea that there is either located at—or emanating from—a given point something which is a "power" seems to me to be based on a misguided analysis, one which at all events fails to account for a considerable number of phenomena. In reality power means relations, a more-or-less organised, hierarchical, co-ordinated cluster of relations. (Foucault 1980c: 198)

Foucault asserts that to understand how power operates in modern society, we must concentrate on its productive effects. This implies a new challenge:

> we must cease once and for all to describe the effects of power in negative terms: it "excludes," it "represses," it "censors," it "abstracts," it "masks," it "conceals." In fact, power produces; it produces reality; it produces domains of objects and rituals of truth. The individual and the knowledge that may be gained of him belong to this production. (Foucault 1979: 194)

In *Discipline and Punish* (1979) Foucault demonstrates this productive aspect of power through an analysis of the relationship between punishment, a technology of power, and the development of the social sciences. He demonstrates that out of the modern practices of punishment (observation, examination, measurement, classification, surveillance, record keeping, etc.) emerged a systematic knowledge of individuals that provided the seed for the development of the human sciences (psychology, criminology, sociology, etc.), a knowledge that allowed for the exercise of power and control over those individuals. Foucault's analysis, therefore, reveals how knowledge, as forms of thought and action, is intricately connected to the operation of power. Indeed, power and knowledge are intimately linked by a process of mutual constitution—one implies the other. Hence Foucault coined the expression "power-knowledge" and set out to investigate the relationship that linked the two practices: "there is no power relation without the correlative constitution of a field of knowledge, nor any knowledge that does not presuppose and constitute at the same time power relations" (Foucault 1979: 27). "Power-knowledge" implies that there can be no assertion without a field of power, or stated differently, that there is no truth without a politics of truth. This concept has methodological implications for the way we approach the study of power. Rather than trying to determine why power exists, which would lead us to define it in terms of an essence, the concept "power-knowledge" invites us to inquire about how power operates, that is about the strategies and procedures through which power is exercised. As Ewald (1975) indicates in his review of *Discipline and Punish*, Foucault approaches the truth claims of the prison reform movements and the discourses they emanate from in a descriptive fashion: Which strategy of production do they come from? Which relations of power do you proceed from? What kinds of subjection or liberation do you produce (Ewald 1975: 1230)?

Recent Foucault-inspired accounts of law reform have ignored Foucault's method of investigating truth claims. While *Discipline and Punish* argues for the existence of a deployment of a micro-physics of power, Foucault does not reify a system of domination. In fact, Foucault's conceptualization of the penal sphere avoids implying a pre-conceived social structure. "Foucault's whole mode of theorizing," Garland states, "seeks to avoid any suggestion that society is a coherent totality which can be analysed by means of structural models or global conceptions" (1990: 133). In an interview preceding the 1977 re-edition of Bentham's *Panopticon*, Foucault is unequivocal about the impossibility of determining power, of revealing its origin:

> But if you ask me, "Does this new technology of power takes its historical origin from an identifiable individual or group of individuals who decide to implement it so as to further their interests or facilitate their utilisation of the social body?" then I would say "No." These tactics were invented and organised from the starting points of local conditions and particular needs. They took shape in piecemeal fashion, prior to any class strategy designed to weld them into vast, coherent ensembles. It should also be noted that these ensembles don't consist in a homogenisation, but rather of a complex play of supports in mutual engagement (of) different mechanisms of power which retain all their specific character. (Foucault 1980a: 159)[4]

Foucault's refusal to think power in terms of its determination, its origin, or its essence implies, Deleuze (1975) argues that power is not a property localized in an institution (the state), subordinated to a structure (the economy), whose mode of action would be instrumental, repressive, and constraining. For Foucault, power is a strategy involving relations of truth, one that is exercised through techniques that constitute both individuals and knowledges.

In order to appreciate better the non-essentialist and non-unitary conception of Foucault's notion of power, it is useful to examine *The History of Sexuality: An Introduction* (1980b). His critique of the "repressive hypothesis" is crucial to understanding how, for him, the constitution of individuals through power is not inscribed in a logic of domination. As we will see, he argues that power is better conceived as a strategy that both constrains and enables action.

b) The History of Sexuality: Subjectification and Resistance

> For their part, the working classes managed for a long time to escape the deployment
> of "sexuality." (Foucault 1980b: 121)

In *The History of Sexuality* Foucault takes issue with the "repressive hypothesis," a view according to which Europeans repressed sexuality, which had hitherto been treated with relative openness. Hence sex, in the Victorian era, became joyless and utilitarian, concealed in the nuclear family and for the reproduction of the species. This narrative is attractive, Foucault argues, because it allows us to associate sexual repression with the rise of capitalism and the bourgeois. In the Victorian era, the argument goes, sex was repressed because it undermined capitalism, which necessitated at this time that all energies be directed toward production rather than pleasure. Sexuality was repressed by the dominant group, by the powers that were.

Rejecting the idea that modern society has somehow dominated sexuality, Foucault argues that over the last three centuries "around and apropos of sex, one sees a veritable discursive explosion" (Foucault 1980b: 17). Rather than silence, we witness more and more talk about sex meant to "yield multiple effects of displacement, intensification, reorientation, and modification of desire itself" (Foucault 1980b: 23). This deployment of discourses on sex has less to do with domination of the masses than to do with a maximization of the public good. In modern society, sexuality has become a thing to classify, specify, categorize, and quantify—in short, to optimize.

> Sex was not something one simply judged; it was a thing one administered. It was
> in the nature of a public potential; it called for management procedures; it had to
> be taken charge of by analytical discourses. (Foucault 1980b: 24)

The deployment of sexuality took place in various discursive sites, such as psychiatry, medicine, demography, biology, politics, and many others. Power operated simultaneously in a number of fields without originating in anyone in particular. Consequently, for Foucault, it makes little sense to talk of power in terms of an expansionary logic of social control.

> So it is not simply in terms of a continual extension that we must speak of this
> discursive growth; it should be seen rather as a dispersion of centers from which
> discourses emanated, a diversification of their forms, and the complex deployment
> of the network connecting them. (1980b: 34)

Foucault's resistance to conceiving power in terms of a continual extension of a single discourse can be partly explained by his refusal to locate power in a specific entity such as "the state." He rejects the analytical importance Marxists in particular give to "the state." In practice, Foucault contends, "the state" is far from being the determining entity. While Foucault's critique is directed at Marxist theories of "the state," it applies equally to accounts of law reform which are founded in a unitary concept of social control centred in "the state."

> We all know the fascination which the love, or horror, of the state exercises today; we know how much attention is paid to the genesis of the state, its history, its advance, its power and abuses, etc. The excessive value attributed to the problem of the state is expressed, basically, in two ways: the one form, immediate, affective and tragic, is the lyricism of the *monstre froid* we see confronting us; but there is a second way of over-valuing the problem of the state, one which is paradoxical because apparently reductionist: it is the form of analysis that consists in reducing the state to a certain number of functions, such as the development of productive forces and the reproduction of relations of production, and yet this reductionist vision, of the relative importance of the state's role nevertheless invariably renders it absolutely essential as a target needing to be attacked and a privileged position needing to be occupied. But the state, no more probably today than at any other time in its history, does not have this unity, this individuality, this rigorous functionality, nor, to speak frankly, this importance; maybe, after all, the state is no more than a composite reality and a mythicized abstraction, whose importance is a lot more limited than many of us think. Maybe what is really important for our modernity—that is, for our present—is not so much the etarisation of society, as the "governmentalization" of the state. (Foucault 1991: 103 emphasis in original)

I will return to this idea of "governmentalization" later. For the moment I want to return to a problem of central importance for Foucault, the constitution of individuals.

While *Discipline and Punish* (Foucault 1979) illustrates the constitution of individuals through mechanisms of objectification—in the sense of subjection to a norm — *The History of Sexuality: An Introduction* (1980b) examines how the individual constitutes him or herself through a process of subjectification[5]—in the sense of resistance to a norm. Foucault contends that the discourses on sex deployed at the end of the eighteenth century were not used initially to repress and regulate the masses. Rather, these discourses were a strategy for the self-affirmation of the emerging bourgeoisie. Through discourses on sex, the bourgeoisie gradually established itself as a body, as a class distinct from both the decadent aristocracy and the ignorant masses.

> It seems to me that the deployment of sexuality was not established as a principle of limitation of the pleasures of others by what have traditionally been called the "ruling classes." Rather it appears to me that they first tried it on themselves. [...]

> The primary concern was not repression of the sex of the classes to be exploited,
> but rather the body, vigor, longevity, progeniture, and descent of the classes that
> "ruled." This was the purpose for which the deployment of sexuality was first
> established, as a new distribution of pleasures, discourses, truths, and powers; it
> has to be seen as the self-affirmation of one class rather than the enslavement of
> another. (Foucault 1980b: 123)

It is clear from Foucault's observation that the deployment of discourses on sexuality did not result simply in the enhancement of social control. In fact, Foucault talks about the production of bio-power: mechanisms that invest, problematize, and manage life so as to maximize it (Foucault 1980b: 143–7). Hence the bourgeoisie, through the organization and elaboration of procedures of "power-knowledge" on sex, not only controlled its own body but "positively" transformed it; the bourgeoisie provided itself with a body which needed to be maximized. The bourgeois subject maximized his or her body by caring for it, preserving it, cultivating it, and protecting it from the other so that it would retain its specificity, status, and value (Foucault 1980b: 123).[6]

Foucault's discussion of peripheral sexualities in *The History of Sexuality: An Introduction* best illustrates how power is implicated in the mechanism by which identity and resistance are constructed and expressed. He argues that the concern for peripheral sexualities underwent a major shift in the nineteenth century. For example, the act of sodomy, according to the ancient civil code, was prohibited because it belonged to a category of forbidden acts. The emphasis on wrongdoing was directed at the act rather than at the perpetrator, who was nothing more or nothing less than the person who engaged in the prohibited act, a sodomite. Foucault contends that this classical vision of sodomy as an act was transformed in the nineteenth century with the emergence of a legal subjectivity embodied in "the perpetrator" of the act. The sodomite gradually became a type of person; he acquired a subjectivity, a case history, a morphology, an anatomy, and a curious physiology: he was a "homosexual." As Foucault astutely puts it, a new creature was born: "the sodomite had been a temporary aberration; the homosexual was now a species" (1980b: 43).

This new species was made intelligible through a variety of power-knowledge strategies that objectified and subjugated. While he was now at the mercy of powerful discourses that named his condition, the homosexual was, nevertheless, in a position to resist these discourses. Foucault contends that once he acquires his new life, the homosexual can use his special positionality and assert his new identity in a variety of ways. He can show off, scandalize, resist—or passively accept that he is sick. The growth of the perversions, of the unorthodox sexualities is therefore, for Foucault, "the real product of the encroachment of a type of power on bodies and their pleasures" (1980b: 48). It is in that sense, then, that Foucault asserts that power is neither an institution nor a structure but "the name that one attributes to a complex strategical situation in a particular society" (Foucault 1980b: 93). This conception of power is different from the thesis of the enhancement and intensification of social control. Power, for Foucault, implies a network, of relations of force between individuals. This relation of force does not suggest confinement; rather, power is a mechanism that both constrains and enables action. In fact, resistance is at the heart of power:

> Where there is power, there is resistance, and yet, or rather consequently, this resistance is never in a position of exteriority in relation to power. (...) [O]ne is always "inside" power, there is no "escaping it." (Foucault 1980b: 95)

Foucault does not negate that power produces control. The effects of this control, however, are neither unifying nor unitary. Inherent in power relations is a "strategic reversibility": power-knowledge strategies function both as instruments to control and as points of resistance. Foucault uses the nineteenth century's discursive construction of homosexuality to show power's dual movement.

> There is no question that the appearance in nineteenth-century psychiatry, jurisprudence, and literature of a whole series of discourses on the species and subspecies of homosexuality, inversion, pederasty, and "psychic hermaphrodism" made possible a strong advance of social controls into this area of "perversity"; but it also made possible the formation of a "reverse" discourse: homosexuality began to speak in its own behalf, to demand that its legitimacy or "naturality" be acknowledged, often in the same vocabulary, using the same categories by which it was medically disqualified. There is not, on the one side, a discourse of power, and opposite it, another discourse that runs counter to it. Discourses are tactical dements or blocks operating in the field of force relations. (Foucault 1980b: 101–2)

* * * * *

c) Power-Knowledge and Government

> Power is not a substance. Neither is it a mysterious property whose origin must be delved into. Power is only a certain type of relation between individuals. Such relations are specific, that is, they have nothing to do with exchange, production, communication, even though they combine with them. The characteristic feature of power is that some men can more or less entirely determine other men's conduct— but never exhaustively or coercively. A man who is chained up and beaten is subject to force being exerted over him. Not power. But if he can be induced to speak, when his ultimate recourse could have been to hold his tongue, preferring death, then he has been caused to behave in a certain way. His freedom has been subjected to power. *He has been submitted to government.* If an individual can remain free, however

little his freedom may be, power can subject him to government. There is no power without potential refusal or revolt. (Foucault 1988: 84; emphasis added)

Foucault nowhere addressed the question of contemporary struggles for rights at any length. Early in his career, he was dismissive of the transformative potential of rights. In his "Two Lectures," presented in Italy in 1976, Foucault affirms that power-knowledge relations are formally delimited by "the rule of right" (1980c: 93). He does not pay much attention to this triangle of power-knowledge-right, except to reduce the rule of right to an ideology that conceals "the element of domination inherent in its techniques" (1980c: 105). Foucault's conception of rights as concealing domination is in some ways similar to that of Marx, although for the latter rights camouflage the power of private property. French political philosopher Claude Lefort criticizes this view of rights as concealment, developing an impressive analysis of the radical indeterminacy of rights in its place (1986: 239–306, 1988: 7–45). While Lefort agrees with Marx that it is not arbitrary to regard the right to property as the only right in the French *Declaration of Rights* of 1791 that is sacred, and the one on which all the others are based, he criticizes Marx for what he is unable to see in the "rights of man":

> Marx falls into and draws us into a trap, which on other occasions and for other purposes, he was very skilful in dismantling: that of ideology. He allows himself to become the prisoner of the ideological version of rights, without examining what they mean in practice, what profound changes they bring to social life. And, as a result, he becomes blind to what, in the very text of the Declaration, appears on the margins of ideology. (Lefort 1986: 248)

Marx is blind to the question of the rights of man, in particular to their symbolic function, because, ironically, he accepts bourgeois ideology. For him, the system of law has no other meaning, therefore, than that which the bourgeois gives to it. Foucault can be accused of similar reductionism. In the lectures of 1976, the system of law in the West has no other meaning than that which he assigns to the theory of sovereignty, that is, a juridical representation of power.

> Right in the West is the King's right. (...) I believe that the King remains the central personage in the whole legal edifice of the West. When it comes to the general organisation of the legal system in the West, it is essentially with the King, his rights, his power and its eventual limitations, that one is dealing. (...) The system of right is centred entirely upon the King, and it is therefore designed to eliminate the fact of domination and its consequences. (Foucault 1980c: 94–5)

For Foucault the rule of right represents the monarchy, a social system where power, knowledge, and right are fused in the body of the sovereign. He suggests that in order to resist disciplinary power one should not invoke the notion of right, but turn instead, "towards the possibility of a new form of right, one which must indeed be anti-disciplinarian, but at the same time liberated from the principle of Sovereignty" (Foucault 1980c: 108).

* * * * *

The nature of the relation between the individual and the political order concerned Foucault in his studies of "bio-power" and "bio-politics." In this work, he implicitly negates his earlier claims that rights in the West were unequivocally linked to the sovereign (1980b, 1988, 1991). Foucault introduced the notion of "bio-power" in his work on sexuality to designate the proliferation of a technology of power-knowledge primarily concerned with life. Bio-power was a mechanism that took charge of life by "investing the body, health, modes of subsistence and habitation, living conditions, *the whole space of existence*" (Foucault 1980b: 143–44, emphasis added). The notion of bio-power is useful for our understanding of the phenomenon of resistance because while it represents a totalizing or universal mechanism—one that interpellates the subject as a member of a population—it also contains the seed for a counter-power or a counter-politics because that mechanism individualizes the subject of a population. It is this aspect of bio-power, its simultaneous totalizing and individualizing tendencies, that is of importance in understanding the strategies by which individual subjects can claim the right to self-determination. Foucault explains that

> against this [bio-] power that was still new in the nineteenth century, the forces that resisted relied for support on the very thing it invested, that is, on life and man as a living being. Since the last century, the great struggles that have challenged the general system of power were not guided by the belief in a return to former rights, or by the age-old dream of a cycle of time or a Golden Age. (...) [W]hat was demanded and what served as an objective was life, understood as the basic needs, man's concrete essence, the realization of his potential, a plentitude of the possible. Whether or not it was Utopia that was wanted is of little importance; what we have seen has been a very real process of struggle; life as a political object was in a sense taken at face value and turned back against the system that was bent on controlling it. It was life more than the law that became the issue of political struggles, even if the latter were formulated through affirmations concerning rights. The "right" to life, to one's body, to health, to happiness, to the satisfaction of needs, and beyond all the oppressions or "alienations," the "right" to rediscover what one is and all that one can be, this "right" (...) was the political response to all these new procedures of power which did not derive, either, from the traditional right of sovereignty. (Foucault 1980b: 144–5)

If life, understood here as "man's concrete essence," is affirmed through rights claims, then, like Foucault, we can no longer conceive law as necessarily linked to the sovereign. It must be linked to a different political rationality, one I believe, in which human rights are at the centre.

While Foucault never specifically addressed the question of human rights, his lectures on "bio-politics" (at the College de France between 1978 and 1979) suggest that struggles for life and for self-determination are to be understood in the context of liberalism. In his lectures, he explores the relation between bio-power—the mechanisms taking charge of life—and the emergence of bio-politics, by which he means

> the way in which a rationalization was attempted, dating from the eighteenth century, for the problems posed to governmental practice by the phenomena specific to an ensemble of living beings: health, hygiene, birthrate, longevity, races ... (1981: 353)

Foucault's statement is significant because it suggests that we cannot dissociate the problems posed by the question of population (bio-power) from the political rationality within which they emerged, liberalism. Far from conceiving it as a political theory or a representation of society, Foucault understands liberalism as an "art of government," that is, as a particular practice, activity and rationality used to administer, shape, and direct the conduct of people (1981: 358). As a rationality of government—a "govern mentality"—liberalism, towards the beginning of the eighteenth century, breaks from reason of state (*la raison d'état*) which since the sixteenth century had sought to "justify the growing exercise of government" (Foucault 1981: 354). What distinguishes liberalism from reason of state as an art of government is that for liberalism "there is always too much government" (Foucault 1981: 354–5). In fact, far from being organized around the principle of a strong state, liberalism upholds the principle of maximal economy with minimal government (Foucault 1981: 354).

The question of liberalism, that of "too much governing," regulates itself, according to Foucault, "by means of a continuing reflection" (1981: 354). The idea of reflexivity here is significant because it refers to a mechanism of self-critique, and self-limitation, inherent in liberalism. Foucault claims that

> Liberalism (...) constitutes—and this is the reason both for its polymorphous character and for its recurrences—an instrument for the criticism of reality, liberalism criticizes an earlier functioning government from which one tries to escape; it examines an actual practice of government that one attempts to reform and to rationalize by a fundamental analysis; it criticizes a practice of government to which one is opposed and whose abuses one wishes to curb. As a result of this, one can discover liberalism under different but simultaneous forms, both as a schema

for the regulation of governmental practice and as a theme for sometimes radical opposition to such practice. (Foucault 1981: 356)

What allows liberalism to oppose state power, then, is not the principle of sovereignty or the idea of a natural right external to the state; rather, it is a rationality, a governmentality of life that takes on "the character of a challenge" (Foucault 1981: 353). People resist the conditions under which they live, they make claims for or against the state, because they have been submitted to government. In other words, the political technologies that seek to render us governable as a population (bio-power and bio-politics) simultaneously make possible the critique of these same technologies.[7]

* * * * *

NOTES

1. Historian David Garland emphasizes this phenomenon in accounts of prison reform: "Foucault's emphatic depiction of punishment as a technology of power-knowledge and his primarily political account of its historical development have produced an instrumental and functionalist conception of punishment in which penal practice is always shaped exclusively by the requirements of social control and in which its design is always calculated to maximize control effects" (Garland 1990: 193).

2. Cohen 1979, 1983, 1985; Ericson 1985, 1987; Ericson and Baranek 1982; Chan and Ericson 1981; Giffen and Lambert 1988; Ben-Yehuda 1985; Small 1988; Smart 1989; Watney 1987.

3. Ericson has since modified his "instrumentalist" account of power. See R.V. Ericson, P. Baranek, and J. Chan (1987), (1989), and (1991).

4. I added "of" to the last sentence because I find the translation awkward. In French it reads: "Il faut noter d'ailleurs que ces ensembles ne consistent pas en une homogénéisation très bien plûtot en un jeu complexe d'appuis que prennent les uns sur les autres, les différents mécanismes de pouvoir, qui restent bien spécifiques" (Foucault 1977b: 124).

5. Foucault used the French word "subjectivation," which is translated either as "subjectification" or "subjectivization." In either case, it is used to refer to the procedure by which the individual constitute him or herself as his or her own master.

6. Throughout much of his early career Foucault explored the relationship between subjectification and power. In *Madness and Civilization* (1967), Foucault contends that the creation of the mad as a special category distinct from the criminal was not initially the result of a mechanism designed to oppress "the other," but corresponded instead to a shift in the practice of confinement and exclusion. In the nineteenth century a new practice of confining insane and criminal people together emerged. Out of this practice, the confined criminals experienced, Foucault claims, an acute sense of difference, antagonism, and injustice, which in turn led to a strategy of resistance on their part.

It was in the name of their differences that the "libertines," the "debauched," and the "prodigal sons" called attention to the *mélange* of categories and demanded their separation from the insane. The criminals resisted the association with the mad because madness, as Foucault demonstrated, became "the specter of the internees, the very image of their humiliation, of their reason vanquished and reduced to silence" (1967: 224–5). What is significant from the point of view of the exercise of power and resistance is that the criminal class demanded *for itself* a separation from "the other." Far from being a strategy of repression, the separation of the sane from the mad was part of a strategy to maximize life, in this case the life of an influential criminal nobility which defined itself as sane.

7. Burchell similarly argues for the centrality of resistance in Foucault's views on liberalism: "it is in the name of forms of existence which have been shaped by political technologies of *government* that we, as individuals and groups, make claims on or against the state" (1991: 217 emphasis in original).

REFERENCES

Ben-Yehuda, N. 1985 *Deviance and Moral Boundaries*. Chicago: University of Chicago Press.

Burchell, G., Gordon, C., and Miller, P. (eds). 1991 *The Foucault Effect: Studies in Governmentality*. Chicago: The University of Chicago Press.

Chan, J. and Ericson, R.V. 1981 *Decarceration and the Economy of Penal Reform*, Research Monograph No. 14. Toronto: Centre of Criminology, University of Toronto.

Cohen, S. 1979 "The Punitive City: Notes on the Dispersal of Social Control," *Contemporary Crisis* 3: 340–55.

_____. 1983 "Social-Control Talk: Telling Stories About Correctional Change," in D. Garland and P. Young (eds) *The Power to Punish: Penality and Social Analysis*. London: Heinemann Educational Books.

_____. 1985 *Visions of Social Control: Crime, Punishment and Classification*. Cambridge: Polity Press.

Deleuze, G. 1975 "Écrivain non: un nouveau cartographe," *Critique* 31(343): 1207–27.

Ericson, R.V. 1985 "Legal Inequality," *Research in Law, Deviance and Social Control* 7: 33–78.

_____. 1987 "The State and Criminal Justice Reform," in R.S. Ratner and J.L. McMullan (eds) *State Control: Criminal Justice Politics in Canada*. Vancouver: University of British Columbia Press.

Ericson, R.V. and Baranek, P.M. 1982 *The Ordering of Justice: A Study of Accused Persons as Dependants in the Criminal Process*. Toronto: University of Toronto Press.

Ericson, R.V. Baranek, P., and Chan, J. 1987 *Visualizing Deviance*. Toronto: University of Toronto Press and Milton Keynes: Open University Press.

_____. 1989 *Negotiating Control*. Toronto: University of Toronto Press and Milton Keynes: Open University Press.

_____. 1991 *Representing Order*. Toronto: University of Toronto Press and Milton Keynes: Open University Press.

Ewald, F. 1975 "Anatomic et corps politiques," *Critique* 31(343): 1228–65.

Foucault, M. 1967 *Madness and Civilization: A History of Insanity in the Age of Reason*, trans. R. Howard. London: Tavistock Publications.

_____. 1977b "Non au sexe roi," interview with Bernard-Henri Levy, *Le Nouvel Observateur* 644, 12 March: 92–130.

_____. 1979 *Discipline and Punish: The Birth of the Prison*, trans. A.M. Sheridan. Harmondwswoth: Penguin.

_____. 1980a "Two Lectures," in C. Gordon (ed.) *Power/Knowledge: Selected Interviews and other Writings 1972–1977*. Sussex: The Harvester Press.

_____. 1980b *The History of Sexuality Vol. 1: An Introduction*. New York: Vintage Books.

_____. 1980c *Power/Knowledge: Selected Interviews and other Writings 1972–1977*, (ed.) C. Gordon. New York: Pantheon Books.

_____. 1981 "History of Systems of Thoughts, 1979," *Philosophy and Social Criticism* 8(3): 352–60.

_____. 1982 "The Subject of Power," in H.L. Dreyfus and P. Rabinow, *Michel Foucault: Beyond Structuralism and Hemeneutics*. Sussex: The Harvester Press.

_____. 1988 "An Aesthetics of Existence," in L. D. Kriezman (ed.), *Foucault: Politics, Philosophy, Culture. Interviews and Other Writings 1977–1984*. New York: Routledge, Chapman & Hail.

_____. 1991 "Governmentality," in G. Burehell, C. Gordon, and P. Miller (eds), *The Foucault Effect: Studies in Govemmentality*. Chicago: The University of Chicago Press.

Garland, D. 1985 *Punishment and Welfare: A History of Penal Strategies*. Aldershot: Gower.

_____. 1986 "Foucault's Discipline and Punish, An Exposition and Critique," *American Bar Foundation Research Journal*: 847–81.

_____. 1990 *Punishment and Modern Society: A Study in Social Theory*. Chicago: The University of Chicago Press.

Giffen, J.P. and Lambert, S. 1988 "What Happened on the Way to Law Reform?," in J.C. Blackwell and P.G. Erickson (eds), *Illicit Drugs in Canada: A Risky Business*. Toronto: Nelson.

Ignatieff, M. 1978 *A Just Measure of Pain: The Penitentiary in the Industrial Revolution*. New York: Pantheon Books.

_____. 1983 "State, Civil Society and Total Institution: A Critique of Recent Social Histories of Punishment," in S. Cohen and A.T. Scull (eds), *Social Control and the State*. Oxford: Martin Robertson.

Lefort, C 1986 *The Political Forms of Modern Society: Bureaucracy, Democracy, Totalitarianism*, edited and introduced by John B. Thompson. Cambridge: The MIT Press.

_____. 1988 *Democracy and Political Theory*. Minneapolis: University of Minnesota Press.

McBarnett, D. 1981 *Conviction: Law, the State and the Construction of Justice*. London: Macmillan.

Melossi D. and Pavarani, M. 1981 *The Prison and the Factory: The Origins of the Penitentiary System*. London: Macmiilan.

Rothman, D. 1971 *The Discovery of the Asylum: Social Order and Disorder in the New Republic*. Boston: Little Brown.

_____. 1980 *Conscience and Convenience: The Asylum and its Alternatives in Progressive America.*
     Boston: Little Brown.
Rushe, G. and Kircheimer, O. 1968 *Punishment and Social Structure.* New York: Russell and
     Russell.
Small, N. 1988 "AIDS and Social Policy," *Critical Social Policy* 21: 9–29.
Smart, C. 1989 *Feminism and the Power of Law.* London: Routledge.
Watney, S. 1987 *Policing Desire: Pornography, AIDS and the Media.* London: Methuen.

CHAPTER 25

The Emergence of Life Politics

ANTHONY GIDDENS

* * * * *

Theodore Roszak has argued that "we live in a time when the very private experience of having a personal identity to discover, a personal destiny to fulfil, has become a subversive political force of major proportions."[1] Critics such as Lasch and others, he goes on to say, mistake the new ethos of self-discovery for the "old-modern" aggrandising individual; they fail to distinguish between new impulses towards personal growth, on the one hand, and capitalistic pressures towards personal advantage and material accumulation on the other. I think this is true, save that the issue has to be theorised rather differently. It is not the reflexive project of the self as such which is subversive; rather, the ethos of self-growth signals major social transitions in late modernity as a whole. [...]

⑤ WHAT IS EMANCIPATORY POLITICS?

From the relatively early development of the modern era onwards, the dynamism of modern institutions has stimulated, and to some extent has been promoted by, ideas of human *emancipation*. In the first place this was emancipation from the dogmatic imperatives of tradition and religion. Through the application of methods of rational understanding, not just to the areas of science and technology, but to human social life itself, human activity was to become free from pre-existing constraints.

If, with appropriate qualifications to cover over-simplification, we recognise three overall approaches within modern politics—radicalism (including Marxism in this category), liberalism, and conservatism—we can say that emancipatory politics has dominated all of them, although in rather differing ways. Liberal political thinkers, like radicals, have sought to free individuals and the conditions of social life more generally from the constraints of pre-existing practices and prejudices. Liberty is to be achieved through the progressive emancipation of the individual, in conjunction with the liberal state, rather than through a projected process of revolutionary upheaval. "Conservatism," the third category, almost by definition takes a more jaundiced view of the emancipatory possibilities of modernity. But conservative thought only exists as a reaction to emancipation: conservatism has developed as a rejection of radical and liberal thought, and as a critique of the disembedding tendencies of modernity.

I define emancipatory politics as a generic outlook concerned above all with liberating individuals and groups from constraints which adversely affect their life chances. Emancipatory politics involves two main elements: the effort to shed shackles of the past, thereby permitting a transformative attitude towards the future; and the aim of overcoming the illegitimate domination of some individuals or groups by others. The first of these objectives fosters the positive dynamic impetus of modernity. The breakaway from fixed practices of the past allows human beings to secure increasing social control over their life circumstances. Of course, major philosophical differences have arisen over how this aim is to be achieved. Some have supposed that the emancipatory drive is governed by causal conditions which, in social life, operate in much the same way as physical causation. For others—and this is surely more valid—the relation is a reflexive one. Human beings are able reflexively to "use history to make history."[2]

The liberating of human beings from traditional constraints has little "content" save for the fact that it reflects the characteristic orientation of modernity—the subjection to human control of features of the social and natural worlds that previously determined human activities. Emancipatory politics only achieves a more substantive content when it is focused on divisions between human beings. It is essentially a politics of "others." For Marx, of course, class was the agency of emancipation as well as the driving force of history. The general emancipation of humanity was to be achieved through the emergence of a classless order. For non-Marxist authors, emancipatory politics gives more far-reaching importance to other divisions: divisions of ethnicity and gender, divisions between ruling and subordinate groups, rich and poor nations, current and future generations. But in all cases the objective of emancipatory politics is either to release underprivileged groups from their unhappy condition, or to eliminate the relative differences between them.

Emancipatory politics works with a hierarchical notion of power: power is understood as the capability of an individual or group to exert its will over others. Several key concepts and orienting aims tend to be especially characteristic of this vision of politics. Emancipatory politics is concerned to reduce or eliminate *exploitation, inequality,* and *oppression.* [...] Exploitation in general presumes that one group—say, upper as compared to working classes, whites as compared to blacks, or men as compared to women—illegitimately monopolises resources or desired goods to which the exploited group is denied access. Inequalities can refer to any variations in scarce resources, but differential access to material rewards has often been given prime importance. Unlike inequalities in genetic inheritance, for instance, differential access to material rewards forms part of the generative mechanisms of modernity, and hence can in principle (not, of course, in practice) be transformed to any desired degree. Oppression is directly a matter of differential power, applied by one group to limit the life chances of another. Like other aspects of emancipatory politics, the aim to liberate people from situations of oppression implies the adoption of moral values. "Justifiable authority" can defend itself against the charge of oppression only where differential power can be shown to be morally illegitimate.

Emancipatory politics makes primary the imperatives of *justice, equality,* and *participation.* In a general way these correspond to the three types of power division just mentioned. All have many variant formulations and can overlap more or less substantially.

* * * * *

⑤ THE NATURE OF LIFE POLITICS

Life politics presumes (a certain level of) emancipation, in both the main senses noted above: emancipation from the fixities of tradition and from conditions of hierarchical domination. It would be too crude to say simply that life politics focuses on what happens once individuals have achieved a certain level of autonomy of action, because other factors are involved; but this provides at least an initial orientation. Life politics does not primarily concern the conditions which liberate us in order to make choices: it is a politics *of* choice. While emancipatory politics is a politics of life chances, life politics is a politics of lifestyle. Life politics is the politics of a reflexively mobilised order—the system of late modernity—which, on an individual and collective level, has radically altered the existential parameters of social activity. It is a politics of self-actualisation in a reflexively ordered environment, where that reflexivity links self and body to systems of global scope. In this arena of activity, power is generative rather than hierarchical. Life politics is lifestyle politics. [...] To give a formal definition: life politics concerns political issues which flow from processes of self-actualisation in post-traditional contexts, where globalising influences intrude deeply into the reflexive project of the self, and conversely where processes of self-realisation influence global strategies.

* * * * *

Life politics, to repeat, is a politics of life decisions. What are these decisions and how should we seek to conceptualise them? First and foremost, there are those affecting self-identity itself. [...] Self-identity today is a reflexive achievement. The narrative of self-identity has to be shaped, altered, and reflexively sustained in relation to rapidly changing circumstances of social life on a local and global

Emancipatory Politics	Life Politics
1. The freeing of social life from the fixities of tradition and custom.	1. Political decisions flowing from freedom of choice and generative power (power as transformative capacity).
2. The reduction or elimination of exploitation, inequality, or oppression. Concerned with the divisive distribution of power/ resources.	2. The creation of morally justifiable forms of life that will promote self-actualisation in the context of global interdependence.
3. Obeys imperatives suggested by the ethics of justice, equality, and participation.	3. Develops ethics concerning the issue "how should we live?" in a post-traditional order and against the backdrop of existential questions.

scale. The individual must integrate information deriving from a diversity of mediated experiences with local involvements in such a way as to connect future projects with past experiences in a reasonably coherent fashion. Only if the person is able to develop an inner authenticity—a framework of basic trust by means of which the lifespan can be understood as a unity against the backdrop of shifting social events—can this be attained. A reflexively ordered narrative of self-identity provides the means of giving coherence to the finite lifespan, given changing external circumstances. Life politics from this perspective concerns debates and contestations deriving from the reflexive project of the self.

In exploring the idea that the "personal is political," the student movement, but more particularly the women's movement, pioneered this aspect of life politics. But they did so in an ambiguous manner. Members of the student movement, especially those associated with "situationalism," tried to use personal gestures and "lifestyle revolts" as a mode of throwing down a challenge to officialdom. They wanted to show not only that daily life expresses aspects of state power, but that by overturning ordinary daily patterns they could actually threaten the power of the state. Seen in this way, however, the politics of the personal only vaguely foreshadows life politics, and remains closer to the emancipatory form. For the objective is to use lifestyle patterns as a means of combating, or sublating, oppression.

Feminism can more properly be regarded as opening up the sphere of life politics—although, of course, emancipatory concerns remain fundamental to women's movements. Feminism, at least in its contemporary form, has been more or less obliged to give priority to the question of self-identity. "Women who want more than family life," it has been aptly remarked, "make the personal political with every step they take away from the home."[3] In so far as women increasingly "take the step" outside, they contribute to processes of emancipation. Yet feminists soon came to see that, for the emancipated woman, questions of identity become of pre-eminent importance. For in liberating themselves from the home, and from domesticity, women were faced with a closed-off social environment. Women's identities were defined so closely in terms of the home and the family that they "stepped outside" into social settings in which the only available identities were those offered by male stereotypes.

When Betty Friedan first spoke of "the problem that has no name," some quarter of a century ago, she meant that being a wife and mother failed to provide the fulfilling life for which many women, almost without knowing it, yearned.[4] Her analysis of this problem led Friedan directly to a discussion of identity and the self. The real "question which has no name" turns out to be "who do I want to be?"[5] Friedan specifically related the issue to her own experiences as a young woman. Having just graduated from college, she felt she had many options open to her, including that of following a professional career as a psychologist. Yet instead of taking up a fellowship she had won for a doctoral programme, she abandoned that possible career without really knowing why. She married, had children, and lived as a suburban housewife—all the while suppressing her qualms about her lack of purpose in life. In the end, she broke away by acknowledging and facing up to the question of her self-identity, coming to see that she needed self-fulfillment elsewhere.

Betty Friedan's deep disquiet about personal identity, she made clear, only came about because there were now more options available for women. It is only in the light of these alternatives that women have come to see that modern culture does not "gratify their basic need to grow and fulfil their potentialities as human beings …"[6] Her book concluded with a discussion of life-planning, the means of helping women create new self-identities in the previously unexplored public domain. Her "new life-plan for women" anticipated many features of self-help manuals that were to come later. The new life-plan involved a commitment to personal growth, a rethinking and reconstruction of the past—by rejecting the "feminine mystique"—and the recognition of risk.

⑤ LIFE POLITICS, BODY, AND SELF

Today, some quarter of a century after Friedan's pathbreaking book first appeared, it has become obvious that many of the issues which at first seemed to concern only women are actually bound up with the relational phenomenon of gender identity. What gender identity is, and how it should be expressed, has become itself a matter of multiple options—ranging up to and including even the choice of whether a person remains anatomically of the same sex into which she or he was born. The politics of self-identity, of course, is not limited to matters of gender differentiation. The more we reflexively "make ourselves" as persons, the more the very category of what a "person" or "human being" is comes to the fore. Many examples can be found to illustrate how and why this is so. For instance, current debates about abortion might seem limited to the body and the rights the body's "owner" might or might not have over its products. But discussions of abortion also turn in some part on whether or not a foetus is a person and, if so, at what point in its development it can be counted as one. In this issue, as so often in the areas of life politics, we find conjoined problems of philosophical definition, human rights, and morality.

As the case of abortion indicates, it is not always easy to distinguish life-political questions concerning self-identity from those that focus more specifically on the body. Like the self the body can no longer be taken as a fixed—a physiological entity—but has become deeply involved with modernity's reflexivity. The body used to be one aspect of nature, governed in a fundamental way by processes only marginally subject to human intervention. The body was a "given," the often inconvenient and inadequate seat of the self. With the increasing invasion of the body by abstract systems, all this becomes altered. The body, like the self, becomes a site of interaction, appropriation, and reappropriation, linking reflexively organised processes and systematically ordered expert knowledge. The body itself has become emancipated—the condition for its reflexive restructuring. Once thought to be the locus of the soul, then the centre of dark, perverse needs, the body has become fully available to be "worked upon" by the influences of high modernity. As a result of these processes, its boundaries have altered. It has, as it were, a thoroughly permeable "outer layer" through which the reflexive project of the self and externally formed abstract systems routinely enter. In the conceptual space between these, we find more and more guidebooks and practical manuals to do with health, diet, appearance, exercise, lovemaking, and many other things.

Reflexive appropriation of bodily processes and development is a fundamental element of life-political debates and struggles. It is important to emphasise this point in order to see that the body has not become just an inert entity, subject to commodification or "discipline" in Foucault's sense. If such were the case, the body would be primarily a site of emancipatory politics: the point would then be to free the body from the oppression to which it had fallen prey. In conditions of high modernity, the body is actually far less "docile" than ever before in relation to the self, since the two become intimately coordinated within the reflexive project of self-identity. The body itself—as mobilised in praxis—becomes more immediately relevant to the identity the individual promotes. As Melucci observes,

> the return to the body initiates a new search for identity. The body appears as a secret domain, to which only the individual holds the key, and to which he or she can return to seek a self-definition unfettered by the rules and expectations of society. Nowadays the social attribution of identity invades all areas traditionally protected by the barrier of "private space."[7]

We can recognise the problem of "ownership" of the body as one distinctive issue posed by its double involvement with abstract systems and the reflexive project of the self. As was mentioned before, "ownership" here is a complex notion bringing in all the problems of defining a "person." In the sphere of life politics, this problem includes how the individual is to make choices concerning strategies of bodily development in life-planning, as well as who is to determine the "disposal" of bodily products and bodily parts.

Body and self are linked in another fundamental domain that has become thoroughly penetrated by the internally referential systems of modernity: reproduction. The term "reproduction" can be used to refer both to social continuity and to the biological continuance of the species. The terminological connection is not accidental: "biological" reproduction is by now wholly social, that is, evacuated by abstract systems and reconstituted through the reflexivity of the self. Reproduction clearly was never solely a matter of external determinism: in all pre-modern cultures various kinds of contraceptive methods, for example, have been used. Nonetheless, for the most part the sphere of reproduction belonged irremediably to the arena of fate. With the advent of more or less fail-safe methods of contraception, reflexive control over sexual practices, and the introduction of reproductive technologies of various kinds, reproduction is now a field where plurality of choice prevails.

The "end of reproduction as fate" is closely tied in to the "end of nature." For until now reproduction has always been at one pole of human involvement with separated nature—death being at the other. Genetic engineering, whose potentialities have only just begun to be tapped, represents a further dissolution of reproduction as a natural process. Genetic transmission can be humanly determined by this means, thus breaking the final tie connecting the life of the species to biological evolution. In this process of the disappearance of nature, emergent fields of decision-making affect not just the direct process of reproduction, but the physical constitution of the body and the manifestations of sexuality. Such fields of action thus relate back to questions of gender and gender identity, as well as to other processes of identity formation.

Reproductive technologies alter age-old oppositions between fertility and sterility. Artificial insemination and *in vitro* fertilisation more or less completely separate reproduction from the traditional categories of heterosexual experience. The sterile can be made fertile, but various permutations of surrogate parenthood are also thus made possible. The opportunity offered for gay couples, for instance, to produce and rear children is only one among various lifestyle options flowing from these innovations. The fact that sexuality no longer need have anything to do with reproduction—or vice versa—serves to reorder sexuality in relation to lifestyles (although, as always, in large degree only through the medium of reflexive appropriation).

The variety of options now introduced, or likely to be developed soon, in the area of reproductive technologies provides a signal example of the opportunities and problems of life politics. The birth of Louise Brown, on 25 July, 1978, marked a new transition in human reproduction. The creation of new life—rather than the negative control of life through contraception—for the first time became a matter of deliberate construction. *In vitro* fertilisation (IVF) uses many techniques which have been around for some while, but certain key innovations have allowed these to be used to fertilise a human egg outside the body. A further development is pre-implantation sex screening. By means of IVF methods, it is possible to transfer an already "sexed" embryo to a woman's womb by DNA amplification techniques. Male and female embryos can be distinguished by such techniques, and an embryo of the desired sex implanted. To these techniques can be added embryo freezing. This process allows embryos to be stored for an indefinite length of time, permitting multiple pregnancies without the need for further ovary stimulation and egg collection. Thus, it is possible, for example, for identical twins to be born years apart from one another.

Further developments which look at least feasible in the control of human reproduction include ectogenesis and cloning. Ectogenesis is the creation of human life entirely outside the body: the production of children without pregnancy. Cloning, the creation of a number of genetically identical individuals, although perhaps more bizarre, appears closer at hand, and has already been achieved in animal experiments.[8]

🖅 PERSONAL LIVES, PLANETARY NEEDS

The discussion thus far draws in the world of social relations external to the self mainly in terms of their reflexive impact on self-identity and lifestyle. However, personal decisions also affect global considerations—the link in this case is from "person" to "planet." Socialised reproduction connects individual decisions to the very continuity of the species on the earth. To the extent to which the reproduction of the species and sexuality become uncoupled, future species reproduction is no longer guaranteed. Global population development becomes incorporated within internally referential systems. A host of individual decision-making processes, linked through these systems, are likely to produce unpredictabilities comparable to those generated by other socialised orders. Reproduction becomes a variable individual decision, with an overall impact on species reproduction which might be imponderable.

We can trace out yet further connections between lifestyle options and globalising influences. Consider the related topics of global ecology and attempts to reduce risks of nuclear war. In broaching ecological issues, and their relation to political debates, we have to ask first of all why they should be so much the focus of attention today. The answer is partly to be found in the accumulating evidence that the material environment has been subject to more far-reaching and intensive processes of decay than was previously suspected to be the case. Much more decisive, however, are the alterations in human attitudes relevant to the issue. For the fact that nature has "come to an end" is not confined to the specialist awareness of professionals;

it is known to the public at large. A clear part of increased ecological concern is the recognition that reversing the degradation of the environment depends upon adopting new lifestyle patterns. By far the greatest amount of ecological damage derives from the modes of life followed in the modernised sectors of world society. Ecological problems highlight the new and accelerating interdependence of global systems and bring home to everyone the depth of the connections between personal activity and planetary problems.

Grappling with the threats raised by the damaging of the earth's eco-systems is bound to demand coordinated global responses on levels far removed from individual action. On the other hand, these threats will not be effectively countered unless there is reaction and adaption on the part of every individual. Widespread changes in lifestyle, coupled with a de-emphasis on continual economic accumulation, will almost certainly be necessary if the ecological risks we now face are to be minimised. In a complicated interweaving of reflexivity, widespread reflexive awareness of the reflexive nature of the systems currently transforming ecological patterns is both necessary and likely to emerge.

The issue of nuclear power is at the centre of these concerns, and, of course, forms a link between ecological issues more generally and the existence of nuclear weapons. Debates about whether or not nuclear power stations should continue to be built and, if so, what their relation should be to existing sources of material power exemplify many of the questions raised in the area of life politics. High-consequence risks are involved, some deriving from long-term, incremental factors, others from more immediate influences. Technical calculations of levels of risk here cannot be completely watertight, because they cannot wholly control for human error and because there may be factors as yet unforeseen. A person who wishes to become informed about debates concerning nuclear power will find that experts are as radically divided in their assessments as in other areas where abstract systems prevail. Unless some other—so far unknown—technological breakthrough is made, the widespread use of nuclear power is likely to be unavoidable if global processes of economic growth carry on at the same rate as today, and even more so if they intensify.

Decreasing dependence on nuclear power, or seeking to eliminate nuclear power sources altogether, either in particular regions and countries or on a wider scale, would involve significant lifestyle changes. As in other areas of the expansion of internally referential systems, no one can be quite sure how much damage to human life and to the physical environment might already have been done by existing nuclear power sources; the evidence is controversial. We come back again to personal questions of socialised biology and reproduction. As one author has put it, "our sperm, our eggs, our embryos and our children" are "in the front line" in the struggle on the "toxic frontier."[9]

As the proponents of "deep ecology" assert, a movement away from economic accumulation might involve substituting personal growth—the cultivation of the potentialities for self-expression and creativity—for unfettered economic growth processes. The reflexive project of the self might therefore be the very hinge of a transition to a global order beyond the current one. The threat of nuclear war is also linked to the reflexive project of the self. As Lasch says, both throw the problem of "survival" into sharp relief. Yet one might equally well say that they both throw into relief the possibility of peace: harmonious human coexistence on the global level and psychologically rewarding self-actualisation on the personal plane. The issue of nuclear weaponry enters life politics as a positive appropriation as well as a negative one. It shows with particular clarity the degree to which the personal and global are interconnected because, as in the case of potential ecological disaster, there is nowhere anyone can go on earth to escape. Military technology has become more and more complex, a series of expert systems about which it is difficult for the layperson to get much specialist knowledge (in some part because of the secrecy with which weapon systems are surrounded). Yet this very process makes the potential outbreak of nuclear war no longer just a specific concern of military tacticians and political leaders, but a matter which impinges on the life of everyone. Operating under a negative sign, the danger of nuclear confrontation coincides with other aspects of the life-political field in stimulating reflexive awareness of the socialisation of nature and its implications for personal life.

* * * * *

NOTES

1. Theodore Roszak, *Person-Planet: The Creative Destruction of Industrial Society* (London: Gollancz, 1979), p. xxviii.
2. Cf. Jürgen Habermas, *Knowledge and Human Interests* (Cambridge: Polity, 1987)—the classic discussion of this issue.
3. Barbara Sichtermann, *Femininity: The Politics of the Personal* (Cambridge: Polity, 1986), p. 2.
4. Betty Frieden, *The Feminine Mystique* (Harmondsworth: Pelican, 1965).
5. Ibid., p. 61.
6. Ibid., p. 68.
7. Alberto Melucci, *Nomads of the Present* (London: Hutchinson Radius, 1989), p. 123.
8. David Suzuki and Peter Knudtson, *Genethics: The Ethics of Engineering Life* (London: Unwin Hyman, 1989).
9. John Elington, *The Poisoned Womb* (Harmondsworth: Penguin, 1986), p. 236.

CHAPTER 26

Introduction: The Cosmopolitan Manifesto

ULRICH BECK

All around the world, contemporary society is undergoing radical change that poses a challenge to Enlightenment-based modernity and opens a field where people *choose* new and unexpected forms of the social and the political. Sociological debates of the nineties have sought to grasp and conceptualize this reconfiguration. Some authors lay great stress on the openness of the human project amid new contingencies, complexities, and uncertainties, whether their main operative term is "postmodernity" (Bauman, Lyotard, Harvey, Haraway), "late modernity" (Giddens), the "global age" (Albrow) or "reflexive modernization" (Beck, Giddens, Lash). Others have prioritized research into new forms of experimental identity (Melucci) and sociality (Maffesoli), the relationship between individualization and political culture (Touraine), the "post-national constellation" (Habermas), or the preconditions of "cosmopolitan democracy" (Held). Others still have contributed a wave of books on the "politics of nature" (Vandana Shiva, Gernot Bohme, Maarten Hajer, John S. Dryzek, Tim Hayward, Andrew Dobson, Barbara Adam, Robin Grove-White, and Brian Wynne). All agree that in the decades ahead we will confront profound contradictions and perplexing paradoxes, and experience hope embedded in despair.

In an attempt to summarize and systematize these transformations, I have for some time been working with a distinction between first modernity and second modernity. The former term I use to describe the modernity based on nation-state societies, where social relations, networks, and communities are essentially understood in a territorial sense. The collective patterns of life, progress and controllability, full employment, and exploitation of nature that were typical of this first modernity have now been undermined by five interlinked processes: globalization, individualization, gender revolution, underemployment, and global risks (as ecological crisis and the crash of global financial markets). The real theoretical and political challenge of the second modernity is the fact that society must respond to all these challenges *simultaneously*.

If the five processes are considered more closely, it becomes clear what they have in common: namely, they are all unforeseen consequences of the victory of the first, simple, linear, industrial modernization based on the national state (the focus of classical sociology from Durkheim, Weber, and Marx to Parsons and Luhmann). This is what I mean by talking of "reflexive modernization." Radicalized modernization undermines the foundations of the first modernity and changes its frame of reference, often in a way that is neither desired nor anticipated. Or, in the terms of system theory: the unforeseen consequences of functional differentiation can no longer be controlled by further functional differentiation. In fact, the very idea of controllability, certainty, or security—which is so fundamental in the first modernity—collapses. A new kind of capitalism, a new kind of economy, a new kind of global order, a new kind of society, and a new kind of personal life are coming into being, all of which differ from earlier phases of social development. Thus, sociologically and politically, we need a paradigm-shift, a new frame of reference. This is not "postmodernity" but a second modernity, and the task that faces us is to reform sociology so that it can provide a new framework for the reinvention of society and politics. Research work on reflexive modernization does not deal only with the *decline* of the Western model. The key question is how that model relates to the *different modernities* in other parts of the world. Which new and unexpected forms of the social are emerging? Which new social and political forces, and which lines of conflict, are appearing on the horizon?

In world risk society, non-Western societies share with the West not only the same space and time but also—more importantly—the same basic challenges of the second modernity (in different places and with different cultural perceptions). To stress this aspect of sameness—and not otherness—is already an important step in revising the evolutionary bias that afflicts much of Western social science to this day, a bias whereby contemporary non-Western societies are relegated to the category of "traditional" or "pre-modern" and thus defined not in their own terms, but as the opposite or the absence of modernity. (Many even believe that the study of pre-modern Western societies can help us understand the characteristics of non-Western societies today!) To situate the non-Western world firmly within the ambit of a second modernity, rather than of tradition, allows a *pluralization of modernity*, for it opens up space for the conceptualization of divergent trajectories of modernities in different parts of the world. This idea of multiple modernities recalls Nehru's image of a "garb of modernity" that can be worn in a number of ingeniously different ways.[1]

The increasing speed, intensity, and significance of processes of transnational interdependence, and the growth in discourses of economic, cultural, political, and societal "globalization," suggest not only that non-Western societies should be included in any analysis of the challenges of the second modernity, but also that the specific refractions and reflections of the global need to be examined in these different sites of the emerging global society.

Reversing Marx's judgement, we could say with Shalini Randeria that many parts of the "Third World" today show Europe the image of its own future. On the positive side, we could list such features as the development of multi-religious, multi-ethnic, and multi-cultural societies, the cross-cultural models and the tolerance of cultural difference, the legal pluralism observable at a number of levels, and the multiplication of sovereignties. On the negative side, we could point to the spread of the informal sector and the flexibilization of labour, the legal deregulation of large areas of the economy and work relations, the loss of legitimacy by the state, the growth of unemployment and underemployment, the more forceful intervention by multinational corporations, and the high rates of everyday violence and crime. All these aspects, together with related questions and arguments, imply that we need a new frame of reference for the world risk society (including non-Western countries) in which we live if we are to understand the dynamics and contradictions of the second modernity (see *Korean Journal of Sociology*, 1998).

As the bipolar world fades away, we are moving from a world of enemies to one of dangers and risks. But what does "risk" mean? Risk is the modern approach to foresee and control the future consequences of human action, the various unintended consequences of radicalized modernization. It is an (institutionalized) attempt, a cognitive map, to colonize the future. Every society has, of course, experienced dangers. But the risk regime is a function of a new order: it is not national, but global. It is rather intimately connected with an administrative and technical decision-making process. Risks presuppose decision. These decisions were previously undertaken with fixed norms of calculability, connecting means and ends or causes and effects. These norms are precisely what "world risk society" has rendered invalid. All of this becomes very evident with private insurance, perhaps the greatest symbol of calculation and alternative security—which does not cover nuclear disaster, nor climate change and its consequences, nor the breakdown of Asian economies, nor the low-probability high-consequences risk of various forms of future technology. In fact, most controversial technologies, like genetic engineering, are not privately insured.

What has given rise to this new prominence of risk? The concept of risk and risk society combines what once was mutually exclusive—society and nature, social sciences and material sciences, the discursive construction of risk and the materiality of threats. Margaret Thatcher, the former British Prime Minister, once said: there is no such thing as society. Most sociologists believe in what can be called a "reverse Thatcherism," namely there is *nothing but society*. This "nothing but society" sociology is blind to the ecological and technological challenges of second modernity. Risk society theory breaks with this self-sufficiency and self-centredness. It argues that there is at the same time the immateriality of mediated and contested definitions of risk *and* the materiality of risk as manufactured by experts and industries world-wide. This has many implications. For example, risk analysis needs an interdisciplinary approach. Risk science without the sociological imagination of constructed and contested risk is *blind*. Risk science that is not informed about the technologically manufactured "second nature" of threats is *naive*. The ontology of risk as such does not grant privilege to any specific form of knowledge. It forces everyone to combine different and often divergent rationality-claims, to act and react in the face of "contradictory certainties" (Schwarz and Thompson, 1990).

* * * * *

Thus, the framework of risk society again connects what have been strictly discrete areas: the question of nature, the democratization of democracy, and the future role of the state. Much political debate over the last twenty years has centred on the decline in the power and legitimacy of government and the need to renew the culture of democracy. Risk society demands an opening up of the decision-making process, not only of the state but of private corporations and the sciences as well. It calls for institutional reform of those "relations of definition," the hidden power-structure of risk conflicts. This could encourage environmental innovations and help to construct a better developed public sphere in which the crucial questions of value that underpin risk conflicts can be debated and judged (see Jacobs, 1997).

But at the same time new prominence of risk connects, on the one hand, individual autonomy and insecurity in the labour market and in gender relations, and, on the other hand, the sweeping influence of scientific and technological change. World risk society opens public discourse and social science to the challenges of ecological crisis, which, as we now know, are global, local, and personal at one and the same time. Nor is this all. In the "global age," the theme of risk unites many otherwise disparate areas of new transnational politics with the question of cosmopolitan democracy: with the new political economy of uncertainty, financial markets, transcultural conflicts over food and other products (BSE), emerging "risk communities," and, last but not least, the anarchy of international relations. Personal biographies as well as world politics are getting "risky" in the global world of manufactured uncertainties.

But the globality of risk does not, of course, mean a global equality of risk. The opposite is true: the first law of environmental risks is: *pollution follows the poor*. In the last decade poverty has intensified everywhere. The UN says more than 2,400 million people now live without sanitation, a considerable increase on a decade ago; 1,200 million have no safe drinking water; similar numbers have inadequate housing, health, and education services; more than 1,500 million are now undernourished, not because there is no food, or there is too much drought, but because of the increasing marginalization and exclusion of the poor.

Not only has the gap between rich and poor grown, but more people are falling into the poverty trap. Free-market economic policies, imposed on indebted countries by the West, worsen the situation by forcing countries to develop expert industry to supply the rich, rather than to protect, educate, or care for the weakest. The poorest countries now spend more servicing their debt to the richest countries than they do on health and education in their own countries.

The past decade has shown that the dogmatic free-market economics imposed throughout the 1980s—and to which every world and nation forum has since signed up—has exacerbated environmental risks and problems just as much as central planning from Moscow ever did. Indeed free-market ideology has increased the sum of human misery. On the back of crucial free-trade pacts like the WTO and NAFTA, for example, consumption is now virtually out of control in the richest countries. It has multiplied six times in less than twenty-five years, according to the UN. The richest 20 per cent of the people are consuming roughly six times more food, energy, water, transportation, oil, and minerals than their parents were.

* * * * *

We live in an age of risk that is global, individualistic, and more moral than we suppose. The ethic of individual self-fulfilment and achievement is the most powerful current in modern Western society. Choosing, deciding, shaping individuals who aspire to be the authors of their lives, the creators of their identities, are the central characters of our time.

This "me-first" generation has been much criticized, but I believe its individualism is moral and political in a new sense. In many ways this is a more moral time than the 1950s and 1960s. Freedom's children feel more passionately and morally than people used to do about a wide range of issues—from our treatment of the environment and animals, to gender, race, and human rights around the world.

It could be that this provides the basis for a new cosmopolitanism, by placing globality at the heart of political imagination, action, and organization. But any attempt to create a new sense of social cohesion has to start from the recognition that individualization, diversity, and scepticism are written into our culture.

Let us be clear what "individualization" means. It does not mean individualism. It does *not* mean individuation—how to become a unique person. It is not Thatcherism, not market individualism, not atomization. On the contrary, individualization is a *structural* concept, related to the welfare state; it means "*institutionalized individualism.*" Most of the rights and entitlements of the welfare state, for example, are designed for individuals rather than for families. In many cases they presuppose employment. Employment in turn implies education, and both of these presuppose mobility. By all these requirements people are invited to constitute themselves as individuals: to plan, understand, design themselves as individuals and, should they fail, to blame themselves. Individualization thus implies, paradoxically, a collective lifestyle.

When this is coupled with the language of ethical globalization, I am convinced that a cosmopolitan democracy is a realistic, if Utopian, project—though in an age of side-effects, we must also reflect on the dark side, on the ways it can be used politically as a front for old-style imperial adventures.

Are we a "me-first" society? One might think so from the catch-phrases that dominate public debate: the dissolving of solidarity, the decline of values, the culture of narcissism, entitlement-oriented hedonism, and so on. On this view, modern society lives off moral resources it is unable to renew; the transcendental "value ecology," in which community, solidarity, justice, and ultimately democracy are "rooted," is decaying; modernity is undermining its own indispensable moral prerequisites.

But this conception of modern society is false. Morality, including Christian morality, and political freedom are not mutually exclusive but mutually inclusive, even if this means that an insoluble contradiction is lodged within Christian traditions.

The question is: what is modernity? And the answer is: not only capitalism (Marx), rationalization (Weber), functional differentiation (Parsons, Luhmann), but also the dynamics of political freedom, citizenship, and civil society. The point of this answer is that morality and justice are not extra-territorial variables for modern society. Quite the reverse is true. Modernity has an independent (simultaneously ancient and very modern) well-spring of meaning in its midst, which is political freedom. This spring is not exhausted by daily use—indeed, it bubbles up all the more vigorously as a result. Modernity, from this point of view, means that a world of traditional certainty is perishing and being replaced—if we are fortunate—by a legally sanctioned individualism for all.

In what we have called the first modernity, the issue of who has and who has not a right to freedom was answered through recourse to such matters as the "nature" of gender and ethnicity; contradictions between universal claims and particular realities were settled by an ontology of difference. Thus, until the early 1970s, even in Western countries, women were denied civil rights such as the control of property and of their own bodies.

In the second modernity, the structure of community, group, and identity loses this ontological cement. After *political* democratization (the democratic state) and *social* democratization (the welfare state) a *cultural* democratization is changing the foundations of the family, gender relations, love, sexuality, and intimacy. Our words about freedom start to become deeds and to challenge the basis of everyday life, as well as of global politics. Being freedom's children, we live under conditions of radicalized democracy for which many of the concepts and formulas of the first modernity have become inadequate.

No one knows how the ever-growing demand for family intimacy can be tied in with the new demands for freedom and self-realization for men, women, and children. No one knows whether the exigencies of mass organization (political parties, trade unions) are compatible with the claims for participation and self-organization.

People are better adapted to the future than are social institutions and their representatives. The decline of values which cultural pessimists are so fond of decrying is in fact opening up the possibility of an escape from the "bigger, more, better" creed, in a period that is living beyond its means both ecologically and economically. Whereas, in the old system of values, the self always had to be subordinated to patterns of the collective, the new orientations towards the "we" are creating something like a cooperative or altruist individualism. Thinking of oneself and living for others—once considered by definition contradictory—are revealed as internally and substantively connected with each other (see Wuthnow, 1991). Living alone means living socially.

* * * * *

With political freedom placed at its centre, modernity is not an age of decline of values but an age *of* values, in which the hierarchical certainty of ontological difference is displaced by the creative uncertainty of freedom. Freedom's children are the first to live in a post-national cosmopolitan world order. But what does this mean politically? Living in an age of side-effects, we have to ask very early what are the unforeseen and unwanted consequences of the new rhetoric of "global community," "global governance," and "cosmopolitan democracy." What are the risks if the cosmopolitan mission succeeds?

The collapse of the Soviet bloc has not only made it easier to effect a collective name-change from "the West" to "global neighbourhood." Its importance is greater than that. For whereas the West's promotion of universal values such as human rights or democracy used always to be open to challenge and was often discredited in practice—in the case of the Vietnam War, for example—today, for the first time, the West has *carte blanche* to define and promote universal values. With the removal of any challenge to the dominance of the world's major economic powers, these moral arguments too can be posited on uncontested grounds. The themes of global civil society and an ethical foreign policy have provided a new ideological cement for the project of Western power.

Globalization implies the weakening of state structures, of the autonomy and power of the state. This has a paradoxical result. On the one hand, it is precisely collapses of the state which have produced most of the really grave human conflicts of the 1990s, whether in Somalia, East Africa, Yugoslavia, Albania, or the former Soviet Union; on the other hand, the idea of "global responsibility" implies at least the possibility of a new Western *military humanism*—to enforce human rights around the globe. Consequently, the greater the success of neoliberal politics on a global level—that is, the greater the erosion of state structures—the more likely it is that a "cosmopolitan façade" will emerge to legitimize Western military intervention. The striking feature here is that imperial power-play can coexist harmoniously with a cosmopolitan mission. For the subordination of weak states to institutions of "global governance" actually creates the space for power strategies disguised as humane intervention.

Of course, there are also double standards of morality involved here. Take the example of cosmopolitan democracy itself. What would happen if the European Union wanted to become a member of the European Union? Naturally it would have to be refused. Why? Because of its glaring lack of democracy! But it must also be asked whether EU member-states such as France, Germany, Britain, or Italy can really be considered democracies, when roughly half the laws passed in their parliaments merely transplant directives issued by Brussels, the World Trade Organization, and so on.

In the age of globalization, there is no easy escape from this democratic dilemma. It cannot be solved simply by moving towards "cosmopolitan democracy." The central problem is that without a politically strong cosmopolitan consciousness, and without corresponding institutions of global civil society and public opinion, cosmopolitan democracy remains, for all the institutional fantasy, no more than a necessary Utopia. The decisive question is whether and how a consciousness of cosmopolitan solidarity can develop. The *Communist Manifesto* was published a hundred and fifty years ago. Today, at the beginning of a new millennium, it is time for a Cosmopolitan Manifesto. The *Communist Manifesto* was about class conflict. The Cosmopolitan Manifesto is about transnational-national conflict and dialogue which has to be opened up and organized. What is to be the object of this global dialogue? The goals, values, and structures of a cosmopolitan society. The possibility of democracy in a global age.

Who will raise this question? The "me-first" generation, freedom's children. We have been witnessing a global erosion of the authority of national states and a general loss of confidence in hierarchical institutions. But at the same time, active intervention by citizens has been growing more common and breaking the bounds of past convention—especially among younger and more educated sections of the population. The spaces in which people think and act in a morally responsible manner are becoming smaller and more likely to involve intense personal relationships. They are also, however, becoming more global and difficult to manage. Young people are moved by issues that national politics largely rules out. How can global environmental destruction be avoided? How can one live and love with the threat of AIDS? What do tolerance and social justice mean in the global age? These questions slip through the political agendas of national states. The consequence is that freedom's children practise a highly political disavowal of politics.

The key idea for a Cosmopolitan Manifesto is that there is a new dialectic of global and local questions which do not fit into national politics. These "glocal" questions, as we might call them, are already part of the political agenda—in the localities and regions, in governments and public spheres both national and international. But only in a transnational framework can they be properly posed, debated, and resolved. For this there has to be a reinvention of politics, a founding and grounding of the new political subject: that is, of *cosmopolitan parties*. These represent transnational interests transnationally, but also work within the arenas of national politics. They thus become possible, both programmatically and organizationally, only as national-global movements *and* cosmopolitan parties.

The underlying basis here is an understanding that the central human worries are "world" problems, and not only because in their origins and consequences they have outgrown the national schema of politics. They are also "world" problems in their very concreteness, in their very location here and now in this town, or this political organization.

Let us take the case of all the various regulation-intensive industries that have been liberalized in recent years: telecommunications is the main example; others include energy, financial services, and food. Increased competition in these areas has brought the domestic regimes that regulate them into conflict, but meanwhile the problems have become global. And this is just the start. Looming ahead are new issues—environmental and labour legislation—in which regulation is even more sensitive, even more crucial. This is the challenge of the years to come. A first wave of national deregulation enforces a second wave of transnational regulation. Without a decisive step towards cosmopolitan democratization, we are heading for a post-political technocratic world society.[2]

* * * *

NOTES

1. For a critique of global capitalism in this respect, see Gray (1998) and Beck (1999a).
2. I thus agree with David Held (1995: 24) when he writes: "Cosmopolitan democracy involves the development of administrative capacity and independent political resources at regional and global levels, as a necessary complement to those in local and national politics."

REFERENCES

Beck, U. (1999a) *What Is Globalization?* Cambridge: Polity.

Beck, U. (1999b) *Schone neue Arbeitswelt.* Frankfurt am Main: Campus. (English edn forthcoming from Polity in 2000.)

Gray, J. (1998) *False Dawn.* London: Granta.

Held, D. (1995) "Democracy and Globalization," in D. Archibugi, D. Held, and M. Köhler (eds), *Reimagining Political Community.* Cambridge: Polity.

Jacobs, M. (ed.) (1997) *Greening the Millennium? The New Politics of the Environment.* Special Issue of *The Political Quarterly.* Oxford: Blackwell.

Korean Journal of Sociology (1998) 39(1), Spring, special issue on Korea: A 'Risk Society'.

Schwarz, M. and Thompson, M. (1990) *Divided We Stand: Redefining Politics, Technology and Social Choice.* New York: Harvester Wheatsheaf.

Wuthnow, R. (1991) *Acts of Compassion.* Princeton, NJ: Princeton University Press.

PART VII

Society, Subjects, and the Self

CRITICAL THINKING QUESTIONS

Lacombe

1. What factors contribute to the formation of social subjectivity, and what social apparatuses exercise a significant influence on subject formation?
2. What did Foucault wish to imply by the concept "mechanisms of life"? Does this imply a straightforward process of subject formation?
3. In what way does Foucault's understanding of subjectification differ from Marx's understanding of the formation of subjects?

Giddens

1. How does Giddens differentiate life politics from life chances?
2. What are some of the ways that life politics can be observed in your daily life in Canada?
3. What is the relationship between life politics and emancipatory politics? If the project of emancipation was once oriented toward freeing individuals from restrictions on their life chances, in what ways has this project changed in "late modernity"?

Beck

1. What does Beck mean by "the cosmopolitan manifesto"? How does he believe that cosmopolitanism is (being) produced?
2. In what ways can we think of cosmopolitianism today? How is it, or how can it be, created, maintained, and reproduced in the context of global communication systems?
3. What do you think is missing from, or what do you think could be added to, Beck's social-structure theory of second modernity?

SUGGESTED READINGS

Althusser, Louis. 1971. "Ideology and Ideological State Apparatuses." In L. Althusser, *Lenin and Philosophy and Other Essays*. New York: Free Press.

In Althusser's famous essay, the concept of the subject is formulated through processes of interpellation or interpellative hailing.

Beck, Ulrich, and Elisabeth Beck-Gernsheim. 2002. *Individualization*. New York: Sage.

Individualization is Beck and Beck-Gernsheim's clarification of one of the major cultural components of the age of second modernity. It is a good book to read alongside A. Giddens's *Modernity and Self-Identity*.

Burchell, Graham, Colin Gordon, and Peter Miller, eds. 1991. *The Foucault Effect: Studies in Governmentality*. Chicago: University of Chicago Press.

For more advanced readers, this book offers original essays concerned with Foucault's understanding of "rationalities" and "technologies" of government. The book continues to have a profound influence on sociological theory.

Foucault, Michel. 1981. *Power/Knowledge: Selected Interviews and Other Writings, 1972–1977*. New York: Pantheon Books.

This book contains Foucault's critical assessment of power. He argues that the exercise of power is caught up in an economy of discourse. This is one of Foucault's texts that undergraduate students may find easiest to understand.

Giddens, Anthony. 1994. *The Transformation of Intimacy*. Stanford, California: Stanford University Press.

In this book, Giddens disputes dominant interpretations of the role of sexuality in modern culture. He argues that the transformation of intimacy holds out the possibility of a radical democratization of the personal sphere.

RELATED WEB SITES

Books by Ulrich Beck
This Web site contains a list of Ulrich Beck's books for further inquiry. *www.campusi.com/author_Ulrich_Beck.htm*

Director's Page (LSE): Anthony Giddens
Although this is an older Web site, there is useful biographical and academic information to be found on Anthony Giddens.

*http://psychology.about.com/gi/dynamic/offsite.htm?site=http%3A%2F%2Fwww.
lse.ac.uk%2FGiddens%2FDefault.htm*

Foucault Info
As the title of the Web site suggests, information on Michel Foucault is
offered.
http://foucault.info/

Foucault Page
This Web site explores some of Foucault's major contributions. A link is
provided to many essays on, by, or about Foucault.
www.csun.edu/~hfspc002/foucault.home.html

Theory.org
This is a somewhat less serious Web site. It offers information on a range of
social theorists, trading cards, "Lego" theorists, and resource links. Students
may enjoy the informal approach to social theory.
www.theory.org.uk/index.htm

REFERENCES

Althusser, Louis. 1971. " Ideology and Ideological State Apparatuses." In *L. Althusser,
    Lenin and Philosophy and Other Essays*. New York: Monthly Review Press.
Butler, Judith, Ernesto Laclau, and Slavoj Žižek. 2000. *Contingency, Hegemony, and
    Universality: Contemporary Dialogues on the Left*. London: Verso.
Foucault, Michel. 1979. *Discipline and Punish: The Birth of the Modern Prison*. New
    York: Vintage Books.
_____. 1982. "The Subject of Power." In *Beyond Structuralism and Hermeneutics*,
    edited by H.L. Dreyfus and P. Rabinow. Sussex: Harvester Press.
Hall, Stuart. 1988. "The Toad in the Garden: Thatcher among the Theorists." In
    Marxism and the Interpretation of Culture, edited by C. Nelson and L. Grossberg.
    Urbana: University of Illinois Press.
Marx, Karl. 1947. *The German Ideology: Collected Works*, vol. 5. New York: International
    Publishers.

PART VIII

Globalization and Global Consciousness

IN THE FINAL CHAPTER OF *CAPITAL* (1976: 931–940), KARL MARX EXPLORED "THE MODERN theory of colonization." He argued that the process of primitive accumulation in Western Europe, the homeland of political economy, was more or less accomplished by 1867. This meant for Marx that the capitalist regime in western Europe had all but obliterated independent producers (those who own or control their conditions of labour). But it was different in the colonies. Systems of independent production, whereby the individual/independent producer enriches herself instead of the capitalist, persisted outside western Europe. For Marx, "Where the capitalist has behind him the power of the mother country, he tries to use force to clear out of the way the mode of production and appropriation which rest on the personal labour of the independent producer" (Marx 1976: 931).

Marx commented only briefly on the imperative for the capitalist mode of production to annihilate forms of production that depend on the labour of the individual producer, as the capitalist chases profitability around the globe. But in the past few decades there has emerged sustained dialogue on the dynamics of globalization and global capitalism. The increasing trends toward studying processes of globalization were influenced in part by the waning of structural functionalism and growing sociological interest in "development theories" and in international capitalism/world system analyses. Although the term "globalization" entered the sociological vocabulary around the 1960s (Waters 1995), it was not until the 1980s, however, that "globalization" as an analytic concept emerged as a central topic in sociological investigation.

While a considerable portion of sociological theorization on globalization pertains to the economic dimensions of the capitalist mode of production, where the nation-state occupies a key role in stabilizing the world capitalist system, recent theoretical work has emphasized at an increasing rate the ethical, moral, environmental, and humanistic dimensions of globalization. In the previous chapter, we saw how Anthony Giddens and Ulrich Beck understand social processes in the recent phase of modernity (late modernity and second modernity, respectively) to release individuals into new forms of life politics or to foster the formation of a cosmopolitan consciousness. In these writings, Giddens and Beck assert that the shared global threats posed by phenomena such as environmental destruction, ozone depletion, nuclear energy, toxic dumping, and deforestation unite people of diverse cultures, territories, and regions through common causes. These themes are extended and elaborated in the readings presented in this chapter.

⑮ SECTION READINGS: ALAN HEDLEY, NAOMI KLEIN, AND NICK STEVENSON

Recent writings on globalization have emphasized that there is no single dimension to global social change. Many contemporary (post 1970) writers recognize that globalizing processes, or at least a particular set of processes, were set in motion with the territorial expansion of northwest Europe in the 16th century. But one of the most prominent differences between sociological theories produced before and after 1980 has been the increasing tendency for writers after 1980 to conflate the local and the global. Modern sociological theorization tended to distinguish between locals and cosmopolitans, *gemeinschaft* and *gesellschaft* (or community and society), public and private, system and lifeworld—what Ulrich Beck identifies as zombie categories. More recent theorization has focused on multidimensional accounts of new life spaces that identify complex configurations that blend together these idealized forms. How these processes emerge, the significance attached to them in everyday life, and the relative importance of their many dimensions remains under sociological debate

In the first reading passage, University of Victoria sociologist Alan Hedley (1940–) addresses the question "What is globalization?" In Hedley's assessment, the term "globalization" comprises a series of interacting human global forces that are currently in motion. The primary motivation for these processes was (and remains) economic, and the primary means of facilitating globalization is technological developments in the form of communications, transportation, and information-processing systems. After 1945, he explains, a complex sequence of technological, organizational, and individual forces intersected to "make the world smaller." These transformations took place in the domains of the public and private sector, as well as in civil society.

The second reading passage is taken from the writings of Naomi Klein. Klein (1970–) is a journalist who is known for her international best seller, *No Logo: Taking Aim at the Brand Bullies* (2000). In that book, Klein focuses on "branding campaigns"—the use of a symbol, such as a logo, to convey information about a product, producer, or service. The use of brands has become ubiquitous since the 1980s. Driven by multinational corporations (e.g., Tommy Hilfiger, McDonald's, Nike), Klein contends, the brand has become more important in the process of production than the actual product being exchanged. The book traces how multinational corporations outsource production to Third-World sweatshops, and it considers increasing trends toward "ad busting," "culture jamming," and anti-corporate activism. In the five years since its first publication in English, *No Logo* has been translated into more than 20 languages and has raised awareness concerning corporate power, social inequality, and possibilities for resisting global capitalism.

Whereas *No Logo* chronicles trends germane to a new set of social movements, *Fences and Windows* (2002), the book to follow *No Logo*, brings together two years of Klein's commentary on demonstrations and summits held around the world. Fences and Windows is not a follow-up book to *No Logo*, but rather a collection of essays, columns, and speeches that were produced mostly as a result of the November 1999 World Trade Organization protests in Seattle. In the reading selection from *Fences and Windows*, Klein highlights an important point about the forces of globalization: they are at once destructive and liberating. Forces of globalization have given rise to exploitation and oppression, she contends, but the forces of globalization have also brought people together more effectively to resist global corporate power.

In the reading passage, Klein addresses a point that is at the heart of contemporary debates in sociological theory and political praxis: political resistance today does not conform to traditional forms of politics and political identification. To whom, Klein asks in the reading, would a plan of action be directed? A second point she makes also speaks to prominent concerns in contemporary sociological theory: there was no political movement or cohesive organization that could easily be identified in the WTO protests. Contemporary political action takes the form of decentralized networks of interacting individuals with diverse targeted agendas. While the protesters share the belief that corporate-driven globalization is a problem, she explains, their views on resistance, strategy, timing, etc., are very different. Klein argues that one of the central forces shaping these "miniature movements," besides a collective feeling of morality and justice, is the Internet. The webs of interactivity observed in protest activity resemble, says Klein, the webs of communicative activity found on the Internet. Driven by more than simply technology (the ability to easily communicate over great distance) or morality, these protest alliances also emerged from the failure of traditional party politics to realize change. The forms of collective action have since educated generations of activists and non-activists, and their potential as a pervasive force of change remains to be seen.

The next reading passage extends these themes. How, asks Nick Stevenson, can new forms of cosmopolitan consciousness be maintained in an age of neo-liberal globalizing politics, conflict, and cultural difference? He begins by arguing that, in order to understand contemporary political cosmopolitanism effectively, it is useful to consider pre-Cold War politics. He draws attention to E.P. Thompson, who argued that, in the context of the ideological deadlock of political elites in the "East" and the "West," the peace movement in Europe was urged to build on common cultural interests of democracy, ecology, and human rights across the bloc system. What was so interesting about Thompson's arguments—and why so many people found inspiration in his words—was that he addressed the ethical and cultural components of world politics beyond ideological constructs of East and West. In other words, Thompson articulated a "third space," a possible vision for the future of democratic alliance. The problem Stevenson identifies is that Thompson's argumentation remained in a nationalistic mindset.

These arguments are important in post-Cold War Europe because cosmopolitan politics have increasingly shifted away from national levels in the context of the forces of globalization. As Stevenson explains, we are currently witnessing calls for the formation of a cosmopolitan polity that breaks from national boundaries to embrace the significance of a range of transcultural problems. How this is to be accomplished, however, remains disputed. While some look to international legal frameworks to usher in the cosmopolitan ideal of unity within diversity, others point to the need for democratic-ethical sensibilities. He contends that global unity will come from the development of alternative spaces beyond state/society dichotomies, and he explains how Ulrich Beck's writings on reflexive modernization help to connect cosmopolitanism to cultural identity. Stevenson also explains how theoretical currents in post-colonial and psychoanalytic writings provide certain key ethical dimensions to cosmopolitan theorization.

CHAPTER 27

Running Out of Control:
Understanding Globalization

R. ALAN HEDLEY

Albert Einstein (1936) once observed that the categories are not inherent in the phenomena. In other words, concepts such as "globalization" and "information and communications technology revolution" are human constructs we have developed in order to understand better the complexities of what we believe is happening in the world. Theories are simplified models of reality, and the first step in theory construction is categorization or classification. Over the past few decades, researchers and social commentators have coined the term "globalization" in order to focus on what they believe are interrelated processes which are having tremendous impacts on our lives in the late twentieth and early twenty-first centuries. Consequently, there is no one correct definition of globalization; it has many different meanings and interpretations, depending upon who is discussing it and in what context. However, there are elements of agreement as to what globalization means.

The derivation of the term "globalization" implies that it involves worldwide processes that are relatively novel and still unfolding. These multidimensional processes are being experienced unevenly throughout the world and in different sectors of social life. *Globalization is a complex set of human forces involving the production, distribution/transmission, and consumption of technical, economic, political, and sociocultural goods and services which are administratively and technologically integrated on a worldwide basis.* This definition highlights the point that globalization comprises technological, economic, political (including military), and sociocultural dimensions. Together these interrelated dimensions make up the (human) global system which operates within the broader global ecological environment.

Concerning the four dimensions of globalization, ... innovations in transportation, communication, and information processing within the past three or four decades have permitted the creation of a technological infrastructure that facilitates the other dimensions of globalization. While technology may be seen as the facilitating means to modern globalization, the primary motivation has been economic—the harnessing of natural and human resources and the establishing of markets and investments worldwide by capitalist enterprise to achieve greater corporate control. In part, to counter the forces of technologically enhanced global capitalism, and to represent civic interests, governments and nongovernmental organizations have also globalized through the formation of international alliances. However, these coalitions have been insufficient to moderate the effects of another important dimension of globalization—the worldwide cultural overlay of Western values, norms, institutions, and practices. Because globalization was initiated predominately by corporations and countries in the Western world, inevitably, what is produced, transmitted, and consumed is monocultural. Thus, globalization as a multidimensional concept involves a worldwide technological infrastructure in which Western-style capitalism predominates.

Finally, if technology facilitates globalization, the ecological biosphere within which we all live represents its outside limits. Certainly during the past few decades, mounting evidence on a variety of fronts such as climate change, pollution, ozone depletion, cumulative environmental degradation, and population growth indicates we are nearing these limits. Consequently, globalization also involves a critical tension between our technological ability to modify the natural environment and the ultimate ecological constraints beyond which human existence is impossible.

In the following section, I describe the various forces instrumental in producing our globalized world.

⬜ FORCES OF GLOBALIZATION

The world has always been a large place, but in some sense it has become much smaller than it was. It measures 25,000 miles in circumference (*Britannica*, 1999). As recently as the late nineteenth century, the great science fiction writer Jules Verne wrote the then unbelievable novel, *Around the World in Eighty Days*. Today, not only can we physically circumnavigate the world in one day, we can electronically orbit the planet in just eight seconds (Phillips, 1996)—three hundred times faster than Shakespeare's magical Puck. Globalization is both feasible and viable now because of technological innovations in transportation, communication, and information processing during the latter part of the twentieth century. In fact, many experts claim that these interrelated innovations constitute the basis for a new technological revolution every bit as significant as the industrial revolution some 250 years earlier.

A major impetus for this recent revolution was World War II, itself a global phenomenon. Government-sponsored research centers produced myriad inventions and discoveries that were applied to the war effort. Some of these, most notably the work in nuclear fission, rocketry, and jet engines, contributed directly to the arsenal of the warring nations, whereas others such as materials development (plastic, superalloys, aluminum, and synthetics) made more indirect contributions. A third area of concentration involved the development of reliable, high-speed support systems, and it was in this context that the computer and telecommunications industries were created and set the stage for the information and communications technology (ICT) revolution that was to follow.

The fact that these technological innovations were organizationally sponsored highlights a second underlying force of globalization. In the years following World War II, organizations in the private, public, and civil sectors all harnessed these innovations to suit their purposes. In the private sector, corporations employed these innovations to secure competitive advantage by becoming transnational in their operations. In the public sector, governments entered into international alliances in attempts to create a stable world order out of the chaos produced by the War. And in reaction to these moves on the part of organizations in the private and public sectors, ordinary citizens—civil society—formed international nongovernmental [NGOs] organizations of their own in order to achieve what they believed were important development objectives. Consequently, technologically enhanced organizations of all types were also instrumental in ushering in the global age.

Finally, on an individual basis, people all over the world also helped to bring about globalization. They enthusiastically adopted the numerous technological innovations in transportation, communication, and information processing to reach out and touch others, both physically and electronically, all around the globe.

Following is a discussion of each of these three main forces of globalization.

Technological Forces

Transportation

Notable innovations in transportation during the past fifty years include the launching of container ships for shipping raw materials and finished manufactured goods worldwide, the introduction of commercial jets, and the debut of space travel. With regard to container ships, Herman (1983: 135) states that "the impact of containerization on the shipping industry can rightly be compared to the impact which steamships had on the field when they were first introduced over a hundred years ago." A container ship has specially designed holds, hatches, and cranes which enable it to take whole truck trailers on board without loading or unloading their contents. This reduces ship time in port (from 65 [percent] to 25 percent annually), cuts stevedoring costs, and virtually eliminates pilferage. It also permits the construction of larger, faster (from fifteen [knots] to twenty-five knots), more fuel-efficient vessels which reduces total operating expenses. For example, Herman (1983: 135) cites comparative statistics on the North Atlantic route for 1970: "fifty containerships provide a tonnage greater by approximately one-third than the one hundred and seventy vessels which operated there only one-half decade before." And given that "over 80 percent of world trade by volume is carried by ship" (Herman, 1983: 3), the inducements offered by containerization are substantial.

The idea of container ships emerged in 1951 when a shipping company "took a converted truck body as deck cargo from Miami to Puerto Rico" (Gilman, 1983:

8). Pearson and Fossey (1983: 220) report that only 106 container ships were built worldwide prior to the 1960s; however, in the 1960s, 478 were constructed, and in the following decade, 1,931 more container ships were launched.

While container ships are important for the efficient and speedy transportation of goods, jet aircraft are invaluable for transporting people and time-sensitive cargo quickly around the globe. The first commercial jet airline service was introduced in Britain in 1952 (Woytinsky & Woytinski, 1955: 500). By 1962, "the difference in speed between the fastest piston-engined transport and a jet was 240 miles an hour, a differential almost as great as all the speed increases made by commercial airplanes between 1918 and 1953" (Serling, 1982: 100). In effect, the world became smaller and more accessible. Recent figures on worldwide air traffic demonstrate this point. According to the International Civil Aviation Organization (ICAO, 2001), in 1999 world airlines carried some 1.6 billion people and 28.2 million metric tons of air cargo (see Box 27.1).

BOX 27.1: FEDEX: A GLOBAL CORPORATION

At 11:45 a.m. on June 11, 2000, I shipped a paper by FedEx from my office in Victoria, Canada, to a colleague in Madras, India. From Victoria, the paper went to Vancouver (4:16 p.m.) and Memphis, Tennessee (6:14 p.m.), FedEx headquarters and central routing hub. My paper left Memphis on 06/12/00 at 2:46 a.m. bound for the European hub city of Paris (8:18 p.m.), and then on to Dubai in the Persian Gulf (2:17 p.m., 06/13/00), and Bombay, India (3:00 a.m., 06/14/00), where it had to wait for commercial customs release (11:00 a.m.). My paper arrived in Madras (9:08 a.m., 06/15/00) and was finally delivered to my Indian colleague (11:30 a.m.).

All of this information I obtained from entering my FedEx tracking number at the FedEx Web site (www.fedex.com). My paper was merely one of millions of shipments that FedEx handles and tracks every day.

According to a July 11, 2000, FedEx Corporation press release posted on its Website:

FedEx Express, a $15 billion subsidiary of FedEx Corp., connects areas that generate 90% of the world's gross domestic product in 24–48 hours with door-to-door, customs cleared service and a money back guarantee. The company's unmatched air route authorities and infrastructure make it the world's largest express transportation company, providing fast, reliable and time-definite transportation of more than 3.3 million items to 210 countries each working day. FedEx employs approximately 145, 000 employees and has more than 43,000 drop-off locations, 663 aircraft and 44,500 vehicles in its integrated global network. The company maintains electronic connections with more than 2.5 million customers via FedEx Powership®, FedEx Ship®, and FedEx InternetShip®.

The concept of globalization received a major boost on October 4, 1957, when the Soviet Union successfully launched Sputnik I, the first-ever space satellite. About the size of a basketball and weighing 183 pounds, it took just ninety-eight minutes to orbit the planet (NASA, 2000). Subsequent space flights provided the first photographs of the Earth as a globe. No longer was it necessary only to conceptualize it in this fashion; now we could actually see it as a spherical whole. Space flight literally produced a new world view of planet Earth. Our world definitely became smaller.

Communication and Information Processing

While technological innovations in transportation reduced the constraints of time and space, advances in communications and information processing technology have virtually eliminated these formerly circumscribing barriers, thus accounting for the claims of a new ICT revolution.

Naisbitt (1982) discusses how developments in information and communications technology have collapsed what he calls the "information float" —the time it takes for a sender of information first to collect and process information, and then to transmit it through some communication channel to a receiver, who also must process it. Whereas the information float was a factor that could not be ignored before the 1970s, today it is trivial. Naisbitt (1982: 23) explains:

> One way to think about the foreshortening of the information float is to think about when the world changed from trading goods and services to standardized currencies. Just imagine how that speeded up transactions. Now, with the use of electrons to send money around the world at the speed of light, we have almost completely collapsed the ... information float. The shift from money to electronics is as basic as when we first went from barter to money.

At the very core of this transformation was the creation of the electronic microchip:

> In the microchip, combining millions of components operating in billionths of seconds in a space the size of the wing of a fly, human beings built a machine that overcame all the conventional limits of mechanical time and space. Made essentially of the silicon in sand—one of the most common substances in earth— microchips find their value not in their substance but in their intellectual content: their design or software. (Gilder, 1989: 12)

Business applications of the microchip took place between 1969 and 1971 at Intel Corporation, which "developed all the key components of the personal computer—the working memory, the software memory, and the microprocessor CPU" (Gilder, 1989: 92). Thus was born the first stage of the ICT microelectronic revolution.

Another stage came into being in 1970 when scientists at Corning Glass Works announced that they had "created a medium [optical fiber] that could transport unprecedented amounts of information on laser beams for commercially viable distances" (Diebold, 1990: 132), thus providing the first revolutionary medium for what is now known as the information highway—the Internet. In parallel with this discovery, work was also proceeding on wireless and satellite connectivity (Bell Labs, 1999).

Coincident with these developments, another momentous event in the creation of the ICT revolution occurred in 1969. In order to withstand the possibility of a nuclear military attack, the U.S. Department of Defense's Advanced Research Projects Agency created a centerless network of supercomputers at major universities and research centers, such that if one computer was struck, the others could still function independently (Flower, 1997; Kahn, 1999). Called ARPNET, this electronic network was the forerunner of the Internet, which was formally established in 1989. "Widespread development of LANS [local area networks], PCs [personal computers] and workstations in the 1980s, [as well as the growing use of e-mail], allowed the nascent Internet to flourish" (Leiner et al., 2000).

All of these developments, taking place at approximately the same time, together formed the foundation for a globalized world little constrained by time and space. And, given recent leading edge developments in transportation, communication, and information processing, there is every reason to expect this trajectory of innovation to continue. In fact, as a result of these innovations the distinction among these terms is becoming blurred. Consider, for example, the relatively new practice of telecommuting—the partial or complete substitution of telecommunications services for transportation to a conventional workplace. In reality, it is a creative and innovative blend of all three of these processes. According to a 2001 survey of the U.S. labor force, 28.8 million workers were transporting themselves both physically and electronically to work (International Telework Association, 2001); worldwide, the number of teleworkers is projected to rise to 137 million by 2003 (Edwards, 2001). Other creative blends of transportation, communication, and information processing include teleconferencing, teleshopping, virtual education, virtual surgery, and space satellites.

Although I have provided specific dates when these various technological innovations were recorded in history, in actual fact they took years to come to fruition. The years following World War II (particularly given the breakup of European colonial empires and the Cold War tensions between capitalism and communism) represented an era of economic reconstruction and scientific enterprise and application. However, as Table 27.1 indicates, a global ICT infrastructure is by no means in place for the vast majority of the world. Most people living in low- and middle-income countries (85 percent of the world's population) are on the other side of what has been termed the digital divide. Substantial proportions of people have yet even to acquire electricity or access a telephone. The World Resources Institute (2000) contends "as much as 80 percent of the world's population has never made a phone call." In addition, it estimates that there are more telephones in New York City than in all of rural Asia, and more Internet accounts in the city of London than in the continent of Africa. Although the Internet connected approximately 513 million people in 2001 (Nua Internet Surveys, 2001), that represents only 8.4 percent of the world's population. In other words, while many significant technological innovations have indeed been achieved since World War II, they have yet to be diffused globally.

Table 27.1: Transportation, Communication, and Information Indicators

Indicators	Income of Countries			
	Low	Middle	High	World
Population (millions, 1999)	2,417	2,667	891	5,975
Percent population	40.5	44.6	15	100
Kilograms of oil equivalent consumption per capita (1997)	563	1,368	5,369	1,692
Air passengers carried (millions, 1998)	54	292	1,121	1,467
Percent air passengers	3.7	19.9	76.4	100
Radios per 1,000 people (1997)	157	359	1,286	418
TV sets per 1,000 people (1998)	76	257	661	247
Telephone main lines/1,000 (1998)	23	109	567	146
Mobile telephones/1,000 (1998)	2	31	265	55
Personal computers/1,000 (1998)	3	23	311	71
Internet hosts/10,000 (Jan./OO)	0.4	10	111	120

Source: Adapted from World Bank, 2001: 275, 293, 309, 311.

Note: According to the World Bank (2001: 271): "Economies are classified into three categories according to income .... The GNP per capita cutoff levels are as follows: low-income, $755 or less in 1999; middle-income, $756–9,265; and high income, $9,266 or more."

Organizational Forces

Transnational Corporations

A transnational corporation (TNC) is "any enterprise that undertakes foreign direct investment, owns or controls income-gathering assets in more than one country, produces goods or services outside its country of origin, or engages in international production" (Biersteker, 1978: xii). Variously termed multinational corporations or multinational enterprises, transnational corporations are formal business organizations that have spatially dispersed operations in at least two countries. One of the most transnational of all major TNCs (see Table 27.2) is Nestle, the Swiss food giant: 84 percent of its total assets, 99 percent of its sales, and 97 percent of its workforce are foreign-based (UNCTAD, 1999: 78).

Although TNCs were in existence prior to the twentieth century (colonial trading companies such as the East India Company, Hudson Bay Company, and the Virginia Company of London were precursors of the modern TNC), it is only since the 1960s that they have become a major force on the world scene (World Bank, 1987: 45). Table 27.3 corroborates this fact by listing the foreign direct investment (FDI) stock of corporations at various intervals during the twentieth century. In 1900, only European corporations were major transnational players, but by 1930 American TNCs had begun to make their presence felt. The year 1960 is pivotal because it marks the new global era in corporate transnationalization. For each of the decades from 1960 to the present, world FDI stock has more than tripled, whereas it only doubled during the entire first half of the twentieth century.

The phenomenal increase in transnational corporate activity during the last four decades may be accounted for in large part by the technological innovations in transportation, communication, and information processing I have just discussed. They permitted corporations to establish profitable worldwide operations and still maintain effective and timely control. Not since before World War II and the Great Depression which preceded it had the corporate sector much opportunity to demonstrate its economic clout. It was in this mood that it eagerly embraced all technological innovations that would give it competitive advantage. Consequently the threefold increase in foreign direct investment between 1960 and 1971 by technologically enhanced, transnationalizing corporations reveals another manifestation of the new global age. Table 27.3 indicates that TNCs from just eleven countries accounted for 82 percent of all foreign direct investment in 1999. American TNCs comprised almost one-quarter of the total foreign investment, and corporations in the Triad (United States, European Union, and Japan) were responsible for nearly 80 percent of world FDI stock (UNCTAD, 2000: 300). Clearly, TNCs mainly operate out of and invest in the developed countries of the global economy.

The magnitude of foreign investment flow in the world is illustrated by the fact that worldwide sales of foreign affiliates in 1999 were $13.6 trillion. This figure is almost twice as high as world exports of goods and services valued at $6.9 trillion (UNCTAD, 2000: 4). This means that global networks of transnational corporations have replaced in importance traditional import-export practices of the past in terms of delivering goods and services to markets worldwide. In 1999, some 63,000 TNCs controlled 690,000 foreign affiliates around the globe (UNCTAD, 2000: 9). These two sets of facts underline the central and growing importance of TNCs in structuring international economic relations.

Table 27.2: Annual Revenues of Leading Corporations and Gross National Products of Selected Countries 1998–99 (billions of US$)

Nation/Corporation	GNP/Revenues
United States (1)	$7,921.3
Japan (2)	4,089.9
Germany (3)	2,122.7
France (4)	1,466.2
United Kingdom (5)	1,263.8
General Motors (1)	176.6
Denmark (23)	176.4
Wal-Mart Stores (2)	166.8
Exxon Mobil (3)	163.9
Ford Motor (4)	162.6
DaimlerChrysler (5)	160.0
Norway (25)	152.1
Greece (31)	122.9
South Africa (32)	119.0
Mitsui (6)	118.6
Mitsubishi (7)	117.8
Toyota Motor (8)	115.7
General Electric (9)	111.6
Iran (33)	109.6
Royal Dutch/Shell Group (11)	105.4
Israel (36)	95.2
Nippon Telegraph and Telephone (13)	93.6
International Business Machines (16)	87.5
BP Amoco (17)	83.4
Volkswagen (19)	80.1
Malaysia (39)	79.8
Hitachi (23)	71.9
Chile (42)	71.3
Matsushita (24)	65.6
Philip Morris (29)	61.8
Sony (30)	60.1
Boeing (32)	58.0
New Zealand (46)	55.8
Honda Motor (34)	54.8
Nissan Motor (36)	53.7
Czech Republic (48)	51.8
Toshiba (38)	51.6
Bank of America (39)	51.4
Nestle (41)	50.0
Hungary (51)	45.6

Sources: For annual revenues of corporations, Fortune, 2000: F1-F2; for GNP, World Bank, 2000: 230-31.

Notes: Gross national product (GNP) measures the total value of goods and services produced by citizens (resident and nonresident) of a particular nation. The numbers in parentheses refer to the overall rank of a nation or corporation in terms of either GNP or revenues.

Table 27.3: Foreign Direct Investment Stock by Country (billions of US$)

Country	1900[a]	1930[a]	1960[a]	1971	1980	1990	1999[b]
United States	0.5	14.7	31.8	82.8	220.2	430.5	1,131.5
United Kingdom	12.1	18.2	13.2	23.1	80.4	229.2	664.1
Germany	4.8	1.1	0.6	7.0	43.1	151.6	420.9
Netherlands	1.1	2.3	1.7	3.5	42.1	109.0	306.4
France	5.2	3.5	2.2	9.2	23.6	110.1	298.0
Japan	neg[c]	neg	neg	4.3	19.6	201.4	292.8
Switzerland	neg	neg	neg	6.5	21.5	66.1	199.5
Canada	neg	1.3	3.0	5.7	23.8	84.8	178.3
Italy	neg	neg	neg	NA[d]	7.3	57.3	168.4
Belgium & Luxembourg	neg	neg	neg	NA	6.0	40.6	159.5
Sweden	neg	0.5	0.5	3.3	3.7	49.5	105.0
Others	neg	neg	neg	13.5	31.9	186.2	834.9
Total[e]	23.8	41.6	53.8	159.2	523.2	1,716.4	4,759.3

Sources: Data for 1970–71 adapted from Buckley, 1985: 200. Data for 1980–1999 from UNCTAD, 2000: 300–5.

Notes:
a. Includes foreign portfolio (individual) investment and foreign direct (TNC) investment.
b. Estimates.
c. Negligible.
d. Not available.
e. World total, excluding Comecon countries, except for 1998.

The rise of modern transnational corporations and the power they hold are reflected in Table 27.2, which compares the annual revenues of some of the world's largest global companies with the gross national products (the annual total value of goods and services produced by resident and nonresident citizens of a particular country) of selected countries. For example, General Motors, the leading corporation in revenues in 1999, had the twenty-third largest economy in the world ($176.7 billion), edging out Denmark at $176.4 billion, and surpassing by far the combined national output of New Zealand, Hungary, and the Czech Republic. These statistics would appear to give some truth to the old saying that "What's good for General Motors is good for the country" (Wilson, 1952). Of the one hundred largest economies in the world, nearly half (forty-nine) are transnational corporations (*Fortune*, 2000: F1-F2; World Bank, 2000: 230–31).

Of the five hundred largest corporations in the world, more than one-quarter (128) are in the financial sector (banks, insurance, and securities) (*Fortune*, 2000: F15–F21). A major reason for this is that most of the services and products financial firms provided can be traded electronically, and consequently these organizations have taken great advantage of the new global ICT infrastructure. As the editors of *Fortune* (2000: F15) state: "Money went global long before 'globalization' became a buzzword. That's why banks have the most entries on the [Global 500] list, as well as the highest revenues and profits." Other firms well represented in the Global 500 are those instrumental in the move toward globalization: modern transportation (aerospace, airlines, and courier services), communication (telecommunications, network communications, and mass media), and information processing (computers, computer services, and electronics). Of these corporations, those in the mass media have been extremely influential in promoting a global perspective in that they transmit content as well as providing infrastructure ....

Environmental Movement

The environmental movement is comprised of many grass-roots and international NGOs, as well as scientific organizations, all over the world. What makes it unique in establishing the case for globalization is the growing realization that our planet and everything on it comprise a very complex, interdependent, living whole. This means that when humans modify their environment in certain ways—such as urbanization, agriculture, forestry, mining and so forth—other consequences, both foreseen and unforeseen, are bound to follow. Approximately thirty years ago, the concept of biological diversity or biodiversity—"the total variability of life on Earth"—was coined, largely in an attempt to focus research on the extent to which human beings are contributing toward environmental degradation, and whether some of the evident trends are reversible (Heywood & Baste, 1995). It was also at this time that the concept of sustainable development originated (Fisher, 1993).

Why is biodiversity important? Aside from being important for the particular natural systems under siege and for providing needed resources such as food, water, shelter, and medicine for human survival, there is a more comprehensive set of reasons relating to globalization as a worldview.

> The sheer diversity of life is of inestimable value. It provides a foundation for the continued existence of a healthy planet and our own well-being. Many biologists now believe that ecosystems rich in diversity gain greater resilience and are therefore able to recover more readily from stresses such as drought or human-induced degradation. When ecosystems are diverse, there is a range of pathways for primary production and ecological processes such as nutrient cycling, so that if one is damaged or destroyed, an alternative pathway may be used and the ecosystem can continue functioning at its normal level. If biological diversity is greatly diminished, the functioning of ecosystems is put at risk. (Biodiversity Unit, 1993)

Contributing to the concept of Earth as an interconnected organism, the American National Aeronautics and Space Administration (NASA), in conjunction with Japan and the European Space Agency, has launched a series of satellites that have established "an international Earth-observing capability" involving "a global-scale examination of the Earth to study the interaction of all the environmental factors—air, water, land, biota—that make up the Earth system" (NASA, 1996). NASA reports that "scientists have been observing the Earth from space for more than 30 years, making measurements of the atmosphere, the oceans, the polar regions and land masses" (NASA, 1996).

Consequently, the environmental movement has been instrumental in altering people's perceptions of the world in which they live. Instead of focusing only on the particular geographical location in which they live, human beings are now coming to realize that their actions may have consequences for the world at large and for the quality of life they and subsequent generations will enjoy.

Individual Forces

Physical Migration
As well as technological innovations and transnational organizations and alliances, individual people also comprise a globalizing force in that the human population, aided largely by improvements in transportation, has become increasingly mobile in a variety of ways.

Mass movements of people around the globe is a post-war phenomenon. During World War II, international travel was restricted, and during the Great Depression before it, the world economy rarely permitted it. With respect to emigration, the most permanent form of human migration, it is only since the war that vast numbers of people have emigrated, mostly from poor to rich countries. The major receiving countries have been the United States, Germany, Canada, and Australia (World Bank, 2000: 38), such that their populations have become increasingly diverse. The World Bank (2000: 37–40) reports that in recent years between two and three million people emigrate annually, with the consequence that now more than 130 million are living outside the countries in which they were born. To these figures must be added international refugees, and as conflicts and natural disasters have risen, so has forced migration. In 1975, the world's international refugees numbered 2.5 million, but just twenty years later, that total had multiplied almost ten times to 23 million (World Bank, 2000: 38).

Less permanent forms of migration include international guest workers (mostly to Europe and the United States), exchange students, and tourists. The demand for guest workers, mainly from North Africa, South Asia, and Mexico, is partly a function of the global economy, but increasingly it is tied to the demographic profile of the industrially developed countries. As a whole, the total fertility rate in the high-income countries is below replacement level (1.7 births per woman), and the population is aging (World Bank, 2000: 243), which could lead to eventual labor shortages. To the extent that these trends continue, demand for foreign labor could increase substantially during the twenty-first century.

Study abroad and foreign exchange are also relatively recent occurrences in terms of the numbers involved and variety of programs offered. For example, at my own mid-sized university, there are currently 118 student and faculty exchange agreements with other universities in 27 different countries (UVic International, 2000). In 1998–99 in the United States, almost half a million foreign students enrolled in colleges and universities, three times more than in the mid-1970s (Open Doors, 1999a). In turn, nearly 114,000 American students studied abroad during 1997–98, a 15 percent increase over the previous year (Open Doors, 1999b). Worldwide, Switzerland has the greatest percentage (15.9 percent) of foreign students at the tertiary level, followed by Australia (12.6 percent), Austria (11.5 percent), and the United Kingdom (10.8 percent) (OECD, 2000c). Clearly, the option to complete at least part of a degree program in another country has become increasingly viable.

International tourism has also expanded enormously during the past fifty years. According to the World Tourism Organization (2000), "Between 1950 and 1999 the number of international arrivals has shown an evolution from a mere 25 million international arrivals to the current 664 million, corresponding to an average annual growth rate of 7 percent." Not only has the number of tourists increased, so too have their destinations. In 1950, almost all of the 25 million tourists went to just fifteen countries; however, in 1999, more than seventy countries hosted at least one million international visitors. Air transport was the most common means of travel (43.7 percent), followed by road (41.4 percent), sea (7.8 percent), and rail (7.0 percent), and France, Spain, the United States, Italy, and China were the most popular destinations. (See Box 27.2 to find out who accompanies these international travelers.)

Not only is international tourism a significant force of globalization, it also contributes in a huge way to the global economy:

> In 1998, international tourism and international fare receipts (receipts related to passenger transport of residents of other countries) accounted for roughly 8 percent of total export earnings on goods and services worldwide. Total international tourism receipts, including those generated by international fares, amounted to an estimated US$532 billion, surpassing all other international trade categories. (World Tourism Organization, 2000)

In other words, international tourism generates more revenue than international trade in either automotive products ($525 billion), chemicals ($503 billion), food ($443 billion), computer and office equipment ($399 billion), fuels ($344 billion), textiles and clothing ($331 billion), or telecommunications equipment ($283 billion).

Box 27.2: MICROBES FLY THE GLOBAL SKIES

A report in my local newspaper (*Times Colonist*, 10/13/00: Al) warned of "a big year for flu" because so many people from all over the world attended the Olympics in Australia, which "had an especially prolonged flu season this year." A check at FluNet, maintained by the World Health Organization (WHO) (http:// oms2.b3e.jussie.fr/FluNet/f_recent_activity. htm) confirmed that there had been a "regional outbreak" of influenza in Australia between September 10 and October 14, 2000.

A search at the WHO site led me to the *WHO Report on Global Surveillance of Epidemic-prone Infectious Diseases* (www.who.int/emc-documents/surveillance/ whocdscsrisr2001c.html), which states: "In the modern world, with increased globalization, and rapid air travel, there is a need for international coordination and collaboration. Everyone has a stake in preventing epidemics." The *Report* focuses on nine infectious diseases (including influenza) all of which have "high epidemic potential."

More recently, with outbreaks of hoof and mouth and mad cow diseases in Europe, especially Britain, customs officers and disease control experts in all countries are taking special precautions to prevent the global spread of these highly infectious diseases via international travelers. These measures include prohibiting passengers from carrying any agricultural products with them, mandatory notification of any farm contact, requiring antibiotic foot baths for the shoe soles of all deplaning passengers, placing additional inspectors and dog teams at airports, and public education programs (www. naturalhealthyliving.com/article1007.html).

The Centers for Disease Control and Prevention headquartered in Atlanta in the United States maintain a comprehensive "Travelers' Health" Web site (www.cdc.gov/ travel).

And considering that international tourism is on an annual growth trajectory of 7 percent, it will only become a more important contributor to the world gross domestic product.

Electronic Migration

Not only are people physically traversing the globe in increasing numbers, they are also orbiting it electronically at a skyrocketing rate. The International Telecommunication Union (ITU, 2000) reports that international telephone calls in 1999 reached a new high of 100 billion minutes, climbing an average of 10 billion minutes per year since 1995. According to the ITU, "the world market for telecommunications (services and equipment) doubled between 1990 and 1999," and is being driven now by the burgeoning mobile cellular communications market. "At the end of 1999, there were more than 450 million subscribers around the world, up from just 11 million in 1990, ... a compound annual growth rate of more than 50 percent per year" (ITU, 2000). The ITU estimates that mobile cellular subscribers will actually exceed conventional fixed-line users during this decade.

Also contributing to the rapid growth of electronic migration is the use of the Internet in general and for e-mail in particular. As I have already reported, Nua Internet Surveys (2001) estimated that 513 million people had accessed the Internet at least once during the three months before August 2001, and this figure is projected to rise to more than 765 million by 2005 (CommerceNet, 2000). In January 2002, the Internet Software Consortium counted more than 147 million host sites on the Internet, almost 38 million more than it enumerated twelve months earlier. Quite clearly, all forms of electronic communication are growing exponentially.

⑤ COUNTERFORCES TO GLOBALIZATION

On at least three levels, huge proportions of humanity are put at risk by the forces of globalization, and consequently, there are growing signs that many people are actively resisting the global age. On the most general level, examine how the world is divided by region. In describing various regions of the world, certain terms come to be adopted, first by official agencies such as the United Nations and national governments, and then more generally by scholars, journalists, and others interested in making sense out of international relations and development. For example, in 1980 Willy Brandt coined the terms "North" and "South" in his *Report of the Independent Commission on International Development Issues* (Brandt Report, 1980). In this report is a map of the world with a bold line dividing it into two parts—North and South .... I have used the terms "developed" and "developing" countries which are categories created by the United Nations to classify all countries in the world. This classification scheme mirrors the North–South dichotomy. These terms are often used as convenient labels to divide the world into two camps—rich and poor. The fact that the global ICT revolution is presently taking place largely in the rich, developed North is generating backlash in the poor, developing South. Many fear that it could broaden the already enormous development gap between North and South (South Commission, 1990).

Paralleling and exacerbating this development gap is a cultural gap which has widened as a result of globalization. On the one side are predominant Western cultural perspectives and values, including Christianity and the global use of English. On the other side are non-Western cultural perspectives and values, including religions other than Christianity and non-European languages. Individual countries and cultural groups within the South are voicing concerns that the forces of globalization could threaten their ethnic, religious, and linguistic heritage and ways of living (Hedley, 2000: 595–97).

Finally, within the developed countries, there is what might be termed a growing class disparity. Studies of the distribution of income and wealth over the last three decades of the twentieth century reveal increasing inequality and polarity (Morris & Western, 1999; Keister & Moller, 2000). It is claimed that global restructuring has caused at least part of this disparity. Consequently, workers and citizens who are not part of the vanguard of the global era, although they are the overwhelming majority, are increasingly disaffected by the promises of globalization.

On each of these three levels of analysis—regional, cultural, and class—it is the larger of the two categories that is at risk from the forces of globalization. Thus, from the perspective of the South, or the non-Western, or the masses, globalization is not viewed with enthusiasm, and consequently active opposition to it could result. These constitute the counterforces to globalization.

... The global technological and organizational infrastructure has been established primarily by corporations, governments, and individuals in rich developed countries for their own benefit. As I mentioned, the overwhelming majority of the world's population has yet to be connected to this infrastructure .... To date, globalization is an exclusionary force, denying active participation to particular regions, cultures, and classes. In turn, this is causing backlash. For many nations, cultures, institutions, organizations, and individuals in the world, modern globalism constitutes an elitist, Northern-based, Western-focused, technologically supported form of economic and cultural imperialism. In order to turn this vicious circle into a virtuous circle, the President of the World Bank (Wolfensohn, 1997: 6) has issued a *Challenge of Inclusion* "to reduce ... disparities across and within countries, to bring more people into the economic mainstream, [and] to promote equitable access to the benefits of development regardless of nationality, race, or gender." Whether this challenge becomes reality remains to be seen; however, until it does, the world as a whole cannot truly be characterized as globalized.

REFERENCES

Bell Labs. 1999. Wireless Milestones. [Online]. Available: www.lucent.com/minds/trends/ trends_v4nl/ timeline.html. Accessed 08/23/00.

Biersteker, T.J. 1978. *Distortion of development? Contending perspectives on the multinational corporation.* Cambridge, Mass.: MIT Press.

Biodiversity Unit, Commonwealth of Australia. 1993. Biodiversity Series, Paper No. 1. [Online]. Available: http://kaos.erin.gov.au/life/generaUnfo/opl.html. Accessed 05/29/00.

Brandt Report. 1980. *North–South: A program for survival. Report of the Independent Commission on International Development Issues.* Cambridge, Mass.: MIT Press.

Britannica. 1999. Earth. [Online]. Available: www.britannica.com/bcom/eb.arti.../ 0,5716,32267+l+31726,00.html. Accessed 10/02/00.

Buckley, P.J. 1985. Testing theories of the multinational enterprise. In *The economic theory of the multinational enterprise,* eds. P.J. Buckley and M. Casson. London: Macmillan.

CommerceNet. 2000. Worldwide Internet Population. [Online]. Available: www.commerce. net/ research/stats/wwstats.html. Accessed 10/05/00.

Diebold, J. 1990. *The innovators: The discoveries, inventions, and breakthroughs of our time.* New York: Truman Talley Books/Plume.

Edwards, J. 2001. Government—help or hindrance to deployment of teleworking? [Online]. Available: www.cefrio.qc.ca/allocutions/presentations/johnedwards.ppt. Accessed 01/18/02.

Einstein, A. 1936. Physics and reality. *Journal of the Franklin Institute* 221(3). Reprinted in *Ideas and opinions by Albert Einstein,* ed. C. Seelig, 1954, 290–323. New York: Wings Books.

Fisher, J. 1993. *The road from Rio: Sustainable development and the non-governmental movement in the third world.* Wesport, Conn.: Praeger.

Flower, J. 1997. The future of the Internet: an overview. In *The future of the Internet*, eds. D. Bender et al., 10–7. San Diego, Calif.: Greenhaven.

Form, W. 1979. Comparative industrial sociology and the convergence hypothesis. *Annual Review of Sociology*, 5: 1–25.

Fortune. 2000. The Fortune Global 500. *Fortune*, 142(3): 227–F24.

Gilder, G. 1989. *Microcosm: The quantum revolution in economics and technology.* New York: Simon & Schuster.

Gilman, S. 1983. *The competitive dynamics of container shipping.* Aldershot, U.K.: Gower.

Hedley, R.A. 2000. Convergence in natural, social, and technical systems: A critique. *Current Science*, 79(5): 592–601.

Herman, A. 1983. *Shipping conferences.* Deventer, Neth.: Kluwer, Law and Taxation.

Heywood, V.H., and I. Baste. 1995. In *Global biodiversity assessment*, eds. V.H. Heywood and R.T. Watson, 1–9. Cambridge: Cambridge University Press.

ICAO. 2001. Growth in air traffic projected to continue. [Online]. Available: www.icao.org/ icao/en/pio200106.htm. Accessed 06/24/01.

International Telework Association. 2001. Telework American 2001. [Online]. Available: www. telecommute.org/twa/twa2001/newsrelease.htm. Accessed 01/18/02.

ITU. 2000. ITU Telecommunication Indicators Update. [Online]. Available: www.itu.int/ journal/200006/E/html/indicat.htm. Accessed 10/10/00.

Kahn, R.E. 1999. Evolution of the Internet. In *World communication and information report 1999–2000*, 157–64. Paris: UNESCO.

Keister, L.A., and S. Moller. 2000. Wealth inequality in the United States. *Annual Review of Sociology*, 26: 63–81.

Leiner, B.M. et al. 2000. A brief history of the Internet. [Online]. Available: www.isoc.org/ internet/ history/brief.shtml. Accessed 05/11/02.

Morris, M., and B. Western. 1999. Inequality in earnings at the close of the twentieth century. *Annual Review of Sociology*, 25: 623–57.

Naisbitt, J. 1982. *Megatrends: Ten new directions transforming our lives.* New York: Warner.

NASA. 1996. The Earth Observing System: Understanding planet Earth.[Online]. Available: http://pao.gsfc.nasa.gov/gsfc/service/gallery/fact_sheets/ earthsci/fs-96(06)-009.htm. Accessed 09/27/00.

NASA. 2000. Sputnik and the dawn of the space age. [Online]. Available: www.hq.nasa. gov/office/pao/History/sputnik/. Accessed 09/27/00.

Nua Internet Surveys. 2001. How many online? [Online] Available: www.nua.ie/surveys/ how_many_online/index.hrml. Accessed 01/18/02.

OECD. 2000c. *OECD in figures.* Paris: Author.

Open Doors. 1999a. Fast facts. [Online]. Available: www.opendoorsweb.org/Press/fast_facts. htm. Accessed 10/05/00.

_____. 1999b. 113,959 U.S. students have studied abroad this year. [Online]. Available: www. opendoorsweb.org/Lead%20Stories/stabl.htm Accessed 10/05/00.

Pearson, R., and J. Fossey. 1983. *World deep-sea container shipping: A geographical, economic and statistical analysis.* Aldershot, U.K.: Gower.

Phillips, P. 1996. *Jules Verne, around the world in eighty days*. [Online]. Available: www.people. virginia.edu/~mtp0f/fiips/review3.html. Accessed 09/26/00.

Serling, R.J. 1982. *The jet age*. Alexandria, Va.: Time-Life.

South Commission. 1990. *The challenge to the South: The report of the South Commission*. New York: Oxford University Press.

UNCTAD. 1999. *World investment report 1999*. New York: United Nations Conference on Trade and Development.

_____. 2000. *World investment report 2000*. New York: United Nations Conference on Trade and Development.

UVic International. 2000. [Online]. Available: www.uvic.ca/international.html. Accessed 09/26/00.

Wilson, C.E. 1952. Statement to the Senate Armed Forces Committee. In *Familiar quotations*, ed. John Bartlett (1980), 817. Boston: Little, Brown.

Wolfensohn, J.D. 1997. *The challenge of inclusion*. Address to the board of governors of the World Bank Group, Hong Kong, China.

World Bank. 1987. *World development report 1987*. New York: Oxford University Press.

_____. 2000. *World development report 1999/2000*. Oxford: Oxford University Press.

_____. 2001. *World development report 2000/2001*. Oxford: Oxford University Press.

World Resources Institute. 2000. WRI conference explores new businesses to transform global digital divide into dividends. [Online]. Available: www.igc.org/wri/press/dd_transform. html. Accessed 10/17/00.

World Tourism Organization. 2000. Tourism highlights 2000. [Online]. Available: www. world-tourism.org/esta/monograf/highligh/HL_MK.htm. Accessed 10/05/00.

Woytinsky, W.S., and E.S. Woytinski. 1955. *World commerce and governments: Trends and outlook*. New York: Twentieth Century Fund.

CHAPTER 28

[Extracts from] *Fences and Windows: Dispatches from the Front Lines of the Globalization Debate*

NAOMI KLEIN

⑤ SEATTLE

The Coming-Out Party of a Movement
December 1999

"Who are these people?" That is the question being asked across the United States this week, on radio call-in shows, on editorial pages, and, most of all, in the hallways of the World Trade Organization meeting in Seattle.

Until very recently, trade negotiations were genteel, experts-only affairs. There weren't protesters outside, let alone protesters dressed as giant sea turtles. But this week's WTO meeting is anything but genteel: a state of emergency has been declared in Seattle, the streets look like a war zone, and the negotiations have collapsed.

There are plenty of theories floating around about the mysterious identities of the fifty thousand activists in Seattle. Some claim they are wannabe radicals with sixties envy. Or anarchists bent only on destruction. Or Luddites fighting against a tide of globalization that has already swamped them. Michael Moore, the director of the WTO, describes his opponents as nothing more than selfish protectionists determined to hurt the world's poor.

Some confusion about the protesters' political goals is understandable. This is the first political movement born of the chaotic pathways of the Internet. Within its ranks, there is no top-down hierarchy ready to explain the master plan, no universally recognized leaders giving easy sound bites, and nobody knows what is going to happen next.

But one thing is certain: the protesters in Seattle are not anti-globalization; they have been bitten by the globalization bug as surely as the trade lawyers inside the official meetings. Rather, if this new movement is "anti" anything, it is anti-corporate, opposing the logic that what's good for business—less regulation, more mobility, more access—will trickle down into good news for everybody else.

The movement's roots are in campaigns that challenge this logic by focusing on the dismal human rights, labour, and ecological records of a handful of multinational companies. Many of the young people on the streets of Seattle this week cut their activist teeth campaigning against Nike's sweatshops, or Royal Dutch/Shell's human rights record in the Niger Delta, or Monsanto's re-engineering of the global food supply. Over the past three years, these individual corporations have become symbols of the failings of the global economy, ultimately providing activists with name-brand entry points to the arcane world of the WTO.

By focusing on global corporations and their impact around the world, this activist network is fast becoming the most internationally minded, globally linked movement ever seen. There are no more faceless Mexicans or Chinese workers stealing "our" jobs, in part because those workers' representatives are now on the same e-mail lists and at the same conferences as the Western activists, and many even travelled to Seattle to join the demonstrations this week. When protesters shout about the evils of globalization, most are not calling for a return to narrow nationalism but for the borders of globalization to be expanded, for trade to be linked to labour rights, environmental protection, and democracy.

This is what sets the young protesters in Seattle apart from their sixties predecessors. In the age of Woodstock, refusing to play by state and school rules was regarded as a political act in itself. Now, opponents of the WTO—even many who call themselves anarchists—are outraged about a lack of rules being applied to corporations, as well as the flagrant double standards in the application of existing rules in rich or poor countries.

They came to Seattle because they found out that WTO tribunals were overturning environmental laws protecting endangered species because the laws, apparently, were unfair trade barriers. Or they learned that France's decision to ban hormone-laced beef was deemed by the WTO to be unacceptable interference with the free market. What is on trial in Seattle is not trade or globalization but the global attack on the right of citizens to set rules that protect people and the planet.

Everyone, of course, claims to be all for rules, from President Clinton to Microsoft's chairman, Bill Gates. In an odd turn of events, the need for "rules-based trade" has become the mantra of the era of deregulation. But the WTO has consistently sought to sever trade, quite unnaturally, from everything and everyone affected by it: workers, the environment, culture. This is why President Clinton's suggestion yesterday that the rift between the protesters and the delegates can be smoothed over with small compromises and consultation is so misguided.

The faceoff is not between globalizers and protectionists but between two radically different visions of globalization. One has had a monopoly for the past ten years. The other just had its coming-out party.

⬚ WHAT'S NEXT?

The Movement against Global Corporatism Doesn't Need to Sign a Ten-Point Plan to Be Effective
July 2000

"This conference is not like other conferences."

That's what all the speakers at "Re-Imagining Politics and Society" were told before we arrived at New York's Riverside Church. When we addressed the delegates (there were about a thousand over three days in May), we were to try to solve a very specific problem: the lack of "unity of vision and strategy" guiding the movement against global corporatism.

This was a very serious problem, we were advised. The young activists who went to Seattle to shut down the World Trade Organization and to Washington, D.C., to protest the World Bank and the International Monetary Fund had been getting hammered in the press as tree-wearing, lamb-costumed, drumbeating bubble brains. Our mission, according to the conference organizers at the Foundation for Ethics and Meaning, was to whip that chaos on the streets into some kind of structured, media-friendly shape. This wasn't just another talk shop. We were going to "give birth to a unified movement for holistic social, economic and political change."

As I slipped in and out of lecture rooms, soaking up the vision offered by Arianna Huffington, Michael Lerner, David Korten, Cornel West, and dozens of others, I was struck by the futility of this entire well-meaning exercise. Even if we did manage to come up with a ten-point plan—brilliant in its clarity, elegant in its coherence, unified in its outlook—to whom, exactly, would we hand down these commandments? The anti-corporate protest movement that came to world attention on the streets of Seattle last November is not united by a political party or a national network with a head office, annual elections, and subordinate cells and locals. It is shaped by the ideas of individual organizers and intellectuals, but doesn't defer to any of them as leaders. In this amorphous context, the ideas and plans being hatched at the Riverside Church weren't irrelevant exactly, they just weren't important in the way that was hoped. Rather than being adopted as activist policy, they were destined to be swept up and tossed around in the tidal wave of information—Web diaries, NGO manifestos, academic papers, homemade videos, cris de coeur—that the global anti-corporate network produces and consumes each and every day.

This is the flip side of the persistent criticism that the kids on the street lack clear leadership—they lack clear followers too. To those searching for copies of efforts from the sixties, this absence makes the anti-corporate movement appear infuriatingly impassive: evidently, these people are so disorganized they can't even get it together to respond to perfectly well-organized efforts to organize them. These are MTV-weaned activists, you can practically hear the old guard saying: scattered, nonlinear, unfocused.

It's easy to be taken in by these critiques. If there is one thing that the left and right agree on, it is the value of a clear, well-structured ideological argument. But maybe it's not quite so simple. Maybe the protests in Seattle and Washington, D.C., look unfocused because they were not demonstrations of one movement at all but rather convergences of many smaller ones, each with its sights trained on a specific multinational corporation (like Nike), a particular industry (like agribusiness), or a new trade initiative (like the Free Trade Area of the Americas). These smaller, targeted movements are clearly part of a common cause: they share a belief that the disparate problems they are wrestling with all derive from corporate-driven globalization, an agenda that is concentrating power and wealth into fewer and fewer hands. Of course, there are disagreements—about the role of the nation-state, about whether capitalism is redeemable, about the speed with which change should occur. But within most of these miniature movements, there is an emerging consensus that decentralizing power and building community-based decision-making potential—whether through unions, neighbourhoods, farms, villages, anarchist collectives, or aboriginal self-government—is essential to countering the might of multinational corporations.

Despite this common ground, these campaigns have not coalesced into a single movement. Rather, they are intricately and tightly linked to one another, much as "hotlinks" connect their Web sites on the Internet. This analogy is more than coincidental and is in fact key to understanding the changing nature of political organizing. Although many have observed that the recent mass protests would have been impossible without the Internet, what has been overlooked is how the communication technology that facilitates these campaigns is shaping the movement in its own Web-like image. Thanks to the Net, mobilizations occur with sparse bureaucracy and minimal hierarchy; forced consensus and laboured manifestos are fading into the background, replaced instead by a culture of constant, loosely structured, and sometimes compulsive information swapping.

What emerged on the streets of Seattle and Washington was an activist model that mirrors the organic, decentralized, interlinked pathways of the Internet—the Internet come to life.

The Washington-based research centre TeleGeography has taken it upon itself to map out the architecture of the Internet as if it were the solar system. Recently, TeleGeography pronounced that the Internet is not one giant web but a network of "hubs and spokes." The hubs are the centres of activity, the spokes the links to other centres, which are autonomous but interconnected.

It seems like a perfect description of the protests in Seattle and Washington, D.C. These mass convergences were activist hubs, made up of hundreds, possibly thousands, of autonomous spokes. During the demonstrations, the spokes took the form of "affinity groups" of between five and twenty protesters, each of which elected a spokesperson to represent them at regular "spokescouncil" meetings. Although the affinity groups agreed to abide by a set of non-violence principles, they also functioned as discrete units, with the power to make their own strategic decisions. At some rallies, activists carry actual cloth webs to symbolize their movement. When it's time for a meeting, they lay the web on the ground, call out "all spokes on the web," and the structure becomes a street-level boardroom.

In the four years before the Seattle and Washington protests, similar hub events had converged outside World Trade Organization, G7, and Asia Pacific Economic Co-operation summits in Auckland, Vancouver, Manila, Birmingham, London, Geneva, Kuala Lumpur, and Cologne. Each of these mass protests was organized according to principles of co-ordinated decentralization. Rather than present a coherent front, small units of activists surrounded their target from all directions. And rather than build elaborate national or international bureaucracies, they threw up temporary structures: empty buildings were turned into "convergence centres," and independent media producers assembled impromptu activist news centres. The ad hoc coalitions behind these demonstrations frequently named themselves after the date of the planned event: J18, N30, A16, and, for the upcoming IMF meeting in Prague on September 26, S26. When these events are over, they leave virtually no trace behind, save for an archived Web site.

All this talk of radical decentralization can conceal a very real hierarchy based on who owns, understands, and controls the computer networks linking the activists to one another. This is what Jesse Hirsh, one of the founders of the anarchist computer network Tao Communications, calls "a geek adhocracy."

The hubs and spokes model is more than a tactic used at protests; the protests are themselves made up of "coalitions of coalitions," to borrow a phrase from Kevin Danaher of Global Exchange. Each anti-corporate campaign is made up of many groups, mostly NGOs, labour unions, students, and anarchists. They use the Internet, as well as more traditional organizing tools, to do everything from cataloguing the latest transgressions of the World Bank to bombarding Shell Oil with faxes and e-mails, to distributing ready-to-download anti-sweatshop leaflets for protests at Nike Town. The groups remain autonomous, but their international co-ordination is deft and, to their targets, frequently devastating.

The charge that the anti-corporate movement lacks "vision" falls apart when looked at in the context of these campaigns. It's true that the mass protests in Seattle and D.C. were a hodgepodge of slogans and causes, that to a casual observer it was hard to decode the connections between the treatment of U.S. death row inmate Mumia Abu-Jamal and the fate of the sea turtles. But in trying to find coherence in these large-scale shows of strength, the critics are confusing the outward demonstrations of the movement with the thing itself—missing the forest for the people dressed as trees. This movement is its spokes, and in the spokes there is no shortage of vision.

The student anti-sweatshop movement, for instance, has rapidly moved from simply criticizing companies and campus administrators to drafting alternative codes of conduct and building a quasi-regulatory body, the Worker Rights

Consortium in partnership with labour activists in the global south. The movement against genetically engineered and modified foods has leaped from one policy victory to the next, first getting many genetically modified foods removed from the shelves of British supermarkets, then getting labelling laws passed in Europe, then making enormous strides with the Montreal Protocol on Biosafety. Meanwhile, opponents of the World Bank's and IMF's export-led development models have produced bookshelves' worth of resources on community-based development models, land reform, debt cancellation, and self-government principles. Critics of the oil and mining industries are similarly overflowing with ideas for sustainable energy and responsible resource extraction—though they rarely get the chance to put their visions into practice.

The fact that these campaigns are so decentralized does not mean they are incoherent. Rather, decentralization is a reasonable, even ingenious adaptation both to pre-existing fragmentation within progressive networks and to changes in the broader culture. It is a by-product of the explosion of NGOs, which, since the Rio Summit in 1992, have been gaining power and prominence. There are so many NGOs involved in anti-corporate campaigns that nothing but the hubs-and-spokes model could possibly accommodate all their different styles, tactics, and goals. Like the Internet itself, both the NGO and the affinity group networks are infinitely expandable systems. If somebody feels that he or she doesn't quite fit into one of the thirty thousand or so NGOs or thousands of affinity groups out there, she can just start her own and link up. Once involved, no one has to give up individuality to the larger structure; as with all things on-line, we are free to dip in and out, take what we want, and delete what we don't. It seems, at times, to be a surfer's approach to activism—reflecting the Internet's paradoxical culture of extreme narcissism coupled with an intense desire for community and connection.

But while the movement's Web-like structure is, in part, a reflection of Internet-based organizing, it is also a response to the very political realities that sparked the protests in the first place: the utter failure of traditional party politics. All over the world, citizens have worked to elect social democratic and workers' parties, only to watch them plead impotence in the face of market forces and IMF dictates. In these conditions, modern activists are not so naive as to believe change will come from the ballot box. That's why they are more interested in challenging the mechanisms that make democracy toothless, like corporate financing of election campaigns or the WTO's ability to override national sovereignty. The most controversial of these mechanisms have been the IMF's structural adjustment policies, which are overt in their demands for governments to cut social spending and privatize resources in exchange for loans.

One of the great strengths of this model of laissez-faire organizing is that it has proven extraordinarily difficult to control, largely because it is so different from the organizing principles of the institutions and corporations it targets. It responds to corporate concentration with fragmentation, to globalization with its own kind of localization, to power consolidation with radical power dispersal.

Joshua Karliner, of the Transnational Resource and Action Center, calls this system "an unintentionally brilliant response to globalization." And because it was unintentional, we still lack even the vocabulary to describe it, which may be why a rather amusing metaphor industry has evolved to fill the gap. I'm throwing my lot in with hubs and spokes, but Maude Barlow of the Council of Canadians says, "We are up against a boulder. We can't remove it, so we try to go underneath it, to go around it and over it." Britain's John Jordan, an activist with Reclaim the Streets, says trans-nationals "are like giant tankers, and we are like a school of fish. We can respond quickly; they can't." The U.S.-based Free Burma Coalition talks of a network of "spiders," spinning a web strong enough to tie down the most powerful multi-nationals. A U.S. military report about the Zapatista uprising in Chiapas, Mexico, even got in on the game. According to a study produced by RAND, a research institute that does contracts for the U.S. military, the Zapatistas were waging "a war of the flea" that, thanks to the Internet and the global NGO network, turned into a "war of the swarm." The military challenge of a war of the swarm, the researchers noted, is that it has no "central leadership or command structure; it is multi-headed, impossible to decapitate."

Of course, this multiheaded system has its weaknesses too, and they were on full display on the streets of Washington during the anti-World Bank/IMF protests. At around noon on April 16, the day of the largest protest, a spokescouncil meeting was convened for the affinity groups that were in the midst of blocking all the street intersections surrounding the headquarters of the World Bank and the IMF. The intersections had been blocked since 6 A.M., but the meeting delegates, the protesters had just learned, had slipped inside the police barricades before 5 A.M. With this new information, most of the spokespeople felt it was time to give up the intersections and join the official march at the Ellipse. The problem was that not everyone agreed: a handful of affinity groups wanted to see if they could block the delegates on their way out of their meetings.

The compromise the council came up with was telling. "Okay, everybody listen up," Kevin Danaher, one of the protest organizers, shouted into a megaphone. "Each intersection has autonomy. If the intersection wants to stay locked down, that's cool. If it wants to come to the Ellipse, that's cool too. It's up to you."

This was impeccably fair and democratic, but there was just one problem—it made absolutely no sense. Sealing off the access points had been a coordinated action. If some intersections now opened up and other rebel-camp intersections stayed occupied, delegates on their way out of the meeting could just hang a right instead of a left, and they would be home free. Which, of course, is precisely what happened.

As I watched clusters of protesters get up and wander off while others stayed seated, defiantly guarding, well, nothing, it struck me as an apt metaphor for the strengths and weaknesses of this nascent activist network. There is no question that the communication culture that reigns on the Net is better at speed and volume than at synthesis. It is capable of getting tens of thousands of people to meet on the same street corner, placards in hand, but is far less adept at helping those same people to agree on what they are really asking for before they get to the barricades—or after they leave.

For this reason, an odd sort of anxiety has begun to set in after each demonstration: Was that it? When's the next one? Will it be as good, as big? To keep up the momentum, a culture of serial protesting is rapidly taking hold. My inbox is cluttered with entreaties to come to what promises to be "the next Seattle." There was Windsor and Detroit on June 4, 2000, for a "shutdown" of the Organization of American States, and Calgary a week later for the World Petroleum Congress; the Republican convention in Philadelphia in July and the Democratic convention in LA. in August; the World Economic Forum's Asia Pacific Economic Summit on September 11 in Melbourne, followed shortly thereafter by anti-IMF demos on September 26 in Prague, and then on to Quebec City for the Summit of the Americas in April 2001. Someone posted a message on the organizing e-mail list for the Washington demos: "Wherever they go, we shall be there! After this, see you in Prague!" But is this really what we want—a movement of meeting stalkers, following the trade bureaucrats as if they were the Grateful Dead?

The prospect is dangerous for several reasons. Far too much expectation is being placed on these protests: the organizers of the D.C. demo, for instance, announced they would literally "shut down" two $30 billion transnational institutions, at the same time as they attempted to convey sophisticated ideas about the fallacies of neo-liberal economics to the stock-happy public. They simply couldn't do it; no single demo could, and it's only going to get harder. Seattle's direct-action tactics worked because they took the police by surprise. That won't happen again. Police have now subscribed to all the e-mail lists. The city of Los Angeles has already put in a request for $4 million in new security gear and staffing costs to protect the city from the activist swarm.

In an attempt to build a stable political structure to advance the movement between protests, Danaher has begun to fundraise for a "permanent convergence centre" in Washington. The International Forum on Globalization, meanwhile, has been meeting since March in hopes of producing a two-hundred-page policy paper by the end of the year. According to IFG director Jerry Mander, it won't be a manifesto but a set of principles and priorities, an early attempt, as he puts it, at "defining a new architecture" for the global economy. [The paper was delayed many times and was still not available at the time of this book's publication.]

Like the conference organizers at the Riverside Church, however, these initiatives face an uphill battle. Most activists agree that the time has come to sit down and start discussing a positive agenda—but at whose table, and who gets to decide?

These questions came to a head at the end of May when Czech President Vaclav Havel offered to "mediate" talks between World Bank president James Wolfensohn and the protesters planning to disrupt the bank's September 26–28 meeting in Prague. There was no consensus among protest organizers about participating in the negotiations at Prague Castle and, more to the point, there was no process in place to make the decision: no mechanism to select acceptable members of an activist delegation (some suggested an Internet vote) and no agreed-upon set of goals to measure the benefits and pitfalls of taking part. If Havel had reached out to the groups specifically dealing with debt and structural adjustment, like Jubilee 2000 or 50 Years Is Enough, the proposal would have been dealt with in a straightforward manner. But because he approached the entire movement as if it was a single unit, he sent those organizing the demonstrations into weeks of internal strife.

Part of the problem is structural. Among most anarchists, who are doing a great deal of the grassroots organizing (and who got on-line way before the more established left), direct democracy, transparency, and community self-determination are not lofty political goals, they are fundamental tenets governing their own organizations. Yet many of the key NGOs, though they may share the anarchists' ideas about democracy in theory, are themselves organized like traditional hierarchies. They are run by charismatic leaders and executive boards, while their members send them money and cheer from the sidelines.

So how do you extract coherence from a movement filled with anarchists, whose greatest tactical strength so far has been its similarity to a swarm of mosquitoes? Maybe, as with the Internet, the best approach is to learn to surf the structures that are emerging organically. Perhaps what is needed is not a single political party but better links among the affinity groups; perhaps rather than moving toward more centralization, what is needed is further radical decentralization.

When critics say that the protesters lack vision, they are really objecting to a lack of an overarching revolutionary philosophy–like Marxism, democratic socialism, deep ecology, or social anarchy–that they all agree on. That is absolutely true, and for this we should be extraordinarily thankful. At the moment, the anti-corporate street activists are ringed by would-be leaders, eager for the opportunity to enlist activists as foot soldiers for their particular vision. At one end there is Michael Lerner and his conference at the Riverside Church, waiting to welcome all that inchoate energy in Seattle and Washington inside the framework of his "Politics of Meaning." At the other, there is John Zerzan in Eugene, Oregon, who isn't interested in Lerner's call for "healing" but sees the rioting and property destruction as the first step toward the collapse of industrialization and a return to "anarcho-primitivism"—a pre-agrarian hunter-gatherer Utopia. In between there are dozens of other visionaries, from the disciples of Murray Bookchin and his theory of social ecology, to certain sectarian Marxists who are convinced the revolution starts tomorrow, to devotees of Kalle Lasn, editor of *Adbusters*, and his watered-down version of revolution through "culture jamming." And then there is the unimaginative pragmatism coming from some union leaders who, before Seattle, were ready to tack social clauses onto existing trade agreements and call it a day.

It is to this young movement's credit that it has as yet fended off all these agendas and has rejected everyone's generously donated manifesto, holding out for an acceptably democratic, representative process to take its resistance to the next stage. Perhaps its true challenge is not finding a vision but rather resisting the urge to settle on one too quickly. If it succeeds in warding off the teams of visionaries-in-waiting, there will be some short-term public relations problems. Serial protesting will burn some people out. Street intersections will declare autonomy. And yes, young activists will offer themselves up like lambs—dressed, frequently enough, in actual lamb costumes—to *The New York Times* op-ed page for ridicule.

But so what? Already, this decentralized, multiheaded swarm of a movement has succeeded in educating and radicalizing a generation of activists around the world. Before it signs on to anyone's ten-point plan, it deserves the chance to see if, out of its chaotic network of hubs and spokes, something new, something entirely its own, can emerge.

CHAPTER 29

Cosmopolitalism and the Future of Democracy: Politics, Culture, and the Self

NICK STEVENSON

If we pause to ask ourselves, at the dawn of the new century, which new political perspectives are likely to play a central role in defining humanity's future, we might reply cosmopolitanism. In a world where instantaneous information, ecological risks and viruses, the financial flows of capital, and refugees are regularly crossing the borders of nation-states, how might we reimagine a radical politics suitable for our current age? Whereas the politics of the twentieth century could for the most part be encapsulated through the interplay of capitalism and socialism, such an argument would be difficult to maintain in respect of our new century. State sovereignty is currently being called into question by the development of the internet, the capacity of long-range weapon systems, the hybridisation of cultures, and environmental erosion. Yet it is currently unclear whether a cosmopolitan politics can indeed emerge between the global ambitions of capitalist financial institutions and the regressive securities of the fundamentalists. How might we maintain a "progressive" political vision for our new century that revives active forms of civic engagement while pointing beyond the cynicism of neoliberalism and the certitudes of the dogmatists?

Cosmopolitanism's strength is that it is able to offer substantial ethical arguments that move political discussion beyond narrower concerns. In this respect, it is my argumentative strategy that cosmopolitanism needs to be able to occupy questions of politics, culture, and selfhood all at once. Cosmopolitanism then resembles an interconnected mosaic of arguments and discourses, rather than predetermined blueprints and plans. That is, cosmopolitanism will only become a substantial ethical vision if it is able to interrelate a number of questions related to politics and society, culture and the self. Without this ability cosmopolitan arguments risk becoming a detached set of political programmes that are unable to articulate the hopes, passions, and projections of a substantial number of the world's people. Within this set of concerns cosmopolitanism becomes as much about issues related to international forms of governance as our capacity to be able to tolerate and engage with the "difference" of the other. If my arguments are followed, universalism and difference are not necessarily in conflict, but are two sides of the same coin. Such views then point towards a new kind of global politics beyond identity politics, narrowly conceived national passions, and enhanced forms of economic competition.

* * * * *

⑤ DISARMAMENT AND EUROPEAN COSMOPOLITANISM

In seeking to understand political cosmopolitanism I want to start before, rather than after, the Cold War. The current debates often suggest that political cosmopolitanism came to fruition after the collapse of the bloc system. This is not only mistaken, but fails to build upon the cultural production of intellectuals and social movements who sought to dismantle the destructive logics of the two main superpowers. As we shall see, unless we tie contemporary political hopes and expectations to a consideration of past understandings we will miss an opportunity to learn from previous mistakes and insights. These considerations can also be connected to what I perceive to be the overt formalism of current political and philosophical versions of cosmopolitanism.[1] That is, while the cosmopolitan ideal remains tied to moral criteria, it also needs to be linked to more ethical and cultural projections.

The fall of the Berlin wall was the biggest political event of my lifetime. As an active member of CND (Campaign for Nuclear Disarmament) since its second coming in the early 1980s, it was the need to dismantle the bloc system that remained at the foreground of mine and others' political imaginations. In particular, an organisation linked to CND called END (European Nuclear Disarmament) was important not only for opposing the destructive logics of the arms race, but for attempting to build an alternative cosmopolitan vision for all European peoples. The key intellectual within this movement was E.P. Thompson, who produced a number of books, pamphlets, and magazine and newspaper articles that sought to elucidate a vision of a democratic Europe that was no longer permanently prepared for war.

Thompson argued that both East and West were involved in an ideological mirror stage, where the threat of the "other" legitimated internal policing and intellectual control.[2] Unlike Halliday,[3] Thompson argued that NATO and the Warsaw Pact mutually reinforced one another. The Cold War was thus better seen as a "conflictual alliance," as after Europe had been divided following the Second World War, there was never any real policy of "roll back" adopted by the superpowers. Instead the Americans hegemonically sealed their dominance through the Marshall Plan, while the Soviet Union depended more on force than consent for its authority. Thompson argued that what tended to be sacrificed in the relationship between the two blocs were the interests of third parties. As the superpowers attempted to hold on to their respective spheres of influence, these interests in areas like Eastern Europe tended to be prioritised over demands for democracy. The Cold War promoted an atmosphere of paranoia and hostility, where democracy was the main casualty. In Thompson's assessment it was the imaginary dimension (or the culturally deformed logic) of the Cold War that was pushing Europe dangerously close to nuclear destruction. By arguing that the Cold War had a reciprocal logic there was a need for the peace movement to articulate a "third space" that could give voice to the common interests of peoples in both East and West. These common interests were for democracy, human rights, and ecological survival. The peace movement within Europe was urged to build alliances and promote cultural understanding and intellectual exchange across the blocs. Hence, given that the political elites of both East and West were locked into the ideology of deterrence, the agency for change would need to come from below. Should the bloc system become dismantled, the hope was that this would provide new opportunities for democratic versions of socialism, peaceful relations between nation-states, and a reduction of the threat of nuclear destruction.

* * * * *

⑤ THE NEW POLITICAL COSMOPOLITANS

Since the fall of the Berlin wall the cosmopolitan view has sought to dispense with specifically national responses. This has largely been due to the argument that processes of globalisation have significantly undermined national forms of citizenship. According to Richard Falk, globalisation has minimised political differences within states by converting elections into trivial rituals, while, simultaneously weakening the internal bonds of community and consideration.[4] Issues such as growing ecological awareness, the impact of global poverty, feminism, and the participation of racial and ethnic minorities cannot readily be integrated into a concern for the declining fortunes of territorial states. Following Beck, Held, and Linklater,[5] there is the view that, without a politically robust cosmopolitan culture, global civil society, and cosmopolitan institutions, we will remain a world at the mercy of the interests of nation-states and economic markets. Democracy has to become a transnational form of governance by breaking with the cultural hegemony of the state. A cosmopolitan political community would thus be based upon overlapping or multiple citizenships connecting the populace into local, national, regional, and global forms of governance. The cosmopolitan polity, guided by the principle of autonomy, would seek to achieve new levels of interconnectedness to correspond with an increasingly global world. These dimensions remain vital, surpassing older divisions in the democratic tradition between direct and representative democracy by seeking to maximise the principle of autonomy across a range of different levels. Within this framework, therefore, the argument for a cosmopolitan democracy is guided by the argument that problems such as HIV, ecological questions, and poverty are increasingly globally shared problems.

We are witnessing growing calls for the democratic ideal to detach itself from national boundaries. This is in response to a number of related developments. For David Held this is both because specifically national democracies have been undermined by more global flows, and because for local forms of accountability to survive and be revived, the democratic ideal must find expression at the transnational level.[6] The task of securing democracy in an increasingly interconnected age must allow for the development of a cosmopolitan democratic law. In this respect, Held has identified the United Nations as an institution that could play a key role in the transformation of governance from a world system built upon the competing ambitions of nation-states to one with a deeper orientation to cosmopolitan forms of democracy. The UN Charter provides a forum where states are in certain respects equal, thereby offering the beginnings of a break with a world order whereby specifically national interests are paramount. However, as Held is well aware, the United Nations is in need of considerable reform before it is able to generate its own political resources and act as an autonomous decision-making centre.

Similarly Habermas and Honneth locate ideas of cosmopolitan democracy in Kant's desire to replace the law of nations with a genuinely morally binding international law.[7] Kant believed that the spread of commerce and the principles of republicanism could help foster cosmopolitan sentiments. As world citizens individuals would act to cancel the egoistic ambitions of individual states. Kant's vision of a peaceful cosmopolitan order based upon the obligation by states to settle their differences through the court of law has gained a new legitimacy in a post-Cold War world. For Habermas, while this vision retains a contemporary purchase, it has to be brought up to date by acknowledging a number of social transformations, including the globalisation of the public sphere and the declining power of states, while also recognising that it is individuals and citizens, not collectivities, who need to become sovereign. Habermas writes: "the community of peoples must at least be able to hold its members to legally appropriate behavior through the threat of sanctions. Only then will the unstable system of states asserting their sovereignty through mutual threat be transformed into a federation of whose common interests take over state functions: it will legally regulate its members and monitor their compliance with the rules."[8]

* * * * *

The key principle here is that multi-level cosmopolitan governance would offer new opportunities for dialogue across a number of levels. Revitalised local and transnational political structures would seek to provide the institutional basis for conversation that would dissolve older divisions between citizens and aliens. In the absence of an Archimedian standpoint that transcends differences of culture, time, and place, such dialogues would provide the basis for a new world society. As

Linklater argues, a cosmopolitan position would need to bring the "other" into an extended dialogue.[9] A genuinely cosmopolitan dialogue would need to avoid the negative representations of "alien" cultures, while deconstructing the assumption that "national" or "local" conversations have the right to override the interests of "insiders" over those of "outsiders." In these terms cosmopolitan moral progress can be accounted for when "they" become "us."

Such arguments are not (as many seem to think) dependent upon the replacement of national democracy with a global state. Cosmopolitan democracy requires the creation of institutions (within and between states as well as at the global level) that enable the voice of the individual to be heard irrespective of its local resonance.[10] Further, and somewhat paradoxically, cosmopolitanism is actually dependent upon the social re-empowerment of the national state while seeking to introduce new voices both internally and externally into the conversation. The downward pressure on public expenditure exerted by financial markets, renewed attempts to include excluded voices within democratic exchange, and a widening of our sense of political community all fall within cosmopolitan concerns. What Anthony Giddens has called the democratisation of democracy means the fostering of a strong participatory civic culture, the building of new institutions across a number of levels, and the development of more global sympathies and horizons.[11]

However, despite the arguments presented thus far, the project for cosmopolitan governance is not without its own internal sympathetic critics. The most pronounced of these has been the voice of Richard Falk.[12] Falk has argued that, rather than being concerned with institution-building as an end in itself, arguments for a cosmopolitan polity need to become focused on the recovery of democratic sensibilities. It is an active citizenry committed to substantive cosmopolitan viewpoints that remains the key agency of change. Cosmopolitanism, therefore, is actually dependent upon the development of a global civil society that is in itself dependent upon pressure and struggle from below. A democratic identity will have to forge itself in opposition to consumerist inclinations, fundamentalism, neoliberalism, and outright cynicism. The recovery of a substantive ethical agenda in a world driven by consumerism, nationalist sentiment, and market calculations is more than a matter of building new institutions. The key to civic momentum in this regard remains the convergence of grassroots activism and the taking of geopolitical opportunities by groups that are mostly organised outside the corridors of social and political elites. Like E.P. Thompson before him, Falk emphasises the importance of carrying the process of democratisation beyond state/society relations to include all areas of power and authority. Such a view breaks with the Utopian sentiment that argues that once the world becomes ordered through the formation of democratic law it automatically becomes a more just place. [...]

* * * * *

⑤ THE CONTRADICTIONS OF COSMOPOLITANISM: CULTURE, RISK, AND THE SELF

Cosmopolitanism as a cultural idea needs to be linked to the ability to live with difference and a healthy respect for "otherness." That is, cosmopolitanism needs to be discursively and emotionally imagined. How do people begin the process of thinking and feeling like cosmopolitans? How might cosmopolitan sensibilities be promoted in communities that are based upon the increased global mobility of some and the more place-specific identities of others?[13] Perhaps more to the point, how can the cosmopolitan project become orientated around the idea that "the messiness of the human predicament is here to stay"?[14]

Arguably the most sustained cosmopolitan vision that has grappled with these concerns has been provided by Ulrich Beck's notion of the risk society. Beck argues that the development of scientific rationality and economic progress have produced a range of ecological risks, from the pollution of the seas to the poisoning of the population.[15] These risks can no longer be dismissed as the side effects of industrialism. Instead, they have become increasingly central to the definition of society at the end of the twentieth century. The risk society evolves through two phases: the first is where the evident dangers of self-destruction are dealt with through the legal and political institutions of industrial society. These might include reliance upon scientific experts, the belief that new laws and policies can effectively deal with pollution, and the idea that ecological questions are secondary to notions of economic distribution. In the contemporary risk society none of these features and claims can be sustained. The emergence of a post-traditional society has seen the axes of family, gender, occupation, and belief in science and economic progress become radically undermined. The "second modernity," therefore, involves an increasingly reflexive questioning of areas of social experience that the Enlightenment failed to problematise. We become ever aware of the fallibility of expert opinion, the "invisible" destruction of nature, and the incalculability of environmental hazards.

Beck brings these questions together through what he calls "reflexive modernisation," which he contrasts with the reflection theory of modernity. Simple reflection theory holds that the modernisation of society leads to the increasing capacity of subjects to ask questions about the society they are living within. Such an optimistic view can be traced back to the Enlightenment (more science, public sphere, and experts equals more self-criticism) and contrasted with the pessimist's view that such developments only result in domination and control. Instead, "reflexive" modernisation can lead to reflection on the forces that are threatening to plunge modernity into self-dissolution, but this is not necessarily the case. Hence Beck is clear that this is not a theory of progress or decline, but one that takes up the ambivalence of modernity by focusing upon "deep-seated institutional crises in the late industrial society."[16] Cosmopolitanisation has to be understood as a relational concept whereby reflexivity becomes linked to fundamentalist attempts to close down questioning and attempts to "construct certitude." This means that fundamentalist attempts to impose gender hierarchies, the belief in expert opinion, and feelings of national superiority are all done in the face of their questioning. As Giddens has argued, to live in a post-traditional culture is to live in a world where tradition becomes one choice amongst others.[17]

The second modernity has given birth to a new form of politics that Beck calls "sub-politics."[18] The humanity-wide project of saving the environment has actually been brought about through the destruction of nature as well as the accompanying culture of risk and uncertainty that have become wrapped around human conceptions of well-being. The politicisation of science and technology is rapidly introducing a reflexive culture whereby politics and morality is gaining the upper hand over scientific experts. This does not mean that scientific research becomes marginalised, rather it actually becomes more central, given the claims and counter claims that become common place in a diversity of areas of public policy. Scientific experts and the public become increasingly aware of the provisional nature of research the more it becomes part of a reflexive democratic dialogue. Thus, a shared environment of global risk enables the formation of an ecological politics that seeks to recover democratic exchange. Whereas struggles for citizenship have historically been organised in material settings like the work place, sub-politics is more likely to be symbolically shaped through the domains of consumption, television media, and the repoliticisation of science.

If the ecological movement asks us to attend to the obligations we have to the earth, it also raises the question of the regeneration of public spaces and democratic dialogue. Beck exhibits an awareness of these dimensions through the possible emergence of an "authoritarian technocracy." Here he argues that industrial society (as we have seen) responded to the problem of ecological risk through the formal development of certain laws, belief in "cleaner" technology, and more informed experts. What is required is a placing of the burden of proof on the agents of money and power that new products and ways of generating electricity are "non-hazardous." Democratic dialogue needs to introduce into its repertoires the principles of doubt and uncertainty. Only when worst-case scenarios and the idea that technical rationality is of itself unsafe are introduced into debate (before we introduce new hazards into public life) can we begin to have a proper discussion on the subject. As Beck argues, "caution would be the mother in the kitchen of toxins."[19] Such a move would break the cycle where state bureaucracies seek to legalise and legitimate public risks, circumventing open forms of democratic dialogue.

These processes are given additional weight through what Beck terms processes of individualisation. By this Beck means that life is increasingly lived as an individual project. The decline of class loyalties and bonds (along with growing income inequalities) means that individuals are increasingly thrown back on their own biographies with human relations increasingly susceptible to individual choice.

For Beck the classic plea of industrial society — "I am hungry" — becomes replaced with "I am afraid." These developments mean that our cultural perceptions become more attuned to what Milan Kundera called the "lightness of our beings," and ethical questions as to how we should live our lives. What Beck does not mean is that the self is being increasingly determined by market individualism or by social isolation more generally. Individualisation means the disembedding of the ways of industrial society and the reinvention of new communal ties and biographies. We are living in the age of DIY biographies. Beck's views contrast with communitarian ideas that suggest that communities need to be remade through the imposition of shared moral rules. That is, it is not the case that individuals are becoming trapped within empty forms of consumer narcissism or a retreat away from politics into the private sphere. Under conditions of welfare industrialism, "people are invited to constitute themselves as individuals: to plan, understand, design themselves as individuals and, should they fail, to blame themselves."[20]

This suggests that modernity has given birth to "freedom's children," who have learnt that fun, mobile phones, and opposition to mainstream politics can be a force for change. The main political dividing line in the struggles that mark the future will be between those who seek to remake civil society and community out of freedom and those who will seek to introduce new forms of discipline and compulsion. Indeed, it is the ethic of individualisation when joined with globalisation that is most likely to lead politics in a cosmopolitan direction. Similarly, Touraine argues that the modern subject must learn successfully to negotiate between the twin traps evident within global networks of production and the return to community.[21] Market hedonism and the drive towards cultural homogeneity denies the ideals of intercultural communication. Whereas the global market has flooded our lives with standardised goods, our increasingly fragmented world has led to the proliferation of sects who reject universal norms. We are then "caught between the calculations of the financiers and the *fatwas* of the *ayatollahs*."[22] We might take the United States as the model for this state of affairs, given it remains the main centre of world markets while being increasingly fragmented into contested communities of opinion. Yet, similarly to Beck, Touraine argues we are living in the age of the Subject. Rather than submitting to the logics of the market or community, the Subject seeks to defend the self against instrumentalism and communalism. The break-up of national-capitalism has led to the weakening of institutions whose aim it is to impose collective norms and identities. This means that where our personal lives are less regulated by norms and hierarchies, this has led to both increasing social inequalities and enhanced possibilities for freedom and creativity. Within this both Beck and Touraine reject the idea that they are merely describing new forms of individualism available to the middle classes. Rather, the Subject's capacity to be creatively involved in dialogue can only be enhanced by recognising the threats to "freedom" posed by communalism and consumerism. The twin dangers of mass culture and cultural nationalism (or indeed communitarianism) are held in check through the rebirth of cosmopolitan politics through individualisation. Here fundamentalism is not defined as universalism (as it tends to be with many poststructuralist writers) but the attempt to close down the reflexivity of the subject. Fundamentalism as cosmopolitanism's "other" appears in the guise of unthinking consumerism, communalism, dogmatisms of both right and left and nationalism.

* * * * *

In terms of a cultural agenda these questions have indeed been most prominently raised by those writing from a postcolonial viewpoint. Notions of hybridisation and mongrelisation have been utilised to claim a radical heterogeneity that resists the essentialisms of racialisation.[23] Rather than embrace the politics of cultural nationalism or the rhetorics of free market liberalism, notions of diaspora have sought to break the simplistic links between place and culture. Processes of transcultural dialogue, difference, and displacement have sought to emphasise how we are all "out of place." Whereas supremacist thinking seeks to fortify boundaries of racial particularity, this is challenged by popular forces that seek to articulate more ambivalent, less settled identities.[24]

In many respects these ideas have already been addressed by Richard Sennett's classic little book on the city.[25] Sennett argues that the desire to bring about the planned and controlled city was an attempt to rationalise and dehumanise the urban landscape. Politically this is often expressed in terms of a search for idealised images of community or an attempt to construct intense feelings of in-group unity. This is actually a way, argues Sennett, of avoiding troubling forms of emotional ambivalence within social relations, and of expelling "otherness" from our community. The city is becoming not so much a zone for "multiple contact points," but a space of "dullness and routine."[26] The desire to live without difference is progressively becoming an everyday feature of urban life as neighbourhoods become increasingly segregated and as urban planners seek to create conflict-free communities. The attempts to flee difference and ambivalence end in violent strategies seeking either to assimilate or expel cultural difference. For Sennett this asphyxiates much about the life of the city that made it exciting in the first place. Similarly, James Donald has argued that urbanity becomes instrumentalised when it is presented as a problem to be solved.[27] This was particularly evident in attempts made within the discourses and practices of urban planners who sought to subject the city to Utopian designs. What is required, then, is an alternative way of imagining urbanity that seeks to foster rather than impose the values of tolerance and difference.

Such projections then break with the idea of the self as embedded within any one community or as atomised and individualistic. Cosmopolitan politics requires a dialogic view of the self. Hence as the social world loses its capacity, once and for all, to fix moral hierarchies through tradition, this opens the cosmos to the difference of others. For Habermas the fully developed ego should in principle be capable of questioning the authority of previously held identities and communally transmitted norms and values.[28] As Habermas recognises, such a notion of selfhood has been most fully outlined by Mead. The self in this account emerges through a three-way conversation between the I, Me, and generalised Other. Mead argues that human selfhood develops out of our capacity to be able to view ourselves from the generalised attitude of other people.[29] Once we learn to take "the attitude of the other," we are able to view ourselves from the position of the community. This is not a description of moral conformity, but the recognition that the dialogic self can only handle community disapproval by setting up moral standards which "out vote" currently held social norms. Hence in cosmopolitan terms, an individual or social movement may be required to come into conflict with the immediate community in the defence of a universalistic morality. Mead in such a view consistently represents individualism as the flip side of universalism.

However, while central to the cosmopolitan project, such a view of the self only takes us so far. The dialogic model of the self is unable to account for the creative productions of the unconscious. According to Elliott, selfhood is not only shaped by the to and fro of conversation between the self and community but is also dependent upon the pre-linguistic configurations of the psyche.[30] Arguably, then, psychoanalysis has a great deal to contribute to a cosmopolitan understanding of the self, given that it has been able to identify much that is creative and destructive about human beings. The dialogic view of the self cannot explain a fear of difference and otherness that may come to obstruct ongoing cosmopolitan conversations. The fear of ambivalence evident within attempts to promote purity or the "objective attitude" could be due to a fear of the feelings that are involved in recognising the complexities of our personal investments within politics and society.[31] The argument here is that whether these are feelings of contradiction, disappointment, or estrangement, they may well be experienced as threatening by the political subject who prefers to take shelter in either the politics of purity or objectivity. The desire to rid the self of ambiguous feelings is indicative of fundamentalist as opposed to cosmopolitan politics. As Christopher Bollas argues, in order to combat fundamentalist politics we need to combat the fascist within each of us.[32] This then offers a different set of political and personal considerations to arguments where authoritarian tendencies are seen as connected to some groups rather than others. The fascist personality will seek to expel doubts and counterviews from the self and replace them with more coherent ideologies. The fascistic mind values the clarity that is to be found in both purifying and purging the self. These violent forms of purification are prefigured within everyday encounters between the self and others, as well as within the self. Each time we denigrate or caricature another, we are participating in a form of emotional violence. By this Bollas is looking at the ways certain political viewpoints are prefigured in the self, not arguing that this is what brings oppressive ideologies into political space. Another way of making this argument is that the purely dialogic view of the self is unable to deal with omnipotence. In this state we are unable to take in the idea that the other person does not want what we want. Hence, while

Habermas and Mead seek to construct an intersubjective view of the self, they do so without paying sufficient attention to the subject's capacity to be destructive.[33] To open up the relationship between the self and other is to ask whether we can avoid assimilating the other to the self. Can we recognise the other's alterity without normalising difference? Similarly, Kristeva has argued that the projection of rage and hatred on to strangers within the community involves the removal of feelings that cannot be held internally.[34] That we are, to borrow her phrase, "strangers to ourselves" may mean we become caught up in destructive psychic processes. As Jung famously put it, "anything that disappears from your psychological inventory is apt to turn up in the guise of a hostile neighbour."[35]

* * * * *

NOTES

1. The argument that many of the Kantian-inspired attempts to reformulate democracy in cosmopolitan terms are overly disconnected from diverse political contexts revisits some of the criticisms made by the early Frankfurt school. In this regard, see Herbert Marcuse, "Philosophy and critical theory," in: David Ingram & Julia Simon-Ingram (eds), *Critical Theory: The Essential Readings* (Paragon, 1992), pp. 5–19.

2. See, for example, Edward P. Thompson, *Zero Option* (Merlin Press, 1982); Edward P. Thompson, *The Heavy Dancers* (Merlin Press, 1985); and Edward P. Thompson, "The Ends of the Cold War," *New Left Review*, No. 182 (1990), pp. 139–46.

3. Fred Halliday, *The Making of the Second Cold War* (Verso, 1983).

4. Richard Falk, "The Decline of Citizenship in an Era of Globalization," *Citizenship Studies*, Vol. 4, No. 1 (2000), pp. 5–17.

5. See, especially, Ulrich Beck, *World Risk Society* (Polity Press, 1999); David Held, *Cosmopolitan Democracy: An Agenda for a New World Order* (Polity Press, 1995); and Andrew Linklater, *The Transformation of Political Community* (Polity Press, 1998).

6. David Held, "Democracy and the international order," in: Daniele Archibugi & David Held (eds), *Cosmopolitan Democracy: An Agenda for a New World Order* (Polity Press, 1995), pp. 96–120.

7. Jürgen Habermas, "Kant's idea of perpetual peace, with the benefit of two hundred years hindsight," in: J. Bohman & M. Lutz-Bachmann (eds), *Perpetual Peace: Essays on Kant's Cosmopolitan Ideal* (MIT Press, 1997), pp. 113–53; and Axel Honneth, "Is universalism a moral trap? The presuppositions of a politics of human rights," in *ibid.*, pp. 155–78.

8. See Habermas, "Kant's idea of perpetual peace," p. 127.

9. See Linklater, *The Transformation of Political Community*.

10. See Daniele Archibugi, "Cosmopolitan Democracy," *New Left Review*, No. 4 (2000), pp. 137–50.

11. Anthony Giddens, *Runaway World: How Globalisation Is Reshaping Our Lives* (Profile Books, 1999).

12. Richard Falk, *On Humane Governance: Towards a New Global Politics* (Polity Press, 1995); and Richard Falk, *Human Rights Horizons: The Pursuit of Justice in a Globalising World* (Routledge, 2000).

13. Zygmunt Bauman, *Liquid Modernity* (Polity Press, 2000); and Manuel Castells, *The Rise of the Network Society* (Blackwell, 1996).

14. See Bauman, *Liquid Modernity*, p. 245.

15. Ulrich Beck, *Risk Society* (Sage, 1992).

16. Ulrich Beck, Anthony Giddens, & Scott Lash, *Reflexive Modernisation: Politics, Tradition and Aesthetics in the Modern Social Order* (Polity Press, 1994), p. 178.

17. Anthony Giddens, *Modernity and Self Identity* (Polity Press, 1991).

18. Ulrich Beck, *The Reinvention of Politics: Rethinking Modernity in the Global Social Order* (Polity Press, 1997).

19. Ulrich Beck, *Ecological Politics in the Age of Risk* (Polity Press, 1995).

20. Beck, *Risk Society.*

21. Alain Touraine, *Can We Live Together? Equality and Difference* (Polity Press, 2000).

22. *Ibid.*, p. 43.

23. Robert J.C. Young, *Colonial Desire: Hybridity in Theory, Culture and Race* (Routledge, 1995).

24. See Paul Gilroy, *Between Camps: Nations, Cultures and the Allure of Race* (Penguin, 2000).

25. Richard Sennett, *The Uses of Disorder: Personal Identity and City Life* (Penguin, 1970).

26. *Ibid.*, p. 135.

27. James Donald, *Imagining the Modern City* (Athlone Press, 1999).

28. Jurgen Habermas, *Communication and the Evolution of Society* (Heinemann, 1979).

29. George Herbert Mead, *Mind, Self and Society: From the Standpoint of a Social Behaviourist* (University of Chicago Press, 1934).

30. Anthony Elliott, *Social Theory and Psychoanalysis in Transition: Self and Society from Freud to Kristeva* (Blackwell, 1992).

31. Andrew Samuels, *The Political Psyche* (Routledge, 1993).

32. Christopher Bollas, *Being a Character* (Routledge, 1992).

33. Jessica Benjamin, *Shadow of the Other: Intersubjectivity and Gender in Psychoanalysis* (Routledge, 1998).

34. Julia Kristeva, *Strangers to Ourselves* (Harvester, 1991).

35. Carl Jung, *Essays on Contemporary Events: Reflections on Nazi Germany*, foreword by Andrew Samuels (Ark, 1988), p. 8.

PART VIII

Globalization and Global Consciousness

CRITICAL THINKING QUESTIONS

Hedley .

1. What are some of the organizational and non-organizational forces that facilitated processes of globalization?
2. In what ways does Hedley see electronic communications facilitating globalization?
3. What are some of the benefits that come with transnational corporations?

Klein

1. How does Klein understand globalization as a contradictory force, as both liberating and constraining?
2. Can the negative and positive aspects of globalization be separated? Use an example to explain your response.
3. Is it useful to think about global activism as a unified social movement today?

Stevenson

1. What is cosmopolitanism?
2. What are some of the ways in which contemporary theories of cosmopolitism differ from theories developed in the context of the Cold War?
3. What are some of the different ways that global democracy may be achieved?

SUGGESTED READINGS

Bauman, Zygmunt. 1998. *Globalization: The Human Consequences*. New York: Columbia University Press.

Bauman argues that the concept of "globalization" is poorly defined. He maintains that the essence of globalization is not electronic communication networks, but rather time/space compression. The book considers the issue of mobility and its implication for social and physical relations.

Bennett, W. Lance. 1999. "Communicating Global Activism Strengths and Vulnerabilities of Networked Politics." *Information, Communication, and Society 6*, 2: 143–168.

Bennett argues that transnational activism is aimed beyond states and directly at corporations, and shows how the Internet is implicated in the new global activism.

Greenberg, Joshua, and Graham Knight. 2004. "Framing Sweatshops: Nike, Global Manufacturing and the American News Media." *Communication and Critical/Cultural Studies 1*, 2: 171–195.

This paper examines U.S. newspaper coverage of sweatshops, focusing on a case study of Nike (1995–2000). The authors argue that activists tended to concentrate on solutions rather than causes, and tended to root the source of the problem in the agency of consumers rather than producers.

Klein, Naomi. 2000. *No Logo: Taking Aim at the Brand Bullies*. Toronto: Vintage Canada.

This is Klein's analysis of branding, corporatization, and resistance. Students will find the book easy to read.

Teeple, Gary. 1995. *Globalization and the Decline of Social Reform*. Toronto: Garamond Press.

This book identifies neo-liberalism as a point of transition from nation-state capitalism to world capitalism. Teeple traces the ascendancy and decline of the welfare state, and some of the problems associated with neo-liberalism and globalization.

RELATED WEB SITES

Centre for Research on Globalization

This site offers many sources from activists and scholars concerned with the negative aspects of globalization.
www.globalresearch.ca/

Essays on Globalization

There are many interesting essays offered on this Web site. Students will find the post September 11th reference point both theoretically interesting and politically relevant.

www.ssrc.org/sept11/essays/globalization.htm

Fences and Windows

Fences and Windows is a not-for-profit organization that provides financial support to grassroots activists who are directly resisting privatization and corporatization around the world.

www.fencesfund.org/

Globalization.com

This is a Web site with many links to resources on globalization generally.

· *www.globalization.com/*

Globalization Web Site

The Globalization Web site offers information on issues, books, organizations, news, and people concerned with the multifaceted nature of globalization.

www.sociology.emory.edu/globalization/about.html

REFERENCES

Marx, Karl. 1976. *Capital*, vol. 1. London: Penguin Books.

Klein, Naomi. 2000. *No Logo: Taking Aim at the Brand Bullies*. Toronto: Vintage Canada.

Waters, Malcolm. 1995. *Globalization* (2nd ed.). New York: Routledge.

PART IX

Postcolonialism, Diaspora, Citizenship, and Identity

THERE ARE TWO GENERAL THEMES DEALT WITH IN THIS FINAL CHAPTER, THE FIRST of which is postcolonialism. The term "colonialism" refers to a sequence of material, economic, political, and cultural forces used by a state or region to claim control over another state or region. Colonialism often takes the form of politico-economic domination (e.g., conquest), and it encompasses ideological forms of domination, including literary, artistic, and cultural modes. The term "postcolonialism" in sociological discourse, then, refers to a set of themes and theories that are concerned with how colonized peoples and nations deal with the legacy of colonialism as they struggle for and develop independence, sovereignty, and national identity. Postcolonial theorists are interested in Western colonialism as it developed since the 16th century, and they investigate the ways in which colonial relations are resisted, challenged, and/or subverted.

Postcolonial theory emerged out of Western colonialism, and since the 1950s it has developed into a critical perspective that analyzes and critiques colonial relations. In the wake of the decolonization movement in regions, including Africa, Asia, and the Middle East, a long list of intellectuals, such as Gayatri Spivak, Aimé Césaire, and C.L.R. James, started to theorize how once-colonized people straddled the cultures of both the colonizing and colonized groups. One of the more prominent contributors to postcolonial theory has been Frantz Fanon (1925–1961) who, in books such as *Black Skin, White Masks* (1967) and *The Wretched of the Earth* (1961), explored not only how colonizing nations justify their domination of colonized nations, but also how colonized people assimilate the language, consciousness, and ideologies that contribute to their continued domination. He argued that colonial ideologies mask relations of domination by normalizing colonial beliefs and values, and that they have a corrosive psychological effect on the souls of the colonized.

The study of postcolonialism has become increasingly popular since the 1970s. Particularly since the publication of Edward Said's *Orientalism* (1978), postcolonial theorists have explored the ways in which race, ethnicity, culture, and human identity have been represented after many colonized countries gained independence. They have theorized the nature of postcolonial hybrid identities, and they have taken interest in sociological concepts such as essentialism, diaspora, nationalism, and subjectivity.

The second general theme dealt with in this chapter is citizenship and identity. Sociological interest in citizenship and identity is by no means unique to 20th- and 21st-century theory, as sociologists have been interested in such issues at least since Durkheim wrote. But recent debates on citizenship and identity have been caught up in theorization about globalization, diaspora, hybridity, and social change. Prominent issues that remain significant in theoretical debates include who qualifies for citizenship and who does not, what national citizenship entails in a globalizing world, and the relationship shared between individuals, on the one hand, and social, national, and international institutions, on the other hand. Citizenship remains a contested category, and the link between identity, citizenship, and struggles for recognition remains salient in social theory.

⑤ SECTION READINGS: EDWARD SAID, STUART HALL, WILL KYMLICKA, AND CHARLES TAYLOR

This section opens with a reading taken from Edward Said's (1978) treatise, *Orientalism*. Said (1935–2003) begins with a theme that should now be familiar to readers: the role that culture, history, literature, and intellectuals play in shaping images, ideologies, and scholarship—in short, the forces involved in the production of knowledge. Said explains that Western knowledge of the Orient is conveyed through cultural media ranging from traditional learning environments (e.g., university) to travel books. Drawing on Nietzsche, he argues that language functions to create images, representations, and impressions about particular places, peoples, and civilizations. These knowledge sets, he continues, become "truths" in the minds of Western viewers, and they sustain the patterns of inequality between the Eastern and Western worlds.

Said distinguishes between "latent" and "manifest" Orientalism. Since the 19th century, he maintains, latent Orientalism has taken the form of an unconscious Western certainty about Oriental existence that conceives of the Orient as backward, separate, and different. In these constructions, Said argues, actual Oriental cultures and peoples are rarely looked at; rather, they are imagined, speculated about, and reified through the Western production of cultural images. By contrast, he refers to manifest Orientalism as overt representations about the Orient. These include language, literature, and history. Through spoken and written discourse, manifest Orientalism is an expression of latent Orientalism. For Said, therefore, the Orient is a social construction based on assumptions, beliefs, images, representations, and attitudes framed by a set of Western cultural forces.

Stuart Hall is the author of the next reading passage. Hall (1932–) is world-renowned for his contributions to cultural studies, media studies, postcolonial studies, and social theory. In the reading, Hall addresses the issues of Caribbean cultural identities, representation, authority, diaspora, and hybridity. Hall contends that scholars tend to explain particular cultural identities based on the social/manifest features exhibited by members of particular cultures. In this sense, manifest cultural identity is understood as a construct that signifies a person's true identity, as the essence of their "pure" identity. For Hall, however, representations of identities are always temporal, partial, fragmentary, and unstable. Certain cultural cinematic representations will resist dominant/hegemonic identities that are imposed external to the community of people in question (colonial identities) by invoking homogeneous representation of "the African experience" or "the Caribbean experience," for example (just as hegemonic colonial representations portrayed the non-Western other as homogeneous and static). But such strategies reduce the complexity of identity formation (class, sex, skin colour, education, etc.) to a singular process of being (of what it means to be "Black" or to be "European" or "White").

Hall also explores a second way to explain cultural identities that accounts for identity constructions as a continual process of negotiation. Identity in this second sense cannot be reduced to an essentialized homogeneous form, and the construct of cultural identity is explained as discontinuous and fragmentary. For this reason, Hall explains cultural identity in the context of diaspora as a process of "enunciation." Identity is never fixed to an essential subject position, he contends; it is never tied to a process of "being." Rather, it entails a process of "becoming" through a series of negotiations, interactions, representations, experiences, and perceptions. In Hall's view, Caribbean cultural identities are better explained in terms of hybrid identities involving the co-existence of cultural differences and dominant cultural representations or forms.

The third reading is excerpted from the writings of Will Kymlicka, Canada research chair (philosophy) at Queen's University, who addresses the arguments of David Held on citizenship and globalization. Recall from the previous chapter (in the Stevenson reading) that David Held believes that the formation of transnational democracy requires the expression of a democratic ideal on a transnational level. Held believes that the development of transnational democracy is necessary because national democracies are undermined by the forces of globalization. He suggests that the realization of transnational citizenship can be accomplished by concentrating on the development of transnational institutions such as the possibilities offered through the United Nations.

Kymlicka begins his critique of Held by exploring citizenship at the domestic level. He argues that Held tends to overstate the degree to which the nation-state has lost control over macro-economic processes, as well as capital mobility, in the era of globalization. According to Kymlicka, there is evidence that countries continue to exercise their autonomy in different ways; he contends that, while globalizing forces do influence domestic policies and politics, the responses of national governments vary.

Kymlicka then turns to the issue of cosmopolitan citizenship. Challenging the argument that the formation of transnational citizenship can be achieved through the formation of transnational institutions, he contends that transnational citizenship presupposes mutual feelings of understanding and trust. He details why he believes the realization of transnational citizenship is not plausible, and concludes that we should expect to witness the formation of democratic-cosmopolitan institutions in the near future. For Kymlicka, it is erroneous to assert that globalization undermines national citizenship.

The final reading comes from the work of Charles Taylor. Taylor (1931–) is Board of Trustees professor of law and philosophy at Northwestern University, former Chicele professor of moral philosophy at Oxford University, and professor emeritus of political science and philosophy at McGill University. The reading begins with the argument that the politics of recognition and mis-recognition occupy a central position in contemporary struggles for social equality and social justice. In one sense, explains Taylor, contemporary struggles for recognition take the form of demands for recognition based on the dignity of all cultures, genders, and peoples. This is a theme that derives from 18th-century notions of the "individualized identity," as well as certain key themes in 18th-century understandings of the formation of the self (and conflicting views of human nature in the context of collapsing social hierarchies and systems of honour). But in the contemporary context, the dynamics of the politics of recognition and difference contain an important philosophical contradiction between the politics of equal dignity (that each person is universally equal) and the politics of identity (that some social groups, and hence individuals claiming membership in those groups, are different from others). As Taylor explains, this contradiction matters: although social groups seek recognition on the basis that they are equal to all others and deserve the dignity afforded to all human beings, they do so on the basis of their inherent differences. The insistence on difference contradicts the principles of dignity and universal sameness because it does not afford groups of people who have been historically excluded from some aspect of social life an equal level of inclusion (or of "difference-blindness"). Instead it maintains and perpetuates a politics of difference. Taylor prompts us to consider what happens when demands for recognition intersect with demands for equal human dignity.

CHAPTER 30

Latent and Manifest Orientalism

EDWARD SAID

* * * * *

[...] Most of us assume in a general way that learning and scholarship move forward; they get better, we feel, as time passes and as more information is accumulated, methods are refined, and later generations of scholars improve upon earlier ones. In addition, we entertain a mythology of creation, in which it is believed that artistic genius, an original talent, or a powerful intellect can leap beyond the confines of its own time and place in order to put before the world a new work. It would be pointless to deny that such ideas as these carry some truth. Nevertheless the possibilities for work present in the culture to a great and original mind are never unlimited, just as it is also true that a great talent has a very healthy respect for what others have done before it and for what the field already contains. The work of predecessors, the institutional life of a scholarly field, the collective nature of any learned enterprise: these, to say nothing of economic and social circumstances, tend to diminish the effects of the individual scholar's production. A field like Orientalism has a cumulative and corporate identity, one that is particularly strong given its associations with traditional learning (the classics, the Bible, philology), public institutions (governments, trading companies, geographical societies, universities), and generically determined writing (travel books, books of exploration, fantasy, exotic description). The result for Orientalism has been a sort of consensus: certain things, certain types of statement, certain types of work have seemed for the Orientalist correct. He has built his work and research upon them, and they in turn have pressed hard upon new writers and scholars. Orientalism can thus be regarded as a manner of regularized (or Orientalized) writing, vision, and study, dominated by imperatives, perspectives, and ideological biases ostensibly suited to the Orient. The Orient is taught, researched, administered, and pronounced upon in certain discrete ways.

The Orient that appears in Orientalism, then, is a system of representations framed by a whole set of forces that brought the Orient into Western learning,

Western consciousness, and later, Western empire. If this definition of Orientalism seems more political than not, that is simply because I think Orientalism was itself a product of certain political forces and activities. Orientalism is a school of interpretation whose material happens to be the Orient, its civilizations, peoples, and localities. Its objective discoveries—the work of innumerable devoted scholars who edited texts and translated them, codified grammars, wrote dictionaries, reconstructed dead epochs, produced positivistically verifiable learning—are and always have been conditioned by the fact that its truths, like any truths delivered by language, are embodied in language, and what is the truth of language, Nietzsche once said, but

> a mobile army of metaphors, metonyms, and anthropomorphisms—in short, a sum of human relations, which have been enhanced, transposed, and embellished poetically and rhetorically, and which after long use seem firm, canonical, and obligatory to a people: truths are illusions about which one has forgotten that this is what they are.[1]

Perhaps such a view as Nietzsche's will strike us as too nihilistic, but at least it will draw attention to the fact that so far as it existed in the West's awareness, the Orient was a word which later accrued to it a wide field of meanings, associations, and connotations, and that these did not necessarily refer to the real Orient but to the field surrounding the word.

Thus, Orientalism is not only a positive doctrine about the Orient that exists at any one time in the West; it is also an influential academic tradition (when one refers to an academic specialist who is called an Orientalist), as well as an area of concern defined by travelers, commercial enterprises, governments, military expeditions, readers of novels and accounts of exotic adventure, natural historians, and pilgrims to whom the Orient is a specific kind of knowledge about specific places, peoples, and civilizations. For the Orient idioms became frequent, and these idioms took firm hold in European discourse. Beneath the idioms there was a layer of doctrine about the Orient; this doctrine was fashioned out of the experiences of many Europeans, all of them converging upon such essential aspects of the Orient as the Oriental character, Oriental despotism, Oriental sensuality, and the like. For any European during the nineteenth century—and I think one can say this almost without qualification—Orientalism was such a system of truths, truths in Nietzsche's sense of the word. It is therefore correct that every European, in what he could say about the Orient, was consequently a racist, an imperialist, and almost totally ethnocentric. Some of the immediate sting will be taken out of these labels if we recall additionally that human societies, at least the more advanced cultures, have rarely offered the individual anything but imperialism, racism, and ethnocentrism for dealing with "other" cultures. So Orientalism aided and was aided by general cultural pressures that tended to make more rigid the sense of difference between the European and Asiatic parts of the world. My contention is that Orientalism is fundamentally a political doctrine willed over the Orient because the Orient was weaker than the West, which elided the Orient's difference with its weakness.

The very presence of a "field" such as Orientalism, with no corresponding equivalent in the Orient itself, suggests the relative strength of Orient and Occident. A vast number of pages on the Orient exist, and they, of course, signify a degree and quantity of interaction with the Orient that are quite formidable; but the crucial index of Western strength is that there is no possibility of comparing the movement of Westerners eastwards (since the end of the eighteenth century) with the movement of Easterners westwards. Leaving aside the fact that Western armies, consular corps, merchants, and scientific and archaeological expeditions were always going East, the number of travelers from the Islamic East to Europe between 1800 and 1900 is minuscule when compared with the number in the other direction.[2] Moreover, the Eastern travelers in the West were there to learn from and to gape at an advanced culture; the purposes of the Western travelers in the Orient were, as we have seen, of quite a different order. In addition, it has been estimated that around 60,000 books dealing with the Near Orient were written between 1800 and 1950; there is no remotely comparable figure for Oriental books about the West. As a cultural apparatus Orientalism is all aggression, activity, judgment, will-to-truth, and knowledge. The Orient existed for the West, or so it seemed to countless Orientalists, whose attitude to what they worked on was either paternalistic or candidly condescending—unless, of course, they were antiquarians, in which case the "classical" Orient was a credit to them and not to the lamentable modern Orient. And then, beefing up the Western scholars' work, there were numerous agencies and institutions with no parallels in Oriental society.

* * * * *

On several occasions I have alluded to the connections between Orientalism as a body of ideas, beliefs, cliches, or learning about the East, and other schools of thought at large in the culture. Now one of the important developments in nineteenth-century Orientalism was the distillation of essential ideas about the Orient—its sensuality, its tendency to despotism, its aberrant mentality, its habits of inaccuracy, its backwardness—into a separate and unchallenged coherence; thus, for a writer to use the word *Oriental* was a reference for the reader sufficient to identify a specific body of information about the Orient. This information seemed to be morally neutral and objectively valid; it seemed to have an epistemological status equal to that of historical chronology or geographical location. In its most basic form, then, Oriental material could not really be violated by anyone's discoveries, nor did it seem ever to be revaluated completely. Instead, the work of various nineteenth-century scholars and of imaginative writers made this essential body of knowledge more clear, more detailed, more substantial—and more distinct from "Occidentalism." Yet Orientalist ideas could enter into alliance with general philosophical theories (such as those about the history of mankind and civilization) and diffuse world-hypotheses, as philosophers sometimes call them; and in many ways the professional contributors to Oriental knowledge were anxious to couch their formulations and ideas, their scholarly work, their considered contemporary observations, in language and terminology whose cultural validity derived from other sciences and systems of thought.

The distinction I am making is really between an almost unconscious (and certainly an untouchable) positivity, which I shall call *latent* Orientalism, and the various stated views about Oriental society, languages, literatures, history, sociology, and so forth, which I shall call *manifest* Orientalism. Whatever change occurs in knowledge of the Orient is found almost exclusively in manifest Orientalism; the unanimity, stability, and durability of latent Orientalism are more or less constant. In the nineteenth-century writers I analyzed […], the differences in their ideas about the Orient can be characterized as exclusively manifest differences, differences in form and personal style, rarely in basic content. Every one of them kept intact the separateness of the Orient, its eccentricity, its backwardness, its silent indifference, its feminine penetrability, its supine malleability; this is why every writer on the Orient, from Renan to Marx (ideologically speaking), or from the most rigorous scholars (Lane and Sacy) to the most powerful imaginations (Flaubert and Nerval), saw the Orient as a locale requiring Western attention, reconstruction, even redemption. The Orient existed as a place isolated from the mainstream of European progress in the sciences, arts, and commerce. Thus, whatever good or bad values were imputed to the Orient appeared to be functions of some highly specialized Western interest in the Orient. This was the situation from about the 1870s on through the early part of the twentieth century—but let me give some examples that illustrate what I mean.

Theses of Oriental backwardness, degeneracy, and inequality with the West most easily associated themselves early in the nineteenth century with ideas about the biological bases of racial inequality. Thus, the racial classifications found in Cuvier's *Le Regne animal*, Gobineau's *Essai sur l'inegalité des races humaines*, and Robert Knox's *The Races of Man* found a willing partner in latent Orientalism. To these ideas was added second-order Darwinism, which seemed to accentuate the scientific validity of the division of races into advanced and backward, or European-Aryan and Oriental-African. Thus, the whole question of imperialism, as it was debated in the late nineteenth century by pro-imperialists and anti-imperialists alike, carried forward the binary typology of advanced and backward (or subject) races, cultures, and societies. John Westlake's *Chapters on the Principles of International Law* (1894) argues, for example, that regions of the earth designated as "uncivilized" (a word carrying the freight of Orientalist assumptions, among others) ought to be annexed or occupied by advanced powers. Similarly, the ideas of such writers as Carl Peters, Leopold de Saussure, and Charles Temple draw on the advanced/backward binarism[3] so centrally advocated in late nineteenth-century Orientalism.

Along with all other peoples variously designated as backward, degenerate, uncivilized, and retarded, the Orientals were viewed in a framework constructed out of biological determinism and moral-political admonishment. The Oriental was linked thus to elements in Western society (delinquents, the insane, women, the poor) having in common an identity best described as lamentably alien. Orientals were rarely seen or looked at; they were seen through, analyzed not as citizens, or even people, but as problems to be solved or confined or—as the colonial powers openly coveted their territory—taken over. The point is that the very designation of something as Oriental involved an already pronounced evaluative judgment, and in the case of the peoples inhabiting the decayed Ottoman Empire, an implicit program of action. Since the Oriental was a member of a subject race, he had to be subjected: it was that simple. The *locus classicus* for such judgment and action is to be found in Gustave Le Bon's *Les Lois psychologiques de l'évolution des peuples* (1894).

But there were other uses for latent Orientalism. If that group of ideas allowed one to separate Orientals from advanced, civilizing powers, and if the "classical" Orient served to justify both the Orientalist and his disregard of modern Orientals, latent Orientalism also encouraged a peculiarly (not to say invidiously) male conception of the world. I have already referred to this in passing during my discussion of Renan. The Oriental male was considered in isolation from the total community in which he lived and which many Orientalists, following Lane, have viewed with something resembling contempt and fear. Orientalism itself, furthermore, was an exclusively male province; like so many professional guilds during the modern period, it viewed itself and its subject matter with sexist blinders. This is especially evident in the writing of travelers and novelists: women are usually the creatures of a male power-fantasy. They express unlimited sensuality, they are more or less stupid, and above all they are willing. Flaubert's Kuchuk Hanem is the prototype of such caricatures, which were common enough in pornographic novels (e.g., Pierre Louys's *Aphrodite*) whose novelty draws on the Orient for their interest. Moreover the male conception of the world, in its effect upon the practicing Orientalist, tends to be static, frozen, fixed eternally. The very possibility of development, transformation, human movement—in the deepest sense of the word—is denied the Orient and the Oriental. As a known and ultimately an immobilized or unproductive quality, they come to be identified with a bad sort of eternality: hence, when the Orient is being approved, such phrases as "the wisdom of the East."

Transferred from an implicit social evaluation to a grandly cultural one, this static male Orientalism took on a variety of forms in the late nineteenth century, especially when Islam was being discussed. General cultural historians as respected as Leopold von Ranke and Jacob Burckhardt assailed Islam as if they were dealing not so much with an anthropomorphic abstraction as with a religio-political culture about which deep generalizations were possible and warranted: in his *Weltgeschichte* (1881–1888), Ranke spoke of Islam as defeated by the Germanic-Romanic peoples, and in his "Historische Fragmente" (unpublished notes, 1893) Burckhardt spoke of Islam as wretched, bare, and trivial.[4] Such intellectual operations were carried out with considerably more flair and enthusiasm by Oswald Spengler, whose ideas about a Magian personality (typified by the Muslim Oriental) infuse *Der Untergang des Abendlandes* (1918–1922) and the "morphology" of cultures it advocates.

What these widely diffused notions of the Orient depended on was the almost total absence in contemporary Western culture of the Orient as a genuinely felt and experienced force. For a number of evident reasons the Orient was always in the position both of outsider and of incorporated weak partner for the West. To the extent that Western scholars were aware of contemporary Orientals or Oriental movements of thought and culture, these were perceived either as silent shadows to be animated by the Orientalist, brought into reality by him, or as a kind of cultural and intellectual proletariat useful for the Orientalist's grander interpretative activity, necessary for his performance as superior judge, learned man, powerful cultural will. I mean to say that in discussions of the Orient, the Orient is all absence, whereas one feels the Orientalist and what he says as presence; yet we must not forget that the Orientalist's presence is enabled by the Orient's effective absence. This fact of substitution and displacement, as we must call it, clearly places on the Orientalist himself a certain pressure to reduce the Orient in his work, even after he has devoted a good deal of time to elucidating and exposing it. How else can one explain major scholarly production of the type we associate with Julius Wellhausen and Theodor Noldeke and, overriding it, those bare, sweeping statements that almost totally denigrate their chosen subject matter? Thus, Noldeke could declare in 1887 that the sum total of his work as an Orientalist was to confirm his "low opinion" of the Eastern peoples.[5] And like Carl Becker, Noldeke was a philhellenist, who showed his love of Greece curiously by displaying a positive dislike of the Orient, which, after all, was what he studied as a scholar.

A very valuable and intelligent study of Orientalism—Jacques Waardenburg's *L'Islam dans le miroir de l'Occident*—examines five important experts as makers of an image of Islam. Waardenburg's mirror-image metaphor for late-nineteenth- and early-twentieth-century Orientalism is apt. In the work of each of his eminent Orientalists there is a highly tendentious—in four cases out of the five, even hostile—vision of Islam, as if each man saw Islam as a reflection of his own chosen weakness. Each scholar was profoundly learned, and the style of his contribution was unique. The five Orientalists among them exemplify what was best and strongest in the tradition during the period roughly from the 1880s to the interwar years. Yet Ignaz Goldziher's appreciation of Islam's tolerance towards other religions was undercut by his dislike of Mohammed's anthropomorphisms and Islam's too-exterior theology and jurisprudence; Duncan Black Macdonald's interest in Islamic piety and orthodoxy was vitiated by his perception of what he considered Islam's heretical Christianity; Carl Becker's understanding of Islamic civilization made him see it as a sadly undeveloped one; C. Snouck Hurgronje's highly refined studies of Islamic mysticism (which he considered the essential part of Islam) led him to a harsh judgment of its crippling limitations; and Louis Massignon's extraordinary identification with Muslim theology, mystical passion, and poetic art kept him curiously unforgiving to Islam for what he regarded as its unregenerate revolt against the idea of incarnation. The manifest differences in their methods emerge as less important than their Orientalist consensus on Islam: latent inferiority.[6]

Waardenburg's study has the additional virtue of showing how these five scholars shared a common intellectual and methodological tradition whose unity was truly international. Ever since the first Orientalist congress in 1873, scholars in the field have known each other's work and felt each others presence very directly. What Waardenburg does not stress enough is that most of the late-nineteenth-century Orientalists were bound to each other politically as well. Snouck Hurgronje went directly from his studies of Islam to being an adviser to the Dutch government on handling its Muslim Indonesian colonies; Macdonald and Massignon were widely sought after as experts on Islamic matters by colonial administrators from North Africa to Pakistan; and, as Waardenburg says (all too briefly) at one point, all five scholars shaped a coherent vision of Islam that had a wide influence on government circles throughout the Western world.[7] What we must add to Waardenburg's observation is that these scholars were completing, bringing to an ultimate concrete refinement, the tendency since the sixteenth and seventeenth centuries to treat the Orient not only as a vague literary problem but—according to Masson-Oursel—as "un ferme propos d'assimiler adéquatement la valeur des langues pour pénétrer les moeurs et les pensées, pour forcer même des secrets de l'histoire."[8]

I spoke earlier of incorporation and assimilation of the Orient, as these activities were practiced by writers as different from each other as Dante and d'Herbelot. Clearly there is a difference between those efforts and what, by the end of the nineteenth century, had become a truly formidable European cultural, political, and material enterprise. The nineteenth-century colonial "scramble for Africa" was by no means limited to Africa, of course. Neither was the penetration of the Orient entirely a sudden, dramatic afterthought following years of scholarly study of Asia. What we must reckon with is a long and slow process of appropriation by which Europe, or the European awareness of the Orient, transformed itself from being textual and contemplative into being administrative, economic, and even military. The fundamental change was a spatial and geographical one, or rather it was a change in the quality of geographical and spatial apprehension so far as the Orient was concerned. The centuries-old designation of geographical space to the east of Europe as "Oriental" was partly political, partly doctrinal, and partly imaginative; it implied no necessary connection between actual experience of the Orient and knowledge of what is Oriental, and certainly Dante and d'Herbelot made no claims about their Oriental ideas except that they were corroborated by a long *learned* (and not existential) tradition. But when Lane, Renan, Burton, and the many hundreds of nineteenth-century European travelers and scholars discuss the Orient, we can immediately note a far more intimate and even proprietary attitude towards the Orient and things Oriental. In the classical and often temporally remote form in which it was reconstructed by the Orientalist, in the precisely actual form in which the modern Orient was lived in, studied, or imagined, the *geographical space* of the Orient was penetrated, worked over, taken hold of. The cumulative effect of decades of so sovereign a Western handling turned the Orient from alien into colonial space. What was important in the latter nineteenth century was not *whether* the West had penetrated and possessed the Orient, but rather *how* the British and French felt that they had done it.

The British writer on the Orient, and even more so the British colonial administrator, was dealing with territory about which there could be no doubt that English power was truly in the ascendant, even if the natives were on the face of it attracted to France and French modes of thought. So far as the actual space of the Orient was concerned, however, England was really there, France was not, except as a flighty temptress of the Oriental yokels. There is no better indication of this qualitative difference in spatial attitudes than to look at what Lord Cromer had to say on the subject, one that was especially dear to his heart:

> The reasons why French civilisation presents a special degree of attraction to Asiatics and Levantines are plain. It is, as a matter of fact, more attractive than the civilisations of England and Germany, and, moreover, it is more easy of imitation. Compare the undemonstrative, shy Englishman, with his social exclusiveness and insular habits, with the vivacious and cosmopolitan Frenchman, who does not know what the word shyness means, and who in ten minutes is apparently on terms of intimate friendship with any casual acquaintance he may chance to make. The semi-educated Oriental does not recognise that the former has, at all events, the merit of sincerity, whilst the latter is often merely acting a part. He looks coldly on the Englishman, and rushes into the arms of the Frenchman.

The sexual innuendoes develop more or less naturally thereafter. The Frenchman is all smiles, wit, grace, and fashion; the Englishman is plodding, industrious, Baconian, precise. Cromer's case is of course based on British solidity as opposed to a French seductiveness without any real presence in Egyptian reality.

> Can it be any matter for surprise [Cromer continues] that the Egyptian, with his light intellectual ballast, fails to see that some fallacy often lies at the bottom of the Frenchman's reasoning, or that he prefers the rather superficial brilliancy of the Frenchman to the plodding, unattractive industry of the Englishman or the German? Look, again, at the theoretical perfection of French administrative systems, at their elaborate detail, and at the provision which is apparently made to meet every possible contingency which may arise. Compare these features with the Englishman's practical systems, which lay down rules as to a few main points, and leave a mass of detail to individual discretion. The half-educated Egyptian naturally prefers the

Frenchman's system, for it is to all outward appearance more perfect and more easy of application. He fails, moreover, to see that the Englishman desires to elaborate a system which will suit the facts with which he has to deal, whereas the main objection to applying French administrative procedures to Egypt is that the facts have but too often to conform to the ready-made system.

Since there is a real British presence in Egypt, and since that presence—according to Cromer—is there not so much to train the Egyptian's mind as to "form his character," it follows therefore that the ephemeral attractions of the French are those of a pretty damsel with "somewhat artificial charms," whereas those of the British belong to "a sober, elderly matron of perhaps somewhat greater moral worth, but of less pleasing outward appearance."[9]

Underlying Cramer's contrast between the solid British nanny and the French coquette is the sheer privilege of British emplacement in the Orient. "The facts with which he [the Englishman] has to deal" are altogether more complex and interesting, by virtue of their possession by England, than anything the mercurial French could point to. Two years after the publication of his *Modern Egypt* (1908), Cromer expatiated philosophically in *Ancient and Modern Imperialism*. Compared with Roman imperialism, with its frankly assimilationist, exploitative, and repressive policies, British imperialism seemed to Cromer to be preferable, if somewhat more wishy-washy. On certain points, however, the British were clear enough, even if "after a rather dim, slipshod, but characteristically Anglo-Saxon fashion," their Empire seemed undecided between "one of two bases—an extensive military occupation or the principle of nationality [for subject races]." But this indecision was academic finally, for in practice Cromer and Britain itself had opted against "the principle of nationality." And then there were other things to be noted. One point was that the Empire was not going to be given up. Another was that intermarriage between natives and English men and women was undesirable. Third—and most important, I think—Cromer conceived of British imperial presence in the Eastern colonies as having had a lasting, not to say cataclysmic, effect on the minds and societies of the East. His metaphor for expressing this effect is almost theological, so powerful in Cramer's mind was the idea of Western penetration of Oriental expanses. "The country," he says, "over which the breath of the West, heavily charged with scientific thought, has once passed, and has, in passing, left an enduring mark, can never be the same as it was before."[10]

In such respects as these, nonetheless, Cromer's was far from an original intelligence. What he saw and how he expressed it were common currency among his colleagues both in the imperial Establishment and in the intellectual community. This consensus is notably true in the case of Cromer's viceregal colleagues, Curzon, Swettenham, and Lugard. Lord Curzon in particular always spoke the imperial lingua franca, and more obtrusively even than Cromer he delineated the relationship between Britain and the Orient in terms of possession, in terms of a large geographical space wholly owned by an efficient colonial master. For him, he said on one occasion, the Empire was not an "object of ambition" but "first and foremost, a great historical and political and sociological fact." In 1909 he reminded delegates to the Imperial Press Conference meeting at Oxford that "we train here and we send out to you your governors and administrators and judges, your teachers and preachers and lawyers." And this almost pedagogical view of empire had, for Curzon, a specific setting in Asia, which as he once put it, made "one pause and think."

> I sometimes like to picture to myself this great Imperial fabric as a huge structure like some Tennysonian "Palace of Art," of which the foundations are in this country, where they have been laid and must be maintained by British hands, but of which the Colonies are the pillars, and high above all floats the vastness of an Asiatic dome.[11]

With such a Tennysonian Palace of Art in mind, Curzon and Cromer were enthusiastic members together of a departmental committee formed in 1909 to press for the creation of a school of Oriental studies. Aside from remarking wistfully that had he known the vernacular he would have been helped during his "famine tours" in India, Curzon argued for Oriental studies as part of the British responsibility to the Orient. On September 27, 1909, he told the House of Lords that

> our familiarity, not merely with the languages of the people of the East but with their customs, their feelings, their traditions, their history and religion, our capacity to understand what may be called the genius of the East, is the sole basis upon which we are likely to be able to maintain in the future the position we have won, and no step that can be taken to strengthen that position can be considered undeserving of the attention of His Majesty's Government or of a debate in the House of Lords.

At a Mansion House conference on the subject five years later, Curzon finally dotted the i's. Oriental studies were no intellectual luxury; they were, he said,

> a great Imperial obligation. In my view the creation of a school [of Oriental studies—later to become the London University School of Oriental and African Studies] like this in London is part of the necessary furniture of Empire. Those of us who, in one way or another, have spent a number of years in the East, who regard that as the happiest portion of our lives, and who think that the work that we did there, be it great or small, was the highest responsibility that can be placed upon the shoulders of Englishmen, feel that there is a gap in our national equipment which ought emphatically to be filled, and that those in the City of London who, by financial support or by any other form of active and practical assistance, take their part in filling that gap, will be rendering a patriotic duty to the Empire and promoting the cause and goodwill among mankind.[12]

To a very great extent Curzon's ideas about Oriental studies derive logically from a good century of British utilitarian administration of and philosophy about the Eastern colonies. The influence of Bentham and Mills on British rule in the Orient (and India particularly) was considerable, and was effective in doing away with too much regulation and innovation; instead, as Eric Stokes has convincingly shown, utilitarianism combined with the legacies of liberalism and evangelicalism as philosophies of British rule in the East stressed the rational importance of a strong executive armed with various legal and penal codes, a system of doctrines on such matters as frontiers and land rents, and everywhere an irreducible supervisory imperial authority.[13] The cornerstone of the whole system was a constantly refined knowledge of the Orient, so that as traditional societies hastened forward and became modern commercial societies, there would be no loss of paternal British control, and no loss of revenue either. However, when Curzon referred somewhat inelegantly to Oriental studies as "the necessary furniture of Empire," he was putting into a static image the transactions by which Englishmen and natives conducted their business and kept their places. From the days of Sir William Jones the Orient had been both what Britain ruled and what Britain knew about it: the coincidence between geography, knowledge, and power, with Britain always in the master's place, was complete. To have said, as Curzon once did, that "the East is a University in which the scholar never takes his degree" was another way of saying that the East required one's presence there more or less forever.[14]

But then there were the other European powers, France and Russia among them, that made the British presence always a (perhaps marginally) threatened one. Curzon was certainly aware that all the major Western powers felt towards the world as Britain did. The transformation of geography from "dull and pedantic" —Curzon's phrase for what had now dropped out of geography as an academic subject—into "the most cosmopolitan of all sciences" argued *exactly* that new Western and widespread predilection. Not for nothing did Curzon in 1912 tell the Geographical Society, of which he was president, that

> an absolute revolution has occurred, not merely in the manner and methods of teaching geography, but in the estimation in which it is held by public opinion. Nowadays we regard geographical knowledge as an essential part of knowledge in general. By the aid of geography, and in no other way, do we understand the action of great natural forces, the distribution of population, the growth of commerce, the expansion of frontiers, the development of States, the splendid achievements of human energy in its various manifestations.
>
> We recognize geography as the handmaid of history .... Geography, too, is a sister science to economics and politics; and to any of us who have attempted to study geography it is known that the moment you diverge from the geographical field you find yourself crossing the frontiers of geology, zoology, ethnology, chemistry, physics, and almost all the kindred sciences. Therefore we are justified in saying

that geography is one of the first and foremost of the sciences: that it is part of the equipment that is necessary for a proper conception of citizenship, and is an indispensable adjunct to the production of a public man.[15]

Geography was essentially the material underpinning for knowledge about the Orient. All the latent and unchanging characteristics of the Orient stood upon, were rooted in, its geography. Thus, on the one hand the geographical Orient nourished its inhabitants, guaranteed their characteristics, and defined their specificity; on the other hand, the geographical Orient solicited the West's attention, even as—by one of those paradoxes revealed so frequently by organized knowledge—East was East and West was West. The cosmopolitanism of geography was, in Curzon's mind, its universal importance to the whole of the West, whose relationship to the rest of the world was one of frank covetousness. Yet geographical appetite could also take on the moral neutrality of an epistemological impulse to find out, to settle upon, to uncover—as when in *Heart of Darkness* Marlow confesses to having a passion for maps.

> I would look for hours at South America, or Africa, or Australia, and lose myself in all the glories of exploration. At that time there were many blank spaces on the earth, and when I saw one that looked particularly inviting on a map (but they all look that) I would put my finger on it and say, When I grow up I will go there.[16]

Seventy years or so before Marlow said this, it did not trouble Lamartine that what on a map was a blank space was inhabited by natives; nor, theoretically, had there been any reservation in the mind of Emer de Vattel, the Swiss-Prussian authority on international law, when in 1758 he invited European states to take possession of territory inhabited only by mere wandering tribes.[17] The important thing was to dignify simple conquest with an idea, to turn the appetite for more geographical space into a theory about the special relationship between geography on the one hand and civilized or uncivilized peoples on the other. But to these rationalizations there was also a distinctively French contribution.

By the end of the nineteenth century, political and intellectual circumstances coincided sufficiently in France to make geography, and geographical speculation (in both senses of that word), an attractive national pastime. The general climate of opinion in Europe was propitious; certainly the successes of British imperialism spoke loudly enough for themselves. However, Britain always seemed to France and to French thinkers on the subject to block even a relatively successful French imperial role in the Orient. Before the Franco-Prussian War there was a good deal of wishful political thinking about the Orient, and it was not confined to poets and novelists. Here, for instance, is Saint-Marc Girardin writing in the *Revue des Deux Mondes* on March 15, 1862:

> La France a beaucoup à faire en Orient, parce que l'Orient attend beaucoup d'elle.
> Il lui demande même plus qu'elle ne peut faire; il lui remettrait volontiers le soin
> entier de son avenir, ce qui serait pour la France et pour l'Orient un grand danger:
> pour la France, parce que, disposée a prendre en mains la cause des populations
> souffrantes, elle se charge le plus souvent de plus d'obligations qu'elle n'en peut
> remplir; pour l'Orient, parce que tout peuple qui attend sa destinée de l'étranger n'a
> jamais qu'une condition précaire et qu'il n'y a de salut pour les nations que celui
> qu'elles se font elles-mêmes.[18]

Of such views as this Disraeli would doubtless have said, as he often did, that France
had only "sentimental interests" in Syria (which is the "Orient" of which Girardin
was writing). The fiction of "populations souffrantes" had, of course, been used by
Napoleon when he appealed to the Egyptians on their behalf against the Turks and
for Islam. During the thirties, forties, fifties, and sixties the suffering populations of
the Orient were limited to the Christian minorities in Syria. And there was no record
of "l'Orient" appealing to France for its salvation. It would have been altogether
more truthful to say that Britain stood in France's way in the Orient, for even if France
genuinely felt a sense of obligation to the Orient (and there were some Frenchmen
who did), there was very little France could do to get between Britain and the huge
land mass it commanded from India to the Mediterranean.

Among the most remarkable consequences of the War of 1870 in France were
a tremendous efflorescence of geographical societies and a powerfully renewed
demand for territorial acquisition. At the end of 1871 the Société de géographie
de Paris declared itself no longer confined to "scientific speculation." It urged the
citizenry not to "forget that our former preponderance was contested from the day
we ceased to compete ... in the conquests of civilization over barbarism." Guillaume
Depping, a leader of what has come to be called the geographical movement,
asserted in 1881 that during the 1870 war "it was the schoolmaster who triumphed,"
meaning that the real triumphs were those of Prussian scientific geography over
French strategic sloppiness. The government's *Journal officiel* sponsored issue after
issue centered on the virtues (and profits) of geographical exploration and colonial
adventure; a citizen could learn in one issue from de Lesseps of "the opportunities in
Africa" and from Garnier of "the exploration of the Blue River." Scientific geography
soon gave way to "commercial geography," as the connection between national
pride in scientific and civilizational achievement and the fairly rudimentary profit
motive was urged, to be channeled into support for colonial acquisition. In the
words of one enthusiast, "The geographical societies are formed to break the fatal
charm that holds enchained to our shores." In aid of this liberating quest all sorts of
schemes were spun out, including the enlisting of Jules Verne—whose unbelievable
success, as it was called, ostensibly displayed the scientific mind at a very high peak
of ratiocination—to head "a round-the-world campaign of scientific exploration,"
and a plan for creating a vast new sea just south of the North African coast, as well

as a project for "binding" Algeria to Senegal by railroad—"a ribbon of steel," as the projectors called it.[19]

Much of the expansionist fervor in France during the last third of the nineteenth century was generated out of an explicit wish to compensate for the Prussian victory in 1870–1871 and, no less important, the desire to match British imperial achievements. So powerful was the latter desire, and out of so long a tradition of Anglo-French rivalry in the Orient did it derive, that France seemed literally haunted by Britain, anxious in all things connected with the Orient to catch up with and emulate the British. When in the late 1870s, the Société académique indo-chinoise reformulated its goals, it found it important to "bring Indochina into the domain of Orientalism." Why? In order to turn Cochin China into a "French India." The absence of substantial colonial holdings was blamed by military men for that combination of military and commercial weakness in the war with Prussia, to say nothing of long-standing and pronounced colonial inferiority compared with Britain. The "power of expansion of the Western races," argued a leading geographer, La Ronciere Le Noury, "its superior causes, its elements, its influences on human destinies, will be beautiful study for future historians." Yet only if the white races indulged their taste for voyaging—a mark of their intellectual supremacy—could colonial expansion occur.[20]

From such theses as this came the commonly held view of the Orient as a geographical space to be cultivated, harvested, and guarded. The images of agricultural care for and those of frank sexual attention to the Orient proliferated accordingly. Here is a typical effusion by Gabriel Charmes, writing in 1880:

> On that day when we shall be no longer in the Orient, and when other great European powers will be there, all will be at an end for our commerce in the Mediterranean, for our future in Asia, for the traffic of our southern ports. *One of the most fruitful sources of our national wealth will be dried up.* (Emphasis added)

Another thinker, Leroy-Beaulieu, elaborated this philosophy still further:

> A society colonizes, when itself having reached a high degree of maturity and of strength, it procreates, it protects, it places in good conditions of development, and it brings to virility a new society to which it has given birth. Colonization is one of the most complex and delicate phenomena of social physiology.

This equation of self-reproduction with colonization led Leroy-Beaulieu to the somewhat sinister idea that whatever is lively in a modern society is "magnified by this pouring out of its exuberant activity on the outside." Therefore, he said,

> Colonization is the expansive force of a people; it is its power of reproduction; it is its enlargement and its multiplication through space; it is the subjection of the universe or a vast part of it to that people's language, customs, ideas, and laws.[21]

The point here is that the space of weaker or underdeveloped regions like the Orient was viewed as something inviting French interest, penetration, insemination—in short, colonization. Geographical conceptions, literally and figuratively, did away with the discrete entities held in by borders and frontiers. No less than entrepreneurial visionaries like de Lesseps, whose plan was to liberate the Orient and the Occident from their geographical bonds, French scholars, administrators, geographers, and commercial agents poured out their exuberant activity onto the fairly supine, feminine Orient. There were the geographical societies, whose number and membership outdid those of all Europe by a factor of two; there were such powerful organizations as the Comité de l'Asie française and the Comité d'Orient; there were the learned societies, chief among them the Societé asiatique, with its organization and membership firmly embedded in the universities, the institutes, and the government. Each in its own way made French interests in the Orient more real, more substantial. Almost an entire century of what now seemed passive study of the Orient had had to end, as France faced up to its transnational responsibilities during the last two decades of the nineteenth century.

In the only part of the Orient where British and French interests literally overlapped, the territory of the now hopelessly ill Ottoman Empire, the two antagonists managed their conflict with an almost perfect and characteristic consistency. Britain was in Egypt and Mesopotamia; through a series of quasi-fictional treaties with local (and powerless) chiefs it controlled the Red Sea, the Persian Gulf, and the Suez Canal, as well as most of the intervening land mass between the Mediterranean and India. France, on the other hand, seemed fated to hover over the Orient, descending once in a while to carry out schemes that repeated de Lesseps's success with the canal; for the most part these schemes were railroad projects, such as the one planned across more or less British territory, the Syrian-Mesopotamian line. In addition, France saw itself as the protector of Christian minorities—Maronites, Chaldeans, Nestorians. Yet together, Britain and France were agreed in principle on the necessity, when the time came, for the partition of Asiatic Turkey. Both before and during World War I secret diplomacy was bent on carving up the Near Orient first into spheres of influence, then into mandated (or occupied) territories. In France, much of the expansionist sentiment formed during the heyday of the geographical movement focused itself on plans to partition Asiatic Turkey, so much so that in Paris in 1914 "a spectacular press campaign was launched" to this end.[22] In England numerous committees were empowered to study and recommend policy on the best ways of dividing up the Orient. Out of such commissions as the Bunsen Committee would come the joint Anglo-French teams of which the most famous was the one headed by Mark Sykes and Georges Picot. Equitable division of geographical space was the rule of these plans, which were deliberate attempts also at calming Anglo-French rivalry. For, as Sykes put it in a memorandum,

it was clear ... that an Arab rising was sooner or later to take place, and that the
French and ourselves ought to be on better terms if the rising was not to be a curse
instead of a blessing ....[23]

The animosities remained. And to them was added the irritant provided by
the Wilsonian program for national self-determination, which, as Sykes himself
was to note, seemed to invalidate the whole skeleton of colonial and partitionary
schemes arrived at jointly between the Powers. It would be out of place here to
discuss the entire labyrinthine and deeply controversial history of the Near Orient
in the early twentieth century, as its fate was being decided between the Powers,
the native dynasties, the various nationalist parties and movements, the Zionists.
What matters more immediately is the peculiar epistemological framework through
which the Orient was seen, and out of which the Powers acted. For despite their
differences, the British and the French saw the Orient as a geographical—and
cultural, political, demographical, sociological, and historical—entity over whose
destiny they believed themselves to have traditional entitlement. The Orient to
them was no sudden discovery, no mere historical accident, but an area to the
east of Europe whose principal worth was uniformly defined in terms of Europe,
more particularly in terms specifically claiming for Europe—European science,
scholarship, understanding, and administration—the credit for having made the
Orient what it was now. And this had been the achievement—inadvertent or not is
beside the point—of modern Orientalism.

There were two principal methods by which Orientalism delivered the Orient
to the West in the early twentieth century. One was by means of the disseminative
capacities of modern learning, its diffusive apparatus in the learned professions,
the universities, the professional societies, the explorational and geographical
organizations, the publishing industry. All these, as we have seen, built upon
the prestigious authority of the pioneering scholars, travelers, and poets, whose
cumulative vision had shaped a quintessential Orient; the doctrinal—or
doxological—manifestation of such an Orient is what I have been calling here latent
Orientalism. So far as anyone wishing to make a statement of any consequence about
the Orient was concerned, latent Orientalism supplied him with an enunciative
capacity that could be used, or rather mobilized, and turned into sensible discourse
for the concrete occasion at hand. Thus, when Balfour spoke about the Oriental to
the House of Commons in 1910, he must surely have had in mind those enunciative
capacities in the current and acceptably rational language of his time, by which
something called an "Oriental" could be named and talked about without danger
of too much obscurity. But like all enunciative capacities and the discourses they
enable, latent Orientalism was profoundly conservative—dedicated, that is, to
its self-preservation. Transmitted from one generation to another, it was a part
of the culture, as much a language about a part of reality as geometry or physics.
Orientalism staked its existence, not upon its openness, its receptivity to the Orient,

but rather on its internal, repetitious consistency about its constitutive will-to-power over the Orient. In such a way Orientalism was able to survive revolutions, world wars, and the literal dismemberment of empires.

The second method by which Orientalism delivered the Orient to the West was the result of an important convergence. For decades the Orientalists had spoken about the Orient, they had translated texts, they had explained civilizations, religions, dynasties, cultures, mentalities—as academic objects, screened off from Europe by virtue of their inimitable foreignness. The Orientalist was an expert, like Renan or Lane, whose job in society was to interpret the Orient for his compatriots. The relation between Orientalist and Orient was essentially hermeneutical: standing before a distant, barely intelligible civilization or cultural monument, the Orientalist scholar reduced the obscurity by translating, sympathetically portraying, inwardly grasping the hard-to-reach object. Yet the Orientalist remained outside the Orient, which, however much it was made to appear intelligible, remained beyond the Occident. This cultural, temporal, and geographical distance was expressed in metaphors of depth, secrecy, and sexual promise: phrases like "the veils of an Eastern bride" or "the inscrutable Orient" passed into the common language.

Yet the distance between Orient and Occident was, almost paradoxically, in the process of being reduced throughout the nineteenth century. As the commercial, political, and other existential encounters between East and West increased (in ways we have been discussing all along), a tension developed between the dogmas of latent Orientalism, with its support in studies of the "classical" Orient, and the descriptions of a present, modern, manifest Orient articulated by travelers, pilgrims, statesmen, and the like. At some moment impossible to determine precisely, the tension caused a convergence of the two types of Orientalism. Probably—and this is only a speculation—the convergence occurred when Orientalists, beginning with Sacy, undertook to advise governments on what the modern Orient was all about. Here the role of the specially trained and equipped expert took on an added dimension: the Orientalist could be regarded as the special agent of Western power as it attempted policy vis-à-vis the Orient. Every learned (and not so learned) European traveler in the Orient felt himself to be a representative Westerner who had gotten beneath the films of obscurity. This is obviously true of Burton, Lane, Doughty, Flaubert, and the other major figures I have been discussing.

The discoveries of Westerners about the manifest and modern Orient acquired a pressing urgency as Western territorial acquisition in the Orient increased. Thus, what the scholarly Orientalist defined as the "essential" Orient was sometimes contradicted, but in many cases was confirmed, when the Orient became an actual administrative obligation. Certainly Cromer's theories about the Oriental—theories acquired from the traditional Orientalist archive—were vindicated plentifully as he ruled millions of Orientals in actual fact. This was no less true of the French experience in Syria, North Africa, and elsewhere in the French colonies, such as they were. But at no time did the convergence between latent Orientalist doctrine and manifest Orientalist experience occur more dramatically than when, as a result of World War I, Asiatic Turkey was being surveyed by Britain and France for its dismemberment. There, laid out on an operating table for surgery, was the Sick Man of Europe, revealed in all his weakness, characteristics, and topographical outline.

The Orientalist, with his special knowledge, played an inestimably important part in this surgery. Already there had been intimations of his crucial role as a kind of secret agent inside the Orient when the British scholar Edward Henry Palmer was sent to the Sinai in 1882 to gauge anti-British sentiment and its possible enlistment on behalf of the Arabic revolt. Palmer was killed in the process, but he was only the most unsuccessful of the many who performed similar services for the Empire, now a serious and exacting business entrusted in part to the regional "expert." Not for nothing was another Orientalist, D.G. Hogarth, author of the famous account of the exploration of Arabia aptly titled *The Penetration of Arabia* (1904),[24] made the head of the Arab Bureau in Cairo during World War I. And neither was it by accident that men and women like Gertrude Bell, T.E. Lawrence, and St. John Philby, Oriental experts all, posted to the Orient as agents of empire, friends of the Orient, formulators of policy alternatives because of their intimate and expert knowledge of the Orient and of Orientals. They formed a band—as Lawrence called it once—bound together by contradictory notions and personal similarities: great individuality, sympathy and intuitive identification with the Orient, a jealously preserved sense of personal mission in the Orient, cultivated eccentricity, a final disapproval of the Orient. For them all the Orient was their direct, peculiar experience of it. In them Orientalism and an effective praxis for handling the Orient received their final European form, before the Empire disappeared and passed its legacy to other candidates for the role of dominant power.

Such individualists as these were not academics. We shall soon see that they were the beneficiaries of the academic study of the Orient, without in any sense belonging to the official and professional company of Orientalist scholars. Their role, however, was not to scant academic Orientalism, nor to subvert it, but rather to make it effective. In their genealogy were people like Lane and Burton, as much for their encyclopedic autodidacticism as for the accurate, the quasi-scholarly knowledge of the Orient they had obviously deployed when dealing with or writing about Orientals. For the curricular study of the Orient they substituted a sort of elaboration of latent Orientalism, which was easily available to them in the imperial culture of their epoch. Their scholarly frame of reference, such as it was, was fashioned by people like William Muir, Anthony Bevan, D.S. Margoliouth, Charles Lyall, E.G. Browne, R.A. Nicholson, Guy Le Strange, E.D. Ross, and Thomas Arnold, who also followed directly in the line of descent from Lane. Their imaginative perspectives were provided principally by their illustrious contemporary Rudyard Kipling, who had sung so memorably of holding "dominion over palm and pine."

The difference between Britain and France in such matters was perfectly consistent with the history of each nation in the Orient: the British were there;

the French lamented the loss of India and the intervening territories. By the end of the century, Syria had become the main focus of French activity, but even there it was a matter of common consensus that the French could not match the British either in quality of personnel or in degree of political influence. The Anglo-French competition over the Ottoman spoils was felt even on the field of battle in the Hejaz, in Syria, in Mesopotamia—but in all these places, as astute men like Edmond Bremond noted, the French Orientalists and local experts were outclassed in brilliance and tactical maneuvering by their British counterparts.[25] Except for an occasional genius like Louis Massignon, there were no French Lawrences or Sykeses or Bells. But there were determined imperialists like Étienne Flandin and Franklin-Bouillon. Lecturing to the Paris Alliance française in 1913, the Comte de Cressaty, a vociferous imperialist, proclaimed Syria as France's own Orient, the site of French political, moral, and economic interests—interests, he added, that had to be defended during this "âge des envahissants impérialistes"; and yet Cressaty noted that even with French commercial and industrial firms in the Orient, with by far the largest number of native students enrolled in French schools, France was invariably being pushed around in the Orient, threatened not only by Britain but by Austria, Germany, and Russia. If France was to continue to prevent "le retour de l'Islam," it had better take hold of the Orient: this was an argument proposed by Cressaty and seconded by Senator Paul Doumer.[26] These views were repeated on numerous occasions, and indeed France did well by itself in North Africa and in Syria after World War I, but the special, concrete management of emerging Oriental populations and theoretically independent territories with which the British always credited themselves was something the French felt had eluded them. Ultimately, perhaps, the difference one always feels between modern British and modern French Orientalism is a stylistic one; the import of the generalizations about Orient and Orientals, the sense of distinction preserved between Orient and Occident, the desirability of Occidental dominance over the Orient—all these are the same in both traditions. For of the many elements making up what we customarily call "expertise," style, which is the result of specific worldly circumstances being molded by tradition, institutions, will, and intelligence into formal articulation, is one of the most manifest. It is to this determinant, to this perceptible and modernized refinement in early twentieth-century Orientalism in Britain and France, that we must now turn.

NOTES

1.   Friedrich Nietzsche, "On Truth and Lie in an Extra-Moral Sense," in *The Portable Nietzsche*, ed. and trans. Walter Kaufmann (New York: Viking Press, 1954), pp. 46–7.

2.   The number of Arab travelers to the West is estimated and considered by Ibrahim Abu-Lughod in *Arab Rediscovery of Europe: A Study in Cultural Encounters* (Princeton, N.J.: Princeton University Press, 1963), pp. 75–6 and passim.

3. See Philip D. Curtin, ed., *Imperialism: The Documentary History of Western Civilization* (New York: Walker & Co., 1972), pp. 73–105.
4. See Johann W. Fück, "Islam as an Historical Problem in European Historiography since 1800," in *Historians of the Middle East*, ed. Bernard Lewis and P.M. Holt (London: Oxford University Press, 1962), p. 307.
5. Ibid., p. 309.
6. See Jacques Waardenburg, *L'Islam dans le miroir de l'Occident* (The Hague: Mouton & Co., 1963).
7. Ibid., p. 311.
8. R. Masson-Oursel, "La Connaissance scientifique de l'Asie en France depuis 1900 et les variétés de l'Orientalisme," *Revue Philosophique* 143, nos. 7–9 (July–September 1953): 345.
9. Evelyn Baring, Lord Cromer, *Modern Egypt* (New York: Macmillan. Co., 1908), 2: 237–8.
10. Evelyn Baring, Lord Cromer, *Ancient and Modern Imperialism* (London: John Murray, 1910), pp. 118, 120.
11. George Nathaniel Curzon, *Subjects of the Day: Being a Selection of Speeches and Writings* (London: George Allen & Unwin, 1915), pp. 4–5, 10, 28.
12. Ibid., pp. 184, 191–2. For the history of the school, see C.H. Phillips, *The School of Oriental and African Studies, University of London, 1917–1967: An Introduction* (London: Design for Print, 1967).
13. Eric Stokes, *The English Utilitarians and India* (Oxford: Clarendon Press, 1959).
14. Cited in Michael Edwardes, *High Noon of Empire: India under Curzon* (London: Eyre & Spottiswoode, 1965), pp. 38–9.
15. Curzon, *Subjects of the Day*, pp. 155–6.
16. Joseph Conrad, *Heart of Darkness*, in *Youth and Two other Stories* (Garden City, N.Y.: Doubleday, Page, 1925), p. 52.
17. For an illustrative extract from de Vattel's work, see Curtin, ed., *Imperialism*, pp. 42–5.
18. Cited by M. de Caix, La Syrie in Gabriel Hanotaux, *Histoire des colonies françaises*, 6 vols. (Paris: Societé de l'histoire nationale, 1929–33), 3: 481.
19. These details are to be found in Vernon McKay, "Colonialism in the French Geographical Movement," *Geographical Review* 33, no. 2 (April 1943): 214–32.
20. Agnes Murphy, *The Ideology of French Imperialism, 1817–1881* (Washington: Catholic University of America Press, 1948), pp. 46, 54, 36, 45.
21. Ibid., pp. 189, 110, 136.
22. Jukka Nevakivi, *Britain, France, and the Arab Middle East, 1914–1920* (London: Athlone Press, 1969), p. 13.
23. Ibid., p. 24.
24. D.G. Hogarth, *The Penetration of Arabia: A Record of the Development of Western Knowledge Concerning the Arabian Peninsula* (New York: Frederick A. Stokes, 1904). There is a good recent book on the same subject: Robin Bidwell, *Travellers in Arabia* (London: Paul Hamlyn, 1976).
25. Edmond Bremond, *Le Hedjaz dans la guerre mondiale* (Paris: Payor, 1931), pp. 242 ff.
26. Le Comte de Cressaty, *Les Intérêts de la France en Syrie* (Paris: Floury, 1913).

CHAPTER 31

Cultural Identity and Diaspora

Stuart Hall

A new cinema of the Caribbean is emerging, joining the company of the other "Third Cinemas." It is related to, but different from the vibrant film and other forms of visual representation of the Afro-Caribbean (and Asian) "blacks" of the diasporas of the West—the new post-colonial subjects. All these cultural practices and forms of representation have the black subject at their centre, putting the issue of cultural identity in question. Who is this emergent, new subject of the cinema? From where does he/she speak? Practices of representation always implicate the positions from which we speak or write—the positions of *enunciation*. What recent theories of enunciation suggest is that, though we speak, so to say "in our own name," of ourselves and from our own experience, nevertheless who speaks, and the subject who is spoken of, are never identical, never exactly in the same place. Identity is not as transparent or unproblematic as we think. Perhaps instead of thinking of identity as an already accomplished fact, which the new cultural practices then represent, we should think, instead, of identity as a "production," which is never complete, always in process, and always constituted within, not outside, representation. This view problematises the very authority and authenticity to which the term, "cultural identity," lays claim.

We seek, here, to open a dialogue, an investigation, on the subject of cultural identity and representation. Of course, the "I" who writes here must also be thought of as, itself, "enunciated." We all write and speak from a particular place and time, from a history and a culture which is specific. What we say is always "in context," *positioned*. I was born into and spent my childhood and adolescence in a lower-middle-class family in Jamaica. I have lived all my adult life in England, in the shadow of the black diaspora—"in the belly of the beast." I write against the background of a lifetime's work in cultural studies. If the paper seems preoccupied with the diaspora experience and its narratives of displacement, it is worth remembering that all discourse is "placed," and the heart has its reasons.

There are at least two different ways of thinking about "cultural identity." The first position defines "cultural identity" in terms of one, shared culture, a sort of collective "one true self," hiding inside the many other, more superficial or artificially imposed "selves," which people with a shared history and ancestry hold in common. Within the terms of this definition, our cultural identities reflect the common historical experiences and shared cultural codes which provide us, as "one people," with stable, unchanging, and continuous frames of reference and meaning, beneath the shifting divisions and vicissitudes of our actual history. This "oneness," underlying all the other, more superficial differences, is the truth, the essence, of "Caribbean-ness," of the black experience. It is this identity which a Caribbean or black diaspora must discover, excavate, bring to light, and express through cinematic representation.

Such a conception of cultural identity played a critical role in all the post-colonial struggles which have so profoundly reshaped our world. It lay at the centre of the vision of the poets of "Negritude," like Aimée Ceasire and Leopold Senghor, and of the Pan-African political project, earlier in the century. It continues to be a very powerful and creative force in emergent forms of representation amongst hitherto marginalised peoples. In post-colonial societies, the rediscovery of this identity is often the object of what Frantz Fanon once called a

> passionate research ... directed by the secret hope of discovering beyond the misery of today, beyond self-contempt, resignation and abjuration, some very beautiful and splendid era whose existence rehabilitates us both in regard to ourselves and in regard to others.

New forms of cultural practice in these societies address themselves to this project for the very good reason that, as Fanon puts it, in the recent past,

> Colonisation is not satisfied merely with holding a people in its grip and emptying the native's brain of all form and content. By a kind of perverted logic, it turns to the past of oppressed people, and distorts, disfigures and destroys it.[1]

The question which Fanon's observation poses is, what is the nature of this "profound research" which drives the new forms of visual and cinematic representation? Is it only a matter of unearthing that which the colonial experience buried and overlaid, bringing to light the hidden continuities it suppressed? Or is a quite different practice entailed—not the rediscovery but the *production* of identity. Not an identity grounded in the archaeology, but in the *re-telling* of the past?

We should not, for a moment, underestimate or neglect the importance of the act of imaginative rediscovery which this conception of a rediscovered, essential identity entails. "Hidden histories" have played a critical role in the emergence of many of the most important social movements of our time—feminist, anti-colonial, and anti-racist. The photographic work of a generation of Jamaican and Rastafarian artists, or of a visual artist like Armet Francis (a Jamaican-born photographer who has lived in Britain since the age of eight) is a testimony to the continuing creative power of this conception of identity within the emerging practices of representation. Francis's photographs of the peoples of The Black Triangle, taken in Africa, the Caribbean, the USA, and the UK, attempt to reconstruct in visual terms "the underlying unity of the black people whom colonisation and slavery distributed across the African diaspora." His text is an act of imaginary reunification.

Crucially, such images offer a way of imposing an imaginary coherence on the experience of dispersal and fragmentation, which is the history of all enforced diasporas. They do this by representing or "figuring" Africa as the mother of these different civilisations. This Triangle is, after all, "centred" in Africa. Africa is the name of the missing term, the great aporia, which lies at the centre of our cultural identity and gives it a meaning which, until recently, it lacked. No one who looks at these textural images now, in the light of the history of transportation, slavery, and migration, can fail to understand how the rift of separation, the "loss of identity," which has been integral to the Caribbean experience only begins to be healed when these forgotten connections are once more set in place. Such texts restore an imaginary fullness or plentitude to set against the broken rubric of our past. They are resources of resistance and identity, with which to confront the fragmented and pathological ways in which that experience has been reconstructed within the dominant regimes of cinematic and visual representation of the West.

There is, however, a second, related but different view of cultural identity. This second position recognises that, as well as the many points of similarity, there are also critical points of deep and significant *difference* which constitute "what we really are"; or rather—since history has intervened—"what we have become." We cannot speak for very long, with any exactness, about "one experience, one identity," without acknowledging its other side—the ruptures and discontinuities which constitute, precisely, the Caribbean's "uniqueness." Cultural identity, in this second sense, is a matter of "becoming" as well as of "being." It belongs to the future as much as to the past. It is not something which already exists, transcending place, time, history, and culture. Cultural identities come from somewhere, have histories. But, like everything which is historical, they undergo constant transformation. Far from being eternally fixed in some essentialised past, they are subject to the continuous "play" of history, culture, and power. Far from being grounded in a mere "recovery" of the past, which is waiting to be found, and which, when found, will secure our sense of ourselves into eternity, identities are the names we give to the different ways we are positioned by, and position ourselves within, the narratives of the past.

It is only from this second position that we can properly understand the traumatic character of "the colonial experience." The ways in which black people, black experiences, were positioned and subjected in the dominant regimes of representation were the effects of a critical exercise of cultural power and normalisation. Not only, in Said's "Orientalist" sense, were we constructed as different and other within the categories of knowledge of the West by those regimes. They had the power to make us see and experience *ourselves* as "Other." Every regime of representation is a regime of power formed, as Foucault reminds us, by the fatal couplet, "power/knowledge." But this kind of knowledge is internal, not external. It is one thing to position a subject or set of peoples as the Other of a dominant discourse. It is quite another thing to subject them to that "knowledge," not only as a matter of imposed will and domination, by the power of inner compulsion and subjective conformation to the norm. That is the lesson—the sombre majesty—of Fanon's insight into the colonising experience in *Black Skin, White Masks*.

This inner expropriation of cultural identity cripples and deforms. If its silences are not resisted, they produce, in Fanon's vivid phrase, "individuals without an anchor, without horizon, colourless, stateless, rootless—a race of angels."[2] Nevertheless, this idea of otherness as an inner compulsion changes our conception of "cultural identity." In this perspective, cultural identity is not a fixed essence at all, lying unchanged outside history and culture. It is not some universal and transcendental spirit inside us on which history has made no fundamental mark. It is not once-and-for-all. It is not a fixed origin to which we can make some final and absolute Return. Of course, it is not a mere phantasm either. It is *something*—not a mere trick of the imagination. It has its histories—and histories have their real, material, and symbolic effects. The past continues to speak to us. But it no longer addresses us as a simple, factual "past," since our relation to it, like the child's relation to the mother, is always-already "after the break." It is always constructed through memory, fantasy, narrative, and myth. Cultural identities are the points of identification, the unstable points of identification or suture, which are made within the discourses of history and culture. Not an essence but a *positioning*. Hence, there is always a politics of identity, a politics of position, which has no absolute guarantee in an unproblematic, transcendental "law of origin."

This second view of cultural identity is much less familiar, and more unsettling. If identity does not proceed, in a straight, unbroken line, from some fixed origin, how are we to understand its formation? We might think of black Caribbean identities as "framed" by two axes or vectors, simultaneously operative: the vector of similarity and continuity; and the vector of difference and rupture. Caribbean identities always have to be thought of in terms of the dialogic relationship between these two axes. The one gives us some grounding in, some continuity with, the past. The second reminds us that what we share is precisely the experience of a profound discontinuity: the peoples dragged into slavery, transportation, colonisation, migration, came predominantly from Africa—and when that supply ended, it was temporarily refreshed by indentured labour from the Asian subcontinent. (This neglected fact explains why, when you visit Guyana or Trinidad, you see, symbolically inscribed in the faces of their peoples, the paradoxical "truth" of Christopher Columbus's mistake: you *can* find "Asia" by sailing west, if you know where to look!) In the history of the modern world, there are few more traumatic ruptures to match these enforced separations from Africa—already figured, in the European imaginary, as "the Dark Continent." But the slaves were also from different countries, tribal communities, villages, languages, and gods. African religion, which has been so profoundly formative in Caribbean spiritual life, is precisely *different* from Christian monotheism in believing that God is so powerful that he can only be known through a proliferation of spiritual manifestations, present everywhere in the natural and social world. These gods live on, in an underground existence, in the hybridised religious universe of Haitian voodoo, pocomania, Native pentacostalism, Black baptism, Rastafarianism, and the black Saints Latin American Catholicism. The paradox is that it was the uprooting of slavery and transportation and the insertion into the plantation economy (as well as the symbolic economy) of the Western world that "unified" these peoples across their differences, in the same moment as it cut them off from direct access to their past.

Difference, therefore, persists—in and alongside continuity. To return to the Caribbean after any long absence is to experience again the shock of the "doubleness" of similarity and difference. Visiting the French Caribbean for the first time, I also saw at once how different Martinique is from, say, Jamaica: and this is no mere difference of topography or climate. It is a profound difference of culture and history. And the difference *matters*. It positions Martiniquains and Jamaicans as both the same *and* different. Moreover, the boundaries of difference are continually repositioned in relation to different points of reference. Vis-à-vis the developed West, we are very much "the same." We belong to the marginal, the underdeveloped, the periphery, the "Other." We are at the outer edge, the "rim," of the metropolitan world—always "South" to someone else's *El Norte*.

At the same time, we do not stand in the same relation of the "otherness" to the metropolitan centres. Each has negotiated its economic, political, and cultural dependency differently. And this "difference," whether we like it or not, is already inscribed in our cultural identities. In turn, it is this negotiation of identity which makes us, vis-à-vis other Latin American people, with a very similar history, different—Caribbeans, *les Antilliennes* ("islanders" to their mainland). And yet, vis-à-vis one another, Jamaican, Haitian, Cuban, Guadeloupean, Barbadian, etc. ...

How, then, to describe this play of "difference" within identity? The common history—transportation, slavery, colonisation—has been profoundly formative. For all these societies, unifying us across our differences. But it does not constitute a common *origin*, since it was, metaphorically as well as literally, a translation. The inscription of difference is also specific and critical. I use the word "play" because the double meaning of the metaphor is important. It suggests, on the one hand, the instability, the permanent unsettlement, the lack of any final resolution. On the other hand, it reminds us that the place where this "doubleness" is most powerfully to be heard is "playing" within the varieties of Caribbean musics. This cultural "play" could not therefore be represented, cinematically, as a simple, binary opposition—"past/present," "them/us." Its complexity exceeds this binary structure of representation. At different places, times, in relation to different questions, the boundaries are re-sited. They become, not only what they have, at times, certainly been—mutually excluding categories, but also what they sometimes are—differential points along a sliding scale.

One trivial example is the way Martinique both *is* and *is not* "French." It is, of course, a *department* of France, and this is reflected in its standard and style of life; Fort de France is a much richer, more "fashionable" place than Kingston—which is not only visibly poorer, but itself at a point of transition between being "in fashion" in an Anglo-African and Afro-American way—for those who can afford to be in any sort of fashion at all. Yet, what is distinctively "Martiniquais" can only be described in terms of that special and peculiar supplement which the black and mulatto skin adds to the "refinement" and sophistication of a Parisian-derived *haute couture*: that is, a sophistication which, because it is black, is always transgressive.

* * * * *

It is possible, with this conception of "difference," to rethink the positionings and repositionings of Caribbean cultural identities in relation to at least three "presences," to borrow Aimée Cesaire's and Leopold Senghor's metaphor: *Présence Africaine, Présence Européenne*, and the third, most ambiguous, presence of all—the sliding term, *Présence Americaine.* Of course, I am collapsing, for the moment, the many other cultural "presences" which constitute the complexity of Caribbean identity (Indian, Chinese, Lebanese, etc). I mean America, here, not in its "first-world" sense—the big cousin to the North whose "rim" we occupy, but in the second, broader sense: America, the "New World," *Terra Incognita.*

Présence Africaine is the site of the repressed. Apparently silenced beyond memory by the power of the experience of slavery, Africa was, in fact present everywhere: in the everyday life and customs of the slave quarters, in the languages and patois of the plantations, in names and words, often disconnected from their taxonomies, in the secret syntactical structures through which other languages were spoken, in the stories and tales told to children, in religious practices and beliefs, in the spiritual life, the arts, crafts, musics, and rhythms of slave and post-emancipation society. Africa, the signified which could not be represented directly in slavery, remained and remains the unspoken, unspeakable "presence" in Caribbean culture. It is "hiding" behind every verbal inflection, every narrative twist of Caribbean cultural life. It is the secret code with which every Western text was "re-read." It is the ground-bass of every rhythm and bodily movement. *This* was—is—the "Africa" that "is alive and well in the diaspora."[3]

When I was growing up in the 1940s and 1950s as a child in Kingston, I was surrounded by the signs, music, and rhythms of this Africa of the diaspora, which only existed as a result of a long and discontinuous series of transformations. But, although almost everyone around me was some shade of brown or black (Africa "speaks"!), I never once heard a single person refer to themselves or to others as, in some way, or as having been at some time in the past, "African." It was only in the 1970s that this Afro-Caribbean identity became historically available to the great majority of Jamaican people, at home and abroad. In this historic moment, Jamaicans discovered themselves to be "black"—just as, in the same moment, they discovered themselves to be the sons and daughters of "slavery."

This profound cultural discovery, however, was not, and could not be, made directly, without "mediation." It could only be made *through* the impact on popular life of the post-colonial revolution, the civil rights struggles, the culture of Rastafarianism, and the music of reggae—the metaphors, the figures, or signifiers of a new construction of "Jamaican-ness." These signified a "new" Africa of the New World, grounded in an "old" Africa: a spiritual journey of discovery that led, in the Caribbean, to an indigenous cultural revolution; this is Africa, as we might say, necessarily "deferred"—as a spiritual, cultural, and political metaphor.

It is the presence/absence of Africa, in this form, which has made it the privileged signifier of new conceptions of Caribbean identity. Everyone in the Caribbean, of whatever ethnic background, must sooner or later come to terms with this African presence. Black, brown, mulatto, white—all must look *Présence Africaine* in the face, speak its name. But whether it is, in this sense, an origin of our identities, unchanged by four hundred years of displacement, dismemberment, transportation, to which we could in any final or literal sense return, is more open to doubt. The original "Africa" is no longer there. It too has been transformed. History is, in that sense, irreversible. We must not collude with the West, which, precisely, normalises and appropriates Africa by freezing it into some timeless zone of the primitive, unchanging past. Africa must at last be reckoned with by Caribbean people, but it cannot in any simple sense be merely recovered.

It belongs irrevocably, for us, to what Edward Said once called an "imaginative geography and history," which helps "the mind to intensify its own sense of itself by dramatising the difference between what is close to it and what is far away."[4] It "has acquired an imaginative or figurative value we can name and feel."[5] Our belongingness to it constitutes what Benedict Anderson calls "an imagined community."[6] To *this* "Africa," which is a necessary part of the Caribbean imaginary, we can't literally go home again.

The character of this displaced "homeward" journey—its length and complexity—comes across vividly, in a variety of texts. Tony Sewell's documentary archival photographs, *Garvey's Children: the Legacy of Marcus Garvey*, tells the story of a "return" to an African identity which went, necessarily, by the long route—through London and the United States. It "ends," not in Ethiopia but with Garvey's statue in front of the St. Ann Parish Library in Jamaica: not with a traditional tribal chant but with the music of Burning Spear and Bob Marley's "Redemption Song". This is our "long journey" home. Derek Bishton's courageous visual and written text, *Black Heart Man*—the story of the journey of a white photographer "on the trail of the promised land"—starts in England, and goes, through Shashemene, the place in Ethiopia to which many Jamaican people have found their way on their search for the Promised Land, and slavery; but it ends in Pinnacle, Jamaica, where the first Rastafarian settlements was [sic] established, and "beyond"—among the dispossessed of 20th-century Kingston and the streets of Handsworth, where Bishton's voyage of discovery first began. These symbolic journies [sic] are necessary for us all—and necessarily circular. This is the Africa we must return to—but "by another route": what Africa has *become* in the New World, what we have made of "Africa": "Africa"—as we re-tell it through politics, memory, and desire.

What of the second, troubling, term in the identity equation—the European presence? For many of us, this is a matter not of too little but of too much. Where Africa was a case of the unspoken, Europe was a case of that which is endlessly speaking—and endlessly speaking *us*. The European presence interrupts the innocence of the whole discourse of "difference" in the Caribbean by introducing the question of power. "Europe" belongs irrevocably to the "play" of power, to the lines of force and consent, to the role of the *dominant*, in Caribbean culture. In terms of colonialism, underdevelopment, poverty, and the racism of colour, the European presence is that which, in visual representation, has positioned the black subject within its dominant regimes of representation: the colonial discourse, the literatures of adventure and exploration, the romance of the exotic, the ethnographic and travelling eye, the tropical languages of tourism, travel brochure and Hollywood, and the violent, pornographic languages of *ganja* and urban violence.

Because *Présence Européenne* is about exclusion, imposition, and expropriation, we are often tempted to locate that power as wholly external to us—an extrinsic force, whose influence can be thrown off like the serpent sheds its skin. What Frantz Fanon reminds us, in *Black Skin, White Masks*, is how this power has become a constitutive element in our own identities.

> The movements, the attitudes, the glances of the other fixed me there, in the sense in which a chemical solution is fixed by a dye. I was indignant; I demanded an explanation. Nothing happened. I burst apart. Now the fragments have been put together again by another self.[7]

This "look," from—so to speak—the place of the Other, fixes us, not only in its violence, hostility, and aggression, but in the ambivalence of its desire. This brings us face to face, not simply with the dominating European presence as the site or "scene" of integration where those other presences which it had actively disaggregated were recomposed—re-framed, put together in a new way; but as the site of a profound splitting and doubling—what Homi Bhaba has called "the ambivalent identifications of the racist world ... the 'otherness' of the self inscribed in the perverse palimpsest of colonial identity."[8]

The dialogue of power and resistance, of refusal and recognition, with and against *Présence Européenne* is almost as complex as the "dialogue" with Africa. In terms of popular cultural life, it is nowhere to be found in its pure, pristine state. It is always-already fused, syncretised, with other cultural elements. It is always-already creolised—not lost beyond the Middle Passage, but ever-present: from the harmonics in our musics to the ground-bass of Africa, traversing and intersecting our lives at every point. How can we stage this dialogue so that, finally, we can place it, without terror or violence, rather than being forever placed by it? Can we ever recognise its irreversible influence, whilst resisting its imperialising eye? The enigma is impossible, so far, to resolve. It requires the most complex of cultural strategies. Think, for example, of the dialogue of every Caribbean filmmaker or writer, one way or another, with the dominant cinemas and literature of the West—the complex relationship of young black British filmmakers with the "avant-gardes" of European and American filmmaking. Who could describe this tense and tortured dialogue as a "one-way trip"?

The Third, "New World" presence, is not so much power, as ground, place, territory. It is the juncture-point where the many cultural tributaries meet, the "empty" land (the European colonisers emptied it) where strangers from every other part of the globe collided. None of the people who now occupy the islands— black, brown, white, African, European, American, Spanish, French, East Indian, Chinese, Portugese, Jew, Dutch—originally "belonged" there. It is the space where the creolisations and assimilations and syncretisms were negotiated. The New World is the third term—the primal scene—where the fateful/fatal encounter was staged between Africa and the West. It also has to be understood as the place of many, continuous displacements: of the original pre-Columbian inhabitants, the Arawaks, Caribs, and Amerindians, permanently displaced from their homelands and decimated; of other peoples displaced in different ways from Africa, Asia, and Europe; the displacements of slavery, colonisation, and conquest. It stands for the endless ways in which Caribbean people have been destined to "migrate"; it is the signifier of migration itself—of travelling, voyaging, and return as fate, as destiny; of the Antillean as the prototype of the modern or postmodern New World nomad, continually moving between centre and periphery. This preoccupation with movement and migration Caribbean cinema shares with many other "Third Cinemas," but it is one of our defining themes, and it is destined to cross the narrative of every film script or cinematic image.

Présence Americaine continues to have its silences, its suppressions. Peter Hulme, in his essay on "Islands of Enchantment,"[9] reminds us that the word "Jamaica" is the Hispanic form of the indigenous Arawak name—"land of wood and water"—which Columbus's re-naming ("Santiago") never replaced. The Arawak presence remains today a ghostly one, visible in the islands mainly in museums and archeological sites, part of the barely knowable or usable "past." Hulme notes that it is not represented in the emblem of the Jamaican National Heritage Trust, for example, which chose instead the figure of Diego Pimienta, "an African who fought for his Spanish masters against the English invasion of the island in 1655"—a deferred, metonymic, sly,

and sliding representation of Jamaican identity if ever there was one! He recounts
the story of how Prime Minister Edward Seaga tried to alter the Jamaican coat-of-
arms, which consists of two Arawak figures holding a shield with five pineapples,
surmounted by an alligator. "Can the crushed and extinct Arawaks represent the
dauntless character of Jamaicans? Does the low-slung, near extinct crocodile, a cold-
blooded reptile, symbolise the warm, soaring spirit of Jamaicans?" Prime Minister
Seaga asked rhetorically.[10] There can be few political statements which so eloquently
testify to the complexities entailed in the process of trying to represent a diverse
people with a diverse history through a single, hegemonic "identity." Fortunately,
Mr Seaga's invitation to the Jamaican people, who are overwhelmingly of African
descent, to start their "remembering" by first "forgetting" something else, got the
comeuppance it so richly deserved.

The "New World" presence—America, *Terra Incognita*—is therefore itself the
beginning of diaspora, of diversity, of hybridity and difference, what makes Afro-
Caribbean people already people of a diaspora. I use this term here metaphorically,
not literally: diaspora does not refer us to those scattered tribes whose identity
can only be secured in relation to some sacred homeland to which they must at all
costs return, even if it means pushing other people into the sea. This is the old, the
imperialising, the hegemonising form of "ethnicity." We have seen the fate of the
people of Palestine at the hands of this backward-looking conception of diaspora—
and the complicity of the West with it. The diaspora experience as I intend it here is
defined, not by essence or purity, but by the recognition of a necessary heterogeneity
and diversity; by a conception of "identity," which lives with and through, not
despite, difference; by *hybridity*. Diaspora identities are those which are constantly
producing and reproducing themselves anew, through transformation and
difference. One can only think here of what is uniquely—"essentially"—Caribbean:
precisely the mixes of colour, pigmentation, physiognomic type; the "blends" of
tastes that is Caribbean cuisine; the aesthetics of the "cross-overs," of "cut-and-mix,"
to borrow Dick Hebdige's telling phrase, which is the heart and soul of black music.
Young black cultural practitioners and critics in Britain are increasingly coming to
acknowledge and explore in their work this "diaspora aesthetic" and its formations
in the post-colonial experience:

> Across a whole range of cultural forms there is a "syncretic" dynamic which
> critically appropriates elements from the master-codes of the dominant culture
> and "creolises" them, disarticulating given signs and re-articulating their symbolic
> meaning. The subversive force of this hybridising tendency is most apparent at the
> level of language itself where Creoles, patois and black English decentre, destabilise
> and carnivalise the linguistic domination of "English"—the nation-language
> of master-discourse—through strategic inflections, re-accentuations and other
> performative moves in semantic, syntactic and lexical codes.[11]

It is because this New World is constituted for us as place, a narrative of displacement, that it gives rise so profoundly to a certain imaginary plenitude, recreating the endless desire to return to "lost origins," to be one again with the mother, to go back to the beginning. Who can ever forget, when once seen rising up out of that blue-green Caribbean, those islands of enchantment? Who has not known, at this moment, the surge of an overwhelming nostalgia for lost origins, for "times past"? And yet, this "return to the beginning" is like the imaginary in Lacan—it can neither be fulfilled nor requited, and hence is the beginning of the symbolic, of representation, the infinitely renewable source of desire, memory, myth, search, discovery—in short, the reservoir of our cinematic narratives.

* * * * *

NOTES

1. Frantz Fanon, "On National Culture," in *The Wretched of the Earth*, London 1963, p. 170.
2. Ibid., p. 176.
3. Stuart Hall, *Resistance through Rituals*, London 1976.
4. Edward Said, *Orientalism*, London 1985, p. 55.
5. Ibid.
6. Benedict Anderson, *Imagined Communities: Reflections on the Origin and Rise of Nationalism*, London 1982.
7. Frantz Fanon, *Black Skin, White Masks*, London 1986, p. 109.
8. Homi Bhabha, "Foreword" to Fanon, ibid., xv.
9. In *New Formations*, no. 3, Winter 1987.
10. *Jamaica Hansard*, vol. 9, 1983–4, p. 363. Quoted in Hulme, *New Formations*, no. 3, Winter 1987.
11. Kobena Mercer, "Diaspora Culture and the Dialogic Imagination," in M. Cham and C. Watkins (eds), *Blackframes: Critical Perspectives on Black Independent Cinema*, 1988, p. 57.

CHAPTER 32

Citizenship in an Era of Globalization

WILL KYMLICKA

The literature is replete with discussions of the impact of globalization on us as workers, consumers, investors, or as members of cultural communities. Less attention has been paid to its impact on us as citizens—as participants in the process of democratic self-government. This is a vitally important issue, for if people become dissatisfied with their role as citizens, the legitimacy and stability of democratic political systems may erode.

David Held is one of the few theorists who has tried to systematically explore the implications of globalization on citizenship, both at the domestic level and at the level of transnational or global institutions (Held 1995: 1999). In effect, Held argues that globalization is eroding the capacity for meaningful democratic citizenship at the domestic level, as nation-states lose some of their historic sovereignty and become "decision-takers" as much as "decision-makers." If meaningful citizenship is to exist in an era of globalization, therefore, it will require democratizing those transnational institutions which are increasingly responsible for important economic, environmental, and security decisions.

While I agree with much of his analysis, I'd like to suggest that there is more room for optimism regarding the prospects for domestic citizenship than he suggests, but perhaps fewer grounds for optimism about global citizenship.

🖻 1. DOMESTIC CITIZENSHIP

First, then, let me consider the impact of globalization on citizenship at the domestic level. Like many commentators, Held argues that globalization is reducing the historic sovereignty of nation-states, and so undermining the meaningfulness of participation in domestic politics. There is obviously some truth in this, but how extensive is the problem? Held gives a nuanced account of this process of globalization, and explicitly distances himself from the more exaggerated claims about the "obsolescence" of the nation-state which are made by the "hyper-globalizers" (Held 1999: 97). Yet I think that Held too, in his own way, may overstate the situation.

It is certainly true that industrialized nation-states have less elbow room regarding macro-economic policy today than they did before. (It is doubtful whether Third World states ever had much elbow room in this area.) This became painfully clear to Canadians when a left-wing government was elected in Canada's largest province (Ontario), and announced a policy of reflationary public spending to reduce unemployment. The response from international financial markets (and bond-rating services) was rapid and severe, and the government quickly dropped the proposal. This made all Canadians aware of how truly dependent we had become on the "men in red suspenders," as our finance minister called Wall Street brokers.

But there are two possible explanations for this phenomenon. Some people see the loss of control by nation-states over macro-economic policy as an inherent and permanent feature of the new world order, which we simply have to learn to live with. This, implicitly at least, is Held's view. But other people argue that the dependence on international financial markets is not an inherent feature of globalization, but rather a contingent result of international indebtedness. On this view, states that run up large foreign debts lose control over their macro-economic policy. We are now so accustomed to governments running up billions of dollars in deficits every year that we take it as normal, even inevitable, that governments owe hundreds of billions of dollars in debt to people outside the country. But it is insane to think that a country can run up such debts for twenty years, and not have it affect their fiscal autonomy. If you put yourself in massive debt to other people, you lose some control over your life.

We will shortly be in a position to test these two hypotheses, since we are witnessing a steep decline in international indebtedness in many countries. What we see in Canada today, for example, as in many other countries, is a shift towards balanced budgets, and a reduction in the debt-to-GDP ratio. As a result, Canada is less dependent on foreign capital today than it has been for any time in the last fifteen years. As of 1998, the Canadian government no longer has to borrow money from the men in red suspenders, and in 1999 actually had a budget surplus. I believe that Canada is now regaining much (though not all) of its earlier macro-economic autonomy, including the option of adopting a jobs-creation programme, which is being seriously debated in Canada.

I think that Held also exaggerates the issue of capital mobility—i.e., the fear that companies will move their operations to whatever country offers the lowest taxes or wages. This is supposed to put dramatic limits on the extent to which countries can adopt more generous unemployment insurance programmes, health and safety legislation, parental leaves, or minimum wages. Here again, there is obviously some truth to this concern, but we need to keep it in perspective. A reporter in a major American city recently selected at random a number of companies in the Yellow Pages and asked each of them whether they had thought about relocating to another country. The number who said yes was negligible. The option of moving overseas is irrelevant for large sectors of the economy — health care, education and training, construction, most retail, most services, agriculture, and so on. The issue of capital mobility is most relevant for mid-to-large manufacturing companies employing low-skilled workers. This is not an insignificant portion of the economy, but it has been a declining percentage for a long time. And it is difficult to see how Third World countries can ever develop except by competing in this sector. The loss of some of these low-skilled manufacturing jobs is inevitable, and perhaps even desirable from the point of view of international justice so long as there are fair transition programmes for those people thrown out of work. But there is no reason to think that large numbers of companies in other sectors will pack up and leave if the government tells them to provide better parental leaves to their workers.

So there remains considerable scope for national policy-making. Moreover, and equally importantly, countries continue to exercise their autonomy in very different ways, reflecting their different political cultures. Even if globalization puts similar pressures on all countries, they need not — and do not — respond in the same way. In his survey of social policy in OECD countries, Keith Banting notes that globalization puts great pressure on nation-states both to respond to the social stresses created by economic restructuring and to the demands of international competitiveness. None the less, despite fears of a race to the bottom or an inexorable harmonization of social programmes, the share of national resources devoted to social spending continues to inch upwards in OECD nations. And while all welfare states are under pressure, "the global economy does not dictate the ways in which governments respond, and different nations are responding in distinctive ways that reflect their domestic politics and cultures" (Banting 1997: 280). I believe that citizens often care deeply about maintaining these national differences in social policy, and they provide considerable motivation for political participation in domestic politics. For example, the differences between Canadian and American approaches to social policy are increasing, not decreasing, and for Canadian citizens, these differences are worth keeping, and fighting for.

This points to another overstatement in Held's analysis. He argues that globalization is undermining the sense that each nation-state forms "a political community of fate" (Held 1999: 102). I think he is vastly overstating the situation here. It is certainly true that "some of the most fundamental forces and processes which determine the nature of life chances" cut across national boundaries (Held 1999: 103). But what determines the boundaries of a "community of fate" is not the forces people are subjected to, but rather how they respond to those forces, and, in particular, what sorts of collectivities they identify with when responding to those forces. People belong to the same community of fate if they *care* about each other's fate, and want to share each other's fate — that is, want to meet certain challenges together, so as to *share* each other's blessings and burdens. Put another way, people belong to the same community of fate if they feel some sense of responsibility for one another's fate, and so want to deliberate together about how to respond collectively to the challenges facing the community. So far as I can tell, globalization has not eroded the sense that nation-states form separate communities of fate in this sense.

For example, as a result of NAFTA, North Americans are increasingly subjected to similar economic "forces and processes." But there is no evidence that they feel themselves part of a single "community of fate" whose members care about and wish to share each other's fate. There is no evidence that Canadians now feel any strong sense of responsibility for the well-being of Americans or Mexicans (or vice-versa). Nor is there any evidence that Canadians feel any moral obligation to respond to these challenges in the same way that Americans or Mexicans do (or vice-versa). On the contrary, Canadians want to respond to these forces *as Canadians*—that is, Canadians debate amongst themselves how to respond to globalization, and they do so by asking what sort of society Canadians wish to live in, and what sorts of obligations Canadians have to each other. Americans ask the same questions amongst themselves, as do the Mexicans. The economic forces acting on the three countries maybe similar, but the sense of communal identity and solidarity remains profoundly different, as has the actual policy responses to these forces. Despite being subject to similar forces, citizens of Western democracies are able to respond to these forces in their own distinctive ways, reflective of their "domestic politics and cultures." And most citizens continue to cherish this ability to deliberate and act as a national collectivity, on the basis of their own national solidarities and priorities.

So I do not accept the view that globalization has deprived domestic politics of its meaningfulness. Nation-states still possess considerable autonomy; their citizens still exercise this autonomy in distinctive ways, reflective of their national political cultures; and citizens still want to confront the challenges of globalization as national collectivities, reflective of their historic solidarities, and desire to share each other's fate. These facts all provide meaning and significance to domestic political participation.

I would not deny that many citizens in Western democracies feel dissatisfied with their political participation. But I would argue that the main sources of dissatisfaction with citizenship in Western democracies have little to do with globalization, and in fact long predate the current wave of globalization. In Canada, for example, we have an electoral system that systematically deprives smaller regions of effective political representation in Canadian political life. We have also been unable to regulate effectively campaign financing, with the result that the political process is increasingly seen as heavily skewed towards wealthy individuals and pressure groups. Nor have we changed party nomination procedures to reduce the systematic under-representation of women, Aboriginals, visible minorities, or the working class.

Moreover, Canada has a ridiculously centralized legislative process, in which the real power rests in the hands of a few people in the inner cabinet. We have no meaningful separation between the executive and legislative functions of government, and we have rigid party discipline. As a result, individual Members of Parliament, whether they are in the governing party or the opposition, have no real input into legislation—at least, much less influence than their counterparts in the American Congress. Parliamentary committees are supposed to provide a forum for input into the legislative process, but they are widely seen as a joke. For most Canadians, therefore, their elected MP is important only for constituency service, not as a conduit to the legislative process. What is the point in making one's views known to one's MP, when individual MPs seem to have no role in the legislative process?

These are the real problems with the political process in Canada—these are at the root of people's increasing sense that they have no real voice in political life. So far as I can tell, they have little to do with globalization. Globalization is not the cause of these problems, nor is there anything in globalization which prevents us from dealing with them. Consider the fate of the recent Canadian Royal Commission on Electoral Reform and Party Financing, which studied these issues in depth, and which issued a number of perfectly sensible recommendations about how to make our political system more equitable, and more responsive to the needs and opinions of Canadians (RCERPF 1991). There is nothing in the discipline of economic globalization or the rules of international regulatory agreements that prevent us from acting on these recommendations. There is nothing in NAFTA, or in our commitments to the UN or the WTO, which prevents us from adopting these recommendations tomorrow.

Yet little has been done to implement them. This is partly because it is rarely in the interest of governing parties to reform a process that put them in power. But it is also partly because we citizens have not demanded that government make it a priority. Whether as individual citizens, members of advocacy groups, or commentators in the media, Canadians have let the government off the hook for improving the democratic process. There is much we can do to protect and enhance our role as citizens, and if we decide not to, the fault lies not in globalization, but in ourselves.

I have focused on the flaws in Canada's political process, but I think we would find very similar problems in other countries—i.e., electoral systems which systemically produce unrepresentative legislatures; over-centralized legislative decision-making; excessive role of wealth in determining power and influence; and so on. These are the real causes of citizen's dissatisfaction with the political process. Globalization is not the cause of these problems, nor does it prevent us from solving them. Indeed, far from depriving domestic citizenship of its meaningfulness, globalization may actually be helping to renew it in important respects. For example, globalization is opening up the political process to new groups. Existing legislative and regulatory processes have been captured by entrenched interest groups for a long time now, but their traditional power bases are being eroded by globalization, and previously excluded groups are jumping in to fill the void (Simeon 1997: 307).

Also, globalization, far from encouraging political apathy, is itself one of the things which seems to mobilize otherwise apathetic people. Consider the vigorous debate over free trade in Canada or the debate in Denmark over the Maastricht Treaty. This should not be surprising since decisions about how to relate to other countries are themselves an important exercise of national sovereignty. This is perhaps clearer in the European context than in North America. It is quite clear, for example, that the desire of Spain or Greece to join the EU was not simply a matter of economic gain. It was also seen as a way of confirming their status as open, modern, democratic, and pluralistic states, after many years of being closed and authoritarian societies. Similarly, the decision about whether to admit new countries from Eastern Europe to the EU will be decided not just on the basis of economic gain, but also on the basis of moral obligations to assist newly democratizing countries, and on the basis of aspirations to create a Europe free of old divisions and hatreds. In other words, decisions by national collectivities to integrate into transnational institutions are, in part, decisions about what kind of societies people want to live in. Being open to the world is, for many people, an important part of their self-conception as members of modern pluralistic societies, and they autonomously decide to pursue that self-conception through various international agreements and institutions. Such decisions are not a denial of people's national identity or sovereignty, but precisely an affirmation of their national identity, and a highly valued exercise of their national sovereignty.

The best example of this, perhaps, is the desire of former Communist countries to join European organizations. It would be a profound misunderstanding to say that the decision by Baltic states to join the Council of Europe is an abridgement of their sovereignty. On the contrary, it is surely one of the most important symbolic affirmations of their new-found sovereignty. One of the most hated things about Communism was that it prevented Baltic nations from entering into such international alliances, and acting upon their self-conception as a "European" country. Latvia's decision to join the Council of Europe was a way of declaring: "now we are a sovereign people, able to act on our own wishes. No longer can anyone tell us who we can and cannot associate with." Sovereignty is valued because it allows nations to act on their interests and identities, and the freedom to enter European organizations is an enormously important example of this sovereignty for Baltic nations.

These examples show, I think, that globalization often provides options which nations value, and decisions about whether and how to exercise these options have become lively topics for national debate. Globalization does constrain national legislatures, although the extent of this is often exaggerated. But globalization also enriches national political life, and provides new and valued options by which nations can collectively promote their interests and identities.

▣ 2. COSMOPOLITAN CITIZENSHIP

So globalization need not undermine the scope for meaningful democratic citizenship at the national level. By contrast, I am rather more sceptical about the likelihood that we can produce any meaningful form of transnational citizenship. I think we should be quite modest in our expectations about transnational citizenship, at least for the foreseeable future.

I heartily agree with many aspects of Held's conception of "cosmopolitan democracy." In particular, I endorse efforts to strengthen the international enforcement of human rights, and I accept Held's idea that the rules for according international recognition to states should include some reference to democratic legitimation. Principles of democracy and human rights should indeed be seen as "cosmopolitan" in this sense—i.e., each state should be encouraged to respect these principles. But I'm more sceptical about the idea that transnational institutions and organizations can themselves be made democratic in any meaningful sense. Can we even make sense of the idea of "democratizing" such institutions? When thinking about this question, it is important to remember that democracy is not just a formula for aggregating votes, but is also a system of collective deliberation and legitimation. The actual moment of voting (in elections, or within legislatures) is just one component in a larger process of democratic self-government. This process begins with public deliberation about the issues that need to be addressed and the options for resolving them. The decisions which result from this deliberation are then legitimated on the grounds that they reflect the considered will and common good of the people as a whole, not just the self-interest or arbitrary whims of the majority.

Arguably, these forms of deliberation and legitimation require some degree of commonality amongst citizens. Collective political deliberation is only feasible if participants understand and trust one another, and there is good reason to think that such mutual understanding and trust requires some underlying commonalities. Some sense of commonality or shared identity may be required to sustain a deliberative and participatory democracy. [...] There are good reasons to think that territorialized linguistic/national political units provide the best and perhaps the only sort of forum for genuinely participatory and deliberative politics.

Held argues that globalization is undermining the territorial basis of politics, and that territory is playing a less important role in the determination of political identity (Held 1999: 99). I think this is simply untrue, at least in the context of multilingual states. On the contrary, all the evidence from multilingual states suggests that language has become an increasingly important determinant of the boundaries of political community within each of these multilingual countries, and territory has become an increasingly important determinant of the boundaries of these language groups.

This is not to deny the obvious fact that we need international political institutions that transcend linguistic/national boundaries. We need such institutions to deal not only with economic globalization, but also with common environmental problems and issues of international security. At present, these organizations exhibit a major "democratic deficit." They are basically organized through intergovernmental relations, with little if any direct input from individual citizens. Held suggests that this is a serious problem, which can only be resolved by promoting new forms of "cosmopolitan citizenship" which enable individuals and non-government groups to participate directly in transnational organizations (Held 1999: 104–8). For example, in the EU, there is considerable talk about increasing the power of the Parliament, which is directly elected by individual citizens, at the expense of the Commission and Council of Ministers, which operate through intergovernmental relations.

I am not so sure that Held's suggestion is realistic. It seems to me that there is no necessary reason why international institutions should be directly accountable to (or accessible to) individual citizens. To be sure, if international institutions are increasingly powerful, they must be held accountable. But why can we not hold them accountable *indirectly*, by debating at the national level how we want our national governments to act in intergovernmental contexts?

It seems clear that this is the way most Europeans themselves wish to reconcile democracy with the growth of the EU. There is very little demand for a strengthened EU Parliament. On the contrary, most people, in virtually all European states, show little interest in the affairs of the European Parliament, and little enthusiasm for increasing its powers. What they want, instead, is to strengthen the accountability of their *national* governments for how these governments act at the intergovernmental Council of Ministers. That is, citizens in each country want to debate amongst themselves, in their vernacular, what the position of their government should be on EU issues. Danes wish to debate, in Danish, what the Danish position should be *vis-à-vis* Europe. They show little interest in starting a European-wide debate (in English?) about what the EU should do. They are keenly interesting in having a democratic debate about the EU, but the debate they wish to engage in is not a debate with other Europeans about "what should we Europeans do?." Rather, they wish to debate with each other, in Danish, about what we Danes should do. To put it another way, they want Denmark to be part of Europe, but they show little interest in becoming citizens of a European demos.

This is not to say that increasing the direct accountability and accessibility of transnational institutions is a bad thing. On the contrary, I support many of Held's suggestions in this regard. I agree that NGOs should have an increased role at the UN and other international bodies (Held 1999: 107–8). And I support the idea of a global civil society, in which people seek to mobilize the citizens of other countries to protest violations of human rights or environmental degradation in their own country. But it is misleading, I think, to describe this as the "democratization" of transnational institutions, or as the creation of democratic citizenship on the transnational level. After all, these proposals would not create any form of collective deliberation and decision-making that connects and binds individuals across national boundaries.

For example, I am a member of Greenpeace, and support their efforts to gain a seat at the table of UN organizations, and their efforts to mobilize people around the world to stop acid rain, the burning of tropical rainforests, or illegal whaling. But this does not really involve democratic citizenship at the transnational level. The fact that Greenpeace has a seat at the table of the UN or the EU, or that Canadian members of Greenpeace write letters protesting Japan's whaling policy, does not change the fact that there is no meaningful forum for democratic deliberation and collective will-formation above the level of the nation-state. I can try to influence Brazil's deforestation policy, but that doesn't mean that Brazilians and Canadians are now citizens of some new transnational democratic community. Transnational activism is a good thing, as is the exchange of information across borders. But the only forum in which genuine democracy occurs is within national boundaries.

Transnational activism by individuals or NGOs is not the same as democratic citizenship. Moreover, attempts to create a genuinely democratic form of transnational citizenship could have negative consequences for democratic citizenship at the domestic level. For example, I am not convinced that it would be a good thing to strengthen the (directly elected) EU Parliament at the expense of the (intergovernmental) EU Council. The result of "democratizing" the EU would be to take away the veto power which national governments now have over most EU decisions. Decisions made by the EU Parliament, unlike those made by the Council, are not subject to the national veto. This means that the EU would cease to be accountable to citizens through their national legislatures. At the moment, if a Danish citizen dislikes an EU decision, she can try to mobilize other Danes to change their government's position on the issue. But once the EU is "democratized" —i.e., once the Parliament replaces the Council as the major decision-making body—a Danish citizen would have to try to change the opinions of the citizens of every other European country (none of which speak her language). And, for obvious and understandable reasons, few Europeans seek this sort of "democratization." For Danish citizens to engage in a debate with other Danes, in Danish, about the Danish position *vis-à-vis* the EU is a familiar and manageable task. But for Danish citizens to engage in a debate with Italians to try to develop a common European position is a daunting prospect. In what language would such a debate occur, and in what forums? Not only do they not speak the same language, or share the same territory, they also do not read the same newspapers, or watch the same television shows, or belong to the same political parties. So what would be the forum for such a trans-European debate?

Given these obstacles to a trans-European public debate, it is not surprising that neither the Danes nor the Italians have shown any enthusiasm for "democratizing" the EU. They prefer exercising democratic accountability through their national legislatures. Paradoxically, then, the net result of increasing direct democratic accountability of the EU through the elected Parliament would in fact be to undermine democratic citizenship. It would shift power away from the national level, where mass participation and vigorous democratic debate is possible, towards the transnational level, where democratic participation and deliberation is very difficult. As Grimm argues, given that there is no common European mass media at the moment, and given that the prospects for creating such a Europeanized media in the foreseeable future "are absolutely non-existent," dramatically shifting power from the Council to the Parliament would "aggravate rather than solve the problem" of the democratic deficit (Grimm 1995: 296).

In short, globalization is undoubtedly producing a new civil society, but it has not yet produced anything we can recognize as transnational democratic citizenship. Nor is it clear to me that we should aspire to such a new form of citizenship. Many of our most important moral principles should be cosmopolitan in scope—e.g., principles of human rights, democracy, and environmental protection—and we should seek to promote these ideals internationally. But our democratic citizenship is, and will remain for the foreseeable future, national in scope.

REFERENCES

Banting, Keith (1997), "The Internationalization of the Social Contract," in Thomas Courchene (ed.), *The Nation State in a Global/Information Era* (John Deutsch Institute for Policy Studies, Queen's University, Kingston, Ont.), 255–85.

Grimm, Dieter (1995), "Does Europe Need a Constitution?," *European Law Journal* 1/3:282–302.

Held, David (1995), *Democracy and the Global Order—From the Modern State to Cosmopolitan Governance* (Polity Press, London).

_____. (1999), "The Transformation of Political Community: Rethinking Democracy in the Context of Globalization" in Ian Shapiro and Casiano Hacker-Cordon (eds.), *Democracy's Edges* (Cambridge University Press, Cambridge), 84–111.

Royal Commission on Electoral Reform and Party Financing (RCERPF) (1995), *Reforming Electoral Democracy: Final Report*, vols. I and II. (Supply and Services, Ottawa).

Simeon, Richard (1997), "Citizens and Democracy in the Emerging Global Order," in Thomas Courchene (ed.), *The Nation State in a Global/Information Era* (John Deutsch Institute for Policy Studies, Queen's University, Kingston, Ont.), 299–314.

CHAPTER 33

The Politics of Recognition

CHARLES TAYLOR

I

A number of strands in contemporary politics turn on the need, sometimes the demand, for *recognition*. The need, it can be argued, is one of the driving forces behind nationalist movements in politics. And the demand comes to the fore in a number of ways in today's politics, on behalf of minority or "subaltern" groups, in some forms of feminism and in what is today called the politics of "multiculturalism."

The demand for recognition in these latter cases is given urgency by the supposed links between recognition and identity, where this latter term designates something like a person's understanding of who they are, of their fundamental defining characteristics as a human being. The thesis is that our identity is partly shaped by recognition or its absence, often by the misrecognition of others and so a person or group of people can suffer real damage, real distortion, if the people or society around them mirror back to them a confining or demeaning or contemptible picture of themselves. Nonrecognition or misrecognition can inflict harm, can be a form of oppression, imprisoning someone in a false, distorted, and reduced mode of being.

Thus, some feminists have argued that women in patriarchal societies have been induced to adopt a depreciatory image of themselves. They have internalized a picture of their own inferiority, so that even when some of the objective obstacles to their advancement fall away, they may be incapable of taking advantage of the new opportunities. And beyond this, they are condemned to suffer the pain of low self-esteem. An analogous point has been made in relation to blacks: that white society has for generations projected a demeaning image of them, which some of them have been unable to resist adopting. Their own self-depreciation, on this view, becomes one of the most potent instruments of their own oppression. Their first task ought to be to purge themselves of this imposed and destructive identity. Recently, a similar point has been made in relation to indigenous and colonized people in general. It is held that since 1492 Europeans have projected an image of such people as somehow inferior, "uncivilized," and through the force of conquest have often been able to impose this image on the conquered. The figure of Caliban has been held to epitomize this crushing portrait of contempt of New World aboriginals.

Within these perspectives, misrecognition shows not just a lack of due respect. It can inflict a grievous wound, saddling its victims with a crippling self-hatred. Due recognition is not just a courtesy we owe people. It is a vital human need.

* * * * *

We can distinguish two changes that together have made the modern preoccupation with identity and recognition inevitable. The first is the collapse of social hierarchies, which used to be the basis for honor. I am using *honor* in the ancien régime sense in which it is intrinsically linked to inequalities. For some to have honor in this sense, it is essential that not everyone have it. This is the sense in which Montesquieu uses it in his description of monarchy. Honor is intrinsically a matter of "préférences."[1] It is also the sense in which we use the term when we speak of honoring someone by giving her some public award, for example, the Order of Canada. Clearly, this award would be without worth if tomorrow we decided to give it to every adult Canadian.

As against this notion of honor, we have the modern notion of dignity, now used in a universalist and egalitarian sense, where we talk of the inherent "dignity of human beings," or of citizen dignity. The underlying premise here is that everyone shares in it.[2] It is obvious that this concept of dignity is the only one compatible with a democratic society, and that it was inevitable that the old concept of honor was superseded. But this has also meant that the forms of equal recognition have been essential to democratic culture. For instance, that everyone be called "Mr.," "Mrs.," or "Miss," rather than some people being called "Lord" or "Lady" and others simply by their surnames—or, even more demeaning, by their first names—has been thought essential in some democratic societies, such as the United States. More recently, for similar reasons, "Mrs." and "Miss" have been collapsed into "Ms." Democracy has ushered in a politics of equal recognition, which has taken various forms over the years, and has now returned in the form of demands for the equal status of cultures and of genders.

But the importance of recognition has been modified and intensified by the new understanding of individual identity that emerges at the end of the eighteenth century. We might speak of an *individualized* identity, one that is particular to me, and that I discover in myself. This notion arises along with an ideal, that of being true to myself and my own particular way of being. Following Lionel Trilling's usage in his brilliant study, I will speak of this as the ideal of "authenticity."[3] It will help to describe in what it consists and how it came about.

One way of describing its development is to see its starting point in the eighteenth-century notion that human beings are endowed with a moral sense, an intuitive feeling for what is right and wrong. The original point of this doctrine was to combat a rival view, that knowing right and wrong was a matter of calculating consequences, in particular, those concerned with divine reward and punishment. The idea was that understanding right and wrong was not a matter of dry calculation, but was anchored in our feelings.[4] Morality has, in a sense, a voice within.

The notion of authenticity develops out of a displacement of the moral accent in this idea. On the original view, the inner voice was important because it tells us what the right thing to do is. Being in touch with our moral feelings matters here, as a means to the end of acting rightly. What I'm calling the displacement of the moral accent comes about when being in touch with our feelings takes on independent and crucial moral significance. It comes to be something we have to attain if we are to be true and full human beings.

To see what is new here, we have to see the analogy to earlier moral views, where being in touch with some source — for example, God, or the Idea of the Good — was considered essential to full being. But now the source we have to connect with is deep within us. This fact is part of the massive subjective turn of modem culture, a new form of inwardness, in which we corne to think of ourselves as beings with inner depths. At first, this idea that the source is within doesn't exclude our being related to God or the Ideas; it can be considered our proper way of relating to them. In a sense, it can be seen as just a continuation and intensification of the development inaugurated by Saint Augustine, who saw the road to God as passing through our own self-awareness. The first variants of this new view were theistic, or at least pantheistic.

The most important philosophical writer who helped to bring about this change was Jean-Jacques Rousseau. I think Rousseau is important not because he inaugurated the change; rather, I would argue that his great popularity comes in part from his articulating something that was in a sense already occurring in the culture. Rousseau frequently presents the issue of morality as that of our following a voice of nature within us. This voice is often drowned out by the passions that are induced by our dependence on others, the main one being *amour propre*, or pride. Our moral salvation comes from recovering authentic moral contact with ourselves. Rousseau even gives a name to the intimate contact with oneself, more fundamental than any moral view, that is a source of such joy and contentment: "le sentiment de l'existence."[5]

The ideal of authenticity becomes crucial owing to a development that occurs after Rousseau, which I associate with the name of Herder — once again, as its major early articulator, rather than its originator. Herder put forward the idea that each of us has an original way of being human: each person has his or her own "measure."[6] This idea has burrowed very deep into modern consciousness. It is a new idea. Before the late eighteenth century, no one thought that the differences between human beings had this kind of moral significance. There is a certain way of being human that is *my* way. I am called upon to live my life in this way, and not in imitation of anyone else's life. But this notion gives a new importance to being true to myself. If I am not, I miss the point of my life; I miss what being human is for *me*.

This is the powerful moral ideal that has come down to us. It accords moral importance to a kind of contact with myself, with my own inner nature, which it sees as in danger of being lost, partly through the pressures toward outward conformity, but also because in taking an instrumental stance toward myself, I may have lost the capacity to listen to this inner voice. It greatly increases the importance of this self-contact by introducing the principle of originality: each of our voices has something unique to say. Not only should I not mold my life to the demands of external conformity; I can't even find the model by which to live outside myself. I can only find it within.[7]

* * * * *

This new ideal of authenticity was, like the idea of dignity, also in part an offshoot of the decline of hierarchical society. In those earlier societies, what we would now call identity was largely fixed by one's social position. That is, the background that explained what people recognized as important to themselves was to a great extent determined by their place in society, and whatever roles or activities attached to this position. The birth of a democratic society doesn't by itself do away with this phenomenon, because people can still define themselves by their social roles. What does decisively undermine this socially derived identification, however, is the ideal of authenticity itself. As this emerges, for instance, with Herder, it calls on me to discover my own original way of being. By definition, this way of being cannot be socially derived, but must be inwardly generated.

But in the nature of the case, there is no such thing as inward generation, monologically understood. In order to understand the close connection between identity and recognition, we have to take into account a crucial feature of the human condition that has been rendered almost invisible by the overwhelmingly monological bent of mainstream modern philosophy.

This crucial feature of human life is its fundamentally *dialogical* character. We become full human agents, capable of understanding ourselves, and hence of defining our identity, through our acquisition of rich human languages of expression. For my purposes here, I want to take *language* in a broad sense, covering not only the words we speak, but also other modes of expression whereby we define ourselves, including the "languages" of art, of gesture, of love, and the like. But we learn these modes of expression through exchanges with others. People do not acquire the languages needed for self-definition on their own. Rather, we are introduced to them through interaction with others who matter to us—what George Herbert Mead called "significant others."[8] The genesis of the human mind is in this sense not monological, not something each person accomplishes on his or her own, but dialogical.

Moreover, this is not just a fact about *genesis*, which can be ignored later on. We don't just learn the languages in dialogue and then go on to use them for our own purposes. We are, of course, expected to develop our own opinions, outlook, stances toward things, and to a considerable degree through solitary reflection. But this is not how things work with important issues, like the definition of our identity. We define our identity always in dialogue with, sometimes in struggle against, the things our significant others want to see in us. Even after we outgrow some of these others—our parents, for instance—and they disappear from our lives, the conversation with them continues within us as long as we live.[9]

Thus, the contribution of significant others, even when it is provided at the beginning of our lives, continues indefinitely. Some people may still want to hold on to some form of the monological ideal. It is true that we can never liberate ourselves completely from those whose love and care shaped us early in life, but we should strive to define ourselves on our own to the fullest extent possible, coming as best we can to understand and thus get some control over the influence of our parents, and avoiding falling into any more such dependent relationships. We need relationships to fulfill, but not to define, ourselves.

The monological ideal seriously underestimates the place of the dialogical in human life. It wants to confine it as much as possible to the genesis. It forgets how our understanding of the good things in life can be transformed by our enjoying them in common with people we love; how some goods become accessible to us only through such common enjoyment. Because of this, it would take a great deal of effort, and probably many wrenching break-ups, to *prevent* our identity's being formed by the people we love. Consider what we mean by *identity*. It is who we are, "where we're coming from." As such it is the background against which our tastes and desires and opinions and aspirations make sense. If some of the things I value most are accessible to me only in relation to the person I love, then she becomes part of my identity.

To some people this might seem a limitation, from which one might aspire to free oneself. This is one way of understanding the impulse behind the life of the hermit or, to take a case more familiar to our culture, the solitary artist. But from another perspective, we might see even these lives as aspiring to a certain kind of dialogicality. In the case of the hermit, the interlocutor is God. In the case of the solitary artist, the work itself is addressed to a future audience, perhaps still to be created by the work. The very form of a work of art shows its character as *addressed*.[10] But however one feels about it, the making and sustaining of our identity, in the absence of a heroic effort to break out of ordinary existence, remains dialogical throughout our lives.

Thus, my discovering my own identity doesn't mean that I work it out in isolation, but that I negotiate it through dialogue, partly overt, partly internal, with others. That is why the development of an ideal of inwardly generated identity gives a new importance to recognition. My own identity crucially depends on my dialogical relations with others.

Of course, the point is not that this dependence on others arose with the age of authenticity. A form of dependence was always there. The socially derived identity was by its very nature dependent on society. But in the earlier age recognition never arose as a problem. General recognition was built into the socially derived identity by virtue of the very fact that it was based on social categories that everyone took for granted. Yet inwardly derived, personal, original identity doesn't enjoy this recognition *a priori*. It has to win it through exchange, and the attempt can fail. What has come about with the modern age is not the need for recognition but the conditions in which the attempt to be recognized can fail. That is why the need is now acknowledged for the first time. In premodern times, people didn't speak of "identity" and "recognition"—not because people didn't have (what we call) identities, or because these didn't depend on recognition, but rather because these were then too unproblematic to be thematized as such.

* * * * *

The importance of recognition is now universally acknowledged in one form or another; on an intimate plane, we are all aware of how identity can be formed or malformed through the course of our contact with significant others. On the social plane, we have a continuing politics of equal recognition. Both planes have been shaped by the growing ideal of authenticity, and recognition plays an essential role in the culture that has arisen around this ideal.

On the intimate level, we can see how much an original identity needs and is vulnerable to the recognition given or withheld by significant others. It is not surprising that in the culture of authenticity, relationships are seen as the key loci of self-discovery and self-affirmation. Love relationships are not just important because of the general emphasis in modern culture on the fulfillments of ordinary needs. They are also crucial because they are the crucibles of inwardly generated identity.

On the social plane, the understanding that identities are formed in open dialogue, unshaped by a predefined social script, has made the politics of equal recognition more central and stressful. It has, in fact, considerably raised the stakes. Equal recognition is not just the appropriate mode for a healthy democratic society. Its refusal can inflict damage on those who are denied it, according to a widespread modern view, as I indicated at the outset. The projection of an inferior or demeaning image on another can actually distort and oppress, to the extent that the image is internalized. Not only contemporary feminism but also race relations and discussions of multiculturalism are undergirded by the premise that the withholding of recognition can be a form of oppression. We may debate whether this factor has been exaggerated, but it is clear that the understanding of identity and authenticity has introduced a new dimension into the politics of equal recognition, which now operates with something like its own notion of authenticity, at least so far as the denunciation of other-induced distortions is concerned.

⑤ II

And so the discourse of recognition has become familiar to us on two levels: First, in the intimate sphere, where we understand the formation of identity and the self as taking place in a continuing dialogue and struggle with significant others. And then in the public sphere, where a politics of equal recognition has come to play a bigger and bigger role. Certain feminist theories have tried to show the links between the two spheres.[11]

I want to concentrate here on the public sphere, and try to work out what a politics of equal recognition has meant and could mean.

In fact, it has come to mean two rather different things, connected, respectively, with the two major changes I have been describing. With the move from honor to dignity has come a politics of universalism, emphasizing the equal dignity of all citizens, and the content of this politics has been the equalization of rights and entitlements. What is to be avoided at all costs is the existence of "first-class" and "second-class" citizens. Naturally, the actual detailed measures justified by this principle have varied greatly, and have often been controversial. For some, equalization has affected only civil rights and voting rights; for others, it has extended into the socioeconomic sphere. People who are systematically handicapped by poverty from making the most of their citizenship rights are deemed on this view to have been relegated to second-class status, necessitating remedial action through equalization. But through all the differences of interpretation, the principle of equal citizenship has come to be universally accepted. Every position, no matter how reactionary, is now defended under the colors of this principle. Its greatest, most recent victory was won by the civil rights movement of the 1960s in the United States. It is worth noting that even the adversaries of extending voting rights to blacks in the southern states found some pretext consistent with universalism, such as "tests" to be administered to would-be voters at the time of registration.

By contrast, the second change, the development of the modern notion of identity, has given rise to a politics of difference. There is, of course, a universalist basis to this as well, making for the overlap and confusion between the two. *Everyone* should be recognized for his or her unique identity. But recognition here means something else. With the politics of equal dignity, what is established is meant to be universally the same, an identical basket of rights and immunities; with the politics of difference, what we are asked to recognize is the unique identity of this individual or group, their distinctness from everyone else. The idea is that it is precisely this distinctness that has been ignored, glossed over, assimilated to a dominant or majority identity. And this assimilation is the cardinal sin against the ideal of authenticity.[12]

Now underlying the demand is a principle of universal equality. The politics of difference is full of denunciations of discrimination and refusals of second-class citizenship. This gives the principle of universal equality a point of entry within the politics of dignity. But once inside, as it were, its demands are hard to assimilate to that politics. For it asks that we give acknowledgment and status to something that is not universally shared. Or, otherwise put, we give due acknowledgment only to what is universally present—everyone has an identity—through recognizing what is peculiar to each. The universal demand powers an acknowledgment of specificity.

The politics of difference grows organically out of the politics of universal dignity through one of those shifts with which we are long familiar, where a new understanding of the human social condition imparts a radically new meaning to an old principle. Just as a view of human beings as conditioned by their socioeconomic plight changed the understanding of second-class citizenship, so that this category came to include, for example, people in inherited poverty traps, so here the understanding of identity as formed in interchange, and as possibly so malformed, introduces a new form of second-class status into our purview. As in the present case, the socioeconomic redefinition justified social programs that were highly controversial. For those who had not gone along with this changed definition of equal status, the various redistributive programs and special opportunities offered to certain populations seemed a form of undue favoritism.

Similar conflicts arise today around the politics of difference. Where the politics of universal dignity fought for forms of nondiscrimination that were quite "blind" to the ways in which citizens differ, the politics of difference often redefines nondiscrimination as requiring that we make these distinctions the basis of differential treatment. So members of aboriginal bands will get certain rights and powers not enjoyed by other Canadians, if the demands for native self-government are finally agreed on, and certain minorities will get the right to exclude others in order to preserve their cultural integrity, and so on.

To proponents of the original politics of dignity, this can seem like a reversal, a betrayal, a simple negation of their cherished principle. Attempts are therefore made to mediate, to show how some of these measures meant to accommodate minorities can after all be justified on the original basis of dignity. These arguments can be successful up to a point. For instance, some of the (apparently) most flagrant departures from "difference-blindness" are reverse discrimination measures, affording people from previously unfavored groups a competitive advantage for jobs or places in universities. This practice has been justified on the grounds that historical discrimination has created a pattern within which the unfavored struggle at a disadvantage. Reverse discrimination is defended as a temporary measure that will eventually level the playing field and allow the old "blind" rules to come back into force in a way that doesn't disadvantage anyone. This argument seems cogent enough—wherever its factual basis is sound. But it won't justify some of the measures now urged on the grounds of difference, the goal of which is not to bring us back to an eventual "difference-blind" social space but, on the contrary, to maintain and cherish distinctness, not just now but forever. After all, if we're concerned with identity, then what is more legitimate than one's aspiration that it never be lost?[13]

So even though one politics springs from the other, by one of those shifts in the definition of key terms with which we're familiar, the two diverge quite seriously from each other. One basis for the divergence comes out even more clearly when we go beyond what each requires that we acknowledge—certain universal rights in one case, a particular identity on the other—and look at the underlying intuitions of value.

The politics of equal dignity is based on the idea that all humans are equally worthy of respect. It is underpinned by a notion of what in human beings commands respect, however we may try to shy away from this "metaphysical" background. For Kant, whose use of the term *dignity* was one of the earliest influential evocations of this idea, what commanded respect in us was our status as rational agents, capable of directing our lives through principles.[14] Something like this has been the basis for our intuitions of equal dignity ever since, though the detailed definition of it .may have changed.

Thus, what is picked out as of worth here is a *universal human potential*, a capacity that all humans share. This potential, rather than anything a person may have made of it, is what ensures that each person deserves respect. Indeed, our sense of the importance of potentiality reaches so far that we extend this protection even to people who through some circumstance that has befallen them are incapable of realizing their potential in the normal way—handicapped people, or those in a coma, for instance.

In the case of the politics of difference, we might also say that a universal potential is at its basis, namely, the potential for forming and defining one's own identity, as an individual, and also as a culture. This potentiality must be respected equally in everyone. But at least in the intercultural context, a stronger demand has recently arisen: that one accord equal respect to actually evolved cultures. Critiques of European or white domination, to the effect that they have not only suppressed but failed to appreciate other cultures, consider these depreciatory judgments not only factually mistaken but somehow morally wrong. When Saul Bellow is famously quoted as saying something like, "When the Zulus produce a Tolstoy we will read him,"[15] this is taken as a quintessential statement of European arrogance, not just because Bellow is allegedly being *de facto* insensitive to the value of Zulu culture, but frequently also because it is seen to reflect a denial in principle of human equality. The possibility that the Zulus, while having the same potential for culture formation as anyone else, might nevertheless have come up with a culture that is less valuable than others is ruled out from the start. Even to entertain this possibility is to deny human equality. Bellow's error here, then, would not be a (possibly insensitive) particular mistake in evaluation, but a denial of a fundamental principle.

To the extent that this stronger reproach is in play, the demand for equal recognition extends beyond an acknowledgment of the equal value of all humans potentially, and comes to include the equal value of what they have made of this potential in fact. [...]

These two modes of politics, then, both based on the notion of equal respect, come into conflict. For one, the principle of equal respect requires that we treat people in a difference-blind fashion. The fundamental intuition that humans command this respect focuses on what is the same in all. For the other, we have to recognize and even foster particularity. The reproach the first makes to the second is just that it violates the principle of nondiscrimination. The reproach the second makes to the first is that it negates identity by forcing people into a homogeneous mold that is untrue to them. This would be bad enough if the mold were itself neutral—nobody's mold in particular. But the complaint generally goes further. The claim is that the supposedly neutral set of difference-blind principles of the politics of equal dignity is in fact a reflection of one hegemonic culture. As it turns out, then, only the minority or suppressed cultures are being forced to take alien form. Consequently, the supposedly fair and difference-blind society is not only inhuman (because suppressing identities) but also, in a subtle and unconscious way, itself highly discriminatory.[16]

This last attack is the cruelest and most upsetting of all. The liberalism of equal dignity seems to have to assume that there are some universal, difference-blind principles. Even though we may not have defined them yet, the project of defining them remains alive and essential. Different theories may be put forward and contested—and a number have been proposed in our day[17]—but the shared assumption of the different theories is that one such theory is right.

The charge leveled by the most radical forms of the politics of difference is that "blind" liberalisms are themselves the reflection of particular cultures. And the worrying thought is that this bias might not just be a contingent weakness of all hitherto proposed theories, that the very idea of such a liberalism may be a kind of pragmatic contradiction, a particularism masquerading as the universal.

* * * * *

NOTES

1. "La nature de l'honneur est de demander des préférences et des distinctions ...." Montesquieu, *De l'esprit des lois*, Bk. 3, chap. 7.
2. The significance of this move from "honor" to "dignity" is interestingly discussed by Peter Berger in his "On the Obsolescence of the Concept of Honour," in *Revisions: Changing Perspectives in Moral Philosophy*, ed. Stanley Hauerwas and Alasdair MacIntyre (Notre Dame, Ind.: University of Notre Dame Press, 1983), pp. 172–81.
3. Lionel Trilling, *Sincerity and Authenticity* (New York: Norton, 1969).
4. I have discussed the development of this doctrine at greater length, at first in the work of Francis Hutcheson, drawing on the writings of the Earl of Shaftesbury, and its adversarial

relation to Locke's theory in *Sources of the Self* (Cambridge, Mass.: Harvard University Press, 1989), chap. 15.

5. "Le sentiment de l'existence dépouillé de toute autre affection est par lui-même un sentiment précieux de contentement et de paix qui suffirait seul pour rendre cette existence chère et douce à qui sauroit écarter de soi toutes les impressions sensuelles et terrestres qui viennent sans cesse nous en distraire et en troubler ici bas la douceur. Mais la pluspart des hommes agités de passions continuelles connoissent peu cet état et ne l'ayant goûté qu'imparfaitement durant peu d'instans n'en conservent qu'une idée obscure et confuse qui ne leur en fait pas sentir le charme." Jean-Jacques Rousseau, *Les Rêveries du promeneur solitaire,* "Cinquième Promenade," in *Oeuvres complètes* (Paris: Gallimard, 1959), 1: 1047.

6. "Jeder Mensch hat ein eigenes Maass, gleichsam eine eigne Stimmung aller seiner sinnlichen Gefühle zu einander." Johann Gottlob Herder, *Ideen,* chap. 7, sec. 1, in *Herders Sämtliche Werke,* ed. Bernard Suphan (Berlin: Weidmann, 1877–1913), 13: 291.

7. John Stuart Mill was influenced by this Romantic current of thought when he made something like the ideal of authenticity the basis for one of his most powerful arguments in *On Liberty*. See especially chapter 3, where he argues that we need something more than a capacity for "ape-like imitation": "A person whose desires and impulses are his own—are the expression of his own nature, as it has been developed and modified by his own culture—is said to have a character." "If a person possesses any tolerable amount of common sense and experience, his own mode of laying out his existence is the best, not because it is the best in itself, but because it is his own mode." John Stuart Mill, *Three Essays* (Oxford: Oxford University Press, 1975), pp. 73, 74, 83.

8. George Herbert Mead, *Mind, Self, and Society* (Chicago: University of Chicago Press, 1934).

9. This inner dialogicality has been explored by M.M. Bakhtin and those who have drawn on his work. See, of Bakhtin, especially *Problems of Dostoyevsky's Poetics,* trans. Caryl Emerson (Minneapolis: University of Minnesota Press, 1984). See also Michael Holquist and Katerina Clark, *Mikhail Bakhtin* (Cambridge, Mass.: Harvard University Press, 1984); and James Wertsch, *Voices of the Mind* (Cambridge, Mass.: Harvard University Press, 1991).

10. See Bakhtin, "The Problem of the Text in Linguistics, Philology and the Human Sciences," in *Speech Genres and Other Late Essays,* ed. Caryl Emerson and Michael Holquist (Austin: University of Texas Press, 1986), p. 126, for this notion of a "super-addressee," beyond our existing interlocutors.

11. There are a number of strands that have linked these two levels, but perhaps special prominence in recent years has been given to a psychoanalytically oriented feminism, which roots social inequalities in the early upbringing of men and women. See, for instance, Nancy Chodorow, *Feminism and Psychoanalytic Theory* (New Haven: Yale University Press, 1989); and Jessica Benjamin, *Bonds of Love: Psychoanalysis, Feminism and the Problem of Domination* (New York: Pantheon, 1988).

12. A prime example of this charge from a feminist perspective is Carol Gilligan's critique of Lawrence Kohlberg's theory of moral development, for presenting a view of human

development that privileges only one facet of moral reasoning, precisely the one that tends to predominate in boys rather than girls. See Gilligan, *In a Different Voice* (Cambridge, Mass.: Harvard University Press, 1982).

13. Will Kymlicka, in his very interesting and tightly argued book *Liberalism, Community and Culture* (Oxford: Clarendon Press, 1989), tries to argue for a kind of politics of difference, notably in relation to aboriginal rights in Canada, but from a basis that is firmly within a theory of liberal neutrality. He wants to argue on the basis of certain cultural needs—minimally, the need for an integral and undamaged cultural language with which one can define and pursue his or her own conception of the good life. In certain circumstances, with disadvantaged populations, the integrity of the culture may require that we accord them more resources or rights than others. The argument is quite parallel to that made in relation to socio-economic inequalities that I mentioned above.

    But where Kymlicka's interesting argument fails to recapture the actual demands made by the groups concerned—say Indian bands in Canada, or French-speaking Canadians—is with respect to their goal of survival. Kymlicka's reasoning is valid (perhaps) for *existing* people who find themselves trapped within a culture under pressure, and can flourish within it or not at all. But it doesn't justify measures designed to ensure survival through indefinite future generations. For the populations concerned, however, that is what is at stake. We need only think of the historical resonance of "la survivance" among French Canadians.

14. See Kant, *Grundlegung der Metaphysik der Sitten* (Berlin: Gruyter, 1968; reprint of the Berlin Academy edition), p. 434.

15. I have no idea whether this statement was actually made in this form by Saul Bellow, or by anyone else. I report it only because it captures a widespread attitude, which is, of course, why the story had currency in the first place.

16. One hears both kinds of reproach today. In the context of some modes of feminism and multiculturalism, the claim is the strong one, that the hegemonic culture discriminates. In the Soviet Union, however, alongside a similar reproach leveled at the hegemonic Great Russian culture, one also hears the complaint that Marxist-Leninist communism has been an alien imposition on all equally, even on Russia itself. The communist mold, on this view, has been truly nobody's. Solzhenitsyn has made this claim, but it is voiced by Russians of a great many different persuasions today, and has something to do with the extraordinary phenomenon of an empire that has broken apart through the quasi-secession of its metropolitan society.

17. See John Rawls, *A Theory of Justice* (Cambridge, Mass.: Harvard University Press, 1971); Ronald Dworkin, *Taking Rights Seriously* (London: Duckworth, 1977) and *A Matter of Principle* (Cambridge, Mass.: Harvard University Press, 1985); and Jürgen Habermas, *Theorie des kommunikativen Handelns* (Frankfurt: Suhrkamp, 1981).

PART IX

Postcolonialism, Diaspora, Citizenship, and Identity

CRITICAL THINKING QUESTIONS

Said

1. What is Orientalism? Can you think of an example from your everyday life?
2. How does Said distinguish between latent and manifest Orientalism?
3. What is the relationship between knowledge and power in Said's understanding of Orientalism?

Hall

1. How does Stuart Hall understand the formation of cultural identity (or identities)?
2. What significance does Hall attach to diaspora and hybridity in the formation of cultural identities?
3. What does Hall mean when he differentiates between a process of being and a process of becoming in cultural identity formation?

Kymlicka

1. In the context of the events of 11 September 2001, what factors do you see contributing to, and subverting, transnational institution building?
2. Is the partial formation of democratic alliances on a transnational level plausible? Think about environmental concerns, for instance.
3. Contrast domestic to cosmopolitan citizenship. Are they incompatible?

Taylor

1. What are the different levels on which identity formation operates today?

2.   What struggles for recognition are prominent in Canada today? Can
     Taylor's arguments be applied to those struggles?
3.   Why do you think Taylor refers to "the politics" of recognition?

SUGGESTED READINGS

Anderson, Benedict. 1991. *Imagined Communities: Reflections on the Origin
and Spread of Nationalism*. London: Verso.
     In this book, Anderson details how nationalism is most effectively
conceptualized as "imagined" because most members of a nation will
never actually know their fellow subjects. He also explores the origins of
perceived national commonalities.

Bissoondath, Neil. 1994. *Selling Illusions: The Cult of Multiculturalism*.
Toronto: Penguin Group.
     This book argues that multicultural policy in Canada produces a form of
cultural ghettoization, and that multiculturalism imports already-contained
cultural categories, thereby failing to facilitate integration in the country.
The book has generated much debate since its original publication.

Carrier, James. 1995. *Occidentalism*. Oxford: Oxford University Press.
     This edited book uses Said's general arguments in Orientialism as a
starting point, but it reflects on images of the Occident produced by the
Orient. The argument problematizes some of the power dynamics theorized
in *Orientalism*.

Eyerman, Ron. 2001. *Cultural Trauma: Slavery and the Formation of African
American Identity*. Cambridge: Cambridge University Press.
     Cultural Trauma is an interesting analysis of the changing nature of
collective identity. Eyerman argues that African American identity and
the significance of slavery change with different generational needs and
desires.

Fanon, Frantz. 1967. *Black Skin, White Masks*. New York: Grove Press.
     This book focuses on language and the body/soul in the context of
colonial relations, racism, and collective psychology. By no means an easy
read, the book nonetheless reveals fascinating insights into identity, culture,
and psychological conflict.

RELATED WEB SITES

Edward Said Archive
A number of diverse links to Said's works and ideas are offered on this
Web site.
www.edwardsaid.org/modules/news/

Nationalism Project

This Web site contains many links to materials on nationalism. Included here are essays, articles, dissertations, book abstracts and reviews, bibliographies, a bibliography, journal articles, and other resources.

www.nationalismproject.org/

Postcolonial Literature

This is a Web guide to postcolonial literature.

www.literaryhistory.com/20thC/Groups/postcolonial.htm

Postcolonial Studies

Postcolonial Studies is a professional journal that takes up issues and contemporary debates in postcolonialism.

www.tandf.co.uk/journals/titles/13688790.asp

Postcolonialism, Nation, Gender

This Web site will introduce a number of terms and concepts such as colonialism, postcolonialism, identity, and diaspora.

www.eng.fju.edu.tw/Literary_Criticism/postcolonism/

REFERENCES

Fanon, Frantz. 1961. *The Wretched of the Earth*. New York: Grove Press.

_____. 1967. *Black Skin, White Masks*. New York: Grove Press.

Said, Edward. 1978. *Orientalism*. New York: Vintage.

Copyright Acknowledgements

Herbert Marcuse, "The New Forms of Control," from *One-Dimensional Man: Studies in the Ideology of Advanced Industrial Society*. Boston: Beacon Press, 1964. Reprinted by permission of Beacon Press.

Jürgen Habermas, "Modernity—An Incomplete Project," from *The Anti-Aesthetic*, New York: The New Press, 1983. Reprinted by permission of The New Press.

Pierre Bourdieu, "The Dynamics of the Fields," from *Distinction: A Social Critique of the Judgement of Taste*, Paris: Les Éditions de Minuit, 1984. Reprinted by permission of Les Éditions de Minuit.

Mariana Valverde, "Moral Capital," from *Canadian Journal of Law and Society* 9:1, 1994. Reprinted by permission of the *Canadian Journal of Law and Society*.

Joan Kelly-Gadol, "The Social Relation of the Sexes: Methodological Implications of Women's History," from *Signs: The Journal of Women in Culture and Society* 1:4, 1976. Reprinted by permission of The University of Chicago Press.

Dorothy Smith, "Feminism and Marxism—A Place to Begin, A Way to Go," from *Feminism and Marxism*, Vancouver: New Star Books, 1977. Reprinted by permission of the author.

bell hooks, "The Significance of Feminism," from *Feminist Theory: From Margin to Center*, Cambridge: South End Press, 2003. Reprinted by permission of South End Press.

David Lyon, "Postmodernity: The History of an Idea," from *Postmodernity*, Buckingham: Open University Press, 1994. Reprinted by permission of Open University Press.

Steven Seidman, "The End of Sociological Theory: The Postmodern Hope," from *Sociological Theory* 9:2, Fall 1991. Reprinted by permission of the American Sociological Association.

Marilyn Porter, "Call Yourself a Sociologist—And You've Never Even Been Arrested?!," from *Canadian Review of Sociology and Anthropology* 32:4, 1995. Reprinted by permission of the *Canadian Review of Sociology and Anthropology*.

Zygmunt Bauman, "Foreword: On Being Light and Liquid," from *Liquid Modernity*. Cambridge: Polity Press, 2000. Reprinted by permission of Polity Press.

Jean Baudrillard, extracts from *The Spirit of Terrorism and Requiem for the Twin Towers*, London: Verso, 2002. Reprinted by permission of Verso Books.

Dany Lacombe, "Reforming Foucault: A Critique of the Social Control Thesis," from *British Journal of Sociology* 47:2, 1996. Reprinted by permission of Blackwell Publishing; published on behalf of the London School of Economics and Political Science.

Anthony Giddens, extracts from *Modernity and Self-Identity*, Palo Alto: Stanford University Press, 1992. Reprinted by permission of Stanford University Press.

Ulrich Beck, "Introduction: The Cosmopolitan Manifesto," from *World Risk Society*, Cambridge: Polity Press, 1999. Reprinted by permission of Polity Press.

R. Alan Hedley, "Running Out of Control: Understanding Globalization," from *Running Out of Control: Understanding Globalization*, Bloomfield: Kumarian Press, 2002. Reprinted by permission of Kumarian Press.

Naomi Klein, "Seattle: The Coming-Out of a Movement; "and "What's Next?: The Movement Against Global Corporatism Doesn't Need to Sign a Ten-Point Plan to Be Effective," from *Fences and Windows: Dispatches from the Front Lines of the Globalization Debate*, Toronto: Vintage Canada, 2002. Reprinted by permission of Vintage Canada.

Nick Stevenson, "Cosmopolitanism and the Future of Democracy: Politics, Culture and the Self," from *New Political Economy* 7:2. London: Carfax Publishing Company, 2002. Reprinted by permission of Carfax Publishing Company / Taylor & Francis.

Edward Said, "Latent and Manifest Orientalism," from *Orientalism*, New York: Pantheon Books, 1978. Reprinted by permission of Pantheon Books/Random House.

Stuart Hall, "Cultural Identity and Diaspora," from *Identity: Community, Culture, Difference,* London: Lawrence & Wishart, Ltd., 1990. Reprinted by permission of Lawrence & Wishart, Ltd.

Will Kymlicka, "Citizenship in an Era of Globalization," from *Politics in the Vernacular: Nationalism, Multiculturalism, and Citizenship*, Oxford: Oxford University Press, 2001. Reprinted by permission of Oxford University Press.

Charles Taylor, "The Politics of Recognition," from *Multiculturalism and the Politics of Recognition*, Princeton: Princeton University Press, 1992. Reprinted by permission of Princeton University Press.